THE SELECTED WRITINGS

OF SIR EDWARD COKE

EDWARD COKE

THE SELECTED WRITINGS

AND SPEECHES OF

Sir Edward Coke

Volume One

EDITED BY

STEVE SHEPPARD

LIBERTY FUND

INDIANAPOLIS, INDIANA

© 2003 Liberty Fund, Inc.

Frontispiece and cover art:
volume I: Reproduced courtesy of the Right Honourable
the Earl of Leicester and the Holkham Estate.
volume II: Collection of the Editor.
volume III: Corbis-Bettmann.

08   07   06   05   04   03   P   5   4   3   2   1

Library of Congress Cataloging-in-Publication Data

Coke, Edward, Sir, 1552–1634.
[Selections. 2003]
The selected writings and speeches of Sir Edward Coke
edited by Steve Sheppard
p.   cm.
Includes bibliographical references and index.
ISBN 0-86597-313-x (pbk.: alk. paper)
1. Law—England.
I. Sheppard, Steve, 1963–
II. Title.
KD358.C65   2003
349.42'092—dc22   2003061935

ISBNs:
0-86597-313-X   volume I
0-86597-314-8   volume II
0-86597-441-1   volume III
0-86597-316-4   set

Liberty Fund, Inc.
8335 Allison Pointe Trail, Suite 300
Indianapolis, Indiana 46250-1684

Summary of Contents

Annotated Table of Contents   vii

Acknowledgments and Dedicatory   xvii

A Note on the Texts, Editions, and Translations   xix

Introduction   xxiii

Chronology of Events Material to the Life, Times, Writings, and
Legacy of Sir Edward Coke from the Death of Henry VIII to the
Opinion in *Marbury v. Madison*   xxxiii

Editions of Coke's Works   lxxiii

Mottoes and Crests of Sir Edward Coke   lxxxix

I. *Reports*   1

II. Coke's Speech and Charge at the Norwich Assizes   521

III. Excerpts from the Small Treatises   555

IV. Excerpts from the *Institutes of the Lawes of England*   573

V. Speeches in Parliament   1185

VI. Appendix I: Official Acts Related to Sir Edward Coke's Career   1305

VII. Appendix II: The Epitaph of Sir Edward Coke   1335

Selected Readings   1341

Table of Regnal Years   1379

Index   1407

Annotated Contents

Mottoes and Crests of Sir Edward Coke   lxxxix
   His Ring as Sergeant of Law
   His Crest
   His Motto

I. *Reports*

Part One of the *Reports*

Preface	Case reports and law study.	4
Shelley's Case	Classic property case; new rule construing language of grant in tail favors marketability over feudal interests in entailment.	6

Part Two of the *Reports*

Preface	The antiquity of the Common Law.	39
Manser's Case	The dangers of legal instruments that are unintelligible to the layman; an illiterate person who transfers by deed must be read the instrument.	42
The Case of Bankrupts	A bankrupt debtor must pay creditors proportionately to their debts and cannot favor one; power of commissioners to avoid disproportionate transfers.	45
The Archbishop of Canterbury's Case	Statutory interpretation; power of religious houses to received tithes.	49

Part Three of the *Reports*
Preface   Reports, history of courts, law study.   59
Heydon's Case   The method and the role of the judge
                          in interpreting statutes; a copyhold case.   78
Fermor's Case   Fraud bars the legal effect of
                          transactions; fraud in a position of trust
                          is particularly odious; public policy
                          problems if fraud is allowed as basis for
                          judicial relief; a fine and copyhold case.   84

Part Four of the *Reports*
Preface   Reports, history, judge's obligations.   94
The Lord Cromwell's   *Qui tam* proceeding in slander; Coke's
  Case   first big case.   105
Cutler v. Dixon   Immunity for acts in judicial
                          proceeding; scandal must be based on
                          acts of impropriety, not good behavior.   111
Vaux's Case   Double jeopardy, being indicted twice
                          for the same felony, is barred   112
Slade's Case   Action on the case allowed; beginnings
                          of commercial and contract law.   116

Part Five of the *Reports*
Preface   The law is important to all citizens, but
                          they do not know it well, which is why
                          Coke writes reports.   126
Foster's Case   Constables may present an arrestee to
                          any justice of the peace, not only the
                          justice who signs an arrest warrant.   128
The Chamberlain of   City taxes; King may grant charters to
  London's Case   ships to load in certain havens.   131
Clark's Case   Local governments may not create
                          imprisonable offences.   134
The Case of   Stolen goods sold in a merchant of a
  Market-Overt   different trade than the goods can still
                          vest good title in a new buyer.   134

Semayne's Case	Rights of homeowner to bar entry; house is to him as his castle; powers of and limits on sheriff to enter.	135
Rooke's Case	Sewer commissioners should tax equally all who are threatened by a riverbank; discretion, administration.	141
Pinnel's Case	Satisfaction of debts.	144
The Case de Libellis Famosis	Rules punishing libel, which include statements that harm reputation, even if true and even if the reputation is of a dead person.	145

Part Six of the *Reports*
Preface	Common Law existed before the Conquest.	150
Jentleman's Case	The King can create judges, but judges determine matters after they are appointed.	157

Part Seven of the *Reports*
Preface	Case of the Post-Nati described; attack on tract from Norwich assize address for misrepresentation.	162
Calvin's Case	Scot born after James VI of Scotland becomes James I of England is entitled to hold lands in England; allegiance, majesty, conquest, natural reason; law of nature cannot be altered.	166
The Case of Swans	Feræ naturæ and Royal beasts are the Queen's; one of Coke's first cases as solicitor.	232
Penal Statutes	Elizabeth I's grant to another to dispense with penal burdens is void; separation of powers and limits of Royal prerogative to avoid a statute.	241

Part Eight of the *Reports*
Preface Antiquity of his sources. 245
Vynior's Case The courts will not enforce an agreement to arbitrate. 260
Dr. Bonham's Case Censors of College of Physicians may not imprison for unlawful practice of medicine, regardless of the College charter and the Act that confirmed it; the common law controls acts of Parliament and may declare them void; judicial review of legislation. 264
The Case of Thetford School Proceeds of trust must be used according to intent of settlor. 284

Part Nine of the *Reports*
Preface More about antiquities. 288
William Aldred's Case Nuisance from a pigsty; environmental law. 308
John Lamb's Case Liability for libel. 313
MacKalley's Case Requirements for criminal indictment, arrest, and juries. 314

Part Ten of the *Reports*
Preface Introduction to cases; antiquities and bibliography. 327
Sutton's Hospital Charter of incorporation; early corporate law case; grant of a power to act in the future is good. 347
The Case of the Isle of Ely Commissioners of Sewers lack powers to decree new rivers; public versus private goods. 378

Part Eleven of the *Reports*
Preface Introduction to cases. 385
The Case of Lord de la Warre Disability of a hereditary member of Lords for life does not disable heir. 388

The Case of the   None may be barred from lawful
   Tailors of Ipswich   employment by an ordinance beyond
                           the limits set by statute.   390
The Case of   Grant by the Crown of monopoly for
   Monopolies   making cards is void; Limits on Royal
                           dispensing power.   394
James Bagg's Case   Citizenship; disenfranchisement must be
                           based on more than subject's impolite
                           words.   404

Part Twelve of the *Reports*
Ford and Sheldon's   Recusancy; retroactivity.
   Case   419
Case of Non Obstante   Custom; Parliament cannot bind King's
                           prerogative.   423
If High   Church courts and the power to
   Commissioners   imprison.
   have Power to
   Imprison   425
Floyd & Barker   Immunity of counsel and judges.   427
Of Oaths before an   No man shall be examined on secret
   Ecclesiastical Judge   opinions.
   Ex Officio   432
Of Pardons   Royal pardon can only waive penalty,
                           not crime.   439
Customs, Subsidies,   Limits on Royal power to tax.
   and Impositions
   (Bates's Case)   441
Buggery   Unlawful sexual acts.   446
Premunire   Writ (similar to prohibition) for use
                           against church court.   447
Nicholas Fuller's Case   No consultation with a judge
                           will be given out of term; construction
                           of jurisdiction of high commission
                           is a judicial matter of Common
                           Law.   454

Sir Anthony Roper's   High Commissioners and habeas
    Case   corpus.   461
The Case of Heresy   Evolution of procedure; indictment of
                         Lollards brought limitation of definition
                         by statute.   465
Langdale's Case   Prohibition does not require a suit in
                         Common Pleas.   471
Mouse's Case   Justification by necessity.   477
Prohibitions del Roy   The King cannot judge any case he
                         chooses.   478
The Lord   Office does not attach at delivery of
    Abergaveny's Case   writ, but in seating at Parliament.   481
Of Convocations   Limits on church convocations, which
                         cannot act contrary to the Common
                         Law, statute, or custom.   484
Proclamations   King cannot change the law.   486
Thomlinson's Case   Habeas corpus case against Court of
                         Admiralty.   490
Walter Chute's Case   Offices created by the King must be to
                         public benefit.   491
Sir Stephen Proctor's   Procedure in Star Chamber.
    Case   494
Exaction of   Voluntary grants demanded by the
    Benevolence   Queen are lawful.   496

Part Thirteen of the *Reports*
    Preface   499
    Prohibitions   Prohibitions.   501
    The Case de Modo   Prohibitions debate.
        Decimandi   505

II. Coke's Speech and Charge at the Norwich Assizes

    Preface   523
    Coke's Preface   525
    Coke's Charge   528

III. Excerpts from the Small Treatises

A. Book of Entries
Preface 558
B. The Compleat Copyholder
Section 33, on Customs 563
C. Little Treatise on Baile & Mainprize
Conclusion, 29–31 569

IV. *Institutes of the Lawes of England*

A. The First Part of the *Institutes;* Coke upon Littleton

Preface   Life and project of Sir Thomas
      Littleton, and some about the law;
      table of consanguinity 577
Sections 1–12, Fee Simple 591
Section 21, Fee Tail, part 2 681
Section 69, Tenant at Will, part 2 683
Section 80, Tenant by the Verge, part 3 684
Section 96, Escuage, part 2 685
Section 108, Knight's Service, part 6 696
Section 138, Frankalmoin, part 5 700
Section 170, Tenure in Burgage, part 9 701
Section 199, Villenage, part 18 711
Section 342, Conditional Estates, part 17 723
Section 366, Conditional Estates, part 41 724
Section 372, Conditional Estates, part 47 731
Section 412, Descents, part 27 731
Section 464, Releases, part 20 734
Section 481, Releases, part 37 737
Section 723, Warranty, part 30 739
Section 728, Warranty, part 35 740
Epilogue 742

B. The Second Part of the *Institutes*

Prologue 746
Magna Carta (complete) 755

Merton, 20 Henry III
  (excerpts)
    Preface   914
    Chapter 9   Common Law, Parliament   916
    Chapter 10   Suits   921
    Chapter 11   924
Marlebridge, 52   Private disputes to be resolved by
  Henry III   law
    Preface   924
Westminster 1,
  3 Edward I (excerpts)
    Preface   History of statute   927
Glocester (excerpts)
    Preface   History of statute   932
Westminster 2,
  13 Edward I (excerpts)
    Preface   History of statute   942
Westminster 3,   Tenants may assign tenancies.
  18 Edward I
    Preface   943

C. The Third Part of the *Institutes*

Table of Offenses   945
Preface   949
Chapter 1, High Treason   952
Chapter 2, Petit Treason   992
Chapter 3, Misprision of Treason   1028
Chapter 4, Conspiring to Kill the King   1029
Chapter 5, Heresy   1033
Chapter 6, Felonie by Conjuration, Witchcraft, Sorcery and
  Inchantment   1041
Chapter 62, Indictments   1048

D. The Fourth Part of the *Institutes*

Table of Courts   1054
Preface   1058

Chapter 1, Of the High and Most Honourable Court of Parliament   1062

Chapter 7, Of the Court of the Kings Bench   1166

V. Speeches in Parliament

A. 1593   Three petitions; Coke as Speaker of the House; liberty of speech, freedom of Parliamentarians from arrest, and free access for Parliamentarians; laws.   1187

B. 1621   Petition of Grievances; privileges of Parliament; impeachments.   1194

C. 1625   Subsidies.   1217

D. 1628   Petition of Right.   1225

VI. Appendix I: Official Acts Related to Sir Edward Coke's Career

A. The High Commission (Coke refuses to appear), 1611   1307

B. *Commendams* and the King's Displeasure, 1616   1310

C. Coke's Hearing, June 26, 1616   1323

D. Coke's Arrest After Parliament, 1621   1329

E. Sir Edward Coke's Case (The Sheriff's Oath), 1626   1332

VII. Appendix II: The Epitaph of Sir Edward Coke   1336

Selected Readings Concerning the Life, Career, and Legacy of Sir Edward Coke   1341

Table of Regnal Years   1379

Index   1407

Acknowledgments and Dedicatory

This project could not have been completed without the support of Liberty Fund, its officers and staff. Second only to their efforts were those of John Baker, whose care has saved, in many ways, this project from an inglorious end. I am profoundly grateful for the counsel and guidance in the development of this project over its many years given by Richard and Morris Arnold, Barbara Black, Marius Bolten, David Bovenizer, Alan Boyer, Dan Coquillette, Garett Fagan, Laura Goetz, Michael Hoeflich, Dan Kirklin, Christian Kopff, Dan Levine, Sam Mortlock, William Nelson, Emilio Pacheco, Mark Anthony Reynolds, and especially James Stoner. Hospitality and assistance in the research were provided by Whitney Bagnall and Kent McKeever at Columbia, David Warrington and his staff at Harvard, Mark Nicholls at Cambridge, Sharon Bradley at Thomas Cooley, and Glen-Peter Ahlers and David Gay at the University of Arkansas. The staff of the Earl of Leicester, particularly Mike Daly and Sam Mortlock, have been terribly gracious and helpful. I am indebted to the good offices of Mr. Mortlock, and of Marjorie and Brian Gill in photographing and confirming the engraving of certain lines in Sir Edward's epitaph in Tittleshall, which made possible the duplication of its inscriptions in these volumes. Danny Abbott, Jenny Adelman, Ingrid Arinez, K. Dement, Jay Atwood, Sylviane Donnadieu, Jessica Gunter, Richard Highsmith, Johnathan Horton, Charlene Kim, Orse Kore, Jackie Long, Al Sleicher, Louisa Vassileva, Shanna Wells, and Brett Worlow provided valuable and tenacious assistance in manuscript production.

This edition is dedicated to my teachers, the first and most influential of whom were my parents, William and Martha, all of whose care and dedication made this edition possible.

S.M.S.
The University of Arkansas
2003

A Note on the Texts, Editions, and Translations

This anthology of the writings of Edward Coke is designed to present a sampling of the works that chronicle his career and its influence on issues of law, constitutions, politics, government, economics, and liberty. In culling from the vast corpus of his writings, some materials, such as cases dealing with the struggle for judicial independence and jurisdictional primacy in the courts of law, are overrepresented as a portion of his works. Other materials, such as his writings on English history, titles, and estates, are quite underrepresented. Regretably, argument and opinions of Coke's reported by others have been omitted owing to the limits of space and cost. It is hoped that a collected scholarly edition of his works may one day remedy these and the other omissions that were necessary to achieve an edition even as short as the present one. The emphasis of this edition being on the influence of his works, it is constructed largely from the writings as they were printed in his generation and the next, without regard to a new comparison to the references that will one day be mandatory for a thorough reappraisal of his works, when such an edition is attempted.

Thus, certain limitations have been accepted in the development of this edition of Coke's writings. The most important was to limit the project to the reproduction of printed materials, without attempting further comparisons of those sources with manuscripts. This limitation also means that certain of Coke's writings that have never been published are not within the scope of this edition.

The texts have been chosen preferring the following criteria: Editions without notes, editing, or annotations by later writers are preferred; later editions that would have been overseen by Coke and corrected by him or under his supervision take precedence over earlier editions; editions that were translated by Coke or by lawyers working in his tradition are preferred to those in French and Latin; and earlier translations are preferred to later translations in order to diminish the degree of anachronism, although corrected editions of early translations have been consulted. Further, certain spelling and typographic conventions have been modernized in order to increase the clarity of the text for the modern reader, and some of these modernizations of the selected texts have been adopted in the light of modernizations employed in later editions. In particular, conventions adopted from the 1793 edition and from the preparation of the Coke volumes of the 1907 English *Reports* have been occasionally applied in the editing of the 1658 *Reports* here, the intent being to present an edition based predominately on the 1658 text, but including such improvements as may enhance its comprehensibility for the modern reader. The orthographic change that will most trouble specialists are the conversions of *i, j, u, v,* and the long *s* to modern usage.

The most significant alteration of the texts occurs in the quotations of statutes, particularly in the excerpts from the Second *Institute.* Coke's original editions quoted the Latin text of statutes in received forms from manuscript and printed editions. Here, the statutes have been replaced with translations from canonical sources produced in the generations following Coke's, which would have been consulted by lawyers employing Coke's materials. Magna Carta is taken from *Magna Charta* (Edward Cooke, trans., London, Printed by the assignees of R. and E. Atkins for T. Simmons, 1680), the translation by Edward Cooke, the barrister. The reader is cautioned that this edition is neither authoritative as a matter of current law nor the most accurate translation as a linguistic exercise, but its selection is consonant with translations that would have reflected the understandings of these texts in the generations immediately following Coke's work. Other statutes are taken from *The Statutes of the Realm,* 1810–28, a nine-volume edition of official, if not always precise, translations into English, or from *The Statutes at Large* of 1743, an edition edited by Owen Ruffhead that was the commercial predecessor to the official edition of 1810.

All other translations are relegated to the notes and have been provided newly for this edition.

Applying these principles, selections have been taken from the following texts:

I. Selections from *The Reports*

Prefaces Vols. I–II   The various first London editions

Reports Vols. 1–11   1658 London edition (with additional text
                            from 1680 and 1793)
Preface & Reports Vol. 12   1655 Bulstrode edition
Preface & Reports Vol. 13   1659 Roycroft edition

II. His Speech and Charge at the Norwich Assizes

From the second edition, 1607

III. Excerpts from the Early Treatises

The Compleat Copyholder   1644 edition
Little Treatise on Baile & Mainprize   1635 edition
Book of Entries   1671 edition

IV. Excerpts from the *Institutes*

First Part   1639 edition
Second Part   1642 edition (see note above regarding statutes)
Third Part   1644 edition
Fourth Part   1644 edition

V. Speeches in Parliament

1593   *Cobbett's Parliamentary History of England,* I (London, 1806)
1621   *Cobbett's Parliamentary History of England,* I (London, 1806), supple-
       mented with private accounts recorded anonymously in *A Journal or
       Diary of the Most Material Passages in the Lower House of the Parliament
       Summoned to be Holden the Sixteenth Day of January Anno Domini 1620
       but by Prorogation Adjourned Till the 23th and then again to 30th of the
       Same Month,* along with *The Notes by Sir Thomas Barrington of the
       House of Commons in 1621.*
1625   *Cobbett's Parliamentary History of England,* II (London, 1807), sup-
       plemented with official manuscript sources for the *H. of C., Draft
       Journal, MS. 3409, H.L.R.O.* and *Committee Book, MS. 3410, H.L.R.O.*
       Also supplemented with private accounts detailed in *Bedford MS. 197*
       and *Petyt MS. 538/8.*

1628   *Cobbett's Parliamentary History of England,* II (London, 1807), supplemented with "Proceedings and Debates of 1628" in *Common Debates
1628* (New Haven, 1977), which was collected from twelve different
sources and also supplemented with materials found in manuscript
sources, *Harleian MS 1601* and *Stowe MS 366,* and *The Diary of Edward
Nicholas S.P. 16/97.*

VI. Appendix I: Official Acts Related to Coke's Career

Orders of Privy Council   Acts of the Privy Council, HMSO, 1906

Introduction

Four hundred years ago, Sir Edward Coke published the first volume of his *Reports*. In time, his publications would include a surprisingly comprehensive set of cases and treatises that would help to modernize the law. Moreover, his decisions as a judge and arguments as a statesman uniquely contributed to the foundation of the law as an institution independent of the political powers of the state and capable of defending the freedom of the citizen. It is fair to say that no one has contributed more to create the modern notion of the rule of law.

Coke, whose name was pronounced "cook," was born in 1552 in Mileham, Norfolk, an eastern, mainly puritan country town of England. He studied at Cambridge, became an influential and wealthy lawyer, served Elizabeth I as Attorney General, and served James I as Chief Justice successively of the two law courts, the Court of Common Pleas and the Court of King's Bench. He opposed the King's interference in judicial affairs and was removed, although he stayed a royal adviser for many years. He entered Parliament and fostered the Petition of Right, a forerunner of the Bills of Rights in England and the United States. (A detailed chronology follows this introduction.)

Coke's influence was great at a pivotal moment in English and American history. Teetering at the end of the 1500s, the Tudor England of which Coke wrote and in which he was the master lawyer had seen the end of the feudal order and the dawn of the commercial age. The Stuart England in which he judged saw the adolescence of the printed book, of King James's Bible and Shakespeare's plays. Moreover, it was an age in which kings sought ever more control over the affairs of state and of individuals but in which individuals had both new ideas about their own opportunities and new money with which to pursue them. The conflicts that emerged to be solved by the law—disputes about property, colonies, commerce, employment, bankruptcy, reputation, natural resources, religion, taxes, crimes, representative and bureaucratic government, and liberty—were taking on many new dimensions.

Coke resolved those conflicts employing the system of law in a way that seemed predictable and consistent and, most important, that was, in the end, without favoritism. He developed books that enshrined not only the results of individual conflicts but also his view of the system, justifying it with a mixture of history and reason. This view of law was a powerful tool, one that also protected certain values of long-lasting influence, especially in the new colonies then being cut into the forests of the Atlantic coast of North America. In these colonies, up to and after the American Revolution, Coke's statements of the law, and of the law's protection of the individual from unreasonable claims by the King or the Parliament, were the central learning of every lawyer.

It has been more than a century since a new edition of any of Coke's writings has been published. More surprisingly, perhaps, there never before has been an anthology that draws from the breadth of his printed works and speeches as justice and parliamentarian. A great need persists for a scholarly edition of all his works. Even so, this edition's goal is much more modest, to present the artifacts of Coke's career, essentially in the printed forms by which they influenced the course of the law, both for reappraisal and for inspiration in considering the recurrent problems of the law.

Coke's Life and Ideas

Edward Coke is a difficult and complicated figure in history, which is un-surprising, as he was a difficult man living in a turbulent time. In his youth, he was a brilliant lawyer but a political hack and a fawning courtier. In his age, he was a scholarly judge and courageous statesman but a venal father. He lived in a time, though, when the compromises of the feudal order were being supplanted on the one hand by absolute monarchy and on the other by ex-ploration and commerce.

Coke forged his views of law not by pondering its niceties but by fighting in its trenches. Coke early acquired a reverence for technique, research, and the honing of a good theory of a case in litigation. He worked hard, had a good memory, and learned the legal precedents as well as anyone ever had. He would turn these techniques and skills to the service of his clients, for whom he deployed a comprehensiveness and lack of reserve that could be breathtaking. As an ambitious young lawyer from a good family (but not a family so good as to tie him initially to the ancient landed interests) and as a protégé of the master politician and royal adviser Lord Burghley, a self-made man who saw his nation's future in its economy, it is not surprising that Coke found himself representing clients who needed new legal remedies and rules.

For Coke to argue for new results from old principles did not require him to believe that he was pursuing change, or arguing for a grand theory, or pursuing a legal revolution. He could merely uphold the rights of Parliament to make law and of the court to apply its traditional principles. By doing so, particularly when those principles included doctrines of reason and remedy, he was pursuing his clients' interests and harvesting "new corn from old fields," in the same manner lawyers had done for generations before him and for all time since. Thus, he could accept, and promote, an idea of law that was at once unchanging but also changing.

His early work therefore pursued a considerable degree of economic liberality in the law, and it is no surprise to see Coke later arguing against monopoly, against lands tied in feudal bonds, and against restraints of trade. Although he did not pursue the wholesale laissez-faire economic regime developed a century later, he was nearer to it than most in his age, and his reforms of the law made its realization all the more possible.

A great lawyer with tremendous skills devoted without reservation to the client can become a tool of tyrannical power if the client is a politician, and as the attorney general of a queen Coke adored, he was hardly immune from abusing his gifts. But when those same skills were turned to the protection of his final client, the law itself, Coke turned loose those gifts in its service.

In this way, Coke applied the same artifice he early used to win property and contract disputes when he later defended the power of Parliament and the bench, the fount and the vessel of the law. He became a tireless advocate of the monopoly of courts of law as the arbiters of disputes, challenging local courts, church courts, private arbitrators, the Chancellor, and even the King.

Coke was ever loyal to James I personally, whom he sincerely called the fountain of justice (as opposed to the fountain of law). Yet this loyalty was not without limit, and Coke argued time and again that Parliament and the Common Law remained the sole sources of the law and that all things must be done by law, particularly the defining of crimes, the levying of tax, and the judgment of cases.

Moreover, the two ideas for which James I, and later Charles I, would most persecute Coke, that judges must act not by command of the King but by the dictates of law and that the law protects the King (as opposed to an all-powerful monarchy subordinate to none but God), can easily be seen in cases he litigated and reported from the time of Elizabeth, which themselves rested on antecedents Coke took pains to enumerate. Simply, the law was not only the means by which the monarch received and gave property but also the tool that protected the monarch's interests in property. The King was powerless to change the nature of a common-law estate in his own lands. Only Parliament could do that, and it could do so only in a manner the courts would accept. In cases turning on means as varied as the common-law standards for the definition of an interest in property, the construction of the meaning of a statute, and the limitations and powers that accrue during judicial process, the monarch's interests in such cases were determined time and again by the preexisting dictates of the law, or at least what the judges proclaimed the law to have been. From such a stage—on which Coke acted practically without a peer as the consummate artist of pleading, precedent, and argument—Coke took all of the tools he would need not only to protect the Queen against her adversaries but also to protect the courts and Parliament from the later kings.

These tools made Coke a dubious courtier. At times, he was embarrassingly ingratiating, but at others his insistence on following his views of the law made him so irritating to the monarch that, had he been a man less useful in so many ways, it would have threatened his life. King James is said to have described Coke as "like a cat: throw her which way you would, she will light upon her feet."

At the height of his career, Coke stood as a barrier against royal power to dictate the outcome of the law. He argued for untrammeled discretion of the judge to "do as a judge ought to do," without royal command or assent. He argued for a single set of laws, common throughout the realm, according to which liberty and property would be reliably regulated, without the recurrent loss of liberty that accompanied courts held as special privileges by local lords, crown administrators, and church officials. The law, as Coke articulated it, protected the individual from tyrannical abuse.

This is, if nothing else, a recipe for the rule of law, of which Coke had a full vision. He saw the rule of law as a complicated amalgam of precedent and argument, reason that brought old laws to answer fresh questions, at least to the practitioner who was both well-skilled in its arcane methods and rules and well-versed in the law's special customs and obligations. The tool most essential to that vision was a comprehensive record of the methods and substance of the law, and this was the chief legacy of his writings.

Coke's Writings

English law for centuries had Year Books and scattered reports collecting cases, statute rolls collecting Acts of Parliament, and a few treatises synthesizing them both on particular topics, primarily the interests of nobles in land. Even so, prior to Coke's *Reports* and *Institutes,* no single written source of English law had managed to strike the balance between the breadth and specificity needed to convey the contours of a whole system of rules and the brevity and selectivity needed to keep the system sufficiently manageable for use. Further, times had changed, and traditional materials required revision to account for both new principles of law and new forms of dispute.

Coke began collecting his private case reports early in his career, not just recording cases he argued (with a decided preference for cases he won), but collecting other cases by watching them, speaking with principals in the opinions and arguments, and amassing a trove of others' notes. He even sent his students to hear arguments and to take notes for him when he couldn't attend, a task on which he seems often to have sent the young student and later colonist Roger Williams. By the time he became Attorney General, the quality of his notes, the range of his reports, and his authority as a lawyer made the *Reports* an instant success.

Coke's writings sometimes slant the bases for his case opinions, occasionally slanting them until, in the opinion of some, his report has turned them upside down. There are times when Coke describes precedents to support a position that would require an unusually idiosyncratic view of the precedent, and he notoriously accepts the authority of earlier law books, particularly the dubious *Mirror,* with a blithe and credulous trust. Most obviously, for all of the reading he did of history (and he read many books on history) Coke seems to have had a very anachronistic eye for the past, often reading the oldest of precedents as if they had been written in his own time, except for the authority they had gained by virtue of their antiquity. Although this anachronistic tendency might have weakened his merit as a legal authority, it also fanned the flames of his imaginative reinterpretations of ancient sources of law, a phenomenon that made possible Coke's wholesale translation of Magna Carta from the contract protecting only the nobility into the law protecting all of the crown's subjects.

Certainly a portion of the authority that Coke cited as a basis for his statements of particular rules of law ranged from questionable to nonsensical. On the other hand, the percentage of Coke's statements for which this is true is nowhere near as high as his detractors sometimes imply; it is just enough to color his enterprise a rather self-authenticating hue. And he did serve as his own authentication. Given his unparalleled personal authority, Coke simply pulled it off. Setting aside his, perhaps inevitable, removal from the bench, it mattered little that the likes of Bacon and Ellesmere griped to the King that Coke's *Reports* misconstrued the cases or that his authorities were weak. Indeed, it has mattered less that historians have plucked at the hem of Coke's gowns over his sources. The fact remained that once Coke—encyclopedia of precedent, virtuoso of pleading, law teacher, Solicitor General, Attorney General, Lord Chief Justice of *both* of the great law benches, Speaker of the House, and proud and incorruptible arbiter of the disputes of King and commoner alike—said that something was the law, almost everyone agreed. In 1824, nearly two centuries after his death, it was explained aptly. "Lord Coke," wrote Chief Justice William Best, often, "had no authority for what he states, but I am afraid we should get rid of a great deal of what is considered law in Westminster hall, if what Lord Coke says without authority is not law. He was one of the most eminent lawyers that ever presided as a judge in any court of justice."

Despite the complaints of those, like Lord Campbell, that Coke was ill-read, his writings are models of prose by a well-read, well-rounded man of his age. He sprinkles his reports with classical allusion; he is particularly fond of Virgil. Moreover, he writes complicated fact patterns with a clarity that still eludes some judges and reporters centuries later. He is a great coiner of epigrams and maxims, and many of his lines have pith, wisdom, and humor. Littered about the *Reports* and especially the *Institutes* are guarded asides to law students, cautions to practitioners, and observations on the rules of the law, some of which are still routinely quoted today. As generations of young lawyers have learned, Coke's prose can be complex and his organization diffuse, but the rewards of careful reading are abundant.

Coke's published works are essentially of three forms: reports, treatises, and speeches. He published his own reports in eleven separate folio volumes, and two appeared posthumously. (There are still more notes for reports that have never been published.) To see the reports as the sum of his judicial works would be to miss his many arguments as a lawyer and opinions as a judge, some of which were reported later by others. His lengthiest project as seen by his successor generations were his treatises, particularly the four *Institutes,* which are usually bound into only three fat folios or six fatter quartos, not including the short treatises on bail and mainprize and copyholding, and the manual on pleading. The extant speeches, other than those reported as case opinions, are largely in the form of records of the debates in Commons and in the Privy Council, although the interesting charge to the jury at Norwich falls into this category as well.

One word is in order when comparing the selections in this book to Coke's writings as a whole. Coke's writings comfortably fill a dozen books with big spines and small print, and an editor choosing what not to include is like Ali Baba in the cave of the forty thieves: there are too many treasures to carry them all away. Although the width of this edition testifies to the patience of the publisher, many wonderful and significant portions of Coke's writings remain untouched. Some of his writings are simply delightful, like his proof that mastiffs are not dogs in a statute punishing dogs that enter the King's woods, or his tale of the judge who built Westminster clock as a penalty for reducing a poor man's fine. Leaving these stories and many of the finer points of early modern common law aside has been rather painful, but those selected stand as testament to the rich domain which this edition only surveys.

Coke's Influence

At the distance of four centuries, it is easy to mistake the significance of Coke's achievements. One might overestimate Coke's contributions by missing the significance in his work of such predecessors as Fortescue, Bracton, and earlier judges, or such allies as Selden and Davies, or such adversaries as Ellesmere and Bacon. It is likewise easy to underestimate Coke's contributions by seeing them as but an articulation of principles that were rarely in doubt or by simply failing to notice their significance, breadth, or novelty.

The arena in which such mistakes are especially regrettable is in appraising Coke's contribution to the modern notion of the rule of law. A controversial and multifaceted notion, the rule of law can be thought of as the idea that no person or group controls the state but that laws are applied to everyone equally and fairly by impartial and independent people who are themselves bound by the laws to do so.

Although it dates from classical Greece, the idea of the rule of law made slow headway in a world personally governed by emperors, popes, and kings. Of course, the compromises among king, lord, and peasant necessary to maintain the feudal order were enshrined in law, but such laws were dependent on an uneasy balance of power and could guarantee neither the stability necessary for justice and predictability nor the mutability necessary for economic change and adaptability. Such a guaranty requires a relatively stable body of laws, sufficiently comprehensive to resolve the complicated questions of human dispute. It also requires methods for determining the existence of those laws and determining precisely which requirements of law govern a particular dispute. It requires tools for enforcing such a determination without regard to the status of the disputants, the biases of the judge, or other factors beyond the dispute and the rules. Last, it requires a near-monopoly of those rules as the source of resolution of disputes. Some of these requirements are terribly problematic, such as determining when a judge acts from bias, what laws may accord status, or what status may not be accorded by laws. Neither those problems nor occasional lapses alter the general requirements of the rule of law, and these requirements were each pursued quite deliberately by Coke.

The influence of this idea of law was in every sense revolutionary, especially in the new balance it struck between monarch and subject. Indeed, notions of a legally limited monarch and of common subjects who held rights, which were, thanks to Coke, now deemed to have existed since Magna Carta, and the idea of a legal machinery independent of all but the authority of the nation's legislature are nearly inextricable from the other causes of the English Civil War, of the American Revolution, and of the American Civil War.

Coke was sponsor or author of many ideas that are now embedded in the structure of the law. England has applied Coke's reports and acknowledged his lessons, and he deeply influenced such writers as Blackstone and Stephen, judges such as Lord Eldon and Lord Denning, and policymakers such as Edmund Burke. He is regularly cited still, and recent surveys of judicial databases yield surprisingly thick lists of citations to Coke's writings from the benches of the common-law world. (A few American citations are listed in the bibliography in volume three.) In all, though, judicial reaction in England and America, centuries after Coke, is now rather like the American response to the writings of Joseph Story; that is, he remains an important figure in the development of the law, whose works are authoritative but not conclusive in arguing for the meaning of ideas and laws.

There are, however, wider circles in the intellectual pool through which Coke's ideas still ripple. Milton and, later, Locke and Montesquieu argued for the protection of the citizen through orderly laws that are independent of the raw power of monarch or parliament. Likewise, Fuller's independence of the law from the church, Harrington's legal limits on the aristocracy, Hobbes's practical view of the state, and Smith's commerce free from oppressive laws are seen by many commentators today as then-novel ideas. Yet these arguments essentially traveled on roads that had been surveyed by Coke. Some, particularly Thomas Hobbes, could hardly have written their greatest works but for Coke's antecedent writing, even if it served mainly to focus their objections.

Writers of philosophical treatises strive to present a comprehensive system, designed to minimize contradiction in a single exposition. By contrast Coke wrote over a long period, encompassing numerous discrete questions, and the whole of his writings present ambiguities and contradictions in a corpus that was not designed on philosophical lines. Simply, Coke was not a philosopher but a lawyer. His works were somewhat inaccessible to the reader who was neither well-skilled in the language of the law nor prepared to become immersed in its study. All of that said, Coke's influence on the political philosophers of the seventeenth and eighteenth centuries, who generally learned the law through his writings, was substantial, and they often acknowledged their debts to him.

His influence on the practical affairs of law and state was rather more direct in America through her colonists, the likes of Roger Williams, James Otis, John Adams, James Madison, George Wythe, Thomas Jefferson, and John Marshall. From Coke, Americans took not abstract notions of government but the tools of law, among them tools of substance—citizens' rights against the state, common law supremacy over local law, legal protections of property from state invasion, limits on monopoly and restraints of trade, the right to habeas corpus, and the right to limit the burdens of taxes and criminal sanctions to those that are enacted only by the people's representatives—and tools of process—judicial independence, judicial review of statutes, judicial review of administrative officials, and judicial impeachment for favoritism or bribery. Americans also acquired the habit of case reporting, treatise writing, and statutory inventory, eventually building a vast body of written and accessible law.

Aristotle's government of laws rather than men was given a practical foundation by Coke's writings and by a career in which, as Maitland said, "The Common Law took flesh." He was an incorruptible judge, a lawyer dedicated to the integrity of law, whose personal authority and legal acumen forever altered the nature of the Common Law.

Chronology of Events

Material to the Life, Times, Writings, and Legacy of
Sir Edward Coke from the Death of Henry VIII to the
Opinion in *Marbury v. Madison*

38 Hen. 8; 1 Edw. 6

January 28, 1547   Henry VIII dies; Edward VI becomes King.

February 1, 1552   Edward Coke is born, to Robert Coke, of Lincoln's Inn, and Winifred Coke (née Knightley), in Mileham, Norfolk. He later said that his birth occurred so suddenly that his mother delivered him on the hearth and not in her bed.

July 6, 1553   Edward VI dies.

July 10, 1553   Lady Jane Grey proclaimed Queen.

1 Mar.; 1&2 Phil. & M.

August 3, 1553   Mary Tudor, a Catholic, proclaimed Queen; Lady Jane is sent to the Tower.

October 1, 1553   Mary crowned Queen.

November 17, 1558   Mary dies. Elizabeth, a Protestant, is pronounced Queen.

1 Eliz.

January 15, 1559   Elizabeth I is crowned Queen.

1561   Robert Coke, Edward's father, dies. Edward is nine.

1561(?)–67   Coke attends the Norwich free school, studying with Mr. Walter Hawe.

October 25, 1567	Coke matriculates at Trinity College, Cambridge; he may have been tutored by Whitgift, Archbishop of Canterbury.
1569	Winifred Coke, Edward's mother, dies.
December? 1570	Coke goes down from Cambridge without an earned degree. An M.A. would later be conferred by grace of the university.
January 21, 1571	Coke enters Clifford's Inn, London.
April 24, 1572	Coke enters Inner Temple as a student of law; he gains particular attention in The Cook's Case, argued on the quality of food served in the Inn.
April 20, 1578	Coke is called to the bar, a year early under the rules of the Inns.
1579	Coke defends a vicar, Mr. Denny, from Lord Cromwell in an action for libel based on a religious dispute and Denny's statement that Cromwell, who hired preachers who abjured the queen's Prayer Book, "like of men who maintain sedition against the Queen's proceedings." Coke wins an arrest of judgment by spotting a pleading by his opponent based on a faulty translation into English of a statute. See The Lord Cromwell's Case, p. 105.
1579–81	Coke is counsel in Shelley's Case, argued by order of Elizabeth I before the Lord Chancellor and all the judges of the realm. The case turns on whether land can be bound up by granting the land to a person for life, with a remainder to that person's heirs. Coke argued successfully that such a limitation ought to be construed to create a single perpetual estate, a fee simple absolute, for the person receiving the land. This allowed the recipient and subsequent grantees greater ability to transfer the land. See Shelley's Case, p. 6.

1579–85	Coke appears as junior barrister in numerous cases under Edmund Plowden and John Popham. He keeps a private notebook with transcriptions of cases earlier reported in manuscripts, a commonplace book, and notes of his own professional and personal life; in time, this notebook will serve as the basis for his *Reports*.
1580–83	Coke appointed Reader, or lecturer, of Lyon's Inn; this appointment is extraordinary, as it usually is made to men ten years or more his senior.
1580–85	Coke purchases manors throughout Norfolk, raising concerns he is monopolizing the whole land market there. He is said to have been allowed by the Crown to purchase only "one acre more" with which he purchases an estate named "Castle Acre," which had as much acreage as he had earlier possessed.
1582	Coke circulates a manuscript of his report of Shelley's Case.
August 13, 1582	Edward Coke marries Bridget Paston, the "first and best wife," whose dowry was £30,000; they would have ten children and happily reside in Huntingfield Hall, Suffolk. Throughout their marriage, Coke would commute from his house in Castle Yard to Huntingfield between terms.
1582	London municipal water is first moved in the city by mechanical pumps.
1583	Coke defends Lacey for murder.
1584	Coke first serves as justice of the peace on the Norfolk Commission of the Peace; he is reappointed in 1586, 1588, and 1591.
	Coke defends Flemming for unorthodox baptism, having the indictment dismissed for failing to state its relationship to an earlier conviction, raising the

chance of double jeopardy. However, he loses a case for a copyholder, despite his arguments from history and pleading requirements.

1585   Coke successfully argues that the Queen's grant of an abbey did not also grant a dependent rectory because the general language of the abbey grant was technically insufficient to grant the rectory as a portion of the abbey.

Coke elected Recorder, a part-time judge, of Coventry.

1585–90   Edward becomes a protégé of William Cecil, Lord Burghley, Elizabeth's Lord Treasurer and great counselor.

April 2, 1586   Coke elected Recorder of Norwich.

1586   Coke represents the Register of the Court of Admiralty in a suit for proceeds from the office of the co-Register. He represents the Vicar of Pancras, arguing *against* a prohibition of a dispute in the Spiritual Court for the payment of tithes. He appeals a partition of property that fails to specify either the statutory basis of the partition or the nature of the estate by which the lands were held.

1587   Christopher Marlowe's play *Tamburlaine the Great* is performed, establishing blank verse as the medium of choice on the stage.

Coke argues Sir Thomas Gresham's Case, on behalf of Lady Gresham, whom he saves from having to pay a fine for alienating a use. He also argues Cooper's Case, an action for the killing of eighteen rabbits.

April 5, 1588	Thomas Hobbes born.
1588–90	Coke begins careful note-taking of a wide range of cases argued by both himself and others, as well as collecting information for reports of unreported cases. By 1591, he appears to have intended to publish his reports, the first of which would appear in print in 1600.
1589	Coke attends Parliament as a burgess for Aldburgh, Suffolk.
	Coke wins Read and Nash's Case, another case involving the Greshams, and The Lord Paget's Case, both of which are cases on the regulation of uses, by which lands could be held by one person for the benefit of another. He loses an unusual case with implications for corporations, in which church wardens sue for the theft of the church bell committed before their tenure, a detail that required Coke to win a difficult argument, but he lost when the court decreed that later wardens must consider the loss to be to the parishioners, not to themselves.
	William Lee invents a knitting machine, allowing mass textile production.
1590 (est.)	The microscope is invented.
1590	Coke defends Guildford, who is charged with the crime of recruiting for the Roman church, securing his release because the charge was brought too late.
	Coke is made Bencher, or a senior lawyer, of the Inner Temple.
October 14, 1591	Coke is unanimously elected Recorder of London, voted £100 pension; he will serve as Recorder only until June of 1592.

1591   Coke invents a defense plea to confess and avoid a
                        plaintiff's title, which is useful in claiming that the
                        defendant is the rightful occupant of property, even
                        though the plaintiff might have a legal right to
                        own it.

1592   Coke is appointed Reader, or lecturer on law, by the
                        benchers of Inner Temple; he lectures particularly on
                        uses. His lectures would be cut short by an
                        evacuation to escape the plague.

June 11, 1592   On the recommendation of Burghley, Elizabeth I
                        appoints Coke Solicitor General. At the time of his
                        appointment, Coke is chastised by Elizabeth for
                        bringing arguments against her interests in taking
                        estates by escheat, to which he tearfully responds,
                        assuring her of his loyalty to her.

1593   The freeholders of Norfolk elect Coke a member of
                        Commons "unanimous, free, and spontaneous,
                        without any solicitation on my part."

February 19, 1593   Coke is elected Speaker of the House of Commons;
                        his opening address as Speaker both recites an
                        ancient tradition of strong monarchical authority
                        and, according to the new custom, asks for freedom
                        of speech in Commons. He is a loyal lieutenant to
                        the Queen throughout the session, burying a bill on
                        reformation of the ecclesiastical courts but delivering
                        up large new subsidies, or taxes, although he did
                        much to protect Parliament's "ancient" rights. See
                        Coke's speeches, p. 1187.

April 10, 1593   Parliament is dissolved; Coke gives a speech on the
                        antiquity of Parliament, extolling its obedience to
                        the sovereign. See p. 1191.

June 1593   Christopher Marlowe dies.

April 1594   Thomas Egerton is made Master of the Rolls,
                        vacating the office of Attorney General. Coke and

Francis Bacon both seek the post. Coke is opposed by the Earl of Essex, the Queen's favorite and a sponsor of Bacon's. Coke is favored by Burghley. This is the period of Bacon's and Coke's first great rivalry; Bacon refers to Coke as "the Huddler."

April 10, 1594

Coke is made Attorney General. Although Coke believes the appointment is the result of Burghley's patronage, he is likely to have been the Queen's own choice. Coke obstructs Bacon's appointment as Solicitor General, performing the duties of both offices for over a year.

1594–95

Romeo and Juliet is first performed.

1595

Attorney General Coke argues for the power of the church court called the High Commission in Cawdrey's Case, in which a priest was barred from preaching. The power of the Commission to employ the penalty for a first offense is upheld, although the penalty had been allowed under the statute only for repeat offenses. Coke's precedent-laden report of the opinion would serve as a basis for asserting royal jurisdiction over all questions of church law. The precedents of this report were strongly attacked by the Jesuit Robert Parsons at the time, and Coke would have his own arguments with the Commission in later years. He also argues a prohibition to assess the tithes owed a rector when a vicar changed the crops in a field from corn to saffron.

1595–1603

Religious dissent from Catholics and Puritan non-conformists grows. Coke leads efforts to suppress pamphlets, attributed to the Jesuit Robert Parsons, promoting the Infanta of Spain as Elizabeth's successor.

Elizabeth's court is plagued by assassination plots, real and rumored. Coke oversees numerous interrogations of defendants, some under torture in prison, some in court, beginning with the trial of a Spanish spy, Elizabeth's physician Roderigo Lopez, for conspiring to kill her.

1596   Coke, as Attorney General, represents the Archbishop of Canterbury, successfully defending him against a prohibition seeking to end tithes owed on lands taken by the Crown in the dissolution of the monasteries. See The Archbishop of Canterbury's Case, p. 49.

Coke is elected Treasurer of the Inner Temple.

1597   Francis Bacon first publishes his *Essayes*. The first book of ten will be enlarged in subsequent editions to thirty-eight, in *The Essaies of Sr Francis Bacon Knight* (1613), and to fifty-eight, in *The Essayes or Counsels, Civill and Morall* (1625).

June 27, 1598   Bridget Coke dies, aged 34.

August 1598   Coke courts Lady Elizabeth Hatton, granddaughter of Burghley, the widow of the nephew and heir of Lord Chancellor Hatton. Bacon is also a suitor for her, being promoted to her by Essex. Coke proposes to her at Burghley's funeral and is accepted, thanks to support for him from her father Thomas Cecil, the new Lord Burghley, and her uncle, Robert Cecil.

November 7, 1598   Coke, aged 50, and Lady Elizabeth, aged 20, are married, "a strange match, and which seemed to afford more amusement to bystanders than comfort to the parties concerned." They are married secretly, violating a church canon against marriages in private houses or without a license or the publication of banns. Archbishop Whitgift moves to excommunicate Edward, Lady Elizabeth, the second Lord Burghley, and the rector who married them. Edward petitions for a dispensation, which is granted on account of Coke's "ignorance of the ecclesiastical law."

August 23, 1599   Frances Coke, the first daughter of Coke and Lady Elizabeth, is born, ten months after their marriage, despite false rumors that Lady Elizabeth was pregnant before her wedding. Queen Elizabeth I is Frances's godmother.

1599   Edmund Spenser, the poet and author of *The Faerie Queene,* dies, aged 47.

1600 or 1601   First performances of *Julius Caesar* and of *Hamlet.*

Summer 1600   Coke argues and wins The Case of Alton Woods, winning a large estate for the Queen, using very technical rules of inheritance and property law, but arguing for a narrow understanding of the estate tail, which would help tie lands up in families and diminish the free trade in lands.

June 1600   The Queen's former favorite, Robert Devereux, Second Earl of Essex, is tried before a special commission following his disastrous attempt to quell a rebellion in Ireland, capped by his making a private truce with the rebel leader, although his real crime was to disobey the Queen in a secret marriage to one of her maids of honor. Essex is confined to his house and then deprived of most of his honors. He loses the Queen's favor and financial support and, apparently, becomes deranged.

1600   The first volume of *Les Reports de Edward Coke* is published by T. Wight. See p. 3.

February 9, 1601   Believing his life endangered following an attack on his friend Henry Wrothesley, Earl of Southampton, Essex accelerates a variety of conspiracies, which

amount to rebellion. He locks four members of the
Privy Council in his house and attempts to rally
Londoners to assault the Queen's guard, resulting in
a few small riots that end when Thomas Cecil
denounces him as a traitor. Essex is arrested the next
day.

February 19, 1601   Coke prosecutes Essex and Southampton for
insurrection. Coke employs savage oratory against
the defendants during the trial. Essex is convicted
and, on February 25, executed. Southampton is
convicted, but his sentence is later commuted to life
in prison.

March 1601   Coke prosecutes other conspirators in the Essex
rebellion.

1601   Bacon issues a book on Essex, *A Declaration of the
Practices & Treasons Attempted and Committed by
Robert, Late Earle of Essex* (1601), which he would
later repudiate in large part in *Sir Francis Bacon His
Apologie, in Certaine Imputations Concerning the Late
Earle of Essex* (1604).

Coke prosecutes Twyne's Case, bringing a criminal
action against a debtor who commits a fraudulent
conveyance to prefer one creditor over another.

1601–10   Coke grows more aloof from the bar; his
professional rivalry with Francis Bacon, K.C., grows
more intense.

August 1601   Elizabeth I visits Coke at his house in Stoke. He
presents her with jewels and gifts worth over £1,000.

1602   *Le Second Part des Reportes del Edward Coke* and *Le
Tierce Part des Reportes* are published by T. Wight.
See pp. 37; 58.

1 Jac.

March 24, 1603   Elizabeth I dies. James VI of Scotland is proclaimed
                   also as James I of England.

May 22, 1603   Edward Coke is knighted. In the months that
                   follow, his wife Lady Elizabeth becomes a confidant
                   of the new Queen, Anne.

Spring 1603   A Catholic plot forms to capture King James and to
                   demand concessions for recusants. The plot includes
                   Lord Cobham, a friend of Sir Walter Raleigh, whom
                   Cobham, after his arrest, implicates in the plot,
                   although Cobham later recants his claim.

July 25, 1603   James VI is crowned James I.

1603   James publishes a manifesto for his rule, *Trewe
                   Lawes of Free Monarchies* (or, "True Laws of Free
                   Monarchies").

                   Thomas Bodley opens the restored library of the
                   Duke Humfrey in Oxford, which in 1610 will
                   become a repository of all copyrighted books in the
                   realm.

1603–5   English deforestation drives lumber prices too high
                   to use wood for industrial fuel, promoting the
                   industrial use of coal.

Summer 1603   London is in the grip of the plague.

November 17, 1603 Coke's nadir. He prosecutes Sir Walter Raleigh for
                   treason, employing disgraceful invective and unfair
                   tactics, which later contribute to the stay of
                   Raleigh's execution. Raleigh is imprisoned in the
                   Tower until 1616, when he is released to prosecute a
                   gold-stealing expedition against Spanish Guyana. It
                   is a politically embarrassing failure, and James in
                   1618 would enforce the suspended death warrant,
                   and Raleigh would be executed.

1604   The fourth volume of the *Reports* is published by
                    T. Wight. See p. 93.

                    Othello is first performed.

1605   The fifth volume of the *Reports* is published by the
                    Companie of Stationers. See p. 125.

                    Argument of the Articuli Cleri. Archbishop Bancroft
                    calls the law judges to answer for prohibitions
                    against the Church. While the written answers are
                    attributed to the law judges, the hand of Attorney
                    General Coke may well have guided their pen.

                    El Ingenioso Hidalgo Don Quixote de la Mancha, the
                    first part of Cervantes's masterpiece, with its ironic
                    but profound homage to the ideals of feudal knight
                    errantry, is published in Spain; it reaches England in
                    translation in 1612.

                    John Cowell publishes his treatise on English law
                    based on Roman law, *Institutiones Juris Anglicani ad
                    Methodum Institutionum Justiniani.*

                    Orlando Gibbons becomes organist of the Chapel
                    Royal.

November 4, 1605   Outside a cellar under the House of Lords, Guy
                    Fawkes is discovered with a slow match and thirty-
                    six barrels of gunpowder, intending to blow up
                    Parliament during James's state opening on
                    November 5. Sir Robert Catesby has devised the
                    plot, carried out with six Roman Catholic
                    conspirators.

January 27, 1606   Coke examines and prosecutes Fawkes, Catesby, and
                    the other Gunpowder plotters; although he develops
                    the clear evidence of their guilt, he also is, again,
                    unusually cruel. They are all executed.

1606

A. Islip for the Companie of Stationers publishes a table summarizing the first five volumes of the *Reports*. A series of updates will follow, culminating in this series in *Fasiculus florum, Or a Handfull of Flowers Gathered out of the Severall Bookes of Sir E. Coke* in 1618.

Ben Jonson's comedy *Volpone* is first performed.

Australia is discovered, by the Dutch.

In Bates's Case, Coke and Chief Justice Popham uphold the power of the King to slap a tariff on imported currants, upholding the opinion of the Barons of Exchequer that the King could regulate trade only if the regulation was in the public interest; this is an opinion that Coke would later regret. See p. 441.

March 28, 1606

Trial of Henry Garnett, English Superior of the Jesuits, for concealing the Gunpowder Plot. Coke prosecutes. Garnett confesses to knowing of the plot under the seal of confession. Based largely on testimony from jail-house spies, Garnett is convicted of misprision of treason and executed.

March–April 1606

Coke assists Popham in drafting the First Royal Charter of the new Virginia Company, a charter that assures that British subjects in the colony and their children born there "shall have and enjoy all Liberties, Franchises, and Immunities, within any of our other Dominions, to all Intents and Purposes, as if they had been abiding and born, within this our Realm of England, or any other of our said Dominions." This promise is renewed in the Charter of 1609 and later charters.

June 20, 1606

Coke is created Serjeant at Law, an honorific granted by the Crown, which was necessary to serve as a senior judge. The memorial rings he had engraved to give to senior lawyers are inscribed *Lex est tutissima cassis,* or "Law is the safest helmet," an abbreviation for a whole maxim: "Law is the safest helmet; under the shield of law no one is deceived."

Coke is made Chief Justice of the Court of Common Pleas, on the same day he is created Serjeant.

August 4, 1606   Coke presides at the Assizes at Norwich. He charges jury to punish corrupt officials. See p. 521.

1607   Sir Moyle Finch's Case is apparently Coke's first case as Chief Justice.

Coke assists the Chancellor in settling the rights of Prince Henry to manors in the Duchy of Cornwall, taking the manors from the grantees who had been given them in fee by Elizabeth. Coke had brought the case as Attorney General.

The sixth volume of the *Reports* is published by the Companie of Stationers. See p. 149.

John Smith leads 120 colonists to settle Virginia.

1607–8   Coke begins judicial battles with the church court called the High Commission, which punishes crimes against church obedience: Prosecutions in the Commission had been stopped by prohibitions from the common law courts. Coke rules that the Commission is limited to ecclesiastical matters and can be prohibited by the law courts from disciplining a lawyer who argued before the Commission, who had applied to the law courts for a prohibition. See High Commission, p. 425,

Langdale's Case, p. 471, Nicholas Fuller's Case,
p. 454, Premunire, p. 447.

1607–12   In a series of cases, Coke and the judges of
Common Pleas rule that the Court of High
Commission has no authority to arrest laymen and
that a layman who resists arrest by a pursuivant, an
official of the Commission, and kills him is not
guilty of murder. They issue prohibitions against the
Commission, enjoining them from imprisoning
people, and they grant release by habeas corpus to
others. See Anthony Roper's Case, p. 461, Case de
Modo Decimandi, p. 505; High Commission, p. 425.
Similar orders are entered against a variety of local
courts, particularly that in York, for exceeding their
jurisdiction or deciding cases without giving the
degree of legal protection required. These
prohibitions will set the law courts on a political
collision course not only with the church and nobles
but also with the King, who was pleased by the
absolutist doctrines of the church courts and whose
courtiers controlled the local courts.

1608   A Parliamentary commission assigned in 1603 to
determine the rights in England of a Scot born after
James's kingship in England fails to resolve the
question, and a test case is created by Parliament to
resolve the issue in the courts. In Calvin's Case, or
the Case of the "Post Nati," Coke, with a large
majority, accepts the King's view and agrees that
Scots born after the accession of James VI as James I
of England are born subject to the same sovereign
and so entitled to the privileges of native English
subjects. This case would have far-reaching effects as
the basis for extending the law over colonial
subjects. See p. 166.

Prompted largely by the significance of Calvin's Case, Coke prepares the seventh volume of the *Reports,* which is published by the Companie of Stationers. See p. 161.

November 10, 1608[1]   In response to the Archbishop of Canterbury's complaint to the King of the prohibitions of the High Commission, James moves to resolve the case himself. Coke both defends his answer in Fuller's Case and argues against the King's acting as a judge of law. Moving from a traditional rationale for such prohibitions that the law judges are agents of the King, Coke asserts that the law is itself the essential measure of such cases and that judges, not the King, interpret the law, which is not based on reason in general but based on the artificial reason of past cases applied by legal custom. In response to Coke's statements a furious James nearly strikes him; Coke falls on all fours and begs his pardon, and Cecil, the Lord Treasurer, intervenes to distract the King. See Prohibitions del Roy, p. 478.

November 24 and   Nicholas Fuller's cause is heard by the King's Bench,
26, 1608   which finds him guilty of schism; he is fined and imprisoned for nine weeks. See p. 454.

December 9, 1608   John Milton is born.

February 1609   Coke is summoned by the King to explain the fifty or sixty prohibitions entered against the court of the President of York, about which the King "had conceived great displeasure." Coke describes the legal

1. The reader is cautioned as to the reliability of specific dates for conferences and hearings, particularly from 1608 to 1613. The official records often conflict; for that matter, so do private accounts and secondary sources. Most dates are recorded here relying on Coke's notebook entries.

infirmities of three or four representative cases, apparently to James's satisfaction. See Prohibitions, p. 501. Later that year, he appears to have been called again to a second conference on the same question.

May–July 1609   The King holds a conference of all the judges and the Privy Council on the jurisdiction of the church court of High Commission and law courts. The particular object of the debate is over the exaction of the modus decimandi, a special form of tithe, or customary tax paid to the church, and the question is whether jurisdiction to enforce this payment is to be in the church courts or the law courts, Coke arguing that only Parliament could put them elsewhere. The debate rages over several meetings, Coke convincing James that the High Commission should rule only on serious offences of church law. See de Modo Decimandi, p. 505.

1609   In Italy, Galileo Galilei develops an improved telescope for measuring heavenly movement.

February 9, 1610   Parliament is in session. Coke is Chief Justice, and so an ex officio adviser to the Lords, but is not active.

1610   Coke rules that a prohibition should not be given to a party after a ruling has been made in the Spiritual Court.

July 7, 1610   Parliament sends an address to the Crown, noting that James's Royal proclamations had affected the liberty and property of subjects and had changed laws and penalties. James agrees to sign a law forbidding new impositions by the Crown without the consent of Parliament.

September 20, 1610   Coke is summoned to the Council by the King to
                     declare whether the King by proclamation can
                     restrict building in London or regulate the trade in
                     starch, necessary for ruffed collars. In one of his
                     most significant attacks on the royal prerogative,
                     Coke, with Chief Justice Fleming, Chief Baron
                     Tanfield, and Baron Altham, refuses to answer
                     without consulting other judges, after which he
                     issues an opinion admitting the King may require
                     subjects to obey the law but cannot extend his
                     prerogative beyond its legal bounds, cannot create
                     new crimes, and cannot enlarge the criminal
                     jurisdiction of Star Chamber. See Proclamations,
                     p. 486.

Fall 1610   The Royal College of Physicians fines Thomas
                     Bonham, a Cambridge medical graduate, for
                     practicing medicine near London without a license
                     from them to do so. The College arrests and jails
                     him when he does not pay the fine and continues to
                     practice. Coke, with Judges Warburton and Daniel,
                     rules that the College could not enforce a monopoly
                     by acting as judge in a case to which it is a party. In
                     discussing the power of the College under its
                     Parliamentary authority, Coke makes one of his
                     most famous statements, "The common law will
                     control Acts of Parliament, and sometimes adjudge
                     them utterly void; for when an Act of Parliament is
                     against common right and reason, or repugnant, or
                     impossible to be performed, the common law will
                     control it and adjudge such Act to be void." See
                     Dr. Bonham's Case, p. 264.

1610–15   Despite the King's exasperation, his respect for Coke
                     remains strong. Coke becomes a friend and mentor
                     to Prince Charles.

1611   The Parliament is finally dissolved on February 9, 1611.

The eighth volume of the *Reports* is published by the Companie of Stationers. See p. 244.

William Byrd publishes his last work, *Psalmes, Songs, and Sonnets.*

In an effort by the new Archbishop and the King to mute Coke's criticism of the High Commission, Coke is appointed to a newly reorganized High Commission. In an October meeting of the Commission, however, Coke refuses to sit with it, claiming not to have seen the articles for the new body, pleading ignorance of what the Commission does and arguing it was a problem not for the Court of Common Pleas but for the King's Bench. While nothing is resolved that day, the matter seems not to have been further pressed by either side. See High Commission, Appendix I, p. 1307.

The authorized edition of the Bible, often called the King James Version, is published.

April 1611   Archbishop Abbot is installed as the new Archbishop of Canterbury.

1612   Coke prohibits extra-jurisdictional proceedings by the Lord President of Wales and by the Lord President of the North, and he reverses attempts in the Court of Marshalsea to act beyond its jurisdiction. He also prohibits the Archbishop of York from suing for a debt in the Court of Exchequer at York.

May 24, 1612   Robert Cecil, Earl of Salisbury, Lord Treasurer, Secretary of State, and Master of Wards, and Coke's friend and supporter, dies. A series of maneuvers in the royal court, in which Bacon moves sharply against Coke, follow over the next year.

1613   The ninth part of the *Reports* is published by the
                        Companie of Stationers. See p. 287.

                        Coke is made a member of the Privy Council.

October 25, 1613   James acts on Bacon's advice to reduce Chief Justice
                        Coke's income and power by a promotion to the
                        superior but less significant Court of the King's
                        Bench, a nominal promotion but actually an attempt
                        to silence him. Attorney General Hobart is
                        promoted to Chief Justice of the Court of Common
                        Pleas, and Bacon becomes Attorney General.

1614   Coke's oldest son, Robert, marries Lady Theophila
                        Berkeley.

                        Chief Justice Hobart rules, in *Day v. Savage,*
                        "Because even an Act of Parliament, made against
                        natural equity, as to make a man Judge in his own
                        case, is void in itself, for *Jura nature sunt
                        immutabilia,* and they are *leges legum.*"

                        The "Addled Parliament" begins session, but the
                        assembly is heavy with Puritans and lasts only a few
                        weeks before being dismissed, accomplishing
                        nothing.

                        James, short of funds without a Parliamentary grant
                        of supply, demands "benevolences," or gifts of
                        money from the great men. Coke gives an unusually
                        large amount, £200. Coke writes that benevolences
                        are not illegal because they are not taxes but
                        offerings of free will. See Exaction of Benevolence,
                        p. 496.

                        Bacon prosecutes Peacham, an old clergyman, for
                        treason, on the basis of a drafted but undelivered
                        sermon found by agents who broke into his house.
                        The sermon held that subjects may, in rare
                        circumstances, resist a sovereign attempting to

subvert their liberties. Peacham refused to confess treason, despite torture on the rack. Bacon seeks from Coke an opinion on the legality of the charge, prior to the trial. Coke refuses to give an opinion that does not follow the forms of argument, conference, and vote of the bench, and when his view is finally given, he decides (much to Bacon's shock) that Peacham has not committed high treason. At a trial six months later before a hostile bench, Peacham is found guilty, although his execution is not carried out, and he dies in prison.

Coke publishes his *Book of Entries,* a collection of forms for pleading. See p. 567.

John Selden publishes his first major book, *Titles of Honour.*

The tenth part of the *Reports* is published by the Companie of Stationers. See p. 326.

Cambridge University elects Coke to be High Steward, an honorary office.

James meets George Villiers, later the Duke of Buckingham, who would become the King's favorite, perhaps his private consort, effectively controlling patronage and royal authority for both James and, later, Charles I. Buckingham's influence was necessary for anyone in Court to advance in title; his influence would lead to several disastrous wars with Spain and France and to the fall from popularity of Charles with the people and nobility, and would hasten the English Civil War.

1615   Coke rules that the Common Law makes treason of suggesting the murder of the King.

The eleventh part of the *Reports,* the last volume of the *Reports* to be published while Coke lived, is published by the Companie of Stationers. See p. 384.

1616   Sir Thomas Overbury is murdered by agents of his
        wife. James seeks to shield the murderers, the
        Countess of Essex and Robert Carr, James I's former
        favorite and Earl of Somerset. Coke examines over
        300 witnesses, proving Essex and Somerset had
        instigated the poisoning. Although his prosecution is
        universally praised, rumors circulate that he has also
        discovered evidence of other crimes and suspicious
        events, including the death in 1612 of Henry, Prince
        of Wales, rumors fanned by Coke's dismissal the
        next year.

        Captain James Smith, the leader of the Virginia
        Colony at Jamestown, publishes *A Description of
        New England.* Besides the regular run, Smith
        specially prints two copies with presentation title
        pages, one copy for Ellesmere and one "For the
        Right Honorable Sir Edward Coke, Lord Chiefe
        Justice of England."

        Ben Jonson writes *Underwoods,* including an homage
        to Coke (at LXV), who of all the King's servants
        there were none "whom fortune aided less nor virtue
        more," when "being the stranger's help and the poor
        man's aid, Thy just defenses made th' oppressor
        afraid."

        Ellesmere, the Lord Chancellor, grants an injunction
        against a judgment obtained by fraud from the
        King's Bench. Coke seeks to have the party who was
        enjoined from his judgment bring an indictment for
        the crime of praemunire (improperly using church
        procedures) against the original defendant. The
        grand jury refuses to indict.

        James asserts the power to grant commendams,
        temporary church appointments that have revenues
        assigned to bishops.

April 1616	Deaths of William Shakespeare and Miguel de Cervantes Saavedra.

April 25, 1616 — Bacon acts for James to assert the prerogative of *Rege inconsulto,* that he has the power to advise judges before they rule, and orders them to stay their judgment until he advises them. Coke and the judges rule, sending a letter to James that they must do the law, and that they did it.

June 6, 1616 — James summons the bench and condemns them all for allowing lawyers' insolence in questioning his power. All twelve, including Coke, fall to their knees and beg his pardon, but in Coke's finest hour, he refuses to admit that the King had a prerogative to command him to stay the proceedings, which would violate his oath as judge. Bacon and Ellesmere argue that Coke was obliged to wait on the King's counsel, a point the other law judges concede. Abandoned by his fellow judges, Coke answers that his obligation is "to do that which shall be fit for a judge to do." James suggests that what the judge should do is to know and administer the ancient law, an injunction that well describes Coke's later project of the *Institutes.* See *Commendams* and the King's Displeasure, p. 1310.

June 20, 1616 — James I rules the Chancellor has jurisdiction for the injunction over the law courts.

Mid-June 1616 — Coke denies Buckingham, the royal favorite, the power to assign a new holder as the office of chief clerk in the Court of Common Pleas, keeping the position for judicial assignment.

June 26, 1616 — Coke is summoned to the Privy Council and charged with various offenses, including failing to pay a debt to the Crown he accepted from his father-in-law, Christopher Hatton, extending his jurisdiction too far through praemunire, and insulting the King in the commendams matter. Coke's defense falls on deaf ears. See Coke's Hearing, 1616, p. 1323.

June 30, 1616 — Lord Treasurer Suffolk, on behalf of the Privy Council, orders Coke to be sequestered in chambers, to be barred from riding as a judge on circuit to hold assizes in outlying cities, to revise his *Reports* and prepare them for censorship by the king, not to call himself "Lord Chief Justice of England" but only Chief Justice of the King's Bench, and not to let his coachman ride without his hat.

October 2, 1616 — Coke reports to the Privy Council that he has repaired the *Reports,* listing five quite minor corrections. The primary charge was against Coke's report in Dr. Bonham's Case, in which he made no real changes. Bacon continues to agitate for his dismissal.

October 17, 1616 — At another hearing, Coke is advised to consider five new points in his *Reports.* Bacon draws up a list of Coke's moves against the King's powers and favorites, which he sends the King.

November 14, 1616 — James resolves to remove Coke from the bench for his "perpetual turbulent carriage."

James issues a *supersedeas,* drafted by Bacon, which removes Coke as Chief Justice of the King's Bench: "For certain causes now moving us, we will that you shall be no longer our Chief Justice to hold pleas before us, and we command you that you no longer interfere in that office, and by virtue of this presence, we at once remove and exonerate you from the same."

November 18, 1616 — Henry Montague is sworn in as Chief Justice of the King's Bench by a triumphant Ellesmere, who admonishes Montague to remember "the removing and putting down of your late predecessor, and by whom: the great King of Great Britain."

1616–21   Coke is given no major positions but is assigned a series of Star Chamber prosecutions of Dutch merchants exporting coin, of Lord Treasurer Suffolk on charges of bribery, and of Attorney General Yelverton, on political grounds. He is assigned to royal commissions on banishing Jesuits and seminarians, on negotiating a treaty with the Dutch regarding East Indian trade, on inquiring into fines owed as taxes on manors, and on examining the trade in weapons to foreign lands.

1617   Coke and Lady Elizabeth have a prolonged, very public fight over the control of their properties.

March–July 1617   In a blatant move to restore his fortunes at court, Coke contrives to marry his daughter Lady Frances to Sir John Villiers, the penniless brother of Buckingham, the royal favorite. Without consulting his wife or daughter, Coke offers her hand to Villiers, who is twice her age but smitten with her beauty and wealth. Lady Elizabeth hides her daughter and tries to marry her to the Earl of Oxford by a ruse based on a forged letter from him. Coke gets a search warrant and leads an armed party to Oatlands, a summer house of his wife's cousins, breaking in and taking Frances by force back to his house, Stoke Pogis. Bacon attempts to intercede with Buckingham and the King to prevent the marriage. Bacon, on a charge by Attorney General Yelverton, prosecutes Coke in the Star Chamber for kidnapping. Lady Elizabeth attempts to take her daughter back but fails, and she also is prosecuted and jailed. The King and Buckingham side with

Coke, and the King chides Bacon for jealousy. Bacon supports the match.

September 29, 1617   Lady Frances and Sir John Villiers are married. James I gives her away. Coke provides a dowry of £10,000. Lady Elizabeth acquiesces, from prison. Lady Frances will later elope with Sir Robert Howard, fleeing the country in man's clothing, give birth to a bastard son, and die abroad.

Late 1617   Coke is restored to the Privy Council.

November 2, 1617   Lady Elizabeth is released from her imprisonment (in a London alderman's house) and renews a life dedicated to ridiculing her husband.

1619 (circa)   William Harvey discovers the role of the heart in the circulation of blood.

1620   Coke is made a Lord Commissioner of the Treasury.

Coke is elected to the new Parliament in an honest election for the borough of Liskeard, Cornwall.

Bacon publishes his book on philosophical method, *Instauratio Magna,* also known as *Novum Organum,* in which he attacks the sufficiency of most general principles as a basis for deduction, to great critical acclaim.

November 21, 1620   A group of 102 radical Puritans of the English Separation Church land well off course from their target in Virginia. They found Plymouth Colony in Massachusetts Bay and would become known as the "Pilgrim Fathers," following a speech by Daniel Webster in the nineteenth century. Tradition suggests that they carried a copy of Coke's First *Institute* among their possessions on their ship, the *Mayflower.*

January 30, 1621   Parliament commences.

January–June 1621   A Bill for Supply, a request by the King for the Commons to grant him funds, is moved by Secretary Calvert. Coke, de facto leader of the opposition in Commons, moves that the request for supply and the petition for grievances against Parliament's privileges be referred together to a committee of the whole House. Coke presents a defense of Parliament based on Magna Carta. He is assisted in his efforts throughout the Parliament by John Selden, who is not then a member.

Coke attacks a parliamentarian named Sheppard, who is expelled from the House for arguing against a Puritan-sponsored bill to ban dancing on the Sabbath, which he held should be Saturday.

Coke assists in several impeachments, including proceedings against Bacon for twenty-eight charges of misconduct as Chancellor, mainly by accepting gifts of money from litigants before him (although many of these donors lost their cases). Bacon is fined £40,000, banished from office and Parliament, and imprisoned in the Tower, although his fine is later remitted and he serves just one day. The King would pardon him in 1624.

Coke supports bills for free trade and against monopolies.

James suggests that Parliament be suspended from May to November, which Coke opposes as against Parliament's privileges to decide on its adjournment, even though the King could dismiss it. Coke succeeds in obstructing a royal commission requiring adjournment of the Commons, after which a majority of the House vote to adjourn. See p. 1194.

June 21, 1621   On Coke's recommendation, Roger Williams, a future champion of religious tolerance and leader of the colony of Rhode Island, is admitted to be a scholar in Sutton's Hospital, a school later named Charter House. Williams would later serve as a copyist for Coke, recording hearings in Star Chamber and elsewhere. He later attends Pembroke College, Cambridge, and appears to have briefly studied law under Coke before emigrating. See Sutton's Hospital, p. 347.

1621   Robert Burton publishes *The Anatomy of Melancholy.*

November–   Parliament returns. Coke moves Parliament to pass
December 1621   resolutions to the King advising him against an alliance, through marriage, with Spain. The King orders the House not to discuss such matters and denies them any privileges by right. Coke authors a protestation arguing for the liberties of Parliament, including parliamentarians' freedom of speech, as "the ancient and undoubted birthright and inheritance of the subjects of England." See p. 1214.

December 14, 1621   Coke is passed over for Lord Treasurer when a raft of new judges is appointed.

December 18, 1621   The Protestation is enrolled in the House Journal.

December 27, 1621   James sends Coke, John Selden, William Prynne, and other leaders of the opposition to the Tower. Coke's house, Holborne, is sealed and his legal papers are seized. See Coke's Arrest after Parliament, p. 1329. His failure to pay Christopher Hatton's debt is again revived, this time in the Court of Wards, but over the following months, no evidence of disloyalty can be produced against him.

December 28, 1621   The King prorogues Parliament, or suspends it until the next term. He orders the Journal be seized, and tears the Protestation Coke had drafted from it with his own hands.

January 6, 1622	James dissolves Parliament.
1622	While in the Tower, after several months' confinement without books, Coke's conditions are mediated; he apparently begins work on his commentary on Littleton's *Tenures,* which will become the First *Institute.*
August 1622	Following intercession by Prince Charles with James, Coke is paroled, but he is dismissed as a privy councillor.
1622	Architect Inigo Jones, Surveyor of the King's Works, completes the new Banqueting House at Whitehall in the Palladian, or Italian Renaissance style, marking the effective end of the age of English perpendicular gothic buildings.
1623	Shakespeare's First Folio is published.
	Coke is named to a commission in Ireland, as a form of banishment. He responds by agreeing to "discover and rectify many great abuses" and is allowed to remain at home.
February 1624	Coke enters the new Parliament as an ally of Buckingham, with whom he is briefly reconciled. Coke successfully promotes acts abolishing monopolies and creating a system of patents for the protection of inventors' rights in their inventions.
May 1624	Coke conducts the impeachment of the Lord High Treasurer Lionel Cranfield, Earl of Middlesex, an opponent of Buckingham, for bribery. Cranfield is banished from office, fined £50,000, and sent to the Tower.
May 29, 1624	Parliament ends. Coke returns to Stoke Pogis to write, although he is restored to the Privy Council.
March 27, 1625	James I dies.

1 Car.

March 27, 1625 | Charles I becomes King, at the age of 24.

1625 | Dutch law scholar Hugo Grotius publishes *De Jure Belli ac Pacis,* or *On the Law of War and Peace.*

London and other cities are in the grip of a severe plague outbreak.

June 22, 1625 | A new Parliament is formed. Coke begins the first Parliament of the new King moderately, without his by-then customary motion for the first day from the last two parliaments, with a motion to appoint a committee of grievances. However, Coke soon opposes heavy taxes and joins opposition to the Duke of Buckingham, the favorite.

November 1625 | Charles I appoints Coke, then aged 73, as Sheriff of Buckinghamshire, thus barring him from sitting in Parliament, because sheriffs are required by statute to remain in their counties. The same trick is played on Edward Alford, William Fleetwood, Sir Francis Seymour, Sir Robert Phelips, Sir Guy Palmes, and Sir Thomas Wentworth, opposition leaders in earlier parliaments. Coke refuses to take the ancient oath as sheriff, which he claims is anti-Protestant. The judges administering it agree with him in part, but he is ordered to take most of it, and so he must serve. See Sir Edward Coke's Case (The Sheriff's Oath), p. 1332.

February 2, 1626 | Charles I is crowned king.

February 10, 1626 | Coke returns to Parliament, elected from Norfolk. The King questions the ability of Coke and other sheriffs to be seated. Parliament appoints a committee to examine their election and privilege, which relies in part on an earlier statement of Coke's to determine that sheriffs cannot sit. Coke returns home and spends his time drafting his *Institutes.*

March 1626   Francis Bacon, while driving through a London
                      suburb wondering whether refrigeration could
                      preserve meat, stops his carriage, purchases a hen,
                      and stuffs it with snow; he contracts bronchitis and
                      dies on April 9.

June 15, 1626   Parliament, including Coke's son Clement, having
                      been fairly obstreperous, is dissolved. On its last day
                      it passes a resolution to consider Coke a *de facto*
                      member, entitled to the privileges of a member
                      against lawsuits.

1627   Charles, embroiled in an expensive and losing war
                      with Spain and in want of money, orders all knights
                      to lend him money and orders the arrest of the
                      many who don't pay as well as those who won't
                      collect it.

November 22, 1627   Argument of The Five Knights' Case, in which four
                      lawyers, led by Selden, defend Sir Thomas Darnel,
                      Sir John Corbet, Sir Walter Earle, Sir John
                      Heveningham, and Sir Edward Hampden, who had
                      been committed to prison for not paying forced
                      loans and who had sought release by habeas corpus,
                      claiming that they could not be imprisoned unless
                      they had violated a law passed by Parliament. Selden
                      and others mount a defense of this point from
                      Magna Carta that would bar the Privy Council from
                      ordering imprisonment without a prior statute. The
                      King's Bench refuses to grant the bail requested
                      under the habeas, and refuses to keep them there
                      without more from the King. The prisoners linger
                      until the seventy-six who refused to pay are all
                      released on January 2, 1628.

1628   The First Part of the *Institutes of the Lawes of
                      England, or, A Commentarie upon Littleton,* is
                      published by the Companie of Stationers. See p. 573.

Coke is elected from Buckinghamshire and, separately, elected from Suffolk to a new Parliament. The Commons is heavy with opposition and legal talent, including Thomas Wentworth, John Selden, William Noye, his co-counsel from the Five Knights' Case, the lawyers John Pym, John Eliot, and Duddley Digges, as well as the young, still-obscure Oliver Cromwell.

March 17, 1628	Charles I's opening address warns members not to be foolish and interfere in his affairs.
March–June 1628	Coke moves for a Parliamentary committee of the whole to consider grievances and supply. He argues for the protection of habeas corpus, moving for a Petition of Right. The House of Lords introduces an amendment to save the "sovereign power of the Crown." Coke persuades Commons to defeat the amendment, and the Lords to agree with its removal. The King, advised by Buckingham, gives an evasive answer that would not amount to acceptance of the Petition as law. Coke denounces Buckingham as the cause of the King's insult to the House. The Lords and Commons make a joint address to Charles I, asking him to assent. Charles I assents to the Petition of Right as a statute of the realm. A supply bill is passed. See p. 1225.
June 26, 1628	Charles I prorogues Parliament.
August 23, 1628	Buckingham, Charles I's favorite and closest adviser, who has been largely responsible for the war with France and has personally led a disastrous military campaign to relieve the Huguenots of La Rochelle, is assassinated. The masses in London celebrate.
January 21, 1629	Parliament recommences briefly. Coke does not attend.

1629–34   Although the idea has long been with him, and
           manuscript parts of the *Institutes,* particularly the
           commentaries on *Magna Carta,* had been written
           prior to 1621, Coke is believed during this period to
           have prepared the manuscripts for the Second,
           Third, and Fourth *Institutes* for publication.

1630   John Winthrop and approximately a thousand
           Puritans sail for Massachusetts.

May 3, 1632   Coke's horse stumbles, pinning him beneath;
               although Coke believes he is not hurt, he is. His
               daughter, the now-reconciled Lady Frances, returns
               home to nurse him.

August 29, 1632   John Locke is born.

1633   Third edition of the First *Institute* is printed by
           M.F.I.H. and R.Y. Assignes of I. More.

           Hearing a rumor that Coke is dead, Lady Elizabeth
           sends her brother to take possession of his house. He
           is not dead, and Lady Elizabeth must wait another
           year and a half.

Summer 1634   Coke grows ill.

September 1, 1634   Secretary of State Sir Francis Windebank and
                     attendants arrive at Stoke Pogis to search for
                     seditious papers on orders of the King and Privy
                     Council. They find Coke on his deathbed and seize
                     his manuscripts, will, and letters.

September 3, 1634   Coke dies, aged 82. He is buried in Tittleshall, next
                     to Bridget, his first wife.

1635   Coke's *A Little Treatise of Baile and Maineprize* is
           first published.

1640	Hobbes circulates his manuscript of *The Elements of Law, Natural and Politic.*
November 3, 1640	The Long Parliament commences.
May 12, 1641	Parliament gives to Coke's heirs the right to publish the later volumes of the *Institutes.*
1641	The colonial General Court of Massachusetts adopts *The Body of Liberties,* which is thought to be based on Coke's view of the law.
	Coke's *The Compleat Copyholder* is first published. See p. 563.
1642	Coke's Second Part of the *Institutes* is first published. See p. 745.
1642–51	English Civil Wars.
1644	Coke's The Third Part of the *Institutes* and The Fourth Part of the *Institutes* are first published. See p. 944 and p. 1053.
1647	General Court of Massachusetts Bay Colony orders the purchase of two copies each of Coke's *Reports,* First *Institute* and Second *Institute,* and *Book of Entries,* as well as of two other law books. Coke's books are the legal mainstay of all colonial libraries.
January 20, 1649	Charles I's last armies and allies have been defeated in the field, and he is brought before a specially constituted high court of justice in Westminster Hall. Charged with high treason and "other high crimes against the realm of England," the king refuses to recognize the court because "a king cannot be tried by any superior jurisdiction on earth." Despite his refusal to plead, he states that he represented the "liberty of the people of England." He is found guilty and, on January 27, sentenced to death.
January 30, 1649	Charles I is executed.

1651	Hobbes publishes *Leviathan, or the Matter, Form, and Power of a Commonwealth, Ecclesiastical and Civil.*
1653–59	Protectorate. Oliver Cromwell rules Britain.
1656	The Twelfth Part of the *Reports* is first published.
	James Harrington publishes *Oceana,* a utopian and imaginative work of political theory, arguing for stable economy, stable laws, and a limited aristocracy.
1658	Oliver Cromwell dies.
1658–59	First English edition of the *Reports,* parts 1–11, is published.
1659	*Certain Select Cases in Law,* the thirteenth volume of Coke's *Reports,* is published. See p. 499.
1 Car. 2 May 29, 1660	The restoration of the monarchy; Charles II is crowned.
1674	*England's Independency upon the Papal Power,* a pamphlet drawn from Coke's and John Davis's writings, is published in London.
1681	*A Dialogue between a Philosopher and a Student of the Common Law* is published anonymously, although it is widely known to be the work of Thomas Hobbes. An extended criticism of Coke's view of law, it presents a more moderate view of sovereignty than *Leviathan.*
1680	Henry Care publishes a tract strongly influenced by the Second *Institute, English Liberties: Or, The Free-Born Subject's Inheritance.* This will go through several printings, including American printings in 1721 and 1774.

1 Jac. 2
February 6, 1684   James II is crowned.

1684   Edward Coke's notes on *Readings on Fines and
                      Recoveries* are first published.

1687   William Penn, the new governor of Pennsylvania,
                      writes *The Excellent Priviledge of Liberty & Property
                      Being the Birth-Right of the Free-Born Subjects of
                      England,* a book heavily influenced by Coke's
                      writings.

1688   The Glorious Revolution.

1 W & M
Feb. 13, 1689   William and Mary are crowned.

1690   John Locke publishes the *Two Treatises of
                      Government.*

1701   Parliament passes the Act of Settlement, which bars
                      Roman Catholics from the crown and, among many
                      other limits on the royal prerogative, establishes
                      judicial independence from royal dismissal.

1 Anne
March 8, 1702   Anne is crowned.

1708   Thomas Wood, who would write his own *Institutes
                      of the Laws of England* in 1720, based on Coke's
                      Institutes, argues for university lectures based on
                      Coke's works in *Some Thoughts concerning the Study
                      of the Laws of England in the Two Universities.* A
                      chair along such lines would be first established in
                      Oxford fifty years later.

1711   The *Conductor Generalis,* a manual for justices of the
                      peace and other legal officials, is first published in
                      New York. As with George Webb's 1736 *The Office
                      and Authority of the Justice of the Peace,* published in
                      Williamsburg, the book is influenced by Coke's

Reports and *Institutes,* as will be later manuals for justices of the peace.

1 Geo.
August 1, 1714   George I is crowned.

1 Geo. 2
June 11, 1727   George II is crowned.

1747   Thomas Coke, Sir Edward's grandson, is made Viscount Coke and Earl of Leicester; this line becomes extinct on the death of Thomas, Lord Coke, and will be re-created in a later Thomas, Lord Coke, in 1837, whence the title continues.

1748   Montesquieu publishes *L'Esprit des Lois,* arguing, among other things, for separation of powers.

1758   Charles Viner's chair in law, the first chair for lecturing on the Common Law in an English university, is filled by William Blackstone.

1 Geo. 3
October 25, 1760   George III is crowned.

1761   James Otis, a Massachusetts lawyer, argues from Bonham's Case, Coke's *Institutes,* the Petition of Right, and Magna Carta that crown writs of assistance (search warrants letting customs officers search any house for smuggled goods without limit) violate fundamental law. The Superior Court in Boston rejects his argument, one of the first causes of the American Revolution. The case is watched and reported by a young John Adams, who later bases the Fourth Amendment requirements of reasonable searches and limited warrants on Otis's argument.

1762   A typical law student of the age, Thomas Jefferson is required to read Coke's *Institutes,* particularly the First, with predictable results: "I do wish the Devil had old Coke, for I am sure I never was so tired of an old dull scoundrel in my life."

1764   A new edition of Coke's *Law Tracts* is published in London by B. W. Hawkins.

1765–69   William Blackstone's four-volume *Commentaries on the Laws of England* is published in Oxford. It is published in 1770 in Philadelphia. The work is original, although it necessarily borrows a great deal from the *Institutes*. It is sufficiently more obliging of the power of Parliament and of the Crown that Thomas Jefferson would later despair when Blackstone is taught in lieu of Coke in the law school at the University of Virginia.

1776   American Declaration of Independence.

1778   The Virginia Supreme Court decides Philips's Case, the first of several considerations of the doctrine of judicial review by state courts and federal circuit judges between independence and 1803.

1779   Judge George Wythe is appointed Professor of Law and Police in the College of William and Mary. He is the first university law lecturer in America. Both he and Judge Tapping Reeve, his later competition in Litchfield, Connecticut, teach their pupils from Coke's *Institutes* and *Reports*.

1782   George Wythe, on the Supreme Court of Virginia, rules that the courts cannot enforce a governor's pardon, or any law, that exceeds the limits of the state's constitution.

1783   The Treaty of Paris ends American Revolution.

1787   U.S. Constitutional Convention. The new Constitution reflects many of the ideas of Coke's arguments, including limits on the executive from legislative and constitutional tasks, limits raising of

	taxes to legislative branch, as well as provision for habeas corpus, impeachment of officials, and judicial independence by appointments for life subject only to legislative impeachment.
1789	The U.S. Constitution comes into force.
1791	The first ten Amendments to the U.S. Constitution are passed.
1796	U.S. Supreme Court in *Hylton v. U.S.* strikes down a tax on carriages as a violation of the uniformity clause of the Constitution of 1789.
1798	U.S. Supreme Court in *Calder v. Bull* posits a limitation of state statutes according to natural law. It is not followed in later cases.
1799	Coke's *Institutes* and *Reports* continue, along with Blackstone's works, to be the standard reading for new law students, although Coke's works are hard going for poorly tutored pupils. Typical of the self-taught clerks studying in law offices, the future justice and professor Joseph Story writes of studying the First *Institute:* "I took it up, and after trying it day after day with very little success, I sat myself down and wept bitterly. My tears dropped upon the book, and stained its pages." Only with tenacious effort did he eventually "comprehend and reason upon the text" and eventually, "when I had completed the reading of this most formidable work, I felt I breathed a purer air, and that I had acquired a new power."
1803	Chief Justice John Marshall announces his opinion in *Marbury v. Madison,* that the U.S. courts cannot enforce an act of Congress that is "repugnant to the Constitution." This case largely confirms judicial review as a principle of American constitutional law.

Editions of Coke's Works

I. The Parts of the *Reports*

A. *First Part of the* Reports

Les Reports de Edward Coke. London: In folio [A. Islip], in aed. T. Wight, 1600. (S.T.C. 5493)

——— [Anr. ed.]. London: In folio [A. Islip], in aed. T. Wight [1601?]. (S.T.C. 5493.4)

——— [Anr. ed.]. London: In folio [A. Islip], in aed. T. Wight, 1601. (S.T.C. 5493.7)

——— [Anr. ed.]. London, 1602. (purported)

——— [Anr. ed.]. London, 1603. (purported)

——— [Anr. ed.]. London: In folio [A. Islip], for the Companie of Stationers, 1609. (S.T.C. 5494)

——— [Anr. ed.]. London: In folio [A. Islip], for the Companie of Stationers, 1619. (S.T.C. 5494.3)

——— [Anr. ed.]. In folio. London: Printed by J. Streater and E. Flesher and H. Twyford, assigns of R. and E. Atkyns; sold by George Sawbridge [etc.], 1672. (S.T.C. 4945)

——— [Anr. ed.]. 1680. (S.T.C. C4944A)

——— [Anr. ed.]. London: By the assigns of J. More, 1636. (S.T.C. 5494.8)

——— [Anr. ed.]. London: By the assigns of R. and E. Atkyns, for S. Keble and J. Walthoe, 1697. (S.T.C. 4947)

B. *Second Part of the* Reports

Le Second Part Des Reportes. . . . London: In folio [A. Islip], in aed. T. Wight, 1602. (S.T.C. 5495)

——— [Anr. ed.]. London: In folio [A. Islip], in aed. T. Wight [1604?]. (S.T.C. 5496)

————— [Anr. ed.]. London: In folio [A. Islip], for the Companie of Stationers, 1610. (S.T.C. 5497)

————— [Anr. ed.]. London: In folio [A. Islip], for the Companie of Stationers, 1618. (S.T.C. 5498)

————— [Anr. ed.]. London: For the Company of Stationers, 1619.

————— [Anr. ed.]. London: By the assigns of J. More, 1635. (S.T.C. 5498.5)

————— [Anr. ed.]. London: By the assigns of R. and E. Atkins, for S. Keble and J. Walthoe, 1697. (S.T.C. 4954)

C. The Third Part of the Reports

Le Tierce Part Des Reportes. . . . London: In folio [A. Islip], in aed. T. Wight, 1602. (S.T.C. 5499)

————— [Anr. ed.]. London: In folio [A. Islip], in aed. T. Wight, 1602. (S.T.C. 5499.2)

————— [Anr. ed.]. London, 1603. (purported)

————— [Anr. ed.]. London: In folio [A. Islip], for the Companie of Stationers, 1610. (S.T.C. 5500)

————— [Anr. ed.]. London: In folio [A. Islip], for the Companie of Stationers, 1619. (S.T.C. 5501)

————— [Anr. ed.]. London: By the assigns of J. More, 1635. (S.T.C. 5501.5)

————— [Anr. ed.]. London: By the assigns of R. and E. Atkyns, for S. Keble and J. Walthoe, 1697. (S.T.C. 4968)

D. The Fourth of the Reports

Le Quart Part Des Reports. . . . London: In folio [A. Islip], in aed. T. Wight, 1604. (S.T.C. 5502)

————— [Anr. ed.]. London: In folio [A. Islip], in aed. T. Wight, 1604. (S.T.C. 5502.3)

————— [Anr. ed.]. London: In folio [A. Islip], for the Companie of Stationers, 1610. (S.T.C. 5503)

————— [Anr. ed.]. London: In folio [A. Islip], for the Companie of Stationers, 1618. (S.T.C. 5503.4)

————— [Anr. ed.]. London: For the Company of Stationers, 1619.

————— [Anr. ed.]. London: By the assigns of J. More, 1635. (S.T.C. 5503.7)

—— [Anr. ed.]. London: By the assigns of R. and E. Atkyns, for S. Keble and J. Walthoe, 1697. (S.T.C. 4942)

E. The Fifth Part of the Reports

Quinta Pars Relationum. . . . the Fifth Part. . . . London: In folio [A. Islip], for the Company of Stationers, 1605. (S.T.C. 5504)

—— [Anr. ed.]. London: In folio [A. Islip], for the Company of Stationers, 1606. (S.T.C. 5505)

—— [Anr. ed.]. London: For the Company of Stationers, 1607.

—— [Anr. ed.]. London: In folio [A. Islip], for the Company of Stationers, 1612. (S.T.C. 5507)

—— [Anr. ed.]. London: In folio [A. Islip], for the Company of Stationers, 1624. (S.T.C. 5508)

—— [Anr. ed.]. London, 1660. (purported)

—— [Anr. ed.]. London: By the assigns of R. and E. Atkyns, for S. Keble and J. Walthoe, 1697. (S.T.C. 4911)

F. The Sixth Part of the Reports

Le Seize Part des Reports. . . . London: In folio [A. Islip], for the Societie of Stationers, 1607. (S.T.C. 5509)

—— [Anr. ed.]. London: In folio [A. Islip], for the Societie of Stationers, 1607. (S.T.C. 5509.5)

—— [Anr. ed.]. London: In folio [A. Islip], for the Societie of Stationers, 1621. (S.T.C. 5510)

—— [Anr. ed.]. London: By the assigns of J. More, 1636. (S.T.C. 5510.5)

—— [Anr. ed.]. London: By the assigns of R. and E. Atkins, for S. Keble and J. Walthoe, 1697. (S.T.C. 4956)

G. The Seventh Part of the Reports

Le Sept Part des Reports. . . . London: In folio [A. Islip], for the Societie of Stationers, 1608. (S.T.C. 5511)

—— [Anr. ed.]. London: In folio [A. Islip], for the Societie of Stationers, 1608. (S.T.C. 5511.2)

—— [Anr. ed.]. London: In folio [A. Islip], for the Societie of Stationers, 1629. (S.T.C. 5512)

———— [Anr. ed.]. London: In folio Printed by J. Streater and H. Twyford, assigns of E. and R. Atkins, 1671. (S.T.C. 4954A)

———— [Anr. ed.]. London: By the assigns of R. and E. Atkins, for S. Keble and J. Walthoe, 1697. (S.T.C. 4955)

H. The Eighth Part of the Reports

Le Huictme Part des Reports. . . . London: In folio [A. Islip], for the Societie of Stationers, 1611. (S.T.C. 5513)

———— [Anr. ed.]. London: In folio [A. Islip], for the Societie of Stationers, 1611. (S.T.C. 5513.2)

———— [Anr. ed.]. London: In folio [A. Islip], for the Societie of Stationers, 1611 [post 1640?]. (S.T.C. 5513.6)

———— [Anr. ed.]. London: In folio [A. Islip], for the Societie of Stationers, 1626. (S.T.C. 5514)

———— [Anr. ed.]. London: By the assigns of R. and E. Atkyns, for S. Keble and J. Walthoe, 1697. (S.T.C. 4937)

I. The Ninth Part of the Reports

Le Neufme Part des Reports. . . . London: In folio [A. Islip], for the Societie of Stationers, 1613. (S.T.C. 5515)

———— [Anr. ed.]. London: In folio [A. Islip], for the Societie of Stationers, 1615. (S.T.C. 5516)

———— [Anr. ed.]. London: In folio [A. Islip], for the Societie of Stationers, 1627. (S.T.C. 5517)

———— [Anr. ed.]. London: By the assigns of R. and E. Atkins, for S. Keble and J. Walthoe, 1697. (S.T.C. 4940)

J. The Tenth Part of the Reports

Le Dixme Part des Reports. . . . London: In folio [A. Islip], for the Societie of Stationers, 1614. (S.T.C. 5518)

———— [Anr. ed.]. London: In folio [A. Islip], for the Societie of Stationers, 1618. (S.T.C. 5519)

———— [Anr. ed.]. London, 1627. (purported)

———— [Anr. ed.]. London: In folio [A. Islip], for the Societie of Stationers, 1629. (S.T.C. 5520)

———— [Anr. ed.]. London: By the assigns of R. and E. Atkins, for S. Keble
and J. Walthoe, 1697. (S.T.C. 4918)

K. The Eleventh Part of the Reports

Le Unzime Part Des Reports.... London: In folio [A. Islip], for the Societie
of Stationers, 1615. (S.T.C. 5521)
———— [Anr. ed.]. London: In folio [A. Islip], for the Societie of Stationers,
1616. (S.T.C. 5522)
———— [Anr. ed.]. London: In folio [A. Islip], for the Societie of Stationers,
1619. (S.T.C. 5523)
———— [Anr. ed.]. London, 1627. (purported)
———— [Anr. ed.]. London: By the assigns of J. More, 1631. (S.T.C. 5524)
———— [Anr. ed.]. London: By the assigns of J. More, 1631. (S.T.C. 5524.3)
———— [Anr. ed.]. London: By the assigns of R. and E. Atkins, for S. Keble
and J. Walthoe, 1697. (S.T.C. 4972)

L. The Twelfth Part of the Reports

The Twelfth Part of the Reports of Sir Edward Coke. London: By T. Roycroft,
for H. Twyford and T. Dring, 1656. (S.T.C. 4969)
———— [Anr. ed.]. London: For H. Twyford and T. Dring, 1658. (S.T.C. 4970)
———— 2d ed. London: By the assigns of R. and E. Atkins, for H. Twyford
and T. Basset, 1677. (S.T.C. 4971)

M. The Thirteenth Part of the Reports

Certain Select Cases in Law. London: By T. Roycroft, for J. Sherley, H. Twyford,
and T. Dring, 1659. (S.T.C. 4909)
———— 2d ed. London: By the assigns of R. and E. Atkins, for H. Twyford,
T. Basset, and B. Sherley, 1677. (S.T.C. 4910)

II. The *Reports*

N.B.: Various editions of the reports were often bound together as a single
set of *Reports*. Entries in this section include only those published apparently
bound for sale as a series.

Les Reports de Sir Edward Coke. [Pts. 1–11 and table] London: Printed by John
    Streater [etc.] sold by George Sawbridge [etc.], 1672 (2 folio; eleven parts
    dated 1671, table dated 1672). (S.T.C. 4945)
———— [Anr. ed.]. 1680. (S.T.C. 4944A)
The Reports of [Pts. 1–11]. London: For W. Lee, M. Walbanck, D. Pakeman,
    and G. Bedell, 1658. (S.T.C. 4944)
———— 2d ed. [Pts. 1–11]. London: By the assigns of R. and E. Atkyns, for
    J. Streater, E. Flesher, and H. Twyford, 1677. (S.T.C. 4945)
———— 2d ed., with 2 tables [Pts. 1–11]. London: For H. Twyford, T. Collins,
    T. Basset, J. Wright, S. Heyrick, T. Sawbridge, M. Pitt, C. Harper, and J.
    Place, 1680. (S.T.C. 4946)
———— [Anr. ed.] [Pts. 1–11]. London: By the assigns of R. and E. Atkins,
    for S. Keble, and J. Walthoe, 1697. (S.T.C. 4947) (also listed under heading
    for each part)
———— [Anr. ed.] [Pts. 1–13]. London: By E. and R. Nutt and R. Gosling,
    1727.
———— Reprint of 1727 ed., London: By E. and R. Nutt and R. Gosling,
    1738.
———— [Anr. ed.] [Pts. 1–11]. London, 1762 (purported)
———— [Anr. ed.] [Pts. 1–13]. Incl. "the respective pleadings." Rev., corr., trans.
    and notes by G. Wilson. London: For J. and F. Rivington, 1776. (7 vols.)
———— [Anr. ed.]. London, for J. and F. Rivington, 1777. (purported)
———— [Anr. ed.]. London, for J. and F. Rivington, 1778. (purported)
———— [Anr. ed.]. Dublin: J. Moore, 1792–93.
———— "New ed.," Rev., corr., trans. and notes by G. Wilson, and notes by
    J. H. Thomas, J. F. Fraser. London: J. Butterworth and son [etc.], 1826. (6
    vols.)
———— [Anr. ed.]. Edinburgh: W. Green & Sons; London: Stevens & Sons,
    1907. (vols. 76, 77 of the *English Reports*)

III. Summaries and Tables of the *Reports*

*Le Necessarie Vse & Fruit De Les Pleadings Conteine En Le Lieur De En Le
    Lieur De Le Tresreuerend Edward Coke Lattorney General La Roigne* . . .
    Richard Cary, ed. London: T. Wright, 1601.
Un Perfect Table a Touts Les Severall Livers Del Reportes. London: In folio [A.
    Islip], for the Companie of Stationers, 1606. (S.T.C. 5525)

———— [Anr. ed.]. London: For the Societie of Stationers, 1618. (S.T.C. 5526)

———— [Anr. ed.]. London: By the assigns of J. More, 1631. (S.T.C. 5526.5)

———— [Anr. ed.]. London: By I. Flesher for W. Lee [and 2 others], 1652.

Fasciculus Florum. Ou Un Briefe & Alphabeticall Collection De Touts Les Memorable Sentences & Texts De Latine, Conteinue En Les Reports Edwardi Coke. Per T. Ashe &c. Lat. 8°. London: G. Eld, 1617. (S.T.C. 5528)

Fasciculus Florum. Or a Handfull of Flowers, Gathered out of the Severall Bookes of Sir E. Coke. London: G. Eld, 1618. (S.T.C. 5529)

Haec epitome undecim librorum relationum. . . . London: By the assigns of J. More, 1640. (S.T.C. 5527)

An Exact Abridgment in English, of the Eleven Books of Reports of. . . . London: By M. Simmons, for M. Walbancke and H. Twyford, 1650. (S.T.C. 4919)

———— 2d ed. London: For M. Walbancke and J. Place, 1651. (S.T.C. 4920)

———— 3d ed. London: By F. Leach, for M. Walbancke and H. Twyford, 1656. (S.T.C. 4920A)

———— "3d" ed. London: By F. Leach, for M. Walbancke, 1657. (S.T.C. 4921)

———— "3d" ed. London: For G. Dawes, 1666. (S.T.C. 4921A)

. . . To Which Is Now Added, an Abridgment of the Twelfth and Thirteenth Books, by John A. Dunlap, 1st American from the 3d London ed., New York: By I. Riley, 1813.

A Perfect Abridgement of the Eleaven Bookes of Reports. London: By I. G. for W. Lee, D. Pakeman, and G. Bedell, 1651. (S.T.C. 4941)

Un Exact Alphabetical Table De Tout. London: For W. Lee and H. Twyford, 1664. (S.T.C. 4923)

An Exact Abridgment of the Two Last Volumes of Reports. London: By H. Twyford and T. Twyford, 1670. (S.T.C. 4922)

An Abridgment of the Reports of the Learned Sir Edward Coke, Knight; the First Eleven Books Abridged by Sir Thomas Ireland, Knight; and the Two Last by Thomas Manley. 4th ed., rev. and cor. Dublin: By H. Watts, 1793.

———— *The Reports, in Verse; Wherein the Name of Each Case and the Principal Points Are Contained in Two Lines.* Edited by J. Worrall. London: By H. Lintot, 1742.

———— [Anr. ed., enl.]. London: J. & W. T. Clarke, 1825.

———— 3d ed., intro., J. Wesley Miller. London: R. Pheney [etc.], 1826.

———— Reprint of 1826 ed., Buffalo, New York: William Hein Corp., 1999.

IV. Declarations and Pleadings (from the *Reports*)

The Declarations and other Pleadings Contained in the Eleven Parts of [his]
Reports. London: For W. Lee, D. Pakeman, and G. Bedell, 1659. (*Decla-rations and Pleadings* contained in his eleven books of *Reports* or abridgments of the *Reports,* which were printed in 1650, 1658, and 1680, were wanting.)
(S.T.C. 4917)

V. The *Institutes* of the Laws of England

A. The *First* Institute *of the Laws of England,* or a Commentary upon Littleton

The First Part of the Institutes of the Lawes of England. Or, a Commentarie upon Littleton. London: In folio [A. Islip], for the Societie of Stationers, 1628. (S.T.C. 15784)
———— 2d ed., corr., with an alphabeticall table. London: By M. Flesher, F. Haviland, and R. Young, 1629. (S.T.C. 15785)
———— 3d ed., corr. London: By M. Flesher, F. Haviland, and R. Young, 1633. (S.T.C. 15786)
———— 4th ed. London: By M. Flesher, F. Haviland, and R. Young, 1639. (S.T.C. 15787)
———— 5th ed. London: For the Companie of Stationers, 1656. (S.T.C. 4924)
———— 6th ed. London: For the Companie of Stationers, 1664. (S.T.C. 4925)
———— 7th ed. London: By J. Streater, J. Flesher, and H. Twyford, 1670. (S.T.C. 4926)
———— 8th ed. London: For the Societie of Stationers, 1670. (S.T.C. 4927)
———— 9th ed., to which is added the Readings on Fines, and Treatise on Bail and Mainprize. London: By W. Rawlins, S. Roycroft, and H. Saw-bridge, 1684. (S.T.C. 4928)
———— 10th ed., with the addition of The Compleat Copyholder and many references. London: By W. Rawlins and S. Roycroft, 1703.
———— 11th ed., to which are annexed *Old Tenures,* and some notes and ad-ditions. London, 1719.
———— 12th ed. London: By the assigns of E. Sayoy, for R. Gosling and H. Lintot, 1738.
———— 13th ed., rev. and corr. by F. Hargrave. London, 1775–88.
———— 13th ed., rev. and corr. by F. Hargrave and C. Butler. London: By T. Wright, for E. Brooke, 1788.

———— 14th ed., by F. Hargrave and C. Butler. London, 1789.

———— 14th ed., Dublin: For J. Moore, 1791.

Additional Notes. Additions to the 13th and 14th eds. London, 1795.

———— *Additional Notes.* Additions to the 13th and 14th eds. Dublin, 1795.

———— 15th ed., by F. Hargrave and C. Butler. London: E. & R. Brooke, 1794–97.

———— 16th ed. London: By L. Hansard & Sons, for E. Brooke, etc., 1809.

———— 17th ed., by C. Butler. London: For W. Clarke, 1817.

———— 18th ed. by C. Butler. London: For J. & W. T. Clarke, 1823.

———— 19th ed., with an analysis of Littleton, written by an unknown hand in 1658–59. Edited by C. Butler. London: For J. & W. T. Clarke, 1832.

———— 1st American ed. from the 16th European ed., rev. and corr. by Ch. Butler and F. Hargrave. Philadelphia: Johnson and Weaver, 1812.

———— 1st American ed. from the 19th London ed., corr. by C. Butler. Philadelphia: R. H. Small, 1853.

———— Reprint of 19th London ed. New York: Garland, 1979.

———— Reprint of 18th London ed. Birmingham, Ala.: Legal Classics Library, 1985.

Littleton's Tenures, in English: printed from the second edition of the Commentary of Sir Edward Coke. London: For W. Clarke and Sons, 1813.

A Systematic Arrangement of Lord Coke's First Institute of the Laws of England: on the plan of Sir Matthew Hale's analysis, with the annotations of Hargrave, Lord Chief Justice Hale, and Lord Chancellor Nottingham, and notes and references, by J. H. Thomas. London: Butterworth, 1818.

———— 1st American ed. from the last London ed., to which are added the notes of Charles Butler. Philadelphia: R. H. Small, 1826–27.

———— 2nd American ed. from the last London ed., to which are added the notes of Charles Butler. Philadelphia, A. Towar, 1836.

———— Reprint of 1836 Philadelphia ed. Buffalo, N.Y.: W. S. Hein Co., 1986.

A Readable Edition of Coke upon Littleton. Edited by Thomas Coventry. London: Saunders and Benning, 1830.

A.1. Tables and Summaries of the First Institute

———— *A Table to the first part of the Institutes.* London, 1629. (S.T.C. 15788)

———— [Anr. ed.]. London: By M. Flesher, F. Haviland, and R. Young, 1630. (S.T.C. 15789)

A.2. *Abridgments of the First* Institute

An Abridgement of the Lord Coke's Commentary on Littleton., 2d ed. London: For W. Lee, D. Pakeman, and G. Bedell, 1651. (S.T.C. 4906)

———— [Anr. ed.]. London: By E. G. for M. Walbancke and H. Twyford, 1652. (S.T.C. 4958)

———— [Anr. ed.]. London: By the assigns of R. and E. Atkyns, 1685. (S.T.C. 4906A)

An Analysis of Littleton. Written by an unknown hand in 1658–59. London: For J. & W. T. Clarke, 1832. (Printed with 15th and later eds. of the First *Institute*)

An Abridgement of the First Part of Coke's Institutes, with additions. London: By the assignee of E. Sayer, for J. Walthoe, 1711.

———— [Anr. ed.]. London, 1714. (purported)

———— 2d ed. London, 1718. (purported)

———— 3d ed., corr. London: E. Nutt and R. Bosling, 1719.

———— 4th ed. London, 1725. (purported)

———— 5th ed. London: By E. Nutt and R. Gosling, for T. Osborne, 1736.

———— 6th ed. London: By H. Lintot, for T. Osborne, 1742.

———— 7th ed. London: H. Lintot, for D. Brown, J. Shuckburgh [etc.], 1751.

———— 8th ed. Dublin: H. Watts and W. Jones, 1792.

———— 8th ed. by J. Rudall. London: S. Sweet, 1822.

———— Photo reprint of 1651 London ed. New York, 1979.

Ritso, Frederick. *An Introduction to the Science of the Law Shewing the Advantages of a Law Education, Grounded on the Learning of Lord Coke's Commentaries upon Littleton's Tenures.* London: W. Clarke and Sons, 1815.

Hobler, Francis. *Familiar Exercises Between an Attorney and His Articled Clerk, On the General Principles of the Laws of Real Property: the First Book of Coke upon Littleton Reduced to Questions. To Which Is Added the Original Text and Commentary.* London: E. Eedle, 1831.

———— 2d ed. 1838.

———— 3rd ed. 1847.

B. *The Second* Institute *of the Laws of England*

The Second Part of the Institutes of the Lawes of England. London: By M. Flesher and R. Young, for E. D., R. M., W. L., and D. P., 1642. (S.T.C. 4948)

———— 2d ed. London: By J. Flesher, for W. L., D. P., and G. B., 1662. (S.T.C. 4949)

———— 3d ed. London: For A. Crooke, 1669. (S.T.C. 4950)

———— 4th ed. London: By J. Streater, H. Twyford, E. Flesher, assigns of R. and E. Atkyns, 1671. (S.T.C. 4951)

———— 5th ed. London: By J. Streater, H. Twyford, E. Flesher, assigns of R. and E. Atkyns, 1671. (S.T.C. 4952)

———— "5th" ed. London: For A. Crooke, W. Leake, A. Roper, F. Tyton, T. Dring, T. Collins, J. Place, W. Place, J. Starkey, T. Basset, R. Pawlett, S. Heyrick, and G. Dawes, 1671. (S.T.C. 4952A)

———— 6th ed. London: By W. Rawlins, for T. Basset, 1681. (S.T.C. 4953)

———— [Anr. ed.]. London: W. Clarke and Sons, 1809.

———— [Anr. ed.]. London: E. and R. Brooke, 1797.

———— [Anr. ed.]. London: W. Clarke and Sons, 1817.

———— Reprint of 1642 ed. New York: Garland, 1979.

———— Reprint of 1797 ed. Buffalo, N.Y.: W. S. Hein Co., 1986.

C. The Third Institute of the Laws of England

The Third Part of the Institutes of the Lawes of England. London: By M. Flesher, for W. Lee, and D. Pakeman, 1644. (S.T.C. 4960)

———— *The Third and Fourth Parts of the Institutes.* London: By M. Flesher, for W. Lee and D. Pakeman, 1648. (S.T.C. 4961)

———— 3d ed. London: By J. Flesher for W. Lee, and D. Pakeman, 1660. (S.T.C. 4962)

———— 4th ed. London: For A. Crooke, W. Leake, A. Roper, F. Tyton, T. Dring, T. Collins, J. Place, W. Place, J. Starkey, T. Basset, R. Pawlett, S. Heyrick, and G. Dawes, 1669. (S.T.C. 4963)

———— "4th" ed. London: By J. Streater, J. Flesher, and H. Twyford, 1670. (S.T.C. 4964)

———— 5th ed. London: For A. Crooke, W. Leake, A. Roper, F. Tyton, T. Dring, T. Collins, H. Place, W. Place, J. Starkey, T. Basset, R. Pawlett, S. Heyrick, and G. Dawes, 1671. (S.T.C. 4965)

———— 6th ed. London: By W. Rawlins, for T. Basset, 1680. (S.T.C. 4966)

———— [Anr. ed.]. London: For E. and R. Brooke, 1797.

———— [Anr. ed.]. London: W. Clarke, 1809.

———— [Anr. ed.]. London: W. Clarke, 1817.

———— Reprint of 1644 ed. New York: Garland, 1979.

———— Reprint of 1797 ed. Buffalo, N.Y.: W. S. Hein, 1986.

D. *The Fourth* Institute *of the Laws of England*

The Fourth Part of the Institutes of the Lawes of England. London: By M. Flesher, for W. Lee and D. Pakeman, 1644. (S.T.C. 4929)

———— 2d ed. London: By M. Flesher, for W. Lee and D. Pakeman, 1648. (S.T.C. 4930)

———— 3d ed. London, 1660. (purported)

———— 4th ed. London: For A. Crooke, W. Leake, A. Roper, F. Tyton, T. Dring, T. Collins, J. Place, W. Place, J. Starkey, T. Basset, R. Pawlett, S. Heyricke, and G. Dawes, 1669. (S.T.C. 4931)

———— 5th ed. London: By J. Streater, H. Twyford, E. Flesher, assigns of R. and E. Atkyns, 1671. (S.T.C. 4932)

———— 6th ed. London: By W. Rawlins, for T. Basset, 1681. (S.T.C. 4933)

———— [Anr. ed.]. London: E. and R. Brooke, 1797.

———— [Anr. ed.]. London: W. Clarke and Sons, 1809.

———— [Anr. ed.]. London: W. Clarke & Sons, 1817.

———— Reprint of 1979 ed. Buffalo, N.Y.: W. S. Hein Co., 1986.

VI. Speech and Charge at Norwich

The Lord Coke his Speech and Charge (at the Assises at Norwich). With a discoverie of the abuses and corruption of officers. Edited by R. Pricket. London: By R. Raworth and N. Okes for C. Pursett, 1607. (S.T.C. 5491)

———— [Anr. ed.]. London: For N. Butter, 1607. (S.T.C. 5492)

———— [Anr. ed.]. London: For N. Butter, 1607. (S.T.C. 5492.2)

———— [Anr. ed.]. London: By R. Raworth and N. Okes, for N. Butter, 1607. (S.T.C. 5492.4)

VII. Book of Entries

A Booke of Entries: Containing Perfect and Approved Presidents of Counts, Declarations, Informations, Pleints. Edited by T. Jones, Common Serjeant of London. London: In folio [A. Islip] for the Societie of Stationers, 1614. (S.T.C. 5488)

———— 2d ed. London: By J. Streater, J. Flesher, and H. Twyford, assigns of R. and E. Atkyns, 1671. (S.T.C. 4908)

———— 2d ed. London: By J. Streater, 1671. (S.T.C. 4908A)

VIII. Little Treatise of Baile and Maineprize

A Little Treatise of Baile and Maineprize. Written by E. C. Knight. London: For W. Cooke, 1635. (S.T.C. 5489)

———— 2d ed., corr. and enl. London: By B. Alsop and T. Fawcet, for W. Cooke, 1637. (S.T.C. 5490)

———— Reprint with 9th ed. of First *Institute.* London: By W. Rawlings, S. Roycroft, and H. Sawbridge, 1684.

———— [Anr. ed.]. London: J. Roberts, 1715.

———— [Anr. ed.]. London: By His Majesty's Law Printers, for T. Cadell, 1783.

———— [Anr. ed.]. Amsterdam, 1973.

———— Reprint of 1635 and 1783 eds., includes indexes. New York: Garland, 1978.

IX. The Complete Copyholder

The Compleat Copyholder, 1630 (presumed; not in S.T.C.)

[Anr. ed.]. London: By T. Cotes, for W. Cooke, 1641. (Reprint of 1st ed., 1630. The forme of keeping a copy-hold court, and court baron is wanting). (S.T.C. 4912)

———— [Anr. ed.]. London: For M. Walbanck, and R. Best, 1644. (S.T.C. 4913)

———— [Anr. ed.]. London: For W. Lee and D. Pakeman, 1650. (S.T.C. 4914)

———— [Anr. ed. w. supp.]. London: By J. Streater, E. Flesher, and H. Twyford, assigns of R. and E. Atkyns, 1668. (S.T.C. 4915)

———— [Anr. ed.]. London: By E. Flesher, J. Streater, and H. Twyford, assigns of R. and E. Atkyns, 1673. (S.T.C. 4916)

———— *A supplement by way of additions to.* London: By E. Flesher, J. Streater, and H. Twyford, assigns of R. and E. Atkyns, 1673. (S.T.C. 4957)

———— Reprint with 10th ed. of First *Institute.* London: W. Rawlins and S. Roycroft, 1703.

X. Three Law Tracts

Three Law Tracts: I. The compleat copyholder; being a discourse of the antiquity and nature of manors and copyholds, & c. II. A reading on 27 Edward the First, called the statute De finibus levatis. III. A treatise of bail and mainprize. Edited by W. Hawkins. London: By His Majesty's Law Printer for J. Worrall, 1764.

———— Reprint. Abingdon, Oxon: Professional Books, 1982.

XI. Later Reprints and Excerpts

Judges Judged Out of their own Mouthes. London: By W. Bentley, for E. Dod & N. Ekins, 1650. (S.T.C. 4938)

———— [Anr. ed.]. London: By W. Bentley, for J. Williams, 1650. (S.T.C. 4939)

Le reading del mon Seignior Coke: sur le statute de 27. E. I. [1299], appelle le statute de Finibus Levatis. London: Excudebat T. R., sumptibus G. Lee, D. Pakeman & G. Bedell, 1662. (S.T.C. 4943)

England's Independency upon the Papal Power Historically and Judicially Stated by Sr. John Davis . . . and by Sr. Edward Coke . . . in Two Reports, Selected from their Greater Volumes. pref. by Sir John Pettus. London: by E. Flesher, J. Streater and H. Twyford, assigns of R. and E. Atkins, 1674.

Magna Charta: Made in the Ninth Year of K. Henry the Third, and Confirmed by K. Edward the First, in the Twenty-Eighth Year of His Reign with Some Short, but Necessary Observations from the L. Chief Just. Coke's Comments upon it, trans., Edward Cooke. London: by the assigns of R. and E. Atkins, for T. Simmons, 1680.

The Great Charter of the Forest, Declaring the Liberties of it Made at Westminster, the Tenth of February, in the Ninth Year of Henry the Third, Anno Dom. 1224, and Confirmed in the Eight and Twentieth of Edward the First, Anno Dom. 1299: with Some Short Observations Taken out of the Lord Chief Justice Coke's Fourth Institutes of the Courts of the Forests. London: Printed by the assignees of R. and E. Atkins for John Kidgell, etc., 1680.

A Declaration of the Libertyes of the English Nation, Principally with Respect to Forests. London: Printed for Richard Janeway, etc., 1681.

Argumentum anti-Normannicum: or an Argument. London: By J. Darby, for M. Keinton, J. Robinson, S. Sprint, 1682. (S.T.C. 4907)

———— [Anr. ed.]. London: By J. Darby, 1682. (S.T.C. 4907A)

The Famous Case of Robert Calvin, A Scots-man: as Contain'd in the Reports of Sir Edward Coke, Lord Chief Justice of the Common-pleas, and as it was Argued in Westminster-Hall by All the Judges of England in the Reign of King James VI of Scotland and I of England. Edinburgh: James Watson, 1705.

A Vindication of the Lord Chancellor Bacon, from the aspersion of injustice, cast upon him by Mr. Wraynham: containing the said Mr. Wraynham's representation of his own case, and the sentence pronounced against him. Together with the learned speeches of the judges, Hubbert, Coke, and other sages in the law. Archbishop Aboot, and other reverend prelates. The Lord Chamberlain, Earl of Arundel, Sir Fulk Crovill, and other noble peers. Now first published from the original manuscript. London: For J. Peele, 1725.

The Corner Stone of the British Constitution Or, the Golden Passage in . . . Magna Charta, with Lord Coke's Remarks. From Second Institute. London: 1789.

Mottoes and Crests of Sir Edward Coke

The inscription on rings, which Edward Coke distributed according to custom to commemorate his being called to become Serjeant at Law:

Lex est tutissima cassis
(Law is the safest helmet)

This is a shorthand for a maxim: "Law is the safest helmet; under the shield of law no one is deceived."

His Crest:

His Motto:

Prudens qui patiens
(The prudent man is patient)

This is an abbreviated form of the fuller motto:

Prudens qui patiens etenim durissima coquit
(The prudent man is a patient man, which aids him in the digestion)

The motto is a pun built on the similarity of Coke's name to the Latin for "digestion," which also accounts for his choice of the ostrich as an heraldic animal. The ostrich was, at that time, believed to have a digestion so strong that it could eat iron, which explains the horseshoe in its beak.

I

Reports

Part One of the *Reports*

The *Reports* are a monumental achievement. Their scope, detail, and organization, particularly in the volumes from four to eleven, created a platform from which the whole organization of the Common Law could be perceived. The emphasis in early volumes of cases in which Coke took part and of cases that were particularly prominent in settling issues of the law governing inheritance and land ownership increased the fame both of Coke and of his *Reports*. For centuries, lawyers of the common law have referred to all reports printed under the name of the reporter by the name of that person, save one. Coke's *Reports* have maintained such a place in the Common Law that they alone are referred to as "The *Reports*."

The First Part of Sir Edward's *Reports* was published in 1600. It was originally entitled *Les Reports De Edvvard Coke L' Attorney Generall Le Roigne De Divers Resolutions, & Judgements Donnes Avec Graund Deliberation, per Les Tres Reverendes Judges, & Sages De La Ley, De Cases & Matters En Ley Queux Ne Fueront Unques Resolve, Ou Ajuges Par Devant, & Les Raisons, & Causes Des Dits Resolutions & Judgements,* which is to say in English *The Reports of Edward Coke, Attorney General of the Realm of Divers Resolutions and Judgements given upon Solemn Arguments, and with great Deliberation, and Conference of the most Reverend Judges, and Sages of the Law; of Cases in Law which never were Resolved or Adjudged Before; And the Reasons and Causes of the Said Resolutions and Judgements.* Coke had circulated manuscript reports of some cases prior to the printing. The whole of the cases in this part presents a series of issues in the control, transfer, and obligations arising from the ownership of property, particularly as these issues had been altered by acts of Parliament, or were limited by ancient rules of the Common Law. There is a considerable emphasis on the style and content of pleading, or its effect on the dispute, and Coke reprinted some of the very extensive pleadings filed in connection with many of the cases.

The Preface to the Reader.

Nothing is or can bee so fixed in mind, or fastened in memorie, but in short time is or may bee loosened out of the one, and by little and little quite lost out of the other: It is therefore necessarie that memorable things should be committed to writing (the witnesse of times, the light and the life of trueth) and not wholly betaken to slippery memorie which seldome yeeldeth a certain reckoning: And herein our present time is of all that ever was to future posterity the most ungratefull; For they of former (though not of such florishing time) to the great benefit of themselves, of us, and our posterity, have faithfully and carefully registred in Bookes, aswell the sayings as the doings which were in their time worthie of note and observation. For omitting others, and taking one example for all, howe carefully have those of our profession in former times reported to ages succeeding, the Opinions, Censures, and Judgements of their reverend Judges and Sages of the Common Lawes: which if they had silenced and not set forth in writing, certainely as their bodies in the bowells of the earth are long agoe consumed, so had their grave Opinions, Censures, and Judgements been with them long sithence wasted and worne away with the worme of oblivion: But wee, as justly to bee blamed, as the thing it selfe to bee bewayled, having greater cause, are lesse carefull, having better oportunity, are lesse occasioned, and being in greater necessitie, are of all others the most negligent, whom neither the excellencie and perfection of knowledge, a thing most pleasant, nor the practise thereof in furtherance of Justice, a thing most profitable (although one great learned and grave man[1] hath made an enterance) can among so many in this flourishing spring time of knowledge move any other to follow his example: The neglect whereof is in mine opinion many waies dangerous, For I have often observed, that for want of a true and certain Report the case that hath been adjudged standing upon the racke of manie running Reports (especially of such as understood not the state of the Question) hath been so diversly drawne out, as many times the true parts of the case have been disordered & disjointed, and most commonly the right reason & rule of the Judges utterly mistaken. Hereout have sprung many absurd & strange opinions, which being caried about in a common charme, & fathered on grave & reverend Judges, many times with the multitude, &

---

1. *Edmundus Plowden.*

sometimes with the learned receive such allowance, as either beguile or bedasil their conceits & judgements. Therfore as I allow not of those that make memory their storehouse, for at their greatest need they shall want of their store; so I like not of those that stuffe their studies with wandring & masterlesse Reports, for they shall find them too soone to lead them to error. In troth, reading, hearing, conference, meditation, & recordation, are necessary I confesse to the knowledge of the common Law, because it consisteth upon so many, & almost infinite particulars: but an orderly observation in writing is most requisite of them all; for reading without hearing is darke and irksome, & hearing without reading is slipperie and uncertaine, neither of them truly yeeld seasonable fruit without conference, nor both of them with conference, without meditation & recordation, nor all of them together without due and orderly observation: *Scribe sapientiam tempore vacuitatis tuae.*[2] And yet he that at length by these meanes shall attaine to be learned, when he shall leave them off quite for his gaine, or his ease, so one shall he (I warrant him) lose a great part of his learning: Therefore as I allow not to the Student any discontinuance at all (for he shall lose more in a month than he shall recover in many:) So doe I commend perseverance to all, as to each of these meanes an inseparable incident. I have sithence the xxii. yeere of her Majesties Raigne, which is now xx. yeeres compleat, observed the true reasons as neere as I could, of such matters in Law (wherein I was of Councell, & acquainted with the estate of the Question) as have been adjudged upon great & mature deliberation; And as I never meant (as many have found) to keepe them so secret for mine owne private use, as to denie the request of any friend to have either view or copy of any of them; So til of late I never could be perswaded (as many can witnes) to make them so publique, as by any intreaty to commit them to print: But when I considered how by her Majesties princely care and choice, her Seates of Justice have beene ever for the due execution of her Lawes, furnished with Judges of such excellent knowledge and wisdome (whereunto they have attained in this fruitfull spring time of her blessed raigne) as I feare that succeeding ages shall not affoord successors equall unto them, I have adventured to publish certaine of their resolutions (in such sort as my little leasure would permit) for the helpe of their memory who heard them, and perfectly knew them, for the instruction of others who knew them not, but imperfectly heard

2. [*Ed.:* Leisure gives the scribe the chance to acquire wisdom. (Taken from Ecclesiasticus 38:25.)]

of them, and lastly, for the common good, (for that is my chiefe purpose) in quieting & establishing of the possessions of many in these generall cases, wherein there hath bin such variety of opinions. In these Reports I have (of purpose) not observed one methode, to the end that in some other Edition (if God so please) I may follow the forme that the Learned shall allowe of, and will sequester mine opinion: For it may be I should preferre those Reports which are lesse paineful, more compendious, and yet (perhaps) no lesse profitable. I have added the pleadings at large: as well for the warrant, and better understanding of the cases and matters in Law, as for the better instruction of the studious Reader in good pleading, which Mast. *Littleton* saith[3] is one of the most honorable, lawdable, and profitable things in the Law: I wish the continuances had bene omitted, and yet some of them also are not without their fruite. To the Reader mine advise is, that in reading of these or any new Reports, hee neglect not in any case the reading of the old Books of yeares reported in former ages, for assuredly out of the old fields must spring and grow the new corne, And so I conclude with the Poet:

> *Cum tua non edas hiis utere & annue Lector:*
> *Carpere vel noli nostra, vel ede tua.*[4]
> *Benĕ vale.*[5]

Shelley's Case.
(1581) Trinity Term, 23 Elizabeth I
In the Court of King's Bench, before all the Justices of England.
First Published in the *Reports*, volume 1, page 93b.*

Ed.: Edward Shelley and his wife Joan were tenants in special tail of a very long-term lease for years, which is to say that they held the right to the land under lease for life, although that right would go to their legal children living at their death and on to their children and so forth either until there

---

3. [*Ed.:* Later editions here note a reference to Littleton §534 and 1st Institute, pp. 303, 332b.]

4. [*Ed.:* Since, reader, you do not publish your own, use and approve these: either do not carp at ours or else publish your own. (Allusion to Martial, *Epigrams*, 1.91.2.)]

5. [*Ed.:* Farewell.]

*[*Ed.:* Coke also reports the pleadings, commencing in volume one at page 88b.]

was a failure of issue (which is to say that the current holder of the lease died and there were no children to take [in which case the lands reverted to Edward or his successors]), or until the lease ran out. Edward and Joan had two sons, Henry and Richard. Joan died. Henry married and had a daughter, Mary, and his wife had conceived a second child, who would be called Henry. Henry the father died before the Henry the younger was born and before his father Edward had died. Edward issued an indenture, or land transfer document, that would recover the old reversion of the fee tail, give the estate to himself for his life, then give it to some people out of the family for 24 years, and then give it to the heirs male of his body lawfully begotten (Edward's legitimate sons or their legitimate sons and so on), with reversion in the event of a failure of issue to the heirs male of the body of John Shelley and of others. Edward died the morning before the procedure to recover the whole interest and enter the indenture was to be completed. Richard, the younger son of Edward, leased the land to a fellow named Wolfe. Henry the younger (the grandson of Edward and nephew of Richard) was born, and lawyers in his name threw Wolfe off the land. Besides the procedural difficulties of whether the action of recovery was good (it was) and whether Henry the younger had an interest (he did), the argument turned on whether Edward's grant in tail was any good; if all of its clauses were in force, Richard could have made his lease. The court ruled that Edward's grant was of an interest for life to Edward with a remainder to Edward's heirs, which amounted to giving himself the whole of the estate, giving the fee tail to himself, thus extinguishing all of the later interests. Henry won.

Richard's interests, in Wolfe, were represented by three serjeants; Henry's interests were represented by Popham, who was then the Solicitor General, as well as Cowper and Coke. The case was heard by the entire bench, the judges of Chancery, the Queen's Bench, the Common Pleas, and the Exchequor. There is considerable discussion of the nature of a grant, the construction of words of a grant, and the vesting of interests in litigants at law. This case has become famous as the origin of the rule now understood that a grant of a life estate to one person, coupled with the grant of a remainder in that person's heirs, becomes a single estate in fee simple absolute. This rule, here advocated by Coke, was a deliberate attempt by the courts to limit feudal restraints on the transfer of land.

Nicholas Wolfe brought an *ejectione firmae*[1] of certain land in B. in the county of Sussex, against Henry Shelley, Esq. defendant, and declared on a lease by Richard Shelley, Esq. to which the defendant pleaded not guilty. And a special verdict was found to the effect following, viz. that Edward Shelley and Joan his wife were seised of the manor of Barhamwick, whereof the said land, wherein the said ejectment was supposed, was and is parcel, in special tail, that is to say, to them and to the heirs of their two bodies lawfully begotten, and shews how, the remainder to the said Edward and his heirs; and it was further found that the said Edward and Joan had issue Henry their eldest son, and the said Richard their younger son, and afterwards the said Joan died, and the said Henry having issue Mary yet living, died in the life of the said Edward, his wife then big with child of the said Henry the now defendant. And afterwards the said Edward Shelley by indenture bearing date the 25th of September, in the first and second year of the late King and Queen Philip and Mary, and first delivered the sixth day of October following, did covenant with Cowper and Martin to suffer a recovery of the said manor, amongst other things: and that the said recovery should be to the use of the said Edward Shelley for the term of his life, without impeachment of waste; and after his decease to the use of Mr. Caril and others for 24 years, and after the said 24 years ended, then to the use of the heirs male of the body of the said Edward Shelley lawfully begotten, and of the heirs male of the body of such heirs male lawfully begotten; and for default of such issue, to the use of the heirs male of the body of John Shelley of Michael Grove, &c. It was also found, that [94 a] the said Edward Shelley, the 9th day of | October, being the first day of the term, between the hours of five and six in the morning died, and afterwards the recovery passed the same day with a voucher over, and immediately after judgment given, an *habere facias seisinam*[2] was awarded, the wife of the said Henry Shelley being at that time great with child with the defendant. And afterwards, that is to say, the 19th day of October next following the recovery was executed; and afterwards the fourth day of December then next following, the wife of the said Henry was delivered of the said Henry now defendant. And it was likewise found that the said manor was in lease for years at the time of the said judgment and recovery, by force of a lease made long before

---

1. [*Ed.:* Ejection from the land. (A writ to commence a suit at law for trespass.)]
2. [*Ed.:* That you cause to have seisin. (The writ of execution in real actions.)]

the original writ purchased, upon which the said recovery was had: and that the said Richard Shelley, second son of the said Edward Shelley, and uncle to the said defendant, entered and made a lease to the said Nicholas Wolfe now plaintiff in the *ejectione firmae;* and that the said Henry Shelley the defendant entered upon the said Nicholas Wolfe and did eject him. And upon the whole matter aforesaid the Jurors pray the advice and judgment of the Court, if the entry of the said Henry the defendant was lawful or not; and if, by the judgment of the Court, the entry of the said Henry should be deemed unlawful, then the jury found that the defendant was guilty, and assessed damages: and if the entry of the defendant should be deemed by the Court to be lawful, then they found for the defendant that he was not guilty, &c.

This case was divided into four principal questions: whereof

1. The first was, if tenant in tail suffers a common recovery with a voucher over, and dies before execution, if execution may be sued against the issue in tail.

2. The second, if tenant in tail makes a lease for years, and afterwards suffers a common recovery, if the reversion be presently by judgment of law in the recoveror, before any execution sued.

3. The third, if tenant in tail having issue two sons, and the elder dies in the life-time of his father, his wife *privement enseint*[3] with a son, and then tenant in tail suffers a common recovery to the use of himself for term of his life, and after his death to the use of A. and C. for 24 years, and after to the use of the heirs male of his body lawfully begotten, and of the heirs male of the body of such heirs male lawfully begotten, and presently after judgment an *habere facias seisinam* is awarded, and before the execution, that is to say, between five and six in the morning of the same day, in | which the recovery [94 b] was suffered, tenant in tail dies, and after his death and before the birth of the son of the elder son, the recovery is executed, by force whereof Richard, the uncle, enters, and after the son of the elder son is born, if his entry upon the uncle be lawful or not.

4. The fourth and last point, if the uncle in this case may take as a purchaser, forasmuch as the elder son had a daughter which was heir general and right heir of Edward Shelley, at the time of the execution of the recovery. And this

---

3. [*Ed.:* secretly pregnant (The 1658 edition translates the phrase into the text as 'young with child.' Later editions restore the French term.)]

case was argued by Anderson the Queen's Serjeant, and Gawdy and Fenner, Serjeants, for the plaintiff, and by Popham, Solicitor-General, Cowper, and Coke, for the defendant.

And as to the first point, the plaintiff's counsel argued, that execution might be sued against the issue in tail; and their principal reason was, because the judgment given against the tenant in tail, and the judgment for the tenant in tail to have in value against the vouchee, bound the right of the estate-tail, and the issue in tail shall not avoid it by the Statute de Donis Conditionalibus, because the law adjudgeth that, in respect of the intended recompense, the issue in tail was not prejudiced: as if tenant in tail grant a rent for the release of one who hath a right to the land, it shall bind the issue in tail, because it is for the benefit of the issue, and so not restrained by the said act, as it is agreed in 44 Edw. 3. 21b. *Octavian Lumbard's Case.* And if the recovery, upon which execution is had in the life of the tenant in tail, shall not be a bar to the issue, it would be mischievous and a great impeachment to common assurances of lands. And further, it was said, that the right of the estate-tail was bound by the judgment, and not by the execution; for if the right of the estate-tail was not bound by the judgment, it could not be bound or barred by the execution had afterwards.

As to the second point, they conceived, that it was not any question, but that the recoverors had not the reversion presently by the judgment, notwithstanding the lands were in lease for years; for they said that the judgment was, that the demandant should recover seisin of the land which was but executory, and could not be executed until execution, entry, or claim. As if a common or reversion, or any other thing which lieth in grant be granted upon condition, if the condition be broken, the thing granted is not in the grantor before claim, for it was said, that when a man may enter, or claim, the law will not adjudge him in possession until entry or claim.

As to the third point, which was the great doubt of the case, they argued, that the said Richard, the uncle, was in by purchase, & *ex consequenti*[4] the entry of the defendant upon him was not lawful; and this in effect was their principal reason:

[95 a]   I Argument. viz., that which originally vests in the heir, and was not in the ancestor, vests in the heir by purchase.

4. [*Ed.:* and as a consequence.]

But this use originally vests in Richard Shelley, and never was [vested] in Edward Shelley.

And therefore the use vests in Richard Shelley by purchase.

And they said, that it was manifest that the use never vested in Edward Shelley, for before the recovery executed no use could be raised, for the use ought to be raised out of the estate of the recoverors, but the recovery was not executed in the life of Edward Shelley, and therefore no use could rise during his life. And Serjeant Anderson said, it was impossible that Richard Shelley should be in by descent, because no right, title, action, use, or other thing touching the uses limited by the said indentures did descend to Richard, but only a thing intended to him, which intent in his life received no perfection; and therefore this case was not like any case where a right, title, action, use, or other thing descendeth from the ancestor to the heir, but is like the case in 5 Edw. 4. 6a. where the wife consents to a ravisher, having issue a daughter, the daughter enters by the statute of 6 Rich. 2. a son is afterwards born, he shall never divest it, for it vested in the daughter by purchase; so is the case agreed in 9 Hen. 7. 25a. If a lease be made to one for life, the remainder to the right heirs of J. S., if J. S. dies having a daughter, his wife with child with a son, the daughter claims it by purchase, and therefore the son born after shall never divest it; but they relied principally upon the case in 9 Hen. 7. 25a. that if a condition descends to the daughter, and she enters for the condition broken, the son born afterwards shall never enter upon her, and yet there she is in by descent, and the title of her entry, that is to say, the condition, she hath as heir: and yet because she was the first in whom it vested, the son born after shall not divest it, which is a stronger case than our case at the Bar.

And further it was said by the plaintiff's counsel, that although the recovery had been executed in the life of Edward Shelley, yet ought the heir male to take by purchase; for they said, that the manner of the limitation of the uses is to be observed in this case, which is first to Edward Shelley for the term of his life, and after his death to the use of others for the term of 24 years, and after the 24 years ended, then to the use of the heirs male of the body of the said Edward Shelley, | lawfully begotten, and of the heirs male of the body   [95 b] of the said heirs male lawfully begotten; in which case they said, that if the heirs male of the body of Edward Shelley should be words of limitation, then the subsequent words, viz. and of the heirs male of the body of the said heirs male lawfully begotten, would be void: for words of limitation cannot be added and joined to words of limitation, but to words of purchase. And they said, that forasmuch as those words, heirs males of the body of Edward Shelley, might be words of purchase, that in this case the law will construe and take them as words of purchase, for otherwise the said subsequent words, "and of the heirs male of their bodies," would be void. And such construction is always to be made of a deed that all the words (if possible) agreeable to reason and conformable to law, may take effect according to the intent of the parties without rejecting of any, or by any construction to make them void. And therefore Anderson put this case, if a man makes a feoffment in fee, to the use of himself for life, and after his decease to the use of his heirs, in this case the fee-simple executed; but in the same case, if the limitation be to the use of himself for life, and after his decease to the use of his heirs, and of their heirs female of their bodies, in this case these words "his heirs" are words of purchase, and not of limitation, for then the subsequent words "and of their heirs female of their bodies" would be void. So they concluded this point, first that no use could rise until execution sued, no execution was sued in the life of Edward Shelley, and then it first vested in Richard as a purchaser before the son of the elder son was born: and for the latter reason, admitting the recovery had been executed, notwithstanding the heirs male of the body of Edward Shelley should take by purchase, and so *quacunque via data,*[5] they concluded, that the use first settled in Richard Shelley as a mere purchaser. And as to the latter point, which in effect (admitting, as hath been said, that the said words were words of purchase) was, that a lease for life is made to A the remainder to the heirs male of the body of Edward Shelley, if in this case Richard may take this estate-tail by purchase as heir male, notwithstanding his elder brother had issue a daughter which is living, and who was his heir general; they said there was no difference as to that, where an estate-tail is limited by gift executed, and when by way of remainder, nor when the heir male of the body claims by descent, nor when by purchase, for if an estate had been made to Edward Shelley, and to the heirs male of his body, in that

[96 a]   case I Richard Shelley without doubt should have had the land by descent, and that by a construction on the Statute *de Donis conditionalibus* to fulfil the mind and intent of the donor.

And so it is, if I give lands to a man, and to his heirs female, and the donee

---

5. [*Ed.:* whichever way you take it,]

hath issue male and female, although the female be not heir general, yet she is heir special to claim *per formam doni.*[6] And this was in effect the substance of the three arguments published and delivered at large on the plaintiff's part before the Justices of the Queen's Bench in Hilary and Easter terms, in the 23d year of the reign of Queen Elizabeth. And on the defendant's part it was argued contrary. As to the first point it was argued, that execution could not be sued against the issue in tail; and therefore as it hath been agreed, that the judgment only against the tenant in tail did not bind, but the judgment to have in recompense, *sequitur a concessis,*[7] that the issue in tail cannot be barred: and for proof that in this case the issue in tail could not have any recompense: first it was said, that if execution could not be sued against the issue in tail, then the issue in tail could not take any benefit of the recompense. For it is agreed in 17 Edw. 2. title Recovery in Value, Fitz. 33. 1 Edw. 3. fo. 12. that he who vouches shall never have execution against the vouchee before execution sued against himself; so that the judgment to recover over in value is not material (as the case is) unless execution may be sued against the issue, which cannot be in this case. For he who is in of an estate in possession, by title paramount a recovery, shall not be bound by the same recovery; but the issue in tail in our case is in of an estate in possession, which he had by title paramount the recovery, and therefore the issue in tail shall not be bound by the recovery. In proof of the first proposition, it hath been adjudged in 28 Hen. 8. reported by Serjeant Bendloes, which case began 26 Hen. 8. in the book at large, where the case was, that an executor having judgment to recover a debt due to the testator, and dying intestate before execution, and the Ordinary committing the administration of the first testator to one, that the administrator could not sue execution upon that recovery, because he deriveth his interest from, and represents the person of the testator, and so before the recovery. So it is, if there be two joint-tenants, and one makes a lease for years, rendering rent, the lessor dies, the other shall not have the rent; because he claims by the first feoffor, which is paramount the lease and the reservation. So if tenant for life makes a lease for years, reserving rent, and afterwards surrenders to him in the reversion, not being in by force of his ancient reversion, he cannot have the rent newly reserved. And in proof that the issue

6. [*Ed.:* by the form of the gift.]
7. [*Ed.:* it follows from these premises, (literally, "from the things granted.")]

in tail was in by a title paramount | the recovery, he said, that the issue in tail shall avoid all charges, leases, and other incumbrances made by his ancestor, because he claims *per formam doni.* And if tenant in fee simple makes a lease for life, and suffers a recovery, he and his heirs are for ever concluded; but he said, if tenant in tail be of a reversion expectant on an estate for life, and he suffers a recovery, and hath judgment to recover over in value, yet his issue shall avoid the recovery, for he shall not be estopped, because he claims in *per formam doni:* but if execution had been sued in the life of tenant in tail, then forasmuch as the estate-tail doth not descend to the issue; and forasmuch as then he may sue execution over, it is good reason to bar the estate-tail; but if the issue in tail be in by lawful descent in possession of the estate-tail before the recovery [is] executed, then the law seems to be otherwise. *Octavian Lumbard's Case* in 44 Edw. 3. which hath been cited on the other side, was not against this opinion, for there the issue in tail reaped the benefit of the release made to his ancestor; but in our case, the issue in tail being in of an estate-tail paramount the recovery, cannot take benefit of the recompense over. And wherefore should not the issue in tail in this case, be at liberty to chuse whether he will take the estate-tail, or otherwise to admit execution to be sued against him, and to sue execution over in value, as well as in 14 Hen. 6. fol. 2. in the case of exchange, in which case although assets of greater value descend to him than the land in tail, yet he may chuse to have the one or the other at his election.

And if tenant in tail be disseised, and levies a fine to the disseisor without warranty and dies, if the issue in tail enters, and is seised by force of the tail before all the proclamations are made, although the proclamations be afterwards made, yet that does not bar the issue: So if tenant in tail levies a fine and disseises the conusee, and dies before all the proclamations are made, and after the proclamations in the time of the issue in tail pass, yet the issue is not bound thereby, by the statute of 32 Hen. 8. and yet the words of the Act are, that all fines after proclamations, &c. shall bar, &c. But it hath always been held, if the issue in tail be remitted and seised by force of the tail before the bar be complete, that is to say, before the proclamation be passed, the issue is not bound; so in this case before execution sued, the issue in tail is seised by force of the tail, and in *per formam doni* before the bar is complete, and therefore the execution cannot be sued against him, nor can any bar after the death of his father be made to the estate tail which is descended to him in possession. And it is agreed in 7 Edw. 3. 335. that if a disseisor at the Common

Law before the Statute | of Non-claim, had levied a fine, or suffered judgment in a writ of right, until execution sued, they were not bars, for the year shall be accounted after the transmutation of the possession by execution of the fine or recovery; and so it is said in *Stowel's Case,* Plow. Com. 357e.; and the books in 28 Ass. pl. 32. 7 Hen. 4. fol. 17. 17b. Plow. Com. 55b. 12 Edw. 4. fol. 20a. were cited, that execution upon a feigned recovery against the father, cannot be sued against the issue in tail.

To the second point they argued, that forasmuch as the land was in lease for years, that the recovery was executed by judgment of law presently after the judgment. And a difference was taken when the lands were in the possession of the tenant at the time of the judgment, and when the lands were in lease for years. And their reason of the difference was, because the recoverors in the one case may sue execution, and in the other case may not; and because the recoverors cannot sue execution, the law will therefore adjudge them in execution presently; the reason thereof is, that otherwise the lessee during the term might commit waste, and would be dispunishable by the recoveror, but if the recoverer may enter or sue execution, then he may prevent it. And therefore, if a fine *sur cognizance de droit tantum*[8] be levied of land in possession, the cognizee hath nothing before entry, as it is agreed 48 Edw. 3. fol. 15b. 10 Hen. 6. fol. 16b. and Littl. in his Chapter of Attornment fol. 131b.: but if a fine *sur cognizance de droit tantum* be levied of a reversion upon an estate for life or years, or of a seignory, or any other thing which lieth in grant, there the reversion, or thing which lieth in grant, passeth presently. And it was said, that a common recovery is in nature of a common conveyance, and so it appears, that a reversion, or thing which lieth in grant, is more easily transferred from one person to another, than an estate of freehold in possession. A condition is executory as well as a judgment, but if the feoffor cannot enter, there the law will adjudge him in possession presently. And therefore it is holden in 20 Hen. 7. fol. 4b. 20 Edw. 4. fol. 19a. & 22 Edw. 4. that if the condition be collateral, and the feoffee makes a lease back again for years to the feoffor, and then the condition is broken, the law shall adjudge the feoffor in of a present fee-simple, because he cannot enter; and yet in that case he

---

8. [*Ed.:* 'upon acknowledgment of right' only (a term of art for the form of fine, or judicial proceeding to sue to convey land, and sometimes to alter the nature of a prior grant; in particular this form was used to convey an estate in reversion or remainder.)]

may say, that forasmuch as he cannot enter, therefore he ought to make claim; yet the law in that case requires no claim to be made; but, in the case before, it is otherwise, where no lease for years had been made back again, and the reason may be for the mischief before-mentioned.

The case of Littleton fol. 84. was likewise cited, where Littleton is of opinion, that in the case of a condition, the fee-simple shall be revested again in the [97 b] lessor, because he cannot enter, and the Law will | adjudge him in possession without entry or claim. It was likewise said, that those things which lie in grant, as in the case before remembered of the fine, they pass to the conusee immediately, by the fine levied: so in the case of a common recovery (which is now become a common assurance and conveyance) such things, which lie in grant, are in the recoveror by the judgment. And therefore, there are some opinions in the Books in 22 Ass. pl. 84. 45 Edw. 3. fol. 26b. & 30 Edw. 3. fol. 33. that if a man hath judgment to recover a rent, or common, or any thing which lieth in grant, there the thing so recovered is in the recoveror by the judgment, for the Books say, that the demandant is in seisin immediately by the judgment. And they cited the case in 27 Hen. 8. fol. 7a. which is direct in the point, that the recovery is executed immediately by the judgment; the land being in lease for years. So they said, first, that execution could not be sued against issue in tail: secondly, if it was necessary that execution should be had in the life of Edward Shelley, that it was executed by the judgment of the law: And if the judgment was executed by operation of the law, then the estate-tail to his heirs male of his body was in Edward Shelley, and consequently the entry of the defendant was lawful without question.

But for the argument of the third point, [which was the great doubt in the case,][9] admitting the Law in both the said points to be against the defendant, that is to say, that execution might be sued against the issue in tail; and that the recovery was not executed in the life of Edward Shelley, but after his death, and before the defendant was born: yet the defendant's counsel argued that the defendant's entry was lawful. The first reason in effect was as followeth: When the Law prescribes a means to perfect or settle any right or estate, if by the act of God, this means in some circumstances (as in our case in time) becomes impossible, yet no party who was to have received benefit, if the means had been, with all circumstances, executed, shall receive any prejudice

---

9. [*Ed.:* This aside was omitted from the 1658 edition; it had been restored by 1793.]

for not executing it in such circumstance which became impossible by the act of God, if every thing be performed without laches that the parties might perform; for it would be unreasonable that those things which are inevitable by the act of God, which no industry can avoid, nor policy prevent, should be construed to the prejudice of any person in whom there was no laches. And therefore the prescript Rule of Law is, that although a man shall not be tenant by the curtesy without actual seisin; yet of a rent, or of an advowson, if the wife dies before the rent-day, or before the avoidance, he shall be tenant by the curtesy, as it is agreed in 7 Edw. 3. | 66a, 66b. & 3 Hen. 7. 5b. for by [98 a] the act of God it is become impossible for him to have actual possession. Also, if lessee for the term of another man's life, be disseised of certain lands, and the disseisor takes the profits of them, now if the disseisee will recover the mean profits, the means which the Law prescribes for the same is, That the tenant for the other man's life shall re-enter, and then he shall recover all the mean profits in an action of trespass; but if the means become impossible by the act of God, by the death of the *cestuy que vie,*[10] so that he cannot re-enter, then he shall have an action of trespass without any re-entry, because the means is become impossible by the act of God, viz. the re-entry, as it is held in 38 Hen. 6. fol. 28e. Also, if a lessee covenants to leave a wood in as good plight as the wood was at the time of the lease, and afterwards the trees are blown down by tempest, he is discharged of his covenant, *quia impotent' excusat legem,*[11] as it is held in 40 Edw. 3. 6a. So if the father be enfeoffed with warranty to him and to his heirs, and afterwards the father enfeoff his son and heir apparent with warranty, and afterwards dies; now in regard the act of God hath destroyed the warranty between the father and the son, the son shall vouch as heir, although he is in by purchase, because the act of God hath determined the warranty between the father and the son, as it is adjudged in 43 Edw. 3. 23b. & 30 Edw. 3. 22. So in this case, when Edward Shelley died the morning of the same day that judgment was given, immediately upon the judgment, the recoverors sued forth an *habere fac' seisinam,* so that no laches was in any party, but it became impossible by the act of God, that execution could be had in the life of Edward Shelley; and therefore execution being had after his decease, shall not prejudice the son born after, who at that time was

10. [*Ed.:* The person whose life measures the duration of the grant, literally, "he for whose life."]

11. [*Ed.:* because impotence (i.e., powerlessness) excuses from the law,]

in utero matris.[12] The second reason was, because the use vested in Richard Shelley although not directly by descent as to have his age, or to toll an entry, &c. yet in the nature and degree of a descent by reason of the original act begun in the life of the ancestor; and their reason, in substance, was to this purpose. Where the heir takes any thing which might have vested in the ancestor, the heir should be *in* by descent; [then, although it first vested in the heir and never in the ancestor, yet the heir shall take it in the nature and course of a descent;][13] but in the case here the use might have vested in Edward Shelley, and if it had vested in Edward, then Richard Shelley would have taken it by descent, and therefore Richard, in this case ought to take this use in the nature and course of a descent. And therefore if a fine had been levied *sur cognisance de droit tantum* to Edward Shelley in fee, and after, and before execution, Edward had died, and Richard had entered before Henry was born; now although Richard be the first who entereth, yet forasmuch as this fine was levied to his ancestor and his | heirs, so that he claimeth by words of limitation; and forasmuch as the first and original act was done in the life of the father, and because it might have vested in the ancestor, and if it had vested in the ancestor, it had descended, for this cause Richard had taken it in course and degree of a descent, and the entry of the defendant had been lawful upon him. And yet, in that case, Richard should not have been in directly by descent, either to be in ward, or to have had his age, or to have tolled the entry of one who had right; but otherwise it is when the remainder is limited to the right heirs of J. S., &c. for there it beginneth in the son by name of purchase, and never could have vested in the brother, as the Book in 9 Hen. 7. 24. cited by the other side is agreed. So in the case of ravishment, 5 Edw. 4. fol. 6. which was cited on the other side; for in these cases, and all the others which have been put by the other side, the estate vested originally by purchase, and no beginning was in the life of the ancestor, which could ever have vested in the ancestor. And 16 Edw. 3 tit. Age Br. 51. if Richard Shelley had a seignory by descent, and afterwards the tenancy had escheated, and after the son is born, in that case the son shall enter upon him; for although the tenancy first vested in him, and never was in the father, yet because the original cause, viz. the seignory, was in the father, therefore the son shall enter upon the uncle. And

[98 b]

---

12. [*Ed.:* in [his] mother's womb.]

13. [*Ed.:* Bracketted text omitted from the 1658 edition; it had been restored by 1793.]

Chapman's Case in Mr. Plowden's new reports, fol. 284. was cited, for there it appears, that a covenant was made with Chapman, that he would make a lease for years to Chapman, &c. and before the lease was made Chapman died, and then the lease was made to his executors, so that the term did first commence in the executors; yet forasmuch as the covenant made to the testator was the cause of the making of the estate to the executors, for that reason the term was assets in the executor's hands, as well as if it had been made to the testator himself. So in our case, although the land first vested in Richard, yet it vested by reason of the recovery had against Edward Shelley, and the indenture made by him, and therefore Richard shall be in course of descent as well as the executors in the course of executors.

Further, admitting that Edward Shelley had exchanged certain land with another, and the other had entered into the land of Edward Shelley, but Edward Shelley had died before the entry, the Law is clear that the heir of Edward Shelley may enter into the land taken in exchange if he will, and so Perkins clearly takes it, fol. 57a.; then admitting that Richard Shelley had entered into the land taken in exchange, now he is the first in whom the land vests, but because it might have vested in Edward Shelley, and because he came to it by words of limitation, the son of the elder son born afterwards shall enter upon him: and yet I no right, title, use, nor action descends in this case; for [99 a] at his election the exchange might have been avoided. And so it is, if a man seised of the manor of S. covenants with another, that when J. S. shall enfeoff him of the manor of D., then he will stand seised of the manor of S. to the use of the covenantee and his heirs; the covenantee dies his heir within age, J. S. enfeoffeth the covenantor; in this case it was holden in *Wood's Case,* 3 Eliz. in the Court of Wards, that the heir shall be adjudged in, in course and nature of a descent; and yet it was neither a right, title, use, nor action that descended, but only a possibility of a use, which could neither be released nor discharged; yet it might, if the condition had been performed, have vested in the ancestor, and then the heir had claimed it by descent. And therefore in that case the heir was not in by purchase, but in by course of descent. And admitting that in all the cases which have been put, as in the case of ravishment, and in the case of the remainder, &c. he who might first enter dies before entry, and the younger son enters, and afterwards the son of the elder son is born, now it is clear, that the son of the elder son shall divest the land from the uncle, for it might have vested in the ancestor; and so to the case which hath been urged by the plaintiff's counsel in 9 Hen. 7. 25. of the condition:

the solicitor and Coke said, that it might be allowed for law, if the true sense thereof be apprehended. And therefore if the condition be, that the feoffor or his heirs pay the sum of 20l. or do any act before a day certain, that they shall re-enter, in that case if the father dies before the day of payment, and the daughter to save the inheritance pays the money, or satisfies the condition; in these cases peradventure the son shall not divest it, for if the daughter had not performed the condition, the land had been utterly lost. And therefore, in that case, a good argument may be made, that the daughter may detain the land, for *qui sentit onus, sentire debet & commodum.*[14] But if the condition was to be performed on the part of the feoffee, or broken in the life of the feoffor, then they said the law was clearly otherwise, for the heir entering for such condition broken shall be in ward, and have his age, and no such special reason as in the case next before.

It was also asked, out of what fountain this use should arise, and who was the mother that conceived this use? and the indenture answers, the recovery. For the indentures say, that the recovery shall be to the uses, &c. Then it was said, if the recovery be the mother which conceived this use, and the fountain out of which the use rose; forasmuch as this recovery was had in the life of Edward Shelley, although the use slept, and was as *embrio in utero matris*[15] until execution sued: yet the execution | being once had, the execution shall respect the recovery and raise the use, which slept before, which use being once awaked, or raised, takes its life and essence from the recovery which was had in the life of Edward Shelley. And thereupon some of the defendant's counsel argued in this manner, The execution of every thing which is executory always respects the original act or cause executory, and when the execution is done, it hath relation to the thing executory, and all makes but one act or record, although it be performed at several times: And therefore if A. by deed indented, covenants with B., that B. shall recover against him the manor of D. within a year next following; and that the recovery and execution thereupon to be had within the said year, shall be had to the recoveror in tail, &c. and after the recovery is had within the year, and the execution is sued after the year, in this case it is clear, that although the covenant is not pursued in time according to the precise form of it, yet the use shall be guided by the said

[99 b]

14. [*Ed.:* who bears the burden ought also to take the benefit.]
15. [*Ed.:* an embryo in [his] mother's womb]

indentures: So in the same case, if the same recovery betwixt the same parties
of the same land was suffered after the year, yet if no other intervenient agreement were between the parties, the recovery shall be intended to be to the
uses of the indentures. For variance in time in such case shall not subvert the
original agreement and contract of the parties. And it is held in 6 Edw. 3. 44b.
that if the presentment to a church by an usurper be in time of war and the
institution and induction, which are but as executions of the presentment be
in time of peace, yet it shall be avoided, for the Law regards the original act
& causa & origo est materia negotii.[16] If a man who is *non compos mentis,*[17]
gives himself a mortal wound, and before he dies he becomes of *sana memoria,*[18]
and afterwards dies of the same wound; in this case, although he dies of *sana
memoria* by reason of his own proper wound, yet because the original cause
of his death, viz. the wound was when he was *non compos mentis,* he shall not
be *felo de se,*[19] because the death, &c. hath relation to the original act which
was the stroke or wound; which see 22 Edw. 3. titula Corone 244. And so it
is 33 Ass. 7. Corone 210. if a servant hath an intent to kill his master, and
before execution of his intent goes out of service, and being out of service,
executes his purpose, and kills him who was his master; this is petit-treason,
for the execution doth respect the original cause, which was the malice conceived when he was servant; and yet if the law should adjudge and make
construction according to the several times, then it would be plain, it would
be no petit-treason. So in our case, the execution of the use relates to the
indentures and recovery.

| It was also asked, when after that the execution was had, so that now the [100 a]
use, which before slept, is raised, what thing is it that governs and directs this
use? And it is to be answered, the indentures. And what is their direction?
That the said Edward Shelley shall have it, and after his death the heirs male
of his body, so that the indentures direct the use to the heirs male of his body
by way of limitation of estate, and not by way of purchase. And from thence
this reason was collected; The indentures direct and govern the manner and
quality of the use, but the indentures direct that the heirs male of the body

16. [*Ed.:* and the substance of the matter lies in the cause and origin.]
17. [*Ed.:* not of sound mind,]
18. [*Ed.:* sound memory (i.e., sane)]
19. [*Ed.:* a suicide,]

of Edward Shelley shall take it by limitation of estate, and not by name of purchase; and therefore Richard ought to have it as heir by limitation of estate, and not by name of purchase; for when the execution was had, the indentures immediately guided the use to Richard, because he was at that time heir male of the body of Edward Shelley, which Richard is not heir after the birth of the son of the elder son. Further it was said, admitting all the matter before would not serve for the defendant (which the defendant's counsel held strongly it would) yet it is to be considered, in this case, that the estate vests in Richard by way of limitation of use and not by any conveyance by the Common Law in possession: and therefore admit our case had been before the making of the stat. of 27 Hen. 8., and that the recoverors had sued execution after the death of Edward, and before the son of the elder son was born, and then the son of the elder son had been born. In that case it was asked, which of them should have the *subpoena?* And the defendant's counsel conceived that the son of the elder son, although the use did first attach in the uncle, should have the *subpoena*. For if the intent of Edward Shelley may appear to the Court, that the son of the elder son should have this use, then that is the rule by which the use is to be guided and directed. For at the Common Law the intent of the parties was the direction of the uses, for they were only determinable, and to be adjudged by the Chancellor who is Judge of Equity, and that in Chancery, which is a Court of Conscience: and as Bracton saith, fol. 18. *Nihil tam conveniens est naturali aequitati quam voluntatem domini volentis rem suam in alium transferre ratam haberi.*[20] And therefore in proof, that uses are directed by the intent and meaning of the parties, divers cases were cited, 31 Hen. 6. titulo Subpoena Fitzherbert 23. Statham Conscience 1. A man being *cestuy que use,* and having an only daughter, declared his intent and meaning to the feoffees, that after his decease his daughter should have his land. And therefore

[100 b] a question I arose in Chancery, whether he might revoke this limitation of the use made to his daughter; and in arguing this case, Fortescue held, That if *cestuy que use* hath issue a daughter, and being sick, declares his intent to his feoffee, that his daughter shall have his land after his decease; and after he recovers his health, and hath issue a son, now he said it is good conscience that the son should have the *subpoena,* for he is his heir. Note the reason of

---

20. [*Ed.:* Nothing is so consonant to natural equity as that the will of an owner wishing to transfer his property to another should be respected.]

Fortescue, because he is his heir. And there Fortescue said, that *Conscientia dicitur a con & scio, quasi simul scire cum Deo,*[21] that is to say, the will of God as near as reason wills. We find likewise in divers other cases in our books, that the intent of the parties is the direction of uses, by a considerable and favourable construction. And therefore it is held in 7 Hen. 6. fol. 4b. if a man be seised of land on the part of his mother, and makes a feoffment in fee, reserving rent to him and his heirs, in that case, by the rule of Common Law, as Littleton says, the rent shall go to the heir on the part of the father; but if a man be seised of lands on the part of the mother, and makes a feoffment in fee to the use of him and his heirs, the book is directly agreed in 5 Edw. 4. fol. 7b. that this use shall not go to the heir at the Common Law, but forasmuch as the land and living move from the part of the mother, therefore in equity, the use which is nothing but a trust and confidence, should go also to the heirs on the part of the mother. Littleton likewise says, that a man shall not have a fee-simple by a feoffment or grant without these words "his heirs." And yet the Law is plain, that if a man had before the statute of 27 Hen. 8. bargained and sold his land for money without these words, "his heirs," the bargainee hath a fee-simple. And the reason is, because by the Common Law nothing passeth from the bargainor, but a use, which is guided by the intent of the parties, which was to convey the land wholly to the bargainee; and forasmuch as the law intends that the bargainee paid the very value of the land, therefore in equity, and according to the meaning of the parties, the bargainee had the fee-simple without these words "his heirs," as it is held in 27 Hen. 8. fol. 5. 4 Edw. 6. Br. Estates 78. 6 Edw. 6. and in the time of Hen. 8. Br. Conscience 25. So in our case, although the use first vested in the uncle, admitting the case to be before the stat. of 27 Hen. 8. yet seeing that the intent of Edward Shelley, was to advance the son of his elder son, and because in equity the general heir is to be favoured, therefore the son after born shall have the *subpoena.*

Moreover the rule in Law is, that if an estate be limited to two, the one capable, and the other not capable, he who is capable shall take the whole, as the cases are agreed in 17 Edw. 3. fol. 29. and 18 Edw. 3. 59. If a man gives land to one *& primogenito filio,*[22] if he hath no son | the father takes the whole: [101 a]

21. [*Ed.:* Conscience is so called from *con* (with) and *scio* (I know), as if to say, to know together with God,]

22. [*Ed.:* [his] firstborn son,]

And so it is 1 lib. Ass. 11. *& tempore*,[23] Edw. 1. Taile 24. if a man gives lands to a man, and to such a woman as shall be his wife, the man takes the whole; but if a man makes a feoffment in fee, to the use of himself and his wife that shall be, and afterwards he marries, his wife shall take jointly with him, as it was held in *The Lord Pawlet's Case*, 17 Eliz. Dyer 340., notwithstanding the whole vested at first in the husband. Also, the rule of Law is, that a remainder cannot stand without a particular estate, and yet the Book is agreed in 37 Hen. 6. fol. 36a. that if a man makes a feoffment in fee to the use of one for life, and after to the use of another in fee, although the particular tenant refuses, yet the remainder is good. And so it is said in the Book in the case of a devise. As if a man devises lands for life, the remainder in fee, and the tenant for life refuses, yet the remainder is good: And so note, that the limitation in uses and estates given by devises resemble one another. So the Judges there took the construction of devises, and of estates conveyed in use to be all one, viz. according to the meaning of the parties: And admitting in the case here, the land had been of the custom of gavelkind,[24] and upon that it had been asked, if Edward Shelley had had sundry other sons, should the elder son only have had the whole use? surely he only should not have it, but all equally, and yet if he had taken it by purchase, then the elder son only ought to have it. Now the intent of Edward Shelley, is to be proved by divers circumstances apparent in the record; first, if Edward Shelley had intended to have given it to the uncle, he never would have given it him by so general a name as "heir male," for if the recovery had been executed in the life of Edward Shelley as was fully intended, then it had been in manner agreed, that Richard Shelley could not have had the land, for the "heirs male" are words of limitation; or if the son of the elder son had been born in the life of Edward Shelley, which was impossible for Edward Shelley to have known the contrary, for the defendant was born within one month after his death, then out of all question the uncle could never have had it; and therefore except you will ground upon absurdities, the one, that Edward Shelley knew that he should die before the recovery executed; the other, that he should die, before the birth of the son of his elder son, which none could know but God; it must be granted, that the intent of

---

23. [*Ed.:* in the time of,]

24. [*Ed.:* "Gavelkind" was a Kentish land-hold by tenure for rents. It descended on the death of the tenant to all of his sons equally, with dower to his widow of one-half rather than one-third of the lands.]

Edward Shelley was to advance his elder son, and by no means to disinherit him. Also, at the time of his death Richard Shelley was eighteen years old: And therefore, if he intended to advance Richard, he would not have given his lands to his trusty friends Mr. Carill and others for twenty-four years; but without doubt he intended that the son of his eldest son should have it; and the same moved him to devise such a term which might be ended when the defendant should be of fit age | to receive and govern his living. The reason why the said Edward Shelley suffered the said recovery was, (as it seems) because Mary, daughter of his elder son named in the special verdict, would have inherited; and if the wife of his elder son had been delivered of a daughter, then had the land gone out of his name, and therefore for the continuance of the land in his name and family, he suffered the said recovery; and therefore it being by way of limitation of use, the son of the elder son ought to have it, and especially inasmuch as no rule in Law in our case is impugned, but it stands well, as hath been proved before, with the rule of the Common Law. And one of the defendant's counsel said, that at the Common Law, a use being but a trust and confidence, and, as is said in 14 Hen. 8., resting only in privity betwixt those who had notice thereof; and forasmuch as the consciences of the feoffees and others who were trusted became too large, and would not perform the confidence reposed in them, but made feoffments upon divers considerations to strangers not having notice of the uses, and by divers other fraudulent devices, did deceive and defraud those to whose uses they were seised: therefore first was the stat. of 1 Rich. 3. made, by which authority was given to the *cestuy que use* to enter and make a feoffment; But after that statute the feoffees oftentimes did prevent the feoffment of *cestuy que use* by subtle and cunning practices, yet defrauding the *cestuy que use,* and not discharging the trust reposed in them; and therefore to take away all the power and means of deceiving by the feoffees, the stat. of 27 Hen. 8. was made. And therefore it is holden for the better opinion at this day, that for the raising of future uses after the stat. the regress of the feoffees is not requisite, and that they have not power to bar these future uses, for the statute hath transferred all the estate out of them. But he said, in our case, if the suing of the execution after the death of Edward Shelley, and before the birth of the son of the elder son, should make the uncle have the land, then it would rest in the disposition and pleasure of the recoverors, whom they would make to inherit; for then it would follow, that if they enter and execute the recovery before the birth of the son of the elder son, then the uncle should have it, and if they would

[101 b]

not enter until after the birth of the son of the elder son, then without all question the son of the elder son should have the land: so that by this construction, the matter would lie in the breast of the recoverers who were but instruments, and not persons in any manner trusted to settle the inheritance in whom they pleased, which was never any part of the meaning of Edward Shelley, and which is very absurd in reason. And it would be mischievous that the inheritance of any man should be at the appointment and discretion of two strangers, who were named only as instruments, and never in any manner [102 a] trusted; and it would be a I greater mischief than any was at the Common Law. Also, as this case is, if the sheriff had executed the recovery upon the day on which the writ of execution was sued forth, then it had been evident that the son of the elder son should have had the land, for then had execution in judgment of law been in the life of Edward Shelley. But by the construction which hath been made, it would likewise be in the power of the sheriff to settle the inheritance in whom he pleased, for if he had executed the recovery the same day, as might have been done, or after the birth of the son of the elder son, then the son of the elder son should have had the land; but *uno absurdo dato infinita sequuntur.*[25] And therefore for the avoidance of these mischiefs and absurdities, the law will adjudge Richard in the land in course and nature of a descent, and then all the mischiefs and absurdities are avoided, and no ground or rule in the law is thwarted.

And note, the stat. of 27 Hen. 8. is, that *cestuy que use* shall have the possession to all intents, constructions, and purposes in law, and of and in such like estates as they had or ought to have in the use; and that he shall have the possession after such quality, manner, form and condition, as they had before had, or have had the use, trust, or confidence; so if the uncle before the statute had had the use, trust or confidence in nature and course of a descent, yet the son of the elder son shall divest the use, and have the *subpoena:* and because the statute executes the possession after such quality, manner, form, and condition, as the use, trust, or confidence was in them; for these causes the possession executed by the statute ought to be subject to the entry of the son of the elder son. And therefore, if *cestuy que use* had issue a daughter, and died before the stat. of 27 Hen. 8. his wife being great with child with a son, and before the birth of the son, the statute had been made, so that the possession

25. [*Ed.:* allow one absurdity, and an infinite number follow.]

had first vested by force of the statute in the daughter, yet the son born after might enter upon her; for the daughter had the possession in the same quality and condition as she had the use, but she had the use by descent, and subject to be divested by the birth of the son, and therefore he ought to have the possession by the statute in the same quality and degree, and that is in the nature and course of descent: But in the case of descent, the son after-born shall enter upon the daughter, and therefore the son in this case shall enter upon the daughter; and the like construction upon the like case hath been made before this time, therefore Justice Mountagu in *Wimbishe's Case*, and Plowden in Plowden's Comm. fol. 56b. held that if a woman hath a jointure made her by her husband in tail, and hath issue a daughter, being great with child with a son, and before the birth of the son she discontinues with warranty; now the stat. of 11 Hen. 7. saith, that such person to whom the title after the death of such wife | doth appertain shall enter into the lands, and shall possess   [102 b] and enjoy the same according to their title to the same, as if no such discontinuance had been made; and therefore he held clearly, that although the daughter after such discontinuance first entereth, yet the son born after shall enter upon her by reason of the words of the stat. of 11 Hen. 7. for the words are, that she ought to enjoy the same according to her title; but her title is in tail, and therefore after the birth of the son, he being next heir in tail, the title of the tail shall be devolved from her to the son.

So in our case the stat. of 27 Hen. 8. saith, that *cestuy que use* shall have the possession in the same quality, manner, form, and condition as he had the use. And therefore if a use were limited before the statute to John S. and Jane at Gappe, and to their heirs, and afterwards they intermarry, and after the statute is made, by which the possession is executed to them and their heirs during the coverture; yet they shall not have a divided estate, but the like moieties as they had in the use. So if *cestuy que use* be of certain lands held by priority and of other land by posteriority, and after the statute is made, by which execution is made of the possession of both at the same time, yet he shall have the possession of both in the same quality as he had the use, and all that by the express words of the statute. And it is to be noted, that the stat. of 27 Hen. 8. doth not speak only of uses, but also of trusts and confidence, so that although no use rose in the time of the life of Edward Shelley, yet there was a trust and confidence expressed in his life. And therefore when the use is once raised, it ought to be vested according to the trust and confidence which Edward Shelley intended and declared by the indentures.

Lastly, the defendant's counsel argued, That the uncle could not have the land as a purchaser, admitting the remainder had been limited to the right heirs male of the body of Edward Shelley, in as much as the eldest son of Edward Shelley had issue Mary his daughter, who is yet alive, as appears by the Record, and who is heir to Edward Shelley. It hath been said, that although Mary at the time of the death of Edward Shelley, was heir general, yet the said Richard was at that time heir male of the body of Edward Shelley. And therefore he might as special heir male of the body of Edward Shelley take the remainder, although Mary is heir general; and therefore it hath been said that if lands had been given to Edward Shelley, and to the heirs male of his body lawfully begotten, that in that case, after his death, Richard Shelley as heir male *per formam doni* shall inherit, although the daughter of the elder son was general heir to Edward Shelley. To that they answered, and took a difference when the heir male of the body claims by descent, and when he claims by purchase; for in descents the law is as hath been alleged, but it is

[103 a] otherwise in cases of purchase. This I difference was proved by the case in 37 Hen. 8. Br. Done 42. If a man makes a gift in tail of lands in gavelkind to a man and his heirs male of his body lawfully begotten, and hath issue four sons, in this case all the sons shall inherit: But if a lease for life be made of lands in gavelkind, the remainder to the right heirs of J. S. and J. S. dies, having issue four sons, in this case the eldest son only shall have the remainder, for there can be but one right heir in the case of purchase.

And so is Ellerker's opinion expresly in 9 Hen. 6. fol. 24a. If a man makes a lease for life, the remainder to the right heirs female of the body of J. S. and J. S. hath issue a son and a daughter, and dieth, in this case the daughter shall not take the remainder, for she is not heir female to take by purchase. And yet it is plain, that if a gift in tail had been made to J. S. himself, and to the heirs female of his body, and J. S. dieth, having issue a son and daughter, the daughter should have had the land by descent. Also in 37 Hen. 8. Br. Done 61. it appears, that the Lord Hussey made a feoffment in fee to the use of Anne his wife for life, and after to the use of the heirs of his body, and after the Lord Hussey was attainted of treason, and although Brook hath not ex-pressed the judgment, yet it was said, it was adjudged, that the right heirs of his body could not as purchaser take the remainder, because he was not heir of his body to take it by purchase, by reason of the attainder of his father. And yet before the stat. of 26 Hen. 8. if tenant in tail had committed high treason the land had descended. And in Brooke's Reports aforesaid it appears, that Hare, the Master of the Rolls, took the difference between a gift in possession to a man and to his heirs female of his body, and a lease for his life, the remainder to the right heirs female of his body; for in case of a remainder (as he said) she ought to be heir indeed, or else she can never claim it by purchase. So it appears by these authorities, that in case of purchase the heir male of the body ought to be heir indeed. And forasmuch as in our case, the uncle was not heir male for a man cannot have two heirs to claim by purchase, therefore as purchaser the uncle cannot claim it. But it hath been said, that the Statute *de Donis Conditionalibus* aids and helps the heir male of the body to take, for that the will of the donor appears, that the heir male of his body should have the land; and the statute saith, *quod voluntas donatoris secundum formam in charta doni sui manifeste expressa, de caetero observetur.*[26] In answer of which, one of the defendant's counsel declared | the reason of the other [103 b] cases and authorities which had been cited, and of the difference which was taken before; and therefore he said that the Statute *de Donis Conditionalibus* did not help this case. Mr. Littleton in his chapter of Estate-tail saith, that every gift in tail within the Statute *de Donis Conditionalibus,* before the making of that statute, was a fee-simple at the Common Law; and therefore he put the case before the Statute *de Donis Conditionalibus,* and examined if the same had been a fee-simple conditional before the said statute, for otherwise it cannot be an estate in fee-tail by the statute. For he said that the Statute *de Donis Conditionalibus* was a nurse, and no mother of estates of inheritances tail, and that it preserved the estates of inheritances in fee-tail, but did not beget or procreate any estates tail, which were not fee-simple conditional before. And therefore he took the law to be clear, that if a man gives land to a man *& semini suo,*[27] or to a man *& liberis suis de corpore,*[28] or *prolibus suis,*[29] or *exitibus suis,*[30] or *pueris suis de corpore,*[31] in these cases the donee hath no estate in fee-tail, but only an estate for term of life; for if such gifts had been made before the statute, they had been no fee-simples conditional; and there-

---

26. [*Ed.:* that the will of the donor be from henceforth observed, according to the form manifestly expressed in the charter of gift.]

27. [*Ed.:* and his seed,]

28. [*Ed.:* and his children of his body,]

29. [*Ed.:* his offspring,]

30. [*Ed.:* his issue,]

31. [*Ed.:* his children (or boys) of his body,]

fore by Mr. Littleton's rule, no estate-tail by the Statute *de Donis Condi-tionalibus.* For the statute creates no new inheritances, which were no in-heritances at the Common Law, but only nurses and preserves those which were estates of inheritance at the Common Law. And therefore the law was taken in the *Case of Martin Hastings* of Norfolk, for the manor of Elsinge, and where an estate was made to one of his ancestors, and to the issue male of his body, that in that case he had but an estate for life. And so it was held by Sir Roger Manwood, then one of the Justices of the Common Pleas, clearly in argument of *Clatch's Case,* anno 16 Eliz. and therefore he examined the case here before the said statute; and he took it without question, that if a lease had been made for life, the remainder to the heirs male of the body of J. S. that in that case, if J. S. had issue two sons, and the eldest son having issue a daughter died in the life of J. S. and then J. S. had died; that in that case the younger son of J. S. after his death cannot take this fee-simple conditional by the Common Law, for he was not heir male of the body to take this fee-simple by purchase; for first he ought to be heir, and secondly he ought to be heir male. And in that case if J. S. had been attainted of treason or felony, the heir male of his body could never have taken the remainder, for he was not heir, which might be the reason of *The Lord Hussey's Case* before cited.

[104 a] And it is holden in 12 Edw. 3. | titulo Variance 77. that where a man makes a gift to the husband and wife, and to the heirs of the body of the husband, and if the husband and wife die without issue of their two bodies, that then it shall remain over; in that case although the will of the donor appears, that the wife shall be also donee in special tail, yet forasmuch as by the order of the Common Law she could not have an estate of fee-simple conditional, for that cause she could not have an estate-tail by the statute. But in the said case where lands are given to a man and the heirs female of his body; here is an estate of inheritance vested in the donee, which estate of inheritance the Statute *de Donis Conditionalibus* directs to the heir female by descent, although there be an issue male.

And as to what hath been objected, that forasmuch as the limitation was to the heirs male of the body of Edward Shelley, and of the heirs male of the body of the heirs male lawfully begotten, that the heirs male of the body of Edward Shelley should be purchasers, for otherwise the subsequent words would be void: The defendant's counsel answered, that it is a Rule in Law, when the ancestor by any gift or conveyance takes an estate of freehold, and in the same gift or conveyance an estate is limited either mediately or immediately to his heirs in fee or in tail; that always in such cases, "the heirs" are words of limitation of the estate, and not words of purchase. And that appears in 40 Edw. 3. fol. 9a, 9b. in *The Provost of Beverley's Case,* in 38 Edw. 3. fol. 31d. 24 Edw. 3. 36b. 27 Edw. 3. fol. 87a. and in divers other books. So inasmuch as in this case Edward Shelley took an estate of freehold, and after an estate is limited to his heirs male of his body, the heirs male of his body must of necessity take by descent, and cannot be purchasers; otherwise is it where an estate for years is limited to the ancestor, the remainder to another for life, the remainder to the right heirs of the lessee for years; there his heirs are purchasers. Or if the remainder be limited to the heir in the singular number upon a lease for life, there the heir takes an estate for term of life by purchase. And if it should be admitted, that in regard of the said subsequent words, the right heirs male should have by purchase to them and the heirs male of their bodies, then a violence would be offered as well to the words as to the meaning of the party, for if the heir male of the body of Edward Shelley should take as purchaser, then all the other issue male of the body of Edward Shelley would be excluded to take any thing by the limitation; and it would be against the express | limitation of the party. For the limitation is   [104 b] to the use of the heirs male of the body of Edward Shelley, and of the heirs male of their bodies begotten, and for default of such issue, to divers other persons in remainder; so if Richard Shelley being the heir male of the body of Edward Shelley at the time of his death should take by purchase, then the heirs male of the body of Richard Shelley only would be inheritable, and no other of the sons of Edward Shelley, nor their heirs male, and consequently, if Richard Shelley should die without issue male, the land would remain over to strangers, and all the other sons of Edward Shelley which he then had and might afterwards have, and their issues, would be utterly disinherited; because the words were in the plural number, "heirs male of the body of Edward Shelley," the former construction will be against the very letter of the indentures, for by that means the plural number will be reduced to the singular number, that is to say, to one heir male of the body of Edward Shelley only: and forasmuch as the first words, viz. ("heirs male of the body of Edward Shelley" include the subsequent words, viz. "the heirs male of their bodies") for every heir male begotten of the body of the heir male of Edward Shelley is, in construction of law, an heir male of the body of Edward Shelley himself; for this reason the subsequent words are words declaratory, and do not restrain the former words. As in the case of Littleton, if a man makes a feoffment in fee, *ita quod*[32] the feoffee shall do such an act, in that case Littleton said it is commonly used in such cases to have also these words, "and if the act be not done, it shall be lawful for the feoffor to re-enter," which he said was more than was necessary, for the first words are sufficient in law, and include them, yet he said they were well put in, to declare and express the law to lay-people.

And lastly in this case, if Richard Shelley should not be in course and nature of a descent, then he could not take at all; for when an estate is made to a man, and after in the same deed, (to limit the quality of the estate) a further limitation is made to his heirs, or to the heirs of his body; in all these cases his heirs, or the heirs of his body, shall never take as purchasers, but in this case these words, "heirs male of the body of Edward Shelley," were words of limitation; and therefore the heir male of the body cannot take as a purchaser. And in proof of the first proposition, it was said, that this is the reason of the book in 40 Ass. pl. 19. and of *Mr. Littleton's Case,* fol. 128. that if a man grants a reversion, or a seignory, by deed to J. S. and his heirs, if the grantee dies before attornment,[33] the attornment to the heir is void, for if the attornment

[105 a] should be good, then the | heir would be in as a purchaser, where by the grant and meaning of the parties, these words, "his heirs," were words of limitation to limit the estate of the grantee himself; and so it was held in *Nichol's Case* in Plow. Com. fol. 483. that if a man leases lands to a man for life, and if the lessor dies without heir of his body, that then the lessee shall have the land to him and to his heirs; in that case, if lessee for life dies, and then the lessor dies without heir of his body, the heir of the lessee shall not have the land, as it was held clearly *causa qua supra.*[34]

And so the law is clear, as it is commonly agreed in our books, if two men exchange lands in fee-simple, or fee-tail, if both the parties die before the exchange be executed, of each part, the exchange is void; for if the heirs should enter, they would be in as purchasers by force of the words, which were words of limitation of the estate, and not of purchase. And upon the same reason is *Brett's and Rigden's Case* adjudged in Plow. Com fol. 342a stronger case than this case is. For a man devised lands to another and to his heirs, and the devisee

---

32. [*Ed.:* so that (i.e., on condition that).]

33. [*Ed.:* "Attornment" was the formal recognition of a transfer of a tenancy in land, by which the new tenant acknowledges his duties, either to a lord, to a grantee, or, for a holder of a future interest, to the present interest holder.]

34. [*Ed.:* for the above reason.]

died in the life of the devisor, and then the devisor died; and it was adjudged, that the heir should not take by the devise, for in that case the heirs are not named as words of purchase, but only to express and limit the estate which the devisee should have; for without the word "heirs," the devisee could not have the fee-simple, and the heirs are named only to convey the land in fee-simple, and not to make any other to be purchaser than the first devisee. So in our case the heirs male of the body of Edward Shelley are named only to give Edward Shelley an estate-tail, and not to make any other purchaser than Edward Shelley only, and without those words he could not have had an estate-tail; and therefore the uncle in our case cannot claim the land as a mere purchaser, but if he takes it in any sort, he shall take it in nature and course of a descent, and therefore *quacunq. via data*,[35] the uncle cannot have the land; and if he take it in nature and course of a descent, (for as a purchaser he cannot take) then the elder son shall enter upon him, and so *quacunq. via data* the son of the elder son ought to have the land. And therefore to conclude: first, no execution could be sued against the issue in tail, because no execution was sued in the life of Edward Shelley. Secondly, admitting execution might have been sued against the issue in tail, and that execution was requisite to be had in the life of Edward Shelley, inasmuch as the lands were in lease for years, that the reversion was immediately vested in the recoveror by the judgment: thirdly, admitting execution might be sued against the issue in tail, and that the recovery was not executed till after the death of Edward Shelley; yet first, I forasmuch as it was impossible by the act of God that execution should be   [105 b] sued in the life of Edward Shelley; secondly, that the indentures guide the use, and direct it to the heirs male of the body of Edward Shelley by words of limitation; thirdly, that the use and estate do not commence originally in the uncle as a mere purchaser, but first vested in the uncle by force of the indentures made by Edward Shelley and the recovery had against him, and might have vested in Edward Shelley, and if it had been vested in Edward Shelley, then without doubt Richard Shelley had taken by descent; fourthly, that the estate is conveyed by way of limitation of use, which is always directed by the intent of the parties; fifthly, that it would be absurd and mischievous to adjudge the whole inheritance to be at the disposal of the recoverors, or of the sheriff, who never were trusted; and lastly, that Richard the uncle ought

---

35. [*Ed.:* Whichever way you take it,]

either to claim in nature or course of descent; and then no question but the entry of the defendant was lawful, or otherwise merely by purchase, which by the rules of law, and for the reasons aforesaid he cannot; and therefore they concluded that the entry of Henry Shelley the defendant was lawful, and that judgment ought to be given against the plaintiff, that he should take nothing by his bill.

After the said case had been openly and at large argued at three several days by the counsel of each side in the King's Bench, the Queen hearing thereof (for such was the rareness and difficulty of the case, being of importance, that it was generally known) of her gracious disposition, to prevent long, tedious, and chargeable suits between parties so near in blood, which would be the ruin of both, being gentlemen of a good and ancient family, directed her gracious letters to Sir Thomas Bromley, Knight, Lord Chancellor of England, who was of great and profound knowledge and judgment in the law, thereby requiring him to assemble all the justices of England before him, and upon conference had between themselves touching the said questions, to give their resolutions and judgments thereof; and thereupon the Lord Chancellor in Easter term, in the 23d year of her reign, called before him at his house, called York-house, Sir Christopher Wray, Knight Lord Chief Justice of England, and all his companions, Justices of the Queen's Bench, Sir James Dyer, Knight Lord Chief Justice of the Court of Common Pleas, and all his companions, justices of the same Court; and Sir Roger Manwood, Knight Lord Chief Baron of the Exchequer, and the Barons of the Exchequer, before whom the questions aforesaid were moved and shortly argued by Serjeant Fenner, on the plaintiff's

[106 a] part, and by one on the defendant's part.[36] At which time the Lord | Chancellor was of opinion for the defendant, and openly declared his opinion before all the justices, that upon the third question the law was for the defendant, and therefore the defendant's entry upon the uncle was lawful: but the said questions were not resolved at that time, the said justices desiring time to consider of the questions. And eight or nine days after in the same term, all the said justices and Barons met together in Serjeant's-Inn, in Fleet Street, for the resolution of the said case, and there the case was again shortly argued by them; after which arguments the justices at that time did confer among themselves, and took further time to consider of the said questions in the next

36. [*Ed.:* Sir Edward Coke.]

vacation, till the beginning of Trinity term then next following; and accordingly in the beginning of Trinity term, after great study and consideration of the said record of the special verdict, all the said justices and Barons met again in Serjeant's Inn, in Fleet Street; at which time upon conference amongst themselves, all the justices of England, the Lord Chief Baron, and the Barons of the Exchequer, except one of the puisne justices of the Court of Common Pleas, agreed that the defendant's entry upon the said Richard the uncle was lawful; and four or five days after their last meeting, one of the defendant's counsel came to the Bar in the Queen's Bench, and moved the justices to know their resolutions in the said case; for their resolution was not before known to the defendant, nor to his counsel. And Sir Christopher Wray, Knight Lord Chief Justice, answered, that they were resolved; and thereupon asked the plaintiff's counsel being then at the Bar, if they could say any more on the plaintiff's part, who answered, That they had said as much as they could: and also demanded of the defendant's counsel, if they had any new matter to say for the defendant, who said, No. And then the said Chief Justice gave judgment, that the plaintiff should take nothing by his bill: And because the counsel of both sides, who were present, were desirous to know upon which of the said points their resolution did depend, the said Chief Justice openly declared, That as to the first point, the better and greater part of all the justices and Barons held that execution might be sued against the issue in tail, because the right of the estate-tail was bound by the judgment against the tenant in tail, and the judgment over to have in value, and that in favour of common recoveries, which are the common assurances of the land.   [106 b]

And as to the second point, they were all agreed, that the reversion was not in the recoverors immediately by the judgment: But he said, that all the justices of England and Barons of the Exchequer, except one of the justices of the Common Pleas, were agreed as to the third point. That the uncle was in, in course and nature of a descent, although he should not have his age, nor be in ward, &c.: First, because the original act, viz. the recovery, out of which all the uses and estates had their essence, was had in the life of Edward Shelley, to which the execution after had a retrospect: Secondly, because the use and possession might have vested in Edward Shelley, if execution had been sued in his life: Thirdly, the recoverors by their entry, nor the sheriff by doing of execution, could not make whom they pleased inherit: Fourthly, because the uncle claimed the use by force of the recovery, and of the indentures by words of limitation, and not of purchase. These were, as the Chief Justice said, the principal reasons of their judgment. And it was resolved by them all, that the recovery, notwithstanding the death of Edward Shelley in the morning between the hours of five and six on the same day, was good enough. And so it was resolved by Sir Thomas Bromley, Knight Lord Chancellor of England, Sir Christopher Wray, Knight Lord Chief Justice of England, Sir James Dyer, Knight Lord Chief Justice of the Court of Common Pleas, Sir Roger Manwood, Knight Lord Chief Baron of the Exchequer, Sir Thomas Gawdy, Knight one of the Justices of Her Highness's Bench, and by all the Justices of the Queen's Bench, and by all the Justices, saving one of the Common Pleas, and by all the Barons of the Exchequer, that the right of the defendant was good, and his entry lawful, and judgment was given accordingly.

Part Two of the *Reports*

The Second Part of Coke's *Reports* was published in 1602. It was originally published in Law French and entitled *Le Second Part Des Reportes Del Edvvard Coke Lattorney General Le Roigne, De Divers matter en Ley, avec graunde & mature consideration resolve, & adjudge, queux ne sueront unques resolve ou adjudge par devant, & les raisons & causes de yceux durant le Raigne de trefillure & renomes Roygne Elizabeth, le fountaine de tout Justice & la vie de la Ley.* In English, *The Second Part of the Reports of Sir Edward Coke, Knight., Her Majesty's Attorney-General, of divers Matters In Law, with great and Mature consideration Resolved and Adjudged, which were never Resolved or Adjudged Before: and the Reasons and Causes thereof: During the Reign of the most Illustrious and Renowned Queen Elizabeth, the Fountain of all Justice, and the life of the Law.* The whole of the cases in this part is a series of issues in the control, transfer, and obligations arising from the ownership of property, including some cases, such as the problem of bankrupts, dealing with satisfaction of debts from property. There is a lesser emphasis in this part on both the style and the content of pleading and on the effect of pleading in deciding the dispute.

Epigrams from the Title Page:

ECCLESIASTICUS CAP. 24.
Videte quod non mihi soli laboravi, sed omnibus exquirentibus scientiam.[1]

PAPIAN. Lib. 1. Definit.
Lex est commune praeceptum, vivorum prudentium consultum, delictorum que sponte vel ignorantia contrabuntur, communis reipublicae sponsio.[2]

---

1. [*Ed.:* Behold, I have not labored for myself only, but for all them that seek wisdom.]

2. [*Ed.:* Law is a universal command, the resolution of prudent men, restraining offences (whether knowingly or unwittingly committed), a general consensus of the common weal.]

ISODORUS.

Lex dicitur a ligando, quia obligat; vel dicitur a legendo, quia publice legatur.[3]

CIC. Lib. 1. de Legibus.

Cum dico legem, a me dici nihil aliud intelligi volo quam imperium; sine quo domus ulla, nec civitas, nec gens; nec gens, nec hominum universum genus stare, nec rerum natura omnis, nec ipse mundus potest.[4]

SENECA AD LUCIL. Epist. 108[5]

Illud tamen prius scribam, quemadmodem tibi ista cupiditas discendi, qua flagrare te video, regenda sit, ne ipsa impediat; nec passim carpenda sunt, nec avide invadenda universa: per partes pervenitur ad totum: aptari onus viribus debet, nec plus occupari, quam cui sufficere possumus: non quantum vis, sed quantum capis hauriendum est: Quo plus recipit animus, hoc se magis laxat.[6]

Idem. Epist. 45.

Lectio certa prodest, varia delectat; qui quo destinavit pervenire vult unam sequatur viam, non per multas vagetur, non ire istud sed errare est.[7]

Idem. ad Lucil. in Epist.

Non refert quam multos, sed quam bonos habeas libros; multitido librorum onerat non instruit, & satius est paucis authoribus te tradere, quam errare per multos.[8]

---

3. [*Ed.: Lex* (law) is so called from *ligando* (binding), because it binds, or it is so called from *legendo* (reading), because it is read out in public.]

4. [*Ed.:* When I say the law, I wish nothing else to be understood to be said by me but *imperium* (authority), without which no house, no city, no people, nor any kind of man, nor the nature of things, nor even the world itself, can stand.]

5. [*Ed.:* These texts were omitted from the 1658 edition, but are included in various others. These translations were included in the 1793 edition.]

6. [*Ed.:* This first will I set down, (which else might hinder thee) how thou art to order that servant desire of learning which I find to be in thee; things are not every where alike gathered, nor universally all greedily snatched: the whole is to be attained unto by parts: burdens must be fitted to the strength of the bearers; neither should we undertake more than we are able to effect: draw out so much as may satisfy not thy mind by thy want: the very mind of man, the more it receiveth, the more it loosens and freeth itself.]

7. [*Ed.:* Certainty in reading is profitable, variety delightful; he that desireth to come to his journey's end must pursue one way, not wander in many, for that is rather to err than to go forward.]

8. [*Ed.:* It matters not how many books thou hast, but how good, multitude of books do rather burden than instruct, and it is far better thoroughly to acquaint thyself with a few Authors, than to wander through many.]

JERO. Epist. 88
Statue tibi quot horis legas, non ad laborem sed ad delictationem.[9]

(Preface)
To the learned Reader.

There are (sayth *Euripides*) three Virtues worthy [of] our meditation; To honour God, our Parents who begat us, and the Common Lawes of Greece: The like doe I say to thee (Gentle Reader) next to thy dutie and pietie to God, and his annointed thy gracious Soveraigne, and thy honour to thy Parents, yeeld due reverence and obedience to the Common Lawes of England: For of all Lawes (I speake of humane) these are most equall, and most certaine, of greatest antiquitie, and least delay, and most beneficiall and easie to be observed; As if the module of a Preface would permit, I could defend against any man that is not malicious without understanding, and make manifest to any of judgement and indifferency, by proofes pregnant and demonstrative, and by Records and Testimonies luculent and irrefragable: *Sed sunt quidam fastidiosi, qui nescio quo malo affectu oderunt Artes antequam pernoverunt.*[1] There is no Jewell in the world comparable to learning; No learning so excellent both for Prince and Subject as knowledge of Lawes; and no knowledge of any Lawes, (I speake of humane) so necessary for all estates, and for all causes, concerning goods, lands, or life, as the Common Lawes of England. If the beauty of other Countries be faded and wasted with bloudy Warres, thanke God for the admirable peace wherein this Realme hath long flourished under the due administration of these Lawes: If thou readest of the tyranny of other Nations, wherein powerfull will and pleasure stands for Law and Reason, and where upon conceit of mislike, men are suddenly poysoned, or otherwise murthered, and never called to answer; Praise God for the Justice of thy gracious Soveraigne, who (to the Worlds admiration,) governeth her people by Gods goodnesse in peace and prosperity by these Lawes, and punisheth not

---

9. [*Ed.:* Tax thyself at so many hours for reading, that thou mayest do it rather with delight than with toil.]

1. [*Ed.:* But there are certain scornful people who—I know not by what ill disposition—hate every profession with which they are unacquainted.]

the greatest offendor, no, though his offence be crimen laese Majestatis,[2] Treason against her sacred person, but by the just and equall proceedings of Law.

If in other Kingdomes, the Lawes seeme to governe: But the Judges had rather misconstrue Law, and doe injustice, then displease the Kings humour, whereof the Poet speaketh, *Ad libitum Regis, sonuit sententia Legis.*[3] Blesse God for Queene Elizabeth, whose continuall charge to her Justices agreeable with her ancient Lawes, is, that for no commandement under the great or privie Seale, writs or letters, common right bee disturbed or delayed. And if any such commandement (upon untrue surmises) should come, that the Justices of her Lawes should not therefore cease to doe right in any point: And this agreeth with the ancient Law of England, declared by the great Charter, and spoken in the person of the King; *Nulli vendemus, nulli negabimus, aut differemus Justiciam vel Rectum.*[4]

If the ancient Lawes of this noble Island had not excelled all others, it could not be but some of the severall Conquerors, and Governors thereof; That is to say, the Romanes, Saxons, Danes, or Normans, and specially the Romanes, who, (as they justly may) doe boast of their Civill Lawes, would (as every of them might) have altered or changed the same.

For thy comfort and encouragement, cast thine eye upon the Sages of the Law, that have beene before thee, and never shalt thou finde any that hath excelled in the knowledge of these lawes, but hath sucked from the breasts of that divine knowledge, honesty, gravity, and integrity, and by the goodnesse of God hath obtained, a greater blessing and ornament then any other profession, to their family and posteritie: As by the page following, taking some for many, you may perceive; for it is an undoubted truth, *That the just shall flourish as the Palme tree, and spread abroad as the Cedars of Libanus.*[5]

Their example and thy profession doe require thy imitation: for hitherto I never saw any man of a loose and lawlesse life, attaine to any sound and perfect knowledge of the said lawes: And on the other side, I never saw any man of excellent judgement in these Lawes, but was withall (being taught by such a Master) honest, faithfull, and vertuous.

If you observe any diversities of opinions amongst the professors of the

---

2. [*Ed.:* Treason; lese majesty was the crime of injuring the dignity of the monarch.]
3. [*Ed.:* Legal decisions were made at the king's whim.]
4. [*Ed.:* To no one shall we sell, to no one deny, to no one delay, Justice or Right.]
5. Psal. 91.12 [AV 92.12].

Lawes, contend you (as it behoveth) to be learned in your profession, and you shall finde that it is *Hominis vitium, non professionis.*[6] And to say the truth, the greatest questions arise not upon any of the Rules of the Common Law, but sometimes upon Conveyances and Instruments made by men unlearned; Many times upon Wills intricately, absurdly, and repugnantly set downe, by Parsons, Scriveners, and such other Imperites: And oftentimes upon Acts of Parliament, overladen with provisoes, and additions, and many times upon a sudden penned or corrected by men of none or very little judgement in Law.

If men would take sound advise and counsell in making of their Conveyances, Assurances, Instruments, and Willes: And Counsellors would take paines to be rightly and truly informed of the true state of their Clyents case, so as their advise and counsell might be apt and agreeable to their Clients estate: And if Acts of Parliament were after the old fashion penned, and by such onely as perfectly knew what the Common Law was before the making of any Act of Parliament concerning that matter, as also how farre forth former Statutes had provided remedie for former mischiefes and defects discovered by experience; Then would very few questions in Law arise, and the learned should not so often and so much perplex their heads, to make atonement and peace by construction of Law betweene insensible and disagreeing words, sentences, and provisoes, as they now doe.

In all my time I have not knowne two questions made of the right of Discents, of escheates by the Common Law, &c. so certaine and sure the Rules thereof bee: Happy were Arts if their professors would contend, and have a conscience to be learned in them, and if none but the learned would take upon them to give judgement of them.

Your kinde and favourable acceptation (gentle Reader) of my former Edition, hath caused me to publish these few cases in performance of my former promise, and I wish to you all no lesse profit in reading of them, then I perswade my selfe to have reaped in observing of them: This onely of the learned I desire:

> *Perlege, sed si quid novisti rectius istis,*
> *Candidus imperti; si non hiis utere mecum.*[7]

6. [*Ed.:* A defect in the men, not in the profession.]

7. [*Ed.:* Read this through, and if you find anything more correct than this, dear Reader, share it; if not, use this with me.]

Manser's Case.
(PAINTER V. MANSER)
(1584) Easter Term, 26 Elizabeth I
In the Court of Common Pleas.
First Published in the *Reports,* volume 2, page 1.*

Ed.: Manser and his son promised Painter to keep certain lands free from legal encumbrances and to sign whatever legal papers Painter required in order to do so. When Painter sent them a legal document to release him of liability, Manser said his son could not read and would not sign it until it had been read to them by a lawyer. When Painter sued Manser, using the appropriate writ of debt, Manser replied in a pleading that he had only delayed to meet with lawyers, that he had maintained the land as promised and that he himself had executed the lease. The court held that a person who cannot read a language asked to sign a document in that language must be allowed to have it read, but this allowance cannot expand the time in which it must be signed and sealed. Manser's other claims were lost for a failure to plead facts necessary to sustain an affirmative pleading, and Painter won the case. The opinion is notable for its discussion of laymen's required knowledge of the law, for its use of relative weights of fact in comparing a precedent, and for its instructions on the requirements of pleading. Look also for Coke's admonition that lawyer's documents should be written to be understood by the parties who need them.

Between Painter and Manser, the case was such: Painter brought an action of debt upon an obligation against Manser, and the defendant pleads the obligation was with condition; *scil.* That whereas the defendant had enfeoffed the plaintiff of certain lands, if the plaintiff shall at all times following enjoy those lands discharged, or otherwise kept indemnified from all incumbrances, &c.; and also, if the defendant and John Manser his son, shall do all acts and devices for the better assurance of those lands to him, as by the plaintiff, or his counsel learned in the law, shall be devised, that then the obligation shall be void; And pleaded that the plaintiff had enjoyed the said lands discharged

---

*[*Ed.:* The pleadings are recorded at Pasch. 26 Eliz. Rot. 1608.]

and kept indemnified from all incumbrances, &c.; And that the plaintiff devised a writing of release to be made by the defendant and John his son, to the plaintiff, which the defendant did seal and deliver as his deed; and because his son was not lettered, and could not read, the said John prayed the plaintiff to deliver it to him, to be shewed to some man learned in the law, who might inform him if it was made according to the condition; and said further, that if it was according to the condition, he would deliver it, which the plaintiff refused; wherefore he did not deliver it, as it was lawful he should not: whereupon the plaintiff demurred; and it was adjudged for the plaintiff. In this case three points were resolved.

1st. If a man, not lettered, be bound to make a deed, he is not bound to seal and deliver any writing tendered to him, unless somebody be present who can read the deed to him, if he requires the writing to be read to him; And if the deed be in Latin, French, or other language (which the party who is to execute the writing doth not understand), in such case, if the | party demands   [3 b] that one should read and interpret the writing to him, and none be present that can read and expound the tenor of the same in that language that the party who is to deliver the deed understands, there the party may well refuse to deliver it. So although the man can read, yet if the deed be in Latin, French, or other such language as the party who is to execute cannot understand, if he require that the writing be read or expounded to him in such language as he may understand it, and nobody be there to do it, the party may refuse to deliver it. And it is to know that *quod ignorantia est duplex, viz. facti & juris; & rursum ignorantia facti (quoad rem nostram attinet) est duplex, videlicet, lectionis & linguae.*[1] Note, reader, that ignorance in reading, or ignorance of the language, *quae sunt ignorantia facti,*[2] may excuse; but as is commonly said, *ignorantia juris non excusat:*[3] For notwithstanding that there it was said, that although the party can read and knows the language also in which the writing was made, yet he does not know the sense and operation of the words in law, and whether they agree with the condition of his obligation, or not; And therefore some of the justices thought that in such case the party shall have

---

1. [*Ed.:* Whereas ignorance is of a dual nature, to wit, of fact and law, and returning to ignorance of fact (to the degree that it is our concern here), it is (also) of a dual nature, that is, of the text and of the language.]

2. [*Ed.:* Which are ignorance of facts.]

3. [*Ed.:* Ignorance of the law does not excuse (its breach).]

reasonable time to shew the writing to his counsel at law to be instructed by them, whether it be according to what he is bound to do, and namely when there is no time limited in which it is to be done, so as in regard that the other party might request the doing of it when he pleased, it is not possible for the party to have his learned counsel at all times with him: and therefore *prima faeie,*[4] it seemed reasonable, that the party shall have reasonable time, as afore said: But at length, upon the view of the record of a judgment in this Court, anno 16 Eliz. in the time of the Lord Dyer, between Sir Anthony Cook and Wotton, that upon such request made to Sir Anthony Cook by Wotton, to seal an indenture, Sir Anthony, who was not learned in the law, was obliged to seal it peremptorily at his peril, and could not obtain convenient time to consult upon it with his counsel; hereupon it was resolved in the case at the Bar according to the said judgment. See the case now reported by the Lord Dyer. Trinit. 16 Eliz. Dier 337, 338. And it was said, that the case at the Bar was stronger than that of Sir Anthony Cook; for in this case the defendant obliged himself, that his son, who was a stranger to the obligation, should do, &c.: in which case he has undertaken that his son shall do it at his peril; for he that is obliged, undertakes more for a stranger than for himself in many cases. *Vide* 33 Hen. 6. 16b. 36 Hen. 6. 8. 2 Edw. 4. 2. 15 Edw. 4. 5b. 22 Edw. 4. 43. and 10 Hen. 7. 14b.

[4 a]   2d. It was resolved, that the [Defendant's] pleading was insufficient: for he hath pleaded, that the plaintiff had enjoyed the | land discharged and kept harmless from incumbrances, where he ought to have shewed how: So if he had pleaded, that he had saved him harmless, he ought to have shewed how; but in such case, if he had pleaded in the negative, *non fuit damnificatus,*[5] there it is otherwise. Secondly, he hath pleaded, *quod quoddam scriptum re-laxationis,*[6] was sealed and delivered, and doth not shew whether the release concerns the lands mentioned in the condition; and for all these causes the plaintiff had judgment to recover.

Note reader, there is great reason, that the writing should be expounded in such language, that the party may understand it, although he could read; because, by the law, he is at his peril to deliver it presently upon request, and hath not time to consult upon it with learned counsel.

---

4. [*Ed.:* on first sight; presumptively,]
5. [*Ed.:* he was not damaged,]
6. [*Ed.:* that a certain deed of release,]

The Case of Bankrupts.

(SMITH v. MILLS)
(1589) Trinity Term, 31 Elizabeth I
In the Court of the King's Bench.
First Published in the *Reports,* volume 2, page 25a.

Ed.: John Cook, a merchant, went bankrupt, owing Robert Tibnam £64 and another group of creditors £273, 12d. The second group of creditors got a commission in bankruptcy against Cook. Cook gave part of his goods to Tibnam in partial payment of his debt, and Tibnam sold them. But the bankruptcy commissioners sold the same goods to the group of creditors in partial satisfaction of their debts. In an important case construing the then-two-decade-old bankruptcy statute, Chief Justice Wray of the King's Bench held that the sale by the commissioners was good, that the purpose of the statute was to protect all of the creditors of a bankrupt, and that a bankrupt debtor cannot give preferential settlements to one creditor, but both debtor and creditors must accept an equal settlement for all of the creditors.

Gregory Smith, Cullamor, and other good merchants of London, brought an action upon the case upon trover and conversion of divers goods, in London, against Thomas Mills, and upon not guilty pleaded, the jury gave a special verdict to this effect: John Cook, of Spalding, was possessed of the same goods, and exercising the trade of buying and selling, 30 Januarii, 29 Eliz. became a bankrupt, and absented himself *secundum formam statuti,*[1] (which was found at large), and the said 30 Januarii was indebted to the plaintiffs, being subjects born, in £273 12d. *pro merchandizis per quemlibet eorum prius venditis;*[2] and then also was indebted to Robert Tibnam, being also a subject born, in £64. Afterwards, 12 February, 29 Eliz. the plaintiffs exhibited a petition to the Lord Chancellor to have a commission upon the Statute of Bankrupts; and 17 February, 29 Eliz. a commission was granted, according to the said statute, under the Great Seal, to William Watson and others. And afterwards, 21 Februarii, 29 Eliz. John Cook gave and delivered the said goods to Tibnam, in satisfaction

---

1. [*Ed.:* according to the form of the statute,]
2. [*Ed.:* for merchandise previously bought from each of them;]

of part of his said due debt, the goods being of the value of £24. And afterwards, *ultimo Martii*,[3] 29 Eliz. the commissioners, by deed indented, sold to the plaintiffs jointly the said goods, and at the same time the said Mills, then factor to Tibnam *in ea parte*,[4] refused to come in as creditor, but claimed the said goods as the proper goods of his master, by the gift aforesaid; and afterwards the goods came to the defendant's hands, and he converted them; but whether the said sale of the said commissioners, notwithstanding the said gift and delivery to Tibnam, be good or not, that was the doubt referred to the consideration of the Court. And judgment was given by Wray, | Chief Justice, and the whole Court, for the plaintiffs. And in this case divers points were resolved:

[25 b]

1st, That the said sale made by the said commissioners, was good; and because the doubt arose only upon the words and intent of the stat. of 13 Eliz. cap. 7., the Court considered the several parts and branches thereof: First, the Act describes a bankrupt, and whom he defrauds, *scil.* the creditors. 2. To whom the creditors should complain for relief, *scil.* to the Lord Chancellor. 3. How, and by what way, relief and remedy is provided, *scil.* by force of a commission under the Great Seal, &c. 4. The authority of the commissioners, *scil.* to sell, &c. that is to say, to every one of the creditors a portion, rate and rate alike, according to the quantity of his or their debt. So that the intent of the makers of the said Act, expressed in plain words, was to relieve the creditors of the bankrupt equally, and that there should be an equal and rateable proportion observed in the distribution of the bankrupt's goods amongst the creditors, having regard to the quantity of their several debts; so that one should not prevent the other, but all should be *in aequali jure.*[5] And so we see in divers cases, as well as the Common Law, as upon the like statutes, such constructions have been made; for, as Cato saith, *Ipsae etenim leges cupiunt ut jure regantur;*[6] And therefore it is held, in 35 Hen. 8. tit. Testaments, Br. 19. a man holdeth three manors of three several lords by knights service, each manor of equal value, he cannot devise two manors and leave the third to

3. [*Ed.:* on the last [day] of March,]
4. [*Ed.:* in that behalf,]
5. [*Ed.:* in the same legal position.]
6. [*Ed.:* The laws themselves desire to be ruled by right;]

descend, according to the generality of the words of the Acts of 32 & 34 Hen. 8. of Wills, for then he should prejudice the other two lords, but, by a favourable and equal construction, he can devise but two parts of each manor, so that equality between them shall be observed. And in 4 Edw. 3. Assize 178. the lord of a town cannot improve it all, leaving sufficient common in the lands of other lords, within the Statute of Merton, cap. 4. And so, in cases at the Common Law, an equality is required; as, in 11 Hen. 7. 12b. a man binds himself in an obligation and his heirs, and hath heirs and lands on the part of his father and on the part of his mother, both heirs shall be equally charged; 48 Edw. 3. 5a, 5b. in dower, if the heir be vouched in three several wards within the same county, he shall not have execution against one only, but all shall be equally charged; 29 Edw. 3. 39. the like case. So here, in our case, there ought to be an equal distribution *secundum quantitatem debitorum suorum;*[7] but if, after the debtor becomes a bankrupt, he may prefer one (who peradventure hath least need), and defeat and defraud many other poor men of their true debts, | it would be unequal and unconscionable, and a great [26 a] defect in the law, if, after that he hath utterly discredited himself by becoming a bankrupt, the law should credit him to make distribution of his goods to whom he pleased, being a bankrupt man, and of no credit; but the law, as hath been said before, hath appointed certain commissioners, of indifferency and credit, to make the distribution of his goods to every one of his creditors, rate and rate alike, a portion, according to the quantity of their debts, as the statute speaketh. Also, the case is stronger, because this gift is an assignment of the bankrupt after the commission awarded under the Great Seal, which commission is matter of record, whereof every one may take conusance.

Lastly and principally, the Court relied upon other words in the Act, *scil.* "And that every direction, bargain and sale, &c. done by the persons so authorised as is aforesaid, in form aforesaid, shall be good and effectual in law, &c., against the said offender, &c., and against all other persons claiming by, from, or under such offender, by any act had, made, or done, after any such person shall become bankrupt, &c.:"

So that, in as much as this assignment and delivery of the said goods was after the said Cook became bankrupt, notwithstanding that, the commis-

---

7. [*Ed.:* according to the amount of their debts:]

sioners may well sell them. And the Court resolved, that the proviso concerning gifts and grants *bona fide*,[8] makes no gift or grant good, which the bankrupt makes after he becomes bankrupt, but excludes them out of the penalty inflicted by the same proviso. And divers exceptions were taken to the verdict by the defendant's counsel.

1. That it was not found, that the said sale by the commissioners of the said goods was by deed enrolled, as they objected the words of the said Act require: but to that, it was answered, and resolved by the Court, that the words of the Act concerning enrolment of the deed coming next after these words, "goods and chattels," are, "or otherwise to order the same for true satisfaction and payment, &c., and that every direction, order, &c., shall be good and effectual;" so this sale, without deed enrolled, is good enough.

2. It was objected, that it was not found that the commissioners had first seen the goods before their sale; for the words of the Act are, *scil.* "to be searched, viewed, &c.:" to that, it was answered, and resolved, that the said words, "or otherwise to order, &c." "and that every direction, &c." refer it to the discretion of the commissioners, and peradventure they cannot come to the sight of them.

3. That the commissioners ought to make several distributions to the several creditors, and not to make a joint sale, or assignment, to several creditors; for [26 b] if I he owed A. £20, B. £20, and C. £5, a joint sale, or assignment, to A. B. and C. is not according to the power given to the commissioners by the said Act; for the Act limits them to make disposition "amongst the creditors, &c., to every one a portion, rate and rate alike, according to the quantity of their debts;" but in this case, he, who hath the least debt, shall have as great interest in the goods, as he who hath the greatest; and so such assignment, in the said case put of several debts, is void, *quod fuit concessum per Curiam.*[9] But to that it was answered, and resolved by the Court, that in the case at the Bar, it appears by the verdict, that the debt due to the plaintiffs was joint, for they found, *ut supra,* that the said John Cook was indebted to the plaintiffs in £273 12d., which shall be intended a joint-debt, and so the sale good, in the case at the Bar.

4. That for as much as the words of the Act are, "To every of the said

8. [*Ed.:* (In or with) good faith,]
9. [*Ed.:* which was granted by the Court.]

creditors a portion, rate and rate alike, distribution ought to be made to all the creditors:" But here it appears, that the said Tibnam was a creditor, and £64 due to him, and yet nothing is allotted or assigned to him, so the sale is void: To that it was answered, and resolved by the Court, that in this case the factor of the said Tibnam, *in ea parte,* refused to come in as a creditor, but claimed all the goods: And this Act gives benefit to those who will inquire and come in as creditors, and not to those, who either out of obstinacy refuse, or through carelessness neglect, to come before the commissioners and pray the benefit of the said statute; for *vigilantibus et non dormientibus jura subveniunt,*[10] for otherwise a debt might be concealed, or a creditor might absent himself, and so avoid all the proceedings of the commissioners by force of the said Act. And every creditor may take notice of the commission, being matter of record, as is aforesaid, and so no inconvenience can happen to any creditor who will be vigilant, but great inconvenience will follow, and the whole effect of the Act be overthrown if other construction shall be made.

| The Archbishop of Canterbury's Case.*   [46 a]
(GREEN V. BALSER)
(1596) Trinity term, 38 Elizabeth I
In the Court of King's Bench.
First Published in the *Reports,* volume 2, page 46a.

Ed.: When Henry VIII dissolved the monasteries and religious houses in England, all of their property went to the Crown under a statute that also freed all such property from the obligation to pay tithes, or religious taxes, which went to the estates of ecclesiastical superiors. A later statute gave the Crown title to these same lands but did not free property from the obligation of tithes. Prior to the dissolution, a religious college had owed tithes to its local rectory. After dissolution, the lands of the college went to Lord Cobham, and the rectory went to the Archbishop, whose tenant, Balser, attempted to collect tithes from Lord Cobham's tenant, Green. Green sought a prohibition against the Archbishop, which is to say an order from the court forbidding the Archbishop to act. The case turns on a statutory anal-

---

10. [*Ed.:* The laws aid those who are vigilant, not those who sleep,]
*[*Ed.:* The 1658 edition spells this, "The Archbishop of Canturburies Case."]

ysis of the language of the two statutes, particularly the later statute, passed in 1547, the first year of Edward VI. The analysis of the statute sets forth many rules on interpretation: a rule requiring two elements does not apply to one; the statement of a burden on an inferior person does not place a burden on a superior person, and that general words regarding the land do not apply to duties not arising from the land. Coke and others represented the Archbishop. The court held that the later statute was held to apply in this case and, because the tithes were owed at the time of the dissolution, the tithes were still owed. The Archbishop won.

In a prohibition in the King's Bench, between Green and Balser; the case was, That in Maidstone was a religious College, to which the Rectory of Maidstone was appropriated. And the said College had divers lands and tenements within the said parish of Maidstone, and all was given to the King by the statute of 1 Edw. 6. And afterwards the rectory was conveyed to the Bishop of Canterbury, and the lands, parcel of the possessions of the said college, were conveyed to the Lord Cobham; and now the farmer of the Lord Cobham brought a prohibition against Balser, farmer of the said rectory, to Whitgift, Archbishop of Canterbury, and in his prohibition he alleged the branch of the statute of 31 Hen. 8. concerning discharge of tithes; and shewed, that the master of the said College was seised of the said lands, and of the said rectory, *simul & semel*,[1] as well at the time of the making of the Act of 31 Hen. 8. as at the making of the said Act of 1 Edw. 6., and held them discharged of tithes; and shewed the said Act of 1 Edw. 6., by which the said college was given to King Edward the sixth; and thereupon the defendant did demur in law. And in this case divers questions were moved.

1. If the said college came to the King as well by the statute of 31 Hen. 8., as by the statute of 1 Edw. 6.; for if this college came to the King by the statute of 31 Hen. 8. then without question the said branch of the said Act concerning the discharge of tithes, extends to it: and it was objected by the plaintiff's counsel, that the words of the said Act are general, *scil.* "that all Monasteries, &c. Colleges, &c. which hereafter shall happen to be dissolved, &c. or by [46 b] any other I means come to the King's Highness &c., shall be vested, deemed, and adjudged by authority of this Parliament in the very actual and real pos-

---

1. [*Ed.:* Together and at one time,]

session of the King, &c." And when this College came to the King by the stat. 1 Edw. 6. it came to the King within these words of the Act "by any mean." But it was answered by the defendant's counsel, and resolved by the Court, That that could not be for several reasons:

1. When the statute speaks of dissolution, renouncing, relinquishing, forfeiture, giving up, &c. which are inferior means, by which such religious Houses came to the King, then the said latter words "or by any other means" cannot be intended of an Act of Parliament: which is the highest manner of conveyance that can be; and therefore the makers of the Act would have put that in the beginning, and not in the end, after other inferior conveyances, if they had intended to extend the Act thereunto. But these words "by other means" are to be so expounded, *scil.* by any other such inferior means. As it hath been adjudged, that bishops are not included within the statute of 13 Eliz. cap. 10, for the statute beginneth with colleges, deans and chapters, parsons, vicars, and concludes with these words, "and others having spiritual promotions;" these latter words do not include bishops, *causa qua supra.*[2] So the statute of West. 2. cap. 41. the words of which are, *statuit Rex, quod si abbates, priores, custodes hospital' & aliarum domorum religiosarum, &c.*[3] These latter words do not include bishops, as it is holden 1 & 2 Phil. and Mary, Dyer, 100. 109. for the cause aforesaid.

2. The said clause of 31 Hen. 8. that the said religious houses shall be in the King by authority of the same Act; and the statute of 1 Edw. 6. enacts, that all colleges; &c. shall be by authority of this Parliament, adjudged and deemed in the actual and real possession of the King; so that the latter Parliament being of as high a nature as the first was, and providing by express words, that the colleges shall be, by authority of the said Act, in the actual possession of the King, the said college cannot come to the King by the Act of 31 Hen. 8. It is said in 29 Hen. 8. Parliament. & Stat. Br. if lands be given to tenant in tail in fee, his issue cannot be remitted, for the latter Act doth take away the Stat. de Donis, &c., 3. The usual form of pleading of them, which came to the King by the statute of 1 Edw. 6., and by the Act of 31 Hen. 8., doth manifest the law clearly, *scil.* to plead surrender or relinquishment,

2. [*Ed.:* for the above reason.]

3. [*Ed.:* the King has laid down that if abbots, priors, keepers of hospitals and other religious houses, etc.]

&c. *virtute cujus ac vigore*[4] of the statute of 31 Hen. 8. the King was seised; but to plead the Act of 1 Edw. 6. of Chauntries, *virtute cujus ac vigore* of the statute of 31 Hen. 8. was never heard or seen: and for all these causes it was resolved, that this college came to the King by the Act of 1 Edw. 6., and not by the Act of 31 Hen. 8.

[47 a]The second question was, forasmuch as the said college came to the King by the Act of 1 Edw. 6., and not by the Act of 31 Hen. 8. | whether the said branch of discharge of tithes extends to such colleges which after came to the King by any other Act, and not by the Act of 31 Hen. 8.; and it was objected, that the said branch should extend to colleges which come to the King by any other Act, for it was said, that although the preamble of the said branch saith, "The late monasteries, &c." yet this is not literally to be understood of monasteries only which were dissolved before the Act, for "late" is to be construed according to the body of the Act, *scil.* of those which were dissolved before, or which should come to the King afterwards by the said Act, so that when they are dissolved and in the King by force of this Act, this Act may call them "late;" *quod fuit concessum per Curiam.*[5] Also they said, that the words of the branch itself are general, *scil.* "any monasteries, &c. colleges, &c. without any limitation, so that they conceived, that the words of the said branch, made for them, and that this clause of discharge should extend to all monasteries, &c. colleges, &c. *quaecunque*,[6] by what means soever they came to the King; and they said, that the intent of the Act was so, for the intent of the Act was to benefit the King, and to make the subject more desirous of purchasing them, &c. Against which it was said by the defendant's counsel, and resolved by the Court, that neither the words, nor the meaning of the said branch, did extend to any monasteries, &c. but to those only, which came to the King by the Act of 31 Hen. 8.; for it would be absurd, that the branch of the Act of 31 Hen. 8. should extend to a future Act of Parliament, which the makers of the Act of 31 Hen. 8., without the spirit of prophecy, could have no foreknowledge of; but this clause of discharge of tithes, shall extend only to those possessions which came to the King by the same Act. And where it was said, that the first words of the branch were general, the same is true, but

4. [*Ed.:* by virtue and by force]
5. [*Ed.:* which was granted by the court.]
6. [*Ed.:* whatsoever,]

the conclusion of that branch is, "in as large and ample manner as the late abbots, &c." So that "late" being so intended, as it hath been agreed on the other side, *scil.* only of religious houses which came to the King by 31 Hen. 8.; it is clear, that that branch cannot extend to this college, which came to the King by the Act of 1 Edw. 6.

The third question was, admitting that the said college had come to the King by the stat. of 31 Hen. 8. If such general allegation of unity of possession of the rectory and of the lands in it, was sufficient; and it was resolved by the Court, That it was not sufficient; for no unity of possession shall be sufficient within the same Act but a lawful and perpetual unity of possession time out of mind, as it was adjudged M. 34 & 35 Eliz. in a prohibition between Valentine Knightly, Esq. plaintiff, and William Spencer, Esq. defendant, where the case was, the plaintiff in the prohibition shewed, that Philip, Abbot of Evesham, and all his predecessors, time out of mind were seised as well of the rectory impropriate of | Badby cum Newman, in the county of Northampton, as of [47 b] the manor of Badby cum Newman, in Badby aforesaid, in his demesne, as of fee, in the right of his monastery, *simul & semel,* until the suppression of the same monastery, *quodque ratione inde,*[7] the said abbot, and all his predecessors, until the dissolution of the same monastery, had held the said manor discharged from the payment of tithes, until the dissolution of the same house; and shewed the branch of the statute of 31 Hen. 8. concerning discharge from the payment of tithes, and conveyed the said manor to Knightly, and the said rectory to Spencer, who libelled in the Spiritual Court for tithes of the demesnes of the said manor, against Knightly, who upon the matter aforesaid brought the prohibition, and it was adjudged, that the prohibition was maintainable; For the said branch of the Act of 31 Hen. 8. was made to prevent two mischiefs, one, that otherwise all the impropriations of rectories to houses of religion, had been disappropriate; for if the body to which the rectory is appropriated, had been dissolved, the impropriation to such body had been dissolved also, as appears by 3 Edw. 3. 21 Edw. 4. 1a. 21 Hen. 7. 4b. F. N. B. 33k, 33l. Another mischief was, that whereas many religious persons were discharged from the payment of tithes, some by their order, as the Cistertians, Templars, Hospitallers of St. John of Jerusalem; as appears by 10 Eliz. Dyer 277; some by prescription, some by composition, some by the Pope's bulls,

---

7. [*Ed.:* and that by reason thereof,]

&c.; and the greater part of religious houses, as the said Abbey of Evesham was, were founded before the council of Lateran; and before time of memory, it would be infinite, and in a manner impossible by any search, to find all the discharges and immunities which such religious houses had. And for this reason also the said branch was made. And the great doubt in the said case, was conceived upon this word "discharge," for it was said, that unity of possession was not any discharge of tithes, and by consequence was not such discharge as was within the intent of the said Act. And for the force of this word "discharge," 18 Edw. 3. Bar. 247. 35 Hen. 6. 10b. 22 Edw. 4. 40B. & 6. Hen. 7. 10b. were cited. But as to that it was resolved by the Court:

1. That the statute doth not say, discharge of tithes, but discharge of payment of tithes.

2. The statute doth not say, discharge of payment of tithes, absolutely, but as freely as the abbot, &c. held it at the day of dissolution; and then this word "discharge" being referred to a certain time, may be intended of a suspension by unity. As if a man seised of a rent disseises the tenant of the land, and makes a feoffment with warranty, the feoffee shall vouch as of land discharged

[48 a] of the rent, and yet the rent was but suspended; | but every suspension is a discharge for a time, and the discharge being referred to the time of the warranty, extends to the suspension. *Quod vide*[8] 30 Edw. 3. 30. 3 Hen. 7. 4. 41a. 21 Hen. 7. 9a. b. F. N. B. 135e.

3. The statute saith, "as freely as the abbot, &c. retained the same." And it was said, that it was the intent of the King, and of the makers of the Act, to discharge the land of payment of tithes in such cases of unity of possession, being a general case, to induce purchasers the rather to purchase the land for greater prices.

4. For the infinite impossibility, and the impossible infiniteness, as hath been said, all the discharges which such religious houses had, could not be known; and the same construction was made in this Court, Hil. 24. Eliz. in a prohibition between John Rose and William Gurling, for tithes in Flixton in the county of Suffolk. See 18 Eliz. Dyer 349. *The Parson of Peykirk's Case.* And it was likewise resolved in the said *Case of Knightly,* that nothing could be traversed but the unity, for *ratione inde, &c.*[9] is but the conclusion and the

8. [*Ed.:* which see, or look up]
9. [*Ed.:* by reason thereof, etc.]

judgment of the law upon the precedent matter; but it was also resolved, that if before the dissolution the farmers of the demesnes had paid tithes, &c. to the abbot, &c., then the intendment of the law, by the reason of the said unity of possession (which ought to be time out of mind), that the land was discharged of the payment of tithes, will not hold place. For as Bracton saith, *stabitur presumptioni donec probetur in contrarium.*[10] But if the lands were always occupied by the abbots, or demised over, and no tithes at any time paid for the same before the Act, although the land be conveyed to one, and the rectory to another, yet the land is discharged of the payment of tithes; And if the farmers of the demesnes had paid tithes before the Act, the same should be pleaded by the defendant in the prohibition, and issue thereupon might be taken, as it was in the like case, Trin. 38 Eliz. in this Court, between Edward Grevil, Esq. possessor of the demesnes of the manor of Nasing, in the county of Essex, plaintiff, and Martin Trot, proprietor of the Rectory of Nasing, defendant, were against such unity of possession in manner and form aforesaid alleged by the plaintiff in the Abbot of Waltham and his predecessors, &c. in the rectory and demesnes, and with like conclusion as aforesaid: The defendant alleged payment of tithes by the farmers of the said demesnes (without any traverse by the rule of the Court) and issue was joined thereupon, and it was tried against Trot, and therefore the prohibition stood. And it was likewise resolved, that although the plaintiff in the case at Bar alleged, that the master of the said college, at the time of the making of the said Act of 1 Edw. 6., held them | discharged of tithes; and although the lands of such [48 b] religious persons may be discharged of tithes by prescription, as it hath been lately adjudged in the case of one Wright in this Court, or by composition, &c.; yet such general allegation that he was discharged of tithes, was not sufficient, without shewing how he was discharged, either by prescription, composition, or other lawful means. But if the land had come to the King by the statute of 31 Hen. 8. then by force of the said branch of discharge of the payment of tithes, such general allegation, that such prior, &c. held the land at the time of the dissolution of the said priory discharged of the payment of tithes, without shewing how, had been sufficient, and so is the common use in prohibitions.

The fourth question, in the case at Bar, was, whether any house which was

---

10. [*Ed.:* a presumption will stand good till the contrary is proved.]

ecclesiastical, and not religious, as bishops, deans and chapters, archdeacons, and the like, shall be within the Act of 31 Hen. 8.; for no house within the Act of 31 Hen. 8. is said religious, but such which was regular, and which consisted of such persons as had professed themselves, and vowed three things, that is to say, obedience, voluntary poverty, and perpetual chastity; and those are called in our law, dead persons in law. For after such profession their heirs shall have their lands, and their executors or administrators their goods, and that was called *mors civilis;*[11] which was the reason that when a lease for life was made, always the *Habendum*[12] was, to have and to hold to him *durante vita sua naturali,*[13] for it was then taken, that if the *Habendum* had been *durante vita sua* (without saying *naturali*) the civil death, that is to say, the entry into religion, had determined it. But it was resolved by the Court, that no ecclesiastical house, if it be not religious, is within the Act of 31 Hen. 8. for divers reasons:

1. The words of the Act are always, through the whole Act, in the copulative, "religious and ecclesiastical," so that if it be ecclesiastical only, it is out of the Act.

2. The makers of the Act, gave the King as well those religious and ecclesiastical houses which were dissolved, &c. as those which should be afterwards dissolved; but none were dissolved before the Act, but only religious houses, and no house ecclesiastical only; for no bishoprick, deanery, archdeaconry, &c. or such-like ecclesiastical and secular corporation was dissolved before; therefore no ecclesiastical house which was not religious, (which after the Act shall be dissolved,) was within the intent and meaning of the said Act.

3. It is enacted by the statute of 31 Hen. 8. that all religious and ecclesiastical houses, which after shall be dissolved, &c. shall be in the actual possession of the King, in the same state and condition as they were at I the time of the making of the said Act; upon which clause of the statute it was adjudged, Pasch. 5. Eliz. Rot. 1029, reported by Serjeant Bendloes, and Mich. 6 & 7 Eliz. Dyer 231., and Plow. Com. 207., that if an abbot after the said Act grants the next avoidance of an advowson, or makes a lease for years, and afterwards surrenders, so that by the Act, the possessions of the abbey ought to be in the King, in the same state and condition as they were at the time of the making

[49 a]

---

11. [*Ed.:* civil death,]
12. [*Ed.:* "To have;" the portion of deed beginning with the words "To have and to hold."]
13. [*Ed.:* during his natural life,]

the Act; and at the time of making of the Act, the land and the advowson were discharged of all interest, for this reason it was adjudged in both cases, that the lease and the grant were void by the said Act. But if a dean and chapter, and other such ecclesiastical and secular corporations should be within the said Act, then if they should surrender their possessions, they would avoid all their own grants and leases, which would be dangerous. And that was one principal reason that the colleges, chantries, &c. which came to the King by the Acts of 37 Hen. 8. or 1 Edw. 6. should not vest in the King by the Act of 31 Hen. 8., for the mischief before, for avoiding of their leases, grants, &c. And to conclude this point, it was held in the Common Pleas, in *Parret's Case,* concerning the Priory of Frideswide, that if the house be not religious and regular, it is not within the Act of 31 Hen. 8.

And as to the opinion of 10 Eliz. Dyer 280. *Corbet's Case,* Concerning the Priory of Norwich, it seems that that differs much from other deans and chapters, for the Dean and Chapter of Norwich was once religious, for they were prior and convent before; and yet that case was denied by Popham Chief Justice, and some other of the Judges, for the reasons and causes aforesaid.

Fifthly, it was held by the Court, that although it is provided by the statute of 1 Edw. 6. that the King shall have the lands of the colleges, &c. "in as ample and large manner as the said priests, wardens, &c. had or enjoyed the same," that these general words should not discharge the land of any tithes, for they are not issuing out of land, but are things distinct from the land. For as the book is in 42 Edw. 3. 13. a. the prior shall have tithes of land against his own feoffment of the same land; and it is no good cause of prohibition, to allege unity of possession in a college, which came to the King by the statute of 1 Edw. 6., as a man may, by the statute of 31 Hen. 8., in an abbot, prior, &c., as aforesaid; for the statute of 1 Edw. 6. hath no such clause of | discharge of [49 b] payment of tithes, as the statute of 31 Hen. 8. hath. And therefore such perpetual unity, as hath been said before, will not serve upon this Act of 1 Edw. 6. And afterwards a consultation[14] was granted: and another consultation was granted the same term in another prohibition sued upon the same matter between Green and Buffken. And Laurence Tanfield and others, were of counsel with the plaintiff, and the Attorney-General and others with the defendant.

---

14. [*Ed.:* A consultation returned an action to a court from which it was removed by the petition for prohibition.]

Part Three of the *Reports*

The Third Part of Coke's *Reports* was published in 1602. It was originally published in Law French and entitled *Le Tierce Part Des Reportes Del Edvvard Coke Lattourney general le Roigne, de Divers Resolutions & Judgements donnes avec graunde deliberaction, per les tresreurened Judges, & Sages dea la ley, de cases & matters en ley queux ne sueront vnques resolve ou adjudge par deuant, & les reasons & causes des dits resolutions & Judgements, durant les tresheureux regiment de tresillustre & renomes Royne Elzabeth, le fountaine de tout Justice & la vie de la ley.* In English, *The Third Part of the Reports of Sir Edward Coke, Knight., Her Majesty's Attorney-General, of divers resolutions and Judgements given with great deliberation, by the most reverend Judges and Sages of the Law, of Cases and matters in law which were never Resolved or Adjudged Before: and the Reasons and Causes of the said resolutions and Judgments, during the most happy Reign of the most Illustrious and Renowned Queen Elizabeth, the Fountain of all Justice, and the life of the Law.* The cases in this part continue to discuss issues of property, with an emphasis on cases of first impression resolving recent issues of statutory construction and the legal definitions of estates in land. There is a greater emphasis in these cases, though, of matters dealing with relations between husband and wife, as well as guardianship and inheritance. There are also more cases considering the nature of leaseholds and the problems of debtors and creditors.

Epigrams from the title page:

In memoria aeterna erit justus, & non tenebit ab auditione mala. PSAL. 105.[1]

---

1. [*Ed.:* The just man shall be in everlasting remembrance, and he shall not be afraid of evil tidings. (Psalms 112:6–7, or 111:7 in the Vulgate.)]

Justicia omnium virtutum princeps est, tuta & fida comes humanae vitae; ea enim imperia, regna, populi, civitates reguntur, quae si de medio tollatur, nec constare possit hominum societas.[2] ISIDOR.

Justicia in sese virtutes continet omnes.[3]

(Preface)
To the Reader.

How profitable and necessarie the Reports of the Judgements and Cases in Law published in former ages have beene, may unto the learned Reader by these two considerations amongst others evidently appeare. First, that the Kings of this Realme, that is to say, Edward the third, Henry the fourth, Henry the fifth, Henry the sixth, Edward the fourth, Richard the third, and Henry the seventh did select and appoint foure discreet and learned professors of Law, to report the judgements and opinions of the Reverend Judges, as well for resolving of such doubts and questions wherein there was (as in all other Arts and Sciences there often fall out) diversitie of opinions, as also for the true and genuine sense and construction of such Statutes and Actes of Parliament, as were from time to time made and enacted. To the end that all the Judges and Justices in all the severall parts of the Realme might as it were with one mouth in all mens cases pronounce one and the same sentence, whose learned workes are extant and digested into Nine severall volumes, wherein if you observe the unitie and consent of so many severall Judges and Courts in so many successions of ages, and the coherence and concordance of such infinite severall and divers cases, (one as it were with sweet consent and amitie proving and approving another) it may be questioned whether the matter be worthy of greater admiration or commendation: For as in nature we see the infinite distinction of things proceed from some unitie, as many flowers from one root, many rivers from one fountain, many arteries in the body of man from one heart, many veyns from one liver, and many sinewes from the braine: So without question, *Lex orta est cum mente divina,*[1] and this admirable unitie

---

2. [*Ed.:* Justice is the prince of all virtues, a safe and faithful companion of human life; indeed it rules empires, kingdoms, peoples, and cities; and, if it is taken away, human society cannot stand firm.]

3. [*Ed.:* Justice contains all the virtues in itself.]

1. [*Ed.:* Law arose by the divine will,]

and consent in such diversitie of things proceed from God the fountaine and founder of all good Lawes and constitutions. Secondly, in consideration of the sweet and delectable fruit that hath beene reaped by those workes for the due administration of justice, and the government of the Realme in peace and tranquilitie. Besides these there bee Reports fit for stronger capacities of equall authority, but of lesse perspicuity then the other, and these bee the judiciall records of the Kings Courts, wherein cases of importance and difficultie are upon great consultation and advisement adjudged and determined, in which Records the reasons or causes of the Judgements are not expressed; For wise and learned men doe before they judge, labour to reach to the depth of all the reasons of the case in question, but in their judgements expresse not any: And in troth, if Judges should set downe the reasons and causes of their judgements within every Record, that immense labour should withdraw them from the necessarie services of the Common-wealth, and their Records should grow to be like *Elephantini libri*[2] of infinite length, and in mine opinion lose somewhat of their present authoritie and reverence; And this is also worthie for learned and grave men to imitate. But mine advise is, that whensoever a man is enforced to yeeld a reason of his opinion or judgement, that then hee set downe all authorities, presidents, reasons, arguments, and inferences whatsoever that may bee probably applied to the case in question; For some will be perswaded, or drawne by one, and some by another, according as the capacitie or understanding of the hearer or reader is. These Records for that they containe great and hidden treasure, are faithfully and safely kept (as they well deserve) in the Kings treasurie: And yet not so kept but that any Subject may for his necessary use and benefite have accesse thereunto, which was the auncient Law of England, and so is declared by an Act of Parliament in 46. *Ed.* 3. in these words "Item pria les Commons, que come recorde & quecunque; chose en la Court le Roy de reason devoient demurr' illonques pur perpetual evidence, & eide de toutz parties a ycelly, & de touts ceux a queux ea nul maner ils atteignent, quant mestier lour fuit. Et ia de novell refusent en la court nostre dit Seign' de serche ou evidence encounter le Roy ou disadvantage de luy; Que pleise ordeiner per estatute, que serche & exemplification soit faitz as toutz gentz, de queconque recorde que les touche en ascun maner', auxybien de ce que chiet encounter le Roy come autres gentz. Le Roy le

---

2. [*Ed.:* Books of elephantine proportions.]

voet":[3] Right profitable also are the auncient bookes of the Common Lawes yet extant; as *Glanvile, Bracton, Britton, Fleta, Ingham,* and *Novae narrationes,* and those also of later times, as the *Old Tenures, Olde Natura brevium, Littleton, Doctor and Student, Perkins, Fitzh. Natura brevium,* and *Stamford,* of which the *Register, Littleton, Fitzherbert,* and *Stamford* are most necessarie and of greatest authoritie, and excellencie; And yet the other also are not without their fruit. In reading of the cases in the Bookes at large, which sometimes are obscure and misprinted, if the Reader after the diligent reading of the case, shall observe how the case is abridged in those two great Abridgements of justice *Fitzherbert,* and *Sir Robert Brooke,* it will both illustrate the case, and delight the Readers; And yet neither that of *Statham,* nor that of the Booke of *Assises* is to be rejected: And for pleading the great Booke of *Entries* is of singular use and utilitie. To the former Reports you may adde the exquisite and elaborate *Commentaries* at large of *Master Plowden,* a grave man and singularly well learned; and the summarie and fruitfull observations of that famous and most reverend Judge and sage of the Law, Sir *James Dyer* Knight, late chiefe Justice of the Court of Common Pleas, and mine owne simple labours: Then have you 15. Bookes or Treatises, and as many volumes of the Reports, besides the Abridgements of the Common Lawes; For I speake not of the Statutes and Actes of Parliament, whereof there bee divers great volumes. And for that it is hard for a man to report any part or branch of any Art or Science justly and truely, which hee professeth not, and impossible to make a just and true relation of any thing that he understands not; I pray thee beware of Chronicle Law reported in our Annales, for that will undoubtedly lead thee to error: For example, they say that *William* the Conquerour decreed that there should be Sheriffes in every Shire, and Justices of Peace to keepe the Countries in quiet, and to see offenders punished, whereas the learned know that Sheriffes were great officers and ministers of justice, as now they are, long before the Conquest, and Justices of Peace had not their being untill almost three hundred yeares after, viz. in the first yeare of *Edward the third.* But the module of a Preface will not suffer mee to enter into that matter, whereat my minde began to kindle: I will onely

---

3. [*Ed.:* Item, by the Commons, that as to records & any actions in the King's Court, reasons must remain there as perpetual evidence and aid for all parties to the same and to all who must know the length of their attaints. And now from recent denials in our lord's courts of search or evidence against the King or to others' disadvantage, that ordinary pleas under statute, that search and precedents be made for all people, of any record that touches in appropriate cases between the King and other people. The King wishes it:]

(to incite the studious Reader to the diligent observation of the Bookes, wherein bee hidden infinite treasure of knowledge,) note unto thee divers excellent things worthie thy observation out of the booke case in *vicesimo sexto libro Assisarum placito* 24.[4] for a president for thee to follow in many other cases: There it appeareth, that in a Writ of Assise the Abbot of B. claimed to have Conusauns of plea, and writs of Assise, and other originall writs out of the Kings Courts by prescription time out of minde of man, in the times of Saint *Edmund,* and Saint Edward the Confessor, Kings of this Realme before the Conquest; and shewed divers allowances thereof, and that King *Henry the first* confirmed their usages, and that they should have conusance of Pleas, so that the Justices of the one Bench, or the other, should not intermeddle, out of which Record (being now above three hundred yeares past) it appeareth, that the predecessors of that Abbot had time out of minde of man in those Kings raignes (that is whereof no man then knew the contrarie, either out of his owne memorie, or by any Record, or other proofe) writs of Assise, and other originall writs out of the Kings Courts. Now albeit that the learned do know that originall writs are directed to the Sheriffe of the Countie where the land doth lie, yet it is not impertinent to set downe the forme of the writ of Assise for the better manifestation of divers things worthy of observation. *Rex Vicecomiti salutem: Questus est nobis. A. quod B. iniuste & sine iudicio disseisiuit eum de libero tenemento suo in E. & c. Et ideo tibi praecipimus, quod si praedict. A. fecerit te securum de clamore suo prosequendo, tunc facias tenementum illud reseisire de catallis quae in ipso capt' fuer', & ipsum tenementum cum catallis esse in pace usque ad primam Assisam cum justiciarii nostri in partes illas venerint, & interim fac'xij, liberos & legales homines de vicineto illo vide-re tenementum illud. Et nomina eorum imbreviar' &'c.*[5] And this forme of writ appeareth in *Bracton lib.4. cap.16.*and in *Glanvile* in his 13. Booke, who wrote not long after the Conquest: Out of which I gather foure things. 1. That time out of minde of man before the Conquest there had been Sheriffes, for the writ of Assise,

4. [*Ed.:* in the sixth book of assizes, plea 24 (i.e., 6 Edw. III, Lib. Ass., pl. 24).]

5. [*Ed.:* The King to the Sheriff, greeting: A. has complained to us that B. has wrongfully and without judgment disseised him of his free tenement in E. etc. Therefore we command you that, if the aforesaid A. shall make you secure for prosecuting his claim, then cause that tenement to be reseised of the chattels which were taken in it, and cause the selfsame tenement with the chattels to be in peace until our Justices shall come to the first Assize in those parts, and in the mean time cause twelve free and lawful men of the neighbourhood to view the tenement; and cause their names to be written down etc.]

and every other originall writ is directed to the Sheriffe, and cannot be directed to any other, unlesse it be in speciall cases to the Coroner, who then stands in the place of the Sheriffe. 2. That likewise by all that time there were trials by the oath of twelve men: for the words of the writ of Assise are, *Et interim fac'*. 12. *liberos & legales homines &'c.*[6] 3. That by like time there had beene writs of Affife and other originall writs retournable into the Kings Courts, which (seeing they be as Justice *Fitzberbert* saith in his preface to his booke of *Natura brevium*, the rules and principles of the science of the Common Law) doe manifestly prove, that the Common Law of England had beene time out of minde of man before the Conquest, and was not altered or changed by the Conquerour. 4. That by all that time there had beene a court of Chauncerie, for all originals doe issue out of that Court, and none other: And in our bookes it appeareth, that all those Mannors that were in the hands of Saint Edward the Confessor, are to this day called Auncient demesne; And that all King *Edward* the Confessors tenants *in Assisis, Iuratis, seu recognitionibus poni non debent;*[7] which immunity and priviledge remaines to the tenants of those manors, to whose hands soever the same bee come, to this day; And this appeareth by the booke of *Domes-day* now remaining in the Eschequer, which was made in the raigne of Saint *Edward* the Confessor, as it appeareth in *Fitzh. Nat. Breuiū fol. 16.* So as without controveisie the triall by Juries, who ever were returned by Sheriffes, was before the Conquest. In the Booke of *Domes-day* you shall also reade, that *Ecclesia sancta Mariae de Worcester habet Hundred' voc' Oswaldshaw, in qua iacent 300. hidae, de quibus Episcopus ipsius Ecclesiae a constitutione antiquorum temporum habet omnes Redditiones Socharum, & omnes consuetudines inibi pertinentes ad dominicum victum, & Regis servitium & suum: Ita ut nullus Vicecomes ullam ibi habere possit quaerelam, nec in aliquo placito, nec in aliqua qualibet causa,*[8] And it appeareth by the Charter it self, that King *Edgar* long before the Conquest, granted to the Church of Worcester the said franchises and hereditaments; whereby it is

---

6. [*Ed.:* And in the mean time cause twelve free and lawful men, etc.]

7. [*Ed.:* ought not to be put into assizes, juries, or recognitions;]

8. [*Ed.:* The Church of St. Mary of Worcester has a hundred called Oswaldshaw, in which lie three hundred hides, from which the Bishop of that Church by an ancient constitution has all the Rents of Socmen and all the customs therein belonging for the lord's maintenance, and the King's service (i.e. knight-service) and his own, in such a way that the Sheriff may have (i.e. hear) any plaint there in any plea or cause whatsoever,]

evident that then there were Sheriffes: And that the Sheriffes had then a Court and determined causes, held Pleas by plaint as to this day they doe, and that there were *Redditiones Socharum,*[9] which prove Socage tenure, and *Regis servitium*[10] knights service, then called *Regis servitium,* because it was done to or for the King, and the Realme: The same King granted the like Charter to the Monasterie of Saint Andrew, in Ely, viz. 2. hundreds within the Isle, and 5. and a halfe without, together with viewes of franke pledge, and by expresse words, that no Sheriffe should intermeddle within the same; But this much (if in a case so evident it be not too much) shall suffice. But if you will give any faith to them, let it be in those things they have published concerning the antiquitie, and honour of the Common Lawes: First, they say that *Brutus* the first king of this land, as soone as hee had settled himselfe in his kingdome, for the safe and peaceable government of his people wrote a book in the Greeke tongue, calling it the lawes of the Britans, and hee collected the same out of the Laws of the Trojans: This king, they say, died after the creation of the World, 2850. yeares, and before the Incarnation of Christ 1130. years, *Samuel* then being Judge of Israel. I will not examine these things in a *Quo warranto,*[11] the ground thereof I thinke was best knowne to the Authors and writers of them; but that the Lawes of the auncient Britans, their contracts and other instruments: and the Records and judiciall proceedings of their Judges were written and sentenced in the Greeke tongue, it is plaine and evident by proofs luculent & uncontrolable: for the proofe whereof I shall be enforced onely to point out the heads of some few reasons, yet so as you may prosecute the same from the fountaines themselves at your good pleasure, and greater leasure. And first take a just testimonie out of the Commentaries of *Julius Caesar,* (whose relations are as true, as the stile and phrase is perfect.) Hee in his 6. Booke of the Warres of France faith, that in antient time the Nobilitie of France were all of two sorts, *Druides* or *Equites;* the one for matters of government at home, the other for martiall empolyments abroad: To the *Druides* appertained the ordering as well of matters Ecclesiasticall, as the admiration of the Lawes and government of the Common-wealth; for so he saith, *De*

---

9. [*Ed.:* Rents of Socmen (Socmen are free tenants who pay socage, or ploughing the lord's land for a set number of days each year. A "soc" was a plough.)]

10. [*Ed.:* King's Service (also "Knight's Service," or tenure in land held by obligation for military service.)]

11. [*Ed.:* A writ of right for the king against anyone who claimed or usurped any office, franchise, or liberty, used here metaphorically.]

omnibus controversiis publicis privatisq; constituunt & c. & si quod est admissum facinus, si caedes facta, si de haereditate, de finibus controversia est, decernunt praemia, poenasq; constituunt.[12] Concerning the mysteries of their Religion, they neither did, nor might commit them to writing, but for the dispatching and deciding of causes, as well publique as private saith hee, *Graecis literis utuntur,*[13] they used to doe it in the Greeke tongue, to the end that their disciplines might not be made common among the vulgar: Now then this being granted that the *Druides* did customarily sentence causes, and order matters publike and private in the Greeke language, it will easily follow, that the very same was likewise used here in Brittanny, and the consequence is evident and necessarie, for that the whole society, and all the discipline of the *Druides* in France, was nothing else but a very Colony taken out from our British *Druides,* as *Caesar* himselfe in the same place affirmeth, from whence they learned and received all their discipline for managing of causes whatsoever. *Disciplina Druidum* (saith he) in *Britannia reperta, atq; inde in Galliam translata: Et nunc qui diligentius illam disciplinam cognoscere volunt, in Britanniam discendi causa proficiscuntur.*[14] The very same witnesseth *Plinie* also *Lib. 3. ca. I.* towards the end. Nay their very name and appellation may serve for a proofe of the use of the Greeke tongue, they being called *Drudes* of δρῦς an Oake, because saith *Plinie* they frequent woods where oakes are, and in all their sacrifices use the leaves of those trees. Adde secondly to this, the daily commerce and trafique betwixt those Britans and French so much spoken of by *Caesar, Strabo,* and *Pliny:* And therefore no doubt but they used one and the same forme of covenanting by writing; which, that it was in Greeke, *Strabo* plainly affirmeth *Lib.4. Geographiae,* that the *Massilienses* a Greek Colonie, and as hystories report the chiefest merchants then in the world next the Phoenicians, so spread abroad the desire of learning their language, that even vulgarly, instancing therein the French Nation, they did τὰ συμβόλαια Ἑλληνιστὶ γράφειν,[15] write saith hee their deeds and obligations in Greeke;

---

12. [*Ed.:* In fact it is they who decide almost all controversies, public and private, etc., and if any crime has been committed, or murder done, or there is a dispute about inheritance, or boundaries, they decide it, appointing the rewards and punishments.]

13. [*Ed.:* use the Greek alphabet,]

14. [*Ed.:* The teaching of the Druids . . . having started in Britain, and having been from thence translated into Gaul, anyone nowadays who wishes to know that discipline more fully must go to Britain in order to learn it.]

15. [*Ed.:* write their contracts or bonds in the Greek language,]

And that there passed continuall traffique likewise betwixt these very *Massiliens* and the *Britaines, Strabo* in the same place directly affirmeth, in that saith he they vied to fetch tin from the British Islands to Massalia ἐκ τῶν Βρεταννικῶν νησῶν εἰς τὴν Μασσαλίαν κομίσεσθαι[16] and for this it is that *Juvenall* who wrote above 1500. yeares past in his 15. Satyre saith, *Gallia caussidicos docuit facūda Britannos:*[17] Not that the French men did teach the Lawyers of England to be eloquent, (which *Caesar* a most certaine Author denieth) but that a Colonel of Grecians residing in France as *Strabo* saith, *Gallia* was said to teach the Professors of the Lawes of England, being written in the Greeke tongue, Eloquence. Now for matters of Religion, *Strabo* in his 4. book observeth that the Britaines worshipped *Ceres* and *Proserpina,* and sacrificed unto them according to the Greeke forme of superstition as they did ἐν τῇ Σαμοθράκη,[18] in Samos. Lastly, that as well the Grecians had trafique here, as that their language was not unknown to the auncient Britaines, the very names given unto this our Countrey doe declare and prove: For *Bret* (from whence our Writers as from an old British word derive the appellation of this Island and inhabitants, because the ancient Britaines were wont to paint their bodies, & in *Juvenall* are called *Picti Britanni,*[19] which was said *Caesar lib.* 5. to make them seem fearfull in fight to their enemies) the same word in that very signification is Greek, and τὸ βρέτας[20] in *Aeschylus* and *Lycophoron* signifies a picture: Now the other part of the word ταινία[21] it is in Greeke as much as Land or Countrey: I omit the name Albion, at the first Olbion, or the happy Island, in Greek, together with a great multitude of English words, as *Chirographer, Prothonot. Ideote & c.* yet tasting of a Greek beginning: For that hereby as I think it is sufficiently proved that the lawes of England are of much greater antiquity than they are reported to be, & than any the Constitutions or Lawes imperiall of Roman Emperors. Now therefore to return to our *Chronologers,* they further say that 441. yeares before the Incarnation of Christ, *Mulmutius,* of some called *Dunvallo M.* of some *Dovebant,* did write 2. Bookes of the Lawes of the Britons, the one called *Stat. Municipalia,* and

16. [*Ed.:* to take from the British islands to Massalia.]
17. [*Ed.:* The Gaulish lawyers taught the Britons eloquence:]
18. [*Ed.:* on Samothrace, (note: not Samos).]
19. [*Ed.:* the Painted Britons,]
20. [*Ed.:* the idols (Coke seems here to mistake the sense of idol from "icon" to be "picture.")]
21. [*Ed.:* (a suffix, which Coke presumes to be of a Hellenic form for "land of.")]

the other *Leges Judiciariae,* for so the same doe signifie in the British tongue, wherein he wrote the same, which is as much to say as the Statute Law, & the Common Law: And 356. yeares before the birth of Christ, *Mercia Proba Queen.* & wife of King Gwintelin wrote a booke of the Lawes of England in the British tongue, calling it *Merchenleg:* King Alfred, or Alured King of the West Saxons, 871. years after Christ wrote a Book of the laws of England, and called the same, *Breviarum quoddam qd' composuit ex diversis legibus, Troianorum, Graecorum, Britannorum, Saxonum, & Dacorum:*[22] In the year after the incarnation of Christ 653. *Sigabert* or *Sigesbert orientalium Anglorum Rex,* wrote a Booke of the Lawes of England, calling it *Legum instituta*[23] King Edward of that name before the Conquest the 3. *Ex immensa Legum congerie, quas Brittanni, Romani, Angli, & Daci condiderunt, optima quaeq; selegit, ac in unam coegit, quam vocari voluit Legem communem:*[24] These and much more to like purpose shall you read in Gildas, Gervasius Tilburien. Galfrid. of Montmouth, Will' of Malmsbury, Hoveden, Matthew of Westminster, Polidor Virgil' of Harding, Caxton, Fabian, Baleus, & others: So as it appeareth by them, that before the Conquest there were amongst others 7. Volumes or bookes intituled, *Leges Britannorum, Statuta Municipalia, Leges Judiciariae, Marchenleg, Breviariŭ legum, Legum Instituta, & Communes Lex. Cum insignis subactor. Angliae Rex Will' ulteriores insulae fines suo subiagasset imperis, & rebelliŭ mentes terribiliŭ perdomuisset et exemplis, ne libera de caetero daretur erroris facultas, decrevit subiectum sibi populŭ Juri scripto legibusq; subiicere: Propositis igitur Legibus Anglicanis secundum tripartitam eorum distinctionem, hoc est, Marchenleg, Daneleg, & West-Saxonleg, quasdam reprobavit, quasdam autĕ approbans transmarinas Newestriae leges, que ad regnipacem tuenda efficacissimae & videbantur adiecit.*[25] This saith *Gervasius Tilburiensis,* one that wrote in the Conquerors time, or shortly after him: Whereby if the same were admitted, it appeareth that some of the English Lawes hee allowed, and such of his owne as he added where *efficacissimae ad Regni pacem tuendā,*[26] and therefore if such

---

22. [*Ed.:* A certain abridgment which is composed from various laws of the Trojans, Greeks, Britons, Saxons, and Danes:]

23. [*Ed.:* Institutes of the Laws.]

24. [*Ed.:* From the immense mass of laws which were left by the Britons, Romans, Angles, and Danes, he selected the best and digested them into one body which he called the Common Law:]

25. [*Ed.:* The laws of the Britons, the municipal statutes, the judge-made laws, the law of Mercia, the breviary of laws, the institute of the laws, and the Common Law . . .]

26. [*Ed.:* most efficacious for protecting the peace of the realm,]

Lawes as he added of his owne had continued (as in troth they did not) they were not so shamelessely and falsly to be slandered, as some maliciously and ignorantly have done; of whom I onely say:

> Aut haec in nostros fabricata est machina muros,
> Aut aliquis latet error, equo ne credite Teucri.[27]

For thy satisfaction herein, heare what *Sir Jo. Fortescue* knight, chief Justice of England, a man of excellent learning and authority, wrote of this matter lib. I. cap. 17. speaking of the Lawes of England; *Quae si optimae & non extitissent, aliqui Regum illorum justitia, ratione, seu affectione cōncitati eas mutassent, aut omnino delevissent, & maxime Romani qui legibus suis quasi totum orbis reliquum judicabant.*[28] After the Conquest, King Henry the first the Conquerors sonne, surnamed *Beauclerke,* a man excellently learned, because he abolished such customs of Normandy as his father added to our Common Lawes, is said to have restored the ancient lawes of England: King Henry the second wrote a book of the Common Lawes and statutes of England, [divided into two tomes,] and according to the same division, intituled the one *pro Republica Leges,*[29] and the other *Statuta Regalia,*[30] whereof not any fragment doth now remaine. And yet by the way I could but smile when I read in some of them, that when *Cardinal Woolsey* at the last perceived untrue surmises and fained complaints for the most part of such poore people as laded him with Petitions, he then waxed weary of hearing their causes, & ordained by the Kings Commission divers under Courts to heare complaints by Bill of poore people; The one was kept in the White hall, the other before the Kings Almoner *Doctor Stokesly,* a man that had more learning then discretion to be a Judge; the third was kept in the Lord *Treasorers* Chamber beside the Starre-chamber: and the fourth at the Rolles at the afternoone: These Courts were greatly haunted for a time, but at the last the people perceived that much delay was used in these Courts, & few matters ended, & when they were ended, they

---

27. [*Ed.:* Either this machine has been made within our walls, or there is some mistake: do not trust the horse of Teucrus (i.e. the Trojan horse).]

28. [*Ed.:* And if these [laws] had not been of the best, some of those kings would have changed them by reason of justice, or merely out of caprice, or totally abrogated them: and especially the Romans, who judged almost the whole of the rest of the world by their laws.]

29. [*Ed.:* laws for the common weal,]

30. [*Ed.:* royal laws,]

bound no man by the Law, then every man was weary of them, and resorted to the Common Law: but *Tractent fabrilia fabri;*[31] and yet it were to be wished, that they had kept themselves within their proper element, for peradventure with wise men some of them have reaped the reward of those that are not beleeved when they say the troth. To the grave and learned writers of Histories my advice is, that they meddle not with any point or secret of any Art or science, especially with the lawes of this realm, before they conferre with some learned in that profession. And where it is reported that it was not lawfull for any common person to use any Seale to any Deed, Charter, or other Instrument in the raigne of Henry the second nor long after, And therefore *Richard Lacie chief Justice* of England in the raigne of Henry the second is said to have reprehended a common person for that he used a patent Seale, when as that pertained as he said to the King and Nobility only; Against which, *Ingulphus* Abbot of Croyland, who is said to have come in with the Conqueror, saith, *Ante Normannorum ingressum chirographa firma erant cum crucibus aureis, aliisque signaculis sed normannos cum cerea impressione uniuscuiusque; speciale sigillum sub intitulatione trium vel quatuor testium conficere chirographa instituere.*[32] By which it appeareth that in the Conquerors time every man might seale with a private seale. But letting these passe, and to beleeve neither till both of them be agreed, in troth it was ever unlawfull for a gentleman to usurpe the armes of seales of another; and to forge or counterfait the seale of any other was unlawfull for any. But otherwise it was never unlawful for any Subject to put his owne seale to any Instrument, as may appeare by infinite Presidents, amongst which for an instance I thought good here to remember one for all, which *Master Joseph Holland* of the Inner Temple a good Antiquary and a lover of learning delivered unto me, and beareth date *Ann. 33. H. 2.* and is sealed at this present with two faire ancient Seales, viz. of Walter of Fridaltorpe and Helias his sonne: and for that it containeth divers matters worthy observation, I thought good to exemplifie it to the Reader *de verbo in verbum. Haec est concordia facta in Comitatu Eborum die Lunae proxime post festum Sancti Hillarii anno regni regis Henrici secundi tricesimo tertio, inter*

31. [*Ed.:* Workmen should stick to their trade;]

32. [*Ed.:* Before the arrival of the Normans, charters were authenticated with gold crosses and other devices; but the Normans began to make charters with wax impressions from the special seals which everyone had, under the names of three or four witnesses.]

Walterum de Fridastorpe & Heliam filium eius, & inter Johannem de Beverlaco, scilicet de une carucata terrae in Fridastorpe, quam predict Joh. clamavit versas eos in eodem Comitatu sicut jus & haereditagium fuum per breve domini Regis, scil, quod praedict Walt & Helias filius eius dederunt, & reddiderunt praedict Joh. pro clameo & recto suo quod in ipsa terra habuit, unam dimid' carucatam terrae in eadem villa, & unam tostum, scilicet illam dimid' carucatam terrae quae iacet inter terram Galfrid' Wanlin & inter praedict' carucatam terrae quam cla- mavit, & illud tostum quod iacet inter terram Adae filie Norman' de Sezevall, & terram Hen. fillii Thom. plenarie cum omnibus pertinentiis suis infra villam & extra, sine ullo retenemento; Hanc vero dimid' carucatam terrae & tostam plenarie cum omnibus pertinentiis suit tenebit predict' Joh. & haered' sui de prae- dict' Heliae heredibus suis: Reddendo inde annuatim praedict' Heliae & haere- dibus suis 12. d. ad terminum Pentecost, pro omnibus servitiis que ad terram illam pertinent: Et praedict' Walterus & Helias & haered' sui warrantizabūt praedict' Jobanni & haeredibus suis praefat' dimit' carucatam terrae & tostum, cum om- nibus pertinentiis contra omnes homines: Hanc vero concordiam ex utraque parte affidaverunt firmiter & fine dolo tenend' ficut praesens chirographum testatur: & saepe dictus Walterus atturnavit praedict' Johannem in eodem Comitat' ad fa- ciendum praedict' servicium praedict' Heliae filio suo, & haeredibus suis; His testibus Remigio Dapifero, Ranulpho de Glanuill' tunc Vicecomite Eborum, Ran- ulpho filio Walteri, Rogero de Badnut, Warino de Rollesby, Alano de Sinderby, Radulpho filio Radulph. Will' de Aton', Nic. de Warham, Roberto de Mara, Alano filio Heliae, Roberto de Melsa, Thom. filio Jodlani, Walram, filio Will' Waltero de Bomadnum, Alano Malebacke, Adamo de Killū, Roberto de Malteby, Gilberto de Torini Willihelmo Agullū, Gilberto filio Richardi, Willihelmo de Backestorpe, Helia Latimer; By which Writ the King commanded the Lord: on *Quod sine dilatione plenum rectum teneat Johanni de Beverlaco de una caracata terrae cū pertinentiis in Fridastorpe quam clamat, & quam Walterus de Fridastorpe, & Helias filius eius ei deforc', Et nisi fecerit Vicecomes Eborum faciat, ne amplius inde clamorem audiamas pro defectu recti.*[33] For thy better understanding,

33. [*Ed.:* . . . word for word: This is the final concord made in the county of York on the Monday next after the feast of St. Hilary in the thirty-third year of the reign of King Henry the second, between Walter of Fridaythorpe and Elias his son, and John of Beverley, namely concerning one carucate of land in Fridaythorpe which the aforesaid John has claimed against him in the same county court as his right and inheritance, by the lord king's writ, that is to say, that the aforesaid Walter and Elias his son have given and rendered to the aforesaid John his claim and the right which he had in that land, half a carucate of

hereby it appeareth that *Joh. de Beverlaco*[34] brought a Writ of Right against Walter of Fridastorpe, and Helias his sonne, of one Ploughland in Fridastorpe, directed to the Lord of the Mannour of whom the said plough land was holden, which Writ was after by a Precept made by the Sherife called a *Tolt*, (because it doth *tollere loquelam*,[35] from the Court Baron to the Countie Court) remooved into the Countie Court, where before *Ranulph de Glanvilla* then Sherife of Yorke, this concord was by consent of parties made in the County Court, by force of the Commission given to the Sherife in default of the Lord by the said Writ, (viz.) That the Sherife in his County Court should see that the demandant should without delay have his full right in the said plough land, upon which Writ in that court this Concord was made, and not onely entred into the Rols of the Countie Court, but by way of Instrument indented, mutually sealed by either partie; So as by this Concord the perclose of the writ, *Ne amplius inde clamorem audiamus pro defectu recti*,[36] was satisfied: And to the end that this concord might be the more firmely kept, each partie bound him selfe to the other by an *Affidavit*. All this is necessarily collected out of

---

land in the same vill, and one toft, that is to say, that half carucate of land which lies between the land of Geoffrey Waulin and the aforesaid carucate of land which he claimed, and that toft which lies between the land of Adam, son of Norman de Sexenall, and the land of Henry, son of Thomas, fully with all their appurtenances within the vill and without, without any withholding, [to hold] this half carucate of land and toft fully with all their appurtenances unto the aforesaid John and his heirs, of the aforesaid Elias and his heirs, rendering thereof annually to the aforesaid Elias and his heirs twelve pence at Whitsun for all services which belong to that land; and the aforesaid Walter and Elias and their heirs shall warrant unto the aforesaid John and his heirs the aforesaid half carucate of land and the toft, with all their appurtenances, against all men; and this concord they have sworn on both sides to keep firmly and without deceit, as the present chirograph witnesses; and the said Walter has often attorned the aforesaid John in the same county to do the aforesaid service to the aforesaid Elias his son, and his heirs. These being witnesses, Remigius Dapifer, Ranulph de Glanvill, then sheriff of Yorkshire, Ranulph son of Walter, Roger de Badnut, Warin de Rollesby, Alan de Sinderby, Ralph son of Ralph, William de Aton, Nicholas de Warham, Robert de Mara, Alan son of Elias, Robert de Melsa (Meaux), Thomas son of Jodlan, Walram son of William, Walter de Bomadnum, Alan Malebacke, Adam de Killum, Robert de Malteby, Gilbert de Torini, William Agullum, Gilbert son of Richard, William de Backestorpe, Elias Latimer. [By which writ the king commanded the lord:] 'that without delay he shall do full right to John of Beverley in respect of one carucate of land with the appurtenances in Fridaythorpe, which he claims, and which Walter of Fridaythorpe and Elias his son deforce from him, so that we may hear no more complaint hereof for want of right'. (A "carucate" was the area of ploughland that could be turned in one day with one plough; also called a "hide," it varied between 60 and 120 acres.)]

34. [*Ed.:* John of Beverley]

35. [*Ed.:* raise up the claim,]

36. [*Ed.:* So that we may hear no more complaint hereof for want of right,]

this auncient & learned Instrument: for *per breve Domini Regis*[37] is expounded
to bee a Writ of Right by these words *clamavit &c. ius suum;*[38] but directly
after when it is said *pro clameo & recto suo:*[39] Also it appeareth that this concord
was made *in comit' Eborum,*[40] and *clamaevit versus eos in eodem comit' &c. per
breve domini regis:*[41] And all this was done *coram Ranulpho de Glanvilla tunc
Vicec':*[42] And the learned do know that a writ of Right cannot be retournable
in the County court, but must of necessitie be remooved thither by *Tolt.* Good
Reader, I dare confidently affirme unto thee, that never any Abbot, Monke,
or Churchman that wrote any of our Annals could have understood this excellent and well indicted concord. But to returne againe to these grave and
learned Reporters of the Lawes, in former times, who (as I take it) about the
end of the raigne of King *Henry the 7.* ceased, betweene which and the cases
reported in the raigne of *Henry the 8.* you may observe no small difference:
So as about the end of the raigne of *Henry the 7.* it was thought by the Sages
of the Law, that at that time the Reports of the Law were sufficient; Wherefore
it may seeme both unnecessarie and unprofitable to have any more Reports
of the Law: But the same causes that mooved the former, doe require also to
have some more added unto them for two speciall ends and purposes. First,
to explaine and expound those Statutes and Actes of Parliament which either
have bin enacted since those Reports, or where not (no occasion falling out)
in Reports expounded at all. Secondly, to reconcile doubts in former Reports
rising either upon diversity of opinions or questions mooved and left undecided, for that it cannot be, but in so many Books written in so many severall
ages, there must be (as the like in all Sciences and Arts both divine and humane
falleth out) some diversitie of opinions, and many doubts left unresolved: For
which only purposes I have published the former two, and this last part of
my Reports, which I trust will be a meane (for so I intended them) to cause
the studious to peruse and peruse againe with greater diligence, those former
excellent and most fruitfull Reports: And in troth these of mine (if so I may
call them, being the Judgements of others) are but in nature of Commentaries,

37. [*Ed.:* by the lord king's writ]
38. [*Ed.:* claimed, etc. his right;]
39. [*Ed.:* for his claim and right:]
40. [*Ed.:* in the county of York,]
41. [*Ed.:* he claimed against them in the same county, etc. by the lord king's writ etc.:]
42. [*Ed.:* before Ranulph de Glanvill, then Sheriff:]

either for the better apprehending of the true construction of certaine generall
Acts of Parliament concerning the whole Realme, in certaine principall points
never expounded before, or for the better understanding of the true sense and
reason of the Judgements and resolutions formerly reported, or for resolution
of such doubts as therein remain undecided. For which purposes in my former
Reports I have reported and published for the explanation & exposition of
the Statute of 23. H. 8. ca. 10. Porters case: Of the broad spreading Statute
of 27. H. 8. cap. 10. of Uses, the cases of Chudleigh, Corbet, Shelley, Albany,
and the Lord Cromwels case: of the Statute of 34. H. 8. cap. 20. of Recoveries,
Wisemans case: Of the Statute of 13. Elizab. cap. 7. of Bankrupts, the case of
Bankrupts: Of the Statute of 34. H. 8. ca. 21. of confirmation of Letters Patents,
Dodingtons case: Of the statute of 31. H. 8. of dissolution of Monasteries:
And of the Statute of 1. Edw. 6. of Chauntries, the Archbishop of Canterburies
case: And of one Branch of the great & generall Statutes of 32. and 34. H. 8.
of Wills, Binghams case. I have reported the Lord Buckhursts case, for the
true understanding and expounding of the auncient and former Booke cases
concerning Charters and Evidences, and to that end the residue of the cases
in those two former parts are published. And seeing the end of these Lawes
is to have Justice duely administred, and Justice distributed is *Ius suum cuique
tribuere*,[43] to give to every one his owne; Let all the professors of the Law, give
to these Books that Justice which these Bookes have in them: that is, to give
to every booke and case his owne true understanding: And not by wresting
or racking, or inference of wit to draw them (no not for approving a troth)
from their proper and naturall sense, for that were a point of great injustice:
For troth and falshood are so opposite, as troth itselfe ought not to be prooved
by any glose or application that the true sense will not beare. Out of all these
Bookes and Reports of the Common Law, I have observed, that albeit sometime by actes of Parliament, and sometime by invention and wit of man, some
points of the auncient Common Law have been altered or diverted from his
due course; yet in revolution of time, the same (as a most skilfull and faithfull
supporter of the common wealth) have bin with great applause for avoyding
of many inconveniences restored againe: As for example, the wisedome of the
Common Law was that all estates of inheritance should be Fee simple, so as
one man might safely alien, demise, and contract, to and with another: But

---

43. [*Ed.:* to give to everyone his right,]

the Statute of *Westminster the second cap.* I. created an estate taile, and made a Perpetuitie by act of Parliament, restraining Tenant in taile from aliening or demising but onely for the life of Tenant in taile, which in processe of time brought in such troubles and inconneniences, that after two hundred yeares, necessitie found out a way by Law for a Tenant in taile to alien. Also by the auncient Common Lawes, freeholds should not passe from one to another but by matter of Record, or solemne Liverie of seisin; But against this were Uses invented, and grew common, and almost universall through the Realme, in destruction of the auncient Common Law in that point: But in time the manifold inconveniences hereof being by experience found, the Statute of 27. *Henr. 8. cap. 10.* was made for restoring of the auncient Common Law againe, as it expresly appeareth by the Preamble of that Statute: And hereof an infinite more of examples might bee added, but hereof this shall suffice: And thus much of the Bookes and Treatises, and of the Reporters and Reports of the Lawes of England. Now for the degrees of the Law: as there bee in the Universities of Cambridge and Oxford divers degrees, as generall Sophisters, Bachellors, Masters, Doctors, of whom bee chosen men for eminent and judiciall places, both in the Church and Ecclesiasticall Courts: So in the Profession of the Law, there are Mootmen, (which are those that argue Readers cases in houses of chauncerie, both in Termes and graund Vacations.) Of Mootemen after eight yeares Studie or thereabouts, are chosen Utterbaristers; of these are chosen Readers in Innes of Chauncerie: Of Utterbarristers, after they have beene of that degree twelve yeares at the least are chosen Benchers, or Auncients, of which one that is of the puisne sort, reades yearely in Summer vacation, and is called a single Readei, And one of the Auncients that have formerly read, reades in Lent vacation, and is called a double Reader, and commonly it is betweene his first and second Reading about nine or tenne yeares, And out of these the King makes choyse of his ATTORNEY, and SOLLICITOR Generall, his ATTORNEY of the Court of Wardes and Liveries, and ATTORNEY of the Duchy: And of these Readers are Serjeants elected by the King, and are by the Kings Writ called *ad statum & gradum Servientis ad Legem:*[44] and out of these the King electeth one, two, or three as pleaseth him to be his Serjeants, which are called the Kings Serjeants; Of Serjeants are by the King also constituted the honorable and reverend Judges, and Sages of

44. [*Ed.:* to the estate and degree of a Serjeant at Law.]

the Law. For the young Student which most commonly commeth from one of the Universities, for his entrance or beginning were first instituted and erected eight houses of Chauncerie, to learne there the Elements of the Law: that is to say, Cliffordes Inne, Lyons Inne, Clements Inne, Barnards Inne, Staple Inne, Furnivals Inne, Davis Inne, and New Inne: And each of these houses consist of fortie or thereabouts. For the Readers, Utterbarristers, Mootemen, and inferiour Students, are foure famous and renowned Colledges, or Houses of Court, called the INNER TEMPLE, to which the first three Houses of Chauncerie appertaine; GRAIES INNE, to which the next two belong; LIN-COLNES INNE, which enjoyeth the last two saving one; and the MIDDLE TEM-PLE, which hath onely the last. Each of the Houses of Court consist of Readers above twentie: Of Utterbaristers above thrice so many: Of yong Gentlemen, about the number of eight or nine score, who there spend their time in Study of Law, and in commendable exercises fit for Gentlemen: The JVDGES of the Law and SERJEANTS being commonly above the number of twentie, are equally distinguished into two higher and more eminent Houses, called Serjeants Inne: All these are not farre distant one from another, and altogether doe make the most famous Universitie for profession of Law onely, or of any one humane Science, that is in the world, and advaunceth it selfe above all others, *Quantum inter viburna Cupressus.*[45] In which Houses of Court and Chauncery, the Readings and other exercises of the Lawes therein continually used, are most excellent and behoovefull for attaining to the knowledge of these Lawes: And of these things this taste shall suffice, for they would require if they should be treated of, a treatise of it selfe. Of the antiquitie of these houses, and how they have beene changed from one place to another, I may say as one said of auncient Cities: *Perpaucae antiquae & civitates Authores Suos norunt.*[46] Now, what Arts or Sciences are necessary for the knowledge & understanding of these Lawes, I say, that seeing these Lawes doe limit, bound and determine, of all other humane lawes, arts, and sciences: I cannot exclude the knowledge of any of them from the professor of these Lawes; the knowledge of any of them is necessary and profitable. But forasmuch as if a man should spend his whole life in the study of these Lawes, yet he might still adde somewhat to

45. [*Ed.:* as great as a cypress among the brushwood. (from Virgil, *Eclogues,* i. 25)]
46. [*Ed.:* our authors have investigated very few ancient cities.]

his understanding of them: Therefore the Judges of the law in matters of difficulty, doe use to conferre with the learned in that Art or Science, whose resolution is requisite to the true deciding of the case in question. Concerning the language or tongue wherein these Lawes are written, for all judiciall Records are entred and enrolled in the Latine tongue: As it appeareth by an Act of Parliament in *Anno 36. cap. 15.* and the words of *Glanvile, Bracton,* and *Fleta, Novae & Narrationes,* and the Booke of *Entries,* and divers of our statutes are set forth in the Latine tongue. Before the raigne of that famous King *Edward the first,* as well all Writs originall and judiciall, as all the bookes of the Law, as *Glanvile, Bracton, & c.* and all the Statutes yet extant were published in the Latine tongue; In the raigne of him and his sonne many Statutes are indited in the Latine: (as some also of the Statutes of *Richard the second* be.) And divers also bee enacted in French, for that they had divers territories and Seigniories that spake French within their dominion, and in respect thereof the better sort learned that language. But forasmuch as the former Reports of the Law, and the rest of the Authors of the Law, (the *Doctor and Student* who wrote in the English tongue excepted) are written in French; I have likewise published these in the same language: And the reason that the former Reports were in the French tongue, was for that they begun in the raigne of King *Edward the third,* who as the world knowes had lawfull right in the Kingdome of France, and had divers Provinces and territories thereof in pro-session: It was not thought fit nor convenient, to publish either those, or any of the Statutes enacted in those dayes in the vulgar tongue, lest the unlearned by bare reading without right understanding might sucke out errors, and trust-ing to their owne conceit might endamage themselves, and sometimes fall into destruction. And it is verily thought that William the Conquerour finding the excellencie and equitie of the Lawes of England, did transport some of them into Normandy, and taught the former Lawes written as they say in Greeke, Latine, British, and Saxon tongues (for the better use of Normans) in the Normane language, and the which are at this day (though in processe of time much altered) called the *Customes of Normandie:* So taught hee En-glishmen the Norman tearmes of hunting, hawking, and in effect of all other playes and pastimes, which continue to this day: And yet no man maketh question but these recreations and disports were used within this Realme before the Conquerours time. But see the Preface of *William de Rouell* of *Allenson* to his Commentary written in Latine upon the booke called, *Le graund Cus-*

tumier de Normandie,[47] entituled in Latine, *Descriptio Normanniae,*[48] where hee sheweth and proveth by other Authors, that most of the Customes of Normandie were derived out of the Lawes of England, in or before the time of the said King Edward the Confessor, from whom William Duke of Normandie did derive the title, by colour whereof he first entred into the crowne of England. If the language or stile doe not please thee, let the excellencie and importance of the matter delight and satisfie thee, and thereby thou shalt wholly addict thy selfe to the admirable sweetnesse of knowledge and understanding: *In lectione non verba sed veritas est amanda, saepe autem reperitur simplicitas veridica, & falsitas composita, quae hominem suis erroribus allicit, & per linguae ornamentum laqueos dulcis aspergit: Et doctrina in multis est, quibus deest oratio.*[49] Certainely the faire outsides of enameled words and sentences, doe sometimes so bedazill the eye of the Readers minde with their glittering shew, as they cause them not to see or not to pierce into the inside of the matter; And he that busily hunteth after affected words, and followeth the strong sent of great swelling phrases, is many times (in winding of them in to shew a little verbal pride) at a dead losse of the matter it selfe, and so *Projicit ampullas & sesquipedalia verba.*[50] To speake effectually, plainely, and shortly, it becometh the gravitie of this profession: And of these things this little taste shall suffice.

Your extraordinary allowance of my last Reports, being freshly accompanied with new desires, have overcome mee to publish these few excellent Judgements and Resolutions of the reverend Judges and sages of the Law, tending either to the true exposition of certaine generall Acts of Parliament, or to the true understanding and sense of our bookes, wherein there seemeth some diversitie of opinion: And albeit they bee few in number, yet many of them consist of divers severall points, and comprehend in them many other Judgements and Resolutions, which never before were reported. If by these labours

---

47. [*Ed.:* The *Grand Coutumier* (i.e. great book of customs) of Normandy.]

48. [*Ed.:* Description of Normandy,]

49. [*Ed.:* "In reading, the truth is to be loved rather than the words; for simplicity is often found to be truthfulness and falseness combined, which lures men into error, while elaborate language scatters snares; and in many matters there is learning which cannot be expressed in speech." (Isidore, de summo bono, lib. 3, Valer. lib. 3.)]

50. [*Ed.:* He throws out bombast and inordinately long words.]

the Common-wealth shall receive any good, and the Reader reape the benefit
that for his reading and study he desireth, I shall have all the reward that for
my writings and paines I require.

Vale.[51]

Heydon's Case.
(1584) Easter Term, 26 Elizabeth I
In the Court of Exchequer.
First Published in the *Reports,* volume 3, page 7a.*

Ed.: This is a construction of leases, life estates, and statutes. Otlery, a
religious college, gave a tenancy in a manor also called "Otlery" to Ware
and his son. The tenancy was established by copyhold, an ancient device
for giving a parcel of a manor to a tenant, usually in return for agricultural
services, which was something like a long-running lease with special privileges for each party. Ware and his son held their copyhold to have for their
lives, subject to the will of the lord and the custom particular to that manor.
The Wares' copyhold was in a parcel also occupied by some tenants at will.
The college then leased the parcel to Heydon for a period of eighty years
in return for rents equal to the traditional rent for the components of the
parcel. The following year, the college was dissolved and lost its lands and
rents to Henry VIII, although the act of dissolution kept in force grants
made within the previous year for a term of life. The Court of Exchequer
found that the grant to the Wares was within the statute's protection but
that the lease to Heydon was void. The ruling was based on an important
discussion of the relationship of a statute to the pre-existing Common Law.
By considering the statute as curing a defect in the Common Law, the
remedy of the statute was limited to curing that defect. Judges are supposed
to construe statutes by seeking the true intent of the makers of the Act,
which is presumed to be *pro bono publico,* or intent for the public good.
[The 1658 and some other editions have the name of the college and manor
as "Ottery."]

---

51. [*Ed.:* Farewell.]
*[*Ed.:* See the initial pleadings at 20 Eliz. Rot. 140.]

In an information upon an intrusion in the Exchequer, against Heydon, for intruding into certain lands, &c. in the county of Devon: upon the general issue, the jurors gave a special verdict to this effect:

First, they found that parcel of the lands in the information were ancient copyholds of the manor of Otlery, whereof the warden and canons regular of the late college of Otlery were seised in the right of the said college; and that the warden and canons of the said college, 22 Hen. 7. at a court of the said manor, granted the same parcel by copy, to Ware the father and Ware the son, for their lives, at the will of the lord, according to the custom of the said manor; and that the rest of the land in the information was occupied by S. and G. at the will of the warden and canons of the said college for the time being, in the time of Henry the Eighth. And further that the said S. and G. so possessed, and the said Ware and Ware so seised as aforesaid, the said warden and canons by their deed indented, dated 12 January anno 30 Hen. 8. did lease the same to Heydon the defendant for eighty years, rendering certain rents severally for several parcels; and found that the said several rents in Heydon's lease reserved, were the ancient and accustomed rents of the several parcels of the lands, and found, that after the said lease they did surrender their college, and all the possessions thereof to King Henry the eighth. And further found the statute of 31 Hen. 8. and the branch of it, *scil.* by which it is enacted, "That if any abbot, &c. or other religious and ecclesiastical house or | place, within one year next before the first day of this present Parliament, [7 b] hath made, or hereafter shall make any lease or grant for life, or for term of years, of any manors, messuages, lands, &c. and in the which any estate or interest for life, year or years, at the time of the making of such grant or lease, then had his being or continuance, or hereafter shall have his being or con-tinuance, and not determined at the making of such lease, &c. Or if the usual and old rents and farms accustomed to be yielden and reserved by the space of twenty years next before the first day of this present Parliament, is not, or be not, or hereafter shall not be thereupon reserved or yielded, &c. that all and every such lease, &c. shall be utterly void." And further found, that the particular estates aforesaid were determined, and before the intrusion Heydon's lease began; and that Heydon entered, &c. And the great doubt which was often debated at the Bar and Bench on this verdict, was, If copyhold estate of Ware and Ware for their lives, at the will of the Lords, according to the custom of the said manor, should, in judgment of law be called an estate and interest for lives, within the said general words and meaning of the said Act.

And after all the Barons openly argued in Court in the same term, *scil.* Pasch. 26 Eliz. And it was unanimously resolved by Sir Roger Manwood, Chief Baron, and the other Barons of the Exchequer, that the said lease made to Heydon of the said parcels, whereof Ware and Ware were seised for life by copy of court-roll, was void; for it was agreed by them, that the said copyhold estate was an estate for life, within the words and meaning of the said Act. And it was resolved by them, that for the sure and true interpretation of all statutes in general (be they penal or beneficial) restrictive or enlarging of the Common Law, four things are to be discerned and considered.

1. What was the Common Law before the the Act.

2. What was the mischief and defect for which the Common Law did not provide.

3. What remedy the Parliament hath resolved and appointed to cure the disease of the commonwealth.

And 4. The true reason and remedy; and then the office of all the Judges is always to make such construction as shall suppress the mischief, and advance the remedy, and to suppress subtle inventions and evasions for continuance of the mischief, and *pro privato commodo,*[1] and to add force and life to the cure and remedy, according to the true intent of the makers of the Act, *pro bono publico.*[2] And it was said, that in this case the Common Law was, that
[8 a] religious and ecclesiastical | persons might have made leases for as many years as they pleased, the mischief was that when they perceived their houses would be dissolved, they made long and unreasonable leases: Now the stat of 31 Hen. 8. doth provide the remedy, and principally for such religious and ecclesiastical houses which should be dissolved after the Act (as the said college in our case was) that all leases of any land, whereof any estate or interest for life or years was then in being, should be void; and their reason was, that it was not necessary for them to make a new lease so long as a former had continuance; and therefore the intent of the Act was to avoid doubling of estates, and to have but one single estate in being at a time: For doubling of estates implies in itself deceit, and private respect, to prevent the intention of the Parliament. And if the copyhold estate for two lives, and the lease for eighty years shall

---

1. [*Ed.:* For private benefit,]
2. [*Ed.:* For the public good. (for the welfare of the whole state and people)]

stand together, here will be doubling of estates *simul & semel*,[3] which will be against the true meaning of Parliament.

And in this case it was debated at large, in what cases the general words of Acts of Parliament shall extend to copyhold or customary estates, and in what not; and therefore this rule was taken and agreed by the whole Court, That when an Act of Parliament doth alter the service, tenure, interest of the land, or other thing, in prejudice of the lord, or of the custom of the manor, or in prejudice of the tenant, there the general words of such Act of Parliament shall not extend to copyholds: But when an Act of Parliament is generally made for the good of the weal public, and no prejudice can accrue by reason of alteration of any interest, service, tenure, or custom of the manor, there many times copyhold and customary estates are within the general purview of such Acts. And upon these grounds the Chief Baron put many cases, where he held, that the Statute of West. 2. De Donis Conditionalibus did not extend to copyholds; for if the statute alters the estate of the land, it will be also an alteration of the tenure, which would be prejudicial to the lord: for of necessity the donee in tail of land ought to hold of his donor, and do him such services (without special reservation) as his donor doth to his lord.

2. Littleton saith, lib. 1. cap. 9. That although some tenants by copy of court-roll have an estate of inheritance, yet they have it but at the will of the lord, according to the course of the Common Law. For it is said, that if the lord put them out, they have no other remedy but to sue to their lord by petition; and so the intent of the Statute de *Donis Conditionalibus* was not to extend (in prejudice of lords) to such base estates, which as the law was then taken, was but at | the will of the lord. And the statute saith, *Quod voluntas* [8 b] *donatoris in carta doni sui manifeste express. de caetero observetur:*[4] so that which shall be entailed, ought to be such an hereditament, which is given, or at least might be given by deed or charter in tail.

3. For as much as great part of the land within the realm, is in grant by copy, it will be a thing inconvenient, and occasion great suit and contention, that copyholds should be entailed, and yet neither fine nor common recovery

---

3. [*Ed.:* Together and at one time,]

4. [*Ed.:* That the will of the donor, manifestly expressed in the charter of his gift, shall be from henceforth observed:]

bar them; so as he who hath such estate cannot (without the assent of the lord by committing a forfeiture, and taking a new estate) of himself dispose of it, either for payment of his debts, or advancement of his wife, or his younger children; wherefore he conceived that the Statute de *Donis Conditionalibus* did not extend to copyholds, *quod fuit concessum per totam Curiam.*[5] But it was said that the statute, without special custom, doth not extend to copyholds; but if the custom of the manor doth warrant such estates, and a remainder hath been limited over and enjoyed, or plaints in the nature of a *formedon*[6] in the descender brought in the court of the manor, and land so entailed by copy recovered thereby, then the custom co-operating with the statute makes it an estate-tail; so that neither the statute without the custom, nor the custom without the statute, can create an estate-tail.

And to this purpose is Littleton, lib. 1. c. 8. for he saith, That if a man seised of a manor, within which manor there hath been a custom which hath been used time out of memory, that certain tenants within the same manor have used to have lands and tenements, to hold to them and their heirs in fee-simple or fee-tail, or for term of life, &c. at the will of the lord, according to the custom of the same manor; and a little after, That *Formedon* in descender lies of such tenements, which writ, as it was said, was not at the Common Law.

To which it was answered by the chief Baron, that if the statute (without custom) shall not extend to copyholds, without question the custom of the manor cannot make it extend to them: for before the statute, all estates of inheritance, as Littleton saith, lib. i. cap. 2., were fee-simple, and after the statute no custom can begin, because the statute being made in 13 Edw. 1. is made within time of memory; *ergo* the estate tail cannot be created by custom; and therefore, Littleton is to be intended (inasmuch as he grounds his opinion upon the custom, that copyholds may be granted in fee-simple, or fee-tail) of a fee-simple conditional at the Common Law: for Littleton well knew, that [9 a] no custom I could commence after the statute of West. 2., as appears in his own book, lib. 2. c. 10. and 34 H. 6. 36. And where he saith, that *formedon* in descender lies, he also saith, that it lies at the Common Law. And it appears in our books, that, in special cases, a *Formedon* in the descender lay at the

5. [*Ed.:* which was granted by the whole court.]
6. [*Ed.:* Writ available for one who had a right to lands or tenements from a gift in tail.]

Common Law, before the statute of Westm. 2., which see 4 Edw. 2. Formedon 50. 10 Edw. 2. Formedon 55. 21 Edw. 3. 47. Plowd. Com. 246b. &c.

And where it was further objected, That the statute of West. 2. cannot without custom make an estate tail of copyholds, because without custom, such estate cannot be granted by copy; for it was said, That estates had been always granted to one and his heirs by copy, that a grant to one and the heirs of his body, is another estate not warranted by the custom: So that in such manors, where such estates of inheritance have been allowed by custom, the statute doth extend to them, and makes them, which before were fee conditional, now by the statute estates in tail, and that the statute cannot, as hath been agreed before, alter the custom, or create a new estate not warranted by the custom.

To that it was answered by the chief Baron, That where the custom of the manor is to grant lands by copy *in feodo simplici*[7] (as the usual pleading is) without question, by the same custom lands may be granted to one and the heirs of his body, or upon any other limitation or condition; for these are estates in fee-simple, *et eo potius*,[8] that they are not so large and ample as the general and absolute fee-simple is, and therefore the generality of the custom doth include them, but not *e converso;*[9] *ad quod non fuit responsum.*[10] But it was agreed by the whole Court, That another Act made at the same Parliament, cap. 18. which gave the *elegit*[11] doth not extend to copyholds, for that would be prejudicial to the lord, and against the custom of the manor, that a stranger should have interest in the land held of him by copy, where by the custom it cannot be transferred to any without a surrender made to him, and by the lord allowed and admitted. But it was agreed by them, that other statutes made at the same Parliament, which are beneficial for the copyholder, and not prejudicial to the lord, may be, by a favourable interpretation, extended to copyholds, as cap. 3. which gives the wife a *cui in vita*,[12] and receipt, and

---

7. [*Ed.:* in fee simple.]

8. [*Ed.:* the rather so,]

9. [*Ed.:* on the contrary.]

10. [*Ed.:* which was not answered.]

11. [*Ed.:* Writ of execution either on a judgment for a debt or damages or on the forfeiture of a recognizance in the king's court.]

12. [*Ed.:* Writ of entry for a widow against a person to whom her husband had in his lifetime alienated his land subject to her inchoate claims.]

cap. 4. which gives the particular tenant a *quod ei deforceat;*[13] and therewith agrees 10 Edw. 4. 2b.

And in this case it was also resolved, That although it was not found that the said rents were the usual rents, accustomed to be reserved within 20 years before the Parliament; yet inasmuch as they have found, that the accustomable rent was reserved, and a custom goes at all times before, for this cause it shall be intended, that it was the accustomable rent within the 20 years, and so it shall be intended, if the contrary be not shewed of the other side. And judgment was entered for the Queen.

Fermor's Case.
(FERMOR v. SMITH)
(1602) Hilary Term, 44 Elizabeth I
In the Court of Chancery, and before all the justices of England.
First Published in the *Reports,* volume 3, page 77a.

Ed.: Richard Fermor leased a messuage, or house and its related buildings and land, to Thomas Smith. The lease was based on a demise, or grant, for a period of 21 years, in return for rents of £3 yearly. Smith held other lands from Fermor as a tenant at will, which means the leases in these lands could be ended any time by Fermor or Smith, for 20s yearly, and he held a copyhold for more lands from Smith for 40s. Smith also held some lands not subject to Fermor. Smith granted all of his lands in the area to Chappell for life, and Smith levied a fine and proclamations, or instituted a proceeding to cut short other interests rather like a modern proceeding to declare an interest by adverse possession, which would cut off Fermor's interests in Fermor's lands possessed by Smith. Smith continued paying all of his rents to Fermor. The five years for the fine to be completed ran. Chappell died, which meant the reversion Smith kept when he gave Chappell the life estate gave possession back to Smith. The 21-year lease expired, and Smith claimed all of the land and barred Fermor from possession. Fermor sued in Chancery, although Egerton the chancellor referred it to

13. [*Ed.:* Writ given to the owners of a particular estate (as for life, in dower, by the courtesy, or in fee-tail) who were barred of the right of possession by a recovery against them through their default or non-appearance in a possessory action.]

the whole bench. The court held that the Parliamentary act that established the use of fines had not been intended for use in such a fraudulent manner. Benefits acquired by fraud cannot bind the people defrauded, particularly when there is a relationship of trust and confidence between the persons defrauding and defrauded. To allow any other result would allow "general mischief to insue." Fermor won.

This case presents good discussions of statutory interpretation based on legislative intent, of fraud and fraud in a position of trust (which Coke seems to have over-emphasized compared to other reporters of the case), and of public policy arguments based on the effect of the ruling on subsequent litigants.

In a case depending in Chancery, between Richard Fermor, Esq. plaintiff, and Thomas Smith defendant, on the hearing the cause before Sir Thomas Egerton, Knight, Lord Keeper of the Great Seal, the case was such; Richard Fermor, the plaintiff, being seised of the manor of Somerton in fee, by indenture 6 Junii 20 Eliz. demised a messuage, parcel of the same manor, to Thomas Smith, the defendant, for twenty-one years, rendering the yearly rent of three pounds during the term, by force of which the defendant entered and was thereof possessed; He was also possessed of divers other parcels of the said manor at the will of the plaintiff, rendering twenty shillings per annum, and held divers other parcels of the said manor by copy of court-roll according to the custom of the said manor, rendering forty shillings rent per annum, all which lay in Somerton: And the said Thomas Smith was seised in his demesne as of fee of divers lands, in the same town, which were his proper inheritance. And afterwards by his deed 15th of October 25 Eliz. demised the said house and all the said land which he held for years, at will, and by copy, to one Chappel for his life, Pasch. 35 Eliz. Smith levied a fine with proclamations of as many messuages and lands, as comprehended as well all the lands which he held for years, at Will, and by copy, as his own inheritance, by covin[1] and practice, to bar the plaintiff of his inheritance; the proclamations and five years passed, Smith at all times, before and after the fine, continued in possession, and paid the said several rents to the plaintiff. Chappel died, the 21 years

---

1. [*Ed.:* Covin ordinarily refers to a secret agreement or conspiracy; here it means by stealthy, or deceitful means.]

[77 b] expired, I and now Smith claimed the inheritance of the land which he held by lease, at will, and by copy, and would have barred the plaintiff by force of the said fine with the proclamations, and five years past. And the Lord Keeper of the Great Seal thinking and considering of the great mischiefs which might ensue by such practices, and on the other side considering that fines with proclamations are the general assurances of the realm, referred this case (being a thing of great importance and consequence) to the consideration of the two Chief Justices Popham and Anderson; and after conference between them, they thought it necessary that all the justices of England and Barons of the Exchequer should be assembled for the resolution of this great case. And accordingly in this same term, all the Judges of England and the Barons of the Exchequer met at Serjeant's Inn in Fleet-street, at two several days, where the case was debated among them. And at length it was resolved, by the two Chief Justices, Popham and Anderson, and by Gawdy and Walmesly, and all the other justices of England and Barons of the Exchequer, (except two) that the plaintiff was not barred by the said fine with proclamations, and that for four causes:

1. The makers of the Act of 4 Hen. 7. cap. 24. did never intend that such fine levied by fraud and practice of lessee for years, tenant at will, or tenant by copy of Court roll, who pretend no title to the inheritance, but intend the disinherison of their lessors or Lords, should bar them of their inheritance, and that appears by the preamble of the Act of 4 Hen. 7. where it is said, "That fines ought to be of greatest strength to avoid strifes and debates, & c." But when lessee for years, or at will, or tenant by copy of Court roll make a feoffment by assent and covin that fine shall be levied, the same is not to avoid strife and debate; but by assent and covin to begin strife and debate where none was; And therefore the Act doth not extend to establish any estate made by such fraud and practice.

2. It was never the intent of the makers of the Act, that those who could not levy a fine, shall by making of an estate by wrong and fraud be enabled by force of the said Act to bar those who had right by levying of a fine: For if they themselves without such fraudulent estate cannot levy a fine to bar them which have the freehold and inheritance, certainly the makers of the Act did not intend that by making of an estate by fraud and practice they should have power to bar them; and such fraudulent estate is as no estate in the judgement of Law.

3. As it is said in *Dalamer's* Case in *Plow. Comm.* 352. if any doubt be

conceived upon the words or meaning of | an Act of Parliament it is good to [78 a] construe the same according to the reason of the Common Law; but the Common Law doth so abhorre fraud and covin, that all Acts as well Judicial as others, and which of themselves are just and lawful, yet being mixt with fraud and deceit, are in judgement of Law wrongful and unlawful: *Quod alias bonum & justum est, si per vim vel fraudem petatur, malum & injustum efficitur:* [2] And therefore if a woman hath title to Dower which is one of the things favoured in Law, and by covin between her & another causeth a stranger to disseise the tenant of the land, to the intent that she may bring a Writ of Dower against him, which is done accordingly, and the woman recover against him upon a just and good title, yet all the same is void and of no force to binde the Terre-tenant; *a fortiori* [3] in the principal Case when the lessee for years maketh a feoffment by covin, which amounteth to a wrong and disseisin, a fine levied by him who is *particeps criminis,* [4] and who had not, nor pretended any right to the land shall not be a barre to the lessor. And that recoveries in Dower, or any other real Action shall be made a good title against the Tenant who cometh to the land by wrong and covin are void and of no force appeareth by 41 Ass. 28. 44 Edw. 3. 25 Ass. 1. 22 Ass. 92. 11 Edw. 4. 15 Edw. 4. 4. 7 Hen. 7. 11. 18 Hen. 8. 5. 12 Eliz. Dyer 295. For although that his right be lawful, and that he hath pursued his Recovery by judgement in the King's Court, yet his covin maketh all that unlawful and wrongful, and yet Recoveries and chiefly upon good title are much favoured in Law: Also the right of inheritance of feme coverts, [5] and infants, are much favoured in Law; and yet if a feme covert or an infant be of covin and consent, that the discontinuee shall be disseised, and that the disseisor shall enfeoff them, and all this is done accordingly, they are not remitted, as appears by Littleton, chap. Remitter 151. & 19 Hen. 8. 12b. And there it is held by six justices, that in such case, if the disseisor enters by covin to the intent to enfeoff the infant, although the infant be not of covin, &c. yet he shall not be remitted, because he who is *in* by him who makes the covin shall be in the same plight as he who did the covinous act. And it is agreed in 19 Hen. 8. 12. b. that if a man makes a disseisin to the

---

2. [*Ed.:* What is otherwise good and just, if it is sought by force and fraud, becomes bad and unjust:]

3. [*Ed.:* with stronger reason.]

4. [*Ed.:* a participant in a crime, (an accomplice).]

5. [*Ed.:* married women.]

intent to make a feoffment with warranty, although he makes the feoffment twenty months after, yet it is a warranty which commences by disseisin.

So if one makes a gift in tail to another, and the uncle of the donor disseises the donee, and makes a feoffment with warranty, the uncle dies, and the warranty descends on the donor, and afterwards the donee dies without issue, the donor brings *Formedon*[6] in the reverter, and the tenant pleads the feoffment

[78 b]   with warranty, the demandant shall | avoid it, because it began by disseisin, and yet the disseisin was not immediately done to the donor, but to the donee; but by it his reversion was devested; and yet warranties are much favoured in law. And it appears in 8 Eliz. 249. Dyer, that a vacat[7] was made of a recovery in the Common Pleas had by covin. The law hath ordained, that he, who will be assured of his goods, shall buy them in open Market, and that sale will bind all strangers, as well as the seller, and yet it is agreed in 33 Hen. 6. 5a, 5b that a sale in Market overt shall not bind him who hath a right to the goods, if the sale be by fraud, or the vendee hath notice that the property of the goods was another's. So the law hath ordained the Court of Common Pleas as an open Market for assurances of land by fine, so that he who will be assured of his land not only against the seller, but all strangers, it is good for him to pass it in this market overt by fine; for, as it is said, *finis finem litibus imponit:*[8] and yet covin and deceit in the case at Bar will void it. In 4 Edw. 2. Cui in Vita 22. it is held, That a resignation made by an abbot by covin should not abate the writ. 34 Edw. 1. Warranty 88. & 19 Edw. 2. Assets 3. & 31 Edw. 1. Voucher 301., a covinous conveyance that assets should not descend, is nothing worth. And it appears in 17 Edw. 3. 59. and 21 Edw. 3. 3. 46. that an estate made to the King, and by his letters patent granted over, and all this by covin between him who granted to the King and the patentee, to make an evasion out of the Statute of Mortmain, shall not bind, but shall be repealed. And 17 Eliz. Dy. 339. a presentation obtained by collusion is void. And 17 Eliz. Dy. 339. letters of administration obtained by collusion are void, and shall not repeal a former administration: see 13 Eliz. Dyer 295. many cases there put concerning covin.

6. [*Ed.:* Writ to take possession by virtue of a grant in tail.]
7. [*Ed.:* cancellation.]
8. [*Ed.:* a fine puts an end to litigation:]

And thereupon it was concluded, That if a recovery in Dower, or other real action, if a remitter to a *feme covert* or an infant, if a warranty, if a sale in market overt, if the King's Letters Patent, if a presentation, administration, &c. *scil.* acts temporal and Ecclesiastical, shall be avoided by covin; by the same reason a fine in the principal case levied by fraud and covin, as is aforesaid, shall not bind; for *fraus & dolus nemini patrocinari debent.*[9]

Note, Reader, in 33 & 34 Eliz. in the King's Bench between Robert Laune plaintiff and William Toker defendant in *Ejectione firmae*[10] of lands in Il-fordcoom in the county of Devon, it was adjudged that where tenant for life levied a fine with proclamation and five years pass in his life, that the lessor should have five years to make his claim after the death of the lessee. And although this statute of 4 Hen. 7. hath a saving for the lessor in such case, yet the saving is of such right "as first shall grow, remain, &c." and the right first accrued to the | lessor after the fine and the forfeiture; but notwithstanding that, in as much as by the covin of the lessee, he in reversion or remainder might be barred of his reversion or remainder (for they do not expect to enter till after the death of the lessee,) and especially when the lessee hath lands of his own inheritance in the same town (as in the case at Bar he had), there the lessor shall have 5 years after the death of the lessee. [79 a]

So it was agreed in the same case, if tenant for life makes a feoffment in fee to one who hath lands in the same town, and the feoffee levies a fine with proclamations; it shall not bind the lessor, but he shall have 5 years after the death of the lessee, for the lessor cannot know of what land the fine is levied, for he is not party to the indenture or agreement between the conusor and conusee;[11] So in the same case, the Judges made a construction against the letter of the statute in salvation of the estate and inheritance of him in the reversion. And so it hath been adjudged before in *Some's Case* in the Common Pleas, in Sir James Dyer's time, as Plowden told me. Also it was said, that if lessee for years makes a feoffment in fee by practice and covin, that the feoffee should levy a fine with proclamations to another (the feoffee having other

---

9. [*Ed.:* fraud and deceit should defend or excuse no man.]

10. [*Ed.:* Writ to recover in trespass lands from a prior present-interest holder whose interest has expired.]

11. [*Ed.:* The conusor, or cognisor, is the person who passes lands through an acknowledgement by fine to the conusee, who receives them.]

lands in the same Town) and all this is done accordingly; and yet the lessee doth continually pay the rent to the lessor, it shall not bind the lessor, for the reasons aforesaid.

Lastly, the Judges in this Resolution did greatly respect the general mischief which would ensue, if such fines levied by practice and covin of those who had the particular interests, should bar those who had the inheritance, and especially in the case at Bar, when after the fine levied, the conusor continually payed the rent to the lessor, which made the fraud and practice apparent, and therefore the lessor was secure, and had no cause of any fear or doubt of such fraud. But it was resolved, that if A. purchases land of B. by feoffment, or bargain and sale, and enrols it, and afterwards perceiving that B. had but a defeasible title, and that C. had right to it, B. levies a fine with proclamations to a stranger, or takes a fine from another with proclamations, to the intent to bar the right of C., this fine so levied by consent should bind; for nothing was done in this case which was not lawful, and the intent of the makers of the Act of 4 Hen. 7. was to avoid strifes and debates, and by the express purview should bind all strangers who do not pursue their right by action, or entry within 5 years. So, if one pretending title to land enters, and disseises another, and afterwards with intent to bind the disseisee, levies a fine with proclamations, this fine shall bind the disseisee by the express purview of the Act, if he neither enters nor I pursues his action within 5 years; and this cannot be called levying by covin, because the levying of the fine is lawful, and the disseisee may re-enter, or bring his action within the 5 years.

[79 b]

The fourth reason was, because the lessee had contrived his fraud and deceit in so secret a manner, that he had deprived the lessor of the remedy which the statute gave him, that is to say, to make his entry, or bring his action within the 5 years: For how could he make his entry, or bring his action, when he knew not of the feoffment which did the wrong? And as to the fine, inasmuch as the lessee had lands in fee-simple in the same town, every one will presume that the fine would be levied of that whereof it might be lawfully levied. And although it contained more acres than his own land, that is usual almost in all fines; and peradventure the lessor did not know the just quantity of the lessee's proper land, for that doth not appertain to him; and therefore it would be unreasonable to give him benefit, in this case, of the non-claim of the lessor, when the wrong and covin of the lessee is the cause of his non-claim. And a man shall not take advantage of his own wrong or covin. The possession of the lessee is not any mean for the lessor to take any notice of this wrong, for he comes to the possession of the land by grant or demise lawfully; and after the feoffment he continues in the possession as a lessee, for he pays his rent as a lessee ought; immo[12] the possession of the lessee, and the payment of the rent, was the cause that the lessor neither knew nor suspected the fraud.

Also it was said, that the fraud and covin in this case made it more odious, because between the lessor and lessee, and the lord and his copyholder, there is a trust and confidence, and therefore a lessee for years and a copyholder shall do fealty, which is a great obligation of trust and confidence; and fraud and deceit by him who is trusted, is most odious in law. And if the makers of this Act had been asked, if their intent was, that such a fine so levied by such practice and covin should bind the lessors, they would have answered, God forbid that they should intend to patronize any such iniquity practised and compassed by those in whom there was trust and confidence reposed. But when a disseisor (although he gains the possession by wrong) levies a fine with proclamation, yet it shall bind as is aforesaid, for a disseisor *venit tanquam in arena,*[13] and it is not possible but that the disseisee to whom the wrong is done, and who hath lost his possession, should be conusant of it; and therefore it will be his own folly, if he makes not his claim; and it is not accompanied with fraud and practice by one who came to the possession lawfully, by grant or demise, and who had a trust reposed in him by his lessor or grantor, which fraud and practice is so secretly contrived, that the | lessor by common pre- [80 a] sumption could not have notice to make his claim, because his lessee continued in possession, and paid his rent, as a lessee ought. And as to that which was objected, That it would be mischievous to avoid fines on such bare averments; It was answered, That it would be a greater mischief, and principally in these days (in which the Poet saith,

——— *Fugere pudor, rectumque, fidesque,*
In quorum subiere locum fraudesque, dolique,
Insidiaeque, & vis, & amor sceleratus habendi.)[14]

---

12. [*Ed.:* more specifically.]

13. [*Ed.:* comes, as it were, into the arena (i.e. into the conflict).]

14. [*Ed.:* Modesty, right and faith were fled away, and in their place came frauds, deceits and snares, and violence, and wicked love of possessions. (quoting Ovid, *Metamorphoses,* I. 129.)]

if fines levied by such covin and practice should bind, And such Objection may be made, if a fine be levied to secret uses to deceive a purchaser, an averment of fraud may be taken against it, by the stat. of 27 Eliz. cap. 4. So if a fine be levied on an usurious contract, it may be avoided by averment, by the statute of 13 Eliz. cap. 8. And Sir Thomas Egerton Lord Keeper of the Great Seal, commended this resolution of the justices, and agreed in opinion with them.

Part Four of the *Reports*

The Fourth Part of Coke's *Reports* was published in 1602. It was originally published in Law French and entitled *Le quart part des reportes del Edward Coke chivalier, l'attorney general le roy: de divers resolutions & judgements dones sur solemnes arguments, & avec graund deliberation & conference des tresreverend judges & sages de la ley de cases difficult, en queux sont graund diversities des opinions, et queux ne fueront unques resolves, ou adjudges, & reporte par devant, et les raisons & causes des dits resolutions & judgements: publies en le primier an (le printemps de tout heureusite) de tresheureux regiment de treshault et tresillustre Jaques roy Dengleterre, Fraunce, & Ireland, & de Escoce le 37., le fountaine de tout pietie & justice, & la vie de la ley.* In English, *The Fourth Part of the Reports of Sir Edward Coke, Knight, the King's Majesty's Attorney-General, of divers Resolutions and Judgments given upon solemn Arguments, and with great Deliberation and Conference of the most reverend Judges and Sages of the Law, of Cases difficult, in which are great diversities of opinions, and which were never Resolved or Adjudged, or Reported before: and the Reasons and Causes of the said Resolutions and Judgements. Published in the first yeare (the springtime of all happiness) of the most happie and prosperous Raigne of the Most High and Most Illustrious James, king of England, France, and Ireland, and of Scotland the 37. the Fountaine of all piety and Justice and the Life of the Law.*

The cases in this part present issues that range further afield from property law than do the first three volumes. Although there are cases on the rights of husbands and wives over property, and on debt collection and many on copyholds (which are akin to modern leases), this part moves into the domains now known as tort law, contract law, criminal law, and civil and appellate procedure.

Epigrams from the title page:

Abominabiles Regi qui agunt impie, quoniam Justicia firmat solium.[1]
PROVERB. 16. 12.

Voluntas Regis labia justa, qui recta loquitur diligetur.[2]
PROVERB. 16. 13.

Custodia innocentiam, & vide aequitatem, quoniam sunt reliquiae homini pacifico.[3]
PSAL. 37. 37.

(Preface)
To the Reader.

There is nothing that can bee said or written of Lawes, although the field bee large, and the common place thereof may seeme to be infinite, but in mine opinion may bee reduced to one of these sixe heades; *Making, Correcting, Digesting, Expounding, Learning, and Observing.* Of Lawes, concerning Making of new, six things amongst many other doe principally fall into consideration. First, under what forme of Common wealth the Lawmakers be governed; For one consideration is requisite where the government is *Monarchicall,* another when it is *Artistocraticall,* and a third where it is *Democraticall.* Secondly, to know the several kinds of the *Muncicipall* Lawes of his owne proper Nation: For the innovation or chaunge of some Laws is most dangerous, and lesse perill in the alteration of others. Thirdly, to understand what the true sence and sentence of the Lawes then standing is and how farre forth former Lawes have made provision in the case that falleth into question. Fourthly, by experience to apprehend what have beene the causes of the danger or hinderance that hath fallen out in that particular to the Common wealth, either in respect of time, place, persons or otherwise. Fifthly, to foresee that a proportionall remedy be applied so, as that for curing of some defects past, there bee not a stirring of more dangerous effects in future. Sixtly, the mean,

---

1. [*Ed.:* It is an abomination to the King to commit wickedness, for the throne is established by righteousness.]

2. [*Ed.:* Righteous lips are the King's desire, for they love him who speak righteously.]

3. [*Ed.:* Mark innocence and behold equity, for they are left to a peaceful man.]

& that only is by authority of the high (that in troth is the highest) Court of Parliament. Concerning the *Correction of olde,* the same respectes are to be observed, that have been said touching the *Making of new.* For *Digesting* of former Laws into Methode and order, three things are requisite: Judgement to know them, Art to dispose them, and Diligence to omit none of them. The *Expounding* of Lawes doth ordinarily belong to the reverend Judges, and *S*ages of the realme: And in cases of greatest difficulty and importance to the high court of parliament: Concerning *Learning* & attaining to the knowledge of these Lawes, I have in the Preface of my first Edition somewhat touched. The observing of Lawes doth concerne all whatsoever; but principally some in particuler, as hereafter shalbe touched, For *Summa sequar fastigia rerum.*[1] Our kingdome is a *Monarchie Sucessive*[2] by inherent birth-right, of all others the most absolute and perfect forme of government, excluding *Interregnum,*[3] and with it infinite inconveniences; The Maxime of the Common Law being, That the king of England never dyeth, which is true in respect of the ever during, and never dying politique capacity. The Lawes of England consist of three parts, The Common Law, Customes, & acts of parliament: For any fundamental point of the ancient Common Lawes and customes of the realme, it is a Maxime in policie, and a triall by experience, that the alteration of any of them is most dangerous; for that which hath beene refined and perfected by all the wisest men in former succession of ages and proved and approved by continuall experience to be good & profitable for the common wealth, cannot without great hazard and danger be altered or chaunged. Infinite were the scruples, suites, and inconveniences that the Statute of 13. *Edw. 1. de Donis conditionalibus*[4] did introduce, which intended to give every man power to create a new found estate in taile, & to establish a perpetuitie of his landes, so as the same should not be aliened nor letten, but only during the life of tenant in taile, against a fundamentall rule of the Common Law; That all estates of inheritance were fee simple, wherupon these inconveniencies insued, purchases defeated, leases evicted, other estates and graunts made upon just and good consideration were avoided, creditors defrauded of the just & due

---

1. [*Ed.:* I will cover the chief points (*Vergil,* Aeneid 1.342).]
2. [*Ed.:* Successive Monarchy.]
3. [*Ed.:* An interval between reigns.]
4. [*Ed.:* concerning conditional gifts.]

debts, Offendors imboldned to commit capital offences, and many other inconveniences followed: Also, what suits and troubles arose by the Statute of *cap.* 34. *Edw.* 3. of *Nonclaime,*[5] enacted against a main point of the Common Law, whereby insued the universall trouble of the Kings subjects, as it was resolved in Parliament in 4.*Hen.* 7. *cap.*24. is apparant to all of least understanding: What intricate and subtile questions in lawe dayly arose upon the validity and construction of willes of lands, which by the rule of law were not devisable before the statuts of 32. and 34.*Hen.* 8. of Wils, dayly experience to the ruine of many, and hinderance of multitudes manifestly teacheth. But above all, certaine late inventions and devises in assurances of lands by limitation of uses, under upstart and wild provisoes and limitations, such as the Common Law never knew, doe breed and multiplie infinite troubles, questions, suits, and difficulties: In the Parliament holden in the 20. yeare of King *Henry* the third, it was mooved that Children borne before mariage (being Bastards by the Common Lawes of this Realme, the wisedome of the Law abhorring clandestine contracts) might be legitimate according to the Civill or Ecclesiasticall lawes, whereunto saith the Statut, *Omnes Comites & Barones una voce responderunt, Nolumus leges Anglia mutare quae hucusque usitatae sunt & approbatae:*[6] In which few words is observable; First, the absolute monaccord and unity, *una voce,* of all the Peeres and Lords of Parliament: Secondly the deniall, *Nolumus leges Anglie,*[7] not of Normandy, or of any other Nation, as is fondly dreamed, as elsewhere I have shewed, but the common Law of England: And thirdly, the reason of their deniall: *Quaehactenus usitate sunt & approbate,*[8] as if they should have said, we will not change the Lawes of England, for that they have been anciently used and approved from time to time by men of most singular wisdome, understanding, and experience. I will not recite the sharpe Law of the *Locrenses*[9] in *magna Graecia,* concerning those that sought innovation in preferring any new Law to be made, you may read it in the glosse of the first booke of *Justinians* Institutes, because it is too sharpe & tart for this age: But take we the reason of that Law, *Quia leges figendi*

5. [*Ed.:* An early statute of limitations.]
6. [*Ed.:* All the Earls and Barons answered with one voice, 'We will not change the old laws of England heretofore used and approved'.]
7. [*Ed.:* We will not [change] the laws of England.]
8. [*Ed.:* [The laws have been] heretofore used and approved,]
9. [*Ed.:* Locrians. . .ancient (great) Greece,]

& refigendi consuetudo est perniciosa.[10] But *Platoes* Law I will recite touching this matter, which you may read in his sixt booke *de Legibus;* If any Citizen doe invent any new thing, which never before was read or heard of, the Inventor thereof, shall first practise the same for the space of tenne yeeres in his owne house, before it be brought into the Common wealth, or published to the people, to the end that if the invention be good, it shall be profitable to the Inventor, and if it were nought, he himselfe and not the Common wealth might taste of the prejudice. And I like well the Edict reported by *Suetonius; Quae praeter consuetudinem & morem maiorum fiunt, neque placent, nec recta videntur,*[11] And I would the commandement of *Honorius* and *Arcadius* were of us Englishmen observed, *Mos fidelissimae vetustatis retinendus est:*[12] And I agree and conclud this point with the Apotheg[m] of *Pereander* of Corinth, *That old Lawes and new meats are fittest for us.* As concerning the correcting of the Common Lawes or antient Customes of England, may be applyed all that hath been said concerning making of Lawes: only this adde; That it hath bin an old rule in Policy and Law, that *Correctio Legum est euitanda.*[13] And yet concerning certaine of our penall statutes, to repeale many that time hath antiquated as unprofitable, and remaine but as snares to intangle the subjects withall; And to omit all those that be repealed, that none by them be deceived, as for example concerning *Drapery,* or such like. To make one plaine and perspicious law divided into articles, so as every subject may know what actes be in force, what repealed, either by particuler or general words, in part or in the whole, or what branches and parts abridged what inlarged, what expounded: so as each man may clearly know what and how much is of them in force, and how to obey them, it were a necessary worke, and worthy of singular commendation: which his Majesty out of his great wisedome and care to the Common wealth, hath commanded to be done: for as they now stand, it will require great paines in reading over all, great attention in observing, and greater judgement in discerning upon consideration of the whole, what the Law is in any one particular point: But with this Caution that there be certaine Statutes concerning the administration of justice, that are in effect

10. [*Ed.:* A custom of enacting and abrogating laws is pernicious.]

11. [*Ed.:* Unless things are done according to custom, and the usage of the majority, they will neither be approved nor seem to be right,]

12. [*Ed.:* A custom of trustworthy antiquity ought to be kept:]

13. [*Ed.:* The amendment of Laws is to be avoided.]

so woven into the Common Law, and so well approved by experience, as it will be no smal danger to alter or change them: And herein according to his Royall commandement (God willing) somewhat in due time shall be performed. For bringing of the Common Lawes into a better Methode, I doubt much of the fruit of that labour. This I know, that abridgements in many professions have greatly profited the Authors themselves; but as they are used have brought no small prejudice to others: For the advised and orderly reading over of the bookes at large in such maner as elswhere I have pointed at, I absolutely determine to be the right way to enduring and perfect knowledge, and to use abridgements as tables, and to trust only to the bookes at large: For I hold him not discreet that will *Sectari rivulos,*[14] when he may *petere fontes.*[15] And certain it is that the tumultuary reading of abridgements, doth cause a confused judgement, and a broken & troubled kind of delivery or utterance: But to reduce the said penall Laws into such methode & order & with such caution as is abovesaid (which cannot be done but in the high court of parliament, nor without the advise of such as before is touched) were an honorable, profitable and commendable worke for the whole common wealth. This fourth part of my Reports doth concerne the true sence & exposition of the lawes in divers & many Cases, never adjudged or resolved before: which for that they may in mine opinion tende to the generall quiet & benefit of many, The onely end (God knoweth) of the edition of them, I thought it a part of my great duty that I owe to the common wealth not to keepe them private, but being withall both incouraged, and in maner thereunto inforced, to publish and communicate them to all, wherein my comfort and contentation is great, both in respect of your singular and favorable approbation of may former labours, as for that I (knowing mine own weakenes) have one great advantage of many famous and excellent men that have taken upon them the great and painfull labour of writing: For they to give their workes the more authority and credite, have much used the figure *Prosopopeia* in faining divers Princes, and others of high authority, excellent wisedom, profound learning, & long experience, to speake such sentences, rules & conclusions, as they intended and desired for the common good, to have obayed and observed; As *Zenophon* the great in his Booke which he wrote of the Institution of Princes, faineth that king *Cambyses* taught and spake many excellent things

14. [*Ed.:* Follow the streams,]
15. [*Ed.:* Seek out the sources.]

to *Cyrus* his sonne; And in another Booke which he wrote of the Art of Chivalry, he saineth how king *Philip* taught and instructed his sonne *Alex[an]der* to fight. But I without figure, or fayning, do report and publish the very true resolutions, sentences, and judgements of the reverend Judges and Sages of the lawes themselves, who for their authoritie, wisedome, learning, and experience, are to be honoured, reverenced, and beleeved. The due *observation* of the said Lawes doth generally without any limitation or exception concerne all: But principally Princes, Nobles, Judges, and Magistrats, to whose custody & charge the due execution (the life and the soule of the Laws) is committed; for that they in respect of their places are more eminent & conspicuous then other men, wherein 3 things are necessarily required, *Understanding, Authoritie,* and *Will: Understanding* concerneth things and persons; That is, first what is right, and just to be done, & what ill, and to be avoyded; Secondly, what persons for merit are to be rewarded, And what for offences to be punished: And both in reward and punishment to observe quantity and qualitie. *Authoritie* to protect the good, and to chastice the ill. *Will* prompt and readie duely, sincerely, and truely to execute the law. But forasmuch as many Adversaries and two open Enemies do continually lie in wait to assault this good and ready will, it must of necessity have two defensive compleat armors of proofe: first *Integrity* against these six secret adversaries, *Gyftes, Affections, Intreatie, Anger, Praecipitation,* and *Morosa cunctatio,* peevish delay. Secondly, *Fortitude* and *Constancie* against the terror of Malice, & feare of danger, two open and violent enemies: *Videte Judices quid faciatis, non enim hominis exercetis judicium sed Domini, & quodcunq; judicaveritis in vos redundabit.*[16] And *Deus est Judex justus, fortis, & patiens,*[17] and so must every Judge bee.[18] *Justus,* without respect to give every man his owne: And therefore *Judicia* are so called, because they are *tanquā Juris dicta*[19] And the law whereby you Judge *est mens quadam nullo perturbata affectu,*[20] Arist. lib. 3°. polit. Fortis against malice and daunger, *Neq; timida probitas, neque improba fortitudo reipublicae est vtilis.*[21] And *Patiens,* when he doth Justice sincerely & with a good conscience, and yet is despised,

16. [*Ed.:* Judges, take heed what you do, for you do not exercise the judgment of man but of God, and whatever you adjudge will redound upon you.]

17. [*Ed.:* God is a just judge, strong and patient.]

18. 1. Paralip. 19. vers. 6.

19. [*Ed.:* like statements of the law.]

20. [*Ed.:* it is for me not to confuse those who are affected (Coke's citation is doubtful).]

21. [*Ed.:* neither provident timidity nor improvident fortitude is useful to the state.]

despited, or disgraced: *Non solum poena, sed patientia acquiret nomen perse-cutionis, & gloriam victoriae*[22] Aristotle lib. 2. Top: *Melius est iudicare secundū leges & literas, quam ex propria scientia & sententia. Ignorantia Judicis est pler-unque calamitas innocentis.*[23] And hereof it proceedeth that the kings of this realme have had such speciall care of calling such men to judiciall places, as have knowledge, and other the incidents inseperable above mentioned. And because these Judges are (if order be observed) taken of such as be Sergeants, especially care is alwaies taken in calling men of Learning, integrity, and living to that state and degree; Never can a Judge punish extortion, that is corrupted himselfe, nor any Magistrate punish any sinne as hee ought, that is known to be an offendor therein himselfe; Therefore it is an incident inseperable to good government, that the Magistrates to whom the execution of Laws is committed be princpall observers of the same themselves. But herein heare what shalbe said, to the which nothing can be added; *Et nunc reges intelligite, erudimini qui iudicatis terram. Seruite Domino in timore, et exultate ei cum tremore, apprehendite disciplinam, ne quando irascatur Dominus, et pereatis de via iusta.*[24] Whosoever wil be compleat Judges, *Intelligite; apprehendite, eru-dimini, seruite, exultate*[25] you must be apparelled with the rich roabes of un-derstanding & learning, you must your selves imbrace discipline, you must observe the lawes your selves, with great feare an humility, which if you will do, *Seruite Domino in timore;*[26] you must be cheerful, & comfort your selves in doing of Justice, for you shall finde many crosses and daungers. *Et exultate,*[27] but yet *cum tremore,*[28] doe all these thinges least ye enter into wrath, and so ye perish from the way of righteousnesse; whereby it appeareth, that the great-est losse a Judge or Magistrate can have, is to give himselfe over to passion and his owne corrupt wil, and to loose the way of righteousnes, *Et pereatis via de justa.*[29] To the whole bodie of the realme concerning this point I say,

---

22. [*Ed.:* Not only pain but suffering acquires the name of persecution and the glory of victory.]

23. [*Ed.:* It is better to judge according to the letter of the law than according to one's own knowledge and feeling. Ignorance in a judge is a great mischief to the innocent.]

24. [*Ed.:* Be wise now therefore, you Kings: be instructed, you judges of the earth. Serve the Lord with fear, and rejoice with trembling. Learn discipline so that the Lord is never angry, and you lose the way of righteousness (Psalms 2:10–12).]

25. [*Ed.:* Understand, learn, be instructed, serve and rejoice.]

26. [*Ed.:* Serve the Lord in fear,]

27. [*Ed.:* And rejoice,]

28. [*Ed.:* with trembling,]

29. [*Ed.:* And you lose the way of righteousness.]

your fault will be the greater, If having a soveraigne so religious, wise, and learned, so great an observer of Laws, so vertuos of his own person, you apply not your selves to his example & presidet; for the heathen Poet could say; *Regis ad exemplum totus componitur Orbis.*[30] But whilest I was intending and going about this Edition, I by commandment attended upon his most excellent Matie for direction about his highnesse affaires that concerned the duty of my place to prosecute; At what time I well perceived what princely care his Matie had taken for execution and expedition of Justice, and that upon consideration thereof hee found two impediments therein: One, that in the two eminent courts of ordinary Justice, the Kings Bench, and the Common pleas, there were foure Judges, and many times in cases of great difficultie the Judges being equally diuided in opinion in either Court, the matter depending long undecided: For preventing whereof his Majestie in this Terme of *Saint Hillarie,* in the first yeere of his most happy and prosperous raigne, added a Judge more to either Bench, Sir *David Williams* Knight, Sergeant at Law, to the King Bench; & Sir *William Daniell* Knight, Sergeant at Law, to the Court of Common pleas, his Majesty saying, that *Numero Deus impare gaudet.*[31] The second impediment was, that divers doubts and questions of law remained undetermined, the same rising partly upon long and ill penned Statuts lately made, partly by reason of late and new devises and inventions in assurances, which the eye of the Law in former ages never beheld, and cannot yet incline to allow them, and partly by conveyances and willes drawne and devised by such as have *Scientiam sciolorum quae est mixta Ignorantia:*[32] which questions and doubts already growne, his Majesty desired might bee resolved and determined according to the true sence of the Lawes of the Realme. And where there have beene som diversity of opinions betweene certain of the Courts of justice, that the same might upon conference & mature consideration be agreed and resolved. And his Majesty understanding (as it seemes) by reason of my former Editions, that I have observed many determinations and judgements of questionable and doubtfull Cases, which upon great study, consideration, conference, and deliberation, have bin resolved and given by the reverend Judges & Fathers of the Law, required mc to proceed, and for the generall good and quiet of the subject to publish them, whose commandement being to me

---

30. [*Ed.:* The whole world was created according to the King's example.]
31. [*Ed.:* God rejoices in an uneven number. (Vergil, Eclogues 8.75)]
32. [*Ed.:* The knowledge of smatterers, which is mixed with ignorance:]

Suprema Lex, hath both incouraged & imposed a necessity upon me to publish
this fourth Edition: Whith conteyneth nothing but his Majesties owne, being
sweet and fruitfull flowers of his Crowne; for the laws of England are indeed
so called, *Jura Coronae, or Jura Regia:* Because as *Bracton lib. I. cap.8.* saith:
*Ipse autem Rex, non debet esse sub homine, sed sub Deo & Lege, quia Lex facit
Regem: attribuat igitur Rex legi, quod Lex attribuit ei, videlicet dominationem
& imperium: Non est enim Rex ubi dominatur voluntas, & non Lex:*[33] that is,
The King is under no man, but onely God and the Law, for the Law makes
the King: Therefore let the king attribute that to the Law, which from the
law he hath received, to wit, power and dominion: for where will, and not
law doth sway there is no King. And in the *Register* the wordes of the writ of
Ad Jura Regia, be, *Rex &c. Salutem: Ad jura nostra Regia ne depereant, seu per
aliquorum vsurpationes indebitas aliqualiter subtra-hantur, quatenus juste po-
terimus, manutenenda, subtractaque & occupata, si quae fuerint ad statum debitum revocanda, necnon ad impugnatores eorundem jurium nostrorum refraen-
andos, & prout convenit iuxta eorum demerita puniendos, eo studiosius nos decet
operam adhibere, & solicitius extendere manum nostram, quo ad hoc vinculo
Juramenti teneri dignoscimur & astringi, pluresque conspicimus indies jura illa
pro viribus impugnare &c.,*[34] 1. "That our Kingly Lawes and rights perish not,
neither be at all withdrawn by undue usurpation of any, which so far forth
as Justly we may, are to be mainteyned, & if any shall be with drawne or
diverted, to be againe restored to their due state; as also for the bridling of
the impugnors of those our said Lawes, & the punishing of them as is meet
according to their deserts, we ought the more diligently to provid, & the more
carefully to extend our hand & authority; for that we are knowne to be thereto
tyed & bound by the bond of an Oath, and for that we daily see very many
to their powers to impugne those said Lawes." And againe, *Rex & c. salutem.
Ad conseruationem jurium Coronae nostrae, eo nos decet studiosius operam adhibere, quoad hoc astringimur vinculo Sacramenti, & alios conspicimus ad ipsorum jurium eneruationem amplius anhelare &c.* concluding thus, *Et sciatis
quod si secus facere presumpseritis, ad vos tanquam violatores Regii juris nostri*

---

33. [*Ed.:* For the King himself ought to be under no man, but under God and the Law, for it is the
Law that makes him King: therefore let the King attribute to the law what the Law attributes to him,
namely lordship and power; for where arbitrary whim rules, and not Law, there is no king.]

34. [*Ed.:* Writ, which was used by a King's clerk to protect a living, or benefice, for someone who
contested the King's title, is translated in the text following this note.]

non immerito grauiter capiemus,[35] which is, "We ought the more earnestly to provid for the conservation of the Lawes & rights of our Crown, as being thereunto tyed by the bond of an Oath; & for that we see others the more greedily to gape after the weakning & subverting of those said Lawes &c. concluding thus; And know ye that if ye shall presume otherwise to do wee shall with griefe not undeservedly hold you as violators of our Kingly rights & Laws." By which ancient writs appeareth: 1. What an exorbitant offence it hath bin ever deemed to impugne or calumniate these Lawes, being the imperiall Lawes of the Crowne. 2. That in all ages, these Lawes have had many that sought to impugne and violate them: And lastly how grieuously such as so presumed to offend should be punished; *Nam & frustra feruntur Leges nisi severe puniantur contemptores;*[36] And it is truely said, that *Non debet Princeps ferre Legum suarum ludibrium:*[37] And wofull experience hath often taught, (which I my selfe have sometimes observed) that many of those men that have strayned their wits, & streched their tongues to scandalize or calumniate these Lawes, had either practised or plotted some hainous crime, and therefore hated, because they feared the just sentence and heavie stroke. The reading of the severall Reports & records of these Lawes, doth not only yeeld immence profit, as elswhere I have noted; but doth conteine the faithfull and true Histories of all successive times, as well concerning the punishment of the evill for their heinous, horrible, and exorbitant offences, as concerning the reward and advancement of men of great merit and vertue for their high and honorable service in the common wealth: And (which is above all) they are memorials to all posterity of the valorous piety, vertues, and victories of the Kings and Princes of this Realme. The first appeareth most evidently amongst other thinges by the creations and erections of men of great desert to eminent places, and degrees of nobility and honour, of such estates, and in such maner and forme, as are warranted by the Lawes of the Realme: The second by the Records of the Attainders in Judiciall proceedings against Capitall and other offendours. And the third by many excellent Records, the most faithfull and perpetuall witnesses, and worthy to be published, and made knowne to all; And therefore at this time least my Preface should exceed his proper module of

---

35. [*Ed.:* This writ is translated in the text following.]
36. [*Ed.:* For the Laws will be rendered useless unless those who disobey them are severely punished;]
37. [*Ed.:* The prince ought not to make a mockery of his Laws:]

that sort; Take one example of a Charter made by *Edgar* King of England, and Recorded, and thereby faithfully continued to this day. "*Altitonantis Dei largiflua clementia, qui est Rex Regum, & Dominus Dominantium: Ego Edgarus Anglorum Basileus, omniumque rerum, Insularum Occani quae Britaniam circumiacent, cunctarumque Nationum quae infra eam includuntur Imperator & Dominus: Gratias ago ipsi Deo omnipotenti Regi meo, qui meum imperium sic ampliauit & exaltauit super Regnum patrum meorom. Qui licet Monarchiam totius Angliae adepti sunt a tempore Athelstani, qui primus Regum Anglorum omnes Nationes quae Britaniam incolunt sibi armis subegit, nullus tamen eorum ultra fines Imperium suum dilatare aggressus est, mihi tamen concessit propitia dininitas cum Anglorum imperio, omnia regna Insularum Oceani cum suis ferocissimis Regibus vsque Norvegiam, maximamque partem Hiberniae, cum sua nobilissima Ciuitate de Dublina, Anglorum regno subiugare; quos etiam omnes meis imperiis colla subdare Dei favente gratia coegi. Quapropter & ego Christi gloriam & laudem in regno meo exaltare, & eius seruitium amplificare deuotus disposui: Et per meos fideles fautores Dunstanum videlicet Archiepiscopum, Ayelyolanum, ac Oswaldum Archiepiscopos, quos mihi patres spirituales & consilatores elegi, magna ex parte disposui &c. Facta sunt haec anno Domini 964. Indictione 8. Regni vero Edgari Anglorum Regis 6. in regia vrbe quae ab incolis Ocleayeccastriae nominatur, in natale Domini festiuitate, sanctorum Innocentium feria 4. &c.* ✠ *Ego Edgar Basileus Anglorum & Imperator Regum gentium, cum consensu & Principum & Archimeorum meorum hanc meam munificentiam signo crucis corroboro.* ✠ *Ego Alfriie Reginacon sensi & signo crucis confirmaui.* ✠ *Ego Dunstun. Archiepiscopus Dorobor. Ecclesiae Christi consensi & subscripsi.* ✠ *Ego Osticel. Archiepiscopus Eboracensis Ecclesia consensi & subscripsi.* ✠ *Ego Alferic. Dux. Ego Bruthnod. Dux. Ego Aridgari Dux.*[38] ✠" Whereby is to be observed, first his piety and devotion towards God the fountaine of all happinesse, the

---

38. [*Ed.:* By the great clemency of Almighty God, who is king of kings, and lord of lords, I, Edgar, king of the English and of everything, emperor and lord of all the islands of the ocean which surround Britain, and of whatever nations they enclose, give thanks to the almighty God himself, my king, who has so amplified and exalted my power over the realm of my fathers etc., who, although they had obtained the monarchy of the whole of England from the time of Æthelstan, the first of the kings of England to subdue with arms all the nations which constitute Britain, though none of them had taken the further step of extending their empire beyond the bounds, and has granted me by his divine favour, to subjugate with English power all the kingdoms of the islands of the ocean, with their fiercest kings, as far as Norway and the greater part of Ireland (with its most noble city of Dublin) to the English kingdom, all of which I have with the grace of God brought together with my power; and on account of this, I have arranged to exalt the glory and praise of Christ in my realm, and to amplify his service of devotion, and by my

true *Summum bonum.*[39] Secondly, the largenesse of his Empery, and the first Conquest of Ireland, long before the Raigne of King Henry the second. To conclud, of the learned Reader my desire is, that he would eithar amend that which herein he shall finde amisse, or at least that he will not finde fault with any part, untill he hath seriously read over the whole, and then it may be he will reprehend the lesse: And although herein I have taken all the labour; yet I unfainedly wish to all the Readers, all, or at the least equall profit.

> *Plura quidem feci, quam quae comprendere dictis*
> *In promptu mihi sit; Rerum tamen ordine ducar.*[40]

> *Interea Lector valeas, & memineris quod quicunque genuinum*
> *Sensum ac vim alicuius legis commento aut techna illuserit,*
> *legis violator habendus est.*[41]

Benè Vale.[42]

The Lord Cromwell's Case.*
(1581) Trinity Term, 23 Elizabeth I
In the Court of King's Bench.
First Published in the *Reports*, volume 4, page 12b.**

Ed.: A case of slander. Lord Cromwell brought some renegade preachers into Northlingham, to preach against the new Book of Common Prayer,

---

faithful supporters, namely Archbishop Dunstan, Archbishops 'Ayelyolanus' and Oswald, whom I have chosen as my spiritual fathers and advisers, I have made great arrangements etc. [. . .] These things were done in the year of the Lord 964, in the eighth year of the indiction, and in the sixth year of the reign of Edgar, king of the English, in the royal town which is called [Gloucester], in the festival period of Christmas, in the feast of the Holy Innocents etc. I, Edgar, king of the English and emperor of the kingdoms of the world, with the consent of my rulers and great men, have confirmed this my munificence with the sign of the cross. I, Queen Ælfrith, have consented and confirmed with the sign of the cross. I, Dunstan, archbishop of Christ's church of Dover, have consented and subscribed. I, Oscytel, archbishop of York, have consented and subscribed. I, Duke Ælfere. I, Duke Brihtnoth. I, Duke Ordgar.]

39. [*Ed.:* Highest good.]

40. [*Ed.:* I have done more things than I can catch in words at the present; Nevertheless, I have set things in order.]

41. [*Ed.:* Meanwhile, farewell Reader; and remember that whoever mocks the genuine sense and force of any law, by scheming or craftiness, is to be considered a violator of the law.]

42. [*Ed.:* Farewell.]

*[*Ed.:* The 1604, 1658, and some other, editions spell this name "Cromwel" in the caption. Both spellings were common, even for this one man, and "Cromwell" is the better known.]

**[*Ed.:* See the original pleadings, at 20 Eliz. Rot. 28.]

which had been required by the Queen to be used in all churches. Edmund Denny, the vicar of Northlingham, complained apparently directly to Lord Cromwell, who replied, "Thou are a false varlet, and I like not of thee." Denny then replied to Lord Cromwell, "It is no marvel that you like not me, for you like of those that maintain sedition against the Queen's proceedings," in other words, Denny accused Cromwell of supporting heresy. Cromwell sued for scandal using a device known as a pleading *qui tam* (literally, "who also") by which a private person may bring a lawsuit for a violation of a criminal law. The jury rejected Denny's argument that his statement was true. Coke defended Denny, demonstrating the faulty pleading of the plaintiff's lawyer, who had cited a poor translation of the statute on which he based his suit from law French into English, which garbled the nature of the claim under the statute as it was in force. This case is interesting for a host of reasons. The use of pleadings *qui tam* has enjoyed a revival in twentieth-century American procedure, and the case is also an example of the courts' voiding of a private act of Parliament. It is an interesting case for the role played by Coke, who throughout his career supported the established Church of England against a host of detractors. It was also Coke's first big case, which Coke won through the careful use of technical pleading standards. Look for his instructions to law students in this regard, near the end of the report. For the fate that awaited Rev. Denny had Coke not found the technical flaw, see The Case de Libellis Famosis, at p. 145.

Henry Lord Cromwell brought an Action *de Scandalis magnatum*[1] against Edmund Denny, Vicar of Northlingham in the county of *Norfolk, tam pro dom' Regina, quam pro seipso;*[2] and declared upon the stat. of 2 R. 2. cap. 5. That if any contrive *aliqua falsa nova, horribilia et falsa nuncia de Praelatis, Ducibus, Comitibus, et aliis Proceribus et Magnatibus Angliae, &c.*[3] by which debate may arise betwixt the Lords and Commons (which God forbid) by which danger, mischief and destruction may happen to the whole Realm, &c.

---

1. [*Ed.:* Concerning the slander of great men.]

2. [*Ed.:* both for the lady Queen and for himself [i.e. in a *qui tam* action].]

3. [*Ed.:* any false news, horrible and false tales concerning the Prelates, Dukes, Earls, and other Peers and great Men of the Realm, etc.]

and *quicunque contra fecerit*,[4] shall incur the penalty of the stat. of W. I. c. 33. And the defendant was charged that he said to the plaintiff, then a baron of the realm, "It is no marvel that you like not of me, for you like of those that maintain sedition against the Queen's proceedings." The defendant justified the words, upon which the plaintiff demurred, and the bar was held insufficient. And term' Trinity 23 Eliz. in arrest of judgment it was moved by the defendant's counsel, that the declaration was insufficient, because the said Act of 2 R. 2. was mis-recited; for the words of the Act are, *Si ascun "controver ascum faux nouvelles et horribles et faux messoinges,"*[5] which word "*messoinges*" he who translated the statutes at large into English, has translated "messages" which was the reason that he who drew the declaration in the case at Bar inserted the said word "*nuncia*" where it should be "*mendacia*". 2. The said Act saith, "and whosoever shall do it, shall incur, &c." And the plaintiff in his declaration saith, *et quicunq; contra fecerit,* which is as much as to say, "who shall not do it;" But against that it was objected, That the said Act was a Private Act, it concerning only the | prelates, nobles, and certain great officers, whereof the Court would not take notice *ex officio;* and therefore the Court ought to take the Act as the party has alleged it: But it was resolved by Wray, Chief Justice, Sir Thomas Gawdy, *et totam Curiam,*[6] that it was such Act, whereof the Court ought to take notice; and *eo magis*[7] because it by a means concerns the King himself.

[13 a]

1. For as much as it touches the Prelates, Nobles, and great Officers, which are of the King's Council, and of eminent qualities, and serve him in so high and honourable Offices, which they have under the King, and by his Royal authority have the administration of justice to his subjects, by which it appears that the slandering of them principally concerns the King himself in his Royal government.

2. In as much as the statute saith, That danger, mischief, and destruction may happen to the whole realm, &c. that also concerns the King, for he is the Head of the Realm; and these are the reasons that always such actions *de scandalis magnatum*[8] have been brought upon the said statute *tam pro domino*

---

4. [*Ed.:* whosoever shall do the contrary.]
5. [*Ed.:* If anyone should fabricate any false news and horrible and false lies.]
6. [*Ed.:* and the whole Court.]
7. [*Ed.:* all the more so.]
8. [*Ed.:* of great scandal (i.e., scandal of the great men).]

Rege quam pro se ipso[9] and of all statutes which concern the King, the Judges ought to take notice of them.

Also, it was likewise resolved that if the Act was private, and that the Court ought to take it to be such as is alleged; Then the said Act was against law and reason, and therefore void; For as the same is alleged those who do not offend shall be punished, and that was *condemnare insontem et demittere reum:*[10] for which cause judgment was given against the plaintiff *quod nihil capiat per billam.*[11] And afterwards the plaintiff brought a new action, and amended the faults of the Declaration: And then the Court was moved that the said words were not Actionable, because it might well be that the plaintiff meant liking of some persons which maintain sedition against the Queen's proceedings, and yet he did not know that they maintain sedition, nor do the words import that the plaintiff knew that they maintained sedition. And it was said, *quod sensus verborum est duplex, scil. mitis et asper; et verba semper accipienda sunt in mitiori sensu:*[12] To which it was said, that sedition is a public thing. *Et dicitur seditio quasi seorsum itio magni populi, quando itur ad manus,*[13] which is notably described by the Poet:

> *Ac veluti magno in populo cum saepe coorta est*
> *Seditio, saevitque animis ignobile vulgus,*
> *Jamque faces et saxa volant, furor arma ministrat.*[14]
>   Virg. Aen.

By which sedition (being so public and violent) it was said that by common intendment the plaintiff had notice of it; and it is not like felony or murder which may be clandestine, and done in secret. But as to that, the Judges did not deliver any opinion, for they said, that upon argument and consideration [13 b] they might alter their opinion | which they now conceived, which would be dangerous to the party; and therefore they said to the defendant's counsel, Be

9. [*Ed.:* also for the lord King as well as for himself [the plaintiff] in some degree.]

10. [*Ed.:* to condemn the innocent and acquit the guilty:]

11. [*Ed.:* that he take nothing by [his] bill.]

12. [*Ed.:* that the sense of words is of two kinds: that is, the mild and the harsh; and words are always to be taken in the milder sense:]

13. [*Ed.:* Sedition is so called as if it were *seorsum itio* (the going asunder) of many people when it takes place.]

14. [*Ed.:* And often, when a disturbance has arisen in a great nation, the base rabble rage angrily, and now flaming brands and stones fly, and madness lends arms. (Virgil, *Aeneid,* 1. 148.)]

well advised, and plead, or demur at your peril; wherefore they pleaded a special justification (well knowing that the other matter should be saved to them) and the effect of the justification was, That the defendant was Vicar of Northlinham, which was a Benefice with Cure, and that the plaintiff procured J. T. and J. G. to preach severally in the church of Northlinham, who in their sermons inveighed against the Book of Common Prayer, which was established by the Queen and the whole Parliament in the first year of her reign, and affirmed it to be superstitious and impious, &c. upon which the plaintiff and defendant speaking in the said church of these sermons, because the vicar knew they had no licence, nor were authorised to preach; when they were ready to preach, before their sermons forbad them, but they by the encouraged by the Plaintiff proceeded. The plaintiff said to the defendant, "Thou art a false varlet, and I like not of thee;" to which the vicar said, "It is no marvel though you like not of me, for you like of these (*innuendo praed*"[15] J. T. and J. G.) that maintain sedition, (*innuendo seditiosam illam doctrinam*[16]) against the Queen's proceedings;" and so justified: And it was moved by the plaintiff's counsel, that this bar was insufficient for divers causes.

1. The matter of justification was insufficient, because (as has been said) sedition cannot be committed by words, but by public and violent action.

2. If the matter of justification was sufficient, then upon the said Dialogue between the plaintiff and defendant the defendant is not guilty: But it was said, that such justification dialogue-wise had not been seen before; but if the truth of the cause is such, he ought to plead not guilty, and give the special matter in evidence.

But if he will justify, he ought to justify the words in the same sense they import upon the matter alleged in the declaration. As if a man bring an Action upon the Case for calling the Plaintiff murderer; The Defendant will say, that he was talking with the plaintiff concerning unlawful hunting, and the plaintiff confessed that he killed several hares with certain engines; to which the defendant answered and said, "Thou art a murderer" (*innuendo* the killing of the said hares) this is no justification, for he does not justify the sense of the words which the declaration imports, and therefore he ought to plead not guilty; But as to that it was answered by the defendant's counsel, and resolved

15. [*Ed.:* meaning, the aforesaid (J. T. and J. G.).]
16. [*Ed.:* meaning, that seditious learning.]

by the whole Court, that the justification was good. For in case of slander by words, the sense of the words ought to be taken, and the sense of them appears by the cause and occasion of speaking of them: for *sensus verborum ex causa* [14 a] *dicendi accipiend' est, et sermones semper accipiendi | sunt secundum subjectam materiam.*[17] Then in this case the defendant's counsel have done well to shew the special matter by which the sense of this word "sedition" appears upon the coherence of all the words, that it was in the defendant's meaning, the said seditious doctrine against the Queen's proceedings, *scil.* the said Act of Parliament *de anno primo,*[18] by which the Book of Common Prayer was established, and that he did not mean any such public or violent sedition as has been described, and as *ex vi termini per se*[19] the word itself imports; and it was said, God forbid that a man's words should be by such strict and grammatical construction taken by parcels against the manifest intent of the party upon consideration of all the words, which import the true cause and occasion which manifest the true sense of them; *quia quae ad unum finem locuta sunt, non debent ad alium detorqueri:*[20] and therefore in the said case of murder, the Court held the justification good; and that the defendant should never be put to the general issue, when he confesses the words and justifies them, or confesses the words, and by special matter shews that they are not actionable. And although he varies from the plaintiff in the sense and quality of the words, yet it is no cause to drive him to the general issue; as in maintenance, the plaintiff charges the defendant with unlawful maintenance, the defendant may justify by reason of a lawful maintenance, and may not plead the general issue: wherefore the plaintiff replied and said, *Quod praed' Edwardus Denny dixit propalavit et praedicta verba, &c. de injuria sua propria absque tali causa,*[21] and thereupon issue was joined; *et postea partes concordaverunt;*[22] and this was the first cause that the author of this book (who was of counsel with the defendant) moved in the King's Bench.

---

17. [*Ed.:* the sense of the words is to be taken from the cause of the speech, and sermons are always to be taken in reference to the subject matter.]

18. [*Ed.:* of the first year,]

19. [*Ed.:* by force of the term by itself.]

20. [*Ed.:* because things that are spoken to one purpose should not be twisted into something else.]

21. [*Ed.:* That the aforesaid Edward Denny spoke and published the aforesaid words etc. of his own wrong, without such cause,]

22. [*Ed.:* and afterwards the parties settled;]

In this case Reader, you may observe an excellent Point of Learning in Actions for Slander, to observe the occasion and cause of the speech, and how the same may be pleaded in excuse of the Defendent.

2. When the matter in fact will clearly serve for your client, although your opinion is that the plaintiff has no cause of action, yet take heed you do not hazard the matter upon a demurrer; in which, upon the pleading, and otherwise, more perhaps will arise than you thought of; but first take advantage of the matters of fact, and leave matters in law, which always arise upon the matters in fact *ad ultimum*[23] and never at first demur in law, when after the trial of the matters in fact, the matters in law (as in this case it was) will be saved to you.

Cutler v. Dixon.
(1585) Michalmass Term, 27 and 28 Elizabeth I
In the Court of King's Bench.
First Published in the *Reports,* volume 4, page 14b.

Ed.: This is a note on the King's Bench's holding that a defendant in an action brought before a justice of the peace may not bring a separate lawsuit against the plaintiffs for allegations made in the pleadings of the initial suit.

It was adjudged, That if one exhibits Articles to Justices of Peace against a person certain, containing divers great abuses and misdemeanors, not only concerning the Petitioners themselves, but many others, and all this to the intent that he should be bound to his good behaviour; In this case the party accused shall not have for any matter contained in such Articles any Action upon the Case, for they have pursued the ordinary course of Justice in such case: And if Actions should be permitted in such cases, those who have just cause for complaint, will not dare to complain for fear of infinite vexation.

---

23. [*Ed.:* to the end.]

Vaux's Case.

(1591) Easter Term, 33 Elizabeth I
In the Court of King's Bench.
First Published in the *Reports*, volume 4, page 44a.

Ed.: William Vaux was arrested for poisoning Nicholas Ridley, which apparently he did at the instigation of Ridley's wife, by having Ridley consume a drink poisoned with ground cantharide beetles. Ridley died. Vaux was indicted, but the form of his indictment neglected to state that Ridley actually drank the poison. The court of assize rendered a judgment that Vaux was a murderer but the indictment was insufficient. Vaux argued he was not guilty, but that anyway he could not be tried twice for the same crime. The King's Bench agreed that the Common Law will not allow double jeopardy, or a person to be twice put in jeopardy of trial for the same offence, but that in this case Vaux had never been truly acquitted because he had never been in danger of punishment. An insufficient indictment cannot be the basis for release even upon a guilty verdict or a confession, but there must be a new trial. Vaux was retried, found guilty, and hanged.

William Vaux at the sessions of peace for the country of Northumberland, held 27 Julii, *anno* 32 Eliz. before the justices of peace of the same county, was indicted of voluntarily poisoning of Nicholas Ridley, which indictment was removed into the King's Bench: and in discharge thereof the said Vaux pleaded, that at another time, *scil.* 12 *Augusti, anno* 30 Eliz. at Newcastle upon Tyne in the county of Northumberland, before the Justices of Assise of the same county the said Vaux was indicted: *quod cum Nich' Ridley nuper de W. in com' praed' Armig' jam defunctus, per multos annos, ante obitum suum nuptus fuisset cuidam Margaretae uxori ejus, et nullum exitum habuit, praed' Will' Vaux nuper de K. in com' C. generos subdolè, cautè, at diabolice intendens mortem, venenationem, et destructionem ipsius Nicolai, et Deum prae oculis non habens, 20 Decembris, anno 28 Eliz. apud W. praedict' felonice, voluntarie, et ex malitia sua precogitata, persuadebat eundem Nichol' recipere et bibere quendam potum mixtum cum quodam veneno vocat' cantharides, affirmans et verificans eidem Nich' quod' praed' potus sic mixtus cum praed' veneno vocat' canth' non fuit intoxicatus (Anglicè* poisoned*) sed quod per reception' inde praed' Nich' exit' de* *corpore dictae Margaretae tunc uxoris suae procuraret, et haberet ratione cujus quidem persuasionis et instigationis praed' Nich' postea, scil. 16 Januarii anno supradicto apud T. in com' N. praed' nesciens praedictum potum cum veneno in forma praedict' fore mixt', sed fidem adhibens praedict' persuasioni dicti Willielmi recepit et bibit, per quod praedictus Nicholaus immediate | post receptionem veneni praedicti per tres horas immediatè sequent' languebat, et postea praed' 16 Jan. anno supradict' ex venenatione et intoxicat' praed' apud T. praed' obiit: et sic praed' Will' Vaux felonicè et ex malitia sua praecogitata praefat' Nich' voluntariè et felonicè modo et forma praed' intoxicavit, interfecit, et murdravit, contra pacem, &c.*[1] Upon which indictment the said Vaux was arraigned before the same justices, and pleaded not guilty: and the jurors gave a special verdict, and found, *quod praed' Nich' Ridley venenatus fuit Anglicè* poisoned, *per receptionem praed' cantharides, et quod praed' Will' Vaux non fuit praesens tempore quo praed' Nich' Ridley recepit praed' canth' sed utrum, &c.*[2] And thereupon judgment was given by the said Justices of Assise in this manner; *super quo visis, et per Cur' hic intellectis omnibus et singulis praemissis, pro eo quod videtur Cur' hic super tota materia per veredictum praed' in forma praed' compert', quod praed' venenatio per reception' canth' et praed' procuratio praed' Will' ad procurand' praed' Nich' ad accipiend' praed' canth' modo et forma prout per verdict' praed' compert' fuit*

[44 b]

---

1. [*Ed.:* That, whereas Nicholas Ridley, late of W. in the aforesaid county, esquire, now deceased for many years, before his death was married to a certain Margaret his wife, and they had no issue, the aforesaid William Vaux, late of K. in the county of C., gentleman, wickedly, advisedly and devilishly intending the death, poisoning and destruction of the selfsame Nicholas, and not having God before his eyes, on the twentieth day of December in the twenty-eighth year of Elizabeth, at W. aforesaid, feloniously, wilfully and of his malice aforethought, persuaded the same Nicholas to accept and drink a certain drink mixed with a certain poison called cantharides, affirming and averring to the same Nicholas that the aforesaid drink, so mixed with the aforesaid poison called cantharides, was not poisoned but that by accepting thereof the aforesaid Nicholas would procure and have issue of the body of the said Margaret then his wife, by reason of which persuasion and instigation the aforesaid Nicholas afterwards, that is to say, on the sixteenth day of January in the above mentioned year, at T. in the county of N. aforesaid, not knowing the aforesaid drink to be mixed with the aforesaid poison, but trusting to the persuasion of the said William, accepted and drank it, whereby the aforesaid Nicholas immediately after receiving the aforesaid poison was ill for three hours immediately following, and afterwards, on the aforesaid sixteenth day of January in the above mentioned year, died from the poisoning and intoxication aforesaid at T. aforesaid, and thus the aforesaid William Vaux feloniously and of his malice aforethought wilfully and feloniously in manner and form aforesaid poisoned, killed and murdered the aforesaid Nicholas, against the peace, etc.]

2. [*Ed.:* that the aforesaid Nicholas Ridley was poisoned by the receiving of the aforesaid cantharides, and that the aforesaid William Vaux was not present at the time when the aforesaid Nicholas Ridley accepted the aforesaid cantharides, but whether, etc.]

non fuit felonia et murdrum voluntar': ideo considerat' est quod praed' Will' Vaux,
de felonia et murdro praed' indictamento praed' superius specificat' necnon de
dicta felonica venenatione praed' Nich' Ridley in eodem indictamento nominati
eidem Will' imposit' eat sine die:[3] and as to the felony and murder he pleaded
not guilty.

And, first, it was resolved *per totam Curiam,*[4] That the said indictment upon
which Vaux was so arraigned was insufficient; and principally because it is not
expressly alleged in the indictment, that the said Ridley received and drank
the said poison, for the indictment is, *praed' Nich' nesciens praed' potum cum*
veneno fore intoxicatum, sed fidem adhibens dict' persuasioni dicti W. recepit et
bibit, per quod, &c.[5] So that it doth not appear what thing he drank, for these
words ("*venenum praed*")[6] are wanting; and the subsequent words, *scilicet per*
quod praedict' N. immediate post receptionem veneni praedict' &c.[7] which words
imply receipt of poison, are not sufficient to maintain the indictment, for the
matter of the indictment ought to be full, express, and certain, and shall not
be maintained by argument or implication, because the indictment is found
by the oath of laymen.

2. It was agreed *per Curiam,* That Vaux was a principal murderer, although
he was not present at the time of the receipt of the poison, for otherwise he
would be guilty of such horrible offence, and yet should be unpunished, which
would be inconvenient and mischievous: for every felon is either principal or
accessary, and if there is no principal there can be no accessory, *quia accessorium*
sequitur principalem;[8] and if any had procured Vaux to do it, he had been

3. [*Ed.:* Whereupon, all and singular the foregoing having been seen and fully understood by the court
here, forasmuch as it seems to the court here upon the whole material found by the aforesaid verdict in
form aforesaid that the aforesaid poisoning by the acceptance of the cantharides, and the aforesaid procuring
by the aforesaid William to procure the aforesaid Nicholas to accept the aforesaid cantharides, as was found
by the aforesaid verdict in manner and form aforesaid, was not felony and wilful murder, therefore it is
decided that the aforesaid William Vaux, with respect to the aforesaid felony and murder specified above
in the aforesaid indictment, and of the said felonious poisoning of the aforesaid Nicholas Ridley named
in the same indictment, as charged against the same William, should go without day.]

4. [*Ed.:* by the whole Court,]

5. [*Ed.:* the aforesaid Nicholas, not knowing the aforesaid drink to be poisoned with venom, but trusting
to the said persuasion of the said William, accepted and drank it, whereby, etc.]

6. [*Ed.:* poison aforesaid.]

7. [*Ed.:* namely, whereby the aforesaid Nicholas immediately after the acceptance of the poison aforesaid,
etc.]

8. [*Ed.:* because the accessory follows the principal;]

accessary before; *quod* | *nota*[9] a special case, where the principal and accessory   [45 a]
also shall both be absent at the time of the felony committed.

3. It was resolved by the Lord Wray, Sir Thomas Gawdy, Clench, and Fenner,
Justices, that the reason of *Auterfoits acquit*[10] was, because where the Maxim
of Common Law is, that the life of a man shall not be twice put in jeopardy
for one and the same offence, and that is the reason and cause that *Auterfoits*
acquitted or convicted of the same offence is a good plea; yet it is intendable
of a lawful acquittal or conviction, for if the conviction or acquittal is not
lawful, his life was never in jeopardy; and because the indictment in this case
was insufficient, for this reason he was not *legitimo modo acquietatus,*[11] and
that is well proved, because upon such acquittal he shall not have an action
of conspiracy, as it is agreed in 9 Edw. 4. 12 a. b. *vide* 20 Edw. 4. 6. And in
such Case in Appeal, notwithstanding such insufficient indictment, the abettor
shall be enquired of as it is there also held; and although the judgment is given
that he shall be acquitted of the felony, yet this acquittal shall not help him,
because he was not *legitimo modo acquietatus;* and when the law saith, that
Auterfoits acquitted is a good plea, it shall be intended when he is lawfully
acquitted; and that agrees with the old book in 19 Edw. 3. Corone 444. where
it is agreed, That if the process upon indictment or appeal is not sufficient,
yet if the party appears (by which all imperfections of the process are saved)
and is acquitted, he shall be discharged; but if the appeal or indictment is
insufficient (as our case is) there it is otherwise: But if one, upon an insufficient
indictment of felony, has judgment, *quod suspend' per coll',*[12] and so attainted,
which is the judgment and end which the law has appointed for the felony,
there he cannot be again indicted and arraigned until this judgment is reversed
by error: But when the offender is discharged upon an insufficient indictment,
there the law has not had its end; nor was the life of the party, in the judgment
of the law, ever in jeopardy; and the wisdom of the law abhors that great
offences should go unpunished, which was grounded without question upon
these ancient maxims of law and state; *maleficia non debent remanere impunita,*
et impunitas continuum affectum tribuit delinquendi, et minatur innocentes qui

---

9. [*Ed.:* which note.]
10. [*Ed.:* previously acquitted.]
11. [*Ed.:* in lawful manner acquitted,]
12. [*Ed.:* that he be hanged by the neck,]

parcit nocentibus:[13] So if a man be convicted either by verdict or confession upon an insufficient indictment, and no judgment thereupon given, he may be again indicted and arraigned, because his life was never in jeopardy, and the law wants its end; And afterwards, upon a new indictment, the said Vaux was tried and found guilty, and had his judgment and was hanged.

Slade's Case.
(1602) Trinity Term, 44 Elizabeth I
In the Court of King's Bench.
First Published in the *Reports,* volume 4, page 92b.*

> *Ed.:* John Slade entered a contract with Humphrey Morley. Slade sold the grains he was growing on eight acres, and Humphrey promised to pay £16. The day for payment came and went with no sign of the money from Humphrey, and Slade sued in assumpsit, a form of contract enforcement action that was then still controversial if an action in debt was available, by bringing an action on the case, which is a special form of pleading that allowed the recovery of special damages (or actual damages that included not only money directly lost by the conduct of the defendant but also money indirectly lost as a result of the defendant's conduct). Thus Slade could seek not only compensation for the damages he suffered but the money lost on the whole debt. Humphrey was represented by Dodderidge and Bacon. Coke represented Slade. The courts were initially divided over whether the action could be maintained, but when the argument was brought before the whole bench of all the courts of England, the King's Bench found that a person harmed by another's breach on a contract could seek an action, and the other benches appear to have acquiesced. Assumpsit and action on the case were allowed, even though the plaintiff could have sued in debt.

---

13. [*Ed.:* Misconduct ought not to remain unpunished, for impunity gives continuous encouragement to offenders and threatens the innocent who suffer harm:]

    *[See the pleadings at Hil. 38 Eliz. Rot. 305.]

John Slade brought an Action upon the Case in the Kings Bench against Humphrey Morley, (which plea began Hill. 38 Eliz. Rot. 305.) And declared, that where as the Plaintiff 10 Nov. 36 Eliz. was possessed of a Close of land in Halberton in the County of Devon called Rack Park, containing by estimation eight acres for term of divers years then and yet to come, and so possessed, the Plaintiff the said 10 Nov. the said Close beforesaid sowed with Wheat and Rie, which Wheat and Rie 8 Maii, 37 Eliz. were grown into blades: The Defendant in consideration that the Plaintiff at the special instance & request of the said Humphrey. bargained and sold to him the said blades of Wheat and Rie growing upon the said Close (the tithes due to the Parson, &c. excepted) did assume and promise to the Plaintiff to pay him 16l. at the Feast of S. John the Baptist then next to come; and for not-payment thereof at the said Feast of S. John Baptist, the Plaintiff brought the Action; The Defendant pleaded *Non assumpsit modo et forma;*[1] and on trial of this issue the Jurors gave a special Verdict, *Scil.* That the Defendant bought of the Plaintiff the Wheat and Rie in blades growing upon the said Close as aforesaid, *prout*[2] in the Declaration is alleged. And further found, that between the Plaintiff and Defendant, there was no other promise or assumption but onely the said bargain; And against the maintenance of this Action divers Objections were made by John Doderidge of Counsel with the Defendant.

1. That the Plaintiff upon this bargain may have ordinary remedy by Action of Debt which is an Action formed in the Register, and therefore he shall not have an Action upon the Case which is an extraordinary Action, and not limited within any certain form in the Register; for *ubi cessat remedium ordinarium, ibi decurritur ad extraordinarium, et nunquam decurritur ad extraordinarium ubi valet ordinarium,*[3] as it appeareth by all our Books; *et nullus debet agere actionem de dolo, ubi alia actio subest.*[4]

The second Objection was that the | maintenance of this Action doth take [93 a] away the Defendants benefit of Wager of Law, and so bereaveth him of the benefit which the Law hath given him as his birthright. For peradventure the Defendant hath paid or satisfied the Plaintiff in private betwixt them, of which

1. [*Ed.:* He did not undertake, in the manner and form [alleged].]
2. [*Ed.:* as.]
3. [*Ed.:* where the ordinary remedy ceases, one shall have recourse to the extraordinary; but one shall never turn to the extraordinary where the ordinary is available,]
4. [*Ed.:* and no one should bring an action for a wrong where another action exists.]

paiment or satisfaction he hath not any witness, and therefore it should be mischievous if he shall not wage his Law in such Case. And that was the cause (as was said) that debts by simple contract shall not be forfeited to the King by outlawry or attainder, because that then by the Kings Prerogative the Subject would be ousted of his wager of Law, which is his birthright as it is holden in 49 Edw. 3. 5a. 50 Ass. 1. 16 Edw. 4. 4 & 9 Eliz. Dyer 262. And if the King shall lose the forefeiture and the debt in such Case, and the debtor by Judgment of the Law shall be rather discharged of his debt, before he shall be deprived of the benefit which the Law hath given to him for his discharge, although that in truth the debt were due and payable; *a fortiori*[5] in the case at Barre, the Defendant shall not be charged in an Action in which he shall be ousted of his Law when he may charge him in an Action of debt, in which he may have the benefit thereof.

And as to these Objections, the Courts of King's Bench and Common Pleas were divided; for the Justices of the King's Bench held that the Action (notwithstanding such Objections) was maintainable; And the Court of Common Pleas held the contrary. And for the honour of the Law, and the quiet of the Subject in the appeasing of such diversity of opinions (*Quia nil in lege intolerabilius est eandem rem diverso jure censeri*)[6] the case was openly argued before all the Justices of England, and Barons of the Exchequer, *Scil.* Sir John Popham Knight Chief Justice of England, Sir Edmund Anderson Knight Chief Justice of the Common Pleas, Sir William Periam Chief Baron of the Exchequer, Clark, Gawdy, Walmesley, Fenner, Kingsmill, Savile, Warberton, and Yelverton, in the Exchequer Chamber, by the Queens Attorney for the Plaintiff, and John Dodderidge for the Defendant; and at another time the Case was argued at Serjeants Inn before all the said Justices and Barons, by the Attorney General for the Plaintiff, and by Francis Bacon for the Defendant; and after many conferences between the Justices and Barons, it was resolved, that the Action was maintainable, and that the Plaintiff should have Judgment. And in this Case these Points were resolved.

1. That although an Action of debt lieth upon the contract, yet the bargainor may have his Action of debt, or Action upon the Case at his election, and that for three reasons or causes. 1. In respect of infinite precedents, (which

5. [*Ed.:* so much the more so.]
6. [*Ed.:* (Nothing is more intolerable in law than to decide the same matter in different ways).]

George Kempe, Esquire Secondary of the Prothonotaries of the King's Bench shewed to me) as well in the Court of Comon Pleas as in the Court of King's Bench, in the reigns of King Hen. 6. Edw. 4. Hen. 7 & Hen. 8. by which it appeareth, That the Plaintiffs declared that the Defendants in consideration of a sale to them made of certain goods, did promise to pay so much money, &c. in which I Cases the Plaintiffs had Judgment. To which precedents and [93 b] Judgments being of so great number, in so many successions of ages, and in the several times of so many reverend Judges, the Justices in this Case gave great regard; and so the Justices in ancient times, and from time to time did as well in matters of form, as in deciding of doubts and questions as well at the Common Law, as in construction of Acts of Parliament: And therefore in 11 Edw. 2. Formedon 32. it is holden, That the ancient forms and manner of precedents are to be maintained and kept; and in 34 Ass. 7. that which hath not been according to usage shall not be suffered, [and in 2 Edw. 3. 29. the ancient form and order is to be observed.]⁷ In 39 H. 6. 30. the opinion of *Prisot' et tot' Cur'*⁸ was, That in a Writ *of mesn*⁹ the Plaintiff ought to surmise the tenure between the Lord paramount and the mesn, as well as between the mesn and the tenant, and shew there divers reasons and causes of their opinions; But when the Justices were informed by the Prothonotaries, that the Book called *les Tales,* contained the form that had always in such Cases been used; the Book saith, That the Justices resolved, that they would not change the usage, notwithstanding that their opinion was to the contrary; and according to the precedent they awarded the Declaration good: 4 Edw. 4. 44. In a Writ of Error brought by John Paston to reverse an outlawry against him, he did not surmise in the Writ at whose suit he was outlawed, and all the Justices said, it was a strange Writ, and no certainty supposed thereby; for by the Writ it did not appear whether he was outlawed at the suit of the party, or at the King's suit, or in what suit, or for what thing; and it might be that he was outlawed for felony, debt, trespass, account or fine to the King; But when the Court was informed that the ancient form was such, then they changed their opinions and awarded the Writ good. And resolved, that common course maketh a Law, although that now as there it was said, perhaps

7. [*Ed.:* Bracketted text omitted from the 1658 edition.]
8. [*Ed.:* and the whole court.]
9. [*Ed.:* An intermediary writ, filed after the initial writ and prior to judgement.]

reason willeth the contrary: But there the Justices said, We cannot change the Law now, for that shall be inconvenient. And therewith agreeth L. 5 Edw. 4. 1. where it is said, That the course of a Court maketh a Law: *vide* Mich. 2 & 3 Phil. & M. 120. the statute of West. 2. cap. 12, *quod justic' coram quib' format' erit' appellum et terminat*[10] shall enquire of damages where the Defendant is acquitted, yet precedents expound the Law against the express letter, *Scil.* That Justices of Nisi Prius (before whom the appeal was not began) shall do it; And many others to this effect are in our Books: But for as much as precedents are not always allowable, for in our Books: the Judges reject some precedents, see a notable Case in L. 5 Edw. 4. 110. for certain rules and differences in this matter; there it is agreed, That where a question was of a return of an Assise, and two or three precedents were shewed, which agreed with the said return; and the Justices said, that two or three retorns or precedents doe not make a Law or custome, especially when there are here in Court 40 and more precedents to the contrary; but if there were no precedent to the contrary it were

[94 a]   another | matter, if not that the Court doe adjudge it against reason, and then it shall be amended, for perhaps the precedents passed without challenge of the party, or debate of the Justices, as then (as it is there recited) of late it was in a Writ of Error for reversing an outlawry in the County of Lancaster, and the Error was because the Sheriff retorned, That *ad com' Lancastriae tent' ibid', &c.*[11] where it should be, *ad com' Lancastriae tent' apud Lancastr',*[12] or other certain place to which this word *ibidem* shall have relation; and although that there were shewed 100 precedents according to the said return, yet the outlawry was reversed: So that in divers Cases precedents do not make a Law; and therefore it was said by the Justices to the parties, That he who would have advantage of precedents ought to search for them at his peril, and for his speed, for the Court would not search for them; for if none, or no usual precedents are not shewn, the Court ought to adjudge according to Law and reason.

Out of which Book, 1. It is to be observed, that two or three or such small number of precedents, doe not make a Law against the generality of precedents in such Case.

2. That the retorn of Sheriffs or Entries of Clerks without challenge of the party, or consideration of the Court being against Common Law and reason,

---

10. [*Ed.:* that the justices before whom the appeal shall be formulated and determined.]

11. [*Ed.:* at the county of Lancaster held there, etc.]

12. [*Ed.:* at the county of Lancaster held at Lancaster,]

are not allowable: But when the precedents are Judicial, *Scil.* where the Justices by divers succession of ages have given in Actions there brought, it shall be intended that some of the Counsel with the Defendant, or some of the Justices before whom the Action was tried, and the Record read would have excepted against it, if in their judgment the Action was not maintainable: but in Case of return of an Outlawry, or entries of Clarks, the Records pass in silence, and without exception of the parties, and therefore are not so authentical as Judgments upon demurrers or verdicts; and therefore in such Cases *Multitudo errantium non parit errori patrocinium,*[13] if such retorns or entries of Clerks and Officers be clearly in the opinion of the Justices against Law and reason: So that in the Case at Barre it was resolved, That the multitude of the said Judicial precedents in so many successions of ages well prove that in the Case at Barre the Action was maintainable.

The second cause of their Resolutions was divers Judgments and Cases resolved in our Books where such Actions upon the Case upon Assumpsit hath been maintainable, when the party might have had an Action of debt, 21 Hen. 6. 55 b. 12 Edw. 4. 13. 13 Hen. 7. 26. 20 Hen. 7. 4 b. & 20 Hen. 7. 8 b. which Case was adjudged as Fitz James citeth it, 22 Hen. 8. Dier 22 b. 27 Hen. 8. 24 & 25 in *Tatams case, Norwood and Read's case* adjudged Plowdens Comm. 180.

3. It was resolved, That every contract executory importeth in it self an *Assumpsit,*[14] for when one agreeth to pay money, or to deliver any thing, thereby he promiseth to pay, or deliver it; and therefore when one selleth any goods to another, and agreeth to deliver them at a day to come, and the other in consideration | thereof promiseth to pay so much money to the other, in this [94 b] Case both parties may have an Action of debt, or an Action upon the Case on *Assumpsit,* for the mutual executory agreement of both parties importeth in it self reciprocal Action upon the Case, as well as Action of debt, and therewith agreeth the Judgment in *Reade and Norwoods Case* Plow Comm. 128.

4. It was resolved, That the Plaintiff in this Action upon the Case upon *Assumpsit* shall not recover onely damages for the special loss (if any be) which

13. [*Ed.:* The multitude of those in error is no defence of the error,]

14. [*Ed.:* Undertaking (An action to enforce a contract not under seal; the plaintiff alleges the defendant undertook an obligation that the law should enforce.)]

he hath, but also for the whole debt, so that recovery or barre in this Action shall be a good barre in an Action of debt brought upon the same contract; so *vice versa,* a recovery or barre in an Action of debt is a good barre in an Action upon the Case upon *Assumpsit. Vide* 12 Edw. 4. 13 a. 2 Rich. 3. 14. (2) 33 Hen. 8. Action sur le Case. Br. 105.

5. In some Cases it shall be mischievous, if an Action of debt shall be only brought, and not an Action upon the Case, as in the Case (*inter*) (Redman and Peck) 2 & 3 Phil. & Mar. Dyer 113. They bargained together that for a certain consideration Redman should deliver to Peck 20 Quarters of Barley yearly during his life, and for not delivery in one year it is adjudged that an Action well lieth, for otherwise it shall be mischievous to Peck, for if he should be driven to his Action of debt, then he himself shall never have it, but his Executors or Administrators, for debt doth not lie in such Case till all the days be incurred, and that shall be contrary to the bargain and intent of the parties, for Peck doth provide it yearly for his necessary use: So (5 Ma. Br. Action sur le Case 108.) that if a sum be given in marriage to be paid at several days, an Action upon the Case lieth for non-payment at the first day, but no Action of debt lieth in such case till all the days are past. Also it is good in these days in as many Cases as may be done by the Law, to oust the Defendant of his Law, and to try the same by the Country, for otherwise it shall be a great occasion of Perjury.

6. It was said, That an Action on the Case on *Assumpsit* is as well a formed Action and contained in the Register, as an Action of debt, for there is its form. Also it appeareth in divers other Cases in the Register, That an Action on the Case will lie, although the Plaintiff may have another formed Action in the Register; F. N. B. 94 g. & Register 103 b. If a man hath a mannor within any Honour, and has a Leet within his mannor of his Tenants, if he or his tenants are distrained by the Lord of the Honour to come to the Leet of the Honour, he who is so distrained may have a general Action of Trespass, or a special Writ upon his Case: So if any Officer take toll of him who ought to be quit of toll, he shall have a general Action of trespass, or an Action upon his Case, as appeareth by Fitz. *ibid.* 94. And if a Prior or other Prelate be

[95 a] riding in his journey, and one distrainth his horse upon which | he rideth when he may distrain other goods. he may have a general Action of Trespass or an Action upon his Case, as appeareth in the Register (100 b. and F. N. B. 93. H.), If the Sheriff suffer one in Execution upon a Statute Merchant to escape, the conusee may have an Action of debt, or an Action upon the case

(H), as appeareth by the *Register, 98 b. and F. N. B. 93. B. C.* So if a man put the Executors of lessee for years out of their term, they may have a special Writ upon their Case, as appeareth *F. N. B. 92. G. & Register 97.* and yet he may have *Ejectione firmae*,[15] or Trespass. And therefore it was concluded that in all cases when the Register hath two Writs for one case, it is in the parties election to take which Writ he will: But the Register hath two several Actions, Action upon the Case upon *Assumpsit,* and also an Action of debt, and therefore the party may elect the one or the other.

And as to the Objection which hath been made, that it shall be mischievous to the Defendant that he shall not wage his Law, forasmuch as he might pay it in secret: To that it was answered, That it shall be accounted his folly that he took not sufficient witnesses to prove the paiment he made; But the mischief shall be rather on the other part, for now experience proves that mens consciences grow so large, that the respect of their private commodity induceth men (and chiefly those who have declining estates) to perjury; for *jurare in propria causa* (as one saith) *est saepenumero hoc seculo praecipitium diaboli ad detrudendas miserorum animas ad infernum.*[16] And therefore in debt, or any Action where Wager of Law is admitted, the Judges doe not admit him to it without good warning, and due examination of the party. And as to the Case which was cited, That debts or duties due by single contract where the party may wage his Law shall not be forfeit by outlawry, because the debtor thereby should be ousted of his Law; To that it was answered by the Attorney General, that in such Cases by Law debts or duties shall be forfeit to the King, and so are the better opinions of the Books *scil 3 Edw. 3. Corone 343. 19 Edw. 2. Avowry 223.* If the tenant of a Prior alien is amerced for want of suit at a Court-Baron, and the King seiseth the temporalties of the Prior alien, yet in an action of debt brought for the same by the prior alien, he shall wage his Law, as it was adjudged *6 Edw. 6. in Serjeant Bendloes Reports, 28 Edw. 3. 92. in Accompt,* and *Stamford Pleas of the Crown 188.* and infinite precedents in all ages in the Exchequer which I have seen approve it. And so it was of late resolved in the Exchequer, and so was holden in this Case by *Popham, Anderson* and all the other Justices with whom I have conferred, against the sudden opinions in

---

15. [*Ed.:* Writ to recover for trespass, literally to throw off of the land,]

16. [*Ed.:* Swearing in one's own cause is often in these times the devil's trapdoor for dragging the souls of the wretched down to Hell.]

[95 b]   *49 Edw. 3. 5. 50 Ass. 1. 16 Edw. 4. 4. & 9 Eliz. 262.* and so you have | a doubt
in our Books well resolved.

And note Reader, that in every *quo minus*[17] brought by the King's debtor
in the Exchequer against one who is indebted to him upon a simple contract,
the Defendant shall not have his Law, for the benefit of the King, as appeareth
in 8 *Hen. 5. Ley 66. 20 Edw. 3. Ley. 52. 10 Hen. 7. 6.* and yet there the King is
not party, *a fortiori*[18] when such debt or duty is forfeit to the King, and the
King is the sole and immediate party: And note, Reader, this Resolution as
to this point with the Judicial Law of God, upon which our Law is in this
point grounded, for it appeareth by the 22 Chapter of *Exodus, ver. 7. Si quis
commendaverit amico pecuniam, &c. et ver. 10. Si quis commendaverit proximo
suo asinum, bovem, ovem, et omne jumentum ad custodiam, et mortuum fuer',
aut debilitatum aut captum ab hostibus, nullusque hoc viderit, jusjurandum erit
in medio quod non extenderit manum ad rem proximi sui, suscipietque Dominus
juramentum et ille reddere non cogetur;*[19] By which it appeareth; that it is in
the election of the party, either to charge the Defendant by witnesses if he
will and to oust him of his Law, or to referre it to the Defendants oath. And
the Text saith, *Nullusque hoc viderit, scil.*[20] if there be no witnesses. So by our
Law in the same Case put in the Text, the owner hath his election either to
bring his Action upon the Case in which the Defendant cannot wage his Law,
or an Action of *detinue*[21] in which he may, *Et jusjurandum in hoc casu est
finis;*[22] for the Plaintiff is bound thereby, and it is the end of all controversie.
And I wonder in these days so little consideration is had of an oath, as I daily
observe; *cum jurare per Deum actus religionis sit, quo Deus testis adhibetur tanquam is qui sit omnium rerum maximus, &c.*[23]

---

17. [*Ed.:* Writ to recover waste brought by one with a right to house-bote or hay-bote in another's
woods,]

18. [*Ed.:* so much the more so.]

19. [*Ed.:* If someone hands over money to his friend etc., and verse 10, if someone hands over to his
neighbour an ass, an ox, or any beast, to look after, and it dies or becomes feeble, or is seized by enemies,
and no one else sees this, there shall be a solemn oath between them that he has not laid hands on his
neighbour's goods, and the owner shall take an oath that he will not compel him to return them. [*Exodus,*
xxii.] (This passage in English in some editions.)]

20. [*Ed.:* And no one sees this.]

21. [*Ed.:* Writ to recover goods in kind or, in the alternative, damages.]

22. [*Ed.:* The oath in this case makes an end of it.]

23. [*Ed.:* since to swear by God is a religious act, whereby God is called to witness, as He who is the
greatest of all things etc.]

Part Five of the Reports

The Fifth Part of Coke's *Reports* was published in 1605. It was originally entitled *Quinta pars Relationum Edwardi Coke Equitis aurati, Regii Attornati Generalis. De variis Resolutionibus & Judiciis, magnâ & maturâ deliberatione in rebus permagni momenti & ponderis, à reverendis Judicibus & Juris-consultissimis latis; unà cum Resolutionum & indiciorum Rationibus & Causis. In lucem aedita anno foelicissimi & florentissimi regni Regis Jacobi, Angliae Franciae & Hiberniae, 3. Scotiae verò 39. augustissimaeq. Majestati eius, justitiae fonti, & legem animae, subiectissima observantiae ergò meritò dedicata & consecrata.* In English, *The Fifth part of the reports of Sr. Edward Coke, Knight, the Kings Attorney Generall. Of divers Resolutions and Judgments given upon great deliberation, in matters of great importance & consequence by the reverend Judges and Sages of the Law; together with the reasons and causes of their Resolutions and Judgements. Published in the yeare of the most happie and prosperous raigne of King James, of England, France and Ireland the 3. and of Scotland the 39. and in all humblenesse, of right, dedicated to his most excellent Majestie, being the fountaine of Justice, and the life of the Law.* The cases in this part are concerned, first, with the administration of law over church matters, particularly the regulation of the clergy and church lands by ecclesiastical and law courts. There are substantial collections of cases on the following: covenants in land, contracts, and leases, including waste and rights to a shipwreck; usury and lending; executions on a debt; the regulation and removal of officeholders; the by-laws and ordinances of cities; city, commercial, and manorial customs; and officials' powers of search and arrest.

Epigram from the title page:

Quid enim laboro, nisi ut veritas in omni questione explicetur;
verum dicentibus facile cedam.[1]
Tul. Tusc. quest. Lib. 3.

(Preface)
To the Reader.

It is truely said (good Reader) that *Error* (*Ignorance* beeing her inseperable twynne) doeth in her proceeding so infinitely multiply her selfe, produceth such monstrous & strange Chimaeraes, floateth in such and so many incerteinties, and sucketh downe such poyson from the contagious breath of ignorance, as all such into whom she infuseth any of her poysoned breath, shee dangerously infects or intoxicates; And that which is wonderfull before shee can come to any end, she bringeth all things (if she be not prevented) by confusion to a miserable and untimely end; *Naturalia & vera artificialia sunt finita, nullus terminus falso, error immensus.*[2] On the other side, Trueth cannot bee supported or defended by any thing but by Trueth her selfe and is of that constitution and constancie, as she cannot at any time or in any part or poynt bee disagreeable to her selfe; she hateth all bombasting and sofistication, and bringeth with her certainty, unity, simplicity and peace at the last; *Putida salsamenta amant origanum, veritas per et placet, honestae per se decent, falsa fucis, turpia phaleris indigent.*[3] Ignorance is so far from excusing or extenuating the error of him that had power to find out the Trueth (which necessarily he ought to know) and wanted only will to seek it, as shee will be a just cause of his great punishment. *Quod scire debes et non vis, non pro ignorantia sed pro contemptu haberi debet.*[4] Error and falshood are of that condition, as without

---

1. [*Ed.:* For why do I labor, if not that the truth in every question be unraveled; to the speakers of Truth, I gladly yield, (Cicero, Tusculan Disputations, 3.46 & 3.51).]

2. [*Ed.:* Natural and artificial truths made by art are finite; but there is no end to falseness, and error is immense.]

3. [*Ed.:* A foul sauce requires seasoning; truth is of itself pleasing, beauty is of itself comely. Falsehood requires cosmetics; ugliness needs adornment.]

4. [*Ed.:* That you refuse to learn what you ought to know should not be accounted ignorance but contempt.]

any resistance they will in time of them selves fade and fall away: But such is the state of Trueth, that though many doe impugn her, yet will shee herself ever prevail in the end, and flourish like the palm-tree; shee may peradventure by force for a time be trodden down, but never by any means whatsoever can shee be trodden out. There is no subject of this Realme, but being instructed by good and plain evidence of his auntient and undoubted patrimony and birthright, (though hee hath for some by ignorance, false persuasion, or vain feare, been deceived or disposed) but will consult with learned and faithfull counsellors for the recovery of the same.

The auntient & excellent Lawes of England are the birth-right and the most auntient and best inheritance that the subjects of this realm have, for by them hee injoyeth not onely his inheritance and goods in peace & quietnes, but his lyfe and his most deare Countrey in safety. And for that I feare that many of my deare Countreymen, (and most of them of great capacitie, and excellent parts) for want of understanding of their own evidence, doe want the true knowledge of their auntient birth-right in some points of greatest importance. I have in the beginning of this my fift work, directed them to those that will not only faithfully counsell, & fully resolve them therein, (such as cannot be daunted with any feare, mooved by any affection, nor corrupted with any reward, but also establish and settle them in quiet possession. Upon just grounds to rectifie an Error in a mans owne mind is a work of a cleare understanding, & of a reformed will, and frequent with such as be good men, & have sober and setled wits. The end of such as write concerning any matter, which by some for want of instruction is called into controversie, should be, with al the candor & charity that can be, used, to perswade and resolve by demonstrative proofes the diligent Reader in the truth. But now adayes those that write of such matters, doe for the most part by their bitter and uncharitable invectives, transported with passion and furie, either beget new controversies, or do as much as in them lye to make the former immortall. Certaine it is; that some Books of that argument, that have had truth for their center, yet because they have wanted temperance, modesty, & urbanity for their circumference, have to the great prejudice of the truth hardened the Adversarie in their errors; and by their bitter invectives, whetted them not onely to defend themselves, and to offend in the like, but many times (beeing thereby urged to write) to defend the error it selfe to the hurt of many, which otherwise might have vanished away without any contradiction. He that against his conscience doth impugne a knowne trueth, doth it eyther in respect of him-

selfe, or of others; of himselfe, in that he hath within him a discontented heart; of others, whom for certaine worldly respects he seeketh to please: Discontented he is, either because hee hath not attayned to his ambitious and unjust desires, or for that in the Eye of the state, he for his vices or wickednes hoth justly deserved punishment & disgrace, & therefore doth oppose himselfe against the current of the present to please others, in respect that his credit or maintenance dependeth upon their favour or benevolence. I Know that at this day all Kingdomes and States are governed by Lawes, & that the particular & approved custome of every nation is the most usuall binding & assured Lawe; I deale only with the municipall lawes of England, which I professe, and where of I have been a Student above these 25. yeres: My only end and desire is, that such as are desirous to see & know (as who will not desire to see & know his own:) may be instructed: such as have been taught amisse (every man beleeving as he hath been taught) may see and satisfie himselfe with the truth, and such as know and hold the truth (by having so ready & easie a way to the fountaines themselves) may be comforted & confirmed.
  Farewell.

> Multaignoramus quae non laterent, si veterum lectio nobis esset familiaris.[5]
>
>   Macrob.lib.6.Satur.

Foster's Case.
(1590) Hilary Term, 32 Elizabeth I
In the Court of King's Bench.
First Published in the *Reports,* volume 5, page 59a.

Ed.: John Lane swore that Ursula Foster was going to injure him or burn down his house, and he sought a general warrant from Nathaniel Bacon, a justice of the peace, who issued it to Robert Smith, the constable. Smith and several other constables arrested Ursula, and the constables offered to take her to Thomas Farmer, another justice of the peace, to post bond. Foster refused to go, but they took her to him anyway, where she entered

---

5. [*Ed.:* We are ignorant of many things which would not be hidden if we were familar with the reading of ancient authors.]

a recognizance to appear in court, after which the constables took her to Nathaniel Bacon, where she refused to post assurances of good conduct. She sued for false imprisonment but lost. The King's Bench found that a constable may take a captive under a general warrant to any available justice.

John Foster and Ursula his wife brought a Writ of false Imprisonment against Robert Smith, and upon the pleading as special verdict, the Case was such; *scil.*[1] That the town of Brancaster is within the Hundred of Smithden, in the County of Norfolk; and that the Defendant was *praed' tempore quo, &c.*[2] one of the Constables of Brancaster. And that Nathaniel Bacon, Esquire, then one of the Justices of Peace within the said County, made a warrant sealed with his seal directed amongst others to the Constables of Brancaster, reciting that John Lane of Brancaster was in fear of his life, mutilation of his members, and burning of his houses by Ursula the Plaintiff, &c. *Vobis, &c. praecipimus quod praed' Ursulam coram aliquo justiciarior' nostrorum ad pacem in com' praedict' assign' venire faciat', seu aliquis vestrám venire faciat' sufficient' man-ucapt', quod ipsa praedict' Ursula praefat' Johann' Lane damnum & malum aliquod, &c. non faciat, nec fieri procurabit. Et si hoc facere recusaverit, tunc ipsam sic recusantem proxim' prison' nostrae in com' praed' duci facias, &c. ibidem moratur' quousque gratis hoc facer' voluer', &c.*[3] By force of which warrant the Defendant did arrest the said Ursula, and that afterwards the Plaintiff and one John Hammond | offered them to goe to Thomas Farmor, Esquire, one   [59 b] of the Justices of Peace of the same County, to be bounden to the Queen according to the purport of the said warrant; And that the said Robert Smith did refuse to goe to the said Thomas Farmor upon which the Plaintiffs went with the said John Hammond to the said Thomas Farmor, and there ac-knowledged a Recognizance to the Queen to appear at the next Sessions to be holden within the Hundred of Smithden (the which was not according to the warrant) and that the Defendant *praedict' tempore quo, &c.* by force of

1. [*Ed.:* that is to say.]

2. [*Ed.:* at the aforesaid time when etc.]

3. [*Ed.:* We command you etc. that you cause the aforesaid Ursula to come before any of our justices assigned to keep the peace in the aforesaid county, or cause any of you to find sufficient mainprise, that the said Ursula should not cause or procure to be caused any damage and harm etc. to the aforesaid John Lane. And if she [they] should refuse this, then cause [the person] so refusing to be led to our nearest prison in the aforesaid county, etc., there to remain until he will do this freely, etc.]

the said warrant brought the said Ursula before the said Nathaniel, before whom she refused to find sureties; for which the said Defendant carried the said Ursula to Gaol by force of the said warrant. And in this Case two Points were resolved by Wray, chief Justice, and the whole Court.

1. That upon the said general Warrant *scil. Coram aliquo Justiciar', &c.*[4] it is at the election of the Constable, who is an Officer and minister of Justice, to carry the party arrested to what Justice he will, for it is more reasonable to give election to the officer, who in presumption of Law is a person indifferent, and sworn to do and execute his Office duly, then to give the election to the Delinquent himself, who by presumption of Law will seek excuses, and perhaps will carry the Constable, being for the most part a poor man, to the farthest part of the County, by reason whereof such Constable would be more negligent and remiss of such Warrants for fear of travel, and loss of their time; Which Judgment is against the opinion of Fineux, 21 Hen. 7. 20. *obiter*,[5] whereof the reporter maketh a *Quaere*.[6] But it agreeth with the opinion of the Lord Brook in abridging the Case of 21 Hen. 7. tit. Faux Imprisonment, 11. Note Reader, the Law adjudged in the point, which never (as I know) was adjudged before.

2. It was resolved, That after the Officer in the Case above, had brought the party before the Justice, and before him she refused to find sureties, the Officer without a new Warrant or commandment may carry the party to Prison, and that by the words of the said Warrant, *Et si hoc facere recusaverint, &c.*[7] And Wray, Chief Justice, said, That a Justice of Peace may in such Case make a Warrant to bring the party before himself, and the same shall be good and sufficient in Law: For, for the most part, he who maketh the Warrant, hath best knowledge of the matter, and therefore most fit to doe Justice in the Case.

4. [*Ed.:* namely, before any of the Justices, etc.]
5. [*Ed.:* by the way.]
6. [*Ed.:* Query.]
7. [*Ed.:* And if they refuse to do this, etc.]

Cases of By-Laws and Ordinances
The Chamberlain of London's Case.
(1590) Michaelmas Term, 32 & 33 Elizabeth I
In the Court of King's Bench.
First Published in the *Reports*, volume 5, page 62b.

Ed.: The city of London passed a by-law requiring taxes on all broad-cloth sold there, and required it to be first approved for sale by city officials at Blackwell Hall, with a penalty for non-compliance. The Chamberlain of London brought an action for debt against the merchants who had not paid. The merchants complained that the tax was a usurpation of Parliament's right to tax, at least over non-City residents, and that the City's right was not unlimited. The action for debt was removed from the city court to the King's Bench, where the tax was upheld as a customary regulation of the City of London. In passing, the Court noted that the King may regulate trade, requiring by charter ships to unload only in certain ports.

The Chamberlain of London brought an Action of Debt in London at the Guildhall there against divers persons, &c. And it was grounded upon an Act of Common Council, or Ordinance made by the Mayor, Aldermen, and Commonalty of the City at their common assembly (which they make by custom, and which amongst others is confirmed by divers Acts of Parliament) by which it was ordained, That if any Citizen, freeman, or stranger within the said City, put any Broad cloth to sale within the City of London before it be brought to Blackwell-hall to be viewed and searched, so that it may appear to be saleable, and that Hallage[1] be paid for the same, *scil.* 1d. for every cloth, that he shall forfeit for every cloth 6s. 8d. And further it was ordained, For such forfeiture the Chamberlain of London for the time being should have an Action of debt, &c. And because the Defendants had broken the said Ordinance, for the penalty inflicted by the said Ordinance, the Chamberlain of London brought an Action of debt in London and the same was removed by Habeas Corpus[2]

---

1. [*Ed.:* "Hallage" is a tax on goods sold in a market.]
2. [*Ed.:* Note, several editions translate this as "corpus cum causa," literally, "body with cause," a variant name for the writ of habeas corpus, a writ directing an officer to present a prisoner to determine the legality

into the King's Bench. And it was moved that those in London cannot make Laws and Ordinances to binde the King's Subjects, and principally strangers, for then they shall have as high authority as an Act of Parliament: And 2. The said Ordinance (as it was urged) was against the Law and the freedom and liberty of the Subject, to compel him to bring his Clothes to any one place. 3. The imposit. of 1d. for Hallage was a charge to the Subject, and by the [63 a]   same reason they may impose 1d. they may impose 2d. and so *in infinit'*:[3] | And one of the Inner Temple of Counsel with the City moved to have a *Procedendo*.[4] It appeareth by many precedents, That it hath been used within the City of London time out of minde for those of London to make Ordinances and Constitutions for the good order and government of the Citizens, &c. consonant to Law and reason, which they call Acts of Common Council. Also all their Customs are confirmed by divers Acts of Parliament, and all such Ordinances, Constitutions, or By-laws are allowed by the Law, which are made for the true and due execution of the Laws or Statutes of the Realm, or for the well government and order of the Body incorporate. And all others which are contrary or repugnant to the Laws or Statutes of the Realm are void and of no effect: And as to such Ordinances and By-laws, these differences were observed; Inhabitants of a Town without any Custome may make Ordinances or By-laws for the reparation of the Church, or a high way, or any such thing which is for the general good of the publick, and in such Case the greater part shall bind all the rest without any Custom. *Vide* 44 Edw. 3. 19. But if it be for their own private profit, as for the well ordering of their Common of pasture, or the like, there, without a Custom they cannot make By-laws: And if be a Custom, then the greater part shall not binde the less, if it be not warranted by the Custom. For as Custom creates them, so they ought to be warranted by the Custom *Vide* 8 Edw. 2. Assise 413. Also Corporations cannot make Ordinances or Constitutions without a Custom, or the King's Charter, if not for things which concern the Commonwealth, as reparations of Church or common high ways, or the like. *Vide* 44 Edw. 3. 19. 8 Edw. 2. Assise 413. 21 Edw. 4. 54. 11 Hen. 7. 13. 21 Hen. 7. 20 & 40. 15 Eliz. Dyer 322.

---

of the prisoner's detention, sometimes used as a means of review of another court's orders. The 1658 edition prints this as "habeas corpus."]

    3. [*Ed.:* infinitely.]

    4. [*Ed.:* Writ directing a lower court to proceed to judgment.]

And as to the Case at Barre many Statutes were made for the true making of woollen Cloth, which is the principal Commodity of this Realm; and to the intent that the said Statutes might be the better executed without any deceit, the said Act of Common Council was made, that they shall be brought to Blackwell-hall, as to a place publick, and known, to the intent they might be searched and viewed, if they were made according to the said Statutes. So the said Ordinance being made for the better keeping and execution of the said Laws, to prevent all frauds and falsities, was good and allowable by the Law. Also the assessing of the said 1d. for Hallage was good, because it was *pro bono publico*,[5] and it was competent and reasonable, having regard to the benefit I which the Subject enjoyed by reason of the said Ordinances, and such assessments being for the maintenance of the publick good, and not *pro privato lucro*,[6] were maintainable by the Law; and it was not to be said a burden or charge to the Subject when he reaped a benefit by it. But it is like Pontage, Murage, Toll, and the like, as appeareth in 13 Hen. 4. 14. b. in which Cases the summe for reparations of Bridges, Walls, &c. ought to be so reasonable, that the Subject shall have more benefit thereby than charge.

[63 b]

Also the penalty inflicted upon the offender, be he Citizen or stranger, is lawful, the offence being done within the City, and the summe being competent and proportionable to the offence, and without a penalty the Ordinance shall be in vain: for *Oderunt peccare mali formidine poenae.*[7] And the appointment of their Chamberlain, being their publick Officer to bring the Action of Debt was well and allowable by Law; and the Ordinance being according to Law, may be put in execution without any other allowance, notwithstanding the Statute of 19 Hen. 7. cap. 7.

And after great deliberation Wray, chief Justice, by the advice of the other Justices, granted a *Procedendo. Vide* 2 Edw. 3. 7. *John de Brittain's Case.* The King granted by his Charter that all manner of Ships coming to such a Haven laden with Merchandizes, should be unladen at a certain place, and not elsewhere, to the intent he might be better answered his Customs and other duties.

5. [*Ed.:* for the public good.]
6. [*Ed.:* for private profit.]
7. [*Ed.:* Evil persons hate to offend for dread of punishment.]

Clark's Case.
(1596) Trinity Term, 38 Elizabeth I
In the Court of Common Pleas.
First Published in the *Reports,* volume 5, page 64a.

Ed.: This note case describes an important limit to the Chamberlain's case, immediately preceding it. A burgess refused to pay tax assessed to pay for civic buildings in the new town of St. Albans and was arrested under the town ordinances. Applying Magna Carta, the Common Pleas held that the town had no authority to inflict imprisonment under a by-law.

In an Action of false Imprisonment brought by Clark against Gape; the Defendant justified the imprisonment, because King Edward the sixth incorporated the town of Saint Alban's by the name of Mayor, &c. and granted to them to make Ordinances; And shewed, that the Queen appointed the Term to be kept there, and that they with the assent of the Plaintiff and other Burgesses, did assess a summe on every inhabitant for the charges in erecting the Courts there; and ordained, That if any refuse to pay it, that he should be imprisoned, &c. and because the Plaintiff being a Burgess, &c. refused to pay, &c. he as Mayor justified; And it was adjudged no plea, for this Ordinance is against the Statute of Magna Charta, cap. 29. *Nullus liber homo imprisonetur;*[1] which Act hath been confirmed above 30 times, and the Plaintiff's assent cannot alter the Law in such Case; But it was resolved, that they might have inflicted a reasonable penalty, but not imprisonment, which penalty they might limit to be levied by distress, or by Action of Debt; and the Plaintiff had Judgment.

The Case of Market-Overt.
(1596) Hilary Term, 38 Elizabeth I
In the Court of Quarter Sessions.
First Published in the *Reports,* volume 5, page 83b.

Ed.: This note case presents a holding of the judges of various courts that stolen goods that are sold by a merchant whose trade is generally in the

---

1. [*Ed.:* No free man shall be imprisoned;]

type of goods sold can create good title in a *bona fide* purchaser, although a sale made after the goods were hidden in a shop or traded in a warehouse would not create good title in the seller. Coke, as Recorder of London, testified to the city custom along these lines.

At the sessions of Newgate now last past, it was resolved by Popham, Chief Justice of England, Anderson, Chief Justice of the Common Pleas, Sir Thomas Egerton, Master of the Rolls, the Attorney General, and the Court, That if Plate be stolen and sold openly in a Scriveners shop on the Market day (as every day is a Market day in London except the Sunday) that this sale shall not change the property, but the party shall have restitution; for a Scriveners shop is not a Market overt for plate: for none will search there for such thing; *& sic de similibus, &c.*[1] But if the sale had been openly in a Goldsmith's shop in London, so that any one that stood or passed by the shop might see it, there it changeth the property. But if the sale be in the shop of a Goldsmith, or behinde a hanging, or behinde a Cupboard upon which his Plate standeth, so that one that stood or passed by the shop cannot see it, it shall not change the property: So if the sale be not in shop, but in the Ware-house, or other place of the house, it shall not change the property, for that is not in Market overt, and none will search there for his goods. So every shop in London is an open market for such things onely which by the trade of the owner are put there to sale; And when I was Recorder of London, I certified the Custome of London accordingly. Note, Reader, the reason of this case extends to all open Markets in England.

Semayne's Case.
(1604) Michaelmas Term, 2 James 1
In the Court of King's Bench.
First Published in the *Reports,* volume 5, page 91a.

Ed.: Peter Semayne held a house in common with George Beriford, who died, leaving his goods in the house. Semayne also held a statute-staple, a type of bond securing a debt from Beriford. Semayne sought a writ to secure

---

1. [*Ed.:* and likewise concerning similar things, etc.]

Beriford's lands and goods in payment of the debt. He gave the writ to the
sheriffs of London, who began forfeiture proceedings against Richard
Gresham, who had succeeded to Beriford's interests at the time of Beriford's
death. The sheriffs offered to enter Gresham's house to seize the goods,
which Gresham opposed. In this famous case, the King's Bench described
the privileges of a house owner, who may defend it as his castle and greatest
refuge. He even has rights against entry and search by the King's sheriffs,
who may break into a house to make an arrest or serve a warrant but who
might commit a trespass if they break in when they do not need. The
standards of entry by sheriffs are also discussed. Semayne lost because in
this non-felony case, Gresham was legally allowed to bar his own door.

In an Action on the Case by Peter Semayne, Plaintiff, and Richard Gresham,
Defendant, the Case was such; The Plaintiff and one George Berisford were
Joynt-tenants of a house in Black Friars in London for years. George Berisford
acknowledged a Recognizance in the nature of a Statute-Staple to the Plaintiff,
and being possessed of divers goods in the said house, died, by which the
Defendant was possessed of the house by survivorship, in which the goods
continued and remained; The Plaintiff sued process of extent upon the Statute
to the Sheriffs of London; The Sheriffs returned the conusor dead, upon which
the Plaintiff had another Writ to extend all the lands which he had at the time
of the Statute acknowledged, or any time after, and all his goods which he
had at the day of his death; which Writ the Plaintiff delivered to the Sheriffs
of London, and told them that divers goods which were the said George Berisford's goods at the time of his death were in the said house: And thereupon
the Sheriffs by virtue of the said Writ, charged a Jury to make enquiry according
to the said writ, and the Sheriff and Jury *accesserunt ad domum praedictam
ostio domus praedict' aperto existen' et bonis praedictis in praedicta domo tunc*
[91 b]   *existen',*[1] and they offered to enter the said house, to extend the | said goods
according to the said Writ; And the Defendant, *praemissorum non ignarus,*[2]
intending to disturb the execution, *ostio proed' domus tunc aperto existen', clau-*

1. [*Ed.:* went to the aforesaid house, the door of the aforesaid house being open, and the aforesaid
goods then being in the aforesaid house,]
   2. [*Ed.:* being not unaware of the foregoing,]

debat contra Vicecom' & jurator' praed,[3] by which they could not enter, and extend the said goods, nor the Sheriff seize them, by which he lost the benefit and profit of his Writ: And in this Case these points were resolved.

1. That the house of every one is to him as his Castle and Fortress as well for defence against injury and violence, as for his repose; and although the life of man is precious and favoured in law; so that although a man kill another in his defence, or kill one *per infortuntun',*[4] without any intent, yet it is felony, and in such case he shall forfeit his goods and chattels, for the great regard which the law hath of a mans life; But if theeves come to a mans house to rob him, or murder, and the owner or his servants kill any of the theeves in defence of himself and his house, it is no felony, and he shall lose nothing, and therewith agreeth 3 Edw. 3. Coron. 303, & 305. & 26 Ass. pl. 23. So it is holden in 21 Hen. 7. 39. every one may assemble his friends or neighbours to defend his house against violence: But he cannot assemble them to goe with him to the Market or elsewhere to keep him from violence: And the reason of all the same is, because *domus sua cuique est tutissimum refugium.*[5]

2. It was resolved, that when any house is recovered by any real Action, or by *Ejectione firmae,*[6] the Sheriff may break the house to deliver possession to the demandent or Plaintiff for the words of the Writ are, *Habere facias seisinam,*[7] or *possessionem, &c.*[8] and after Judgment it is not the house in right and judgment of Law of the tenant or defendant.

3. In all Cases when the King is party, the Sheriff (if the doors be not open) may break the parties house, either to arrest him, or to doe execution of the Kings process, if otherwise he cannot enter. But before he break it, he ought to signify the cause of his coming, and to make request to open doors; and that appeareth by the Statute of Westm. 1. c. 17. (which is but an affirmance of the Common Law) as it hereafter appeareth, for the Law without default in the owner abhorre destruction or breaking of any house which is for the habitation and safety of a man, by which great damage and inconvenience

3. [*Ed.:* the door of the aforesaid house then being open, closed [the door] against the sheriff and jurors aforesaid.]

4. [*Ed.:* by misfortune.]

5. [*Ed.:* everyone's house is his safest refuge ("Every man's home is his castle.")]

6. [*Ed.:* Writ of ejectment, or removal from land.]

7. [*Ed.:* cause [the plaintiff] to have seisin.]

8. [*Ed.:* [cause the plaintiff to have] possession etc.]

may follow to the party, when no default is in him; for perhaps he doth not know of the process, which, if he had notice of it is presumed that he will obey it, and that appeareth in 18 Edw. 2. Execut. 252 where it is said, That the Kings Officer who cometh to doe execution, &c. may open the doors which are shut, and break them, if he may not have the keys; which proveth, that he ought first to demand them: 17 Edw. 3. 16. J. hurteth R. so as he is in danger of death, J. flieth, and thereupon Hue and Cry is made, J. getteth into the house of T. those who pursue him, if the house be kept and defended [92 a] with force (which proveth that first request ought I to be made) may lawfully break the house of T. for it is at the Kings suit. 27 Ass. p. 66. The Kings Bailiff may distrain for issues in a Sanctuary, 27 (28) Ass. p. 35. By force of a *capias*[9] upon indictment of Trespass the Sheriff may break his house to arrest the party; but in such Case, if he break the house when he may enter without breaking it, (that is, on request, or if he may open the door without breaking) he is a trespasser, 41 Ass. 17. upon issue joyned on a traverse of an Office in Chancery, *Venire facias*[10] was awarded returnable in the Kings Bench, without mentioning *non omittas propter aliquam libertatem;*[11] yet for as much as the King is party, the Writ of itself is *non omittas propter aliquam libertatem,* 9 Edw. 4. 9. That for felony, or suspicion of felony, the Kings Officer may break the house to apprehend the felon, and that for two reasons: 1. For the Commonwealth, for it is for the Commonwealth to apprehend felons. 2. In every felony the King hath interest, and where the King hath interest there the Writ is *non omittas propter aliquam libertatem;* and so the liberty or privilege of the house doth not hold against the King.

4. In all Cases when the door is open the Sheriff may enter the house, and do execution at the suit of any Subject, either of the body, or of the goods; and so may the Lord in such case enter the house to distrain for his rent, or service, 38 Hen. 6. 26. a. 8 Edw. 2. Distr. 21 & 33 Edw. 3. Avow. 256. the Lord may distrain in the house, although he holds lands in which he may distrain. *Vide* 29 As. 49. But the great question in this Case was, if by force of a *Capias* or *Fieri Facias*[12] at the suit of the party the Sheriff after request made to open

---

9. [*Ed.:* Writ of capias; a predeccessor to the arrest warrant.]
10. [*Ed.:* Writ acting as a summons to appear.]
11. [*Ed.:* do not omit on account of any liberty.]
12. [*Ed.:* Writ of execution for collection of a debt (literally, "that you cause to be made.").]

the door, and denial made, may break the Defendants house to doe execution if the door be not opened. And it was objected, That the Sheriff had well do it for divers causes: 1. Because it is by process of Law; and it was said, That it would be granted that a house is not a liberty, for if a *Fieri fac.* or a *Capias* be awarded to the Sheriff at the suit of a common person, and that he make a mandate to the Baily of a liberty who hath return of Writs, that *nullum dedit responsum*[13] in this Case another Writ shall issue with *non omittas propter aliquam libertatem* yet (it will be said on the other side) that he shall not break the defendants house, as he shall doe of another liberty; As in the county of Suffolk there are two liberties, one of S. Edmund Bury, and the other of S. Etheldred of Ely, put case a *Capias* comes at the suit of A., to the Sheriff of Suffolk to arrest the body of B. the Sheriff maketh a mandate to the Bailiff of the liberty of S. Etheldred, who maketh no answer, in this Case the Plaintiff shall have a Writ of *non omittas* by force at which he may arrest the Defendant within the liberty of Bury, although that no fault be in him: 2. Admit it be a liberty, the Defendant himself shall not take advantage of a liberty: As | if   [92 b] the Bailiff of a liberty be Defendant in any Action, and process of *Capias* or *Fieri facis* come to the Sheriff against him, the Sheriff shall execute the process against him, for a liberty is always for the benefit of a stranger to the Action. 3. For necessity the Sheriff shall break the Defendants house after a denial as is aforesaid, for at the Common Law a man shall not have any execution for debt, but only of the Defendants goods. Put case then the Defendant will keep all his goods in his house, and so the Defendant by his own act shall prevent not onely the Plaintiff of his just and true debt, but it shall be also a great imputation to the Law, that there should be so great defect in it, that in such Case the Plaintiff by such shift without any default in him should be barred of his execution. And the Book in 18 Edw. 2. Execute 252. was cited to prove it, where it is said That it is not lawful for any one to disturb the execution of the Kings Officer, who cometh to execute the Kings process; for if a man might stand out in such manner, a man shall never have execution; but there it appeareth (as hath been said) that there ought to be request made before the Sheriff break the house. 4. It was said, that the Sheriff is an Officer of great authority, in whom the law reposeth great trust and confidence, and are of sufficiency to answer all wrongs which shall be done; And they have

---

13. [*Ed.:* gave no answer.]

custodiam Comitatus,[14] and therefore it shall not be presumed that they will abuse the house of any one by colour of doing their office in execution of the Kings Writs, against the duty of their office, and their Oath also: But it was resolved, That it is not lawful for the Sheriff (upon request made and denial) at the suit of a common person, to break the Defendants house *scil.* to execute any process at the suit of any Subject, for thereof would follow great inconvenience that men in the night as in the day should have their houses (which are their Castles) broken by force of which great damage and mischief may follow, for by colour thereof, upon a feigned suit, the house of any man at any time might be broken when the Defendant might be arrested elsewhere, and so men should not be in safety or rest in quiet in their own houses: And although the Sheriff be an Officer of great authority, and trust, yet it appeareth by experience, that the Kings Writs are executed by Bailiffs, persons of little or no value: And it is not to be presumed, that all the substance a man hath is in his house, nor that a man will lose his liberty, which is so inestimable, if he hath sufficient to satisfy his debt. And all the said Books, which prove, that when the process toucheth the King, that the Sheriff may break the house, implies that at the suit of the party, the house may not be broken, otherwise the addition (at the suit of the King) should be vain and frivolous. And with this Resolution agreeth the Book in 9 (13) E. 4. 9. and the express difference there appeareth between the Case of felony, which (as hath been said) con-

[93 a] cerneth the Commonwealth, and the suit | of any other subject, which is for the particular interest of the party, as there it is said in 18 El. 4. 4. a. by Littleton and all his Companions it is resolved, That the Sheriff cannot break the Defendants house by force of a *Fieri Facias,*[15] but he shall be a trespasser by the breaking, and yet the execution which he then doth in the house is good. And it was said, that the said book of 18 Edw. 2. was but a Nota, and not any judicial Judgment, and it doth not appear at whose suit the Case is intended, but it is an observation or collection (as it seemeth) of the Reporter. And if it be of a *Quo minus*[16] or other Action in which the King is party, or is to have benefit, the Book is good Law.

5. It was resolved, That the house of any one is not a Castle or privilege

14. [*Ed.:* custody of the county.]
15. [*Ed.:* Writ to execute a judgment.]
16. [*Ed.:* Writ brought against delinquent debtor of the King (literally, "by which the less.").]

but for himself, and shall not extend to protect any person who flieth to his house, or the goods of any other which are brought and conveyed into his house, to prevent a lawful execution, and to escape the ordinary process of Law; for the privilege of his house extends onely to him and his family, and to his own proper goods, or to those which are lawfully and without fraud or covin there; And therefore in such Cases after denial upon request made, the Sheriff may break the house; and that is proved by the Statute of West. 1. c. 17. by which it is declared, That the Sheriff may break a house or Castle to make Replevin, when the goods of another which he hath distrained are by him conveyed to his house or Castle, to prevent the owner to have a Replevin of his goods; which Act is but an affirmance of the Common Law in such points. But it appeareth there, that before the Sheriff in such Case break the house, that he is to require the goods to be delivered to him; for the words of the Statute are, After that the castle shall be solemnly demanded by the Sheriffs &c.

6. It was resolved, admitting that the Sheriff after denial made may break the house, as the Plaintiffs Councel pretend he may, then it followeth that he hath not done his duty, for it doth not appear, that he made any request to open the door of the house. Also the Defendant, as this Case is, hath done that which he may well doe by the Law, *scil.* to shut the door of his own house.

Lastly, the general allegation, *praemissorum non ignarus,*[17] was not sufficient in this Case where the notice of the premises is so material; but in this cause it ought have been certainly, and directly alledged, for without notice of the process of the Law, and of the coming of the Sheriff with the Jury to execute it, the shutting of the door of his own house was lawful. And Judgment was given against the Plaintiff.

Rooke's Case.
(1598) Hilary Term, 40 Elizabeth I
In the Court of Common Pleas.
First Published in the *Reports,* volume 5, page 99b.

Ed.: The Commissioners of Sewers assessed Carter a fee of 8s for every acre he had adjoining the River Thames, to pay for maintaining the bank from

---

17. [*Ed.:* being not unaware of the foregoing.]

collapsing and causing floods. They assessed him because there was an ancient prescriptive obligation of the holder of his lands to maintain the bank, but there were many landowners whose lands would be flooded, from whom the commissioners did not assess any fees at all. Coke asserts that Justice Walmsley in the Common Pleas held even though the prescription existed, the statute required that the commissioners should have assessed the costs to everyone who benefitted from the flood prevention, not just the bank-owner. This case is one of the earliest examples of judicial review of an administrative act and often thought to be a foundation of modern administrative law. See also Case of the Isle of Ely, p. 378.

In Replevin in the Common Pleas by Rooke against Withers; The Defendant justified the taking by authority of Commission of Sewers directed to B. S. and others; to survey all walls (*prout*[1] in the Commission) in the River of Thames, in the Country of Kent and Essex, because that one Carter, &c. was assessed to every acre for repairing of a Bank, &c. for the not-paiment of which he took the distress; To which the Plaintiff replied, Of his own wrong, without such cause. And the Jurors found the Commission and the Statutes of 6 Hen. 6. cap. 5. & 23 Hen. 8. cap. 5. And that the Commissioners did impanel a Jury to inquire of defaults, who presented that 7 acres of meadow in which the distress was taken, was next adjoining to the River; and that the bank of the River was adjoining to the said 7 acres, for which they taxed Carter to pay 8s. for every acre: And the Jury further found, that the occupiers of the said 7 acres have used always to repair the said bank, sometimes voluntarily, and sometimes by presentment. And further that divers other persons had lands to the quantity of 800 acres within the same level, and subject to drowning, if the said bank be not repaired: And if this assessment of the owner of the land next adjoining onely, without any assessment of the other who had lands subject to the like danger of drowning, was lawful or not, was the Question. And in this Case three Points were resolved.

1. That the finding of the repairing, &c. by the occupiers of the said 7 acres was not material, because the occupiers might be tenants at will, or other

---

1. [*Ed.:* as.]

particular tenants, who by their Act cannot binde him who hath the inheritance.

2. That the Commissioners ought to tax all who are in danger of being endamaged by the not repairing equally, and not he who has the land next adjoining to the River onely; for the statute of 6 Hen. 6. cap. 5. in which the Commission of Sewers is formed and specified, hath precise words in the same Commission, That no person of any estate or condition shall be spared. *Ita quod aliquibus tenentibus terrarum sive tenementorum, &c. diviti vel pauperi, vel alteri cujuscunque conditionis, statûs, vel dignitat' fuerit, qui defensionem, commodum, & salvationem per praed' Wallias, fossata, guttera, pontes, calceta, & gurgites, &c. habent vel habere poterint nullatenus parcatur in hac parte.*[2] And if the Law shall be otherwise, inconvenience may follow, for it may be that the rage and force of the water shall be so great, that the value of the land adjoining will not serve to make the banks, And therefore the Statutes will have all which are in danger and who are to take commodity by the making of the banks, to be contributory; for *qui sentit commodum sentire debet & onus:*[3] and the said Statutes require equality, which well agreeth with the rule of Equity: see the *Case of Bankrupts* in the second Part of my Reports. *Et vide* 35 Hen. 8. Br. tit. Testam. 19. 4 Edw. 3. Assise 178. 11 Hen. 7. 12. 29 Edw. 3. 39. & *Sir William Herbert's Case* in the third Part of my Reports; Cases of equality grounded upon reason and equity, *Ipsae etenem leges cupiunt ut jure regantur;*[4] And notwithstanding the said words of the said Commission give authority to the Commissioners to do according to their discretions, yet their proceedings ought to be limited and bound with the rule of reason and Law. For discretion is a science or understanding to discern between falsity and truth, between right and wrong, and between shadows and substance, between equity and colourable glosses and pretences, and not to doe according to their wills and private affections; for as one saith, *Talis discretio discretionem confundit.*[5] And Walmesley, Justice held, and it was not denied by any, That if the owner of the land were bound by prescription to repair the River bank,

2. [*Ed.:* So that no tenants of lands or tenements etc., rich or poor, nor any persons, of whatever condition, estate, or dignity, who have or could have any protection, benefit and safeguard by the aforesaid walls, ditches, gutters, bridges, causeways and weirs, shall be in any way spared in this behalf.]

3. [*Ed.:* he who takes the benefit should also bear the burden:]

4. [*Ed.:* And the laws desire that they be ruled by right;]

5. [*Ed.:* Such a discretion confounds discretion.]

that yet upon such Commission awarded, the Commissioners ought not to charge him onely, but ought to taxe all who had land in danger: And to this purpose the Statutes were made; for otherwise it might be that all the land shall be drowned before that one person onely could repair the bank, and that appeareth by the words of the Statutes: for which cause Judgment was given for the Plaintiff.

Pinnel's Case.
(1602) Trinity Term, 44 Elizabeth I
In the Court of Common Pleas.
First Published in the *Reports,* volume 5, page 117a.*

Ed.: Cole owed £8 10s to Pinnel, and paid £5 2s. 2d. Cole claimed Pinnel accepted the lesser amount in satisfaction of the whole debt. Pinnel sued. The court held that, although a debtor can choose the terms of repayment, and the debt may be satisfied by something of value like a horse, a payment for a lesser amount cannot satisfy the debt.

Pinnel brought an Action of Debt upon an Obligation against Cole of 16 l. for the paiment of 8 l. 10 s. the 11 day of Nov. 1600. The Defendant pleaded, that he at the instance of the Plaintiff, before the said day, *scil.* 1 *Octob.* 44. *apud West solvit querenti* he paid to the Plaintiff, *5l. 2s. 2d. quas quidem 5l. 2s. 2d.,*[1] the Plaintiff accepted in full satisfaction of the 8 l. 10 s. And it was resolved by the whole Court, That paiment of a lesser summe in satisfaction of a greater, cannot be any satisfaction for the whole, because it appeareth to the Judges that by no possibility, a lesser summe can be a satisfaction to the Plaintiff for a greater summe: But the gift of a Horse, Hawk, &c. in satisfaction is good. For it shall be intended that a Horse, Hawk, &c. shall be more beneficial to the Plaintiff than the money in respect of some circumstance, or otherwise the Plaintiff would not have accepted of it in satisfaction. But when the whole summe is due, by no intendment the acceptance of parcel can be a satisfaction to the Plaintiff: But in the Case at Bar it was resolved, that the paiment and acceptance of parcel before the day in satisfaction of the whole,

---

*The initial pleadings in this case are recorded at 44 Eliz. Rot. 501.

1. [*Ed.:* which is precisely 5L. 2s. 2d.]

shall be a good satisfaction in regard of circumstance of time; for peradventure parcel of it before the day, shall be more beneficial to him than the whole at the day, and the value of the satisfaction is not material: So if I be bounden in 20 l. to pay you 10 l. at Westminster and you request me to pay you 5 l. at the day at York, and you will accept it in full satisfaction of the whole 10 l. it is a good satisfaction | for the whole: for the expenses to pay it at York, is [117 b] sufficient satisfaction: But in this Case the Plaintiff had Judgment for the insufficient pleading; for he doth not plead that he had payed the 5 l. 2 s. 2 d. in full satisfaction (as by the Law he ought) but pleaded the paiment of part generally; and that the Plaintiff had accepted of it in full satisfaction. And always the manner of tender and of the paiment, shall be directed by him who made the tender or paiment, and not by him who accepteth it. And for this cause Judgment was given for the Plaintiff.

See Reader 36 Hen. 6. Barre 37. in debt upon an Obligation of 10 l. the defendant pleaded, that one F. was bound by the said deed with him, and each in the whole, and that the Plaintiff had made an acquittance to F. bearing date before the obligation, and delivered after, by which acquittance he did acknowledge himself to be paid 20 s. in full satisfaction of the 10 l. And it was adjudged a good barre; for if a man acknowledge himself to be satisfied by deed, it is a good barre, without any thing received. *Vide* 12 Rich. 2. Barre 243. 26 Hen. 6. Barre 37. 10 Hen. 7, &c.

| The Case *de Libellis Famosis.* [125 a]
(1605) Easter Term, 3 James I
In the Court of Star Chamber.
First Published in the *Reports,* volume 5, page 125a.

Ed.: Coke, as Attorney General, prosecuted in the Star Chamber the publisher of poems making fun of two Archbishops of Canterbury. This opinion delineates the standards for a libel. A person may libel another person by harming their reputation, even by saying things that are true, whether the person is a private or public figure, and whether the person is dead or alive. A libeller may be punished by fine, imprisonment, or the amputation of the ears. See also the Lord Cromwell's case, at p. 105 and Lamb's case, p. 313.

In the Case of *L. P.* in the Starre-chamber this Term, against whom the Attorney General proceeded *ore tenus*[1] on his own confession, for composing and publishing an infamous Libel in verse, by which *John* Archbishop of *Canterbury* (who was a Prelate of singular piety, gravity, and learning, *now dead*) by circumlocutions and descriptions, and not in express terms; and *Richard* Bishop of Canterbury who now is, were traduced and scandalized: In which these Points were resolved:

1. That every Libel which is called *famosus Libellus, seu infamatoria scriptura*,[2] is made either against a private man, or against a Magistrate or publick person. If it be against a private man it deserveth a severe punishment, for although the Libel be made against one, yet it inciteth all those of the same family, kindred, or society to revenge, and so may be the cause of *per consequens* to quarrels and breach of the peace, and may be the cause of shedding of blood, and of great inconvenience: if it be against a Magistrate, or other public person, it is a greater offence; for it concerneth not onely the breach of the peace, but also the scandal of government; for what greater scandal of government can there be than to have corrupt or wicked Magistrates to be appointed and constituted by the King to govern his Subjects under him? And greater imputation to the State cannot be, than to suffer such corrupt men to sit in the sacred seat of Justice, or to have any medling in or concerning the administration of Justice.

2. Although the private man or Magistrate be dead at the time of the making of the Libel, yet it is punishable for in the one Case it stirreth up others of the same family, blood, or society to revenge, and to breach the peace and in the other the Libeller doth traduce and slander the State and government, which dieth not.

3. A Libeller (who is called *famosus defamator*) shall be punished either by indictment at the Common Law, or by Bill, if he deny it, or *ore tenus* upon [125 b] his confession | in the Starre-chamber, and according to the quality of the offence he may be punished by fine or imprisonment, and if the Case be exorbitant, by Pillory and loss of his Ears.

4. It is not material whether the Libel be true, or whether the party against

1. [*Ed.:* Literally, "by word of mouth," a case heard ore tenus despite a confession determines liability, considering the available defenses as if they had been raised in demurrer.]
2. [*Ed.:* Scandalous libel or scandalous writing.]

whom the Libel is made, be of good or ill fame; for in a setled state of Government the party grieved ought to complain for every injury done him in an ordinary course of Law, and not by any means to revenge himself, either by the odious course of libelling, or otherwise: He who killeth a man with his sword in fight is a great offender, but he is a greater offender who poisoneth another, for in the one case he who is the party assaulted may defend himself, and knoweth his adversary, and may endeavour to prevent it: But poisoning may be done so secret that none can defend himself against it; for which cause the offence is the more grievous, because the offender cannot easily be known; And of such nature is libelling, it is secret, and robbeth a man of his good name, which ought to be more precious to him than his life, & *difficillimum est invenire authorem infamatoriae scripturae;*[3] because that when the offender is known, he ought to be severely punished. Every infamous libel, *aut est in scriptis, aut sine scriptis;*[4] a scandalous libel *in scriptis*[5] when an Epigram, Rhime, or other writing is composed or published to the scandal or contumely of another, by which his fame and dignity may be prejudiced. And such libel may be published, 1. *Verbis aut cantilenis:*[6] As where it is maliciously repeated or sung in the presence of others. 2. *Traditione,*[7] when the libel or copy of it is delivered over to scandalize the party. *Famosus libellus sine scriptis*[8] may be, 1. *Picturis,* as to paint the party in any shameful and ignominious manner. 2. *Signis,* as to fix a Gallows, or other reproachful and ignominious signs at the parties door or elsewhere. And it was resolved, Mich. 43 & 44 Eliz. in the Starre-chamber in *Halliwood's* Case, That if anyone finds a Libel (and would keep himself out of danger), if it be composed against a private man, the finder either may burn it, or presently deliver it to a Magistrate: But if it concerns a Magistrate, or other public person, the finder of it ought presently to deliver it to a Magistrate, to the Intent that by examination and industry, the Author may be found out and punished. And libelling and calumniation is an offence against the Law of God. For Leviticus 17, *Non facias calumniam proximo.* Exod. 22 ver. 28, *Principi populi tui non maledices.* Ecclesiastes 10, *In cogitatione* | *tua* [126 a]

---

3. [*Ed.:* and has troubled himself and comes across the publisher of inflammatory writings.]
4. [*Ed.:* either is in writing, or without writing.]
5. [*Ed.:* in writing.]
6. [*Ed.:* Words or songs.]
7. [*Ed.:* Communication (literally "handing over" or "passing on").]
8. [*Ed.:* A scandalous libel without writing.]

ne detrahas Regi, nec in secreto cubiculi tui diviti maledices, quia volucres coeli portabunt vocem tuam, & qui habet pennas annuntiabit sententiam. Psal. 69. 13, *Adversus me loquebantur qui sedebant in porta, & in me psallebant qui bibebant vinum.* Job. 30. ver. 7. & 8, *Filii stultorum & ignobilium, & in terra penitus non parentes, nunc in eorum canticum versus sum, & factus sum eis in proverbium.*[9] And it was observed, that Job, who was the Mirrour of patience, as appeareth by his words, became *quodammodo*[10] impatient when Libels were made of him; And therefore it appeareth of what force they are to provoke impatience and contention. And there are certain marks by which a Libeller may be known: *Quia tria sequuntur defamatorem famosum:*[11] 1. *Pravitatis incrementum,* increase of lewdness: 2. *Bursae decrementum,* decrease of money, and beggary: 3. *Conscientiae detrimentum,* shipwreck of conscience.

---

9. [*Ed.:* Thou shalt not defraud thy neighbor (Lev. 17). Thou shalt not curse the leader of thy people (Exod. 22:8). Curse not the King, No, not in thy thought and curse not the rich in thy bed chamber: for a bird of the air shall carry the voice, and that which hath wings shall tell the matter (Eccles. 10). They that sit at the gate speak against me, and I was the song of drunkards (Psal. 69:13). They were the children of fools, Yea, children of base men: they were viler than the earth. And now I am their song, I am their byword (Job 30:7,8).]

10. [*Ed.:* in a manner.]

11. [*Ed.:* because three things follow from scandalous libel:]

Part Six of the *Reports*

The Sixth Part of Coke's *Reports* was published in 1607. It was originally entitled *Le Size Part Des Reportes Del Edw. Coke Chivalier, Chief Justice del Common Bank. Des Divers Resolutions & Judgments dones sur solemne Arguments, & avec grand deliberations & conferences des tres-reverend Judges & Sages de la Ley, de Cases en Ley queux ne sueront unques resolve ou adjudges par devant: Et les Raisons & Causes des dits Resolutions & Judgments. Pulblies en le cinq' An de treshuat & tres-illustre Jacques Roy Deengleterre, France & Ireland, & de Escosse le 41, le Fountain de tout Pietie & Justice, & la vie de la Ley.* In English, *The Sixth Part of the Reports of Sr. Edward Coke, Knight, Lord Chief Justice of Common Pleas, of divers Resolutions and Judgments given with great deliberation, by in matters of great importance & consequence by the reverend Judges and Sages of the Law; together with the reasons and causes of their Resolutions and Judgements. Published in the fifth yeare of the most beloved and most illustrious King James, of England, France and Ireland and of Scotland the 41, the Fountain of all piety and Justice, and the life of the Law.* The cases in this part cover a wide range of topics without quite the organization of the earlier volumes. Part Six includes cases on the maintenance of wards (infants or others under the protection of the king), feudal obligations, the rights of nobility, the powers of judges, procedural bars to repeat litigation, the interests in land to protect from the waste of it by others, as well as issues regarding estates and future interests.

Epigrams from the title page:

Neminem oportet esse Legibus Sapientiorem.
Non aliunde floret Resp. quam si Legum vigeat Authoritas.[1]

---

1. [*Ed.:* It is necessary that no one is wiser than the law. Nowhere does a state flourish unless the authority of the law thrives.]

(Preface)
To The Reader.

Since the Publishing of the Fifth Part of my Reports, a good Student of the Common Laws desired to be satisfied in one special Point in my Epistle to the second Part of my Reports,[2] where I affirmed, *That if the ancient Laws of this noble Island, had not excelled all others (speaking of humane) it could not be but some of the several Conquerors and Governors thereof, that is to say, the Romans, Saxons, Danes or Normans; and especially the Romans, (who as they justly may) do boast of their Civil Laws, would (as every of them might) have altered or changed the same.* And (saith he) some of another Profession are not perswaded, that the Common Laws of *England* are of so great Antiquity, as there superlatively is spoken. True it is, that the said Period was mine own Opinion, but not out of mine own Head; for it is the Judgment of that most Reverend and Honourable Judge, Sir *John Fortescue* Knight, Chief Justice of *England* in the Reign of King *Henry the Sixth;* who (besides his profound knowledge in the Law, being also an excellent Antiquary) in his Book intituled, *De Politica administratione & Legibus Civilibus florentissimi Regni Angliae Commentarius,*[3] *cap. 17.* saith thus: [4] *The Realm of* England *was first inhabited of the* Britans, *next after them the* Romans *had the Rule of the Land, and then again the* Britans *possessed it; after whom the* Saxons *invaded it, who changing the Name thereof, did for* Britain, *call it* England: *after them, for a certain time, the* Danes *had the Dominion of the Realm, and then* Saxons *again, but last of all the* Normans *subdued it, whose Descent continueth in the Government of the Kingdom at this present. And in all the times of these several Nations, and of their Kings, this Realm was still ruled with the self same Customs that it is now governed withal; which if they had not been right good, some of these Kings, moved either with Justice, or with Reason or Affection, would have changed them, or else altogether abolish them, and especially the* Romans, *who did judge all the rest of the World by their own Laws. Likewise would other of the aforesaid Kings have*

---

2. Praef. i. Co. Rep.

3. [*Ed.:* Commentary on the political government and civil laws of the most flourishing realm of England.]

4. Praef. 8 Co. Rep.

done, which by the Sword only possessing the Realm of England, might by the like Power and Authority have extinguished the Laws thereof. And touching the Antiquity of the same, neither are the Roman Civil Laws, by so long continuance of ancient times confirmed; nor yet the Laws of the Venetians, which above all other are reported to be of most Antiquity, forasmuch as their Island in the beginning of the Britans was not then inhabited, as Rome then also unbuilded, neither the Laws of any Nation of the World which worshippeth God, are of so old and ancient years; whereof the contrary is not to be said nor thought, but that the English Customs are very good, yea of all other the very best.

And albeit, I had so good a Warrant for the said Assertion (for every Man that writes ought to be so careful of setting down truth, as if the Credit of his whole Work consisted upon the certainty of every particular period) yet was I right glad to hear of any exception, to the end that such as were not perswaded, might either be rightly instructed, and the Truth confirmed; or that I might upon true grounds be converted and the Error reformed: I desired that they would propose some Particulars, as many as they would (for Generalities never bring any thing to a conclusion.) At length (for this was remembred when I had almost forgotten it) their great desire was to see some Proofs, that the Common Law in these four particular Cases was before the Conquest, as now it is.

¶ First, That the Queen, being Wife to a King Regnant, was a person sole by the Common Law to sue and be sued, to give and take, &c. solely without the King.[5]

¶ Secondly, That a Man seised of Lands in Fee-simple, shall forfeit his Lands and Goods by Attainder of Felony by Outlawry, and that thereby his Heirs should be disinherited.

¶ Thirdly, That a Woman being attainted of Petty Treason, should be burnt.

¶ Fourthly, Whether the ancient Laws of *England* did permit any Appeal to *Rome* in Causes Spiritual or Ecclesiastical.

I had no sooner seen these Questions, but instantly I found direct and demonstrative Answers to the same. For the first, behold an ancient Charter made long before the Conquest, which followeth in these Words.

---

5. *Co. Lit. 133. a. Seld. Tit. of Honor 86. 20 E. 3. Fitz. Nonhability 9. 4 Co. 23.b. 9 Co. 47.a. Co.Lit.3.a. Plowden 231. a. Seld. Epinomis 11.*

Our Lord Jesus Christ reigning for ever. I Aethelswith[6] *Queen of the* Mercians *by Gods Grant, with the Consent of my Ealdermen, will give by Grant to* Cuthwolph *my most faithful Servitor, a certain piece of Land, being part of my peculiar power (that is to say) a piece of Land of fifteen Manses, in a place which is called* Laking, *for his Obedience, and payable Mony in this manner, that is to say, a thousand five hundred Shillings of Silver and Gold, or fifteen hundred Sicles, that he may have, possess and enjoy at his pleasure, as long as he liveth; and after his end and limit of his days, he may leave it to whomsoever he will, for everlasting Power and perpetual Inheritance. And this my Donation is covenanted in the year of our Lords Incarnation DCCCLXVIII. the first Indiction. And we do charge all Secular Powers, in the Name of God the Father, the Son and the Holy Ghost, to observe the foresaid inviolate. These Witnesses subscribing and consenting thereunto, whose Names here recited are under-written. I* Ethelred *King of the* West-Saxons *have consented and subscribed. I* Burghred *King of the* Mercians *have consented and subscribed. I* Aethelswitth *Queen, have consented and subscribed, &c.*

I have here set down another Charter of Record made also long before the Conquest, *de verbo in verbum,*[7] for a direct Answer to the second.

I Ethelred *by Gods Providence Emperor of all* Albion, *do grant to my welbeloved Servitor, whose Nobility of Parentage hath given* Ulfric *for Name, for the faithful Service wherewith he hath courteously served me, a certain parcel of Land, that is to say, two Manses and an half, in a place where the Inhabitants call* Aet Dunmalton, *in perpetual Inheritance, that he may well enjoy and prosperously possess the same, as long as he is seen to run the race of this Life with vital breath, and may leave the same to what Successor he please, after his departure from this transitory Life. Let the said Land situated in a certain Common be free from all wordly impediment, with all which are known to belong to the said place, as well in great matters as in small, in Fields, Pastures, Meadows, Woods; Expedition, building of Bridge and Castle being excepted. Such as shall diminish and violate this my Gift (which I wish may be far from the Minds of all faithful) let them have their part with them, of whom it shall be resounded,* Depart from me ye

---

6. *Seld. Epinomis 11.* This *Ethelswith* was Wife to *Burgh,* King of the *Marches,* and it appeareth that King *Burgh* was alive at this time, for he was a Witness to the Grant; and this Law continueth so to this day.

7. [*Ed.:* word for word.]

cursed into everlasting fire, which is prepared for Sathan and his Angels, *unless they do make amends by lawful satisfaction, obtaining Pardon by due Penance towards God. Whereas that which Mans Memory doth overpass, the diligent search of writing doth preserve. This is to be notified to the Readers, that the said Land came to the disposition of my right, by the crime of a certain Mans unspeakable Presumption, wherewith boldly and feloniously he hath not abhorred to incumber himself, which Man his Parents named* Ethelsig, *albeit he hath discredited his Name by a foul fault. And by me (as is aforesaid) the said Land is bestowed upon my reverend Servitor. The manner of whose fault we thought good to note here in English.*

This was the Land forfeited at *Dunmalton*,[8] that *Ethelsig* forfeited to King *Ethelreds* Hands. It was so then, that he stole *Ethelwins* Swine, who was Son to *Ethelmere* Ealderman. Then his Man did ride to him, and took the things stoln out of *Ethelsigs* House; but he burst out to the Woods, and Men outlawed him, and Men brought to King *Ethelred* his Lands and his Goods. Then gave he that Land to his servant *Hawes* for a perpetual Inheritance. And *Wulfric,* Son to *Wulfrun,* after had it of him in exchange for other Lands that pleased him better; and this was with the Kings leave, and with the Testimony of his Wise Men.

This Donation was made in the year from the Incarnation of our Lord DCCCCXCV the eighth Indiction, in the seventeenth year of the said King. This Charter was witten with the consent of them whose Names are here underwritten. I Ethelred *King of* Englishmen *have constantly consented and ratified this Donation under the Sign of the Holy Cross. I* Alfrick *by Gods Grace elected unto the Archbishoprick of* Canterbury, *have established this Gift with the Sign of the Cross, &c.*

Touching the Third,[9] Caesar in his Commentaries, *Lib. 6. p. 68.* (who wrote before the Incarnation of Christ above 1600 years past) affirmeth, That if the Wife be suspected of the death of her Husband, *Es si compertum est, igni, &c. interficiunt:*[10] that is, and if she be found guilty of the death of her Husband, which is Petty-Treason, the Wife is burnt to death, as she is (in that Case) at this day.

---

8. *Seld. Epinomis 11.*

9. *See in the Preface to the third Part of my Reports out of* Caesars Com. Disciplina Druydū in Britannia reperta, atque in Galliā translata, &c. Seld. Janus Angl. 17.

10. [*Ed.:* And if it is proved, she shall be put to death by fire, etc.]

For the last, by an Act of Parliament holden in the tenth year of King *Henry the Second*, which was in *Anno Domini* 1164. it is enacted as followeth.

As concerning Appellations if any shall arise from the Archdeacon, they must proceed to the Bishop, from the Bishop to the Archbishop;[11] *and if the Archbishop do fail in doing Justice, it must lastly come to the King, that by his Precept the Controversie may be ended in the Archbishops Court, so that there ought not to be any proceeding farther without assent of the King.* And that this amongst many other might not tast of Innovation, the Record saith, *This Recognition or Record was made of a certain part of the Customs and Liberties of the Predecessors of the King, to wit, of King* Henry *his Grandfather, and of other Kings, which ought to be observed in the Kingdom, and held of all for the Dissentions and Discords often arising between the Clergy and our Lord the Kings Justices, and the Peers of the Realm; and all the Archbishops, Bishops, Abbots, Priors, Clergy, with the Earls, Barons, and all the Nobles, &c. have sworn and assuredly promised in the Word of Truth, with one consent to keep and observe the said Recognition toward the King and his Heirs in good sooth without evil meaning for ever.*

But herein I perswaded my self, that every Man that had advisedly and with an equal mind read *Caudries* Case, published in my last Reports, would therewith in this point have been satisfied. And I must freely acknowledge, that I never expected, that any Divine would have attempted to have made such an Answer to that Case, as lately hath been published for two causes. First, for that it is (exceeding all bounds of Truth and Charity) full of Maledictions and Calumniations, nothing pertinent to the state of the Question. It becometh not Divines to be of fiery and Salamandrine Spirits; neither are bitter Invectives fomed out of an hot mouth, ever fretting it self upon the Bit of Discontentment (the Seeds of Hatred, and means of making Controverversies immortal) beseeming the Lips of any man of that profession. Sure I am, that neither Quicksands having no stedfast ground, nor Quicksets of Brambles or Briers, are fit either for foundations, or for fences or defences, especially for him that usurpeth the sublime and broad spreading Name of *The Catholick Divine*.[12] He that will make any Answer out of Conscience and Charity, to persuade the adverse Party, should repeat his Authorities, his Arguments, his Reasons and Categorically and Christianly answer the Matter *ad idem*,[13] without any In-

---

11. Seld. Janus Angl. 72. Rog. Hovenden f. 303.
12. *Father* Parsons *the Jesuit.*
13. [*Ed.:* to the same effect.]

vective against the person, whom his end is (or should be) to convert to his Opinion. Young Sophisters are wont to rail (and by that means keep themselves from a Nonplus) when they are not able to answer the Argument inforced against them. Secondly, for that (as I published in my Epistle to the Reader) I dealt only with the Municipal Laws of *England,* as a subject proper to my Profession.

Expect not from me (good Reader) any reply at all, for I will not answer unto his Invectives, and I cannot make any reply at all to any part of his Discourse. True it is, that Calumniations be great Motives of Revenge, and consequently of breach of Charity, and of Gods Commandment: And therefore *David* prayed, *Redime me a calumniis hominum, ut custodiam mandata tua.*[14] But it is far unbeseeming a man of my Vocation, *Convitium convitio regerere:*[15] For that were *Lutum luto purgare.*[16] And God hath left a president of a Judge, (who also was the first Reporter of Law) that he[17] was *Mitissimus super omnes homines qui morantur in terra;*[18] whose Example all Judges (though they be provoked every day) ought as much as they can to imitate and follow. This only will I say in this Cause, to him and of him, *Ille didicit maledicere, & ego maledicta contemnere.*[19] The cause that I cannot reply is, for that I have only reported the Text, and as it were the very Voice of the ancient Laws of this Realm proved and approved in all successions of Ages, as well by universal consent in Parliaments, as by the Judgments and Resolutions of the Reverend Judges and Sages of the Common Laws, in their Judicial proceeding, which they gave upon their Oaths and Consciences.

I quoted the Year, the Leaf, the Chapter and other certain References for the ready finding thereof. And I could have added more, if the Report of that Case (being very long, as it is) should not have been drawn to an extraordinary Prolixity. But when I looked into the Book, ever expecting some Answer to the Matter; in the end I found the Author utterly ignorant (but exceeding bold, as commonly those qualities concur) in the Laws of the Realm, the only subject of the Matter in hand, but could not find in all the Book any Authority

---

14. [*Ed.:* Rescue me from the calumnies of men, that I may keep thy commands.]
15. [*Ed.:* to make a reproach with a reproach.]
16. [*Ed.:* to clean dirt with dirt.]
17. *Moses.* because it is for the defence of the realm.
18. [*Ed.:* The mildest above all men who dwelt on the earth.]
19. [*Ed.:* He denied speaking ill, and I condemn ill speaking.]

out of the Books of the Common Laws of this Realm, Acts of Parliament, or
any legal and judicial Records quoted or cited by him for the Maintenance
of any of his Opinions or Conceits: Whereupon (as in Justice I ought) I had
Judgment given for me; upon a *Nihil dicit*,[20] and therefore cannot make any
replication. For his Divinity and Histories cited by him, only published in
the said Book *Ad faciendum populum*,[21] (but how truly and sincerely his own
Conscience knowing, he thought it best for the salving of his Credit, to conceal
his Name) I will not answer, for then, I should follow him in his Error, and
depart from the state of the question, whose only subject is the Municipal
Laws of this Realm.

I have (good Reader) brought this sixth Work to a Conclusion, and published it for thy private Instruction, for the publick good and quiet of many,
and for preventing of Danger, the Daughter of Error. I confess that *Englishmens*
Actions have been renowned in the Ear of the whole World, but far better
done than they have been told, for want of a good History; and their Laws
most excellent, but far better than they seem to any Eye (unless he can look
in the visual line) for want of good Stile, and fair falling Sentences (which
never were at so high a price as now they bear) but wise Men will embrace
the secrets of Skill, though they be written with an evil Pen, and will not
refuse precious Jewels, though they be brought in a plain and homely recep-
tacle.

The reporting of particular Cases or Examples is the most perspicuous
course of teaching, the right rule and reason of the Law; for so did Almighty
God himself, when he delivered by *Moses* his Judicial Laws, *Exemplis docuit
pro Legibus*,[22] as it appeareth in *Exodus, Leviticus, Numeri* and *Deuteronomi*.
And the Glossographers, to illustrate the Rule of the Civil Law, do often reduce
the Rule into a Case, for the more lively expressing and true application of
the same. In reading these and other of my Reports, I desire the Reader, that
he would not read (and as it were swallow) too much at once; for greedy
Appetites are not of the best digestion; the whole is to be attained to by parts,
and Nature (which is the best Guide) maketh no leap, *Natura non facit sal-
tum*.[23] And true it is that *Seneca* saith, (as in another place I have said) *Quo*

---

20. [*Ed.:* he says nothing, [a form of confession of the action].]
21. [*Ed.:* to make popular,]
22. [*Ed.:* He taught the laws with examples]
23. [*Ed.:* Nature does not make a leap.]

plus recipit animus, hoc se magis laxat.[24] The Mind, the more it suddenly receiveth, the more it loseth, and freeth it self. A cursory and tumultuary reading doth ever make a confused Memory, a troubled Utterance and an uncertain Judgment. If these or any other of my Works may in any sort (by the goodness of Almighty God, who hath enabled me hereunto) tend to some discharge of that great Obligation of duty wherein I am bound to my Profession, and give directions for the establishment of Inheritances, Possessions and Interests in peace and quietness, I shall reap some fruits of the Tree of Life; for my desire shall be accomplished, and I shall receive sufficient Recompence for all my Labours; for their true and final end shall be effected.

Accipe, quo semper finitur Epistola verbo,
Et vigeant Jura, & (Lector amice) Vale.[25]

Jentleman's Case.
(Between Crosby and Jentleman)
(1583) Easter Term, 25 Elizabeth I
In the Court of King's Bench.
First Published in the *Reports,* volume 6, page 11a.

> *Ed.:* In this opinion, which foreshadows many of Coke's arguments with James I, the judges of the King's Bench consider when various officials are Judges, who are appointed by writ, by the king, or by statute, to hear certain causes of action, or who are suiters seeking a writ of right, to which they are automatically entitled, or a writ of justicies, which require a sheriff to hear a dispute over a debt. The King cannot abolish courts of the common law but may create new courts, and appoint Judges to courts, but once he has made the appointment, the judge ought to determine matters in the court.

It is to be observed, that the words of a Writ of Right directed to the Lord of a Mannor are, *Pracipimus tibi, quod plenum rectum teneas A de B de uno*

---

24. [*Ed.:* the more the mind takes in [suddenly], the more it loses it.]

25. [*Ed.:* Accept—the word with which a letter always ends—and let the laws flourish, and (dear reader) Farewell.]

messuagio, &c.[1] And the words of a Writ of *Justicies* are, *Rex vic. S. Salutem. Praec. tibi quod Justicies A. quod juste & sine dilatione reddat*[2] B 20l. &c. And so of other Writs which are Vicountiel. So the Writ of Droit close is directed to the Lord of the Mannor; *Pracipimus tibi quod secundum consuetudinem manerii, &c. plenum rectum teneas, &c. de uno messuagio.*[3] And the Writs are in the same words when they are directed to the Bailifs of a Mannor. And upon the words aforesaid it was objected, that in such cases the Lord, or the Baylifs, or the Sherif, are Judges, for they have authority by the Kings Writ, and the Writs are directed to them, and not to the suters; and therefore it was

said, That the difference is, when the plea is in ancient | Demesne, Court Baron, or County Court without writ, there the suters are Judges; but when the writ is directed to the Lord, or Baylifs, or Sherif, by which they are commanded to doe Right and Justice to the parties, there they are Judges. Also it was said, that by force of *Justicies*[4] a plea may be holden in the Countie above forty shillings, and therefore it is reason that Judge should be appointed than the suters, who of common right are Judges of small things under forty shillings. And to this purpose are some opinions *in temp.*[5] Edw. 1. tit. Det. 177. 21 Edw. 4. 66. b. & 21 Hen. 6. tit. Retorne. 17. 21 Hen. 6. 34. a. 44 Edw. 3. 10. where Finchden holdeth, where the admeasurement of power[6] is made before the Sherif, the Sherif is Judge. But upon consideration of all the Books it was resolved, that in none of the said Cases, the Lord of a Mannor, or the Baylifs, or Sherif, are Judges; but bee the plea holden by writ, or without writ the suters are Judges. And the reason why the writ shall bee directed to the Lord, or Sherif, &c. is, because the Court Baron is the Lords Court, and the County Court is the Sherif's Court; and therefore it is great reason the writ be directed to him to whom the Court doth belong, to the end he see two things performed. 1. To hold his Courts that Justice and Right be therein done to the parties. 2. That he answered the profits of his Court which belong to

---

1. [*Ed.:* We command you that you hold full right to A. B. concerning one messuage, etc.]

2. [*Ed.:* The king to the sheriff of S., greeting. We command you that you justice A. that rightly and without delay he render . . .]

3. [*Ed.:* We command you that according to the custom of the manor etc. you hold full right, etc. concerning one messuage.]

4. [*Ed.:* Writ giving a sheriff unusually greater powers in a debt collection.]

5. [*Ed.:* in the time.]

6. [*Ed.:* The 1658 edition has here "power"; the 1607 has "dower."]

him. But in case where they hold plea by force of the Kings writ, it doth not change the nature and jurisdiction of the Court: For as these without writs are not Courts of Record, so when the plea is holden by writ, the Courts are of the same nature; for upon a Judgement given in both cases, a writ of false Judgement lyeth, and not a writ of Error: But if the writ which of record should constitute a new Judge, *viz.* the Lord in the one case, and the Sherif &c. in the other, then the authority of the Judge being by the Kings Writ, which is of Record, the Court as to this purpose shall be also of record, quod est perspicue falsum.[7] For without question, as it appeareth by F. N. B. and all the books, a writ of false Judgement lyeth in such Case, although the plea be held by writ: Also the Kings writ cannot alter the jurisdiction of the Court Baron, County, Hundred, &c. which are all Courts at the Common Law, and have Judges authorised and appointed in them by the Law; and therefore all things determinable in those Courts ought to be determined by the Judges of the same Courts; but it is true, the King may create a new Court, and appoint new Judges in it; but after the Court is established and created, the Judges of the Court ought to determine the matters in the Court. And therefore neither the Lord of ancient demesne, nor of a Court Baron, nor the Sherif in the County Court, when the | plea is holden by writ of Right, Justicies, [12 a] Admeasurement, &c. are Judges, but the Suters, who are by the Common Law are the Judges of the Court. And therewith agree the books in 34 Hen. 6. 35. 39 Hen. 6. 5. a. 7 Edw. 4. 23. a. 6 Edw. 4. 3. b. 12 Hen. 7. 16, &c. And observe well the words of the writ in the Register, 10. b. *Rex sectatoribus, Cur. J. Manerii de G. quae est de antiquo dominico Coronae Angliae, ut dicitur, Salutem. Cum secundum legem & consuetudinem infra maneria, quae hujusmodi antiquo dominico Coronae Angliae hactenus existunt, ut dicitur, usitat' in placitis in Curia eorundem Maneriorum pendentibus, cum ad judicium inde reddendum sit placitatum, sectatores hujusmodi curiae ad judicia in placitis inde reddend. licite procedere debeant & consueverunt totis temporibus retroactis.*[8] And there it

---

7. [*Ed.:* which is obviously false. In English in 1658, but in Latin in most editions.]

8. [*Ed.:* The King to the suitors of the court of J. of the manor of G., which is of the ancient demesne of the crown of England, as it is said, greeting. Whereas according to the law and custom until now used within the manors which are of the ancient demesne of the crown of England, as it is said, in pleas depending in the court of the same manors, when pleaded as far as judgment to be given therein, the suitors of such court ought, and have been accustomed in all times past, lawfully to proceed to render the judgments in the pleas therein.]

appeareth, that the plea did there depend by a writ of Droit close, &c. *Vobis mandamus, &c. ad judicium inde reddendum cum omni celeritate procedatis, &c.*[9] by which it appeareth, that although the plea is holden by writ, yet the suters are the only Judges. It appeareth also by the said books, That in a Hundred Court, the suters are judges, and so the Law is well resolved in a Case, wherein there was variance in opinions in our books. But in some case, the sheriff is made Judge by Parliament, as in Redisseisin, by the Statute of Merton, cap. 3. And all his proceeding, by force of that Act, is of record; and a writ of Error lyeth of a judgement given against him, &c. *vide* 44 Edw. 3. 10. In a Court of Pipowders the Steward is Judge, 6 Hen. 4. 3. acc. 7 Edw. 4. 23. a. In the Leet the Steward, and in the torn the Sheriff judge, 10 Hen. 6, 7. 7 Hen. 6. 12. 12 Hen. 7. 15. In the Court of Marshalsea, the steward and marshal of the King's house are Judges, 19 Edw. 4. 8. b. F. N. B. 241. B. 20 Edw. 4. 16. b. 7 Hen. 6. 30. 4 Hen. 6. 8. Artic. super Chartas, cap. 3.

---

9. [*Ed.:* We command you, etc. to proceed with all speed to render judgment therein, etc.]

Part Seven of the *Reports*

The Seventh Part of Coke's *Reports* was published in 1608. It was originally entitled *La sept part des reports Sr. Edw. Coke chivaler, chiefe Justice del Common Banke: des divers resolutions & judgements done sur solemne arguments & avec grand deliberation & conference des tresreverend judges & sages de la ley, de cases en ley queux ne fueront unques resolve ou adiudges par deuant: et les raisons & causes des dits resolutions & judgements. Publies en le size an del treshaut & tresillustre Jaques roy d'Engl. Fr. & Irel. & de Escoce le 42. Le fountaine de tout Pietie & Justice, & la vie de la Ley.* In English, *The Seventh Part of the Reports of Sir Edward Coke, Knight, Lord Chief Justice of Common Pleas, of divers Resolutions and Judgments given upon solemn Arguments, and with great deliberation and Conference of the reverend Judges and Sages of the Law, of Cases in law which were never Resolved or Adjudged Before: and the Reasons and Causes thereof. Published in the Sixth year of the most high and Most Illustrious James, King of England, France, and Ireland, and of Scotland the 42., the Fountain of all Justice, and the life of the Law.* Coke maintained that he had not intended to publish another part of the Reports so quickly, but the significance of the first case in Part Seven, *Calvin's Case,* convinced him to bring it to print. *Calvin's Case* was of great importance to the constitution of Great Britain in the relationship among its constituent nations and with her new colonies. The case was also important in determining the role of the courts, the Parliament, and the King and in determining the status of the subject to the King. Besides *Calvin's Case,* this part of the *Reports* covers a wide range of mainly more recent cases, of local enforcement of criminal laws, property, appointment to offices, uses (a predecessor to the modern trust), wild animals, estates, inheritance, procedure, the powers of the Queen, and the effects of divorce.

Epigrams from the Title Page:

Frequentibus Argumentis & Collationibus latens veritas aperitur, cum
sub eisdem verbis saepe lateat multiplex intellectus.

Veritas saepius agitata magis splendescit in lucem.[1]

(Preface)
Deo, Patriae, Tibi.[2]

I had no sooner (good Reader) made an end of the Sixth Part of my Commentaries or Reports, but the greatest Case that ever was argued in the Hall of Westminster began to come in question, and afterwards was Argued by all the Judges of England. This great Case (for that Memory is *infida & labilis*[3]) whiles the Matter was recent and fresh in mind, and almost yet sounding in the Ear, I set down in writing, out of my short Observations which I had taken of the effect of every Argument, (as my manner is, and ever hath been) a summary memorial of the principal authorities and reasons of the Resolutions of that Case, for mine own private solace and instruction. I never thought to have published the same, for that it was not like to give any direction in like Cases that might happen, (the chiefest end of publishing Reports) it is of his own nature so like the Phoenix, and so singular and rare in accident, as the union of two famous and ancient Kingdoms in ligeance and obedience under one great and mighty Monarch. Now when I had ended it for my private, I was by commandment to begin again (a matter of no small labour and difficulty) for the publick. For certainly, that succinct method and collection that will serve for the private memorial or repertory, especially of him that knew and heard all, will nothing become a publick Report for the present and all posterity, or be sufficient to instruct those Readers, who of themselves know nothing, but must be instructed by the Report only in the right rule and reason of the case in question. And as *unda gignit undam,*[4] so commonly one

---

1. [*Ed.:* The hidden truth is opened up by frequent argument and conference, since hiding beneath the same words there is often a manifold understanding. The truth being frequently considered shines greater in the light.]

2. [*Ed.:* To God, to the country, to you.]

3. [*Ed.:* untrustworthy and unstable.]

4. [*Ed.:* a wave begets a wave,]

labour cometh not alone: This brought on another with it; for seeing this Case was of so rare a quality, I thought good as well for thine instruction and use (good Reader) as for the repose and quiet of many, in resolving of Questions and Doubts (wherein there hath been great diversity of Opinions) concerning their estates and possessions, to publish some others that are common in accident, weighty in consequent, and yet never resolved or adjudged before: So as it is now verified in this, that which hath been said of old, *Labor labori laborem addit.*[5]

With this Seventh Work or part of my Reports (whereunto Almighty God of his goodness hath in this short time, amongst many other publick Employments, enabled me) I have out of my love unto all my dear Countrymen, of what perswasion in Religion soever they be, thought good to give them all a caveat or fore-warning in a Case of great importance, that deeply and dangerously concerns them all in so high a point, that in the first degree it is a *Praemunire,*[6] and in the second High Treason. And yet many men, without all fear (by reason I think they know not the Law) run into the danger thereof almost every day. I must confess, that this is a writing or a scribling World, *quotidie plures, quotidie pejus scribunt.*[7] And sure I am, that no man can either bring over those Books of late written (which I have seen) from *Rome* or Romanists, or read them, and justifie them, or deliver them over to any other with a liking and allowance of the same (as the Authors end and desire is they should) but they run into desperate dangers and downfalls; for the first offence is a *Praemunire,* which is to be adjudged to be out of the Kings protection, to lose all their Lands and Goods, and to suffer perpetual Imprisonment, and they that offend the second time therein, incur the heavy danger of high Treason. These Books have glorious and goodly Titles, which promise directions for the Conscience, and remedies for the Soul, but there is *mors in olla:*[8] They are like to Apothecaries Boxes, *quorum tituli pollicentur remedia, sed pixides ipsae venena continent,*[9] whose Titles promise remedies, but the Boxes themselves contain Poyson. This forewarning I give out of conscience and

---

5. [*Ed.:* Labour adds work to work.]

6. [*Ed.:* The offence of introducing a foreign power into the Kingdom, used particularly to regulate Roman Catholics in the Kingdom.]

7. [*Ed.:* every day more people write, and every day worse.]

8. [*Ed.:* death in a jar.]

9. [*Ed.:* the labels whereof promise remedies, but the boxes themselves contain poison,]

care of their safety, that blindfold might fall into so great danger by their means whom they so much reverence. I am not afraid of Gnats that can prick and cannot hurt, nor of Drones that keep a buzzing, and would, but cannot sting.

Non metuo pulicis stimulos, fucique susurros.[10]

And little do I esteem an uncharitable and malicious practise in publishing of an erroneous and ill spelled Pamphlet, under the name Pricket, and dedicating it to my singular good Lord and Father in Law the Earl of Excester, as a Charge given at the Affises holden at the City of Norwich, 4 *Augusti* 1606. Which I protest was not only published without my privity, but (besides the omission of divers principal matters) that there is no one period therein expressed in that sort and sense that I delivered it: Wherein it is worthy of observation how their expectation (of scandalizing me) was wholly deceived, for behold the catastrophe. Such of the Readers as were learned in the Laws, finding not only gross Errors and Absurdities in Law, but palpable mistakings in the very words of Art, and the whole context of that rude and ragged Stile, wholly dissonant (the Subject being legal) from a Lawyers dialect, concluded, that *inimicus & iniquus homo superseminavit zizania in medio tritici:*[11] The other discreet and indifferent Readers, out of Sense and Reason, found out the same conclusion, both in respect of the vanity of the phrase, and for that, I publishing about the same time one of my Commentaries, would, if I had intended the publication of any such matter, have done it my self, and not to have suffered any of my works to pass under the name of Pricket, and so *una voce conclamaverunt omnes,*[12] That it was a shameful and shamless practice, and the Author thereof, to be a wicked and malicious falsary.

Circumvertit enim vis & injuria quemque,
Atque unde exorta est, ad eum plerumq; revertit.[13]

In these and the rest of my Reports, I have (as much as I could) avoided Obscurity, Ambiguity, Jeopardy, Novelty and Prolixity. 1. Obscurity, for that

---

10. [*Ed.:* I am not afraid of the sting of the flea and the humming of the drone.]

11. [*Ed.:* an enemy and a wicked man has scattered tares in the midst of the wheat.]

12. [*Ed.:* they all shouted with one voice.]

13. [*Ed.:* For force and wrong turn themselves around, and most often return to him from whence they came.]

is like unto Darkness, wherein a Man for want of Light, can hardly with all his industry discern any way. 2. Ambiguity, where there is Light enough, but there be so many winding and intricate ways, as a Man, for want of direction, shall be much perplexed and intangled, to find out the right way. 3. Jeopardy, either in publishing of any thing, that might rather stir up Suits and controversies in this troublesome World, than stablish quietness and repose between Man and Man (for a Commentary should not be like unto the Winterly Sun; that raiseth up greater and thicker Mists and Fogs, than it is able to disperse) or in bringing the Reader, by any means, into the least question of peril or danger at all. 4. Novelty, For I have ever holden all new or private interpretations, or opinions, which have no Ground or Warrant out of the Reason or Rule of our Books, or former Presidents, to be dangerous, and not worthy of any Observation: For *periculosum existimo quod honorum virorum non comprobatur exemplo.*[14] 5. Prolixity, For a Report ought to be no longer than the matter requireth, and as *Languor prolixus gravat medicum, ita relatio prolixa gravat lectorem.*[15]

The Case of Postnati, I confess, is longer than any of the rest, and that for three Causes. 1. For that it was an Exchequer-chamber Case, for deciding whereof all the Judges of England (as the Law doth require) did argue openly and at large. 2. For that never any Case within Mans Memory, was argued by so many Judges in the Exchequer-chamber, as this was, there having argued the Lord Chancellor and 14 Judges. 3. For the variety as well of the important matter, as of the several kinds of excellent Learning and knowledge, delivered in the Arguments of this Case.

Finally, With these Wishes and Desires I conclude. 1. That the Studious Reader might indeed receive as great profit and delight in Reading this work, as I did (unless mine own judgment deceive me) in composing and framing thereof. 2. That *quoad ejus fieri possit, quaiam plurima legibus ipsis difiniantur, quam paucissima vero Judicis arbitrio relinquantur.*[16]

---

14. [*Ed.:* I consider anything dangerous that is not proved by the example of good men.]

15. [*Ed.:* just as a prolonged illness grieves the doctor, so a prolix report grieves the reader.]

16. [*Ed.:* as far as may be, most things should be defined by the laws themselves and little should be left to the discretion of the judge.]

Calvin's Case, or the Case of the Postnati.[1]

(1608) Trinity Term, 6 James I
In the Court of King's Bench, heard in the Exchequer
by the Chancellor and all the Judges of England.
First Published in the *Reports,* volume 7, page 1a.

Ed.: Under the feudal system, the absolute loyalty owed by a subject to the King, an allegiance enforced by duties that were tied to the holding of interests in land, made unthinkable, and illegal, the ownership of land by one person in two different kingdoms. When King James VI of Scotland assumed the English throne, both the Scots and the English were beholden to the same monarch, and the traditional reason for prohibiting a foreigner to own lands in the kingdom, which would have barred a Scot from holding lands in England and vice versa, was considerably weakened. It was particularly difficult when applied to someone who was born after James had taken the new throne, who were called the *post-nati,* a phrase by which the case is often known. The issue in this case arose when Robert Calvin, who was a Scot born three years after James's coronation in England, came by land in England. His lands were entered by Richard and Nicholas Smith, and when Calvin's guardians sued, the Smith's defense was that Robert could not own the land.

The case was heard by all of the judges of England, while Coke was Chief Justice of Common Pleas, with arguments by Bacon as Solicitor General and Hobart as Attorney General. Coke was very active in this case, arguing the King's position throughout and presenting, here the last argument, for Calvin, before the Court's judgment. The Court, considering arguments based on the nature of allegiance, majesty, conquest, natural reason, and an unalterable law of nature, held that Calvin was not an alien, and he could hold land in England. This case had tremendous implications for James's view of forging a single nation of Great Britain, as well as for the rights of subjects living in the new colonies overseas. For the effects of citizenship on a local level, see James Bagg's Case, p. 404.

---

1. [*Ed.:* Those born after [the accession of James VI of Scotland to the throne of England].]

James by the grace of God of England, Scotland, France, and Ireland, King, defender of the faith, &c. To the Sheriff of Middlesex greeting: Robert Calvin, gent. hath complained to us, that Richard Smith and Nicholas Smith, unjustly, and without judgment, have disseised him of his freehold in I Haggard, otherwise Haggerston, otherwise Aggerston, in the parish of St. Leonard, in Shoreditch, within thirty years now last past; and therefore we command you, that if the said Robert shall secure you to prosecute his claim, then that you cause the said tenement to be reseised with the chattels which within it were taken, and the said tenement with the chattels to be in peace until Thursday next after fifteen days of Saint Martin next coming; and in the mean time, cause twelve free and lawful men of that neighbourhood to view the said tenement, and the names of them to be inbreviated; and summon them by good summoners, that they be then before us wherever we shall then be in England, ready thereof to make recognition; and put, by sureties and safe pledges, the aforesaid Richard and Nicholas, or their bailiffs, (if they cannot be found), that they be then there, to hear the recognition; and have there the summoners, the names of the pledges, and this writ. Witness ourself at Westminster, the 3d day of November, in the 5th year of our reign of England, France, and Ireland, and of Scotland the one-and-fortieth.

The writ of Assize.

[1 b]

For 40s. paid in the hamper,

KINDESLEY.

Middlesex, ss. The assize cometh to recognise, if Richard Smith, and Nicholas Smith unjustly, and without judgment, did disseise Rob. Calvin, gent. of his freehold in Haggard, otherwise Haggerston, otherwise Aggerston, in the parish of St. Leonard in Shoreditch, within thirty years now last past: and whereupon the said Robert, who is within the age of twenty-one years, by John Parkinson, and William Parkinson, his guardians, by the Court of the said King here to this being jointly and severally specially admitted, complaineth that they disseised him of one messuage with the appurtenances, &c. And the said Richard and Nicholas, by William Edwards, their attorney, come and say, that the said Robert ought not to be answered to his writ aforesaid, because they say that the said Robert is an alien born, on the 5th day of Nov. in the 3rd year of the reign of the King that now is, of England, France, and Ireland, and of Scotland the thirty-ninth, at Edinburgh within his kingdom of Scotland aforesaid, and within the allegiance of the said lord the King, of the said kingdom of Scotland, and out of the allegiance of the said lord the

The Count.

Aliance pleaded in bar.

King of his kingdom of England; and at the time of the birth of the said Robert Calvin, and long before, and continually afterwards, the aforesaid kingdom of Scotland, by the proper rights, laws, and statutes of the same kingdom, and not by the rights, laws, or statutes of this kingdom of England, was and yet is ruled and governed. And this he is ready to verify, and thereupon prayeth judgment, if the said Robert, to his said writ aforesaid, ought to be answered,

Demurrer. &c. And the aforesaid Robert Calvin saith, that the aforesaid plea, by the aforesaid Richard and Nicholas above pleaded, is insufficient in law to bar him, the said Robert from having an answer to his writ aforesaid; and that the said Robert to the said plea in manner and form aforesaid pleaded, needeth not, nor by the law of the land is bound to answer; and this he is ready to verify, and hereof prayeth judgment; and that the said Richard and Nicholas to the aforesaid writ of the said Robert may answer. And the said Richard and

Joinder. Nicholas, forasmuch as they have above alleged sufficient matter in law to bar him the said Robert from having an answer to his said writ, which they are ready to verify; which matter the aforesaid Robert doth not gainsay, nor to the same doth in any ways answer, but the said averment altogether refuseth to admit as before pray judgment, if the aforesaid Robert ought to be answered

Continu- to his said writ, &c. And because the Court of the lord the King here are not
ances. yet advised of giving their judgment of and upon the premises, day thereof is given to the parties aforesaid; before the lord the King at Westminster until Monday next after eight days of St. Hilary, to hear their judgment thereof, because the Court of the lord the King here thereof are not yet, &c. And the assize aforesaid remains to be taken before the said lord the King, until the same Monday there, &c. And the sheriff to distrain the recognitors of the assize aforesaid: and in the *interim* to cause a view, &c.; at which day, before

Curia advi- the lord the King at Westminster, come as well the aforesaid Robert Calvin,
sare valt. by his guardians aforesaid, as the aforesaid Richard Smith and Nicholas Smith

[2 a] by their attorney aforesaid; and because the Court of the Lord the King | here of giving their judgment of and upon the premises is not yet advised, day thereof is given to the parties aforesaid before the lord the King at Westminster, until Monday next after the morrow of the Ascension of our Lord, to hear their judgment: because the Court of the lord the King here are not yet, &c. And the assize aforesaid remains further to be taken, until the same Monday there, &c.: and the sheriff, as before, to distrain the recoguitors of the assize aforesaid, and in the *interim* to cause a view, &c. At which day, before the lord the King at Westminster, come as well the aforesaid Robert Calvin by

his guardians aforesaid, as the aforesaid Richard Smith and Nicholas Smith, by their attorney aforesaid, &c.: and because the Court of the lord the King here, &c.

The question of this case as to matter in law was, whether Robert Calvin the Plaintiff (being born in Scotland since the Crown of England descended to His Majesty) be an alien born, and consequently disabled to bring any real or personal action for any lands within the realm of England. After this case had been argued in the Court of King's Bench at the barre, by the counsel learned of either party, the Judges of that Court, upon conference and consideration of the weight and importance thereof, adjourned the same (according to the ancient and ordinary course and order of Law) into the Exchequer Chamber, to be argued openly there; first by the counsel learned of either party, and then by all the Judges of England: where afterwards the case was argued by Bacon Solicitor General, on the part of the Plaintiff, and by Laur. Hide for the Defendant: and afterward by Hobart Attorney-General for the Plaintiff, and by Serjeant Hutton for the Defendant: and in Easter term last, the case was argued by Heron puisne Baron of the Exchequer, and Foster puisne Judge of the Court of Common Pleas: and, on the second day appointed for this case, by Crook puisne Judge of the King's Bench, and Altham Baron of the Exchequer: the third day by Snigge Baron of the Exchequer, and Williams one of the Judges of the King's Bench: the fourth day by Daniel one of the Judges of the Court of Common Pleas, and by Yelverton one of the Judges of the King's Bench: And in Trinity Term following, by Warbarton one of the Judges of the Common Pleas, and Fenner one of the Judges of the King's Bench: and after argued Walmesley one of the Judges of the Common Pleas, and Tanfield chief Baron: and, at two several days in the same Term, Coke, chief Justice of the Common Pleas, Fleming, ch. Justice of the King's Bench, and Sir Thomas Egerton, Lord Ellesmere, Lord Chancellor of England, argued the case (the like plea in disability | of Robert Calvin's person being pleaded *mutatis mutandis*[2] in the Chancery in a suit there for evidence concerning lands of inheritance, and by the Lord Chancellor adjourned also into the Exchequer chamber, to the end that one rule might overrule both the said cases). And first (for that I intend to make as summary a Report as I can) I

The Question.

[2 b]

2. [*Ed.*: changing what ought to be changed.]

will at the first set down such arguments and objections as were made and drawn out of this short record against the Plaintiff, by those that argued for the Defendants. It was observed, that in this plea there were four nouns, *quatuor nomina*,[3] which were called *nomina operativa*,[4] because from them all the said arguments and objections on the part of the Defendants were drawn; that is to say, 1. *Ligeantia*[5] (which is twice repeated in the plea, for it is said, *Infra ligeantiam domini regis regni sui Scotiae, et extra ligeantiam domini regis regni sui Angliae*.)[6] 2. *Regnuum*[7] (which also appeareth to be twice mentioned, viz. *regnum Angliae*, and *regnum Scotiae*.)[8] 3. *Leges*[9] (which are twice alleged, viz. *Leges Angliae*, and *leges Scotiae*,[10] two several and distinct Lawes). 4. *Alienigena*[11] (which is the conclusion of all, viz. that Robert Calvin is *Alienigena*).

1. *Ligentia*. By the first it appeareth, that the Defendants do make two ligeances, one of England, and another of Scotland, and from these several ligeances two arguments were framed, which briefly may be concluded thus: Whosoever is born *infra ligeantiam*, within the ligeance of King James of his kingdom of Scotland, is *Alienigena*, an alien born, as to the kingdom of England: but Robert Calvin was born at Edinburgh, within the ligeance of the King of his kingdom of Scotland; therefore Robert Calvin is *Alienigena*, an alien born, as to the kingdom of England. 2. Whosoever is born *extra ligeantiam*, out of the ligeance of King James of his kingdom of England, is an alien as to the kingdom of England: but the plaintiff was born out of the ligeance of the King of his kingdom of England; therefore the Plaintiff is an alien, &c. Both these arguments are drawn from the very words of the plea, viz. *Quod praedictus Robertus est alienigena, natus 5 Novembris anno regni domini regis nunc Angliae, &c. tertio, apud Edenburgh infra regnum Scotiae, ac infra*

3. [*Ed.:* four nouns.]
4. [*Ed.:* operative nouns.]
5. [*Ed.:* allegiance.]
6. [*Ed.:* Within the allegiance of the Lord King of his realm of Scotland and outside the allegiance of the Lord King of his realm of England.]
7. [*Ed.:* the realm.]
8. [*Ed.:* the realm of England [and] the realm of Scotland.]
9. [*Ed.:* laws.]
10. [*Ed.:* laws of England [and] laws of Scotland.]
11. [*Ed.:* alien born.]

ligeantiam dicti domini regis dicti regni sui Scotiae, ac extra ligeantiam dicti domini regis regni sui Angliae.[12]

2. *Regna.* From the several kingdoms, viz. *regnum Angliae,* and *regnum Scotiae,* three arguments were drawn: 1. *Quando duo jura (imo duo regna) concurrunt in una persona, aequum est ac si essent in diversis:*[13] but in the King's person there concurr two distinct and several kingdoms; therefore it is all one as if they were in divers persons, | and consequently the Plaintiff is an alien as all the *Antenati*[14] be for that they were born under the ligeance of another King. 2. Whatsoever is due to the King's several politic capacities of the several kingdoms is several and divided: but ligeance of each nation is due to the King's several politique capacities of the several kingdoms; *Ergo,* The ligeance of each nation is several and divided, and consequently the Plaintiff is an alien, for that they that be born under several ligeances are aliens one to another. 3. Where the King hath several kingdoms by several titles and descents, there also are the ligeances several: but the King hath these two kingdoms by several titles and descents; therefore the ligeances are several. These three arguments are collected also from the words of the plea before remembered.

3. *Leges.* From the several and distinct lawes of either kingdom, they did reason thus; 1. Every subject that is born out of the extent and reach of the Laws of England, cannot by judgment of those laws be a natural subject to the King, in respect of his kingdom of England: but the Plaintiff was born at Edinburgh, out of the extent and reach of the Laws of England; therefore the Plaintiff by the judgment of the lawes of England cannot be a natural subject to the King, as of his kingdom of England. 2. That subject, that is not at the time and in the place of his birth inheritable to the laws of England, cannot be inheritable or partaker of the benefits and privileges given by the laws of England: but the plaintiff at the time, and in the place of his birth was not inheritable to the Laws of England, (but only to the Laws of Scotland;) therefore he is not inheritable, or to be partaker of the benefits or privileges

[3 a]

12. [*Ed.:* That the aforesaid Robert is an alien born, born on the fifth of November in the third year of the reign of the present Lord King of England, etc. at Edinburgh within the realm of Scotland and within the allegiance of the said Lord King of his said realm of Scotland and outside the allegiance of the said Lord King of his realm of England.]

13. [*Ed.:* when two rights (nay two realms) come together in one person, it is the same as if they were in several.]

14. [*Ed.:* born before [the union].]

of the Laws of England. 3. Whatsoever appeareth to be out of the jurisdiction of the laws of England, cannot be tried by the same Laws: but the Plaintiff's birth at Edenborough is out of the jurisdiction of the laws of England; therefore the same cannot be tried by the Laws of England. Which three arguments were drawn from these words of the plea, viz. *Quodque tempore nativitatis praeedictus Roberti Calvin, ac diu antea, et continuè postea, praedictum regnum Scotiae per jura, leges et statuta ejusdem regni propria, et non per jura, leges, seu statuta hujus regni Angliae regulat' et gubernat' fuit, et adhuc est.*[15]

4. *Alienigena.* From this word *Alienigena* they argued thus Every subject that is *alienae gentis (id est) alienae ligeantiae, est alienigena:*[16] but such a one is the plaintiff; therefore, &c. And to these arguments, all that was spoken learnedly and at large by those that argued against the Plaintiff may be reduced.

[3 b] | But it was resolved by the L. Chancellor and twelve Judges, viz. the 2. chief Justices, the chief baron, Justice Fenner, Warbarton, Yelverton, Daniel, Williams, baron Snig, baron Altham, Justice Crooke, and baron Heron, that the Plaintiff was no alien, and consequently that he ought to be answered in this Assise by the Defendant.

How this case was argued by the Lord Chancellor and the Judges.

This case was as elaborately, substantially, and judicially argued by the Lord Chancellor, and by my brethren the Judges, as I ever read or heard of any; and so in mine opinion the weight and consequence of the cause, both *in praesenti et perpetuis futuris temporibus*[17] justly deserved: for though it was one of the shortest and least that ever we argued in this Court, yet was it the longest and weightiest that ever was argued in any court; the shortest in syllables, and the longest in substance; the least for the value (and yet not tending to the right of that least) but the weightiest for the consequent, both for the present, and for all posterity. And therefore it was said, that those that had written *de fossilibus*[18] did observe, that gold hidden in the bowels of the earth, was in respect of the masse of the whole earth, *parvum in magno:*[19] but of this short

---

15. [*Ed.:* And that at the time of the birth of the aforesaid Robert Calvin, and long before, and continuously thereafter, the aforesaid realm of Scotland was ruled and governed by the proper written and unwritten laws and statutes of the same realm and not by the written and unwritten laws and statutes of this realm of England, and it still is.]

16. [*Ed.:* of an alien people, that is, of an alien allegiance, is an alien born.]

17. [*Ed.:* at the present and in the future in perpetuity.]

18. [*Ed.:* of things which may be dug from the earth.]

19. [*Ed.:* a small thing in a great.]

plea it might be truly said (which is more strange) that here was *magnum in parvo*.[20] And in the arguments of those that argued for the Plaintiff, I specially noted, That albeit they spake according to their own heart, yet they spake not out of their own head and invention: wherein they followed the counsel given in God's book, *Interroga pristinam generationem*[21] (for out of the old fields must come the new corn) *et diligenter investiga patrum memoriam*,[22] and diligently search out the judgments of our forefathers: and that for divers reasons. First on our own part, *Hesterni enim sumus et ignoramus, et vita nostra sicut umbra super terram:*[23] for we are but of yesterday, (and therefore had need of the wisdom of those that were before us) and had been ignorant (if we had not received light and knowledge from our forefathers) and our daies upon the earth are but as a shadow, in respect of the old ancient dayes and times past, wherein the Laws have been by the wisdom of the most excellent men, in many successions of ages, by long and continual experience (the trial of right and truth) fined and refined, which no one man (being of so short a time) albeit he had in his head the wisdom of all the men in the world, in any one age could ever have effected or attained unto. And therefore it is *optima regula, qua nulla est verior aut firmior in jure, Neminem oportet esse sapientiorem legibus:*[24] no man ought to | take upon him to be wiser than the   [4 a] laws. Secondly, in respect of our forefathers: *Ipsi*[25] (saith the text) *docebunt te, et loquentur tibi, et ex corde suo proferent eloquia*,[26] they shall teach thee, and tell thee, and shall utter the words of their heart, without all equivocation or mental reservation; they (I say) that cannot be daunted with fear of any power above them, nor be dazzled with the applause of the popular about them, nor fretted with any discontentment (the matter of opposition and contradiction) within them, but shall speak the words of their heart, without all affection or infection whatsoever.

Also in their arguments of this case concerning an alien, they told no strange

---

20. [*Ed.:* a great thing in a small [matter].]

21. [*Ed.:* Examine the first generation.]

22. [*Ed.:* and diligently investigate the memory of [your] fathers.]

23. [*Ed.:* for we are yesterday's men, and our life is but a shadow upon the earth.]

24. [*Ed.:* the best rule, than which nothing is more true or more settled in law, that no one ought to consider himself wiser than the laws.]

25. [*Ed.:* they.]

26. [*Ed.:* [they] will teach you and tell you, and speak eloquently from their heart.]

histories, cited no foreign laws, produced no alien precedents, and that for two causes: the one, for that the Laws of England are so copious in this point, as God willing by the report of this case shall appear: the other, lest their arguments concerning an alien born, should become forein, strange, and an alien to the state of the question, which being *quaestio juris,*[27] concerning freehold, and inheritance in England, is only to be decided by the laws of this Realm. And albeit I concurred with those that adjudged the Plaintiff to be no alien, yet do I find a mere stranger in this case, such a one as the eye of the Law (our books, and book cases) never saw, as the ears of the Law (our Reporters) never heard of, nor the mouth of the Law (for *Judex est lex loquens*[28]) the Judges our forefathers of the Law never tasted: I say, such a one, as the stomack of the Law, our exquisit and perfect Records of pleadings, entries, and judgments, (that make equal and true distribution of all cases in question) never digested. In a word, this little plea is a great stranger to the Laws of England, as shall manifestly appear by the resolution of this case. And now

The method that the reporter doth use.

that I have taken upon me to make a report of their arguments, I ought to do the same as truly, fully, and sincerely as possibly I can: howbeit, seeing that almost every Judge had in the course of his argument a peculiar method, and I must only hold myself to one, I shall give no just offence to any, if I challenge that which of right is due to every Reporter, that is, to reduce the summe and effect of all to such a method, as upon consideration had of all the arguments, the Reporter himself thinketh to be fittest and clearest for the right understanding of the true reasons and causes of the judgment and resolution of the case in question.

What things did fall into consideration in this case.

[4 b]

In this case 5. things did fall into consideration. 1. *Ligeantiu.* 2. *Leges.* 3. *Regna.* 4. *Alienigena.* 5. What legal inconveniences would ensue on either side.

| 1. Concerning ligeance: 1. It was resolved what ligeance was: 2. How many kinds of ligeances there were: 3. Where ligeance was due: 4. To whom it was due: and lastly, How it was due.

2. For the Laws: 1. That ligeance, or obedience of the subject to the Sovereign, is due by the Law of nature: 2. That this Law of nature is part of the Laws of England: 3. That the Law of nature was before any judicial or municipal

27. [*Ed.:* a question of law.]
28. [*Ed.:* A judge is the law speaking.]

Law in the world: 4. That the Law of nature is immutable and cannot be changed.

3. As touching the kingdomes: How farr forth by the act of Law the Union is already made, and wherein the kingdomes doe yet remain separate and divided.

4. Of *Alienigena*, an alien born: 1. What an alien born is in Law: 2. The division and diversity of aliens: 3. Incidents to every alien: 4. Authorities in Law: 5. Demonstrative conclusions upon the premises, that the Plaintiff can be no alien.

5. Upon due consideration had of the consequent of this case: What inconveniences legal should follow on either party.

And these several parts I will in this Report pursue in such order as they have been propounded: and first *de Ligeantia*.

1. Ligeance is a true and faithful obedience of the subject due to his Sovereign. This ligeance and obedience is an incident inseparable to every subject; for as soon as he is born he oweth by birth right ligeance and obedience to his Sovereign. *Ligeantia est vinculum fidei;* and *Ligeantia est quasi legis essentia. Ligeantia est ligamentum, quasi ligatio mentium: quia sicut ligamentum est connexio articulorum et juncturarum, &c.*[29] As the ligatures or strings do knit together the joints of all the parts of the body, so doth ligeance joyn together the Sovereign and all his Subjects, *quasi uno ligamine.* Glanvil, who wrote in the reign of Hen. 2. lib. 9. cap. 4. speaking of the connexion which ought to be between the Lord and Tenant that holdeth by homage, saith, That *mutua debet esse dominii et fidelitatis connexio, ita quod quantum debet domino ex homagio, tantum illi debet dominus ex dominio, praeter solam reverentiam,*[30] and the Lord (saith he) ought to defend his tenant. But between the Sovereign and the subject there is without comparison a higher and greater connexion: for as the subject oweth to the King his true and faithful ligeance and obedience, so the Sovereign is to govern and protect his Subjects, | *regere et protegere subditos suos:*[30] so as between the Sovereign and subject there is *duplex et*

The 1st general part what ligeance is.

[5 a]
Note.

29. [*Ed.:* Allegiance is a bond of faith. Allegiance is, as it were, the essence of law. Allegiance is a ligament, as it were a tying together of minds, just as a ligament is a connection of limbs and joints, etc.]

30. [*Ed.:* the bond of trust arising from lordship should be mutual, so that the lord owes as much to [his man] on account of lordship as he owes to his lord on account of lordship, save only reverence. *Ed.:* to rule and protect the subjects.]

reciprocum ligamen; quia sicut subditus regi tenetur ad obedientiam, ita rex sub-dito tenetur ad protectionem: merito igitur ligeantia dicitur a ligando, quia con-tinet in se duplex ligamen.[31] And therefore it is holden in 20 H. 7, 8. that there is a liege or ligeance between the King and the subject. And Fortescue, cap. 13. *Rex ad tutelam legis, corporum, et bonorum subditorum erectus est.*[32] And in the Acts of Parliament of 10 Rich. 2. cap. 5. and 11 Rich. 2. cap. 1. 14 Hen. 8. cap. 2. &c. Subjects are called liege people: and in the acts of Parliament in 34 Hen. 8. cap. 1. and 35 Hen. 8. cap. 3., &c. the King is called the liege Lord of his Subjects. And with this agreeth M. Skene in his book DE EXPOSITIONE verborum (which book was cited by one of the Judges which argued against the Plaintiff) Ligeance is the mutual bond and obligation between the King and his subjects, whereby subjects are called his liege subjects, because they are bound to obey and serve him, and he is called their liege Lord, because he should maintain and defend them. Whereby it appeareth, that in this point the Law of England, and of Scotland is all one. Therefore it is truly said that *protectio trahit subjectionem, et subjectio protectionem.*[33] And hereby it plainly appeareth, that ligeance doth not begin by the oath in the Leet; for many men owe true ligeance that never were sworn in a Leet, and the swearing in a Leet maketh no denization, as the book is adjudged in 14 Hen. 4. fol. 19. This word ligeance is well expressed by divers several names or *synonymia* which we find in our books. Sometime it is called the obedience or obeysance of the subject to the King, *obedientia regi,* 9 Edw. 4. 7. 9 Edw. 4. 6. 2 Rich. 3. 2. in the book of entries, *Ejectione Firm'.* 14 Hen. 8. cap. 2. 22 Hen. 8. cap. 8., &c. Sometime he is called a natural liege man that is born under the power of the King, *sub potestate regis,*[34] 2. Hen. 3. tit. Dower. *Vide* the Statute de 11 Edw. 3. cap. 2 Sometimes ligeance is called faith *Fides, ad fidem Regis, &c.* Bracton who wrote in the reign of Hen. 3. lib. 5. tractat' de exceptionibus, cap. 24. fol. 427. *Est etiam alia exceptio quae competit ex persona quaerentis, proper defectum nationis, ut si quis alienigena qui fuit ad fidem Regis Franc', &c.*[35] And Fleta (which book

---

31. [*Ed.:* a dual and reciprocal tie, because just as the subject is bound in obedience to the king, so the king is bound to the protection of the subject; and therefore allegiance is properly so called from *ligando* (tying) because it contains within itself a two-way tie.]

32. [*Ed.:* the King is made in order to safeguard the law, the bodies and the goods of the subjects.]

33. [*Ed.:* protection attracts subjection, and subjection protection.]

34. [*Ed.:* under the power of the King.]

35. [*Ed.:* There is also an exception with respect to the person of the plaintiff, on account of a defect of birth, as where he is an alien born who owed allegiance ["was to the faith of"] the King of France, etc.]

was made in the reign of E. 1.) agreeth therewith; for lib. 6. c. 47. *de exceptione ex omissione participis,* it is said, *vel dicere potuit, quod nihil juris clamare poterit tanquam particeps eo quod est ad fidem regis Franciae, quia alienigenae repelli debent in Anglia ab agendo, donec fuerunt ad fidem regis Angliae.*[36] *Vide* 25 Edw. 3. *de natis ultra mare.*[37] [faith and ligeance of the King of England; and Litt. lib. 2. cap. Homage, saving the faith that I owe to our Sovereign Lord the King] and Glanvil, lib. 9. cap. 1. *Salva fide debita dom' Regi et haeredibus suis.*[38] Sometimes ligeance is | called ligealty, 22 Ass. Pl. 25. By all which it evidently appeareth, that they that are born under the obedience, power, faith, ligealty, or ligeance of the King, are natural subjects, and no aliens. So as, seeing now it doth appear what ligeance is, it followeth in order, that we speak of the several kinds of ligeance. But herein we need to be very wary, for this caveat the law giveth, *ubi lex non distinguit nec nos distinguere debemus;*[39] and certainly *lex non distinguit,*[40] but where *omnia membra dividentia*[41] are to be found out and proved by the law itself. [5 b]

2. There is found in the law four kinds of ligeances: the first is, *ligeantia naturalis, absoluta, pura, et indefinita,*[42] and this originally is due by nature and birthright, and is called *alta ligeantia*[42a] and he that oweth this is called *subditus natus.*[43] The second is called *ligeantia acquisita,*[44] not by nature but by acquisition or denization, being called a denizen, or rather donaizon, because he is *subditus datus.*[45] The third is *ligeantia localis*[46] wrought by the law, and that is when an alien that is in amity cometh into England, because as long as he is within England, he is within the King's protection; therefore so long as he is there, he oweth unto the King a local obedience or ligeance,

How many kinds of Ligeonces there be.

36. [*Ed.:* or [the plaintiff] may say that he can claim no right as a parcener because he owes allegiance to [literally, is to the faith of] the King of France, because aliens born ought to be barred from suing in England until they owe allegiance to [are to the faith of] the king of England.]

37. [*Ed.:* concerning those born overseas.]

38. [*Ed.:* Saving the faith due to the lord king and his heirs.]

39. [*Ed.:* where the law makes no distinction, we ought not to distinguish.]

40. [*Ed.:* the law makes no distinction.]

41. [*Ed.:* all the points of difference.]

42. [*Ed.:* natural, absolute, pure and unlimited allegiance.]

42a. [*Ed.:* high allegiance.]

43. [*Ed.:* subject born.]

44. [*Ed.:* acquired allegiance.]

45. [*Ed.:* a subject made by gift.]

46. [*Ed.:* local allegiance.]

for that the one (as it hath been said) draweth the other. The fourth is a legal obedience, or ligeance which is called legal, because the municipal laws of this realm have prescribed the order and form of it; and this to be done upon oath

Ligeantia naturalis.

at the Torn or Leet. The first, that is, ligeance natural, &c. appeareth by the said Acts of Parliament, wherein the King is called natural liege Lord, and his people natural liege subjects]; this also doth appear in the indictments of treason (which of all other things are the most curiously and certainly indicted and penned) for in the indictment of the Lord Dacre, in 26 Hen. 8. it is said, *praed' Dominus Dacre debitum fidei et ligeant' suae, quod praefato domino Regi naturaliter et de jure impendere debuit, minime curans, &c.*[47] And Reginald Pool was indicted in 30 Hen. 8. for committing treason *contra dom' Regem supremum et naturalem dominum suum.*[48] And to this end were cited the indictment of Edward Duke of Somerset in 5 Edw. 6. and many others both of ancient and later times. But in the indictment of treason of John Dethick in 2 and 3 Ph. and Mar. it is said, *quod praed' Johannes machinans, &c. praedict' dominum Philippum et dominam Mariam supremos dominos suos,*[49] and omitted (*naturalis*) because King Philip was not his natural liege Lord. And of this point

Ligeantia acquisita.

more shall be said when we speak of local obedience. The second is *ligeant' acquisita,* or denization: and this in the books and records of the law appeareth to be threefold; 1. absolute, as the common denizations be, to them and their

[6 a]

I heires, without any limitation or restraint: 2. limited, as when the King doth grant letters of denization to an alien, and to the heirs males of his body, as it appeareth in 9 Edw. 4. fol. 7. in *Baggot's case;* or to an alien for term of his life, as was granted to John Reynel, 11 Hen. 6. 3. It may be granted upon condition, for *cujus est dare, ejus est disponere,*[50] whereof I have seen divers precedents. And this denization of an alien may be effected three manner of wayes: by Parliament, as it was in 3 Hen. 6. 55. in Dower: by letters patents, as the usual manner is: and by conquest, as if the King and his subjects should conquer another Kingdome or dominion, as well *Antenati* as *Postnati,* as well they which fought in the field, as they which remained at home for defence

47. [*Ed.:* the aforesaid Lord Dacre, not regarding the duty of his faith and allegiance which naturally and rightfully he ought to have borne to the lord king, etc.]

48. [*Ed.:* against the Lord King, his sovereign and natural lord.]

49. [*Ed.:* that the aforesaid John, scheming, etc. the aforesaid Lord Philip and Lady Mary his sovereign lords.]

50. [*Ed.:* whose is to give, his is to dispose.]

of their countrey, or employed elsewhere, are all denizens of the kingdom or dominion conquered. Of which point more shall be said hereafter.

3. Concerning the local obedience, it is observable, that as there is a local protection on the King's part, so there is a local ligeance of the subject's part. And this appeareth in 4 Mar. Br. 32. and 3 and 4 Ph. and Mar. Dyer 144. Sherley a Frenchman, being in amity with the King, came into England, and joyned with divers subjects of this realm in treason against the King and Queen, and the indictment concluded *contra ligeant' suae debitum;*[51] for he owed to the King a local obedience, that is, so long as he was within the King's protection: which local obedience, being but momentary and incertain, is strong enough to make a natural subject; for if he hath issue here, that issue is a natural born subject: *a fortiori*[52] he that is born under the natural and absolute ligeance of the King (which as it hath been said, is *alta ligeantia*) as the plaintiff in the case in question was, ought to be a natural born subject; for *localis ligeantia est ligeantia infima et minima, et maxime incerta.*[53] And it is to be observed, that it is *nec coelum, nec solum,*[54] neither the climate nor the soyl, but *ligeantia* and *obedientia* that make the subject born: for if enemies should come into the realm, and possess a town or fort, and have issue there, that issue is no subject to the King of England, though he be born upon his soyl, and under his meridian, for that he was not born under the ligeance of a subject, nor under the protection of the King. And concerning this local obedience, a president was cited in Hill. 36. Eliz. when Stephano Ferrara de Gama, and Emanuel Lewes Tinoco, two Portugals born, coming into England under Queen Elizabeth's safe-conduct, and living here under her protection, joyned with Doctor Lopez in treason within | this Realm against her Majesty: and in this case two points were resolved by the Judges. First, that their indictment ought to begin, that they intended treason *contra dominam Reginam, &c.*[55] omitting these words (*naturalem domin' suam*)[56] and ought to conclude *contra ligeant' suae debitum.* But if an alien enemy come to invade this realm, and be taken in warr, he cannot be indicted of treason: for the indictment cannot

Ligeantia localis.

[6 b]

51. [*Ed.:* against the duty of his allegiance.]
52. [*Ed.:* so much the more so.]
53. [*Ed.:* local allegiance is something mean and small, and extremely uncertain.]
54. [*Ed.:* neither the climate (lit. sky) nor the soil.]
55. [*Ed.:* against the Lady Queen, etc.]
56. [*Ed.:* his natural lady.]

conclude *contra ligeant' suae debitum,* for he never was in the protection of the King, nor ever owed any manner of ligeance unto him, but malice and enmity, and therefore he shall be put to death by martial law. And so it was in anno 15 Hen. 7. in *Perkin Warbeck's case,* who being an alien born in Flanders, feigned himself to be one of the sons of Edward the fourth, and invaded this realm with great power, with an intent to take upon him the dignity royall: but being taken in the warr, it was resolved by the Justices, that he could not be punished by the Common law, but before the Constable and Marshal (who had special commission under the great Seal, to hear and determine the same according to martial law) he had sentence to be drawn, hanged, and quartered, which was executed accordingly. And this appeareth in the book of Griffeth Attorney general, by an extract out of the book of Hobart, Attorney general to King Hen. 7.

Ligeantia legalis.

4. Now are we to speak of legal ligeance, which in our books, *viz.* 7 Edw. 2. tit. Avowry 211. 4 E. 3. fol. 42. 13 E. 3. tit. Avowry 120, &c. is called Suit Royall, because that the ligeance of the subject is only due unto the King. This oath of ligeance appeareth in Britton, who wrote in anno 5 Edw. 1. cap. 29. (and is yet commonly in use to this day in every Leet) and in our books; the effect whereof is: "You shall swear, that from this day forward, you shall be true and faithfull to our Sovereign Lord King James; and his heires, and truth and faith shall bear of life and member, and terrene honour, and you shall neither know nor hear of any ill or damage intended unto him, that you shall not defend. So help you Almighty God." The substance and effect hereof is (as hath been said) due by the law of nature, *ex institutione naturae,*[57] as hereafter shall appear: the form and addition of the oath is, *ex provisione hominis.*[58] In this oath of ligeance five things were observed. First, That for the time it is indefinite, and without limit, "from this day forward." Secondly, Two excellent qualities are required, that is, to be "true and faithful." Third, To whom? "to our Sovereign Lord the King and his heirs": (And albeit Britton doth say, to the King of England that is spoken *proper excellentiam,* to design the person, and not I to confine the ligeance: for a Subject doth not swear his ligeance to the King, only as King of England and not to him as King of Scotland, or of Ireland, &c. but generally to the King). Fourth. In what man-

[7 a]

57. [*Ed.:* from the law of nature, or custom.]
58. [*Ed.:* the ordinance of man.]

ner? "and faith and troth shall bear, &c. of life and member;" that is, until the letting out of the last drop of our dearest heart blood. Fifth. Where, and in what places ought these things to be done? in all places whatsoever; for, "you shall neither know nor hear of any ill or damage," &c. that you shall not defend, &c. so as natural ligeance is not circumscribed within any place. It is holden 12 Hen. 7. 18b. That he that is sworn in the Leet, is sworn to the King for his ligeance, that is, to be true and faithful to the King: and if he be once sworn for his ligeance, he shall not be sworn again during his life. And all Letters patents of denization be, that the Patentee shall behave himself *tanquam verus et fidelis ligeus domini Regis.*[59] And this oath of ligeance at the Tourne and Leet was first instituted by King Arthur; for so I read, *Inter leges Sancti Edwardi Regis ante conquestum 3 cap. 35. Et quod omnes principes et comites, proceres, milites et liberi homines debent jurare, &c. in Folkemote, et similiter omnes proceres regni, et milites et liberi homines universi totius regni Britann' facere debent in pleno Folkemote fidelitatem domino Regi, &c. Hanc legem invenit Arthurus qui quondam fuit inclytissimus Rex Britonum, &c. hujus legis authoritate expulit Arthurus Rex Saracenos et inimicos a regno, &c. et hujus legis authoritate Etheldredus Rex uno et eodem die per universum regnum Danos occidit. Vide Lambert inter leges Regis Edwardi, &c. fol. 135 et 136.*[60] By this it appeareth, when and from whom this legal ligeance had his first institution within this realm. *Ligeantia* in the case in question is meant and intended of the first kind of ligeance, that is, of ligeance natural, absolute, &c. due by nature and birth-right. But if the Plaintiff's father be made a denizen, and purchase lands in England to him and his heirs, and die seised, this land shall never descend to the Plaintiff, for that the King by his Letters Patents may make a denizen, but cannot naturalize him to all purposes, as an Act of Parliament may doe; neither can Letters Patents make any inheritable in this case, that by the common Law cannot inherit. And herewith agreeth 36 Hen. 6. tit. Denizen Br. 9.

59. [*Ed.:* as a true and faithful liege of the Lord King.]

60. [*Ed.:* And that all princes and earls, peers, knights and free men ought to swear, etc. in the folk-moot, and likewise all peers of the realm and the knights and free men of the whole realm of Britain ought to do fealty to the lord king in full folk-moot, etc. This law was introduced by Arthur, who was once a most famous king of the Britons, [and] by authority of this law King Arthur expelled the Saracens and enemies from the realm, etc.; and by authority of this law King Ethelred on one and the same day killed the Danes throughout the realm. See Lambarde, under the laws of King Edward, etc., ff. 135 and 136.]

Homage is
two-fold.

[7 b]

Homage in our book is twofold, that is to say, *Homagium Ligeum,*[61] and that is as much as ligeance, of which Bracton speaketh, lib. 2. c. 35. fol. 79. *Soli Regi debet' sine dominio, seu servitio:*[62] | and there is *Homagium feodale,*[63] which hath his original by tenure. In Fit. Nat. Brev. 269. there is a writ for respiting of this later homage (which is due *ratione feodi sive tenurae:) Sciatis quod respectuamus homagium nobis de terr' et tenementis quae tenentur de nobis in capite debit'.*[64] But *Homagium ligeum, i.e. Ligeantia,* is inherent and insep-arable, and cannot be respited.

Where nat-
ural legi-
ance is
due.

3. Now are we come unto (and almost past) the consideration of this cir-cumstance, where natural ligeance should be due: For by that which hath been said it appeareth, that ligeance, and faith and truth which are her members and parts, are qualities of the mind and soul of man, and cannot be circum-scribed within the predicament of *ubi*[65] for that were to confound predica-ments, and to goe about to drive (an absurd and impossible thing) the pre-dicament of Quality into the predicament of *ubi. Non respondetur ad hanc quaestionem, ubi est?* to say, *Verus et fidelis subditus est; sed ad hanc quaestionem, qualis est? Recte et apte respondetur, verus et fidelis ligeus, &c. est.*[66] But yet for the greater illustration of the matter, this point was handled by itself, and that ligeance of the subject was of as great an extent and latitude, as the royal power and protection of the King, *et è converso.*[67] It appeareth by the statute of 11 Hen. 7. cap. 1. and 2 Edw. 6. cap. 2. that the subjects of England are bound by their ligeance to goe with the King, &c. in his wars, as well within the Realm, &c. as without. And therefore we daily see, that when either Ireland or any other of his Majesty's dominions be infested with invasion or insur-rection, the king of England sendeth his subjects out of England, and his subjects out of Scotland also into Ireland, for the withstanding or suppressing of the same, to the end his rebels may feel the swords of either nation. And

61. [*Ed.:* Liege Homage.]

62. [*Ed.:* it is owed to the King alone, without lordship or service.]

63. [*Ed.:* feudal Homage.]

64. [*Ed.:* by reason of fee or tenure: Know ye that we have respited the homage due to us from the lands and tenements which are held of us in chief.]

65. [*Ed.:* where.]

66. [*Ed.:* It is not an answer to the question 'Where is he?' to say that he is a true and faithful subject. However, the question 'What kind of person is he?' is rightly and aptly answered by saying that he is a true and faithful liege.]

67. [*Ed.:* and conversely.]

so may his subjects of Guernsey, Jersey, Isle of Man, &c. be commanded to make their swords good against either rebel or enemy, as occasion shall be offered: whereas if natural ligeance of the subjects of England should be local, that is, confined within the realm of England or Scotland, &c. then were not they bound to goe out of the continent of the realm of England or Scotland, &c. And the opinion of Thirninge in 7 Hen. 4. tit. Protect' 100. is thus to be understood, that an English subject is not compellable to go out of the realm without wages, according to the statutes of 1 Edw. 3. c. 7. 18 Edw. 3. c. 8. 18 Hen. 6. c. 19, &c. 7 Hen. 7. c. 1. 3 Hen. 8. c. 5, &c. In anno 25 Edw. 1. Bigot Earl of Norfolk and Suffolk, and Earl Marshal of England, and Bohun Earl of Hereford and High Constable of England, did exhibit a petition to the King in French (which I have seen anciently recorded) on | the behalf of [8 a] the Commons of England, concerning how and in what sort they were to be employed in his Majesty's warrs out of the realm of England: and the Record saith, that, *post multas et varias altercationes*,[68] it was resolved, they ought to go but in such manner and form as after was declared by the said Statutes, which seem to be but declarative of the common Law. And this doth plentifully and manifestly appear in our books, being truly and rightly understood. In 3 H. 6. tit. Protection 2. one had the benefit of a protection, for that he was sent into the King's wars *in comitiva*,[69] of the protector; and it appeareth by the Record, and by the Chronicles also, that this employment was into France; the greatest part thereof then being under the King's actual obedience, so as the subjects of England were employed into France for the defence and safety thereof: In which case it was observed, that seeing the protector, who was *Prorex*,[70] went, the same was adjudged a voyage royal, 8 Hen. 6. fol. 16. the Lord Talbot went with a company of Englishmen into France, then also being for the greatest part under the actual obedience of the King, who had the benefit of their protections allowed unto them. And here were observed the words of the writ in the Register, fol. 88. where it appeareth, that men were employed in the King's warrs out of the realm *per praeceptum nostrum*,[71] and the usual words of the writ of protection be *in obsequio nostro*.[72] 32 Hen. 6.

---

68. [*Ed.*: after many and various altercations.]
69. [*Ed.*: in the company.]
70. [*Ed.*: viceroy.]
71. [*Ed.*: by our command.]
72. [*Ed.*: in our following.]

fol. 4. it appeareth, that Englishmen were pressed into Guyenne, 44 Edw. 3. 12. into Gascoyn with the Duke of Lancaster, 17 Hen. 6. tit. Protection, into Gascoyn with the Earl of Huntington, steward of Guienne, 11 Hen. 4. 7. into Ireland, and out of this realm with the Duke of Gloucester and the Lord Knolles: *Vide* 19 Hen. 6. 35. And it appeareth in 19 Edw. 2. tit. Avowrie 224. 26 Ass. 66. 7 Hen. 19, &c. that there was *forinsecum servitium*[73] foreign service, which Bracton, fol. 36. calleth *regale servitium;*[74] and in Fitz. N. B. 28. that the King may send men to serve him in his warrs beyond the sea. But thus much (if it be not in so plain a case too much) shall suffice for this point for the King's power, to command the service of his Subjects in his wars out of the Realm. Whereupon it was concluded, That the ligeance of a natural-born subject was not local, and confined only to England. Now let us see what the Law saith in time of peace, concerning the King's protection and power of command, as well without the realm, as within, that his Subjects in all places may be protected from violence, and that justice may equally be administered to all his Subjects.

[8 b] ¶ In the Register, fol. 25 b. *Rex universis et singulis admirall', castellan', custodibus castrorum, villar', et aliorum fortalitiorum praepositis, vicecom' majoribus, custumariis, custodib' portuum, et alior' locor' maritimor' ballivis, ministr', et aliis fidel' suis, tam in transmarinis quam in cismarinis partib' ad quos, &c. salutem. Sciatis, quod suscepimus in protectionem et defension' nostram, necnon ad salvam et securam gardiam nostram W. veniendo in regnum nostrum Angl', et potestatem nostram, tam per terram quam per mare cum uno valetto suo, ac res ac bona sua quaecunque ad tractand' cum dilecto nostro et fideli L. pro redemptione prisonarii ipsius L. infra regnum et potestatem nostram praed' per sex menses morando et exinde ad propria redeundo. Et ideo, &c. quod ipsum W. cum valetto, rebus et bonis suis praed' veniendo in regn' et potestat' nostram praed' tam per terr' quam per mare ibid' ut praedict' est ex causa antedicta morando, et exinde ad propria redeundo, manuteneatis, protegatis, et defendatis; non inferentes, &c. seu gravamen. Et si quid eis forisfactum, &c. reformari faciatis. In cujus, &c. per sex menses duratur'. T. &c.*[75] In which writ 3. things are to be observed: 1. that

73. [*Ed.:* foreign service.]
74. [*Ed.:* royal service.]
75. [*Ed.:* The King to all and singular admirals, chatelains, keepers of castles, vills and other fortresses, provosts, sheriffs, mayors, customers, keepers of ports and other maritime places, bailiffs, ministers, and others his faithful subjects, both overseas and on this side of the seas, to whom [these presents shall come],

the King hath *fidem et fideles in partib' transmarinis.*[76] 2. that he hath *protection'*
in partib' transmarinis.[77] 3. that he hath *potestatem in partibus transmarinis.*[78]
In the Register fo. 26. *Rex universis et singulis admirallis, castellanis, custodibus*
castrorum, villarum, et aliorum fortalitiorum praepositis, vicecom' majoribus,
custumariis, custodib' portuum, et alior' locor' maritimorum ballivis, ministris,
et aliis fidelibus suis, tam in transmarinis quam in cismarinis partibus ad quos,
&c. salutem. Sciatis quod suscepimus in protectionem et defensionem nostram,
necnon in salvum et securum conductum nostr' I. valettum P. et L. Burgensium
de Lyons obsidum nostrorum, qui de licentia nostra ad partes transmarinas pro-
fecturus est, pro finantia magistrorum suorum praedict' obtinenda vel deferenda,
eundo ad partes praedictas ibidem morando, et exinde in Angl' redeundo. Et ideo
vobis mandamus, quod eidem I. eundo ad partes praed' ibidem morando, et exinde
in Angl' redeundo, ut praed' est, in persona, bonis, aut rebus suis, non inferatis,
seu quantum in vobis est ab aliis inferri permittatis injuriam, molestiam, &c. aut
gravamen. Sed eum potius salvum et securum conductum, cum per loca passus,
seu districtus vestros transierit, et super hoc requisiti fueritis, suis sumptibus habere
faciatis. Et si quid eis forisfactum fuerit, &c. reformari faciatis. In cujus, &c. per
tres ann' durat' T. &c.[79] And certainly this was, when Lyons in France (bor-

---

greeting. Know ye that we have taken into our protection and defence, and also under our security and
safeguard, W., on his coming into our realm of England and into our power, both by land and by sea,
with one yeoman (or valet), and whatsoever his things and goods, to remain for six months in order to
treat with our beloved and faithful L. for the redemption of a prisoner of him the said L. within our realm
and power, and then to return from thence to his own country. And therefore [we command you] etc.
that you support, protect and defend the selfsame W. with his yeoman, things and goods aforesaid, coming
into our realm and power aforesaid both by land and by sea and there remaining as aforesaid for the
aforesaid cause, and returning from thence to his own country, not imposing [upon them injury] etc. or
grievance. And if any wrong is done to them etc. you shall reform it. In [witness] whereof etc.; to last for
six months. Witness, etc.]

76. [*Ed.*: allegiance (literally "faith") and faithful subjects in parts [lands] beyond the seas.]

77. [*Ed.*: protection in parts [lands] beyond the seas.]

78. [*Ed.*: power in parts [lands] beyond the seas.]

79. [*Ed.*: The king to all and singular admirals, chatelains, keepers of castles, vills and other fortresses,
provosts, sheriffs, mayors, customers, keepers of ports and other maritime places, bailiffs, ministers, and
others his faithful subjects, both overseas and on this side of the seas, to whom [these presents shall come],
greeting. Know ye that we have taken into our protection and defence, and also under our sure and safe
conduct, J. the yeoman (or valet) of P. and L., burgesses of Lyons, our hostages, who by our licence is
setting out to parts beyond the seas to obtain or bring his masters' money, while he is going to the parts
aforesaid, staying there, and returning from thence into England. And therefore we command you not to
lay any injury, molestation etc. or grievance upon the same J. while going to the parts aforesaid, staying

dering upon Burgundy, an ancient friend to England) was under the actual
obedience of King Henry the 6. For the King commanded *fidelibus suis,*[80] his
faithfull Magistrates there, I that if any injury were there done, it should be
by them reformed and redressed, and that they should protect the party in
his person and goods in peace. In the Register, fol. 26. two other writs: *Rex
omnibus seneschallis, majoribus, juratis, paribus praepositis, ballivis et fidelibus
suis in ducatu Aquitaniae ad quos, &c. salutem. Quia dilecti nobis T. et A. cives
civitat' Burdegal' coram nobis in Cancellar' nost' Angl' et Aquitan' jura sua pro-
sequentes, et metuentes ex verisimilibus conjecturis per quosdam sibi comminantes
tam in corpore quam in rebus suis, sibi posse grave damnum inferri, supplicaverunt
nobis sibi de protectione regia providere: nos volentes dictos T. et A. ab oppres-
sionibus indebitis praeservare, suscepimus ipsos T. et A. res ac justas possessiones
et bona sua quaecunque in protectionem et salvam gardiam nostram specialem.
Et vobis et cuilibet vestrum injungimus et mandamus, quod ipsos T. et A. familias,
res ac bona sua quaecunque a violentiis et gravaminibus indebitis defendatis, et
ipsos in justis possessionibus suis manuteneatis. Et si quid in praejudicium hujus
protectionis et salvae gardiae nost' attentatum inveneritis, ad statum debitum
reducatis. Et ne quis se possit per ignorantiam excusare praesentem protectionem
et salvam gardiam nostram faciatis in locis de quibus requisiti fueritis infra district'
vestrum publice intimari, inhibentes omnibus et singulis sub poenis gravibus, ne
dictis A. et T. seu famulis suis in personis seu rebus suis, injuriam molestiam,
damnum aliquod inferant seu gravamen: et penocellas nostras in locis et bonis
ipsorum T. et A. in signum protectionis et sal' gard' memorat', cum super hoc
requisiti fueritis, apponatis. In cujus, &c. dat' in palatio nostro Westm' sub Magni
Sigilli testimonio, sexto die Augusti anno 44 E. 3.*[81] *Rex universis et singulis sen-*

[9 a]

---

there, and returning from thence into England, as above, in his person, goods or things, nor (so far as you
are able) to permit others to do so, but rather cause him to have at his own costs safe and sure conduct
as he goes through your districts and as you are thereupon requested. And if any wrong is done to them
etc., cause it to be reformed. In [witness] whereof etc.; to last for three years. Witness, etc.]

　80. [*Ed.:* to his faithful [subjects].]

　81. [*Ed.:* The king to all his stewards, mayors, jurats, peers, provosts, bailiffs and faithful subjects in
the duchy of Aquitaine to whom [these presents shall come], greeting. Because our beloved T. and A.,
citizens of the city of Bordeaux, pursuing their rights before us in our chancery of England and Aquitaine,
and fearing by reasonable conjectures the possibility of suffering grave damage through certain people
threatening them, both in their bodies as in their goods, have made supplication unto us to provide royal
protection: we, wishing to preserve the said T. and A. from undue oppression, have taken them the said
T. and A., their things and rightful possessions, and whatsoever their goods, into our special protection

eschallis, constabular' castellanis, praeposit', minist', et omnib' ballivis et fidelibus
suis in dominio nostro Aquitan' constitutis ad quos, &c. salut'. Volentes G. et R.
uxorom ejus favore prosequi gratiose, ipsos G. et R. homines et familias suas ac justas
possessiones, et bona sua quaecunque, suscepimus in protectionem et defensionem
nostram, necnon in salvam gardiam nostram specialem. Et ideo vobis et cuilibet
vestrum injungimus et mandamus, quod ipsos G. et R. eorum homines, familias
suas, ac justas possessiones et bona sua quaecunque manuteneatis, protegatis, et
defendatis: non inferentes eis seu quantum in vobis est ab aliis inferri permittentes,
injuriam, molestiam, damnum, violentiam, impedimentum aliquod seu grava-
men. Et si quid eis forisfact', injuriatum vel contra cos indebite attentatum fuerit,
id eis sine dilatione corrigi, et ad statum debitum reduci faciatis, prout ad vos et
quemlibet vestrum noveritis pertinere: penocellas super domibus suis in signum
praesentis salvae gardiae nostrae (prout moris erit) facientes. In cujus, &c. per
unum annum duratur' T. &c.[82] | By all which it is manifest, that the protection [9 b]
and government of the King is general over all his dominions and kingdoms,
as well in time of peace by justice, as in time of warr by the sword, and that

---

and safeguard. And we enjoin and command you, and each of you, that you defend them the said T. and A., their servants, things, and whatsoever their goods, from violence and undue grievance, and maintain them in their rightful possessions. And if anything in prejudice of this our protection and safeguard should come to your attention, return things to their due condition. And that no one may excuse themselves by ignorance of our present protection and safeguard, cause it to be publicly announced in places where you shall be requested within your districts, forbidding all and singular under grievous penalties that they should not inflict any injury, molestation, damage or grievance upon the said A. and T., or their servants, in their persons or things; and, when you are thereunto requested, put our pensells (i.e. little banners or labels) on the places and goods of the selfsame T. and A., as a sign of protection and safeguard being remembered. In [witness] whereof, etc. Given in our palace of Westminster under the witness of the great seal, on the sixth day of August in forty-fourth year of Edward III.]

82. [*Ed.:* The king to all and singular his stewards, constables, chatelains, provosts, ministers and all bailiffs and faithful subjects in our lordship of Aquitaine to whom [these presents shall come], greeting. We, wishing graciously to favour G., and R. his wife, have taken them the said G. and R. and their servants and rightful possessions, and whatsoever their goods, into our protection and defence and into our special safeguard. Therefore we enjoin and command you, and each of you, that you support, protect and defend them the said G. and R., their men and servants, their rightful possessions, and whatsoever their goods, not inflicting upon them or (as far as you are able) permitting others to inflict upon them any injury, molestation, damage, violence, hindrance or grievance. And if any wrong is done to them or unduly committed against them, you are to correct it without delay and cause things to be returned to their due condition, as far as you know to belong to you and each of you, making pensells (i.e. little banners) upon their houses, as the custom is, as a token of our present safeguard. In [witness] whereof, etc.; to last for one year. Witness, etc.]

all be at his command, and under his obedience. Now seeing power and protection draweth ligeance, it followeth, that seeing the King's power, command
and protection, extendeth out of England, that ligeance cannot be local, or
confined within the bounds thereof. He that is abjured the Realm, *Qui abjurat
regnum amittit regnum, sed non Regem, amittit patriam, sed non patrem patriae*[83]: for notwithstanding the abjuration, he oweth the King his ligeance,
and he remaineth within the King's protection; for the King may pardon and
restore him to his country again. So as seeing that ligeance is a quality of the
mind, and not confined within any place; it followeth, that the plea that doth
confine the ligeance of the Plaintiff to the kingdom of Scotland, *infra ligeantiam Regis regni sui Scotica, et extra ligeantiam regis regni sui Angliae*,[84]
whereby the Defendants do make one local ligeance for the natural subjects
of England, and another local ligeance for the natural subjects of Scotland,
is utterly unsufficient, and against the nature and quality of natural lineage,
as often it hath been said. And Coke, chief Justice of the Court of Common
pleas, cited a ruled case out of Hingham's Reports, *Tempore* E. 1. which in his
argument he shewed in Court written in parchment, in an ancient hand of
that time. Constance de N. brought a writ of Ayel against Roger de Cobledike,
and others, named in the writ, and counted that from the seisin of Roger her
grandfather it descended to Gilbert his son, and from Gilbert to Constance,
as daughter and heir. *Sutton dit, Sir, el ne doit este responde, pur ceo que el est
Francois et nient de la ligeance ne a la foy Dengliterre, et demaund judgement
si el doit action aver:*[85] that she is not to be answered, for that she is a French
woman, and not of the ligeance, nor of the faith of England, and demand
judgment, if she this action ought to have. Bereford (then chief Justice of the
Court of Common Pleas) by the rule of the Court disalloweth the plea, for
that it was too short, in that it referred ligeance and faith to England, and
not to the King: and thereupon Sutton saith as followeth; *Sir, nous voilomous
averre, que el ne est my de la ligeance Dengliterre, ne a la foy le Roy et demaund*

---

83. [*Ed.:* He who abjures the realm leaves the realm but not the king; he leaves the country, but not
the father of the country.]

84. [*Ed.:* within the allegiance of the king of his realm of Scotland, and outside the allegiance of the
king of his realm of England.]

85. [*Ed.:* Sutton said: Sir, she ought not to be answered, because she is French and not of the allegiance
or faith of England, and he demanded judgment whether she ought to have an action.]

jugement, et si vous agardes que el doit este responde, nous dirromus assets: [86] that
is, Sir, we will aver, that she is not of the ligeance of England, nor of the faith
of the King, and demand judgment, &c. | Which later words of the plea (nor   [10 a]
of the faith of the King) referred faith to the king indefinitely and generally,
and restrained not the same to England and thereupon the plea was allowed
for good, according to the rule of the Court: for the book saith, that afterward
the plaintiff desired leave to depart from her writ. The rule of that case of
Cobledike, did (as Coke chief Justice said) over-rule this case of *Calvin,* in
the very point now in question; for that the plea in this case doth not referre
faith or ligeance to the King indefinitely and generally, but limiteth and res-
traineth faith and ligeance to the kingdom: *Extra ligeantiam regis regni sui*
Angliae, [87] out of the ligeance of the King of his kingdom of England; which
afterwards the Lord Chancellor and the chief Justice of the king's Bench,
having copies of the said ancient Report, affirmed in their arguments. So as
this point was thus concluded, *Quod ligeantia naturalis nullis claustris coercetur*
nullis metis, refraenatur, nullis finibus premitur. [88]

4 & 5. By that which hath been said it appeareth, that this ligeance is due   To whom
only to the King; so as therein the question is not now, *cui, sed quomodo*   and how
ligeance is
debetur. [89] It is true, that the King hath two capacities in him: one a natural   due.
body, being descended of the blood royal of the Realm; and this body is of
the creation of Almighty God, and is subject to death, infirmity, and such
like; the other is a politic, body or capacity, so called, because it is framed by
the policy of man (and in 21 Edw. 4. 39. b. is called a mysticall body;) and
in this capacity the King is esteemed to be immortal, invisible, not subject to
death, infirmity, infancy, nonage, &c. Vide Pl. Com. in the case of *The Lord*
Barkley, 238. and in the case of *The Duchy* 213. 6 Edw. 3. 291. and 26 Ass pl.
54. Now seeing the King hath but one person, and several capacities, and one
politique capacitie for the Realm of England, and another for the Realm of
Scotland; it is necessary to be considered, to which capacity ligeance is due.

---

86. [*Ed.:* Sir, we will aver that she is not of the allegiance of England, nor of the king's faith, and we
demand judgment. And if you award that she should be answered, we will have enough to say.]

87. [*Ed.:* Outside the king's allegiance of his realm of England.]

88. [*Ed.:* That natural allegiance is not confined by any enclosures, nor restrained by any bounds, nor
constrained by any limits.]

89. [*Ed.:* [not now] to whom, but in what way, it is owed.]

And it was resolved, that it was due to the natural person of the King (which is ever accompanied with the politique capacity, and the politique capacity as it were appropriated to the natural capacity) and it is not due to the politique capacity only, that is, to his crown or kingdom distinct from his natural capacity, and that for divers reasons. First, every subject (as it hath been affirmed by those that argued against the Plaintiff) is presumed by Law to be sworn to the King, which is to his natural person; and likewise the King is sworn to his subjects (as it appeareth in Bracton, lib. 3. de actionibus, cap. 9. fol.

[10 b]   107.) which oath he taketh in his natural | person: for the politique capacity is invisible and immortal; nay, the politique body hath no soul, for it is framed by the policy of man. 2. In all indictments of Treason, when any doe intend or compass *mortem et destructionem domini Regis*[90] (which must needs be understood of his natural body, for his politique body is immortal, and not subject to death) the indictment concludeth, *contra ligeantiae suae debitum;*[91] ergo, the ligeance is due to the natural body. *Vid* Fit. Justice of Peace 53. et Pl. Com. 384. in *The Earl of Leicester's case.* 3. It is true, that the King *in genere*[92] dieth not, but, no question, *in individuo*[93] he dieth: as for example, Henry the eighth, Edward the sixth &c. and Queen Elizabeth died, otherwise you should have many kings at once. In 2 et 3 Ph. et Mar. Dyer 128. one Constable dispersed divers bills in the streets in the night, in which was written, that King Edward the sixth was alive, & in France, &c: and in Coeman street in London, he pointed to a young man, and said, that he was King Edward the sixth. And this being spoken *de individuo* (and accompanied with other circumstances) was resolved to be high Treason; for the which Constable was attainted and executed. 4. A body politique (being invisible) can as a body politique neither make nor take homage: *Vide* 33 Hen. 8. tit. Fealty, Brook. 5. *In fide,*[94] in faith or ligeance nothing ought to be feigned, but ought to be *ex fide non ficta.*[95] 6. The King holdeth the kingdom of England by birthright inherent, by descent from the blood royal, whereupon succession doth attend; and therefore it is usually said, to the King, his heirs, and successors, wherein heirs is first

90. [*Ed.:* the death and destruction of the lord king.]
91. [*Ed.:* against the duty of his allegiance.]
92. [*Ed.:* in the abstract (or literally, "of his genus").]
93. [*Ed.:* in the individual.]
94. [*Ed.:* In faith.]
95. [*Ed.:* from unfeigned faith.]

named, and successors is attendant upon heirs. And yet in our ancient books, succession and successor are taken for hereditance and heirs. Bracton lib. 2. de acquirendo rerum dominio c. 29. *Et sciend' est quod haereditas est successio in universum jus quod defunctus antecessor habuit, ex causa quacunque acquisitionis vel successionis, et alibi affinitatis jure nulla successio permittitur.*[96] But the title is by descent, by Queen Elizabeth's death the crown and kingdom of England descended to his Majesty, and he was fully and absolutely thereby King, without any essential ceremony or act to be done *ex post facto:*[97] for coronation is but a royal ornament and solemnization of the royal descent, but no part of the title. In the first year of his Majesties reign, before his Majesties coronation, Watson and Clarke, Seminary priests, and others, were of opinion, that his Majesty was no complete and absolute King before his coronation, but that coronation did add a confirmation and perfection to the descent; and therefore (observe their damnable and damned consequent) that they by | strength and power might before his coronation take him and his [II a] royal issue into their possession, keep him prisoner in the Tower, remove such counsellors and great officers as pleased them, and constitute others in their places, &c. And that these and other acts of like nature could not be Treason against his Majesty, before he were a crowned King. But it was clearly resolved by all the Judges of England, that presently by the descent his Majesty was completely and absolutely King, without any essential ceremony or act to be done *ex post facto,* and that coronation was but a Royal ornament, and outward solemnization of the descent. And this appeareth evidently by infinite precedents and book cases, as (taking one example in a case so clear for all) King Henry the Sixth was not crowned until the eighth year of his reign, and yet divers men before his coronation were attainted of Treason, of Felony, &c. and he was as absolute and complete a King, both for matters of judicature, as for grants, &c. before his coronation, as he was after, as it appeareth in the Reports of the 1, 2, 3, 4, 5, 6, and 7 years of the same King. And the like might be produced for many other Kings of this Realm, which for brevity in a case so clear I omit. But which it manifestly appeareth, that by the Laws of England

---

96. [*Ed.:* And it is to be known that inheritance is a succession to all the right that the deceased ancestor had, by reason of whatsoever acquisition or succession, and elsewhere no succession is permitted by right of affinity.]

97. [*Ed.:* afterwards.]

there can be no *inter regnum* within the same. If the King be seised of land by a defeasible title, and dieth seised, this descent shall toll the entry of him that right hath, as it appeareth by 9 Edw. 4. 51. But if the next King had it by succession, that should take away no entry, as it appeareth by Littleton fol. 97. If a disseisor of an infant convey the land to the King who dieth seised, this descent taketh away the entry of the Infant, as it is said in 34 Hen. 6. fol. 34. 45. lib. Ass. pl. 6. Plow. Com. 234. where the case was: King Henry the third gave a Mannor to his brother the Earl of Cornwall in tail (at what time the same was a fee simple conditional) King Henry the third dyed, the Earl before the Statute of *Donis conditional'* (having no issue) by deed exchanged the Mannor with warranty for other lands in fee, and died, without issue, and the warranty and assets descended upon his nephew King Edward the first; and it was adjudged, that this warranty and assets, which descended upon the natural person of the King, barred him of the possibility of reverter. In the reign of Edward the second the Spencers, the father and the son, to cover the Treason hatched in their hearts, invented this damnable and damned opinion, That homage and oath of ligeance was more by reason of the King's Crown [11 b] (that is, of his politic capacity) than by reason of the person of the | King, upon which opinion they inferred execrable and detestable consequences: 1. If the King do not demean himself by reason in the right of his Crown, his lieges are bound by oath to remove the King: 2. Seeing that the King could not be reformed by suit of Law that ought to be done *per aspert.*[98] 3. That his lieges be bound to govern in aid of him, and in default of him. All which were condemned by two Parliaments, one in the reign of Edward the second called *Exilium Hugonis le Spencer,* and the other in Anno 1. Ed. 3. cap 1. Bracton lib. 2. *de acquirendo rerum dominio,*[99] c. 24. fol 55, saith thus, *Est enim corona Regis facere justitiam et judic', et tenere pacem, et sine quibus corona consistere non potest nec tenere; hujusmodi autem jura sive jurisdictiones ad personas vel tenementa transferri non poterunt, nec a privata persona possideri, nec usus nec executio juris, nisi hoc datum fuit ei desuper, sicut jurisdictio delegata delegari non poterit quin ordinaria remaneat cum ipso Rege. Et lib. 3. de actionibus, cap. 9. fol. 107. Separare autem debet Rex, cum sit Dei vicarius in terra,*

---

98. [*Ed.:* by the sword.]

99. [*Ed.:* The banishment of Hugh Despenser; of Acquiring the Dominion of Things.]

jus ab injuria, oequam ab iniquo, ut omnes sibi subjecti honeste vivant, et quod nullus alium laedat, et quod unicuique quod suum fuerit recta contributione reddatur.[100] In respect whereof one saith, That *Corona est quasi cor ornans, cujus ornamenta sunt misericordia et justicia.*[101] And therefore a King's Crown is an Hieroglyphick of the Lawes, where Justice, &c. is administered; for so saith P. Val. lib. 41. pag. 400. *Coronam dicimus legis judicium esse, propterea quod certis est vinculis complicata, quibus vita nostra veluti religata coercetur.*[102] Therefore if you take that which is signified by the Crown, that is, to do Justice and Judgment, to maintain the Peace of the Land, &c. to separate right from wrong, and the good from the ill; that is to be understood of that capacity of the King, that *in rei veritate*[103] hath capacity, and is adorned and indued with indowments as well of the soul as of the body, and thereby able to doe Justice and Judgment according to right and equity, and to maintain the peace, &c. and to find out and discern the truth, and not of the invisible and immortal capacity that hath no such indowments; for of itself it hath neither soul nor body. And where divers Books and Acts of Parliament speak of the Ligeance of England, as 31 Edw. 3. tit. Cosinage 5. 42 Edw. 3. 2. 13 Edw. 3. tit. Br. 677. 25 Edw. 3. Statut. de natis ultra mare. All these and other speaking briefly in a vulgar manner (for *loquendum ut vulgus*[104]) and not pleading (for *sentiendum ut docti*[105]) are to be understood of the Ligeance due by the people of England to the King; for no man will affirm, that England itself, taking it for the Continent thereof, doth owe any | ligeance or faith, or that any faith or ligeance   [12 a]

---

100. [*Ed.:* For the king's crown is to do justice, give judgment, and keep the peace, and without these things the crown can neither subsist or endure. These rights or jurisdictions cannot be transferred to persons or tenements, nor possessed by a private person—neither the usage nor the execution of the right—unless it was given to him from above as a delegated jurisdiction; and jurisdiction cannot be delegated without an ordinary jurisdiction remaining in the king himself.

And in book III, ch. 9, fo. 107: The king, since he is the vicar of God on earth, must distinguish right from wrong, equity from iniquity, that all his subjects may live uprightly, that none of them should injure each other, and that by a just award each may be restored to that which is his.]

101. [*Ed.: Corona* (the crown) is, as it were, *cor ornans* (an ornamenting heart), the ornaments whereof are mercy and justice.]

102. [*Ed.:* We call the judgment the crown of the law, because it is tied up with certain bonds whereby our lives are coerced as if by ties.]

103. [*Ed.:* in truth.]

104. [*Ed.:* we must speak as the common people.]

105. [*Ed.:* we must plead as the learned.]

should be due to it: but it manifestly appeareth, that the ligeance or faith of the Subject is *proprium quarto modo,*[106] to the King, *omni, soli, et semper.*[107] And oftentimes in the Reports of our Book cases, and in Acts of Parliament

also, the Crown or Kingdome is taken for the King himself, as in Fitzh. Natur. Brev. fol. 5. *Tenure in capite*[108] is a Tenure of the Crown, and is a Seignorie in grosse, that is, of the person of the King: and so is 30 Hen. 8. Dyer fol. 44, 45. a Tenure in chief, as of the Crown, is merely a Tenure of the person of the King, and therewith agreeth 28 Henry 8. tit. Tenure Br. 65. The Statute of 4 Hen. 5. cap. *ultimo* gave Priors aliens, which were conventual to the King and his heirs, by which gift saith 34 Hen. 6. 34. the same were annexed to the Crown. And in the said Act of 25 Edw. 3. whereas it is said in the beginning, within the Ligeance of England, it is twice afterward said in the same Act within the Ligeance of the King, and yet all one Ligeance due to the King. So in 42 Edw. 3. fol. 2. where it is first said, the Ligeance of England, it is afterward in the same case called, the Ligeance of the King; wherein though they used several manner and phrases of speech, yet they intended one and the same Ligeance. So in our usual Commission of Assise, of Gaol delivery, of Oyer and Terminer, of the Peace, &c. power is given to execute Justice, *Secundum legem et consuetudinem regni nostri Angliae;*[109] and yet Littleton lib. 2. in his chapter of Villenage, fol. 43. in disabling of a man that is attainted in a *Praemunire*[110] saith, That the same is the King's Law; and so doth the

Register in the Writ of *ad jura regia*[111] style the same.

The reasons and cause wherefore by the policy of the Law the King is a body politique, are three, viz. 1. *causa majestatis,*[112] 2. *causa necessitatis,*[113] and 3. *causa utilitatis.*[114] First, *causa majestatis,* the King cannot give or take but by matter of Record for the dignity of his person. Secondly, *causa necessitatis,*

---

106. [*Ed.:* appropriate in the fourth way. (legal allegiance)]
107. [*Ed.:* all, only and always.]
108. [*Ed.:* in chief.]
109. [*Ed.:* according to the law and custom of our realm of England.]
110. [*Ed.:* procedure for conviction for premunire.]
111. [*Ed.:* Writ to enforce crown rights in a living.]
112. [*Ed.:* by reason of majesty.]
113. [*Ed.:* by reason of necessity.]
114. [*Ed.:* by reason of utility.]

as to avoyd the attainder of him that hath right to the Crown, as it appeareth in 1 Hen. 7. 4. lest in the *interim* there should be an *Interregnum*,[115] which the Law will not suffer. Also by force of this politique capacity, though the King be within age, yet may he make Leases and other Grants, and the same shall bind him; otherwise his Revenue should decay, and the King should not be able to reward service, &c. Lastly, *causa utilitatis,* as when lands and possessions descend from his collateral Ancestors, being Subjects, as from the Earl | of March, &c. to the King, now is the King seised of the same *in jure coronae*,[116] in his politique capacity; for which cause the same shall go with the Crown; and therefore, albeit Queen Elizabeth was of the half blood to Queen Mary, yet she in her body politique enjoyed all those fee simple lands, as by the Law she ought, & no collateral cousin of the whole blood to Queen. Mary ought to have the same. And these are the causes wherefore by the policy of the Law the King is made a body politique: So as for these special purposes the Law makes him a body politique, immortal, and invisible, whereunto our liegance cannot appertain. But to conclude this point, our liegance is due to our natural liege Sovereign, descended of the blood Royal of the Kings of this Realm. And thus much of the first general part *de Ligeantiâ*.[117]

[12 b]

Now followeth the second part, de Legibus, wherein these parts were considered: First, That the ligeance or faith of the Subject is due unto the King by the Law of Nature: Secondly, That the Law of Nature is part of the Law of England: Thirdly, That the Law of Nature was before any Judicial or Municipal Law: Fourthly, That the Law of Nature is Immutable.

De legibus. The second general part.

The Law of Nature is that which God at the time of creation of the nature of man infused into his heart, for his preservation and direction; and this is *lex aeterna*,[118] the Moral Law, called also the Law of Nature. And by this Law, written with the finger of God in the heart of man, were the people of God a long time governed, before that Law was written by Moses, who was the first Reporter or Writer of Law in the world. The Apostle in the second Chapter to the Romans saith, *Cum enim gentes quae legem non habent naturaliter ea*

The Law of Nature.

---

115. [*Ed.:* interregnum (interval between kings).]
116. [*Ed.:* by the law of the Crown,]
117. [*Ed.:* concerning allegiance.]
118. [*Ed.:* eternal law.]

quae legis sunt faciunt.[119] And this is within that commandment of the Moral Law, *Honora patrem,*[120] which doubtless doth extend to him that is *pater patriae*[121] And the Apostle saith, *Omnis anima potestatibus sublimioribus subdita sit.*[122] And these be the words of the great Divine, *Hoc Deus in Sacris Scripturis jubet. hoc lex naturae dictari, ut quilibet subditus obediat superio,*[123] And Aristotle, Nature's Secretary, Lib. 5. Aethic. saith, That *jus naturale est, quod apud omnes homines eandem habet potentiam.*[124] And herewith doth agree Bracton, lib. 1. cap. 5. and Fortescue, cap. 8, 12, 13, and 16. Doctor and Student, cap. 2. and 4. And the reason hereof is, for that God and Nature is one | to all, and therefore the Law of God and Nature is one to all. By this Law of Nature is the Faith, Ligeance, and Obedience of the Subject due to his Sovereign or Superiour. And Aristotle 1. Politicorum proveth, that to Command and to Obey is of Nature, and that Magistracy is of Nature: For whatsoever is necessary and profitable for the preservation of the society of man, is due by the Law of nature: But Magistracy and Government are necessary and profitable for the Preservation of the society of man; therefore Magistracy and Government are of Nature. And herewith accordeth Tully lib. 3. *de legibus, Sine imperio nec domus ulla, nec civitas, nec gens, nec hominum universum genus stare, nec ipse denique mundus potest.*[125] This Law of Nature, which indeed is the eternal Law of the Creator, infused into the heart of the creature at the time of his creation, was two thousand years before any Laws written, and before any Judicial or Municipal Laws. And certain it is, That before Judicial or Municipal Laws were made, Kings did decide causes according to natural equity, and were not tied to any rule or formality of Law, but did *dare jura.*[126] And this appeareth by Fortescue, cap. 12 & 13. and by Virgil that Philosophical Poet, 7th Aeneid.

[13 a]

---

119. [*Ed.:* for people who have no law naturally do those things which are of law.]

120. [*Ed.:* Honour [thy] father.]

121. [*Ed.:* father of the country.]

122. [*Ed.:* Every soul is subject to more sublime powers.]

123. [*Ed.:* Here God in the holy scriptures wills it to be laid down as the law of nature that every subject should obey the sovereign.]

124. [*Ed.:* The law of nature is that which has the same power among all men.]

125. [*Ed.:* Without government, no house, no city, no people, no kind of man, can stand, nor in the course of time can the world itself.]

126. [*Ed.:* give the laws.]

Hoc Priami gestamen erat, cum jura vocatis
More daret populis.[127]

And 5th Aeneid.

——— Gaudet regno Trojanus Acestes,
Indicitque forum et patribus dat jura vocatis.[128]

And Pomponius lib. 2. cap. de origine juris, affirmeth, that in Tarquinius Superbus's time there was no Civile Law written, and that Papirius reduced certain observations into writing, which was called Jus Civile Papirianum. Now the reason wherefore Laws were made and published, appeareth in Fortescue cap. 13. and in Tully lib. 2. officiorum: *At cum jus aequabile ab uno viro homines non consequerentur, inventae sunt leges.*[129] Now it appeareth by demonstrative reason, that Ligeance, Faith, and Obedience of the Subject to the Sovereign, was before any Municipal or Judicial Laws: 1. For that Government and Subjection were long before any Municipal or Judicial Laws: 2. For that it had been in vain to have prescribed Laws to any, but to such as owed Obedience, Faith, and Ligeance before, in respect whereof they were bound to obey and observe them: *Frustra enim | feruntur leges nisi subditis et obe-*   [13 b] *dientibus.*[130] Seeing then that Faith, Obedience, and Ligeance, are due by the Law of Nature, it followeth that the same cannot be changed or taken away; for albeit Judicial or Municipal Laws have inflicted and imposed in several places, or at several times, divers and several punishments and penalties for breach or not observance of the Law of Nature (for that law onely consisted in commanding or prohibiting, without any certain punishment or penalty), yet the very Law of Nature itself, never was nor could be altered or changed. And therefore it is certainly true, that *Jura naturalia sunt immutabilia.*[131] And herewith agreeth Bracton lib. 1. cap. 5. and Doctor and Student cap. 5 and 6. And this appeareth plainly and plentifully in our Books.

127. [*Ed.:* This was Priam's burden, when, after his wont, he gave laws to the assembled peoples. [Virgil, *Aeneid,* 7. 246.].]

128. [*Ed.:* Trojan Acestes delights in his kingdom, proclaims a court, and gives laws to the assembled senate (lit. fathers). [Virgil, *Aeneid,* 5. 757.].]

129. [*Ed.:* Since men will not follow a law devised by one man, though it is equitable, [written] laws have been invented.]

130. [*Ed.:* It is in vain to make laws unless there are subjects and persons who will obey them.]

131. [*Ed.:* The laws of nature are immutable.]

If a man hath a Ward by reason of a Seigniory, and is Outlawed, he forfeiteth the Wardship to the King: But if a man hath the Wardship of his own Son or Daughter, which is his heir apparent, and is Outlawed, he doth not forfeit this Wardship; for nature hath annexed it to the person of the Father, as it appeareth in 33 Hen. 6. 55. *Et bonus Rex nihil a bono patre differt, et patria dicitur a patre, quia habet communem patrem, qui est pater patriae.*[132] In the same manner, *maris et foeminae conjunctio est de jure naturae,*[133] as Bracton in the same book and chapter, and St. Germin in his book of the Doctor and Student, cap. 5., do hold. Now, if he that is attainted of Treason or Felony, be slain by one that hath no authority, or executed by him that hath authority, but pursueth not his warrant, in this case his eldest son can have no appeal, for he must bring his appeal as heir, which being *ex provisione hominis,*[134] he loseth it by the attainder of his Father: but his Wife (if any he have) shall have an appeal, because she is to have her appeal as Wife, which she remaineth notwithstanding the attainder, because *maris et foeminae conjunctio*[135] is *de jure naturae,*[136] and therefore (it being to be intended of true and right Matrimony) is indissoluble: and this is proved by the book in 33 Hen. 6. fol. 57. So if there be Mother and Daughter, and the Daughter is attainted of felony, now cannot she be heir to her Mother for the cause aforesaid; yet after her attainder if she kill her Mother, this is Paricide and Petit treason; for she remaineth her daughter, for that is of nature, and herewith agreeth 21 Edw. 3. 17. b. If a man be attainted of Felony or Treason, he hath lost the King's legal protection, for he is thereby utterly disabled to sue any action real or personal (which is a greater disability than an alien in league hath) and yet [14 a] such a person so attainted hath not lost that | protection which by the law of nature is given to the King; for that is *indelebilis et immutabilis,*[137] and therefore the King may protect and pardon him, and if any man kill him without warrant, he shall be punished by the Law as a Manslayer; and thereunto accordeth 4 Edw. 4. and 35 Hen. 6. 57. 2 Ass. pl. 3. By the statute of 25 Edw.

132. [*Ed.:* A good king is not different from a good father, and *patria* (country) is so called from *pater* (father), because it has a common father who is *pater patriae* (father of the country).]

133. [*Ed.:* The union of husband and wife is by the law of nature,]

134. [*Ed.:* by the provision of man.]

135. [*Ed.:* the union of husband and wife.]

136. [*Ed.:* by the law of nature,]

137. [*Ed.:* indelible and immutable.]

3. cap. 22. a man attainted in a *Praemunire*,[138] is by expresse words out of the King's protection generally; and yet this extendeth onely to legal protection, as it appeareth by Littleton, fol. 43. for the Parliament could not take away that protection which the Law of Nature giveth unto him; and therefore, notwithstanding that Statute, the King may protect and pardon him. And though by that Statute it was further enacted, That it should be done with him as with an enemy, by which words any man might have slain such a person (as it is holden in 24 Hen. 8. tit. Coron. Br. 197.) until the statute made anno 5 Eliz. cap. 1. yet the King might protect and pardon him. A man Outlawed is out of the benefit of the Municipal Law; for so saith Fitzh. Nat. Brev. 161. *Utlagatus est quasi extra legem positus:*[139] and Bracton lib. 3. tract. 2. cap 11. saith, that *caput geret lupinum;*[140] and yet is he not out either of his natural ligeance, or of the King's natural protection; for neither of them are tyed to Municipal Laws, but is due by the Law of Nature, which (as hath been said) was long before any Judicial or Municipal Laws. And therefore if a man were Outlawed for Felony, yet was he within the King's natural protection, for no man but the Sheriff could execute him, as it is adjudged in 2 lib. Ass. pl. 3. Every subject is by his natural Ligeance bound to obey and serve his Sovereign, &c. It is enacted by the Parliament of 23 Hen. 6. that no man should serve the King as Sheriff of any County, above one year, and that, notwithstanding any clause of *non obstante*[141] to the contrary, that is to say, notwithstanding that the King should expressly dispense with the said Statute: howbeit it is agreed in 2 Hen. 7. that against the expresse purview of that act, the king may by a special *Non obstante* dispense with that act, for that the act could not barr the King of the service of his subject, which the law of nature did give unto him. By these and many other cases that might be cited out of our books, it appeareth, how plentiful the authorities of our Laws be in this matter. Wherefore to conclude this point (and to exclude all that hath been or could be objected against it) if the obedience and ligeance of the subject to his Sovereign be due by the Law of nature, if that law be parcel of the Laws, as well of England, as of all other nations, and is immutable, and that *Post-*

---

138. [*Ed.:* Writ against those who introduce a foreign power to the Kingdom; used to regulate Roman Catholics.]

139. [*Ed.:* An outlaw is, as it were, put outside the law.]

140. [*Ed.:* he bears the head of the wolf.]

141. [*Ed.:* notwithstanding, words commencing a writ relieving someone of an obligation or power.]

[14 b]   *nati*[142] and we of England are united by birth right, I in obedience and ligeance
            (which is the true cause of natural subjection) by the law of nature; It followeth,
i.e. of   that Calvin the Plaintiff being born under one ligeance to one King, cannot
Scotland.   be an alien born; And there is great reason, that the Law of nature should
            direct this case, wherein five natural operations are remarkable; First the King
            hath the crown of England by birth right, being naturally procreated of the
            blood royal of this Realm; Secondly, Calvin the Plaintiff naturalized by pro-
            creation and birth right, since the descent of the Crown of England; Thirdly,
            ligeance and obedience of the subject to the Sovereign, due by the law of
            nature; Fourthly, protection and government due by the law of nature; Fifthly,
            this case, in the opinion of divers, was more doubtful in the beginning, but
            the further it proceeded, the cleerer and stronger it grew; and therefore the
            doubt grew from some violent passion, and not from any reason grounded
            upon the law of nature, *quia quanto magis violentus motus (qui fit contra na-*
            turam) appropinquat ad suum finem, tanto debiliores et tardiores sunt ejus motus;
            sed naturalis motus, quanto magis appropinquat at suum finem, tanto fortiores
            et velociores sunt ejus motus.[143] Hereby it appeareth how weak the objection
            grounded upon the rule of *Quanto duo jura concurrunt in una personû, &c.*[144]
            is: For that rule holdeth not in personal things, that is, when two persons are
            necessarily and inevitably required by law, (as in the case of an alien born there
            is;) and therefore no man will say, that now the King of England can make
            warr or league with the King of Scotland, *et sic de caeteris:*[145] and so in case
            of an alien born, you must of necessity have two several ligeances to two several
            persons. And to conclude this point concerning laws, *Non adservatur diversitas*
            regnor' sed regnant', non patriarum, sed patrum patriar', non coronarum, sed
            coronatorum, non legum municipalium, sed regum majestatum.[146] And therefore
            thus were directly and clearly answered, as well the objections drawn from
            the severalty of the kingdoms, seeing there is but one head of both, and the
            Postnati and us joyned in ligeance to that one head, which is *copula et tanquam*

---

        142. [*Ed.:* those born after [the union].]

        143. [*Ed.:* Because a violent passion (one made contrary to nature) becomes slower and weaker the
    closer it approaches its end, whereas a natural motion becomes faster and stronger.]

        144. [*Ed.:* When two rights come together in one person, etc.]

        145. [*Ed.:* and thus the union.]

        146. [*Ed.:* a distinction is not to be made of realms, but of rulers; not of countries, but of fathers of
    countries; not of crowns, but of the crowned; not of municipal laws, but of king's majesties.]

oculus[147] of this case; as also the distinction of the Laws, seeing that ligeance of the subjects of both kingdoms, is due to their Sovereign by one law, and that is the Law of nature.

For the third, It is first to be understood, that as the law hath wrought four unions, so the law doth still make four separations. The first union is of both kingdoms under one natural liege sovereign King, and so acknowledged by the Act of | Parliament of recognition. The second is an union of ligeance and obedience of the subjects of both kingdoms, due by the law of nature to their Sovereign: And this union doth suffice to rule and over rule the case in question; and this in substance is but a uniting of the hearts of the subjects of both kingdoms one to another, under one head and sovereign. The third union is an union of protection of both kingdoms, equally belonging to the subjects of either of them: And therefore the two first arguments or objections drawn from two supposed several ligeances, were fallacious, for they did *disjungere conjungenda*.[148] The fourth union and conjunction is, of the three Lions of England, and that one of Scotland, united and quartered in one escutcheon.

Concerning the separations yet remaining: First, England and Scotland remain several & distinct kingdoms; 2. They are governed by several judicial or municipal laws; 3. They have several distinct and separat Parliaments; 4. Each kingdom hath several Nobilities; For albeit a *Postnatus* in Scotland, or any of his posterity, be the heir of a Nobleman of Scotland, and by his birth is legitimated in England, yet he is none of the Peers or Nobility of England: for his natural ligeance and obedience, due by the law of nature, maketh him a subject, and no alien within England: but that subjection maketh him not noble within England; for that Nobility had his original by the King's creation, and not of nature. And this is manifested by express authorities, grounded upon excellent reasons in our books. If a Baron, Viscount Earl, Marquess, or Duke of England, bring any action real or personal, and the defendant pleadeth in abatement of the writ, that he is no Baron, Viscount, Earl, &c. and thereupon the demandant or Plaintiff taketh issue; this issue shall not be tried by Jury, but by the record of Parliament, whether he or his ancestor, whose heir he is, were called to serve there as a Peer, and one of the Nobility of the Realm. And so are our books adjudged in 22 Ass. 24. 48 Edw. 3. 30. 35 H. 6. 40. 20

The 3d general part concerning both kingdoms.

[15 a]

---

147. [*Ed.*: a coupling, and, as it were, an eye.]
148. [*Ed.*: separate things which ought to be conjoined.]

Eliz. Dyer. 360. *Vide* in the 6 part of my *Reports*, in *The Countess of Rutland's case*. So as the man, that is not *de jure* a Peer, or one of the Nobility, to serve in the upper house of the Parliament of England, is not in the legal proceedings of law accounted Noble within England. And therefore if a Countee of France or Spain, or any other foreign kingdom, should come into England, he should not here sue, or be sued, by the name of Countee, &c. for that he is none of the Nobles that are members of the | upper house of the Parliament of England: and herewith agree the book cases of 20 Edw. 4. 6. and 11 Edw. 3. tit. Bre. 473. Like law it is, and for the same reason, of an Earl or Baron of Ireland, he is not any Peer, or of the Nobility of this Realm: and herewith agreeth the book in 8 Rich. 2 tit. Proces. pl. ultim. where in an action of Debt process of Outlawry was awarded against the Earl of Ormond in Ireland; which ought not to have been, if he had been noble here. *Vide* Dyer 20 Eliz. 360.

[15 b]

But yet there is a diversity in our books worthy of observation, for the highest and lowest dignities are universal; for if a King of a forein nation come into England, by the leave of the King of this Realm (as it ought to be) in this case he shall sue and be sued by the name of a King: and herewith agreeth 11 Edw. 3. tit. Br. 473. where the case was, that Alice, which was the wife of R. de O. brought a writ of Dower against John Earl of Richmond, and the writ was, *Praecip. Johann' Comiti Richmondiae custodi terr' et haeredis*[149] of William the son of R. de. O. the tenant pleaded, that he is Duke of Britain, not named Duke, judgment of the writ? But it is ruled, that the writ was good, for that the Dukedom of Brittain was not within the Realm of England. But there it is said, that if a man bring a writ against Edward Baliol, and name him not King of Scotland, the writ shall abate for the cause aforesaid. And hereof there is a notable precedent in Fleta lib. 2. cap. 14. where treating of the jurisdiction of the King's Court of Marshalsea it is said, *Et haec omnia ex officio suo licite facere poterit (ss. seneschal' aul' hospitii Regis) non obstante alicujus libertate, etiam in alieno regno dum tamen reus in hospitio Regis poterit inveniri secundum quod contigit Paris. anno 14 Ed. 1. de Engelramo de Nogent capto in hospitio Regis Angl' (ipso rege tunc apud Parisiam existente) cum discis argenti furatis recenter super facto, rege Franc' tunc presente, et unde licet curia Regis Franc' de praed' latrone per castellanum Paris. petita fuerit, habitis hic et inde tractatibus in Consilio Regis Franc', tandem consideratum fuit; quod Rex Angl'*

---

149. [*Ed.:* command John, earl of Richmond, guardian of the land and heir.]

illa regia praerogativa, et hospitii sui privilegio uteretur, et gauderet, qui coram Roberto Fitz-John milite tunc hospitii Regis Angl' seneschallo de latrocinio convictus, per considerationem ejus cur. fuit suspensus in patibulo sancti Germani de Pratis.[150] Which proveth, that though the king be in forein kingdom, yet he is judged in law a king there. The other part of the said diversity, is proved by the book case in 20 Edw. 4. fol. 6. where, in a writ of debt brought by Sir John Douglas knight, against Elizabeth. Molford, the defendant, demanded judgment of the writ, for that I the Plaintiff was an Earl of Scotland, but not [16 a] of England; and that our Sovereign Lord the king had granted unto him safe conduct, not named by his name of dignity, judgment of the writ, &c. And there Justice Littleton giveth the rule: the Plaintiff (saith he) is an Earl in Scotland, but not in England; and if our Sovereign Lord the king grant to a Duke of France a safe conduct to merchandise, and enter into his Realm, if the Duke cometh and bringeth merchandise into this land, and is to sue an action here, he ought not to name himself Duke, for he is not a Duke in this land, but only in France. And these be the very words of that book case: out of which I collect three things. First, that the Plaintiff was named by the name of a knight, wheresoever he received that degree of dignity. *Vide* 7 Hen. 6. 14 b. accord. Second. That an Earl of another nation or kingdom is no Earl (to be so named in legal proceedings) within this Realm: and herewith agreeth the book of 11 Edw. 3. *The Earl of Richmond's case* before recited. Third. That albeit the king by his Letters Patents of safe conduct doe name him Duke, yet that appellation maketh him no Duke, to sue or to be sued by that name within England: So as the law in these points (apparent in our books) being observed, and rightly understood it appeareth how causeless their fear was that the adjudging of the Plaintiff to be no alien should make a confusion of the Nobilities of either kingdom.

---

150. [*Ed.:* And he (namely the steward of the hall of the king's household) may lawfully do all these things by virtue of his office, notwithstanding any liberty—even in someone else's realm—provided that the offender may be found in the king's household. For example, in Paris in the fourteenth year of Edward I, Ingelram de Nogent happened to be arrested in the household of the king of England (the king himself then being in Paris) with discs of stolen silver recently made, the king of France being then present: and although the [jurisdiction of the] court of the king of France was claimed by the châtelain of Paris in respect of the aforesaid thief, whereupon a discussion occurred in the council of the king of France, at length it was decided that the king of England should use and enjoy that royal prerogative, and the privilege of his household; and he was convicted of larceny before Robert FitzJohn, knight, then steward of the household of the king of England, by judgment of the court, and hanged on the gallows of St Germain des Pres.]

The 4th
general
Part. De
alienigena.

Now are we in order come to the fourth Noun (which is the fourth general part) *Alienigena;* wherein six things did fall into consideration. 1. Who was *Alienigena,* an alien born by the laws of England. 2. How many kinds of aliens born there were. 3. What incidents belonged to an alien born. 4. The reason why an alien is not capable of inheritance or freehold within England. 5. Examples, resolutions, and judgments, reported in our books in all succession of ages, proving the Plaintiff to be no alien. 6. Demonstrative conclusions upon the premises, approving the same.

Who is an
alien.

1. An Alien is a subject that is born out of the ligeance of the king, and under the ligeance of another, and can have no real or personal action for or concerning land; but in every such action the tenant or defendant may plead that he was born in such a Country which is not within ligeance of the king, and demand judgment if he shall be answered. And this is in effect the description which Littleton himself maketh, lib. 2. cap. 14. Villen. fol. 43. *Al-*

[16 b]

ienigena est alienae gentis seu alience ligeantiae, qui etiam | dicitur peregrinus, alienus, exoticus, extraneus, &c. Extraneus est subditus, qui extra terram, i.e. potestatem regis natus est.[151] And the usual and right pleading of an alien born doth lively and truly describe and express what he is. And therein two things are to be observed; 1. That the most usual and best pleading in this case is, both exclusive and inclusive, viz. *extra ligeantiam domini Regis, &c. et infra ligeantiam alterius Regis,*[152] as it appeareth in 9 Ed. 4. 7. Book of Entries, fol. 244, &c. which cannot possibly be pleaded in this case, for two causes; First for that one king is Sovereign of both kingdoms; second, One ligeance is due by both to one Sovereign, and in case of an alien there must of necessity be several kings, and several ligeances. Secondly, no pleading was ever *extra regnum,*[153] or *extra legem,*[154] which are circumscribed to place, but *extra ligeantiam,*[155] which (as it hath been said) is not local or tied to any place.

It appeareth by Bracton lib. 3. tract. 2. cap. 15. fol. 134. that Canutus the Danish king, having settled himself in this kingdom in peace, kept notwithstanding (for the better continuance thereof) great Armies within this Realm.

151. [*Ed.:* An alien born is of foreign birth or foreign allegiance, and is also called *peregrinus* (foreigner), alien, exotic, stranger, etc. A stranger is a subject who is born outside the land, that is, outside the king's power.]
152. [*Ed.:* outside the allegiance of the lord king, etc. and within the allegiance of the other king.]
153. [*Ed.:* outside the kingdom.]
154. [*Ed.:* outside the law.]
155. [*Ed.:* outside allegiance.]

The Peers and Nobles of England, distasting this government by arms and armies, (*Odimus accipitrem quia semper vivit in armis*)[156] wisely and politikely persuaded the king, that they would provide for the safety of him and his people, and yet his armies, carrying with them many inconveniencies, should be withdrawn; And therefore offered, that they would consent to a law, that whosoever should kill an alien, and be apprehended, and could not acquit himself, he should be subject to justice: but if the manslayer fled, and could not be taken, then the Town where the man was slain should forfeit 66 marks unto the King: and if the Town were not able to pay it, then the Hundered should forfeit and pay the same unto the King's treasure; whereunto the King assented. This law was penned *Quicunque occiderit Francigenam, &c.*[157] not excluding other aliens, but putting *Francigena,* a Frenchman for example, that others must be like unto him, in owing several ligeance to a several Sovereign, that is, to be *extra ligeantiam Regis Angl',*[158] and *infra ligeanitiam alterius Regis.*[159] And it appeareth before out of Bracton and Fleta, that both of them use the same examples (in describing of an alien) *ad fidem Regis Franciae.*[160] And it was holden, that except it could be proved that the party slain was an Englishman, that he should be taken for an alien; and this was called Englesherie, *Englesheria,* that is, a proof that the party slain was an Englishman. (Hereupon I Canutus presently withdrew his armies, and within a while after lost his crown, and the same was restored to his right owner.) The said law of Englesherie continued until 14 Edw. 3. cap. 4. and then the same was by Act of Parliament ousted and abolished. So amongst the laws of William the First, (published by Master Lambert. fol. 125.) *Omnis Francigena*[161] (there put for example as before is said, to express what manner of person *alienigena* should be) *qui tempore Edvardi propinqui nostri fuit particeps legum et consuetudinum Anglorum*[162] (that is, made denizen) *quod dicunt ad scot et lot persolvat secundum legem Anglorum.*[163]

[17 a]

156. [*Ed.:* We hate the hawk because he always lives in arms.]
157. [*Ed.:* Whosoever should find a Frenchman, etc.]
158. [*Ed.:* outside the allegiance of the king of England.]
159. [*Ed.:* within the allegiance of the other king.]
160. [*Ed.:* owing allegiance to (literally, "to the faith of") the king of France.]
161. [*Ed.:* Every Frenchman . . .]
162. [*Ed.:* . . . who in the time of our kinsman Edward had a share in the law and custom of the English . . .]
163. [*Ed.:* . . . paid what was called Scot and lot according to the law of the English.]

Every man is either *Alienigena,* an *Alien* born, or *subditus,*[164] a subject born. Every Alien is either a friend that is in league, &c. or an enemy that is in open war. &c. Every Alien enemy is either *pro tempore,* temporary for a time, or *perpetuus,* perpetual, or *specialiter permissus,* permitted especially. Every subject is either *natus,* born, or *datus,* given or made: And of these briefly in their order. An alien friend, as at this time, a German, a Frenchman, a Spaniard, &c. (all the Kings and Princes in Christendom being now in league with our Sovereign, but a Scot being a Subject, cannot be said to be a friend, nor Scotland to be *solum amici*[165]) may by the Common Law have, require, and get within this Realm, by gift, trade, or other lawfull means, any treasure, or goods personal whatsoever, as well as any Englishman, and may maintain any action for the same: But Lands within this Realm, or houses (but for their necessary habitation onely) Alien friends cannot acquire, or get, nor maintain any action real or personal, for any land or house, unless the house be for their necessary habitation. For if they should be disabled to acquire and maintain these things, it were in effect to deny unto them trade and traffique, which is the life of every Island. But if this Alien become an enemy (as all Alien friends may) then is he utterly disabled to maintain any action, or get any thing within this Realm. And this is to be understood of a temporary Alien, that being an enemy may be a friend, or becoming a friend may be an enemy. But a perpetual enemy (though there be no wars by fire and sword between them) cannot maintain any action, or get any thing within this Realm. All Infidels are in Law *perpetui inimici*[166] perpetual enemies (for the Law presumes not that they will be converted, that being *remota potentia,*[167] a remote possibility) for between them, as with the devils, whose subjects they be, and the

[17 b]   Christian, there is perpetual I hostility, and can be no peace; for as the Apostle saith, 2 Cor. 15. *Quae autem conventio Christi ad Belial, aut quae pars fideli cum infideli,* and the Law saith, *Judaeo Christianum nullum serviat mancipium, nefas enim est quem Christus redemit blasphemum Christi in servitutis vinculis detinere.* Register 282. *Infideles sunt Christi et Christianorum inimici.*[168] And

---

164. [*Ed.:* subject.]

165. [*Ed.:* friendly soil.]

166. [*Ed.:* perpetual enemies.]

167. [*Ed.:* a remote possibility.]

168. [*Ed.:* 2 *Corinthians* 6, 15: And what covenant has Christ with Belial? Or what has a believer to do with an infidel?

[And the law says]: No Christian should be sold in slavery to a Jew, for it is unlawful that one whom

herewith agreeth the Book in 12 Hen. 8. fol. 4. where it is holden that a Pagan cannot have or maintain any action at all.

And upon this ground there is a diversity between a conquest of a kingdom of a Christian King, and the conquest of a kingdom of an Infidel; for if a King come to a Christian kingdom by conquest, seeing that he hath *vitae et necis potestatem,*[169] he may at his pleasure alter and change the Laws of that kingdom, but untill he doth make an alteration of those Laws, the ancient Laws of that kingdom remain. But if a Christian King should conquer a kingdom of an Infidel, and bring them under his subjection, there *ipso facto*[170] the Laws of the Infidel are abrogated, for that they be not only against Christianity, but against the Law of God and of Nature, contained in the Decalogue; and in that case, untill certain Laws be established amongst them, the King by himself, and such Judges as he shall appoint, shall judge them and their causes according to natural equity, in such sort as Kings in ancient time did with their kingdoms, before any certain Municipal Laws were given as before hath been said. But if a king have a kingdom by title of descent, there, seeing by the Laws of that kingdom he doth inherit the kingdom, he cannot change those Laws of himself, without consent of Parliament. Also if a king hath a Christian kingdom by conquest, as King Henry the second had Ireland, after King John had given unto them, being under his obedience and subjection, the Laws of England for the government of that country, no succeeding king could alter the same without Parliament. And in that case while the Realm of England and that of Ireland were governed by several Laws, any that was born in Ireland was no Alien to the Realm of England. In which precedent of Ireland three things are to be observed: 1. That then there had been two descents, one from Henry the second to King Richard the first, and from Richard to King John, before the alteration of the Laws. 2. That albeit Ireland was a distinct Dominion, yet the title thereof being by Conquest, the same by judgment of law might by expresse words be bound by the Parliaments of England. 3. That albeit no | reservation were in King John's Charter, yet by judgment of Law a Writ of Error did lye in the king's bench in England, of an erroneous Judgment in the king's bench of Ireland. Furthermore, in the

Margin notes:

By what laws kingdoms gotten by conquest, &c. shall be governed.

Ireland.

[18 a]

Christ has redeemed should be held in the bonds of servitude to someone who blasphemes against Christ.
    [Register, fo. 282:] Infidels are enemies of Christ and of Christians.]
    169. [*Ed.:* power of life and death.]
    170. [*Ed.:* by that fact.]

case of the conquest of a Christian kingdom, as well those that served in Wars at the Conquest, as those that remained at home for the safetie and peace of their country, and other the King's subjects, as well *Antenati* as *Postnati,* are capable of Lands in the kingdom or country conquered, and may maintain any real action, and have the like privileges and benefits there, as they may have in England.

The third kind of enemy is, *inimicus permissus,* an Enemy that cometh into the Realm by the King's safe conduct, of which you may read in the Register fol. 25. Book of Entries, Ejectione Firmae 7, 32 Hen. 6. 23. &c. Now what a Subject born is, appeareth at large by that which hath been said *de ligeantia:* and so likewise *de subdito dato,*[171] of a *donaison;*[172] for that is the right name, so called, because his legitimation is given unto him; for if you derive denizen from *deins nee,*[173] one born within the obedience or ligance of the King, then such a one should be all one with a natural born subject. And it appeareth before out of the laws of King William the First of what antiquity the making of denizens by the King of England hath been.

Of the incidents to an alien. 3. There be regulary (unlesse it be in special cases) three incidents to a subject born. 1. That the parents be under the actual obedience of the king. 2. That the place of his birth be within the king's dominion. And 3. the time of his birth is chiefly to be considered; for he cannot be a subject born of one kingdom, that was born under the ligeance of a king of another kingdom, albeit afterwards one kingdom descend to the king of the other. For the first, it is termed actual obedience, because though the King of England hath absolute right to other kingdoms or dominions, as France, Aquitain, Normandy, &c. yet seeing the King is not in actual possession thereof, none born there since the Crown of England was out of actual possession thereof, are Subjects to the king of England. 2. The place is observable, but so as many times ligeance or obedience without any place within the king's dominions may make a subject born, but any place within the king's dominions may make a subject born, but any place within the king's dominions without obedience can never produce a natural subject. And therefore if any of the king's Ambassadors in forein Nations, have children there of their wives, being English women, by

171. [*Ed.:* a subject by reason of gift.]
172. [*Ed.:* gift.]
173. [*Ed.:* born within [the allegiance].]

the Common Laws of England they are natural born subjects, and yet they are born out of the king's dominions. But if Enemies should come into any of the king's dominions and surprise any Castle or Fort, and I possess the same [18 b] by hostility, and have issue there, that issue is no subject to the king, though he be born within his dominions, for that he was not born under the king's ligeance or obedience. But the time of his birth is of the essence of a subject born; for he cannot be a subject to the king of England, unlesse at the time of his birth he was under the ligeance and obedience of the king. And that is the reason that *Antenati* in Scotland (for that at the time of their birth they were under the ligeance and obedience of another king) are Aliens born, in respect of the time of their birth.

4. It followeth next in course to set down the reasons, wherefore an Alien born is not capable of inheritance within England, and that he is not for three reasons. 1. The secrets of the Realm might thereby be discovered. 2. The revenues of the Realm (the sinews of War, and Ornament of Peace) should be taken and enjoyed by strangers born. 3. It should tend to the destruction of the Realm. Which three reasons do appear in the Statutes of 2 Hen 5. cap. and 4 Hen. 5. cap. ultimo. But it may be demanded, Wherein doth that destruction consist; Whereunto it is answered; First, it tends to destruction *tempore belli;* [174] for then strangers might fortify themselves in the heart of the Realm, and be ready to set fire on the Commonwealth, as was excellently shadowed by the Trojan horse in Virgil's second Book of his Aeneid, where a very few men in the heart of the City, did more mischief in a few hours, than ten thousand men without the walls in ten years. Secondly, *tempore pacis,* [175] for so might many aliens born get a great part of the inheritance and freehold of the Realm, whereof there shall follow a failure of Justice (the supporter of the Commonwealth) for that Aliens born cannot be returned of Juries for the trial of Issues between the king and the subject, or between subject and subject. And for this purpose, and many other see a Charter (worthy of observation) of King Edw. and the third written to Pope Clement, *Datum apud Westm' 26. die Sept. ann. regni nostri Franciae 4 regni vero Angliae 17.* [176]

> Wherefore an alien born is not capable of lands.

---

174. [*Ed.:* in time of war.]

175. [*Ed.:* in time of peace.]

176. [*Ed.:* given at Westminster on the twenty-sixth day of September in the fourth year of our reign of France and in the seventeenth year of our reign of England.]

Examples
and au-
thorities in
law.

5. Now are we come to the Examples, Resolutions, and Judgments of former times; wherein two things are to be observed, First, how many Cases in our Books do over-rule this Case in question for *ubi eadem ratio ibi idem jus, et de similibus idem est judicium.*[177] 2. That for want of an express Text of Law *in terminis terminantibus*[178] and of examples and precedents in like cases (as was objected by some) we are driven to determine the question by natural reason: for it was said, *si cesset lex scripta id custodiri | oportet quod moribus et consuetudine inductum est, et si qua in re hoc defecerit, recurrendum est ad rationem.*[179] But that receiveth a threefold answer: First, that there is no such rule in the Common or Civile Law; but the true rule of the Civile Law is, *Lex scripta si cesset, id custodiri oportet quod moribus et consuetudine inductum est, et si qua in re hoc defecerit, tunc id quod proximum et consequens ei est, et si id non appareat, tunc jus quo urbs Romana utitur, servari oportet.*[180] Secondly, if the said imaginative rule be rightly and legally understood, it may stand for truth: for if you intend *ratio* for the legal and profound reason of such as by diligent study and long experience and observation are so learned in the Laws of this Realm, as out of the reason of the same they can rule the case in question, in that sense the said rule is true: But if it be intended of the reason of the wisest man that professeth not the Laws of England, then (I say) the rule is absurd and dangerous; for *cuilibet in sua arte perito est credendum et quod quisque norit in hoc se exerceat. Et omnes prudentes illa admittere solent quae probantur iis qui in sua arte bene versati sunt,*[181] Arist. 1. Topicorum, cap. 6. Thirdly, there be multitudes of Examples, Precedents, Judgments, and Resolutions in the Laws of England, the true and unstrained reason whereof doth decide this question; for example: the Dukedom of Acquitain, whereof Gascoin was parcel, and the Earldom of Poitiers, came to King Henry the second

[19 a]

---

177. [*Ed.:* where the reason is the same, the law is the same; and where things are similar, the judgment is the same.]

178. [*Ed.:* in terms to be determined.]

179. [*Ed.:* if a written law ceases [to be in force], it is necessary to observe that which has been brought in by usage and custom; and, if that is lacking, recourse may be had to reason.]

180. [*Ed.:* If a written law ceases [to be in force], it is necessary to observe that which has been brought in by usage and custom; and, if that is lacking, then that which is nearest and consequent upon it; and, if that is not apparent, then it behoves to observe the rule used by Roman law.]

181. [*Ed.:* credit is to be given to anyone who is an expert in his craft and therefore in each by how he has practiced [the law]. And all prudent persons are accustomed to admit those things which are approved by those who are well versed in their craft.]

by the marriage of Elianor, daughter and heir of William Duke of Acquitain, and Earl of Poitiers, which descended to Richard the First, Henry the Third, Edward the First, Edward the Second, Edward the Third 3., &c. In 27 lib. Ass. pl. 48. in one case there appear two Judgments and one Resolution to be given by the Judges of both Benches in this case following. The possessions of the Prior of Chelsey in the time of war were seised into the king's hands, for that the Prior was an alien born: The Prior by petition of right sued to the king, and the effect of his Petition was, That before he came Prior of Chelsey, he was Prior of Andover, and whiles he was Prior there, his possessions of that Priory were likewise seised for the same cause, supposing that he was an alien born; whereupon he sued a former petition, and alleged that he was born in Gascoin within the ligeance of the king: which point being put in Issue and found by Jury to be true, it was adjudged he should have restitution of his possessions generally without mentioning of advowsons. After which restitution, one of the | said advowsons became voyd, the Prior presented, [19 b] against whom the king brought a *Quare Impedit*,[182] wherein the king was barred, and all this was contained in the later petition. And the Book saith, that the Earle of Arundel, and Sir Guy de B. came into the Court of Common Pleas, and demanded the opinion of the Judges of that Court concerning the said Case, who resolved, that upon the matter aforesaid the king had no right to seize. In which case, amongst many notable points, this one appeareth to be adjudged and resolved, that a man born in Gascoin under the king's ligeance, was no alien born, as to lands and possessions within the Realm of England, and yet England and Gascoin were several and distinct countries. 2. Inherited by several and distinct titles. 3. Governed by several and distinct Municipal Laws, as it appeareth amongst the Records in the Tower, Rot. Vasc. 10. Edw. 1. Num. 7. 4. Out of the extent of the Great Seal of England, and the jurisdiction of the Chancery of England. 5. The like objection might be made for default of tryal, as hath been made against the Plaintiff. And where it was said that Gascoin was no kingdom, and therefore it was not to be matched to the case in hand, it was answered, that this difference was without a diversity as to the case in question; for if the plea in the case at the Bar be good, then without question the Prior had been an alien; for it might have

---

182. [*Ed.*: Writ to recover a presentation; a real action to determine a disputed title to an advowson, which was the control of the patronage of an ecclesiastical office that controlled land.]

been said, (as it is in the Case at Bar) that he was born *extra ligeantiam regis regni sui Angliae, et infra ligeantiam dominii sui Vasconiae,*[183] and that they were several dominions, and governed by severall Laws: But then such a conceit was not hatched, that a king having several dominions should have several ligeances of his subjects. Secondly, it was answered, that Gascoin was sometime a kingdome, and likewise Millain, Burgundy, Bavaria, Brittain, and others were, and now are become, Dukdoms. Castile, Arragon, Portugal, Barcelona, &c. were sometime Earldoms, afterwards Dukedoms, and now kingdoms. Bohemia and Polonia were sometime dukedoms, and now kingdoms, and (omitting many other, and coming nearer home) Ireland was before 32 Henry the eighth a Lordship, and now is a kingdom, and yet the King of England was as absolute a Prince and Sovereign when he was Lord of Ireland, as now, when he is styled King of the same. 10 Edw. 3. 41. an exchange was made between an Englishman and a Gascoyn, of lands in England and in Gascoin; *ergo,* the Gascoin was no alien, for then had he not been capable of lands in England, 1 Hen. 4. 1. the King brought a Writ of right of ward against one [20 a] Sybill, whose husband was exiled into Gascoin; | *ergo* Gascoin is no parcel or member of England, for *exilium est patriae privatio, natalis soli mutatio, legum nativarum amissio*[184] 4 Edw. 4. 10. the king directed his Writ out of the Chancery under the Great Seal of England, to the Maior of Burdeaux (a city in Gascoin) then being under the king's obedience, to certify, whether one that was outlawed here in England, was at that time in the king's service under him *in obsequio Regis*[185] whereby it appeareth, that the king's Writ did run into Gascoin, for it is the trial that the common Law hath appointed in that case. But as to other cases, it is to be understood, that there be two kinds of Writs, viz. *brevia mandatoria et remedialia, et brevia mandatoria et non remedialia: brevia mandatoria et remedialia,*[186] as Writs of Right, of *Formedon, &c.*[187] of Debt, Trespasse, &c. and shortly, all Writs real and personal, whereby the party wronged is to recover somewhat, and to be remedied for that wrong

183. [*Ed.:* outside the king's allegiance of his realm of England and within the allegiance of his lordship of Gascony.]

184. [*Ed.:* exile is a deprivation of country, a change of native soil, a loss of native laws.]

185. [*Ed.:* in the king's following.]

186. [*Ed.:* mandatory and remedial writs, and mandatory but not remedial writs. Mandatory and remedial writs . . .]

187. [*Ed.:* Writ brought by a person claiming a gift in tail.]

that was offered unto him, are returnable or determinable in some Court of Justice within England, and to be served and executed by the Sheriffs, or other ministers of Justice within England; and these cannot by any means extend into any other kingdom, Country, or Nation, though that it be under the king's actual ligeance and obedience. But the other kind of Writs that are mandatory, and not remedial, are not tyed to any place, but doe follow subjection and ligeance, in what Country or Nation soever the Subject is, as the king's Writ to command any of his subjects residing in any forein Country to return into any of the king's own Dominions, *Sub fide et ligeantia quibus nobis tenemini.*[188] And so are the aforesaid mandatory Writs cited out of the Register of Protection for safety of body and goods, and requiring, that if any injury be offered, that the same be redressed according to the Laws and Customs of that place. *Vide* le Register fol. 26. Stamford Praerog. cap. 12. fol. 39. saith, That men born in Gascoin are inheritable to lands in England. This doth also appear by divers Acts of Parliament: for by the whole Parliament, 39 Edw. 3. cap. 16. it is agreed, that the Gascoins are of the ligeance and subjection of the King. *Vide* 42 Edw. 3. cap. 2. & 28 Hen. 6. cap. 5. &c.

Guyen was another part of Aquitain, and came by the same title: and those of Guyen were by act of Parliament in 13 Hen. 4. not imprinted, *ex Rot. Parliament. eodem anno,*[189] adjudged and declared to be no aliens, but able to possess and purchase, &c. lands within this Realm. And so doth Stamford take the law, praerog. c. 12. f. 39. | And thus much of the Dukedom of Aquitaine, which (together with the Earldom of Poitiers) came to King Henry the second (as hath been said) by marriage, and continued in the actual possession of the Kings of England by ten descents, viz. from the first year of King Henry the second, unto the two and thirtieth year of King Henry the sixth, which was upon the very point of three hundred years, within which Dutchie there were (as some write) 4. Archbishopricks, 24. Bishopricks, 15. Earldoms, 202 Baronies, and above a thousand Captainships and Bailiwicks; and in all this long time, neither book case nor record can be found wherein any plea was offered to disae any of them that were born there, by forein birth, but the contrary hereof directly appeareth by the said book case of 27 lib. Ass. 48.

The Kings of England had sometimes Normandy under actual ligeance and

Marginal notes:
Guyen, Guienne.
[20 b]
Normandy, Normenia, Normandia.

---

188. [*Ed.:* under the faith and allegiance by which you are held to us.]
189. [*Ed.:* from the rolls of the parliament of that year.]

obedience. The question is then, whether men born in Normandy, after one King had them both, were inheritable to lands in England; and it is evident by our books that they were: for so it appeareth by the declaratory act of 17 Edw. 2. de praerog. Regis, c. 12. that they were inheritable to, and capable of lands in England: for the purview of that Statute is *quod Rex habebit escaetas de terris Normannorum, &c.*[190] *ergo* Normans might have lands in England: *et hoc similiter intelligendum est, si aliqua haereditas descendat alicui nato in partibus transmarinis, &c.*[191] Whereby it appeareth, that they were capable of lands within England by descent. And that this Act of 17 Edw. 2. was but a declaration of the Common Law, it appeareth both by Bracton who (as it hath been said) wrote in the reign of Henry the third, lib. 3. tract. 2. c. 1. f. 116. and by Britton who wrote in 5 Edw. 1. c. 18. that all such lands as any Norman had either by descent or purchase, escheated to the King for their treason, in revolting from their natural liege Lord and Sovereign. And therefore Stamford praerog. cap. 12. fol. 39. expounding the said Statute of 17 Edw. 2. cap. 12. concludeth, that by that chapter it should appear (as if he had said, it is apparent without question) that all men born in Normandy, Gascoin, Guyen, Anjou, and Brittain, (whiles they were under actual disobedience) were inheritable within this realm as well as Englishmen. And the reason thereof was, for that they were one ligeance due to one Sovereign. And so much (omitting many other authorities) for Normandy: saving I cannot let passe the Isles of Jernsey and Gersey, parts and parcels of the Dukedom of Normandy, yet remaining under the actual ligeance and obedience of the King. I think no man will

[41 a]

Guernsey and Jesey.

doubt, but those that are | born in Jernsey and Gersey (though those Isles are no parcel of the Realm of England, but several dominions, enjoyed by several titles, governed by several laws) are inheritable and capable of any lands within the Realm of England, 1 Edw. 3. fo. 7. Commission to determine the title of lands within the said Isles, according to the Laws of the Isles: and Mich. 41 E. 3. in the Treasury, *Quia negotium praed' nec aliqua alia negotia de insula praed' emergentia non debent terminari nisi secundum legem insulae praed', &c.*[192]

---

190. [*Ed.*: that the king shall have escheats of Norman lands, etc.]

191. [*Ed.*: and this is likewise to be understood, if any inheritance descends to anyone born in parts beyond the seas, etc.]

192. [*Ed.*: because neither the aforesaid business nor any other business arising from the aforesaid island ought to be determined except in accordance with the law of the aforesaid island, etc.]

And the Register, fol. 22. *Rex fidelibus suis de Jernsey et Gersey.*[193] King William the first brought this Dukedom of Normandy with him, which by five descents continued under the actual obedience of the Kings of England, and in or about the sixth year of King John, the Crown of England lost the actual possession thereof, until King Henry the fifth recovered it again, and left it to King Henry the sixth, who lost it in the 28th year of his reign: wherein were (as some write) one Archbishoprick, and six Bishopricks, and an hundred strong towns and fortresses, besides those that were wasted in warre. Maud the Empresse, the only daughter and heir to Henry the first, took to her second husband Jeffrey Plantaginet, Earl of Anjou, Tourain, and Mayne, who had issue King Henry the second to whom the said Earldom by just title descended, who, and the kings that succeeded him, stiled themselves by the name of *Comes Andeguv,*[194] *&c.* untill King Edward the third became king of all France: and such as were born within that Earldom, so long as it was under the actual obedience of the King of England, were no aliens, but natural born subjects, and never any offer made that we can find to disable them for forein birth. But leave we Normandy and Anjou, and speak we of the little, but yet ancient and absolute kingdom of the Isle of Man, as it appeareth by diverse ancient and authentike records; as taking one for many. Artold King of Man sued to King Henry the third to come into England to conferr with him, and to perform certain things which were due to King Henry the third thereupon King Henry the third 28. *Decemb. ann. regn. sui* 34, at Winchester, by his letters patents gave license to Artold King of Man, as followeth; *Rex omnibus salutem. Sciatis, quod licentiam dedimus, &c. Artoldo Regi de Man veniendo ad nos in Angl', ad loquend' nobisc' et ad faciend' nobis quod facere debet, et ideo vobis mandamus quod ei Regi in veniendo ad nos iu Angl', vel ibi morando, vel inde redeundo nullum faciat' aut fieri permittatis damnum, injur', molestiam, aut gravamen, vel etiam hominib' suis quos secum ducet et si aliquid eis forisfact' fuerit, id eis sine dilat' faciat' emendari. In cujus, &c. duratur' usque ad fest' S. Mich.*[195] Wherein | 2 things are to be observed; 1. That seeing that Artold King

Man,
Mannia.

[21 b]

193. [*Ed.:* The king to his faithful [subjects] of Jersey and Guernsey.]

194. [*Ed.:* Earl of Anjou.]

195. [*Ed.:* The king to all [etc.], greeting. Know ye that we have given licence etc. to Artold, king of Man, to come to us in England to speak with us and to do for us what ought to be done; and therefore we command you that you do not cause, or allow to be caused, any damage, injury, molestation, or grievance,

of Man sued for a licence in this case to the King, it proveth him an absolute King for that a Monarch or an absolute Prince cannot come into England without licence of the King, but any subject being in league, may come into this Realm without licence; 2. That the King in his licence doth stile him by the name of a King. It was resolved in 11 Hen. 8. that where an office was found after the decease of Thomas Earl of Darby, and that he died seised, &c. of the Isle of Man, that the said office was utterly void, for that the Isle of Man, Normandy, Gascoin, &c. were out of the power of the Chancery, and governed by several laws; and yet none will doubt, but those that are born within that Isle, are capable and inheritable of lands within the Realm of England. Wales was sometimes a kingdom, as it appeareth by 19 Hen. 6. fol. 6. and by the act of Parliament of 2 Hen. 5. cap. 6. but whilst it was a kingdom, the same was holden, and within the fee, of the King of England: and this appeareth by our books. Fleta lib. 1. cap. 16. 1 Edw. 3. 14. 8 Edw. 3. 59. 13 Edw. 3. tit. Jurisdict'. 10 Hen. 4. 6. Plow. Com. 368. And in this respect, in divers ancient Charters, Kings of old time styled themselves in several manners, as King Edgar, *Britannia* Βασιλεὺς; *Etheldredus, totius Albionis dei providentia Imperator; Edredus magnae Britanniae monarcha,*[196] which among many other of like nature I have seen. But by the Statute of 12 Edw. 1. Wales was united and incorporated into England, and made parcel of England in possession; and therefore it is ruled in 7 Hen. 4. fol. 1. 4. that no protection doth lie *quia moratur in Wallia,*[197] because Wales is within the realm of England. And where it is recited in the act of 27 H. 8. that Wales was ever parcel of the Realm of England, it is true in this sense, viz. that before 12 E. 1. it was parcel in tenure, and since it is parcel of the body of the Realm. And whosoever is born within the fee of the King of England, though it be in another kingdom, is a natural born subject, and capable and inheritable of lands in England, as it appeareth in Plow. Com. 126. And therefore those that were born in Wales before 12 Edw. 1. whilst it was onely holden of England, were capable and inheritable of lands in England.

Wales, Cambria, Wallia. (margin)

to the same king while coming to us in England, staying there, or returning from thence, nor to his men whom he brings with him, and if any wrong is done to them you are to cause it to be put right without delay. In [witness] whereof, etc.; to last until the feast of St Michael.]

196. [*Ed.:* King; Ethelred, of all Albion the provident Emperor; Edredy great monarch of the Britons.]
197. [*Ed.:* because he is staying in Wales.]

Now come we to France and the members thereof, as Callice, Guynes, France, Gallia, Francia. Tournay, &c. which descended to King Edward the third as son and heir to Isabel, daughter and heir to Philip le Beau, King of France. Certain it is, whiles I King Henry the sixth had both England and the heart and greatest part of [22 a] France under his actual ligeance and obedience (for he was crowned King of France in Paris) that they that were then born in those parts of France, that were under actual ligeance and obedience, were no aliens, but capable of, and inheritable to lands in England. And that is proved by the writs in the Register, fol. 26. cited before. But in the inrolment of Letters Patents of denization in the Exchequer, *int' originalia,*[198] Anno 11 Hen. 6. with the Lord Treasurer's Remembrancer, was strongly urged and objected: for (it was said) thereby it appeareth, that King Henry the sixth in Anno 11 of his reign, did make denizen one Reynel, born in France: Whereunto it was answered, that it is proved by the said Letters Patents, that he was born in France before King Henry the sixth had the actual possession of the Crown of France, so as he was *Antenatus:* and this appeareth by the said Letters Patents, whereby the King granteth, that *Magister Johannes Reynel serviens noster, &c. infra regnum nostrum Franc' oriundus pro termino vitae suae sit ligeus noster, et eodem modo teneatur sicut verus et fidelis noster infra regnum Angl' oriundus, ac quod ipse terras infra regnum nostrum Angl' seu alia dominia nostra perquirere possit et valeat.*[199] Now if that Reynel had been born since Henry the sixth had the quiet possession of France (the King being crowned King of France about one year before) of necessity he must be an infant of very tender age, and then the King would never have called him his servant, nor made the Patent (as thereby may be collected) for his service, nor called him by the name of *Magister Johannes Reynel:* But without question he was *Antenatus,* born before the King had the actual and real possession of that Crown.

Callice [Calais] is a part of the kingdom of France, and never was parcell Calice, Calecia, Caletum. of the kingdom of England, and the kings of England enjoyed Callice in and from the reign of King Edward the third, until the losse thereof in Queen Maries time, by the same title that they had to France. And it is evident by

198. [*Ed.:* amongst the 'originalia' rolls.]

199. [*Ed.:* Master John Reynel, our servant, etc., born within our realm of France, shall be our liege for term of his life, and shall keep himself in the same manner as a true and faithful subject of ours born within the realm of England, and that he may and shall have power to acquire lands within our realm of England or other our dominions.]

our books, that those that were born in Callice, were capable and inheritable to lands in England, 42 Edw. 3. cap. 10. *Vide* 21 Hen. 7. 33. 19 Hen. 6. 2 Edw. 4. 1. 39 Hen. 6. 39. 21 Edw. 4. 18. 28 Hen. 6. 3 b. By all which it is manifest, that Callice being parcel of France, was under the actual obedience and commandment of the King, and by consequent those that were born there, were natural born subjects, and no aliens. Callice from the reign of King Edward the third until the fifth year of Queen Mary, remained under the actual obe-

[22 b]   dience of the king of England. | Guines also, another part of France, was under the like obedience to King Henry the sixth, as appeareth by 32 Hen. 6. fol.

Guynes,   4. And Tournay was under the obedience of Henry the eighth., as it appeareth
Tournay.   by 5 Eliz. Dyer, fol. 224. for there it is resolved, that a bastard born at Tournay, whiles it was under the obedience of Henry the eighth, was a natural subject, as an issue born within this realm by aliens. If then those that were born at Tournay, Callice, &c. whiles they were under the obedience of the king, were natural subjects, and no aliens, it followeth, that when the kingdom of France (whereof those were parcels) was under the king's obedience, that those that were then born there, were natural subjects, and no aliens.

Ireland,   Next followeth Ireland, which originally came to the kings of England by
Hibernia.   conquest but who was the first conqueror thereof, hath been a question. I have seen a Charter made by King Edgar, in these words: *Ego Edgarus Anglorum Βασιλεὺς, omniumque insularum oceani, quae Britanniam circumjacent, Imperator et Dominus, gratias ago ipsi Deo omnipotenti Regi meo, qui meum imperium sic ampliavit et exaltavit super regnum patrum meorum, &c. mihi concessit propitia divinitas, cum Anglorum imperio omnia regna insularum oceani, et cum suis ferocissimis Regibus usque Norvegiam, maximamque partem Hibern', cum sua nobilissima civitate de Dublina, Anglorum regno subjugare, quapropter et ego Christi gloriam et laudem in regno meo exaltare, et ejus servitium amplificare devotus disposui, &c.*[200] Yet for that it was wholly conquered in the reign of Henry the second, the honour of the conquest of Ireland is attributed to him,

200. [*Ed.:* I, Edgar, king of the English, and emperor and lord of all the islands of the ocean which surround Britain, give thanks to the almighty God himself, my king, who has amplified and exalted my power over the realm of my fathers etc. and by whose divine favour it has been granted to me to subjugate with English power all the kingdoms of the islands of the ocean, with their fiercest kings, as far as Norway and the greater part of Ireland (with its most noble city of Dublin), to the English kingdom, on account of which I have arranged to exalt the glory and praise of Christ in my realm, and to amplify his service of devotion, etc.]

and his style was, *Rex Angl' Dominus Hibern' Dux Normann' Dux Acquittan' et Comes Andegav',*[201] King of England, Lord of Ireland, Duke of Normandy, Duke of Aquitain, and Earl of Anjou. That Ireland is a dominion separate and divided from England, it is evident from our books, 20 Hen. 6. 8. *Sir John Pilkington's case.* 32 Hen. 6. 25. 20 Eliz. Dyer 360. Plow. Com. 360. And 2 Rich. 3. 12. *Hibernia habet Parliamentum, et faciunt leges, et nostra statuta non ligant eos, quia non mittunt milites ad Parliamentum* (which is to be understood, unlesse they be especially named) *sed personae eorum sunt subjecti regis, sicut inhabitantes in Calesia, Gasconia, et Guyan.*[202] Wherein it is to be observed, that the Irishman (as to subjection) is compared to men born in Calice, Gascoin, and Guyan. Concerning their Laws, *Ex rotulis patentium de Anno* 11 *Regis Hen. 3.*[203] there is a Charter which that king made, beginning in these words, *Rex, &c., Baronibus, militibus, et omnibus libere tenentibus L. salutem, satis ut credimus* | *vestra audivit discretio, quod quando bonae memoriae*   [23 a] *Johannes quondam Rex Angl' pater noster venit in Hiberniam ipse duxit secum viros discretos et legis peritos, quorum communi consilio et ad instantiam Hibernensium statuit et precepit leges Anglicanas in Hibern' ita quod leges easdem in scripturas redactas reliquit sub sigillo suo ad Scaccarium Dublin'.*[204] So as now the Laws of England became the proper Laws of Ireland; and therefore, because they have Parliaments holden there, whereat they have made divers particular Laws concerning that dominion, as it appeareth in 20 Hen. 6. 8. & 20 Eliz. Dyer 360. and for that they retain unto this day divers of their ancient customs, the book in 20 Hen. 6. 8. holdeth, that Ireland is governed by laws and customs, separate and diverse from the Laws of England. A voyage royal may be made into Ireland. *Vide* 11 Hen. 4. 7. & 7 Edw. 4. 27. which proveth it a distinct Dominion. And in Anno 33 Reg. El. it was resolved by all the Judges of England

201. [*Ed.:* King of the English, Lord of Ireland, Duke of Normandy, Duke of Acquitain, and Count of Anjou.]

202. [*Ed.:* Ireland has a parliament, and they make laws, and our statutes do not bind them because they do not send knights to parliament . . . but their persons are the king's subjects, just as the inhabitants in Calais, Gascony and Guienne.]

203. [*Ed.:* Out of the patent rolls for the eleventh year of King Henry III.]

204. [*Ed.:* The king etc. to the barons, knights, and other free tenants of L., greeting. We believe your discretion has sufficiently heard that when John, our father of good memory, lately king of England, came into Ireland he took with him discerning men who were learned in the law, by whose common advice and at the instance of the Irish he laid down and ordained the English laws in Ireland, so that he left the same laws edited in writing under his seal at the Exchequer in Dublin.]

in the case of Orurke an Irishman, who had committed high Treason in Ireland, that he by the statute of 33 Hen. 8. c. 23. might be indicted, arraigned, and tried for the same in England, according to the purview of that statute: the words of which statute be, *That all Treasons, &c. Committed by any person out of the realm of England, shall be from henceforth inquired of, &c.* And they all resolved (as afterward they did also in *Sir John Perrot's case*) That Ireland was out of the Realm of England, and that Treasons committed there, were to be tried within England by that Statute. In the Statute of 4 Hen. 7. cap. 24. of Fines, provision is made for them that be out of this land, and it is holden in Pl. Com. in *Stowel's case* 375, that he that is in Ireland, is out of this land, and consequently within that proviso. Might not then the like plea be devised as well against any person born in Ireland, as (this is against Calvin that is a *Post-natus*[205]) in Scotland? For the Irishman is born *extra ligeantiam regis regni sui Angl', &c.*[206] which be *verba operativa*[207] in the plea: But all men know, that they are natural born Subjects, and capable of and inheritable to lands in England. Lastly, to conclude this part with Scotland itself; in ancient time part of Scotland (besides Berwick) was within the power and ligeance of the King of England, as it appeareth by our Books 42 Edw. 3. 2. *The Lord Beaumont's case,* 11 Edw. 3. c. 2, &c. and by precedents hereafter mentioned; and that part (though it were under the king of England's ligeance and obe-

[23 b] dience) yet was it governed by the Laws of Scotland. | *Ex rotulis Scotiae,* Anno 11 Edw. 3. amongst the records in the Tower of London. *Rex, &c. Constituimus Rich. Talebot Justiciarium nostrum villae Berwici super Twedam, ac omnium aliarum terrarum nostrarum in partibus Scot', ad faciend' omnia et singula quae ad officium justiciarii pertinent, secundum legem et consuetudinem regni Scot'.*[208] And after Anno 26 Edw. 3. *ex eodem rot. Rex Henrico de Percey, Ricarda de Nevil, &c. Volumus et vobis et alteri vestrum tenore praesentium committimus et mandamus, quod homines nostri de Scot' ad pacem et obedientiam nostram existentes, legibus, libertatibus, et liberis consuetudinibus, quibus ipsi et antecessores sui tempore celebris memoriae Alexandri quondam Regis Scot' rationabiliter usi*

---

205. [*Ed.:* person born after [the union].]

206. [*Ed.:* outside the king's allegiance of his realm of England, etc.]

207. [*Ed.:* operative words.]

208. [*Ed.:* The king, etc. We have constituted Richard Talbot our justice of the vill of Berwick upon Tweed and of all our other lands in the parts of Scotland, to do all and singular the things which belong to the office of a justice according to the law and custom of the realm of Scotland.]

fuerunt, uti ut gaudere deberent, prout in quibusdam indenturis, &c. plenius dicitur contineri.[209] And there is a Writ in the Register 295 a. *Dedimus potestatem recipendi ad fidem et pacem nostram homines de Galloway.*[210] Now the case in 42 Edw. 3. 2. (which was within sixteen years of the said grant, concerning the Lawes in 26 Edw. 3.) ruleth it, That so many as were born in that part of Scotland, that was under the ligeance of the King, were no aliens, but inheritable to lands in England; yet was that part of Scotland in another Kingdome governed by several Lawes, &c. And if they were natural Subjects in that case, when the King of England had but part of Scotland, what reason should there be why those that are born there, when the King hath all Scotland, should not be natural Subjects, and no aliens? So likewise Barwick is no part of England, nor governed by the Lawes of England; and yet they that have been born there, since they were under the obedience of one King, are natural born Subjects, and no aliens, as it appeareth in 15 Rich. 2. cap. 7, &c. *Vide* 19 Hen. 6. 35. & 39 Hen. 6. 39. And yet in all these cases and examples, if this new devised plea had been sufficient, they should have been all aliens against so many judgments, resolutions, authorities, and judicial Precedents in all successions of ages. There were sometimes in England, whiles the Heptarchy lasted, seven several crowned Kings of several and distinct Kingdomes, but in the end the West Saxons got the Monarchy, and all the other Kings melted (as it were) their Crowns to make one imperial Diadem for the King of the West Saxons over all. Now when the whole was under the actual and real ligeance and obedience of one King, were any that were born in any of those several and distinct Kingdomes, aliens one to another? Certainly they being born under the obedience of one King and Sovereign were all natural born subjects, and capable of and inheritable unto any lands in any of the said Kingdomes.

| In the holy History reported by St. Luke, *Ex dictamine spiritus sancti, cap.*   [24 a]
21 *et* 22 *Act. Apostolorum,*[211] it is certain, that St. Paul was a Jew, born in Tarsus,

---

209. [*Ed.:* The king to Henry de Percy, Richard de Nevil, etc., [greeting]. We will and, by the tenor of the presents, we commit and command you and each of you that our men of Scotland, being in peace and in our obedience, ought to use and enjoy the laws, liberties and free customs which they and their ancestors reasonably used in the time of Alexander of celebrated memory, king of Scots, as in certain indentures etc. is said to be more fully contained.]

210. [*Ed.:* We give authority to receive the men of Galloway into our faith and peace.]

211. [*Ed.:* By the word of the Holy Spirit, in chapters 21 and 22 of the Acts of the Apostles.]

a famous City of Cilicia: for it appeareth in the said 21st chapter, 39 verse, by his own words: *Ego homo sum quidem Judaeus a Tarso Ciliciae non ignotae civitatis municeps.*[212] And in the 22d chapter, 3. verse, *Ego sum vir Judaeus natus Tarso Ciliciae, &c.*[213] and then made that excellent Sermon there recorded, which when the Jews heard, the Text saith, verse 22. *Levaverunt vocem suam dicentes, tolle de terra hujusmodi, non enim fas est eum vivere: vociferantibus autem eis et projicientibus vestimenta sua, et pulverem jactantibus in aerem,*[214] Claudius Lysias the popular Tribune, to please this turbulent and profane multitude (though it were utterly against justice and common reason) the Text saith, *Jussit Tribunus induci eum in castra, 2. flagellis caedi, et 3. torqueri eum (quid ita?) ut sciret propter quam causam sic acclamarent:*[215] and when they had bound Paul with cords, ready to execute the Tribune's unjust commandment, the blessed Apostle (to avoid unlawfull and sharp punishment) took hold of the law of a heathen Emperour, and said to the Centurion standing by him, *Si hominem Romanum et indemnatum licet vobis flagellare?*[216] Which when the Centurion heard, he went to the Tribune and said, *Quid acturus es? Hic enim homo civis Romanus est.*[217] Then came the Tribune to Paul, and said unto him: *Dic mihi si tu Romanus es? At ille dixit, etiam.*[218] And the Tribune answered, *Ego multa summa civitatem hanc consequutus sum.*[219] But Paul not meaning to conceal the dignity of his birth-right, said, *Ego autem et natus sum:*[220] as if he should have said to the Tribune, you have your freedom by purchase of money, and I (by a more noble means) by birth-right and inheritance. *Protinus ergo* (saith the text) *decesserunt ab illo qui illum torturi erant. Tribunus quoque timuit postquam rescivit, quia civis Romanus esset, et quia alligasset eum.*[221] So

212. [*Ed.:* I am a man, a certain Jew of Tarsus in Cilicia, a free citizen of no mean city.]

213. [*Ed.:* I am a man, a Jew born in Tarsus in Cilicia, etc.]

214. [*Ed.:* They raised their voices, saying, 'Take him from this earth, he is not fit to live,' shouting and casting off their clothes and throwing dust in the air.]

215. [*Ed.:* the tribune ordered him to be put in a fortress, and examined with whipping and torture, in order to know the reason why they cried out against him.]

216. [*Ed.:* If he is a Roman and uncondemned, is it lawful for you to whip him?]

217. [*Ed.:* Take heed what you do. For this man is a Roman citizen.]

218. [*Ed.:* Tell me if you are a Roman. And he said, 'Yes'.]

219. [*Ed.:* I obtained my citizenship (freedom of the city) with a great sum.]

220. [*Ed.:* But I was born so.]

221. [*Ed.:* Then forthwith those who were about to torture him departed; and the tribune also was afraid, after he knew that he was a Roman, because he had tied him up.]

as hereby it is manifest, that Paul was a Jew, born at Tarsus in Cilicia, in Asia Minor, and yet being born under the obedience of the Roman Emperour, he was by birth a citizen of Rome in Italy in Europe that is, capable of and inheritable to all privileges and immunities of that city. But such a plea as is now imagined against Calvin might have made St. Paul an Alien to Rome. For if the Emperour of Rome had several ligeances for every several Kingdome and Countrey under his obedience, then might it have been said against St. Paul, that he was *extra | ligeantiam Imperatoris regni sui Italiae, et infra li-*   [24 b] *geantiam Imperatoris regni sui Ciliciae, &c.*[222] But as Saint Paul was *Judaeus patria et Romanus privilegio, Judaeus natione et Romanus jure nationum;*[223] so may Calvin say, that he is *Scotus patriae et Anglus privilegio; Scotus natione, et Anglus jure nationum.*[224]

Samaria in Syria was the chief City of the ten Tribes: but it being usurped by the king of Syria, and the Jews taken prisoners, and carried away in captivity, was after inhabited by the Panyms. Now albeit Samaria of right belonged to Jurie, yet because the people of Samaria were not under actual obedience, by the judgment of the chief Justice of the whole world they were adjudged *Alienigenae,* Aliens: For in the Evangelist St. Luke, c. 17. when Christ had cleansed the ten Lepers, *Unus autem ex illis* (saith the Text) *ut vidit quia mundatus esset, regressus est, cum magna voce magnificans Deum, et cecidit in faciem ante pedes ejus gratias agens, et hic erat Samaritanus. Et Jesus respondens dixit, Nonne decem mundati sunt, et novem ubi sunt? Non est inventus qui rediret et daret gloriam Deo nisi hic alienigena.*[225] So as by his judgment this Samaritan was *Alienigena,* a Stranger born, because he had the place, but wanted obedience. *Et si desit obedientia non adjuvet locus.*[226] And this agreeth with the Divine, who saith, *Si locus salvare potuisset, Satan de coelo pro sua inobedientia*

222. [*Ed.:* outside the emperor's allegiance of his realm of Italy, and within the emperor's allegiance of his realm of Cilicia, etc.]

223. [*Ed.:* A Jew by country and a Roman by privilege, a Jew by birth and a Roman by the law of nations.]

224. [*Ed.:* A Scot by country and an Englishman by privilege.]

225. [*Ed.:* And one of them, when he saw that he was healed, went back and with a loud voice glorified God, and fell down on his face at his feet, giving him thanks: and he was a Samaritan. And Jesus answering said, 'Were there not ten that were cleansed? Where are the other nine? None of them is found to come back and give glory to God except this foreigner.']

226. [*Ed.:* And, if obedience is lacking, the place does not help.]

non cecidisset. Adam in paradiso non cecidisset, Lot in monte non cecidisset, sed potius in Sodom.[227]

6. Now resteth the sixth part of this division, that is to say, six demonstrative illations, or conclusions, drawn plainly and expressly from the premises.

1. Every one that is an Alien by birth, may be, or might have been, an enemy by accident; but Calvin could never at any time be an enemy by any accident; *ergo* he cannot be an alien by birth. *Vide* 33 Hen. 6. fol. 1. the difference between an alien enemy and a subject traytor. *Hostes sunt qui nobis, vel quibus nos bellum decernimus, caeteri proditores, praedones, &c.*[228] The *major* is apparent, and is proved by that which hath been said. *Et vide* Magna Charta, cap. 30. 19 Edw. 4. 6. 9 Edw. 3. c. 1. 27 Edw. 3. c. 2. 4 Hen. 5. c. 7. 14 Edw. 3. stat. 2. c. 2. &c.

2. Whosoever are born under one natural ligeance and obedience, due by the Law of Nature to one Sovereign are natural born Subjects: But Calvin was born under one natural ligeance and obedience, due by the Law of Nature to one Sovereign; *ergo* he is a natural born subject.

[25 a] | 3. Whosoever is born within the King's power or protection, is no Alien: But Calvin was born under the King's power and protection; *ergo* he is no Alien.

4. Every stranger born must at his birth be either *amicus*,[229] or *inimicus:*[230] But Calvin at his birth could neither be *amicus* nor *inimicus; ergo* he is no stranger born. *Inimicus* he cannot be, because he is *subditus,* and for that cause also he cannot be *amicus;* neither now can *Scotia* be said to be *solum amici,*[231] as hath been said.

5. Whatsoever is due by the law or constitution of man, may be altered: But natural ligeance or obedience of the subject to the Sovereign cannot be altered; *ergo* natural ligeance or obedience to the Sovereign is not due by the law or constitution of man. Again, whatsoever is due by the Law of Nature, cannot be altered: But ligeance and obedience of the subject to the Sovereign is due by the law of Nature; *ergo* it cannot be altered. It hath been proved before, that ligeance or obedience of the inferior to the superior, of the subject

---

227. [*Ed.:* If the place could save, Satan would not have fallen from heaven for his disobedience, Adam would not have fallen in paradise, Lot would not have fallen on the mountain but rather in Sodom.]

228. [*Ed.:* Enemies are those who wage war with us; others are traitors, robbers, etc.]

229. [*Ed.:* friend.]

230. [*Ed.:* enemy.]

231. [*Ed.:* friendly territory.]

to the Sovereign, was due by the Law of Nature many thousand years before any Law of man was made: Which ligeance or obedience (being the onely mark to distinguish a subject from an alien) could not be altered; therefore it remaineth still due by the Law of Nature. For *Leges naturae perfectissimae sunt et immutabiles, humani vero juris conditio semper in infinitum decurrit, et nihil est in eo quod perpetuo stare possit. Leges humanae nascuntur, vivunt, moriuntur.*[232]

Lastly, whosoever at his birth cannot be an alien to the King of England, cannot be an alien to any of his subjects of England: But the Plaintiff at his birth could be no alien to the king of England; *ergo* the Plaintiff cannot be an alien to any of the subjects of England. The *major* and *minor* both be *propositiones perspicue verae.*[233] For as to the *major* it is to be observed, that whosoever is an alien born, is so accounted in Law in respect of the King: And that appeareth first by the pleading so often before remembered, that he must be *extra ligeantiam Regis,* without any mention making of the subject. 2. When an alien born purchaseth any lands, the King onely shall have them, though they be holden of a subject, in which case the subject loseth his Seigniorie. And as it is said in our Books, an Alien may purchase *ad proficuum Regis;*[234] but the act of Law giveth the alien nothing: And therefore if a woman alien marrieth a subject, she shall not be endowed, neither shall an alien be tenant by the courtesy. *Vide* 3 Hen. 6. 55. 4 Hen. 3. 179. 3. The subject shall plead, that the defendant is an | alien born, for the benefit of the king, that [25 b] he upon office found may seize, and 2. that the Tenant may yield to the King the land, and not to the alien, because the king hath best right thereunto. 4. Leagues between our Sovereign and others are the onely means to make aliens friends, *et foedera percutere,*[235] to make Leagues, onely and wholly pertaineth to the king. 5. Wars do make aliens enemies, and *bellum indicere*[236] belongeth onely and wholly to the king, and not to the subject, as appeareth in 19 Edw. 4. fol. 6. 6. The King onely without the subject may make not onely Letters

---

232. [*Ed.:* The laws of nature are most perfect and immutable, whereas the condition of human law always runs into the infinite and there is nothing in them which can stand for ever. Human laws are born, live, and die.]

233. [*Ed.:* propositions of obvious truth.]

234. [*Ed.:* to the king's profit.]

235. [*Ed.:* and make treaties.]

236. [*Ed.:* proclaiming war.]

of Safe conduct, but Letters Patents of Denization, to whom, and how many he will, and enable them at his pleasure to sue any of his Subjects in any action whatsoever, real or personal, which the king could not doe without the subject, if the subject had any interest given unto him by the Law in any thing concerning an alien born. Nay, the Law is more precise herein than in number of other cases, of higher nature: for the king cannot grant to any other to make of strangers born, denizens, it is by the Law itself so inseparably and individually annexed to his royal person (as the book is in 20 Hen. 7. fol. 8.) For the Law esteemeth it a point of high Prerogative, *Jus majestatis, et inter insignia summae potestatis*[237] to make aliens born subjects of the Realm, and capable of the lands and inheritances of England, in such sort as any natural born subject is. And therefore by the Statute of 27 Hen. 8. cap. 24. many of the most ancient Prerogatives and royal Flowers of the Crown, as authority to pardon Treason, Murther, Manslaughter, and Felony, power to make Justices in Eyre, Justices of Assise, Justices of Peace and Gaol Delivery, and such like, having been severed and divided from the Crown, were again reunited to the same: But authority to make Letters of Denization, was never mentioned therein to be resumed, for that never any claimed the same by any pretext whatsoever, being a matter of so high a point of Prerogative. So as the pleading against an alien, the purchase by an alien, leagues and wars between aliens, denizations, and safeconducts of aliens, have aspect onely and wholly unto the king. It followeth therefore, that no man can be alien to the subject that is not an alien to the king, *Non potest esse alienigena corpori, qui non est capiti, non gregi qui non est Regi.*[238]

   The authorities of Law cited in this case for maintenance of the Judgment, 4 Hen. 3. tit. Dower. Bracton lib. 5. fol. 427. Fleta, lib. 6. cap. 47. *In temps* E. 1. Hingham's Report. 17 Edw. 2. cap. 12. 11 Edw. 3. | cap. 2. 14 Edw. 3 Statut. de Franciââ. 42 Edw. 3. fol. 2. 42 Edw. 3. cap. 10. 22 Lib. Ass. 25. 13 Rich. 2. cap. 2. 15 Rich. 2. cap. 7. 11 Hen. 4 fol. 19 13 Hen. 4. fol. 26. 14 Hen. 4. fol. 19. 13 Hen. 4. Statutum de Guyan. 29 Hen. 6. tit. Estoppel 48. 28 Hen. 6. cap. 5. 32 Hen. 6. fol. 23. 32 Hen. 6. fol. 26. Littl. *temps* Edw. 4. lib. 2. cap. Villenage. 15 Edw. 4. fol. 15. 19 Edw. 4. 6. 22 Edw. 4. cap. 8. 2 Rich. 3. 2. and

[26 a]

---

237. [*Ed.:* A right of majesty, and among the ensigns of the highest power.]

238. [*Ed.:* One cannot be an alien to the body who is not so to the head, an alien to the people who is not so to the king.]

12. 6 Hen. 8. fol. 2. Dyer. 14 Hen. 8. cap. 2. No manner of stranger born out
of the King's obeysance, 22 Hen. 8. cap. 2. Every person born out of the Realm
of England, out of the King's obeysance, 32 Hen. 8. cap. 16. 25 Hen. 8. cap.
15, &c. 4 Ed. 6. Plowd. Comment. fol. 2. *Fogasse's* case. 2 and 3 Phil. and Mar.
Dyer 145. *Shirley's* case. 5 Eliz. Dyer 224. 13 Eliz. cap. 7. de Bankrupts. All
Commissions ancient and late, for the finding of offices, to entitle the King
to the lands of the Aliens born: Also all Letters Patents of Denization of ancient
and later times do prove, That he is no alien that is born under the king's
obedience.

Now we are come to consider of legal inconveniences: And first of such as
have been objected against the Plaintiff, and, secondly of such as should follow,
if it had been adjudged against the Plaintiff.

The 5th
general
part con-
cerning
inconve-
niences.

Of such inconveniences as were objected against the Plaintiff, there remain
onely four to be answered; for all the rest are clearly and fully satisfied before:
1. That if *Postnati* should be inheritable to our laws and inheritances, it were
reason that they should be bound by our Laws; but *Postnati* are not bound
by our Statute or Common Laws; for they having (as it was objected) never
so much freehold or inheritance, cannot be returned of Juries, nor subject to
scot or lot, nor chargeable to Subsidies or Quinzimes, nor bound by any Act
of Parliament made in England. 2. Whether one be born within the kingdom
of Scotland, or no, is not tryable in England, for that it is a thing done out
of this Realm, and no Jury can be returned for the tryal of any such Issue:
And what inconvenience should thereof follow, if such pleas that wanted tryal
should be allowed (for then all aliens might imagine the like plea) they that
objected it, left it to the consideration of others. 3. It was objected, that this
Innovation was so dangerous, that the certain event thereof no man could
foresee, and therefore some thought it fit, that things should stand and continue as they had been in former time, for fear of the worst. 4. If *Postnati* were
by Law legitimated in England, it was objected what inconvenience and con-
fusion should | follow, if (for the punishment of us all) the King's royal Issue
should faile, &c. whereby those kingdomes might again be divided. All the
other arguments and objections that have been made, have been answered
before, and need not to be repeated again.

[26 b]

1. To the first it was resolved, That the cause of this doubt was the mistaking
of the Law: For if a *Postnatus* do purchase any lands in England, he shall be
subject in respect thereof, not onely to the Laws of this Realm, but also to all
services and contributions, and to the payment of Subsidies, Taxes, and pub-

lique charges, as any Denizen or Englishman shall be; nay, if he dwell in England, the King may command him by a Writ of *Ne exeat Regnum,*[239] that he depart not out of England. But if a *Postnatus* dwell in Scotland, and have lands in England, he shall be chargeable for the same to all intents and purposes, as if an Englishman were owner thereof, and dwelt in Scotland, Ireland, in the Isles of Man, Jernsey, or Gersey, or elsewhere. The same Law is of an Irishman that dwells in Ireland, and hath land in England. But if *Postnati,* or Irishmen, men of the Isles of Man, Jernsey, Gersey, &c. have lands within England, and dwell here, they shall be subject to all services and publique charges within this Realm, as any Englishman shall be. So as to services and charges, the *Postnati* and Englishmen born are all in one predicament.

2. Concerning the tryal, a threefold answer was thereunto made and resolved. 1. That the like objection might be made against Irishmen, Gascoins, Normans, men of the Isles of Man, Jernsey, and Gersey, of Berwick, &c. all which appear by the rule of our books to be natural born subjects; and yet no Jury can come out of any of those countries or places, for trial of their births there. 2. If the demandant or plaintiff in any action concerning lands be born in Ireland, Jernsey, Gersey, &c. out of the Realm of England, if the tenant or defendant plead, that he was born out of the ligeance of the king, &c. the demandant or plaintiff may reply, that he was born under the ligeance of the King at such place within England; and upon the evidence the place shall not be material, but only the Issue shall be, whether the demandant or plaintiff were born under the ligeance of the King in any of his kingdoms or dominions soever; And in that case the Jury (if they will) may find the special matter, viz. the place where he was born, and leave it to the judgment of the [27 a] Court: and that Jurors may take knowledge of things done I out of the Realm in this and like cases, *vide* 7 Hen. 7. 8. b. 20 Edw. 3. Averment 34. 5 Ric. 2. tit. Trial 54. 15 Edw. 4. 15. 32 Hen. 6. 25. Fitz. Nat. Br. 196. *Vid Dowdales* case in the sixth part of my Reports, fol. 47. and there divers other judgments be vouched. 3. Brown in Anno 32 Hen. 6. reporteth a Judgment then lately given, that where the defendant pleaded, That the plaintiff was a Scot, born at St. John's Town in Scotland, out of the ligeance of the King; whereupon they were at Issue, and that Issue was tried where the Writ was brought, and that

---

239. [*Ed.:* Literally, "that he should not leave the realm," a writ issued in chancery forbidding travel out of the kingdom without leave of the King or a court.]

appeareth also by 27 Ass. pl. 24. that the Jury did find the Prior to be born in Gascoin: for so much is necessarily proved by the words *trove fuit*[240] And 20 Ed. 3. tit. Averment 34. in a *juris utrum*,[241] the death of one of the vouchees was alleged at such a Castle in Britain, and this was inquired of by the Jury: And it is holden in 5 Rich. 2. tit. Trial 54. That if a man be adhering to the enemies of the King in France, his Land is forfeitable, and his adherency shall be tried where the land is, as oftentimes hath been done, as there it is said by Belknap: And Fitz. Nat. Bre. 196 in a *Mortdanc*,[242] if the ancestor died *in intinere peregrinationis sum vers. Terram sanctam*[243] the Jury shall inquire of it. But in the case at barr, seeing the Defendant hath pleaded the truth of the case, and the Plaintiff hath not denied it, but demurred upon the same, and thereby confessed all matters of fact, the Court now ought to judge upon the especial matter, even as if a Jury upon an issue joyned in England, as it is aforesaid, had found the especial matter, and left it to the Court.

3. To the third it was answered and resolved, That this judgment was rather a renovation of the judgments and censures of the reverend Judges and Sages of the law in so many ages past, than any innovation, as it appeareth by the books and book cases before recited: neither have Judges power to judge according to that which they think to be fit, but that which out of the laws they know to be right and consonant to law. *Judex bonus nihil ex arbitrio suo faciat, nec proposito domesticae voluntatis, sed juxta leges et jura pronuntiat.*[244] And as for *timores*,[245] fears grounded upon no just cause, *Qui non cadunt in constantem virum, vani timores aestimandi sunt.*[246]

4. And as to the fourth, it is less than a dream of a shadow, or a shadow of a dream: for it hath been often said, Natural legitimation respecteth actual obedience to the Sovereign at the time of the birth: for as the *Antenati* remain aliens as to the Crown of England, because they were born when there were

---

240. [*Ed.:* it was found.]

241. [*Ed.:* Writ by which the incumbent holder of an interest in lands of the Church seeks recovery of that interest from another.]

242. [*Ed.:* Mort'd ancestor, a writ to recover real property lost at the death of an ancestor.]

243. [*Ed.:* in going on his pilgrimage to the Holy Land.]

244. [*Ed.:* A good judge does nothing by his own whim, nor by the suggestion of his own will, but pronounces according to statutes and laws [*leges et jura*].]

245. [*Ed.:* fears.]

246. [*Ed.:* Fears are to be accounted trifling if they would not operate upon a constant man.]

[27 b] several Kings of the several kingdoms, and the | uniting of the kingdoms by descent subsequent, cannot make him a Subject to that Crown to which he was an alien at the time of his birth: So albeit the kingdoms (which Almighty God of his infinite goodness and mercy divert) should by descent be divided, and governed by several Kings; yet it was resolved, That all those that were born under one natural obedience, whiles the Realms were united under one Sovereign, should remain natural born Subjects, and no aliens; for that naturalization due and vested by birthright, cannot by any separation of the Crowns afterward be taken away: nor he that was by judgment of Law a natural Subject at the time of his birth, become an alien by such a matter *ex post facto*. And in that case, upon such an accident, our *Postnatus* may be *ad fidem utriusque Regis,*[247] as Bracton saith in the afore remembered place, fol. 427. *Sicut Anglicus non auditur in placitando aliquem de terris et tenement, in Francia ita nec debet Francigena et alienigena, qui fuerit ad fidem Regis Franciae, audiri placitando in Angiui: sed tamen sunt aliqui Francigenae in Francia qui sunt ad fidem utriusque: et semper fuerunt ante Normaniam deper ditam et post, et qui placitant hic et ibi, ea ratione qua sunt ad fidem utriusque, sicut fuit Willielmus comes mareschallus et manens Angiui, et M. de Gynes manens in Francia, et alli plures.*[248] Concerning the reason drawn from the Etymologies, it made against them, for that by their own derivation, *alienae gentis*[249] and *alienae ligeantiae*[250] is all one: But arguments drawn from Etymologies, are too weak and too light for Judges to build their judgments upon: for *Saepenumero ubi proprietas verborum attenditur, sensus veritatis amittitur:*[251] and yet when they agree with the Judgment of Law, Judges may use them for ornaments. But on the other side, some inconveniences should follow, if the plea against the Plaintiff should be allowed: for first it maketh Ligeance local: *videlicet, Ligeantia Regis regni*

247. [*Ed.:* in the allegiance (literally, "to the faith") of either king.]

248. [*Ed.:* Just as an Englishman shall not be heard to implead anyone for lands and tenements in France, so should not a Frenchman and an alien born, who owes allegiance to [lit. is to the faith of] the king of France, be heard to plead in England; yet there are some Frenchmen in France who owe allegiance to both kings, and always did, both before the loss of Normandy and after, and who plead here and over there, by reason that they owe allegiance to both, as was William, earl marshal, living in England, and M. de Gynes, living in France, and many others.]

249. [*Ed.:* of foreign birth.]

250. [*Ed.:* of foreign allegiance.]

251. [*Ed.:* Often where the precise meaning of words is attended to, the true sense is lost.]

sui Scotiae, and *Ligeantia Regis regni sui Angliae:*[252] whereupon should follow, First, That faith or ligeance, which is universal, should be confined within locall limits and bounds; Secondly, That the Subject should not be bound to serve the King in peace or in warre out of those limits; Thirdly, it should illegitimate many, and some of noble blood, which were born in Gascoign, Guyen, Normandie, Callice, Tournay, France, and divers other of his Majesties Dominions, whiles the same were in actual | obedience, and in Berwick, Ire- [28 a]
land, Jernsey, and Gersey, if this plea should have been admitted for good. And thirdly, this strange and new devised plea inclineth too much to countenance that dangerous and desperate error of the Spencers, touched before, to receive any allowance within Westminster Hall.

In the proceeding of this case, these things were observed, and so did the chief Justice of the Common pleas publiquely deliver in the end of his argument in the Exchequer Chamber. First, That no commandment or messuage by word or writing was sent or delivered from any whatsoever to any of the Judges, to cause them to incline to any opinion in this case: which I remember, for that it is honourable for the State, and consonant to the Laws and Statutes of this Realm. Secondly, there was observed, what a concurrence of Judgments, Resolutions, and Rules, there be in our books in all ages concerning this case, as if they had been prepared for the deciding of the question of this point: and that (which never fell out in any doubtfull case) no one opinion in all our books is against this judgment. Thirdly, That the five Judges of the King's Bench, who adjourned this case into the Exchequer Chamber, rather adjourned it for weight than for difficulty, for all they in their arguments *una voce*[253] concurred with the judgment. Fourthly, That never any case was adjudged in the Exchequer Chamber with greater concordance and lesse variety of opinions, the Lord Chancellor and twelve of the Judges concurring in one opinion. Fifthly, That there was not in any remembrance so honourable, great, and intelligent an auditory at the hearing of the arguments of any Exchequer Chamber case, as was at this case now adjudged. Sixthly it appeareth, that *Jurisprudentia legis communis Angliae est scientia socialis et copiosa:*[254] so-

---

252. [*Ed.:* namely, the King's allegiance of his realm of Scotland, [and] the King's allegiance of his realm of England.]

253. [*Ed.:* with one voice.]

254. [*Ed.:* The jurisprudence of the common law of England is a sociable and a copious science.]

ciable, in that it agreeth with the principles and rules of other excellent Sciences, divine and human: copious, for that *quamvis ad ea quae frequentius accidunt jura adaptantur*,[255] yet in a case so rare, and of such a quality, that losse is the assured end of the practice of it (for no alien can purchase lands, but he loseth them; and *ipso facto* the King is entitled thereunto, in respect whereof a man would think few men would attempt it) there should be such a multitude and *farrago* of authorities in all successions of ages, in our books and book cases, for the deciding of a point of so rare an accident. *Et sic determinata et terminata est ista quaestio.*[256]

     | *The Judgment in the said Case, as entered on Record, &c.*

"Whereupon all and singular the premises being seen, and by the Court of the Lord the now King here diligently inspected and examined, and mature deliberation being had thereof; for that it appears to the Court of the Lord the now King here, that the aforesaid plea of the said Richard Smith and Nicholas Smith above pleaded, is not sufficient in law to bar the said Robert Calvin from having an answer to his aforesaid writ: therefore it is considered by the Court of the lord the now King here, that the aforesaid Richard Smith and Nicholas Smith to the writ of the said Robert do further answer."

The Case of Swans.
(1592) Trinity Term, 34 Elizabeth I
Before the Queen's Commissioners.
First Published in the *Reports*, volume 7, page 15b.

Ed.: Joan Young and Thomas Saunger received a writ from the Exchequer, directing the sheriff of Dorset to round up 400 loose swans from the rivers of the county. Swans are Royal fowl, however, and a wild swan is the property of the monarch. The right to these swans in Dorset was once held by the local abbot, who lost the right along with the abbey to Henry VIII at the dissolution. Henry then granted the estate to Giles Strangeways, whose heir gave them a right to the swans for one year. The question is whether

---

255. [*Ed.:* although the laws are adapted to those things that more frequently happen.]
256. [*Ed.:* And thus is this question determined and ended.]

the swans were Strangeways's or remained the Queen's. Coke, as Solicitor General, represented the Queen. The Court held that the swans that are *ferae naturae,* or wild animals, cannot be given by transfer or taken by prescription.

Between the Queen, and the Lady Joan Young, late the wife of Sir John Young Knight deceased and Thomas Saunger defendants, the Case was such. An Office was found at W. in the County of Dorset, 18th of September Ann. 32 Eliz. before Sir Matthew Arundel and other Commissioners of the Queen under the great Seal, *Quod a villa de Abbotsbury, in praed' com' Dorset, usque ad mare per insulam de Portland in eodem Com' est quaedam aestuaria, Anglicè* a Mere or Fleet, *in quam mare fluit et refluit, in qua quidem aestuaria sunt* 500 *cigni, quorum* 410. *sunt albi, et* 90 *cignetti, et quod omnes praedicti cigni et cignetti sunt in possessione J. Young & Tho. Saunger, & quod quilibet eorum est valoris* 2s. 6d. *quodque major pars tempore captionis dictae inquisitionis minime fuer' signat':*[1] which Office being certified into the Exchequer, a writ was directed to the Sheriff of the same County to seise all the said white Swans not marked, by force whereof the Sheriff returned, that he had seised 400 white Swans, &c. To which afterwards, Hil. 34 Eliz. the said | Joan Young and   [16 a] Thomas Saunger pleaded; *Quod praedict' aestuaria sive aqua, jacet in paroch' de Abbotsbury in Com. Dorset*[2] (and abutted it) and that before the Inquisition taken, the Abbot of Abbotsbury was seised *de praed' aestuaria, et de ripis et solo ejusdem*[3] in fee, and that at the time of the inquisition, and time out of mind, *fuit et adhuc est quidam volatus cignorum et cignettor' feror', vocat'* a game of wild swans, &c. *in aestuaria sive aqua illa, et ripis, et solo ejusdem nidificant', gignen' et frequentant' Anglice* haunting, *de quo quidem volatu cignor' et cignettor' praed' abbas et omnes praedecessores sui Abbates Monasterii praed', per totum tempus praedict' habuere et gavisi fuerunt, et habere et gaudere consueverunt, tot'*

1. [*Ed.:* that from the vill of Abbotsbury in the aforesaid county of Dorset as far as the sea, by the island of Portland in the same county, there is a certain estuary, called in English a 'mere' or 'fleet', in which the sea ebbs and flows, in which estuary there are five hundred swans, whereof four hundred and ten are white and ninety are cygnets, and that all the aforesaid swans and cygnets are in the possession of Joan Young and Thomas Saunger, and that each of them is worth two shillings and sixpence, and that the greater part of them at the time of the taking of this inquisition were unmarked.]

2. [*Ed.:* That the aforesaid estuary or water lies in the parish of Abbotsbury in the county of Dorset.]

3. [*Ed.:* of the aforesaid estuary and of the banks and soil of the same.]

profic' et increment' omnium et singulor' cignor' et cignettor' feror', in aestuaria praed' nidificant', gignen' et frequent' qui quidem cigni et cignetti per totum tempus praed' fuerunt ferae naturae, et infra idem tempus iidem cigni et cignetti seu eorum aliqui aliquo signo non usi fuissent, nec consuevissent signari, nisi quod praed' nuper Abbas et praedecessores sui praed' per totum tempus praed' ad eorum libitum quosd' seu aliquos de minorib' cignettis annuatim pullulant' quos ad usum et culinae et hospitalitatis suae statuerunt expendend', in hunc modum annuatim signare consueverunt, et usi fuerunt viz. amputare mediam juncturam unius alae, Anglice, to cut off the pinion of one wing, *cujuslibet talis cignetti, ea intentione, quod cignetti sic amputati minime valerent avolare.*[4] And afterwards the Abbot surrendered the premises to King Henry the eighth who *anno* 35 of his Reign granted to Giles Strangways, Esq. by his Letters Patent *inter alia, totam illam liberam Piscariam nostr' in aqua, vocat'* the Fleet Abbotsbury *praed', ac omnia messuag', aquas, piscat' et caetera haereditam' nostr' quaecunque in Abbotsbury, in dict' Com' Dorset dict' nuper Monasterio, &c. adeo plene et integre, &c. et in tam amplis modo et forma &c.*[5] and that the said Giles died, and that the same descended to Giles Strangways his Cousin and heir, who demised to the Defendants the said Game of swans for one year, &c. and prayed *quod manus dictae dominae Reginae amoveantur.*[6] Upon which the Queen's Attorney did demur in the law.

---

4. [*Ed.:* there was and still is a certain flock of wild swans and cygnets called 'a game of wild swans' in that estuary or water, nesting, breeding and congregating— in English 'haunting'—in the banks and soil of the same, of which same game of swans and cygnets the aforesaid abbot and all his predecessors, as abbots of the aforesaid monastery, for the whole time aforesaid, have had and enjoyed and have been accustomed to have and enjoy all the profit and gain of all and singular the wild swans and cygnets nesting, breeding and haunting in the estuary aforesaid, which swans and cygnets for the whole time aforesaid were *ferae naturae* (of a wild nature), and within the same time neither the same swans and cygnets nor any of them were used or accustomed to be marked with any mark, save that the aforesaid late abbot and his aforesaid predecessors for the whole time aforesaid have been accustomed annually to mark at their free pleasure some of the smaller cygnets coming forth each year which were to be spent in his kitchen and hospitality, in this manner, namely to amputate the middle joint of one wing—in English 'to cut off the pinion of one wing'—of every such cygnet, with the intention that the cygnets so amputated should not be able to fly away.]

5. [*Ed.:* amongst other things, all that our free fishery in the water called 'the fleet' in Abbotsbury aforesaid, and all messuages, waters, fisheries and other our hereditaments whatsoever in Abbotsbury in the said county of Dorset [belonging] to the said late monastery etc., as plainly and fully etc. and in as ample a manner and form, etc.]

6. [*Ed.:* that the hands of the lady queen be ousted.]

1. It was Resolved, That all white Swans not marked, which having gained their natural liberty, and are swimming in an open and common River, might be seised to the King's use by his prerogative, because that *Volatilia, (quae sunt ferae naturae) alia sunt regalia, alia communia:* and so *Aquatilium, alia sunt regalia, alia communia:*[7] as a Swan is a Royal fowl; and all those, the property whereof is not known, do belong to the King by his prerogative: and so Whales and Sturgeons are Royal Fishes, and belong to the King by his Prerogative. And there hath been an ancient Officer of the King's, called *Magister deductus cignorum,*[8] | which continueth to this day. But it was Resolved also, That the [16 b] subject might have property in white Swans not marked, as some may have swans not marked in his private waters, the property of which belongs to him, and not to the King; and if they go out of his private waters into an open and common River, he may bring them back and take them again. And therewith agreeth Bracton, lib. 2. cap. 1. fo. 9. *Si autem animalia fera facta fuerint man-sueta, & ex consuetudine eunt, & redeunt, volant, & revolant, (ut sunt Cervi, Cigni, Pavones, et Columbae, et hujusmodi) eousque nostra intelligantur, quam-diu habuerint animum revertendi.*[9] But if they have gained their natural liberty, and are swimming in open and common Rivers, the King's Officer may seise them in the open and common River for the King: for one white Swan, without such pursuit as aforesaid, cannot be known from another, and when the property of a swan cannot be known, the same being of its nature a Fowl Royal, doth belong to the King; and in this case the book of 7 Hen. 6. 27. was vouched, where Sir John Tiptoft brought an action of Trespass for wrongful taking of his Swans; the Defendant pleaded that he was seised of the Lordship of S. within which Lordship, all those whose estate he hath in the said Lordship, had had time out of mind, &c. all estreies being within the said Manor; and we say that the said Swans were estraying at the time in the place where, &c. and we as Landlords did seise and make proclamations in Fairs and Markets, and so soon as we had notice that they were your Swans, we delivered them to you at such a place. The Plaintiff replied, That he was seised of the Manor of B. joining to the Lordship of S. and we say, that we and our Ancestors,

7. [*Ed.:* because fowl, which are of a wild nature, are sometimes royal and sometimes common.]

8. [*Ed.:* master of the game of swans.]

9. [*Ed.:* But if wild animals are made tame, and are accustomed go and return, or fly away and fly back, as do deer, swans, peacocks and pigeons, and the like, they shall be understood to be ours so long as they have *animus revertendi* (the intention of returning).]

and all those, &c. have used time out of mind, &c. to have Swans swimming through all the Lordship of S. and we say, that long time before the taking we put them in there, and gave notice of them to the Defendant that they were our Swans; and prayed his Damages. And the opinion of Strange there was well approved by the Court, that the Replication was good: For when the Plaintiff may lawfully put his swans there, they cannot be estrays, no more than the Cattle of any can be estrays in such place where they ought to have Common; because they are there where the Owner hath an interest to put them, and in which place they may be without negligence or *laches*[10] of the Owner. Out of which Case, these points were observed concerning Swans, 1. That every one who hath Swans within his Manor, that is to say, within his private waters, hath a property in them, for the Writ of Trespass was of wrongful taking his Swans; *scil. Quare cignos suos &c.*[11] 2. That one may prescribe to have a game of Swans within his Manor, as well as a Warren, or Park. 3. That he who hath such a game of Swans may prescribe, that his Swans may swim

[17 a]   within the I Manor of another. 4. That a swan may be an Estray, and so cannot any other Fowl, as I have read in any Book. In 2 Rich. 3. 15 & 16. The Lord Strange and Sir John Charlton brought an Action of Trespass against 3, because the Defendants had taken and carried away 40 Cygnets of the Plaintiff's in the County of Bucks, to his damages of 10 l. One of the Defendants pleaded, That the water of the Thames ran through the whole realm, and that the County of Buckingham is adjoining to the Thames, and that the custom of the said County of Buckingham is, and hath been time out of mind, &c. That every Swan (for Cignet in the book is taken for a Swan) which hath course in any water, which water runs to the Thames within the same County, That if any Swan cometh on the land of any man, and there builds, and hath Cignets on the same land, that then he who hath the property of the Swan shall have 2 of the Cignets, and he who hath the land shall have the third Cignet, which shall be of less value than the other 2; and that was adjudged a good custom, because the possessor of the Land suffers them to build there, where he may drive them off. And by this Judgment it also appears, That a man may allege a Custom or Prescribe in Swans or Cignets. And in the same Case it is said, That the truth of the matter was, that the Lord Strange had certain Swans

10. [*Ed.:* unreasonable delay.]
11. [*Ed.:* that is to say, why [he took] his swans, etc.]

which were Cocks, and Sir John Charleton certain Swans which were Hens, and they had Cignets between them; and for these Cignets the owners did join in one Action, for in such case by the general custom of the Realm, which is the Common Law in such case, the Cignets do belong to both the owners in common equally, *scil.* to the owner of the Cock, and the owner of the Hen; and the Cignets shall be divided betwixt them. And the Law thereof is founded on a reason in nature; for the Cock Swan is an emblem or representation of an affectionate and true Husband to his Wife above all other Fowle; for the Cock Swan holdeth himself to one female only; and for this cause nature hath conferred on him a gift beyond all others; that is, to die so joyfully, that he sings sweetly when he dies; upon which the Poet saith,

> Dulcia defecta modulatur carmina lingua,
> Cantator, cygnus, funeris ipse sui, &c.[12]

And therefore this case of the Swan doth differ from the case of Kine, or other brute beasts. *Vide* 7. Hen. 4. 9. And it was agreed that none can have a Swan mark, which in Latin is called *cigninota*[13] if it not be by the grant of the King, or of his Officers authorised thereto, or by prescription. And if he hath a lawful Swan-mark, and hath Swans swimming in open and common Rivers, lawfully marked therewith, they belong to him *ratione privilegii*.[14] But none shall have a Swan-mark, or Game of Swans, if he hath not Lands or Tenements of an Estate of Freehold of the yearly value of five Marks, above all charges, on pain of forfeiture of his Swans, whereof the King shall have one moiety, and he who seises shall have the other moiety: and that is by the stat. of 22 Edw. 4. cap. 6. And he who hath such Swan-mark may grant it over. And thereof I have seen a notable precedent in the time of Henry the sixth which is such, *Notum sit omnib' hominib' praesentib' et futuris, quod ego J. Steward Miles, dedi et | concessi Tho' fil' meo primogenito, et haeredib' suis, cigninot' meam armor' meor', prout in margine laterali pingitur, quae mihi jure haereditar' descendeb' post mort' J. Steward mil' patris mei: Habend' sibi et haeredib' suis, una cum omnib' cignis et cignicul' cum dicta nota baculi nodati signat',* [17 b]

---

12. [*Ed.:* The swan, chanter of its own death, modulates sweet songs with failing tongue [Martial, *Epigrams*, 13. 77. 1.].]

13. [*Ed.:* swan mark.]

14. [*Ed.:* by reason of privilege.]

sub condit' quod quilib' feria solis durante vita a gula Augusti, usque ad Cornis-
privium apud dom' meam de Darford, unum cigniculʼ bene signat' mihi aut meis
deliberet, quod si defecerit, tunc volo, quod hoc praesens chirographum cassetur
penitus, et pro nihilo habeatur. In cuj' rei testimon' ad instant' Matildae uxor'
meae, meum sigil' secret' Christi crucifixi praesentib' feci apponi. Hiis testib' R.
Clerico, J. D. Conyers, Alano Fabro, et al' Dat. apud dom' meam mansional' de
Darf. in vigilia S. Dunst' ep' an' regni Regis Hen' post conquest' Angliae sexti.[15]

14. And in the Margent was printed a little ragged staff. And in this case it
was resolved, that in some of them which are *ferae naturae,*[16] a man hath *jus*
proprietatis,[17] a right of property, and in some of them a man hath *jus priv-*
ilegii,[18] a right of privilege. And there are three manner of rights of property,
scil. property absolute, property qualified, and property possessory. A man
hath not absolute property in any thing which is *ferae naturae,* but in those
which are *domitae naturae.*[19] Property qualified and possessory a man may
have in those which are *ferae naturae;* and to such property a man may attain
by two ways, by industry, or *ratione impotentiae et loci;*[20] by industry as by
taking them, or by making them *mansueta, i.e. manui assueta,* or *domesticae,*
i.e. domui assueta:[21] But in those which are *ferae naturae,* and by industry are
made tame, a man hath but a qualified property in them, *scil.* so long as they
remain tame, for if they do attain to their natural liberty, and have not *animum*
revertendi,[22] the property is lost, *ratione impotentiae et loci:* As if a man has

---

15. [*Ed.:* Be it noted by all men present and to come that I, J. Steward, knight, have given and granted
to Thomas, my firstborn son, and his heirs, my swan-mark of my arms, as painted in the side-margin,
which descended to me by hereditary right after the death of J. Steward, knight, my father, to have and
to hold unto him and his heirs, with all the swans and cygnets marked with the said sign of a knotted
staff, upon condition that every Sunday during his lifetime between the gule of August [i.e., Lammas] and
Carnisprivium [i.e., the beginning of Lent] he shall deliver to me or mine at my house of Darford one
cygnet well marked; and, if he defaults, then I will that this my present chirograph should be utterly quashed
and had for naught. In witness whereof, at the instance of my wife Maud, I have caused my privy seal
with the crucifix to be set to the presents, these being witnesses: R. Clerk, J. [de] Conyers, Alan Smith,
and others. Given at my mansion house of Darford on the vigil of St Dunstan the Bishop in the fourteenth
year of the reign of King Henry the sixth after the conquest.]

16. [*Ed.:* of a wild nature.]
17. [*Ed.:* right of property.]
18. [*Ed.:* right of privilege.]
19. [*Ed.:* domesticated by nature.]
20. [*Ed.:* by reason of powerlessness and place.]
21. [*Ed.:* domesticated, that is, habituated to the house.]
22. [*Ed.:* intention of returning.]

young Shovelers or Goshawks, or the like, which are *ferae naturae,* and they build in my land, I have possessory property in them, for if one takes them when they cannot fly, the owner of the soil shall have an action of Trespass, *Quare boscum suum fregit, et tres pullos espervor' suor',* or *aidear' suar' pretii tantum, nupe in eod' bosco nidificant', cepit, et asportav';*[23] and therewith agreeth the regist. and F. N. B. 86. (D) L. & 89. K. 10 Edw. 4. 14. 18 Edw. 4. 8. 14 Hen. 8. 1 b. Stamf. 25 b. &c. *vide* 12 Hen. 8. 4. & 18. Hen. 8. 12. But when a man hath savage beasts *ratione privilegii,* as by reason of a Park, Warren, &c. he hath not any property in the Deer, or Conies, or Pheasants, or Partridges, and therefore in an action, *Quare Parcum Warrennum, &c. fregit et intrav', et 3. damas, lepores, cuniculos, phasianos, perdices, cepit et asportavit,*[24] he shall not say (*suos*)[25] for he hath no property in them, but they do belong to him *ratione privil'* for his game and pleasure, so long as they remain in the privileged place; for if the owner of the Park dies, his heir shall have them, and not his Executors or Administrators, because without them the Park, which is an | Inheritance, is not complete; nor can Felony be committed of [18 a] them, but of those which are made tame, in which a man by his industry hath any property, Felony may be committed. And therewith agrees the rule of the book in 3 Hen. 6. 55 b. 8 Edw. 4. 5 b. 22 Hen. 6. 59. which is ill reported, and 43 Edw 4. 24. *vide* 22 Ass. 12 Hen. 3. 13 Eliz. Dyer 306. 38 Edw. 3. 19. *Vide* 2 Edw. 2. tit. Distress. 2 Edw. 3. Avowry 182. But a man may have property in some things which are of so base nature, that no Felony can be committed of them; and no man shall lose life or member for them, as of a Blood-hound or Mastiff, *molessus,*[26] 12 Hen. 8. 3. *Vide* 18 Hen. 8. 2. But he who steals the Eggs of Swans out of the Nest shall be imprisoned for a year and a day, and fined at the will of the King; one moiety to the King, the other to the owner of the Land where the eggs were so taken, and that is by the Statute of 11 Hen. 7. cap. 17. And it hath been said of old time, That he who steals a Swan in an open and common River, lawfully marked, the same Swan (if it may be) or another swan, should be hung in a house by the beak, and he who stole

23. [*Ed.:* [to show] Why he broke his wood, and took and carried away three sparrowhawk chicks, of such and such a price, lately nesting in the same wood.]
24. [*Ed.:* [to show] Why he broke and entered the park, warren, etc., and took and carried away three does [or] hares, rabbits, pheasants, partridges.]
25. [*Ed.:* his.]
26. [*Ed.:* mastiff.]

it shall in recompence thereof be obliged to give the owner so much Wheat that may cover all the swan, by putting and turning the Wheat on the head of the Swan, until the head of the Swan be covered with the Wheat. And it was resolved, That in the principal case the prescription was insufficient; for the effect of the prescription is to have all wild Swans, which are *ferae naturae*,[27] and not marked *nidificant, gignent, et frequentant*,[28] within the said Creek. And such prescription for a Warren would be insufficient, *scil.* to have all Pheasants and Partridges, *nidificantes, gignentes*,[29] and frequenting within his Manor. But he ought to say, to have free Warren of them within his Manor: For although they are *nidificantes, gignentes,* and frequenting within the manor, he cannot have them *jure privilegii*,[30] but so long as they are within the place. But it was resolved, That if the defendants had alleged, that within the said Creek there had been time out of mind &c. a game of wild Swans not marked, building and breeding; and then had prescribed, that such Abbot and all his Predecessors, &c. had used at all times to have and take to their use some of the said Game of wild Swans and their Cignets within the said creek, it had been good; for although Swans are royal Fowls, yet in such a manner a man may prescribe in them: for that may have a lawful beginning by the King's grant: For in Rot. Parliam 16 Rich. 2. part. 1. numero. 3a. like grant was of wild Swans unmarked in the County of Cambridge, to B. Bereford, Knight. The like grant in Rot Parl. anno 30 Edw. 3 part 2. num. 20. the King granted to C. W. all his wild Swans unmarked between Oxford and London for seven years. In Rot. Parl. an. 1 Hen. 4. part. 6. numer. 14. A grant was made to John Fenne, to survey and keep all wild swans unmarked; *ita quod de proficuo res-* [18 b] *pondeat ad Scaccarium.*[31] | By which it appear, that the King may grant wild Swans unmarked; and by consequence a man may prescribe in them within a certain place, because it may have a lawful beginning. And a man may prescribe to have Royal Fish within his Manor, as it is held in 39 Edw. 3. 35. for the reason aforesaid. And yet without prescription they do belong to the King by his Prerogative.

27. [*Ed.:* of a wild nature.]
28. [*Ed.:* nesting, breeding and haunting.]
29. [*Ed.:* nesting, breeding.]
30. [*Ed.:* by right of privilege.]
31. [*Ed.:* so that he answer for the profit to the Exchequer.]

Penal Statutes.
(1605) Hilary Term, 2 James I.
Before all the Justices of England.
First Published in the *Reports,* volume 7, page 36b.

Ed.: Queen Elizabeth issued a grant that would allow its recipient to be free of the burdens of a penal statute, giving the grant before there was a judgment against the recipient for violating the statute. The grant also allowed the recipient to give similar dispensations to others. This is contrary to the law and will not be allowed, a view that would be reflected in the seventeenth century in England's Bill of Rights. This case is an important illustration of common law limits on Royal authority and is essentially an enforcement of separation of powers between the Parliament and the Crown. Look for wonderful metaphors on the King's powers in law, and their limits.

This Term upon Letters directed to the Judges to have their Resolution concerning the validity of a Grant made by Queen Elizabeth, under the great Seal, of the penalty and benefit of a penal Statute, with power to dispense with the said statute, and to make a warrent to the Lord Chancellor, or Keeper of the great Seal, to make as many dispensations, and to whom he pleased; And upon great Consideration and deliberation by all the Judges of England, It was Resolved, That the said grant was utterly against Law. And in this case these points were Resolved, 1. That when a Statute is made by Parliament for the good of the Commonwealth, the King cannot give the penalty, benefit, and dispensation of such Act to any subject; Or give power to any subject to dispense with it, and to make a warrant to the great Seal for Licences in such case to be made: For when a Statute is made *pro bono publico,*[1] and the King (as the head of the Commonwealth, and the fountain of Justice and Mercy) is trusted the whole Realm with it; this confidence and trust is so inseparably joined and annexed to the person of the King in so high a point of Sovereignty, that he cannot transfer the same to the disposition or power of any private person, or to any private use: for it was committed to the King by all his

---

1. [*Ed.:* for the public good.]

Subjects for the good of the Commonwealth. And if he may grant the penalty of one Act, he may grant the penalty of Two, and so *in infinitum.*[2] And such grant of a penalty was never seen in our Books. But it is true, the King may (upon any cause moving him in respect of time, place, or person, &c.) make

[37 a]   a *Non Obstante*[3] | to dispense with any particular person, that he shall not incur the penalty of the Statute, and therewith agree our books. But the King cannot commit the Sword of his Justice, or the Scale of his Mercy, concerning any penal Statute to any subject, as is aforesaid. 2. It was also Resolved, That the penalty of an Act of Parliament cannot be levied by any grant of the King, but only according to the purpose and purview of the Act: for the Act which gives the penalty ought to be followed only in the prosecution and levying thereof: and great inconveniences would thereon follow, if penal Laws should be transferred to subjects. 1. Justice thereby should be scandalized; for when such Forfeitures are granted, or promised to be granted before they are recovered, the same is the cause of a more violent and undue proceeding. 2. When it is publicly known, that the Forfeiture and penalty of the Act of Parliament is granted, it is a great cause that the Act itself is not executed; for the Judge and Jurors, and every other, is thereby discouraged. 3. Thereupon would follow, that no penalty should by any Act of Parliament be given to the King, but limited to such uses with which the King could not dispense. And hereupon divers who had sued to have the benefit of certain penal Laws, were upon this Resolution denied. And the Certificate of all the Judges of England concerning such grants of penal Laws and Statutes was in these words. "May it please your lordships, we have (as we are required by your honourable Letters of the 21st of October last) conferred and considered amongst ourselves (calling to us his Majesty's Counsel learned) of such matters as were thereby referred unto us, and have thereupon, with one consent, resolved for Law and conveniency as followeth: First, That the prosecution and execution of any penal Statute cannot be granted to any, for that the Act being made by the policy and wisdom of the Parliament for the general good of the whole Realm, and of trust committed to the King, as to the head of Justice, and of the weal public, the same cannot by Law be transferred over to any subject; neither can any penal Statute be prosecuted or executed by his Majesty's grant, in

2. [*Ed.:* infinitely.]

3. [*Ed.:* Notwithstanding; an order relieving a person of a power or a liability.]

other manner or order of proceeding, than by the Act itself is provided and prescribed: Neither do we find any such grants in any former ages: And of late years, upon doubt conceived, that penal Laws might be sought to be granted over, some Parliaments have forborn to give forfeitures to the Crown, and have disposed thereof to the relief of the Poor, and other charitable uses, which cannot be granted or employed otherwise. We are also of opinion, That it is inconvenient, that the Forfeitures upon penal Laws or others of like nature. should be granted to any other before the same be recovered or vested in his Majesty by due and lawful proceeding; for that in our experience | it maketh   [37 b] the more violent and undue proceeding against the subject, to the scandal of Justice, and the offence of many. But if by the industry or diligence of any, there accrueth any benefit to his Majesty, after the recovery, such have been rewarded out of the same at the King's good pleasure, &c. Dated 8 November, 1604." And to this Letter all the Judges of England set their hands.

Part Eight of the *Reports*

The Eighth Part of Coke's *Reports* was published in 1611. It was originally entitled *La huictime part des Reports de Sr. Edvv. Coke. Chevalier, Chiefe Justice del Common Banke: des divers resolutions & jugements donez sur solennes arguments & avec grand deliberation & conference des tresreverends juges & sages de la ley, des cases en ley queux ne fueront unques resolus ou adjudgez par devant: Et les raison & causes des dits resolutions & jugements: publie en le neufme an de treshaut & tresillustre Jaques roi Dengl. Fr. & Irel. & de Escoce le 44. Le Fountaine de tout Pietie & Justice, & la vie de la Ley.* In English, *The Eighth Part of the Reports of Sir Edward Coke, Knight, Lord Chief Justice of Common Pleas, of divers Resolutions and Judgments given upon solemn Arguments, and with great deliberation and Conference of the reverend Judges and Sages of the Law, of Cases in law which were never Resolved or Adjudged Before: and the Reasons and Causes thereof. Published in the Ninth year of the most high and Most Illustrious James, King of England, France, and Ireland, and of Scotland the 44., the Fountain of all Justice, and the life of the Law.* This rather long part surveys a broad range of cases, particularly presenting cases on the privileges of nobility, the privileges of the City of London and the regulation of professions, although there are cases dealing with issues of property and inheritance.

Epigrams from the Title Page:

Magna Charta, cap. 29.
Nulli vendemus, nulli negabimus, aut differemus justitiam aut rectum.[1]

---

1. [*Ed.:* To no one shall be sell, to no one shall we deny or delay, justice or right.]

Westm̄ 1. cap. 1.
Rex praecipit ut pax Sacrosanctae Ecclesiae, & Regni solidè conservetur & colatur in omnibus, & quod Justitia singulis, tam pauperibus quam divitibus, administretur, nulla habita personarum ratione.[2]

(Preface)
Deo, Patriae, Tibi.[3]

That which I have written as you know (learned Reader) in some of my former prefaces of the Antiquitie & excellencie of our laws of England, hath produced these two questions: First whether Historiographers do concurre with that which there so constantly hath beene affirmed: Secondly, seeing so great and so often rehersall is made of the common Laws of England, what the body or text of the common lawe is, and consequently where a man may finde it. To both which in the end I yeelded to make answere. For the first: albeit the books and records (which are *& vetustatis & veritatis vestigia*)[4] cited by me in the prefaces to the third and sixt parts of my Commentaries, are of that authority that they need not the aide of any Historian: yet will I with a light touch set downe out of the consent of Storie some proofes of the Antiquitie, and from the censure of those persons who in respect of their profession (for they were Monkes and Clergie men) may rather fall into a Jealousie of referuednes then flatterie, somewhat of the equitie and excellencie of our Lawes; And that it doth appeare most plaine in successiue authoritie in storie what I have positiuely affirmed out of record, That the grounds of our common laws at this day were beyond the memorie on register of any beginning, & the same which the Norman conqueror then found within this realm of England.[5] The laws that *Wil.* Conqueror sware to observe, were *bonae & approbatae antiquae regni leges,*[6] that is, the lawes of this kingdome were in the beginning of the Conquerours raigne good, approved, and auncient. And, that

2. [*Ed.:* The King commands that the peace of Holy Church and the realm be firmly preserved and kept in all respects, and that justice be administered to all, both poor and rich, with no respect of persons.]
3. [*Ed.:* To God, to the country, to you.]
4. [*Ed.:* records of age and truth.]
5. Ex vita Abbatis sancti Albabani.
6. [*Ed.:* the good, approved, and ancient laws of the Kingdom.]

the people might the better observe their duetie and the Conquerour his oath,[7] he caused *twelve of the most discreete and wise men in everie shire throughout all England,* to be sworne before himself, that, without swarving, either *ad dextram* or *sinistram,*[8] That is, neither to flatter prerogative or extend priviledge, *they should declare the integritie of their lawes without concealing, adding, or in any sort varying from the truth.* And *Aldred* the Archbishop that had crowned him, and *Hugh* the Bishop of London, *by the Kings commandement wrote that which the said Jurats had delivered:* And these (as saith *Ingulphus*[9]) *by publike proclamation, hee declared to bee authentike, and, for ever, under grievous punishment, to bee inviolably observed.*[10] The summe of which, composed by him into a *Magna Charta* (the groundworke of all those that after followed) hee blessed with the seale of securitie & wish of eternitie, closing it up with this generall: *And wee further commaunde that all men keepe and observe duely the Lawes of King Edward:* rearing up the frontispice of his gratious worke with his glorious stile, *Willielmus Dei gratia Rex Anglorum, Dux Normannorum, Omnibus hominibus suis Francis & Anglicis Salutĕ. Statuimus imprimis super omnia vnum Deum per totum regnum nostrum venerari, vnam fidem Christi semper inuiolatam custodiri, pacem & securitatem et concordiam, iudicium & Iusticiam inter Anglos & Normannos, Francos & Britones Walliae & Cornubiae, Pictos & Scotos Albaniae, similiter inter & Insulanos, provinoias et patrias quae pertinent ad coronam et dignitatem, defensionem & obseruationem & honorem regni nostri, et inter omnes nobis subiectos per vniuersam Monarchiam regni Britaniae firmitèr & inuiolabilitèr obseruari.*[11] *W. Ruf.* that succeeded his father,[12] so exceeded himself in misrule & oppression, that there is left no register of his goodnes in this kind, for in his time *the kingdom was oppressed*

7. Ex lib. Monast. de Lichfield.
8. [*Ed.:* to the right [or] the left,]
9. Ex Ingulpho Abbate Crowlandense. Ex libro Antiquarum legum.
10. Ex libro manuscripto de legibus antiquis.
11. [*Ed.:* William, by the grace of God king of the English, duke of the Normans, to all his men, French and English, greeting. We command firstly, above all things, that God be venerated throughout our realm, the faith of Christ kept for ever inviolate, and peace, security and concord, judgment and justice between English and Normans, French and Britons, Welsh and Cornish, Picts and Scots of Albany, likewise between [*blank*] and the islanders, the province and countries which belong to the crown and dignity, defence, notice and honour of our kingdom, and among all our subjects throughout the whole monarchy of the kingdom of Britain, be firmly and inviolably observed.]
12. Ex Math. Par. monacho sancti Albani.

with unjust exactions, & the Justice corrupted with evill usages, as appeareth by the great charter of his succeeding brother, king *Henrie* the first,[13] who therby tooke away *all the evill customes wherewith the kingdome of England was unjustly oppressed, and restored the Lawe of King Edward,* (such Lawe as was in the time of the holy Confessor) *with those amendments which his father added by the advise of his barons.* What these were *Math. Paris*[14] (who hath inserted the Charter in his storie) declareth to be *the ancient Liberties and Customes which flourished in this kingdome in the time of holy king* Edw. And herewith agreeth *Hoveden*[15] in these words: *King* H. *the first took away all the evil customes & unjust exactions wherwith the kingdome of England was unjustly oppressed: he setled an assured peace in his whole kingdome, and commanded the law of king* Edward *to be observed, he restored to all &c.* The which, almost in the same phrase, *Florentius*[16] a Monke of Worcester, and living in the raigne of *Henry* the first, observeth. And by whome the Injustice of the foregoing age proceeded, and by whome and how redressed *William*[17] the Monk of Malmesbury delivereth in these words: Henrie *born in England, of kinglie birth, &c. by his proclamation speedily sent through England: restrained the injustice brought in by his brother and* Ranulph &c. *and abolished the unwonted lenitie of some lawes, giving assurance by his owne and all the Nobilities oth, that they should not be deluded &c.* K. *Stc.* that succeeded his uncle, confirmeth in his great Chartre of liberties *to the barons & commons of Eng.* in these words,[18] *All the Liberties and good lawes which* H. *king of England my Uncle graunted unto them: And I graunt them all the good lawes and good customes which they enjoyed in the raigne of K.* Edw. and was so jealous of invocation, as *Roger Bacon*[19] the learned Frier saith in his book, *de impediments sapientiae: King* Stephen *forbad by publicke edict that no man should reteine the Lawes of Italie formerly brought into England.* The next to this man was *Hen.* 2. who in another great Charter established the former Lawes in these words.[20] Henrie *by the*

---

13. Ex Rogero Hoveden presbitero.
14. Ex Mat. Par.
15. Ex Roger Hoveden.
16. Ex Florentio-monach. Wigorn.
17. Ex Willielmo monacho Malmesbur.
18. Ex libro legū Antiquarum.
19. Ex libro Rogeri Bacon de impedimentis sapientie.
20. Ex libro legū Antiquarum.

grace of God King of England, duke of Normandie, and Aquitaine, Earle of Aniou,
to all Earles, Barons, and his faithful Subiects of France, and England, Greeting,
Know ye that I, to the honour of God & holy Church, & for the common amend-
ment of my whole kingdome, have graunted and restored, And by my Charter
confirmed to God and holy church, and to all Earles and Barons, and to all my
Subjects, All grants and donations, & liberties and free customes, which king Henry
my Grandfather gave and graunted unto them. And all those evill customes which
he abolished and remitted, I likewise doe remit, and for me and my heires doe
agree shall be abolished. By which words it appeareth, that he had reference to
that Charter of his Grandfather that abolished the unjust exaction and usages
of his brothers raigne, and confirmed the old and excellent laws under Saint
Edwards government. And no lesse ancient, even by the like authorities will
appeare the customes of some of our Cities: For of London saith *Fitzstephen*[21]
(a Monke of Canterburie) *it was built before that of Remus and Romulus* (meaning Rome) *wherefore even to this day they use the same ancient laws publike*
Ordinances &c. Let us descend a little lower to the times of King *John* the son
of *Henrie* the 2. He in the 17. yere of his raign made the two great Charters,
the one called *Magna charta* (not in respect of the quantitie but of the weight)
& the other *Charta de Foresta,* which are yet extant to this day. Of which the
Monk of Saint Albons faith,[22] *Quae ex parte maxima leges antiquas & regni*
consuetudines continebant: that is, which for the most part did conteine the
ancient lawes and customes of this Realme. And soone after he saith: *And*
those lawes and liberties which the Nobilitie of the Realme did there seeke to
confirme, are partly in the above said Charter of king Henrie, *and partly taken*
out of the ancient lawes of King Edward: not that king *Ed.* the Confessor did
institute them, but that he *out of the huge heape of the lawes, &c. chose the best*
and reduced them into one, as in the preface to the third part of my reports
more at large it appeareth. The said great charters made by king *John* are set
downe *in haec verba* in *Math. Par. pa.* 246.[23] and in effect doe agree with
Magna Charta[24] and *Charta de Foresta* established & confirmed by the great
charter made in 9. *H.* 3. which for their excellencie have since that time beene

21. Ex Stephanide monacho Cát.
22. Math. Par. an. domini 1215. pa.246. 247.
23. Math. Par. pa. 246.
24. Magna Carta. 9.H.3.

confirmed & commanded to be put in execution by the wisdome & authoritie of 30. severall parliaments and above. And these Laws are in the *Register* in many writs called *Liberties,* for there it is said, *according to the tenor of the great charter of the liberties of England,* so called of the effect, *because they make free:* And *Math. of Par.* and others (as it appeareth before) stileth them by the same name. So as the antiquitie and excellencie of our common lawes doe not only appeare by Historians of our owne persuasion in Religion, but by these monasticall writers: the which I have added the more at large in this point to that which I affirmed in my former prefaces, to the end that they agreeing together, may the better persuade both parties to agree to the truth manifestly proved by many unanswerable arguments in the said preface to the third part, and by the authoritie of Sir *John Fortescue* chiefe Justice in the raign of K. Henry the sixth amongst others at large cited in my preface to the 6. part, by all which it is manifest, that in effect the verie bodie of the common lawes before the conquest are omitted out of the fragments of such acts and ordinances as are published under the title of the Laws of king *Alured, Edward* the I. *Edward* the second, *Ethelstane, Edward, Edgar, Etheldred, Canutus, Edward* the Confessor, or of other kings of England before the Conquest. And those few chapters of Lawes yet remaining, are for the most part certaine acts and ordinances established by the said severall kings by assent of the common councell of their kingdome. As for the excellencie of our municipall lawes I will adde to that which hath been said before, that the monk of Crowland[25] calleth them *the most just lawes,* and *Math.* of Westmn[26] of them saith: *They being by the appointment of king* Knute *translated out of English into Latine, were by him for their equity commanded to be observed as well in* Denmarke *as in England.* And of this matter thus much shall suffice. But yet before I take my leave of these Historians, I must incounter some of them in two maine points. First, that the trial by Juries of 12. men (which is one of the invincible arguments of the antiquitie of the common laws, being only appropriated to them) was not instituted by the powerful wil of a Conqueror, as some of them peremptorily affirme they were. The 2. that the Court of common pleas was not erected after the statut of *Magna Charta* (which was made in the 9. yere of king Henry the third) contrary to that which others do hold. For the first, I

25. Ex Monache Crowlandiae.
26. Ex Math. Westm.

referre the learned Reader to the preface before the 3. part of my Reports, where he shall receive full & cleare satisfaction herein, and will onely adde the judgement of the great ornament (in his kinde) of this kingdome in his *Britania pag.* 109. with which I wil conclude this point: *But wheras* Polidore Virgil writeth, *that* Wil. *the Conqueror first brought in the trial by 12. men, there is nothing more untrue, for it is most certaine and apparent by the laws of* Etheldred, *that it was in use many yeres before: Neither hath hee any cause to terme it a terrible Judgement; for free-borne and lawfull men, are duly by order impanelled & called forth of the neighborhood; these are bound by othe to pronounce and deliver up their verdit touching the fact; they heare the counsell plead on both sides before the bench or Tribunal, and the depositions of witnesses, the taking with them the evidences of both parties, they are shut up together and kept from meat drink and fire (unlesse peradventure some one of them bee in danger of death) until they be agreed of the matter in fact: which when they have pronounced before the Judge he according to Law giveth sentence. For this manner of triall our most wise & provident ancestors thought the best to finde out the truth, to auoid corruption, & to cut off all partiality & affections.* And for the excellencie and indifferencie of this kinde of triall, and why it is onely appropriated to the common lawes of England, reade Justice *Fortescue* cap. 25. 26. 27. 28. 29. 30. 31. 32.&c. which being worthy to be written in letters of gold for the weight and worthines thereof, I will not abridge any part of the same, but referre the learned Reader to the fountaine it selfe.

As to the second, it is clearer then the light at noon day, that the court of Common pleas was not erected after the statute of 9. *H. 3. Cap.* 1. 1. *Common pleas shall not follow our Court, but shal be holden in some place certaine.* First, at the same time, and in the same great Charter, and in the next Chapter saving one, the Court of common pleas is expresly named; *Assises of Darreine presentment shall alwaics bee taken before the Justices of the Bench,* & no man doubteth but *Justiciarÿ de Banco* are Justices of the Common pleas. 2.King *Henry* the first, the sonne of the Conquerour, by his Charter, graunted to the Abbot of B. a Charter of confirmation of all his usages &c. And further graunted, that hee should have Conusance of all manner of pleas, so that the Justices of the one bench, or of the other, or Justices of Assise, should not meddle &c. and this Charter appeareth in 26. *lib. Ass. pl.* 24.[27] 3. In the booke

----

27. 26. lib. Assi. pl. 24.

case of 6. *Edw. 3. fol.* 54. 55[28] it appeareth, that 15.[29] *Mich.* in the sixt yere of king *Richard* the first, a fine was levied betweene the Abbot of S. and *Theoband* C. of the advowson of the Church of Preston, before the Archbishop of Canterbury, the Bishop of Rochester and others (Justices *del Banke,* that is, of the court of common Pleas.) And it appeareth in Master *Plowdens Com. in Stowels case,*[30] that fines were levied before the Conquest. In the Treasorie there are yet remaining some fragments of records and judgements in the raigne of king *Rich.* the 1. as wel *coram Justiciariis de Banco, as coram Rege. Martin de Pateshull was made* Justiciarius de Banco *in the first yere of H.3.*[31] which was before the statute of *Magna Charta.* And *in an.* 10. Ed. 4. *fo.* 53[32] all the Judges of England did affirme, that the Chauncery, Kings Bench, Common-place, and Eschequer, be all the kings Courts, and have bene time out of memory of man; so as no man knoweth which of them is the most auncient. But in a case so clere this shall suffice. And yet let me observe, that divers Bishops and other Ecclesiasticall persons in ancient time, did studiously reade over the lawes of England, and thereby attained to great and perfect knowledge of the same. And the saide *Martin de Pateshull* who was, as before is saide, chiefe Justice of the Court of Common pleas in the first yere of king *Hen.* the third, was also Deane of Paules; of whome it is said that he was *a man of great wisdome and exceeding well learned in the Lawes of this Land.* And *John Britton*[33] bish. of Hereford, wrote an excellent worke in the daies of King *Edward* the 1. of the common lawes of England, which remaine to this day. And many Noblemen have been excellently learned in the laws of England, as taking one example for many, least this preface should grow too large, *Ranulphus de Meschives* the great and worthy Earle of Chester and the third and last of that family, (having as mine Author saith) great knowledge and understanding in the lawes of this Land, compiled a Booke of the same Lawes, as a witnesse of his great skill therein: of whom *Mathew Par. pag. 350.*[34] reporteth (as an effect of his learning and knowledge in the Lawes of this Realme:) *But* Ranulph *Earle of Chester alone*

---

28. 6. Ed. 3. 54. 55.
29. 15. Mich. 6. Ric. primi.
30. Pl. Com. in Stowels case.
31. Ex. rot. Pat. de anno 1.H.3.
32. 10. Ed. 4. 53.
33. Joh. Briton Episcopus Heref.
34. Math. Par. pa. 350.

valliantly resisted, as not willing to bring his Countrey into servitude (by paying of Tenths to the Pope:) And would not suffer the religious or Clerkes of his fee to pay the sayde Tenths, although all England and Wales, Scotland and Ireland, were compelled to pay them. And at a partiament holden in the twentieth yeare of king *Henry* the third,[35] the Act saith: *All the Bishops desired the Lordes that they would consent, That all such as were borne afore Matrimony should be legitimate as well as they that be borne within Matrimony, as to the succession if inheritance, forasmuch as the Church accepteth such for legitimate: And all the Earles and Barons with one voyce answered, That they would not change the laws of this Realme, which hitherto have beene used and approved.* Which uniforme and resolute answere of all the nobilitie of England, *nullo contradicente,*[36] doth shew the inward and affectionate love & reverence they bare unto the common Lawes of their deere Countrie. The certaine and continual practise of the common lawes of England soone after the Conquest, even in the time of King *Henry* the first the Conquerours sonne (which almost was within the smoake of that fierie Conquest) and continued ever since, doe plainely demonstrate that those lawes were before the dayes of *William* the Conquerour. For it had not beene possible to have brought the Lawes to such a perfection as they were in the raigne of King *Henry* the second succeeding, if the same had beene so sodainely brought in or instituted by the Conquerour: Of which lawes this I will say, That there is no humane Lawe within the circuit of the whole world, by infinite degrees, so apt and profitable for the honorable, peaceable, and prosperous governement of this kingdome, as these auntient and excellent lawes of England be.

Ranulphus de Glanuilla chiefe Justice, in the raigne of King *Henry* the second, learnedly and profoundly wrote of part of the Laws of England (whose workes remaine extant at this day:) and in his preface he writeth, That the king did governe this realme *By the lawes of the kingdome, and by customes founded upon reason, & of antient time obtained.* By which words spoken so many hundred yeres since, it appeareth, that then there were Lawes and Customes of this kingdome grounded upon reason and of antient time obtained, which hee neither could nor would have affirmed, if they had beene so recently and almost presently before that time instituted by the Conquerour. And in

---

35. St. Merton c.9.
36. [*Ed.:* no one speaking against.]

token of my thankfulnes to that worthy Judge,[37] whom I cite many times in these Reports, (as I have done in my former) for the fruit, which I confesse my selfe to have reaped out of the faire fieldes of his labors, I will, for the honor of him, and of his name and posteritie, which remaine to this day (as I have good cause to know) impart and publish both to all future and succeeding ages which I have found of great antiquity, & of undoubted verity; the original wherof remaineth with me at this day, and followeth in these words. Ranulphus de Glanvilla *Justiciarius Angliae,*[38] *fundator fuit domus de Butteley*[39] *in com' Suff. quae fundata erat anno Regis* H. *filii imperatricis* 17. & *anno dom'* 1171. *quo anno* Tho. Becket *Cantuar' archiepiscopus erat occisus. Et dictus* Ranulphus *nascebatur in villa de Stratford in com' Suff. & habuit manerium de Benhall cum toto dominio ex dono dicti regis*[40] H. *Et duxit in uxorem quandam*[41] Bertam *filiam domini* Theobaldi de Valeymz *senioris, dom' de Parham, qui* Theobald *per cartam suam dedit dicto* Rañ & Bertae *uxori suae totam terram de Brochous cum pertin', in qua domus de Butteley sita est, cum aliis terris & tenementis in libero maritagio. Pradictus verò* Ranulphus *procreavit tres filias de dicta*[42] Berta, *viz.* Matildam, Amabiliam, & Helewisam, *quibus dedit terram suam ante progressum suum versus terram sanctam.*[43] Matilda, *prima soror, habuit ex dono patris sui totam villam de Benhall integralitèr unà cum advocatione ecclesiae five monasterii beatae Mariae de Butteley, & nupsit cuidam militi nomine* Will de Auberuille, *de quibus processit* Hugo de Auberuille, *de ipso* Hugone Will de Auberuille, *de ipso* Willielmo *processit quaedam* Johanna *filia unica & haeres, quae nupsit cuidam militi de Cancia nomine* Nicholao Kyryell *qui duxit in uxorem Margaretam filiam dom'* Galfridi Peche; & *ille* Nich' *vendidit dom'* Guidoni Ferī *praedict' manerium de Benhall: & tum ille* Nich' *de uxore sua genuit alium dom'* Nich' *militem in Cancia, qui vixit ante primam pestilentiam. Ipse autem* Guido *talliavit praedictum maner' in cur' dom' Regis apud* Westm' *in crastin' Ascensionis dom', anno regni regis* E. *filij* E. *primo, sibi* & Alianorae

37. He did beare azure, a chiefe indented or: which coatearmor the *Pastons* of Norf: doe quarter at this day.

38. Justiciarius Angliae. [*Ed.:* For translations of notes 38–50 see note 51.]

39. Fundator prioratus de Butteley.

40. Donum Regis.

41. Uxor eius.

42. Filiae eius.

43. Nuptie et dotationes filiarū, & earum posteritas.

uxori suae & haeredib' dese exeunt': Et si ipse Guido *sine haerede decederet, rem'* Wil' de S. Quintino & *haeredibus.* Amabilia, *secunda soror, habuit ex dono patris sui medietatem vill' de Bawdeseia & medietatem vill' de Fynbergh.* Amabilia *praedicta habuit virum nomine* Radulphum de Ardern, *de quo processit* Tho. de Ardern *filius & haeres, De* Th' Radul *filius & haeres, qui feossauit priorem & conuentum de Butteley de medietate villae de Bawdesey. De predicto* Radulpho *processit quidam* Tho. Ardern *filius & haeres.* Helewisa, *tertia soror, habuit ex dono patris sui aliam medietatem villae de Bawdesey praedicta, et aliam medietatem villae de Fynbergh praedicta.* Helewisa *praedicta habuit virum nomine* Robertū *filium* Rob. *de quo processit* Rad' *filius et haeres, qui feoffavit* Warinum de Insula *de medietate praedicta villae de Fynbergh. De* Rad' *processit* Rob' *filius & haeres qui feoffavit* Ran' *fratrem suum de medietate praedicta villae de Bawdesey. Et nota, quod praefatus* Ranulp' *de Glanuilla fuit vir praeclarissimus genere, utpote de nobili sanguine,*[44] *vir insuper strenuissimus*[45] *corpore,*[46] *qui provectiori aetate ad terram sanctam properauit,*[47] *& ibid' contra inimicos crucis Christi*[48] *strenuissimè usq; ad necem dimicauit. Fuit autem* Berta[49] *ex illustri prosapia orta, filia dom'* Theobaldi Valeymz *senioris domini de Parham, quorum* & Ranulphi & Bertae[50] *consanguinei multi, de quibus plures milites, omnes vero gentiles & generosi, istam partem Suff. eorum incolatu & generosa carnis propagine honorificè illustrabant annis multis.*[51] And *Henr' de Bracton* a Judge of this realm,

44. Vir preclariffimus de nobili sanguine.
45. Vir strenuissimus.
46. Vide Pl. com. f.
47. 368. b. obijt apud Acres.
48. Ad terram sanctam peregrinatus.
49. Effusio sanguinis contra inimicos Christi.
50. Prosapia uxoris Bertae.
51. [*Ed.:* Ranulph de Glanville, Justiciar of England, was founder of the house of Buttely in county Suffolk, which was founded in year 17 of the reign of Henry the son of the empress, and in the year of the Lord 1171, the same year that Thomas Becket the Archbishop of Canterbury was slain. And said Ranulph was born in the vill of Stratford in county Suffolk and held the manor of Benhall with full dominion, by gift of the said king Henry. And he took to wife Berta, the daughter of Lord Theobald Valeymz senior, Lord of Parham, and this Theobald gave by his charter to said Ranulph and Berta his wife all the land of Brochous, where the home of Butteley is situated, with its appurtenances, along with other lands and tenements, Said Ranulph sired three daughters from said Berta, namely Matilda, Amabilia and Helewisa, to whom he gave his land before his pilgrimage to the Holy Land. Matilda, the first sister, had as a gift from her father the whole vill of Benhall along with a claim on the church or monastery of Holy Mary of Butteley, and she wed a certain knight by the name of Will de Auberville, from whom was born Hugo of Auberville, from whom was born Will de Auberville, from whom was born a certain Joan, sole daughter

in the raigne of K. *Henry the third* in his first chapter of his first Booke *Nu-merotertio* saith: *I* Henry de Bracton *have set my mind to serch out diligently the ancient Judgements of the just, not without much paines and labor &c.* So as he stileth the laws of England by the name of *The auncient Judgements of the Just.* The author of the Booke called *Fleta* (who wrote in the raigne of king *Edward the first*) in his Preface to his Worke agreeth with *Glanvill* concerning the Antiquity and honor of the lawes of England, and there sheweth the reason wherefore he intitled his book by the name of *Fleta: But this Treatise which may worthily be called* Fleta, *because it was compiled, in the Fleete, of the Lawes of England.* I have a Register of our Writs originall, written in the raigne of K. *H.*2. (in whose time *Glanvill* wrote) containing the originall Writs which were long before the Conquest, as in the said Preface to the third part appeareth, and yet also remaining in force, such excepted as have been instituted or altered by Acts of parliamént since that time, which is the most ancient booke yet extant of the Common law, and so ancient, as the beginning whereof cannot be shewed. To the 2. question I doe affirme, That the Statutes of *Magna Charta, Charta de Foresta, Merton, Marlebridge, Westm'* I. *De Bigamis, Gloc', Westm'* 2, *Articuli super cartas, articuli Cleri, statutum Eboraic, Praerogativa*

---

and heir, who wed a certain knight from Kent by the name of Nicholas Kyryell, who took to wife Margaret the daughter of Lord Galfridus Peche; and that Nicholas sold to Lord Guido Ferr said manor of Benhall: and then Nicholas sired from his wife another Lord Nicholas, a knight in Kent, who lived before the first plague. And said Guido entailed said manor in the court of the Lord King at Westminster on the morrow of the Ascension of the Lord, in the first year of the reign of king Edward the son of Edward I, to him and his wife Eleanor and the heirs proceeding from him. And if Guido himself died without an heir, he bequeathed the estate to Will de S. Quintinus and his heirs. Amabilia, the second daughter, had as a gift from her father half of the vill of Bawdesia and half of the vill of Fynbergh. Amabilia had a husband by the name of Radulph de Ardern, from whom was born Thomas de Ardern his son and heir, and Thomas in turn sired Radulph his son and heir, who enfeoffed the prior and convent of Butteley with half of the vill of Bawdesey. Said Radulf sired a certain Thomas Ardern his son and heir. Helewisa, the third sister, had as a gift from her father half of the said vill of Bawdesey, and also half of the said vill of Fynbergh. Said Helewisa had a husband by the name of Robert son of Robert, and from him was born Radulph his son and heir, who enfeoffed Warinus de Insula with said half of the vill of Fynbergh. From Radulph was born Robert his son and heir, who enfeoffed Ranulph his brother with said half of the vill of Bawdesey. And note, that said Ranulph de Glanville was a man of very distinguished birth, of noble blood and enormous strength of body, who at an advanced age made a pilgrimage to the Holy Land, and there battled vigorously to the death against the enemies of Christ. Moreover, Berta was of an illustrious family, the daughter of Lord Theobald Valeymz senior, Lord of Parham, and Ranulph and Berta had many kinsmen, many of whom were knights, and all of whom were gentlemen of noble birth, and they and their illustrious progeny for many years gave great honor to county Suffolk.]

regis, and some few others, that be auncient, amongst which, the statute of 25. *E.* 3. is not to be omitted, touching tresons (which for the most part are but declarations of the Common law) together with the original writs contained in the *Register* concerning comon pleas, and the exact & true formes of Inditements & Judgements thereupon in criminall causes, are the very body, & as it were the very text of the common lawes of England. And our yeare Bookes and Records yet extant for above these 400. yeares, are but Commentaries and Expositions of those lawes, originall writs, inditements and judgements. By two cases, the one of *Jebu Webbe,* & the other called *Blackamores case* now among others published & resolved in this blessed & florishing spring time of his Majesties Justice, specially (among many others) it appeareth, that our Booke cases and Records are also right Commentaries, and true Expositions of Statutes and Acts of parliament. And for an example of an originall writ, among many other, I referre the studious Reader especially to *Calyes case* in *Pasc'* 26. of the raigne of the late Queene *Eliz.* of ever blessed memorie, now published, whereby it more clerely appeareth how iudicious the opinion of Justice *Fitzh.* is in his preface to his *N.B.* where he saith, that originall writs are the foundations whereupon the Law dependeth, & how truly he calleth thé the Principles of the law, & fortifieth also the opinion of *Bracton li.* 5. *fo.* 413. where he faith, that (*Breue formatum est ad similitud' regulae iuris:*[52]) which Case I have reported in that forme to this end, that Students seeing the singuler use of original writs, wil in the beginning of their study learn them, or at least the principallest of them without booke, whereby they shal attaine unto 3. things of no smal moment: 1. to the right understanding of their books: 2. to the true sense & judgement of law; & lastly, to the exquisit forme & maner of pleding. And the Case of *Barretry* standeth for an example of an inditement. The neglect of Assises & reall actions hath produced 2. inconueniences in the Common wealth, & a 3. is (if it be not stept on already) like to insue: 1. the multitude of suits in personall actions, wherein the realty of freehold & inheritance is tried, to the intollerable charge and vexation of the subject: 2. multiplicitie of suits in one and the same Case, wherein oftentimes there are divers verdits on the one side, and divers on thother, and yet the pf. or def. can come to no finite end, nor can hold the possession in quiet, though it be often tried & adjudged for either party. And

---

52. [*Ed.:* A formed writ is like a rule of law.]

this groweth, for that the right institution of the Lawe is not obserued, to the uniust slander of the common law, & to the intollerable hindrance of the common wealth. In personall actions concerning debts, goods, & chattels, a recovery or bar in one action is a bar in another, and there is an end of the controversie. In reall actions for freehold & inheritance, being of a higher & worthier nature, & standing upon greater variety of titles & difficulties in law, there could not be above 2. trials, or at the most (& that very rarely) 3. and in the mean time, after one recovery, the possession resteth quiet. 3. The discontinuance of real actions will produce in the end 2. dangerous effects, viz. want of true judgement in the Professors of the Law, & grosse ignorance in Clerks of the right entries & proceedings in those Cases. We see that workes of Nature are best preserved from their owne beginnings, frames of Policy are best strengthned from the same ground they were first founded, & justice is ever best administred when Laws be executed according to their true and genuine institution. And therefore to the end the ancient & excellent institution of the Common Law might be recontinued for the good of the common wealth, (*For it is convenient for the commonwealth, that there be an end of controversies.*) I have therfore reported 2. Cases of *Assises,* for that the writ of *Assise* (in case where it lieth) is *optimum & maxime festinum remedium:* [53] And the cases of *Buckmere & Syms* of writs of Formedon in remainder: & *Ed. Altuams* case of a writ of Dower. And we, that are Judges of the Realm, have resolved to cut off al superfluous & unjust delaies, & as much as we can, all fained dilatory & curious pleadings: the admittance whereof, of late time, hath bin a great cause why reall actions, & specially writs of *Assise,* have not bin so frequent as they have been. And though in reall actions, as the weight of the cause requireth, there are longer times given in the proceeding, then in personall actions, as appeareth in Justice *Fortescues* booke *ca.* 53. (where it appeareth that those times are neither overlong, nor without just cause; *For many times in deliberations judgements grow to ripenes, but in over hastie processe never:*) yet shal the demaundant come to a timely finall end by these reall actions, which he shall never do by prosecution of personall actions for the triall of freehold or inheritance. And they that well observe the three parts of the Reports in the raigne of king *E.* 3. shal find few or no actions of trespas or personal actions brought concerning any lands or tenements, but either where

53. [*Ed.:* the best and most speedy remedy.]

no title of freehold or inheritance came in question, or where the plaintife could not have any reall action: and therfore amongst many others it appeareth in an action of trespas *Quare clausum fregit*[54] brought by the B. of Coventry & Lichfield in 6. *Ed.* 3. *fo.* 34. *b.* exception was taken to the replication of the B. for that he pleaded in the realty, for alwaies in those daies real cases were determined in real actions, which made the Judges in those times to merit that honorable testimony which *Thirning* chiefe Justice attributeth to them in the 12. yere of the raigne of K. *Henry the fourth* that they were the greatest Sages that ever were: & that in the raigne of K. *Edward the third* the law was of the greatest perfection that ever it was; & that pleding (the greatest honor & ornament of the law) grew in the raigne of that king to that excellency, as that the pleading in former times having regard to the pleadings in the raigne of king *E.*3. are holden by *Thirning* to be but feeble. I have reported the great case of the duchy of Cornwall for divers causes. 1. Although this very case hath bin long since (as shal appere in this Report) judicially adjudged, yet hath the same of late bin called in question againe, partly for that the said judgements remain privatly amongst the rest of the kings Records, unknown but to a few, & partly, for that the resons & causes of the judgements being (according to law) not expressed in the Record it self, gave no ful & cleere satisfaction: but principally, for that there was no report made & published of the true causes & resons of those resolutions & judgements. 2. To the end that such as have not any part therof, may hereby be instructed of the true state of the possessions of this duchy, & by this means be admonished how they deale with any that have bought or purchased any of these possessions; & that such as have acquired or gotten any of them, knowing that the judgement was given in this case, both upon many direct authorities in the point, & upon plain & demonstrative reason (the 2. main causes of true satisfaction) may therwith rest satisfied. The last, but not the least, is, for that the most noble & excellent Prince, who is *omine nomine numine magnus,*[55] & the greatest that ever was before him, hath in his first Cause *in hoc forensi dicendi genere*[56] gotten victorie. I have for some respects reported the same in Latin, wherein I have been contented *potiùs scribere propriè quam Latinè;*[57] & for that the

---

54. [*Ed.:* [to show] why he broke his close (the writ of trespass).]
55. [*Ed.:* great by omen, by name, by power.]
56. [*Ed.:* in this forensic manner of speaking.]
57. [*Ed.:* to speak rather in my own language than in Latin.]

words of art which wil beare no translation, are herein so many & so frequent,
I have added the report therof in the vulgar language, that the reader may use
either of them at his pleasure. There are certein other cases now published
by me, concerning some of the most abstruse darke & difficult points in the
law, & yet very necessary to be known, as in *Arthur Blackamores* case concerning Amendments, *Beechers* case of a *Retraxit,* departure in despite of the
Court, & of Fines and Amercements, *Greisleyes* case of affearing of Amercements, & some others. And I have of purpose done these as plainly and cleerly,
and therewith as briefly as I could. For the lawes are not like to those things
of Nature, *which shine much brighter through Cristall or Amber, then if they be*
beheld naked: nor like to Pictures that ever delight most when they are gar-
nished & adorned with fresh and livelie colors, and are much set out & graced
by artificial shadowes. And, whether it be in respect of the matter, or my yeres
growing fast on, being now in the 60. yere of mine age, or for what other
respect soever it be, sure I am I have felt this eighth Work much more painfull
then any of the other have been unto me. And yet hath almighty God of his
great goodnes (amidst my publike imploiments) enabled me hereunto. And
as the Naturalists say, that there is no kinde of bird or fowle of the wood or
of the plaine that doth not bring somewhat to the building & garnishing of
the Eagles nest, some, cinnamon and other things of price, and some, juniper
and such like of lesser value, every one according to their quality, power, and
ability: so ought every man according to his power, place, and capacity to
bring somewhat, not onely to the profit and adorning of our deere Conntrey
(our great Eagles nest) but therein also, as much as such mean instruments
can to expres their inward intention & desire, to honor the peaceable days of
his Majesties happy & blessed government to al posterity. And for that I have
been called to this place of Judicature by his Majesties exceeding grace & favor,
I hold it my duty, having observed many things concerning my profession,
to publish amongst others certaine Cases that have been adjudged and resolved
since his Majesties raigne in his highest Courts of ordinary Justice in this calme
and florishing spring time of his Majesties justice, amounting with those of
my former edition in al to 84. And (if it shall please God) I intend hereafter
to set out an other Worke, whereof I have onely collected the materials, but
not reduced them to such a forme as I intend, left if I should leave it as it is,
it might, after my death, be published (as hath bin done in the like case) before
it be perfected. Your extraordinary alowance of my former Works, together
with your continuall and earnest desire of other Editions, have much in-

couraged me to undertake these paines: And if you shall reape in your studies such profit thereby, as I from my heart desire, and as you (from your desire of knowledge) doe expect, then shall my Labors seeme light unto me, for my expectation shall be satisfied.

Benè vale.[58]

Vynior's Case.*
(1609) Trinity Term, 7 James I
First Published in the *Reports,* volume 8, page 81b.**

> *Ed.:* William Wilde and Robert Vynior had agreed on a bond, by which Wilde owed Vynior £20 15s, with a variety of accompanying obligations and under which any disagreement about performance of the terms of the bond would be decided by William Rugge as arbitrator. Vynior sued Wilde for breach of his obligations, and Vynior argued that Wilde should rely on a decision of Rugge's. In this case, the power to enter into a binding agreement to arbitration is rejected under the view that the power to revoke an authority in another person to arbitrate was irrevocable. Vynior won.

Robert Vynior brought an action of debt against William Wilde upon an obligation of 20 1. 15 *Julii anno* 6 of the same king. The Defendant demanded Oyer of the Bond and of the Condition endorsed, which was, *That if the above bounden William Wilde do, and shall from time to time, and at all times hereafter, stand to, abide, observe, perform, fulfil, and keep, the rule, order, judgment, arbitrament, sentence, and final determination of William Rugge, Esquire, Arbitrator indifferently named, elected, and chosen, as well on the part of the said William Wilde, as on the part of the said Robert Vynior, to rule, order, adjudge, arbitrate, and finally, determine all matters, suits, controversies, debates, griefs, and contentions, hereto moved and stirred, and now depending between the said parties, touching or concerning the sum of Two and twenty pence heretofore taxed upon the said William Wilde, for divers kinds of Parish business, within the parish*

---

58. [*Ed.:* Farewell.]

*The 1658 edition spelled these names "Vinyor" and "Wylde"; the names here have been set as to conform to later citations.

**See the pleadings at Trinit. 7 Jac. Rot. 2629.

of Themilthorpe in the county of Norfolk, so as the said award be made and set down in writing under the hand and seal of the said William Rugge, at or before the Feast of St. Michael the Archangel next ensuing, after the date of these presents, That then, &c. And the Defendant pleaded, That the said Will. Rugge, *nullum fecit arbitrium de et super praemissis, &c.*[1] The Plaintiff replyed, That after the making of the said Writing obligatory, and before the said Feast of St. Michael, *scil.* 22 *Aug. Anno* 6, *supradicto apud Themilthorpe praed' praedict' Willihelm' Wilde per quodd' script' suum cujus datus est eisdem die et anno revocavit et |* [82 a] *abrogavit, Anglice,* did call back, *omnem authoritatem quamcunque quam idem Willielmus Wilde per praed' scriptum obligatorium dedisset, et commisisset praefat' Willielmo Rugge arbitratori suo, et adtunc totaliter deadvocavit, et vacuum tenuit totum et quicquid dict' Willielmus Rugge post deliberationem ejusdem scripti sibi faceret in et circa dict' arbitrium regulam, &c. unde ex quo praed' Wil'mus Wilde post confectionem praed' scripti, et ante praed' Festum Sancti Michaelis tunc prox' sequen' in forma praed' exoneravit, et abrogavit arbitratorem praed' de omni authoritate arbitrandi de et super praemissis in conditione praed' superius specific' contra formam et effectum conditionis illius, et submissionis in ead' mention' idem Robertus petit judicium, &c.*[2] Upon which the Defendant did demur in law. And in this case 3. points were resolved.

1. That although William Wilde the Defendant was bound in a Bond *to stand to, abide, observe, the rule, &c. arbitrament, &c.* yet he may countermand the same; for a man cannot by his act make such authority, power, or warrant not countermandable, which by the Law and of his nature is countermandable; As if I make a Letter of Attorney to make livery, or to sue an Action in my name; or if I assign Auditors to take an account; or if I make one my Factor; or if I submit myself to an Arbitrament; although that these are done by express

---

1. [*Ed.:* made no arbitration upon and concerning the foregoing.]

2. [*Ed.:* namely on the twenty-second day of August in the above-mentioned sixth year, at Themilthorpe aforesaid, the aforesaid William Wilde by a certain writing of his dated the same day and year revoked and abrogated—in English 'did call back'—all the authority whatsoever which the same William Wilde had, by the aforesaid bond, given and committed to the said William Rugge, his arbitrator, and then wholly disavowed and held as void all and whatever the said William Rugge [had awarded] for him in and about the said arbitration, rule, etc., after the delivery of the same writing, wherefore, inasmuch as the aforesaid William Wilde after the making of the aforesaid writing and before the aforesaid feast of Michaelmas then next following discharged and abrogated the aforesaid arbitrator in form aforesaid from all authority to arbitrate upon and concerning the foregoing specified above in the aforesaid condition, against the form and effect of that condition and the submission mentioned therein, the same Robert prays judgment, etc.]

words irrevocably, yet they may be revoked: So if I make my Testament and last Will irrevocably, yet I may revoke it, for my act or my words cannot alter the judgement of the Law to make that irrevocable, which is of its own nature revocable. And therefore (where it is said in 5 Edw. 4. 3. b. If I be bounden to stand to the award which I. S. shall make, I could not discharge that arbitrament, because I am bound to stand to his award, but if it be without Obligation it is otherwise) it was Resolved, that in the one case or the other the authority of the Arbitrator may be revoked; but then in the one case I shall forfeit my bond, and in the other I shall forfeit nothing; for, *ex nuda submissione non oritur actio:*[3] and therewith agreeth Brooke in abridging the said book of 5 Edw. 4. 3. b. and so the book of 5 Edw. 4. is well explained. *Vide* (31 Hen. 6. 30 28, Hen. 6. 6b. 49 Edw. 3. 9a. 18 Edw. 4. 9. 8 Edw. 4. 10.)

2. It was Resolved, That the Plaintiff need not aver, that the said William Rugge had notice of the said Countermand, for that is implied in these words, *revocavit et abrogavit omnem authoritatem, &c.*[4] for without Notice it is no revocation or abrogation of the authority: and therefore if there was no Notice, [82 b] then the Defendant might take issue, *quod | non revocavit, &c.*[5] and if there was no notice, it shall be found for the Defendant; as if a man plead, *quod feoffavit, dedit,*[6] or *demisit pro termino vitae,*[7] the same implieth Livery, for without Livery, it is no Feoffment, gift, or demise; But there is a difference when 2 things are requisite to the performance of an act, and both things are to be done by one and the same party, as in case of Feoffment, gift, demise, revocation, countermand, &c. And when two things are requisite to be performed by several persons; as of a grant of a Reversion, attornment is not implied in it, and yet without attornment the grant hath not perfection, but for as much as the grant is made by one, and the attornment is to be by another, it is not implied in the pleading of the grant of one; but in the other case both things are to be done by one and the same party, and that maketh the difference. And therewith agreeth 21 Hen. 6 30a. where William Bridges brought an action of debt for 200l upon an arbitrament against William Bent-

---

3. [*Ed.:* no action arises from a void submission [to arbitration].]
4. [*Ed.:* revoked and abrogated all authority, etc.]
5. [*Ed.:* that he did not revoke, etc.]
6. [*Ed.:* that he enfeoffed, gave [demised for life].]
7. [*Ed.:* [that he enfeoffed, gave] demised for term of life.]

ley; the Defendant pleaded, that before any Judgment, or Award made by the Arbitrators, the said William Bentley discharged the Arbitrators at Coventry, in the county of Warwick; and the same was holden a good barr and yet he did not averr any Notice to be given. So it is adjudged in (28 Hen. 6. 6 6 Hen. 7. 10, &c.)

3. It was Resolved, That by this Countermand or revocation of the power of the Arbitrator, the Obligee shall take benefit of the Obligation and that for two causes. 1. because he hath broken the words of the Condition, which are *That he should stand to, and abide, &c. the rule, order, &c.* and when he countermands the Authority of the Arbitrator, *he doth not stand to and abide, &c.* which words were put in such Conditions, to the intent that there should be no countermand, but that an end should be made by the Arbitrator of the Controversie, and that the power of the Arbitrator should continue till he had made an Award; and when the Award is made, then there are words to compel the parties to perform it, *scil. observe, perform, fulfil, and keep the rule, order, &c.* and this form was invented by prudent Antiquity; and it is good to follow in such cases the ancient forms and precedents, which are full of knowledge and wisdom; and with this Resolution agreeth the said book of 5 Ed. 4. 3b. which is to be intended, as above said, *ut supra,* That the Obligor cannot discharge the Arbitrament, but that he shall forfeit his bond, and the book giveth the reason, which is the cause of this Resolution, *scilicet,*[8] because I am bound to stand to his award *scil. to stand to his award,* which I do not when I discharge the Arbitrator. The other reason is, because the Obligor by his own act hath made the Condition of the Obligation (which was endorsed for the benefit of the Obligor, to save him from the penalty of the Obligation) impossible | to be performed, and by Consequence his Obligation is become [83 a] single, and without the benefit or help of any Condition, because he hath disabled himself to perform the Condition *Vide* (21 Edw. 4. 55 per Choke, & 18 Edw. 4. 18b & 20a) If one be bounden in a Obligation, with Condition that the Obligor shall give leave to the Obligee for the time of 7 years to carry wood, &c. in that case although he gives him leave, yet if he Countermands it, or disturbs the Obligee, the obligation is forfeited. And afterwards Judgement was given for the Plaintiff.

8. [*Ed.:* that is to say.]

Dr. Bonham's Case.

(1610) Hilary Term, 7 James I.
In the Court of Common Pleas.
First Published in the *Reports,* volume 8, page 113 b.

Ed.: This is, perhaps, Coke's most famous case and most famous report, although he likely did not see it as startling as it would be thought in later generations. The College of Physicians held a concession in their charter under an act of Parliament giving it the sole right to license anyone who would practice medicine in London. Thomas Bonham was a medical doctor educated in the University of Cambridge, who began to practice medicine in London in 1606. He was examined by the College of Physicians, who refused to qualify him to practice. Bonham continued in practice and the censors fined him £5 and ordered him to stop. He continued and refused to obey the College's orders. The president and censors of the college and their two servants arrested Bonham. Bonham sued them for false imprisonment. Coke, sitting in Common Pleas but with the agreement of Fleming, the Chief Justice of the King's Bench, ruled that the language of the charter was not designed to give the college the right to imprison for unlicensed practice in order to benefit the public but to maintain the monopoly of its members and graduates, that the president did not have the power to fine, that proceedings of such a body should be recorded in writing and not done by voice alone, that any fines they collected belonged to the King and not to the College, and that the provision of the charter that allowed imprisonment must be read very strictly in order to prevent the loss of a subject's liberty at the pleasure of others. In reaching these conclusions, Coke noted that the College cannot be a judge in a case to which it is a party. He then considered whether the censors were judges, and stated that in many cases the common law will void acts of Parliament when they are "against common right and reason, or repugnant, or impossible to be performed." This is often thought to be the first judicial statement of a power of judicial review over legislation. As to other invalid restraints from professions, see *Case of the Tailors of Ipswich,* p. 390, and for restraints of trade, see *Case of the Monopolies,* p. 394.

| Thomas Bonham, Doctor in Philosophy and Physick brought an action [114 a] of false imprisonment against Henry Atkins, George Turner, Thomas Mound-ford, and John Argent, Doctors in Physick, and John Taylor, and William Bowden Yeomen, For that the Defendants, the 10 of *Novemb. anno 4 Jacobi,* did imprison him, and detain him in prison by the space of 7 days. The Defendants pleaded the Letters Patents of King Henry the 8. bearing date the 23 of Septemb. in the 10 year his reign, by which he reciteth, *Quod cum regii officii sui munus arbitrabatur ditionis suae hominum faelicitati omni ratione consulere, id autem vel imprimis fore si improborum conatibus tempestive oc-curreret, &c.*[1] By the same Letters Patents the King granted to *John Chambre, Thomas Linacre, Ferdinando de Victoria, John Halswel, John Frances,* and *Robert Yaxley, quod ipsi omnesque homines ejusdem facultatis de et in civitat' London sint in re et nomine unum corpus et communitas perpetua, per nomen praesidentis et Collegii, sive communitatis facultatis medicinae London, &c.*[2] And that they might make meetings and Ordinances, &c. But the case at Bar doth principally consist upon two Clauses in the Charter. The first, *Concessimus etiam eisdem praesidenti et Collegio seu Communitati et successoribus suis, quod nemo in dicta Civitate, aut per septem milliaria in circuitu ejusdem, exerceat dictam facultatem Medicinae, nisi ad hoc per dicts praesidents et Communit. seu successores suos, qui tempore fuerint, admissus sit per ejusdem praesidentis et Collegii Literas sigillo suo communi sigillat. sub poena centum | solidorum pro quolibet mense quo non* [114 b] *admissus eandem facultatem exercuerit, dimidium inde Domino Regi et haere-dibus suis, et dimidium dict' praesidenti et Collegio applicand', &c.*[3] The second clause is, which immediately followeth in these words, *Praeterea voluit et con-cessit pro se et successoribus suis, quantum in se fuit, quod per praesident' Collegium*

1. [*Ed.:* That whereas the function of his royal office was considered to have regard, by virtue of his authority, to the happiness of men of all kinds, but first and foremost to oppose opportunely the undertakings of the wicked, etc.]

2. [*Ed.:* that they and all men of the same faculty of and in the city of London be in fact and in name a corporation and perpetual community by the name of the president and college or community of the faculty of medicine of London, etc.]

3. [*Ed.:* We also grant to the same president and college or community, and their successors, that no one within the same city or within seven miles thereof should exercise the said faculty of medicine unless he has been admitted thereto by the said president and community, or their successors for the time being, by the letters of the same president and college sealed with their common seal, under pain of one hundred shillings for every month in which they exercise the same faculty while not admitted, one half thereof to be paid to the lord king and his heirs and one half to the said president and college, etc.]

praedict' Communitat' pro tempore exist' et eorum successores imperpetuum, qua-
tuor, singulis annis per ipsos eligerent qui haberent supervisum et scrutinium,
correctionem et gubernationem omnium et singulorum dict' Civitatis Medicorum,
utentium facultat' medicinae in eadem Civitate, ac aliorum Medicorum forin-
secorum quorumcunque facultatem illam Medicinae, aliquo modo frequentan-
tium et utentium infra eandem Civitatem et suburbia ejusdem, sive infra septem
milliarii in circuitu ejusdem Civitatis, ac punitionem eorundem pro delictis suis
in non bene exequend' faciend' et uten' illa: necnon supervisum et scrutinium
omnium medicinarum, et earum receptionem per dictos Medicos seu aliquem
eorum hujusmodi ligeis dicti nuper Regis pro eorum infirmitatibus curand' et
sanand' dand' imponend', et utend' quoties et quando opus fuerit, pro commodo
et utilitat' eorundem ligeorum dicti nuper Regis: Ita quod punitio eorundem Med-
icorum utentium dicta facultate Medicinae sic in praemiss' delinquentium per
fines, amerciamenta et imprisonament' corporum suorum, et per alias vias ra-
tionabiles et congruas exequeretur, as by the said Charter more fully appeareth.
And that by force of said Letters Patents, The said John Chambre, Thomas Linacre,
&c. and all the men of the same faculty in the said City were unum corpus et
communitas perpet' sive collegium perpetuum.[4] And afterwards by Act of Parliament *An.* 14 *Hen.* 8. It was enacted, That the said corporation, and every
grant, article, and other things in the said Letters Patents contained and specified, should be approved, granted, ratified, and confirmed, *in tam amplo et*
largo modo prout poterit acceptari, cogitari, et construi per easdem Literas Pa-

---

4. [*Ed.:* He further willed and granted for himself and his successors, as much as in him was, that every year four persons should be elected by the president [and] college [or] community aforesaid for the time being, and their successors for ever, who should have the supervision and scrutiny, correction and governance of all and singular the physicians [*medici*] of the said city using the faculty of medicine in the same city, and of all other foreign physicians [i.e. from outside the city] whatsoever frequenting and using in any way the faculty of medicine within the same city, and the suburbs thereof, or within seven miles of the same city, and the punishment of the same for their offences in not well executing, performing and using the same, and also the supervision and scrutiny of all medicines and of their receipt by the said physicians, or any of them, to be given to, imposed on and used for the said late king's lieges for curing and healing their infirmities as often and whenever the need arises, for the benefit and utility of the same lieges of the said late king, so that the punishment of the same physicians using the said faculty of medicine who thus offend in the foregoing respects shall be carried out by fines, amercements and imprisonment of their bodies, and by other reasonable and suitable ways, as by the said charter more fully appears. [And that by force of said letters patent the said John Chambre, Thomas Linacre, etc., and all the men of the same faculty in the said City, were] one corporation and perpetual community or college for ever.]

tentes.[5] And further it was enacted, That the said 6 persons named in the said Letters Patents, as Principal of the said College, and 2 others of the said College, who should be named *Electi,*[6] and that the said Elects should choose one of them to be President, as by the said Act appeareth: And further they pleaded the Act of 1 *Mariae,* by which it is enacted, *Quod quaedam concessio per Literas Patents de incorporatione facta per praedict' nuper Regem Medicis* London. *Et omnes clausulae et articuli content' in eadem concessione approbarentur, concederentur, ratificarentur et confirm' per praedict' Parl'; in consideratione cujus inactitat' fuit authoritate ejusdem Parliamenti. Quod praed' statut' et actum Parliamenti in omnibus articulis et clausulis in eodem content' extunc imposterum starent et continuarent in pleno robore, &c.*[7] And further it was enact-l-ed, *That* [115 a] *whensoever the President of the College, or Commonalty of the faculty of Physick of* London *for the time being, or such as the said President and College shall yearly, according to the tenor and meaning of the said Act, authorize to search, examine, correct, and punish all offenders and transgressors in the said faculty, &c. shall send or commit any such offender or offenders for his or their offence or disobedience, contrary to any article or clause contained in the said grant or Act, to any ward, gaol, or prison within the same City (the Tower of* London *except) that then from time to time the Warden, Gaoler, or keeper, &c. shall receive, &c. such person so offending, &c. and the same shall keep at his proper charge, without bail or mainprize, until such time as such offender or disobedient be discharged of the said imprisonment by the said President, and such persons as shall be thereunto authorised, upon pain that all and every such Warden, Gaoler, &c. doing the contrary, shall lose and forfeit the double of such fines and amerciaments as such offender and offenders shall be assessed to pay, by such as the said President and College shall authorise as aforesaid, so that the fine and amerciament be not at any one time above the sum of 20 l., the one moiety to the King, the other moiety*

5. [*Ed.:* in as ample and large a manner as it may be accepted, intended and construed by the same letters patent.]

6. [*Ed.:* chosen, the elected.]

7. [*Ed.:* That the grant by letters patent of incorporation made by the aforesaid late king to the physicians of London, and all the clauses and articles contained in the same grant, be approved, granted, ratified and confirmed by the aforesaid parliament; in consideration whereof it was enacted by authority of the same parliament that the aforesaid statute and act of parliament, [and] all the articles and clauses contained in the same, should thenceforth stand and continue in full force, etc.]

to the President and College, &c. And further pleaded, That the said Thomas Bonham the 10th of April, within *London,* against the form of the said Letters Patents, and the said Acts, *exercebat artem Medicinae, non admissus per literas praed' praesidentis et Collegii sigillo eorum communi sigillat' ubi revera praed'* Tho. Bonham *fuit minus sufficiens ad artem Medicinae exercend'*.[8] By force of which, the said Thomas Bonham 30 April 1606, was summoned in London by the Censors or Governours of the College, to appear before the President and Censors, and Governours of the College aforesaid at the College, &c. the 14th day of April next following, *super praemissis examinand'*.[9] At which day the said Thomas Bonham came before the President and Censors, and was examined by the Censors *de scientia sua in facultate sua in Medicin' administrand'. Et quia praed'* Thomas Bonham *sic examinatus minus apte et insufficienter in praed' arte medicinae respondebat, et inventus fuit super examinationem praed' per praed' Praesident' et Censores minus insufficiens et inexpert' ad artem Medicinae administrand' ac pro eo quod praed'* Thomas Bonham *multotiens ante tunc examinatus, et interdictus per ipsum praesident' et Censores, de causis praed' ad artem medicinae administrand' per unum mensem et amplius post talem interdictionem facultatem illam in* Lond' *praed' sine licentia, &c. ideo adtunc et ibid' consideratum fuit per praed. Praesident' et Censores, quod praed'* Thomas Bonham *pro inobedientia et contempt' suis praed' amerciaretur to* 100s. *in proximis comitiis praed' praesident' et Collegii persolvend' et deinceps abstineret,*

[115 b] *&c. quousque inventus fuerit sufficiens, &c. sub poena | conjiciendi in Carcerem si in praemissis delinqueret.*[10] And that the said Thomas Bonham, 30 *Octob.* 1606, within *London* did practise Physick, and the same day he was summoned

---

8. [*Ed.:* exercised the art of medicine, not being admitted by letters of the aforesaid president and college sealed with their common seal, whereas in truth the aforesaid Thomas Bonham was insufficiently qualified to exercise that art.]

9. [*Ed.:* for examination of the foregoing.]

10. [*Ed.:* And because the aforesaid Thomas Bonham, being so examined, answered ineptly and insufficiently in the aforesaid art of medicine, and was found upon the aforesaid examination by the aforesaid president and censors to be insufficient and inexpert to practise the art of medicine, and forasmuch as the aforesaid Thomas Bonham has often previously been examined and banned by the president and censors, for the causes aforesaid, from practising the art of medicine, he for one month and more after such interdiction [exercised] that faculty in London aforesaid without licence, etc., therefore it was then and there decided by the aforesaid president and censors that the aforesaid Thomas Bonham should be amerced one hundred shillings for his aforesaid disobedience and contempt, to be paid at the next meeting of the aforesaid president and college, and in the meantime to abstain etc. until he should be found sufficient, etc., on pain of being put in prison if he should offend in the premises.]

by the Censors to appear before the President and them the 22 of Octob. then next following, at which day Bonham made default. *Ideo consideratum fuit per praed' Censores,*[11] that for his disobedience and contempt he should be amerced to 10 l. and that he should be arrested and committed to custody, And afterwards 7 *Novemb.* 1606. the said Thomas Bonham at their assembly came before the President and Censors, and they asked him if he would satisfy the College for his dis-obedience and contempt, and submit himself to be examined; and obey the censure of the College, who answered, That he had practised Physick and would practice Physick within *London,* asking no leave of the College, and that he would not submit himself to the President and Censors; and affirmed, that the President and censors had no authority over those who were Doctors in the University; For which cause, the said 4 Censors, *scil.* Dr. Turner, Dr. Moundforde, Dr. Argent, and Dr. Dun, then being Censors or Governors, *pro offensis et inobedientia praed' adtunc et ib' ordinaverunt et decreverunt, quod praed'* Thomas Bonham *in carcerem mandaretur ib' remansur' quousque abinde per praesident' et censores, seu gubernatores Collegii praed' pro tempore existen' deliberaretur,*[12] And there then by their warrant in writing, under their Common Seal, did commit the Plaintiff to the prison of the Counter in London, *&c. without bail or mainprise, at the costs and charges of the said Thomas Bonham, until the said Thomas Bonham by the warrant of the President and Censors of the said college, or their Successors, was delivered.* And Dr. Atkins then President, and the Censors, and Bowden and Taylor as their servants, and by the commandment of the said President and Censors, did carry the Plaintiff with the warrant, to the Gaol, &c. which is the same imprisonment. The Plaintiff replied and said, That by the said Act of 14 H. 8. it was further enacted, *And where that in the Dioces of* England, *out of* London, *it is not like to find always men able sufficiently to examine (after the Statute) such as shall be admitted to exercise Physick in them, that it may be enacted in this present Parliament, That no person from henceforth be suffered to exercise or practise Physick through* England, *until such time that he be examined at* London *by the said President and 3 of the said Elects, and to have from them*

---

11. [*Ed.:* Therefore it was decided by the aforesaid censors,]

12. [*Ed.:* for the aforesaid offences and disobedience then and there ordained and decreed that the aforesaid Thomas Bonham be sent to prison, there to remain until he should be delivered from thence by the president and censors, or governors, for the time being, of the aforesaid college.]

Letters Testimonial of their approving and examination, Except he be a graduate of Oxford *or* Cambridge, *which have accomplished all things for his form without grace:* And that the Plaintiff, in the year of our Lord 1595. was a Graduate, *scil.* a Doctor in the University of *Cambridge,* and had accomplished all things concerning his degree for his form without grace, by force whereof he had exercised and practised Physick within the City of *London* until the Defendants had imprisoned him, &c. upon which the Defendant did demurr in Law. And [116 a] this case was often I argued by the Serjeants at Bar in diverse several Terms; And now this Term, the case was argued by the Justices, and the effect of their arguments who argued against the Plaintiff (which was divided into three parts) shall be first reported. The first was, Whether a Doctor of Physick of the one University or the other, be by the Letters Patents, and by the body of the Act of 14 H. 8. restrained to practice Physick within the City of *London,* &c. The second was, If the Exception in the said Act of 14 H. 8 hath excepted him or not. The third was, That his imprisonment was lawful for his said dis-obedience. And as to the first, they did relie upon the Letter of the grant, ratified by the said Act of 14 H. 8. which is in the negative, *scil. Nemo in dicta civitate, &c. exerceat dictam facultatem nisi ad hoc per praedict' praesidentem et communitatem, &c. admissus sit, &c.*[13] And this proposition is a general negative, and *Generale dictum est generaliter intelligendum;*[14] and *nemo*[15] excludeth all; and therefore a Doctor of the one University or the other, is prohibited within this negative word *Nemo.* And many cases were put, where negative Statutes shall be taken *stricte et exclusive,*[16] which I do not think necessary to be recited. Also they said, that the Statute of 3 H. 8 *cap.* 11. which in effect is repealed by this Act of 14 H. 8. hath a special proviso for the Universities of *Cambridge* and *Oxford,* which being here left out, doth declare the intention of the makers of the Act, that they did intend to include them within this general prohibition, *Nemo in dicta Civitate, &c.*[17] As to the two points they strongly held, that the said latter clause, And where that in the Dioceses of *England* out of *London,* &c. this clause according to the words doth extend only to places out of *London*

---

13. [*Ed.:* Namely, no one in the said city, etc. should exercise the same faculty unless thereto admitted, etc. by the aforesaid president and community, etc.]

14. [*Ed.:* a general statement shall be understood generally.]

15. [*Ed.:* no one.]

16. [*Ed.:* strictly and exclusively.]

17. [*Ed.:* No one in the said city, etc.]

and so much the rather, because they purview for *London* before, *Nemo in dicta Civitate, &c.* Also the makers of the Act put a distinction betwixt those who shall be licensed to practise Physick in *London,* &c. for they ought to have the admittance and allowance of the President and College in writing, under their Common Seal; but he who shall be allowed to practise Physick throughout *England* out of *London* ought to be examined and admitted by the President and 3 of the Elects; and so they said, that it was lately adjudged in the Kings Bench, in an Information exhibited against the said Doctor Bonham for practising of Physick in *London* for divers Months. As to the third point they said, That for his contempt and dis-obedience before them in their College, they might commit him to prison, for they have authority by the Letters Patents and Act of Parliament, And therefore for his contempt and misdemeanor before them they may commit him. Also the Act of—1 Mariae has given them power to commit them for every offence or dis-obedience contrary to any article or clause contained in the said grant or act, But there is an express Negative Article in the said grant, and ratified by the Act of 14 H. 8 | *Quod Nemo in dicta Civitate, &c. exerceat, &c.*[18] And the Defendants [116 b] have pleaded, that the Plaintiff hath practised Physick in London by the space of one moneth, &c. And therefore the Act of 1 Mariae hath authorised them to imprison him in this case; for which cause they did conclude for the Defendants against the Plaintif. But it was argued by Coke Chief Justice, Warburton and Daniel Justices at the Common Pleas, to the contrary. And Daniel conceived, That a Doctor of Physick of the one University or the other, &c. was not within the body of the Act, and if he was within the body of the Act, that he was excepted by the said latter clause: but Warburton argued against him for both the points: and the Chief Justice did not speak to those points, because he and Warburton and Daniel did agree, that this action was clearly maintainable for 2 other points. But to the 2 other points he and the said 2 other Justices, (Warburton) and (Daniel) did speak, *Scil.* 1. Whether the censors have power for the Causes alleged in their barr, to fine and imprison the Plaintif. 2. Admitting that they have power to doe it, if they had pursued their power. But the Chief Justice before he argued the points in Law, because that much was said in the Commendations of the Doctors of Physick of the said College within *London* and somewhat (as he conceived,) in derogation of the

18. [*Ed.:* That no one in the said city, etc. should exercise, etc.]

Dignity of the Doctors of the Universities, he first attributed much to the Doctors of the said College within *London,* and did confess that nothing was spoken, which was not due to their merits; but yet that no Comparison was to be made, between that private College, and any of the Universities of *Cambridge* and *Oxford* no more than between the Father and his Children, or between the Fountain and the small Rivers which descend from thence: The University is *Alma mater,*[19] from whose breasts those of that private College have sucked all their science and knowledge (which I acknowledge to be great and profound) but the Law saith, *Erubescit lex filios castigare parentes:*[20] the University is the fountain, and that and the like private Colleges are *tanquam rivuli,*[21] which flow from the Fountain, *et melius est petere fontes quam sectari rivulos.*[22] Briefly, *Academiae Cantabrigiae et Oxoniae sunt Athenae nostrae nobilissimae regni soles, oculi et animae regni, unde Religio, humanitas, et doctrina in omnes regni partes uberrimé diffunduntur:*[23] but it is true, *nunquam sufficiet copia laudatoris, quia nunquam deficiet materia laudis;*[24] & therefore, these Universities exceed and excell all private Colleges, *quantum inter viburna cupressus.*[25] And it was observed in the said Letters Patents, and the King, and the Parliament in the Act of 14 H. 8. in making of a Law concerning Physicians, for the more safety and health of men therein, followeth the order of a good Physician (*Rex enim omn'artes censetur habere in scrinio pect'sui*[26]) for, *Medicina est duplex, removens, et promovens; removens morbum, et promovens ad salutem;*[27] And, therefore, 5. manner of persons (who more hurt the body of men than the disease itself[28]) are to be removed:—1. *improbi.*[29] 2. *avari, qui med-*

[117 a]

---

19. [*Ed.:* Literally, "nursing mother," usually thought of in the sense of a foster mother.]

20. [*Ed.:* The law blushes when children chastise [their] parents:]

21. [*Ed.:* like streams.]

22. [*Ed.:* it is better to seek out the sources than to follow the streams.]

23. [*Ed.:* The universities of Oxford and Cambridge alone are the noblest Athens of the kingdom, the eyes and minds of the realm, whence religion, humanity and learning are best diffused into all parts of the kingdom.]

24. [*Ed.:* there can never be enough praise, because there never wants matter to praise.]

25. [*Ed.:* like a cypress among the bushes.]

26. [*Ed.:* (For the king is reckoned to have all the arts encased in his breast)]

27. [*Ed.:* physic is of two kinds, remotive and restorative: that is, removing illness, and restoring to health.]

28. [*Ed.:* The 1658 edition omits here this line: one of which said of one of their patients, "fleeing from the disease, he meets a physician."]

29. [*Ed.:* bad.]

icinam magis avaritiae suae causa quam ullius bonae conscientiae fiducia prof-
itentur.[30] 3. *malitiosi.*[31] 4. *temerarii.*[32] 5. *inscii.*[33] and of the other part, 5. manner
of persons were to be promoted, as appeareth by the said Act, *scil.* those who
were, 1., *profound,* 2. *sad,* 3. *discreet,* 4. *groundedly learned,* 5. *profoundly studied.*
And it was well ordained, That the Professors of Physick should be profound,
sad, discreet, &c. and not youths, who have no gravity and experience; for as
one saith, *In juvene Theologo conscientiae detrimentum, in juvene legista bursae
detrimentum, in juvene medico caemiterii incrementum.*[34] And it ought to be
presumed, every Doctor of any of the Universities to be within the Statutes,
scil. to be profound, *sad, discreet, groundedly learned,* and *profoundly studied,*
for none can there be Master of Arts (who is a Doctor of Philosophie) under
the study of 7. years, and cannot be Doctor in Physick under 7. years more
in the study of Physick: and that is the cause that the Plaintiff is named in
the Declaration, Doctor of Philosophy, and Doctor of Physick, *quia oportet
Medicum esse Philosophum, ubi enim Philosophus desinit, incipit Medicus.*[35] As
to the 2. points upon which the Chief Justice, Warburton and Daniel, gave
judgment. 1. It was Resolved by them, That the said censors had not the power
to commit the Plaintif for any of the Causes mentioned in the barr, and the
cause and reason thereof shortly was, That the said clause, which giveth power
to the said Censors to fine and imprison, doth not extend to the said Clause,
scil. Quod nemo in dicta Civitate, &c. exerceat dictam facultatem, &c.[36] which
prohibiteth every one to practise Physick in *London,* &c. without licence of
the President and College; but extendeth only to punish those who practise
Physick within *London, pro delicitis suis in non bene exequendo, faciendo et
utendo facultate Medicinae,*[37] by fine and imprisonment: So that the Censors
have not power by the Letters Patents, and the Act to fine or imprison any
for practising Physick within *London,* but only *pro delictis suis in non bene*

30. [*Ed.:* greedy, who profess physic more by reason of avarice than any reliance on good conscience.]
31. [*Ed.:* malicious.]
32. [*Ed.:* timorous.]
33. [*Ed.:* ignorant.]
34. [*Ed.:* In a young theologian there is loss of conscience, in a young lawyer loss of money, in a young physician a filling of the cemetery.]
35. [*Ed.:* because it behoves a physician to be a philosopher, but where the philosopher leaves off the physician begins.]
36. [*Ed.:* Namely, that no one in the said city, etc., should exercise the said faculty, etc.]
37. [*Ed.:* for their offences in not well executing, exercising and using the faculty of medicine.]

exequendo, &c.[38] *scil.* for ill and not good use and practise of Physick. And that was made manifest by 5. reasons, called *vividae rationes,*[39] because they had their vigour and life from the Letters Patents and the Act itself. And the best Expositor of all Letters Patents, and Acts of Parliament, are the Letters Patents and the Acts of Parliament themselves, by construction, and conferring

[117 b] all the parts | together, *Optima Statuti interpretatrix est (omnibus particulis ejusdem inspectis) ipsum Statutum;*[40] And *In ustum est nisi tota lege inspecta una aliqua ejus particula proposita judicare vel respondere.*[41] The first reason was, that these two were two absolute, perfect, and distinct Clauses, and as parallels, and therefore the one did not extend to the other; for the second beginneth, *Praeterea voluit et concessit, &c.*[42] and the branch concerning fine and imprisonment, is parcel of the second clause. 2. The first Clause prohibiting the practicing of Physick, &c. doth comprehend 4. certainties;—1. certainty of the thing prohibited, *scil.* practice of Physick. 2. Certainty of the time, *scil.* practice for one moneth. 3. Certainty of penalty, *scil.* 5 l. 4. Certainty in distribution, *scil.* one moyety to the King, and the other moyety to the College; and this penalty he who practiseth Physick in *London* doth incurr, although he practices and uses Physick well, and profitably for the body of man; and upon this branch the Information was exhibited in the Kings Bench. But the clause to punish *delicta in non bene exequendo, &c.* upon which branch the case at barr stands, is altogether incertain, for the hurt which may come thereby may be little or great, *leve vel grave,*[43] excessive or small, &c. And therefore the King and the makers of the Act, cannot, for so uncertain offence impose a certainty of the fine, or time of imprisonment, but leave it to the Censors to punish such offences, *secundum quantitatem delicti,* which is included in these words, *per fines, amerciamenta, imprisonamenta corporum suorum, et per alias vias rationabiles et congruas;*[44] 2. The harm which accrueth by *non bene*

---

38. [*Ed.:* for their offences in not well executing, etc.]

39. [*Ed.:* vivid reasons.]

40. [*Ed.:* The best interpreter of a statute, once all the points thereof have been looked into, is the statute itself.]

41. [*Ed.:* Unless the whole of the law has been looked into, it is unjust to adjudge or answer in any one point that has been propounded.]

42. [*Ed.:* He moreover wills and grants, etc.]

43. [*Ed.:* light or serious.]

44. [*Ed.:* according to the seriousness of the offence . . . by fines, amercements, imprisonment of their bodies, and by other reasonable and suitable ways.]

exequendo, &c.[45] doth concern the body of man; and, therefore, it is reasonable that the offender should be punished in his body, *scil.* by imprisonment; but he who practiceth Physick in *London* in a good manner, although he doth it without leave, yet it is not any prejudice to the body of man. [3. He who practises physic in London doth not offend the statute by his practice, unless he practises it by the space of a month.][46] But the clause of *non bene exequendo, &c.* doth not prescribe any time certain, but at what time soever he ministereth Physick *non bene, &c.* he shall be punished by the said 2. branch: And the Law hath great reason in making this distinction, for divers Nobles, Gentlemen, and others come upon divers occasions to London, and when they are here they become subject to diseases, and thereupon they send for their Physicians in the Country, who know their bodies and the cause of their diseases; now it was never the meaning of the Act to barr any one of his own Physician; and when he is here he may practise and minister Physick to another by 2. or 3. weeks, &c. without any forfeiture; for any one who practiseth Physick well in *London* (although he has not taken | any degree in any of the Universities) shall forfeit nothing, if not that he practise it by the space of a month; and that was the cause, that the time of a month was put in the Act. 4. The Censors, cannot be Judges, Ministers, and parties; Judges, to give sentence or judgment; Ministers to make summons; and Parties, to have the moyety of the forfeiture, *quia aliquis non debet esse Judex in propria causa, imo iniquum est aliquem sui rei esse judicem:*[48] and one cannot be Judge and Attorney for any of the parties, Dyer 3 E. 6. 65. 38 E. 3. 15. 8 H. 6. 19b. 20a. 21 E. 4. 47a. &c. And it appeareth in our Books, that in many Cases, the Common Law doth controll Acts of Parliament, and somtimes shall adjudge them to be void: for when an Act of Parliament is against Common right and reason, or repugnant, or impossible to be performed, the Common Law will controll it, and adjudge such Act to be void; and, therefore, in 8 E. 3. 30 a, b. *Thomas Tregor's Case* upon the Statute of *West* 2. Cap 38. *and Artic' Super Chartas, cap* 9. Herle saith, Some Statutes are made against Common Law and right, which

[118 a]

45. [*Ed.:* not well executing, performing [medicine], etc.]

46. [*Ed.:* The clause here bracketted was omitted from the 1658 edition.]

47. [*Ed.:* not well executing, etc.]

48. [*Ed.:* because no one ought to be a judge in his own cause, it is wrong for anyone to be the judge of his own property.]

those who made them, would not put them in execution: The Statute of *West* 2. *Cap.* 21. giveth a Writ of *Cessavit haeredi petenti super haeredem tenent' et super eos quibus alienatum fuerit hujusmodi tenementum:*[49] and yet it is adjudged in 33 Edw. 3 *Cessavit*[50] 42. where the Case was, Two Coparceners Lords and Tenant by Fealty and certain Rent, one Coparcener had issue and dyeth; the Aunt and the Niece shall not join in a *Cessavit,* because the heir—shall not have a *Cessavit* for the cesser in the time of his ancestor. F. N. B. 209. F. and therewith agreeth Plow. Com. 110a.; and the reason is, because in a *Cessavit* the Tenant before Judgment may render the arrearages and damages, and hold his Land again, and that he cannot doe when the heir bringeth a *Cessavit* for the cesser in the time of his auncestor, for the arrearages incurred in the life of the auncestor do not belong to the heir: and because it shall be against right and reason, the Common Law shall adjudge the said Act of Parliament as to that point void. The Statute of *Carlisle,* made *anno* 35 *E.* 1. enacteth, That the Order of the *Cistercians,* and *Augustines* who have a Covent and Common Seal, that the Common Seal shall be in the keeping of the Prior, who is under the Abbot, and 4. others of the most grave of the house; and that any deed sealed with the Common Seal, which is not so in keeping, shall be void: and the opinion of the Court (*Anno 27 H. 6 Annuity* 41.) was, that this Statute was void, for it is impertinent to be observed, for the Seal being in their keeping, the Abbot cannot seal any thing with it, and when it is in the Abbots hands, it is out of their keeping *ipso facto;*[51] and if the Statute should be observed, every Common Seal shall be defeated upon a simple [118 b]   surmise, which cannot be tryed. Note Reader the words | of the said Statute of *Carlisle,* which was made 35 E. 1. which is called *Statutum Religiosorum* are, *Et insuper ordinavit Dominus Rex et statuit, quod Abbates Cisterc' et Praemonstraten' ordin' religiosorum, &c. de caetero habeant sigillum Commune, et illud in Custodia Prioris Monasterii seu domus, et quatuor de dignioribus et discretioribus ejusdem loci conventus sub privato sigillo Abbatis ipsius loci custod' depo', &c. Et si forsan aliqua scripta obligationum, donationum, emptionum, venditionum, alienationum, seu aliorum quorumcunque, contractuum alio sigillo quam*

---

49. [*Ed.:* "To the heir of the plaintiff against the heir of the tenant, and against those to whom such a tenement should be alienated," opening words of the writ of cessavit.]

50. [*Ed.:* Writ by a fee-holder to recover lands from a tenant who owed rents or services that had been withheld for two years or more; a form of eviction.]

51. [*Ed.:* by that fact.]

tali sigillo communi sicut praemittit' custodit' inveniant' a modo sigillat', pro nullo penitus habeantur omnique careant firmitate.[52] So the Statute of 1 E. 6. c. 14. giveth Chauntries, &c. to the King, saving to the Donor, &c. all such rents, services, &c. and the Common Law doth controll it, and adjudges the same void as to services, and the Donor shall have the Rent, as a Rentseck, distrainable of Common right, for it should be against common right and reason that the King should hold of any, or do service to any of his subjects, 14 Eliz. Dyer 313. and so it was adjudged Mich. 16 & 17 Eliz. in Common Pleas in *Strowd's* case. So if any Act of Parliament giveth to any to hold, or to have Conusans of Pleas of all manner of pleas arising before him within his Mannor of D., yet he shall hold no plea, to which he himself is party; for, as hath been said, *iniquum est aliquem suae rei esse judicem.*[53] 5. If he should forfeit 5 l. for one month by the first clause, and shall be punished for practising at any time by the second clause, two absurdities would follow, 1. that one should be punished not only twice but many times for one and the same offence. And the Divine saith, *Quod Deus non agit bis in idipsum;*[54] and the Law saith, *Nemo debet bis puniri pro uno delicto.*[55] 2. It should be absurd, by the first clause to punish practising for a moneth, and not for lesser time, and by the 2. to punish practising not only for a day, but at any time, so he shall be punished by the first branch for one moneth by the forfeiture of 5 l. and by the 2. by fine and imprisonment, without limitation for every time of the moneth in which anyone doth practise Physick. And all these reasons were proved by two grounds, or Maxims of Law; 1. *Generalis Clausula non porrigitur ad ea quae specialiter sunt comprehensa:*[56] And the Case between *Carter* and *Ringstead, Hil.* 34 *Eliz. Rot.* 120. in Common Pleas, was cited to this purpose, where the case in effect was, That A. seised of the Mannor of Staple, in *Odiham,* in the

---

52. [*Ed.:* And moreover the lord King has ordained and laid down that abbots of the Cistercian and Premonstratensian orders [and other] religious orders etc. from henceforth should have a common seal, in the custody of the prior of the monastery or house and four of the more worthy and discerning men of the convent of the same place, to be laid up in safe keeping under the private seal of the abbot of the same place etc. And if it should happen that any writings of bonds, donations, purchases, sales, alienations, or any other contracts, be hereafter sealed with any other seal than such common seal kept as aforementioned, they are to be deemed void and to lack all force.]

53. [*Ed.:* it is wrong to be a judge of one's own property.]

54. [*Ed.:* God does not proceed twice against the same person.]

55. [*Ed.:* No one ought to be punished twice for one offence.]

56. [*Ed.:* A general clause is not to be extended to something which is specially mentioned.]

county of *Southampton* in Fee, and also of other Lands in *Odiham* aforesaid
in Fee, suffered a Common Recovery of all, and declared the use by Indenture,
That the Recoverer should stand seised of all the Lands and Tenements in
Odiham to the use of A. and his wife, and to the heirs of his body begotten;
[119 a]   and further, that the Recoveror | should stand seised to the use of him, and
to the heirs of his body, and died, and the wife survived, and entered into the
said Mannor by force of the said general words. But it was adjudged, That
they did not extend to the said Mannor which was specially named: and if it
be so in a deed, *a fortiori,*[57] it shall be so in an Act of Parliament, which (as
a Will) is to be expounded according to the intention of the makers. 2. *Verba
posteriora propter certitudinem addita ad priora quae certitudine indigent sunt
referenda.*[58] 6 E 3. 12 a, b. Sir Adam de Clydrow, Knight, brought a *praecipe
quod reddat*[59] against John de Clydrow; and the Writ was, *Quod juste, &c.
reddat Manerium de Wicombe et duas carucatus terrae cum pertinentiis in Clydrow,*[60] in that case the Town of Clydrow shall not relate to the Mannor, *quia
non indiget,*[61] for a Mannor may be demanded without mentioning that it
lyeth in any town; but *cum pertinentiis,*[62] although it cometh after the Town,
shall relate to the Mannor, *quia indiget. Vide* 3 E. 4. 10. the like case. But it
was Objected, That where by the second Clause it was granted, that the Censors should have *supervisum et scrutinium, correctionem et gubernationem omnium et singulorum Medicorum, &c.*[63] they had power to fine and imprison.
To that it was Answered, 1. That the same is but part of the sentence, for by
the entire sentence it appeareth in what manner they shall have power to
punish, for the words are, *ac punitionem eorum pro delictis suis in non bene
exequendo, faciendo, vel utendo illa facultate:*[64] so that without Question all
their power to correct and punish the Physicians by this clause is only limited

57. [*Ed.:* so much the more so.]

58. [*Ed.:* Subsequent words, added for the purpose of certainty, are to be referred back to the previous
words which lack certainty.]

59. [*Ed.:* Writ commanding the defendant to act or show cause why he had not acted; a predecessor
to the injunction.]

60. [*Ed.:* that rightfully, etc. he render the manor of Wicomb and two carucates of land with the
appurtenances in Clydrow. (A carucate is approximately 100 acres.)]

61. [*Ed.:* because [this inference] is not needed.]

62. [*Ed.:* with the appurtenances.]

63. [*Ed.:* supervision and scrutiny, correction and governance of all and singular the physicians, etc.]

64. [*Ed.:* and their punishment for their offences in not well executing, exercising, or using that faculty.]

to these 3. cases, *scil. in non bene exequendo, faciendo, vel utendo, &c.*[65] Also
this word *punitionem,* is limited and restrained by these words, *Ita quod punitio
eorundem Medicorum, &c. sic in praemissis delinquentium, &c.*[66] which words,
sic in praemissis delinquentium, limit the first words in the first part of this
sentence, *ac punitionem eorum pro delictis suis in non bene exequendo, &c.*[67] 2.
It shall be absurd, That in one and the same sentence the makers of the Act
shall give them a general power to punish without limitation; and a special
manner how they shall punish, in one and the same sentence. 3. *Hil.* 38 *Eliz.*
in a *Quo warranto*[68] against the Mayor and Commonalty of London, it was
holden, that where a grant is made to the Mayor and Commonalty, that the
Mayor for the time being should have *plenum et integrum scrutinium, gubernationem, et correctionem omnium et singulorum Mysteriorum, &c.*[69] without
granting them any Court, in which should be legal proceedings, that the same
is good for search, by which discovery may be made of offences and defects,
which may be punished by the Law in any Court; but it doth not give, nor
can give them any irregular or absolute power to correct or punish any of the
| Subjects of the kingdom at their pleasures. 2. It was Objected, That it is   [119 b]
incident to every Court created by Letters Patents, or Act of Parliament, and
other Courts of Record, to punish any misdemeanors done in Court, in disturbance or contempt of the Court, by imprisonment. To which it was answered, That neither the Letters Patents nor the Act of Parliament hath granted
them any Court, but only an authority, which they ought to pursue, as it shall
be afterwards said. 2. If any Court had been granted them, they could not by
any incident authority *implicitè*[70] granted unto them for any misdemeanor
done in Court, commit him to prison without bayl or mainprise, until he
shall be by the commandment of the President and Censors, or their Successors, delivered, as the Censors have done in this case. 3. There was not any
such misdemeanor for which any Court might imprison him, for he only
shewed his case to them, to which he was advised by his Counsel, he may
justifie, which is not any offence worthy of Imprisonment.

65. [*Ed.:* in not well executing, exercising or using, etc.]
66. [*Ed.:* so that the punishment of the same physicians, etc., thus offending in the premises, etc.]
67. [*Ed.:* and their punishment for their offences in not well executing, etc.]
68. [*Ed.:* Writ against one who exceeds or usurps a prerogative granted by the crown.]
69. [*Ed.:* the full and entire scrutiny, governance and correction of and singular the crafts, etc.]
70. [*Ed.:* implicitly.]

The Second point. Admitting that the Censors had power by the Act, if they had pursued their Authority, or not? And it was Resolved by the Chief Justice, Warburton and Daniel, that they have not pursued it for 6. causes. 1. By the Act the Censors only have power to impose a fine, or amercement; and the President and Censors imposed the amercement of 5 l. upon the Plaintif. 2. The Plaintiff was summoned to appear before the President and Censors, &c. and did not appear and therefore he was fined 10 l. whereas the President hath not any authority in that case. 3. The fines or amercements to be imposed by them by force of the Act, do not belong to them, but to the King, for the King hath not granted the fines or amercements to them, and yet the fine is appointed to be paid to them *in proximis Comitiis,*[71] and they have imprisoned the Plaintif for nonpayment thereof. 4. They ought to have committed the Plaintif presently by construction of Law, although that no time be limited in the Act, as in the Statute of *West* 2. cap. 12. *De Servientibus, Ballivis, &c. qui ad compotum reddend' tenentur, &c. cum Dom' hujusmodi servientium dederit eis auditores compoti, et contingat ipsos in arrearagiis super compotum suum omnibus allocatis et allocandis, arrestentur corpora eorum, et per testimonium auditorum ejusdem compoti mittantur et liberentur proximae gaolae Domini Regis in partibus illis, etc.*[72] in that case, although no time be limited when the Accomptant shall be imprisoned, yet it ought to be done presently, as it is holden in 27 H. 6. 8 a. and the reason thereof is given in *Fogassaes case,* Plowd. Com. 17 b. that the generality of the time shall be restrained to the present time, for the benefit of him upon whom the pain shall be inflicted, and there-
[120 a]   with agreeth Plow. Com. 206 b. in *Stradling's* | *case.* And a Justice of Peace upon view of the force, ought to commit the offender presently. 5. For as much as the Censors had their authority by the Letters Patents and Act of Parliament, which are high matters of Record, their proceedings ought not to be by word, and so much the rather, because they claimed authority to fine and imprison. And therefore if judgment be given against one in the Common Pleas in a Writ of Recaption, he shall be fined and imprisoned; but if the Writ be Vi-

---

71. [*Ed.:* at the next meeting.]

72. [*Ed.:* Concerning servants, bailiffs, etc., who are bound to render an account, etc., when the lords of such servants appoint auditors of their account, and they happen to be in arrears upon the account, everything being allowed which ought to be allowed, their bodies are to be arrested and, by the evidence of the auditors of the same account, sent and delivered to the next gaol of the lord king in those parts, etc.]

contiel[73] in the Countie, there he shall not be fined or imprisoned, because that the Court is not of Record, F. N. B. *in bre Recaption.* so in F. N. B. 47 a. a plea of Trespasse *vi et armis*[74] doth not lie in the County Court, Hundred Court, &c. for they cannot make Record of fine and imprisonment; and regular those who cannot make a Record, cannot fine and imprison. And therewith agreeth 27 H. 6. 8. Book of Entries: The auditors make a Record when they commit the Defendant to prison; A Justice of peace upon view of the force may commit, but he ought to make a record of it. 6. Because the Act of 14 H. 8. hath given power to imprison until he shall be delivered by the President and the Censors, or their Successors, reason requireth that same be taken strictly for the liberty of the Subject (as they pretend) is at their pleasure: And the same is proved by a Judgment in Parliament in this Case; For when this Act of 14 H. 8. had given power to the Censors to imprison, yet it was taken so literally, That the Gaoler was not bound to receive them which they committed to him, and the reason thereof was because they had authority to do it without any Court: And thereupon the Statute of 1 *Ma. cap.* 9. was made, that the Gaoler should receive them upon a pain, and none can be committed to any prison, if the Gaoler cannot receive him: but the first Act, for the cause aforesaid was taken so literally, that no necessary incident was implyed. And where it was objected, that this very Act of 1 *Mariae c.* 9. hath enlarged the power of the Censors, and upon the word of the Act; It was clearly resolved, that the said Act of 1 Mariae did not enlarge the power of the Censors to fine or imprison any person for any cause for which he ought not to be fined or imprisoned by the said Act of 14 H. 8. For the words of the Act of Queen Marie are according to the tenor and meaning of the said Act: Also shall send or commit any offender or offenders for his or their offence or dis-obedience, contrary to any article or clause contained in the said grant or Act, to any Ward, Gaol, &c. But in this case Bonham hath not done any thing which appeareth within this Record, contrary to any article or clause contained within the Grant or Act of 14 H. 8. Also the Gaoler who refuseth shall forfeit the double value of | the fines and amerciaments that any offender or dis-obedient [120 b] shall be assessed to pay; which proveth that none shall be received by any Gaoler by force of the Act of 14 H. 8. but he who may be lawfully fined or

73. [*Ed.:* Writ triable in the court of the sheriff, the old county court.]
74. [*Ed.:* with force and arms.]

amerced by the Act of 14 H. 8. and for that was not Bonham, as by the reasons and causes aforesaid it appeareth. And admit that the Replication be not material, and the Defendants have demurred upon it; yet forasmuch as the Defendants have confessed in the Bar, that they have imprisoned the Plaintif without cause, the Plaintif shall have Judgement: And the difference is, when the Plaintif doth reply, and by his replication it appeareth that he hath no cause of action, there he shall never have Judgement: But when the Bar is insufficient in matter, or amounteth (as this case is) to a confession of the point of the action, and the Plaintif replieth, and sheweth the truth of the matter to enforce his case, and in judgment of Law it is not material; yet the Plaintiff shall have Judgement; for it is true that sometimes the Count shall be made good by the Bar, and sometimes the Bar by the Replication, and sometimes the Replication by the Rejoynder, &c. But the difference is when the Count wanteth time, place, or other circumstance, it may be made good by the Bar, so of the Bar, Replication, &c. as appeareth in 18 E. 4 16b. But when the Count wanteth substance, no Bar can make it good, so of the Bar, Replication, &c. and therewith agree 6 Edw. 4. 2. a good case, and mark there the words of Choke[75] *Vide* 18 Edw. 3. 34 b. 44 Edw. 3. 7 a. 12 Edw. 4. 6. 6 Hen. 7. 10. 7 Hen. 7. 3. 11 Hen. 4. 24. &c. But when Plaintiff makes Replication, sur-rejoinder, &c. and thereby it appeareth, that upon the whole matter and Record the Plaintif hath no cause of action, he shall never have judgement, although the Bar or Remainder be insufficient in matter, for the Court ought to judge upon the whole Record, and every one shall be intended to make the best of his own case. *Vide Rigeway's case,* in the 3 part of my Reports 52 b. And so these differences were resolved and adjudged between *Kendall and Helyer,* Mich. 25 & 26 *Eliz.* in the Kings Bench. And Mich. 29 & 30 Eliz. in the same Court, between *Gallys and Burbry.* And Coke chief Justice, in the conclusion of his argument did, observe 7 things for the better direction of the President and Commonalty of the said College in time to come. 1. That none can be punished for practising of Physick in London, but by forfeiture of 5 l. by the month, which is to be recovered by the Law. 2. If any practise Physick there for a lesse time than a moneth, that he shall forfeit nothing. 3. If any person prohibited by the Statute offend in *non bene exeq',* &c.[76] they

75. [*Ed.:* The French here is "nota la dictum Choke."]
76. [*Ed.:* not well executing, etc.]

may punish him according to the Statute within the month. 4. Those who may commit to prison by the Statute ought to commit presently. 5. The fines which they I set, according to the Statute, doe belong to the King. 6. They cannot impose a fine, or imprison, without a Record of it. 7. The cause for which they impose fine and imprisonment ought to be certain, for it is traversable; For although they have the Letters Patents and an Act of Parliament, yet because the party grieved hath no other remedy, neither by Writ of Error, or otherwise, and they are not made Judges, nor a Court given to them, but have an authority only to doe, the cause of their commitment is traversable in an action of false imprisonment brought against them; as upon the Statute of Bankrupts, their warrant is under the Great Seal, and by Act of Parliament; yet because the party grieved hath no other remedy if the Commissioners doe not pursue the Act and their Commission, he shall traverse, That he was not a Bankrupt, although the Commissioners affirm him to be one; as this Term it was resolved in this Court, in Trespass between *Cutt and Delabarre,* where the issue was, whether William Piercy was Bankrupt or not, who was found by the Commissioners to be a Bankrupt; *à fortiori*[77] in the Case at Bar, the cause of the imprisonment is traversable; for otherwise the party grieved may be perpetually, without just cause, imprisoned by them: But the Record of a force made by one Justice of Peace is not traversable, because he doth it as Judge, by the Statutes of 15 Rich. 2. and 8 Hen. 6. and so there is a difference when one maketh a Record as a Judge, and when he doth a thing by special authority, as they did in the case at Bar and not as a Judge. And afterwards for the said two last points, Judgement was given for the Plaintif, *nullo contradicente*[78] as to them. And I acquainted Sir Thomas Fleming, Chief Justice of the Kings Bench with this Judgement and with the reasons and causes thereof, who approved of the Judgement which we had given: And this is the first Judgement upon the said Branch concerning fine and imprisonment, which hath been given since the making of the said Charter and Acts of Parliament, and therefore I thought it worthy to be Reported and published.

[121 a]

77. [*Ed.:* so much the more so.]
78. [*Ed.:* no one opposing.]

The Case of Thetford School, &c.

(1609) Easter Term, 7 James 1.

First Published in the *Reports,* volume 8, page 130b.

Ed.: This case is a consideration of the interpretation of a trust for charitable purposes. Thomas Fulmerston gave lands to "certain people" so that the income from the lands could support a preacher for four days a year, the erection of a free school and maintenance of four poor people. The land grew in value so that there was greater income than necessary, and the people acting as trustee wanted to keep the excess. The Lords ruled that the excess must be used in accord with the grantor's intent, and the excess was used to support more poor people.

Upon a private bill exhibited in the Parliament for erection of a Free-school, maintenance of a Preacher, and of 4 poor people, *Scil.* 2 poor men, and 2 poor women according to the Will of Sir Thomas Fulmerston, Knight a Question was moved by the Lords, and was such: Land of the value of 35 £. *Anno 9 Eliz.* was devised by Will in writing to certain persons and their heirs, for the maintenance of a Preacher four days in the year; Of a Master and Usher of a Free Grammar School and of certain poor people, and a special distribution was made by the Testator himself, in the same Will, amongst them, of the Revenues, *scil.* To the Preacher a certain sum, and certain sums, to the School-master and Usher, and to the Poor people, amounting in the whole to 35 £ *per annum,* which was the yearly profit of the Land at that time; and afterwards the lands became of greater value; *viz.* the value of 100 £ *per annum.* Now 2 Questions were moved.

—1. if the Preacher, School-master, Usher, and Poor, should have only the certain sums appointed to them by the Founder, or that the Revenew and profit of the Land should be imployed to the increase of the Stipend of the Preacher, School-master, Usher, and Poor?

[131 a]   2. If any surplusage I doth remain, how it should be imployed?

And it was Resolved, on hearing of Councel learned on both parts several dayes at *Serjeants Inn,* by the two Chief Justices, and Justice Walmsey (to whom the Lords referred the consideration of the Case) That the Revenew and profit of the said Lands should be imployed to the encrease of the Stipend of the Preacher, School-master, &c. and Poor; and if any surplusage doeth remain, it should be expended for the maintenance of a greater number of Poor, &c. and nothing should be converted by the Devisees to their own uses. So in the Case in Question, Where Lands in *Croxton,* in the County of Norfolk, were devised by Sir Richard Fulmerston, to his Executors, to find the said works of Piety and Charity, with such certain distribution as is aforesaid; and now the value of the Mannor was greatly encreased, that it shall be employed in performance and encrease of the said works of Piety and Charity instituted and erected by the Founder: for it appears by his distribution of the profits, that he intended all should be imployed in works of Piety and Charity, and nothing should be converted to the private use of the Executors or their heirs. And this Resolution is grounded on evident and apparent reason; for, as if the Lands had fallen in value, the Preacher, School-master, &c. and Poor people should lose, so when the Lands doe increase in value, by the same reason they shall gain. And they said, that this Case did concern the Colleges in the Universities of Cambridge and Oxford, and other Colleges, &c. For in old time when Lands were of small value, (victuals then being cheap,) and were given for the maintenance of poor Scholars, &c. and that every scholar, &c. should have 1 *d.* or 1 *d. ob.* a day, that then such small allowance was Competent in respect of the price of victuals, and the yearly value of the Land; and now the price of victuals being encreased, it shall be injurious to allow a Poor scholar 1 *d.* or 1 *d. ob.* a day, which cannot keep him, and to convert the residue to private uses, where, in right it ought to be imployed to the maintenance or encrease (if it may be) of such works of Piety and Charity which the Founder has expressed, and nothing to any private use; for every College is seised *in jure Collegii, scil.*[1] to the intent that the members of the College, according to the intent of the Founder, should take the benefit thereof and that nothing should be converted to private uses. *Panis | egentium vita*   [131 b] *pauperum, et qui defraudat eos homo sanguinis est.*[2] And afterwards upon Conference had with the other Justices, they were of the same opinion; and according to their opinions the Bill passed in both Houses of Parliament, and

---

    1. [*Ed.:* in law of the College, that is to say.]
    2. [*Ed.:* The bread of the needy is their life; who defrauds them of it is a man of blood (murderer). Eccles. 34:25).]

afterwards was confirmed by the Kings assent. Note, Reader, there is a good Rule in the Act of Parliament called Statutum Templariorum: *Ita semper quod pia et celeberrima voluntas Donatoris in omnibus teneatur et expleatur, et perpetuo sanctissime perseveret.*[3]

---

3. [*Ed.:* In such a way that the intent of the Donor be faithfully and continuously observed in all things, be carried out in full, and remain forever inviolate.]

Part Nine of the *Reports*

The Ninth Part of Coke's *Reports* was published in 1613. It was originally entitled *La Neufme part des reports del Sr. Edw. Coke chivalier, chief justice del common bank: divers resolutions & judgments dones fur solemne arguments, & avec grand deliberation & conference des tres-reverend judges & sages de la ley, de cases en ley queux ne fueront unques resolve ou adjudges par devant: et les raisons & causes des dits resolutions & judgments: publie en le dixiesme an de treshaut & tres-illustre Jaques Roy Dengleterre, France & Ireland, & de Escosse le 46, le fountain de tout Pietie & Justice, & la vie de la ley.* In English, *The Ninth Part of the Reports of Sir Edward Coke, Knight, Lord Chief Justice of Common Pleas, of divers Resolutions and Judgments given upon solemn Arguments, and with great deliberation and Conference of the reverend Judges and Sages of the Law, of Cases in law which were never Resolved or Adjudged Before: and the Reasons and Causes thereof. Published in the tenth year of the most high and Most Illustrious James, King of England, France, and Ireland, and of Scotland the 46., the Fountain of all Justice, and the life of the Law.* Coke here presented another wide-ranging series of topics, including cases in property, criminal law, delivery of an instrument, copyhold, ravishment of a ward, libel, trespass, debt, trusts, leases, and procedure. A large number of these cases were decided in the Court of Wards.

Epigrams from the Title Page:

Marleb. Ann. 52 H. 3. cap. 1.
Provisum est concordatum & concessum, quod tam majores quam minores Justitiam habeant & recipiant in Curia Domini Regis.[1]

Westm. 1. Ann. 3 Ed. 1. cap. 50.
Summa Charitas est unicuiq; facere justiciam omni tempore cum opus fuerit.[2]

---

1. [*Ed.:* It is provided, agreed, and granted that both great and small should have and receive justice in the lord king's court.]

2. [*Ed.:* It is the most charitable thing to do justice at all times when it is needed.]

(Preface)
Deo, Patriae, Tibi.[3]

Seeing the light touch I gave in my preface to mine eight worke[s] out of consent of historie, hath with the judicious Reader (finding it consonant to judiciall record) wrought so good effect, I will adde somewhat thereunto, which I am persuaded will adde to their satisfaction and solace therein, who do reverence and love (as all men ought) the nationall Lawes of their native countrey. I have a very auntient and learned treatise of the Lawes and usages of this kingdome whereby this Realme was governed about 1100. years past, of the title and subject of which booke the Author shal tel you himeselfe in these words. *Which summary I have intituled,* The Mirror of Justices, *according to the vertues and* substances embellies *which I have observed, and which have been used by holy Customs since the time of King* Arthur, *&c.* And soon after. *The Law whereof this Summary is made, is of antient Usages warranted by holy Scripture; and because it is generally given to all, it is therefore called Common. And for that there is no other Law but this, this alone of Antiquities is by general Councils or Parliaments permitted to be used by holy Usages,* &c.

In this Book in effect appeareth the whole frame of the ancient Common Laws of this Realm, as by these few particulars shall appear: As the diversity and distinction of the Courts of Justice (which are *Officinae Legis.*[4])

And first of the High Court of Parliament, which Court is mentioned before by the name of Council general, or Parliament, and *cap.* 1. § 3. *King* Alfred *ordaineth for a Usage perpetual, that twice in the year, or oftner if need be, they shall assemble themselves at* London *to treat in Parliament of the Government of the People of God, how they should keep themselves from sin, should live in quiet, and should receive right by certain Laws and holy judgments,* &c.

2. The Court of Chancery. *It was ordained, that every one upon complaint, should have out of the Kings Chancery a Writ remedial, without any difficulty,* &c. *In the time of King* Alfred *there was no Writ of Grace, but all Writs were remedial, grantable (as of duty) by vertue of an Oath,* &c.

3. The Kings Bench. *Chief Justices holding Pleas of the King.* And soon after. *To the Office of the Chief Justices belongeth, to redress and punish by Writ the*

In Proemio The Book called *The Mirror of Justices. Cap.* I. §. 1.

The Laws warranted by holy Scripture.

Why they be called the Common Laws Counsels general or Parliaments.

The High Court of Parliament. Cro. Arg. 54.

Cap. 1. §. 3. The Court of Chancery. 5. §. 1.

Cap. 4. Of Jurisdiction. The Kings Bench.

---

3. [*Ed.:* To God, to the Country, to you.]
4. [*Ed.:* the workshops of the law.]

wrongful Judgments, Wrongs and Errors of other Justices; and to cause to come before the King the Parties and the Record with the original Writ. And before these Justices are all Writs pleadable, returnable and determinable, where it is mentioned, Before the King himself, &c. It belongeth, also to their Office to hear and determine all Plaints of personal Wrongs done within twelve miles of the King: And to deliver the Gaol of Prisoners deliverable; and to determine all that is determinable by Justices in Eyre, and more or less, according to the nature of their Commission.

4. The Court of Common Pleas. *To the Justices of the Bench power is given to take Fines, to hear and determine grand Assizes, Common Pleas, &c.*

5. The Court of Exchequer. *Moreover the Barons of the Exchequer have Jurisdiction over the Kings Receivers and Bailiffs and of the alienation of the fiefs (or fees) and Rights belonging to the King, and to the Rights of his Crown, &c.*

6. *Justiciarii itinerantes,*[5] or Justices in Eire. *The Kings do Right to all Men by their Justices, Commissioners itinerant, assigned to have Conusans of all Pleas. In aid of such Eires, the Sheriffs Turns and Views of Frankpledges are necessary. And all those whom the good Men of such Enquests did endite of a capital offence, the Kings were wont to destroy without any Answer; which Usages are yet in practise in Almaigne: But by Warrant of Pity and Mercy (because the frailty of Man cannot refrain from sin, unless God of his Grace give him abstinence) It is accorded, That no Appellee or Inditee shall be destroyed without Answer.*

7. The Sheriffs Turn, whereof mention is made before. *The Sheriffs, of ancient Ordinance, do hold general Assemblies twice a year in every Hundred, whither all the Freeholders, within the Hundred are bound to come by the service of their Fiefs (or Fees) that is to say, once after Michaelmas, and another time after Easter. And because the Sheriffs, for the doing hereof, make their Turns (or Courses) through the Hundred, such Assemblies are called the Sheriffs Turns. Where, it belongeth to the Sheriffs, to enquire of all Offences personal, and of all the circumstances of Offences done in those Hundreds; and of Wrongs done by the Kings and Queens Ministers; and of Wrongs done to the King and to the Commonalty, according to the Articles aforesaid in the Divisions of Offences.*

8. Leets on Courts des Views de Frankpledge. *Concerning these Assemblies, first it is thus ordained, That every Hundredor shall assemble once a year; and not only Freeholders, but all of the Hundred, as well Strangers as Denizens, from*

Cap. 4.
§. eodem.
The Court
of Common Pleas.

Eodem c.
§. eodem.
The Court
of Exchequer.

Cap. 1.
§. 3. The
Office of
Justices in
Eire.

Cap. §. 16.
The Sheriffs Turn.

Cap. 1.
§. 17. De
Views de
Frankpledge.

5. [*Ed.:* itinerant justices.]

twelve years upwards (except Archbishops, Bishops, Abbots, Priors and all Religious People and Clerks, Eàrls, Barons and Knights, married Women, persons dumb and deaf, Diseased, Bastards and Lepers, and those that are Deciners elsewhere) to enquire of the points aforesaid, and of the Articles following; and that not by Bondmen or Women, but by the Oaths of twelve Free-men at the least; for a Bondman cannot indite a Free-man, nor no other that is not receivable to do suit in the same Courts. And because it was anciently ordained, That none should abide in the Realm, if he were not in some Decine (or Tything) and undertaken for by Free-men, the Hundredors are once a year to view the Frankpledges and the Sureties: And therefore are such Views called Views of Frankpledges.

Cap. 1. §. 15. The County Court.

9. The County Court. *The Sheriffs hold a Court from Month to Month, or from five Weeks to five Weeks, according to the greatness and largeness of the Country; and these Courts are called Counties, where the Judgments are given by the Suitors, if there be no Writ: And this warranted by ordinary Jurisdiction.*

Cap. 1. §. 15. Court Baron and Hundred Court.

10. Court Barons and Hundred Courts. *The other mean Courts, are the Courts of every Lord of the Fee, &c.*

Court of Pipowders. Cap. 1. §. 3. & §. 15. of mean Courts.

11. Courts de Pipowders. *And that from day to day speedy Justice be done to Strangers in Fairs and Markets, as of Pipowders according to the Law of Merchants.*

Cap. 1. §. 3. Court of Admiralty.

12. Court de Admiralty. *The King hath Sovereign Jurisdiction upon the Sea.*

Cap. 1. §. 13. Courts of the Forest.

13. Courts of the Forest. *The Kings Ministers of his Forest have power, by authority of their Office, to swear Men without the Kings Writ for the safegard of the Peace, and for the Kings Right and the common good, &c.*

Cap. 2. §. 5. Of Countors.

He also treateth of the Professors of the Law, as of the Countors, that is, of the Serjeants and other Pleaders, *There are many that cannot prosecute nor defend their own Causes in Judgment, and many which may not: And therefore are Countors necessary, that that which the Plaintiffs and Actors may not or cannot do by themselves, they may do by their Serjeants, Proctors or Friends. Countors are Serjeants skilful in the Law of the Realm, which serve the common people to prosecute and defend their Actions in Judgment (when need is) for their Fee.*

And also of Attornies, where amongst other things it is said, *None may be an Attorny, which may not be a Countor, &c.*

Cap. 1. §. 3.

Of the Ministers of Justice, as Viscounts, Coroners, Escheators, Bailiffs of Hundreds, &c. *Also by the ancient Kings, Coroners were ordained in every County, and Sheriffs to keep the Peace when the Earls were absent from their Charges, and Bailiffs in lieu of Hundredors, &c.*

Ca. eodem §. eodem.

Of the Prerogatives of the King: *As of Deodands, Alienation to Aliens, Treasure found, Wreck, Waif, Estray, Chattels of Felons and Fugitives, Counties, Honors, Hundreds, Sokes, Gaols, Forests, chief Cities, chief Ports of the Sea, great Maners:*

These held the first Kings as their Right, and of the residue of the Land did enfeoff the Earls, Barons, Knights, Serjeants and others to hold of the Kings, by services provided and ordained for defence of the Realm. It was ordained, that the Knights Fee should come to the eldest by Succession of Heritage; and that Socage Fee should be partable between the male Children: And that the Liege Lords should have the Marriage.

He treateth in the first Chapter of Crimes, and their Divisions of the Crime of Majesty, of Fausonnery,[6] of Treason, of Burning, of Homicide, of Felony, of Burglary, of Rape, *&c.* In the second, of Actions, of Judges, of Actors, *&c.* In the third, of Exceptions dilatory and peremptory, that is, Pleas to the Writ and in Barr, *&c.* of Trials by Juries and by Battail, of Attaints, of Challenges, of Fines, *&c.* In the fourth, of Judgments, and therein of Jurisdiction, of Proces in criminal Causes, and in Actions real, personal and mixt. So as in this Mirror you may perfectly and truly discern the whole Body of the Common Laws of *England.* In Mr. *Plowdens* Commentaries, *fol.* 8*a.* in *Fogasses* Case, *Bradshaw* Attorny General citeth this Book by the Name of *Mirror des Justices, le quel* (saith he) *fuit fait devant le Conquest.* The meaning of *Bradshaw* was, not that the Book was made before the Conquest, but that the Text of Law which he titeth out of that Book was the Law of this Realm, before the Conquest.

But here, though *summa sequar fastigia rerum,*[7] yet I will stay my foot and fix my staff a while, for this grave and learned Author will shew us in this Mirror the great Antiquity of the said Courts of the Common Law, and particularly of the high Court of Parliament ever since the time of King *Arthur,* who reigned about the year of our Lord 516. not that this Court and the rest were instituted then, but that the reach of his Treatise extendeth no higher than to write of the Laws and Usages of this Realm continued since the Reign of that King. He citeth (as you have heard) a Statute of King *Alfred,* as well concerning the holding of this Court of Parliament twice every year at the City of *London,* as to manifest the threefold end of this great and honorable Assembly of Estates. 1. That the Subject might be kept from offending, that is, that Offences might be prevented both by good and provident Laws and by the due Execution thereof. 2. That men might live safely in quiet: And 3. That all Men might receive Justice by certain Laws and holy Judgments, that is, to the end that Justice might be the better administred, that Questions and

---

6. [*Ed.:* Falsifying or counterfeiting a seal or coin.]
7. [*Ed.:* which was made before the conquest. . . . I will only cover the main points.]

defects in Laws might be by this high Court of Parliament explained, reduced to certainty, and adjudged.

This Court, being the most supream Court of this Realm, is a part of the frame of the Common Laws, and in some Cases doth proceed legally according to the ordinary course of the Common Law, as it appeareth in 39 Edw. 3. f. To be short, of this Court it is truly said, *Si vetustatem spectes est antiquissima, si dignitatem est honoratissima, si Jurisdictionem est capacissima.*[8]

And where Question hath been made whether this Court of Parliament continued during the Heptarchy, let the Records themselves make answer. King *Ina* began his Parliament thus, as hath been anciently translated into Latin (which Translation I have:) *Ego* Ina *Dei gratia* West Saxonum *Rex, exhortatione & doctrina* Cenredes *patris mei, &* Heddes *Episcopi mei, &* Erkenwaldes *Episcopi mei, & omnium Aldremannorum meorum & seniorum Sapientum Regni mei, multaq; congregatione Servorum Dei sollicitus de salute animarum nostrarum & statu Regni mei, Constitui rectum conjugium, & justa judicia, pro stabilitate & confirmatione populi mei, benigna sedulitate celebrari: Et nullo Aldremanno vel alicui de toto regimine nostro conscripto liceat abolere judicia.*[9]

The like Parliament was holden by *Offa* King of the *Mercians,* and by *Etherbert* King of *Kent,* and the rest of the seven Kings. After the Heptarchy, taking some few Presidents for many, King *Edward,* Son of the aforenamed King *Alfred,* before the Conquest the first, held a Parliament at *Exeter,* and called thither all his Wisemen: Edwardus *Rex admonuit omnes Sapientes suos qui fuerint* Exoniae *ut investigarent simul & quaererent quomodo pax eorum melior esse possit quam ante fuit, &c.*[10] And it shall evidently appear hereafter, that this *Conventus Sapientum*[11] included the Lords and Commons of the Parliament.

King *Ethelstaen apud Grateleiane,*[12] where all the Noblemen and Wisemen

8. [*Ed.:* If you seek antiquity, it is ancient; if dignity, it is most honorable; if jurisdiction, it is very broad.]

9. [*Ed.:* I, Ine, by the grace of God king of the West Saxons, by the exhortation and teaching of Cenrede my father, and Hedde my bishop, and Erkenwald my bishop, and of all my ealdormen and wise elders of my kingdom, and by a great gathering of the servants of God, being solicitous of the health of our souls and the estate of my kingdom, have appointed right union and just judgments to be laid down with benign diligence for the establishment and strengthening of my people; and it shall be lawful for no ealdorman or other person of our whole realm to abolish judgments.]

10. [*Ed.:* King Edward warned all his wise men to be at Exeter to investigate together and enquire how their peace might be made better than before etc.]

11. [*Ed.:* meeting of wise men.]

12. [*Ed.:* at Grateley.]

of the Realm were gathered together; here was *Conventus omnium Nobilium & Sapientum.*[13] In the Reign of the same King other of his Acts of Parliament are stiled and anciently translated thus. *Haec sunt Judiciae* Exoniae *quae Sapientes consilio* Ethelstani *Regis instituerunt, & iterum apud Fresresham & tertia vice apud ubi haec difinita simul & confirmata sunt.*[14]

King *Edgar,* sirnamed Pacification, at several places enacted many Laws by the Counsel of his Wisemen, here was *Consilium Sapientum,*[15] whose Acts of Parliament, being antiently translated into Latin, were intuled thus, *Haec sunt instituta quae* Edgarus *Rex consilio Sapientum suorum instituit, &c.*[16]

King *Etheldred* at *Woodstock;* and there Laws ordained by him and his Wisemen: *Hoc est Consilium quod Etheldredus Rex & omnes Sapientes sui condixerunt, ad emendationem pacis omnis populi, apud* Woodstock:[17] And another Parliament by him and his Wisemen, both Spiritual and Lay: Here was *Consilium Spiritualium & Laicorum.*[18] And stiled another thus, *Haec sunt verba pacis & prolocutionis quae* Etheldredus *Rex & omnes Sapientes ejus cum exercitu firmaverunt, qui cum Anulano,* Justinio & Guemundo Stigrani *filio venit.*[19] And held another Parliament at *Habam: Haec instituerut*[20] *Etheldredus Rex & Sapientes ejus apud* Habam.[21]

King *Edmund* at *London,* where he summoned both the Spiritualty and Temporalty, and called them by one general Name of Wisemen: Here was *Conventus Sapientum Spiritualium & Temporalium.*[22] But it is best to hear the ancient Translator himself, *Edmundus Rex congregavit magnam Synodum divini ordinis & seculi apud Londoniae Civitatem, in Sancto Paschae solenni, &c.*[23]

---

13. [*Ed.:* a meeting of all the noble and wise men.]

14. [These are the judgments of Exeter which were instituted by the wise men of the council of King AEthelstan, and again at 'Fresresham', and a third time at [*blank*] where these were defined and confirmed together.]

15. [*Ed.:* council of wise men.]

16. [*Ed.:* These are the constitutions which King Edgar instituted by the council of his wise men.]

17. [*Ed.:* This is the advice which King AEthelred and all his wise men brought in for the improvement of the peace of the whole people.]

18. [*Ed.:* council of spiritual and lay men.]

19. [*Ed.:* These are the words of peace and of the speech which King AEthelred and all his wise men confirmed with the army which came with Anulanus, Justinius and Guemundo son of Stigranus.]

20. [*Ed.:* These things were instituted [NB belongs with next passage].]

21. [*Ed.:* by King AEthelred and his wise men at 'Habam'.]

22. [*Ed.:* a meeting of wise men, spiritual and temporal.]

23. [*Ed.:* The king assembled a great synod of the clergy [literally, divine order] and of secular persons at the city of London at the holy feast of Easter.]

And another of his Parliaments beginneth thus, *Hae sunt institutiones quas* Edmundus *Rex & Episcopi sui cum sapientibus suis instituerunt apud Culincona, &c.*[24] And soon after, *Ego* Edmundus *Rex mando & praecipio omni populo Seniorum & Juniorum qui in regione mea sunt, qui investigans investigavi cum sapientibus Clericis & Laicis.*[25]

King *Canutus* at *Winchester;* by the King and the reverend Council of his Wisemen. There was *Venerandum Concilium Sapientum.*[26] For so was that Parliament being of ancient time translated into Latin, called, but hear the Title itself: *Haec sunt Statuta Canuti Regis Anglorum, Danorum, Norvegarum venerando Sapientum ejus consilio, ad laudem & gloriam Dei, & sui regalitatem, & commune commodum, habita in Sancto Natali Domini apud Wintoniam, &c.*[27]

All which and many more are extant and publickly known, but I will add that which I read in the legier Book of the late Monastery of Saint *Edmonds Bury,* now in my hands, of an ancient handwriting, wherein is cited a Parliament holden in the fifth year of this King *Canutus* Reign; but I will keep silence, and let the Book it self speak. *Rex* Canutus *anno Regni sui quinto,* videlicet,[28] *Per centum & triginta annos ante compilationem Decretorum quae anno Domini* 1150. *fuer' compilat', anno septimo Pontificatus Papae* Eugenii *tertii, & ante compilationem aliorum Canonum quorumcunq; cunctos Regni sui Praelatos, Proceresq; ac Magnates ad suum convocans Parliamentum in suo publico Parliamento persistentibus personaliter in eodem* Wulstano & Adelnodo *Archiepiscopis* & Ailwino *Episcopo* Elmhamense, & *aliis Episcopis ipsorum suffraganeis, septem Ducibus cum totidem Comitibus, necnon diversorum monasteriorum nonnullis Abbatibus, cum quumplurimis gregariis militibus, ac cum populi multitudine copiosa, ac omnibus adhuc in eodem Parliamento personaliter existentibus, votis Regiis unanimiter consentientibus praeceptum & decretum fuit,*

24. [*Ed.:* These are the institutions which King Edmund and his bishops, with their wise men, instituted at 'Culincona', etc.]

25. [*Ed.:* I, King Edmund, command and order all people, both old and young, who are within my jurisdiction, that I have sought out with wise clerks and laymen . . .]

26. [*Ed.:* Venerable council of wise men.]

27. [*Ed.:* These are the statutes of Canute, king of the English, Danes and Norse, with the venerable advice of his wise men, to the praise and glory of God, and his regality, and the common profit, made at the feast of Christmas at Winchester etc.]

28. Pryn sur 4 Institut. f. 78. [*Ed.:* in the fifth year of his reign, namely.]

quod Monasterium Sancti Edmundi, *&c. sit ab omni Jurisdictione Episcoporum Comitatus illius extunc imperpetuum funditus liberum & exemptum, &c. Illustris Rex* Hardicanutus *praedicti Regis* Canuti *filius, haeres & successor, ac sui patris vestigiorum devotus imitator, &c. cum laude & favore* Aegelnod' Dorobornensis, *nunc* Cantuariensis, & Alfrici Eborac' *Episcoporum, aliorumq; Episcoporum suffragan', necnon cunctoruns Regni sui mundanorum principum descriptum constituit roboravitq; praeceptum.*[29] Which immunity I know that the said Monastery held until the dissolution thereof in the 31st year of the Reign of King *Henry the eighth.*

But let us proceed, and yet omit many, and touch only that which hath been controverted. It is said, that *Silent leges inter arma,*[30] and that during all the time of the Conqueror no Parliament was lawfully assembled, &c. for *Silent leges inter arma,* and during all his Reign, either the Sword was not put up into the scabbard, or if it were, the Hand was always upon the hilt ready to draw it again. But that a Parliament was assembled and holden according to the common Laws of *England,* in *William* the Conquerors time, it is evident, for that an Act established at a Parliament holden in the Reign of *W.* the Conqueror was pleaded and adjudged to be firm and good and accordingly put in execution by the Judges of the Realm, which they neither would nor could have done, if it had been commanded by the powerful Will of the Conqueror, and not established by a Parliament duly assembled, according to the form and frame of the Common Law. And therefore as well for manifestation hereof; as for proof of that which hath been said, you shall read in

29. [*Ed.:* For one hundred and thirty years before the compilation of the decretals which were compiled in the year of our Lord 1150, in the seventh year of the pontificate of Pope Eugenius III, and before the compilation of any other canons whatsoever, [King Canute] summoned the whole body of prelates, peers and magnates of his realm, in his public parliament; and archbishops Wulstan and Adenoldo, bishop Ailwin of Elmham, and other bishops their suffragans, seven dukes, with all the earls, and many abbots of various monasteries, and great crowds of knights, personally appeared there with a copious multitude of people; and, while all of them were still in the same parliament, it was ordered and decreed by the royal will, everyone consenting, that the monastery of St. Edmund, etc. should thenceforth for ever be free and exempt for ever from all jurisdiction of the bishops of that county etc. The illustrious King Hardicanute, son of the aforesaid King Canute, his heir and successor, and a devoted imitator of the ways of his father, with the praise and favour of bishops Aegelnod of Dover, now of Canterbury, and Aelfric of York, and other bishops their suffragans, and also of the whole body of people of his realm, have constituted and confirmed the above mentioned command of worldly princes.]

30. [*Ed.:* The laws are silent amidst arms [during war].]

the Book Case of 21 *E. 3. f. 60a., 60b.*[31] *That the King sued a Writ of Attachment upon a Prohibition against the Bishop of* Norwich, *for that where the Abby of St.* Edmonds Bury *in the County of* Suffolk *was founded by the Progenitors of the King, and exempt from all Jurisdiction of the Ordinary, and that no Ordinary should visit there, and that none should go against the said ordinance and the foundation aforesaid: That upon controversie between* Arfastus *late Bishop of* Norwich, *and B. late Abbot of* Bury, *of the Exemptions aforesaid; in the time of* William *the Conqueror, at his Parliament on a certuin day holden, it was ordained by the King, the Archbishop of* Canterbury, *and all the other Bishops of the Land, the Earls, Barons,* &c. *That at what time the Bishop of* Norwich, *or any of his successors, should go against the points of the foundation, and exemptions aforesaid, that the Bishop for the time being should pay to the King or to his Heirs thirty Talents of Gold: And declared further, how the King sent a Prohibition to the Bishop, that he should not enter into the said Franchise, nor attempt any thing against the priviledge of the said Church of St.* Edmund, *and that notwithstanding the said Prohibition, the then Bishop of* Norwich *had visited the Abby aforesaid, and had summoned the Abbot to shew the Charters of their Foundation, wrongfully and in despight of our Sovereign Lord the King: whereunto the then Bishop pleaded not guilty, and he was found guilty by the Verdict of the Enquest. Whereupon it was adjudged, that the Temporalties of the Bishop should be seised into the Kings Hands. But it was advised and resolved by all the Judges, that in right of the Talents they could not give Judgment; for two causes:* 1. *For that the Prohibition was the original Suit, and that was determined by the Judgment in the Prohibition, that the Temporalties of the Bishop should be seised into the Kings Hands, which then was the proper Judgment in the Suit.* 2. *Concerning the Talents they were a penalty ordained by Parliament in that case, so that the Penalty had no dependency upon the Prohibition, which is the original Suit. But it was advised and resolved by the Judges, that the Bishop of* Norwich *had forfeited the said Penalty of the Talents to the King, and that they ought to grant a* Scire facias[32] *to the then Bishop for that purpose, which was granted accordingly, upon which Writ the Bishop appeared and pleaded, and thereupon Judgment was given, that the King should recover the said Talents, as by the said Book Case judicially adjudged appeareth.*

---

31. Pryn sur 4 Institut. 1, 7. 4 Inst. 12.

32. [*Ed.:* Writ to require a person to act or show cause to avoid acting on the basis of a record, such as a judgment.]

Which Case if the Opponents had seen or known, they would have therewith rested satisfied. And this notable Judgment giveth credit to that ancient Treatise, intituled thus, (a)[33] *Modus tenendi Parliamentum. Hic describitur modus quomodo Parliamentum Regis* Angliae, & Anglicorum *suorum tenebatur tempore Regis* Ed. *filii Regis* Etheldredi, *qui quidem modus fuit per discretiores Regni, coram* Williel' *Duce* Normaniae, & *Conquestore & Rege* Angliae, *ipso Conquestore hoc praecipiente, & per ipsum approbat' & suis temporibus & successoribus, suorum Regum* Angl' *usitat':*[34] Wherein the Assembly of the Kings, the Lords and Commons, according to the manner continued to this day, is set down, which I have in a fair and very ancient written hand, whereby it is manifest that *Conventus Nobilium & Sapientum, &c.*[35] included both the Lords and the Commons of the Parliament.

It is evident[36] that there were Tenants in ancient demesne before the Conquest, and for a certainty therein, and to know of what Manors such Tenants did hold, it appears by the Book of Domesday, that all the Tenants that did hold any of those Manors that were in the hands of King *Ed.* the Son of King *Etheldred,* or of King *W.* the Conqueror, were Tenants in ancient demesne. And these Tenants then had and yet have these priviledges amongst others, for that they were bound by their tenure to plow and husband, *&c.* the Kings demesns before and in the Conquerors time, therefore they were not to be returned Burgesses to serve in Parliament, to the end they might intend the Kings Husbandry the better. 2. They were not to be contributory to the Fees of the Knights of Shires that served in Parliament; which Priviledges (though the cause ceaseth) continueth to this day; therefore there were Parliaments unto which the Knights and Burgesses were summoned both before and in the Reign of the Conqueror. For your satisfaction herein, see *F.N.B. 14.e.* 49 *Edw.3.22.b.2.3.a.* 40 *Edw.3.25.* 11*Hen.4.2. &c.* Also the ancient Towns called Boroughs are the most ancient Towns within *England,* for those Towns which now are Cities and Counties, in ancient time were Burghs, and called Burghs, for out of those ancient Towns called Burghs came the Burgesses to the Parliament, which are the very words of *Littleton lib.* 2. *c.* 10. *Vide* 40 *Ass. p.* 27.

---

33. a) Pryn sur Inst. 1, 2, 3, tc. 78, &c. Inst. 12.
34. [*Ed.:* The Method of Holding Parliament . . . , the title of the treatise.]
35. [*Ed.:* a meeting of noble and wise men, etc.]
36. *F.N.B. 14. d.*

11 *Hen.4.2.* 22 *Edw.4.11. &c.* So as it appeareth that the ancient Burghs are the most ancient Towns of *England,* and consequently long time before the Conquest; and I have found many of them since the Conquest incorporated into Cities, and distinguished into Counties since the Conquest, but had been ancient Burghs (from whence came the Burgesses to the Parliament) time out of mind before the Conquest: Nay divers of the most ancient Burghs, that yet send Burgesses to the Parliament, flourished before the Conquest, and have been of little or no account to have any such privileges newly granted to them at any time since. And I could yet never find when any of them, or any other the ancientest Burghs, were of ancient time since the Conquest endowed with that privilege.

King *Henry* the first *Anno Domini* 1100[37] *cum suorum consilio decrevit ut monetagium commune quod capiebatur per Civitates vel Comitatus quod non fuer' tempore* Edwardi *Regis, hoc ne amodo fiet. Item quod Ecclesius non venderet nec ad forman daret, mortuo Episcopu vel Abbate.*[38] And this King assembled another Parliament[39] on *Candlemas* Day at *London Anno Domini* 1123.

King Henry the Second in the year of our Lord God 1185. (as testifieth *Mathew Paris*) *Convocavit Clerum Regni & populum cum omni Nobilitate ad fontem Clericorum.*[40]

King *John* held a Parliament in the sixth year of his Reign, as it appeareth by his Writs of the Chancery in these words: *Rex Vicecomiti, &c. Sciatis quod consensum est cum assensu Archiepiscorum, Comitum, Baronum & omnium fidelium nostrorum* Angliae, *quod novem Milites per totam* Angliam *invenient decimum Militem bene paratum equis & armis ad defensionem Regni nostri, &c.*[41] But to proceed any further were but to gild Gold, or to add a little Drop to the great Ocean.

Concerning the name of the Parliament two things fall into consideration,

---

37. *Richardus Hagustadensis* & *Math. Paris.* in brevi Historia.

38. [*Ed.:* In the year of our Lord 1100, [King Henry I] with his council decreed that the common mint which was undertaken by the citizens or the county, which was not in the time of King Edward, should not from thenceforth be done. Also that he would not sell or let to farm churches on the death of the bishop or abbot.]

39. Ex Chronico de *Peterburgo.*

40. [*Ed.:* Called together the clergy and people of the realm, with all the nobility, to Clerkenwell.]

41. [*Ed.:* The King to the Sheriff etc. Know ye that it is agreed, with the assent of the archbishops, earls, barons and all our faithful subjects of England, that every nine knights throughout England should find the tenth knight ready with horses and arms for the defence of our kingdom, etc.]

1. What the Word signifieth. 2. When this supream Court was christened by the name of Parliament: Touching the first, it is so called for two causes, 1. Because that every Member of that high Court hath judicial place, and for that every Man there should without any Spirit, either of contradiction or smoothing, *Parler la ment,*[42] speak judicially his mind, it is called Parliament.[43] 2. The Laws there made are called Acts of Parliament, because they are to be expounded, being part of the Laws of the Realm, by the Judges of the Law, according to the mind and true meaning of the speakers that were the makers of these Acts; as *Testamentum*[44] is to be expounded *secundum mentem Testatoris,*[45] and *Arbitramentum secundum mentem Arbitatoris.*[46] As to the 2d,[47] the *Saxons* called this Court *micel gemott,*[48] the great Assembly, *wittena gemott,*[49] the Assembly of Wise Men, the Latin Authors of those times called it *Commune Concilium, magna Curia, generalis Conventus, &c.*[50] And let it be granted, that *W.* the Conqueror changed the name of this Court, and first called it by the name of a Parliament, yet manifest it is by that which hath been said, that he changed not the frame or jurisdiction of this Court in any point. And the very Names in substance that were attributed to this Court before the Conquest, are continued after the Conquest to this day. For in the *Mirror* of Justices, as appeareth before, it is called *Concilium generale,* Fleta lib.2.*c.*2. *Habet etiam Rex Curiam Suam in Concilio Suo in Parliamentis Suis, praesentibus Praelatis, Comitibus, Baronibus, Procerib', & aliis viris peritis.*[51] 8 R.2. Avowry 260. and in many other Books it is called *Rex & Concilium:* In the Original Regist.f.280. it is called *Magnum Concilium.* In Dorso claus.16 E.2. M. 5. Henricus *de bello monte* Baro *de magno & Secreto Concilio Regis:*[52] and *Rot. Parliam' an.* 3 E. 4. *parte prima* M. 2. it is called *Magnum Concilium.* Bracton

---

42. [*Ed.:* to speak the mind.]

43. *Co. Lit. 110. b.*

44. [*Ed.:* testament.]

45. [*Ed.:* according to *mentum testatoris* (the mind of the testator).]

46. [*Ed.:* arbitration according to the mind of the arbitrator.]

47. *Tay. Hist. Gav. 65. Co. Lit. 110. a.*

48. [*Ed.:* the great meeting.]

49. [*Ed.:* the meeting of wise men.]

50. [*Ed.:* The common council, great court, general meeting, etc.]

51. [*Ed.:* The King also has his court in his council in his parliaments, in the presence of the prelates, earls, barons, peers and other learned men.]

52. [*Ed.:* Henry, baron de Beaumont, of the king's great and secret council.]

lib. 1. c. 2. termeth it *Magna Curia.* Anno 17 E. 2. de Templariis, *Super quo convocatis Majoribus de Concilio Domini Regis tam Justiciariis quam Laicis personis in Parliamentum, concordatum est in Parliamento, &c.*[53] And in many Statutes in the Reigns of *Henry the third Edward the first* and succeeding Kings, it is called *Commune Concilium,* and *Commune Concilium Regis,* and *Commune Concilium Regni,*[54] and so runneth the Writ of *Wast,*[55] and many other original and judicial Writs. But if any be desirous to see more of this King, let him look into the eighth part of my Reports in the Princes Case. So as I conclude, that the nature and name of the Court, in use before the Conquest, continueth to this day. And where some do suppose, that in the Parliament holden at *Westminster,* in the third year of the Reign of King *Edward the first* called *Westm'* the 1. this Word Parliament first crept in, where it is called the first general Parliament by the assent of the Archbishops, Bishops, Abbots, Priors, Earls, Barons and all the Comminalty of the Land summoned to the same, *&c.* It is manifest that the name was long before that time, as well by that which hath already been said, as for that in the 9th year of *Edward* 2. Son and immediate Successor to King *Edward* 1. at a Parliament then holden, it is said thus, *Sciatis quod iam dudum temporibus progenitorum nostrorum quondam Regum* Angliae *in diversis Parliamentis suis, &c.*[56] which could not have truly been said if the Name had first begun in the Reign of his Father.[57,58] This is not that Court that in *France* bear the Name of Parliaments, for they are but ordinary Courts of Justice which (if you believe *Paulus Jovins*) were by us first setled there: But this is that which both *England* and *Scotland* agree in naming of it a Parliament, which the *French* doth term *Assemblee des Estats,* or *les Estats,* and the *German* a Dyet.[59]

Fleta ubi Supra a saith of this Court, *Ubi terminatae sunt dubitationes ju-*

---

53. [*Ed.:* Whereupon, the leading members of the lord king's council, both justices and lay persons, having been called into parliament, it is agreed in parliament, etc.]

54. [*Ed.:* Common council, and the king's common council, and the common council of the realm.]

55. [*Ed.:* Waste]

56. Pryn sur 4 Institut. 2, &c.

57. [*Ed.:* Be it known that not long since, in the times of our forebears formerly kings of England, in their various parliaments, etc.]

58. Co. Lit. 110.a.

59. [*Ed.:* assembly of the estates, or the estates.]

diciorum, & novis injuriis emersis nova constituuntar remedia, & unisuique jus-
ticia prout meruerit retribuetur ibidem.[60]

In Master *Plowdens Commentaries* 388.[61] *Le Parliament est Court de tresgrand*
honour & justice, de que nul doit imaginit chose dishonourable.[62] I will pretermit
Fortescue sometime Chief Justice of *England*, in his Treatise *De Laudibus Legum*
Angliae,[63] and many others, and will conclude this Point with him that is the
chief Antiquary of his time, because he concludeth the sum of all aptly, dis-
tinctly and eloquenly,[64] *sol.* 128. *b. Quod ad* Angliae *Tribunalia, Curias, five*
Juris fora attinet, in triplici sunt apud nos differentia, alia enim sunt Ecclesiastica,
alia temporalia, & unum mixtum, quod maximum, & longe amplissimum, non
ita vetusto nomine e Gallia *mutuato Parliamentum dicitur. Majores nostri Anglo-*
Saxones Wittena gemott, *i. Prudentum Conventus, &* Geredniss, *i. Concilium,*
& Micel synod *(a Graeca dictione, synodus) i. Magnus Conventus, Latini ejus*
& Subsequentis aevi Scriptores, Commune Concilium, Curiam altissimam, ge-
nerale placitum, Curiam magnam, Magnatum Conventum, praesentiam Regis,
Praelatorum, Procerumque collectorum, commune totius Regni Concilium, &c.
vocarunt. Utque universum AEtoliae *Concilium* Panetolium Livio *nominatur,*
ita Pananglium, *recte dici possit. Ex Rege enim, Clero, Nobilibus, Majoribus,*
Equitibus & Burgensibus electis; sive ut significantius dicam stylo forensi, ex Rege,
Dominis spiritualibus, & temporalibus, atque ex Communitate constat, qui univ-
ersae Angliae *corpus repraesentant. Statis autem temporibus non habetur, sed a*
Rege pro arbitrio indicitur, quoties de rebus arduis & urgentibus, ne quid detri-
menti Respublica capiat, consultandum, ejusdemq; solius arbitrio dissolvitur. Sum-
mam autem & sacrosanctam authoritatem habet in legibus ferendis, confirmandis,
antiquandis, interpretandis, proscriptis in integrum restituendis, litibus inter pri-
vatos difficilioribus decidendis, & ut semel dicam, in omnibus quae ad reipublicae
salutem, vel etiam privatum quemcunq; spectare possint.[65]

---

60. [*Ed.:* where doubtful judgments are determined and new remedies appointed for new injuries, and
there everyone who should merit it is given justice.]

61. Plowd. 398. b. 11 Co. 14. a.

62. [*Ed.:* the parliament is a court of the greatest honour and justice, of which no one ought to imagine
a dishonourable thing.]

63. [*Ed.:* In praise of the laws of England.]

64. Camden.

65. [*Ed.:* There are with us three distinctions with respect to the tribunals, courts or jurisdictions of

In this ancient Mirror you may also clearly discern as far as the Reign of the often named King *Arthur,* the great Antiquity of the Officers and Ministers of the Common Law, and of their inferior Courts, as for example, of the Offices of the Keepers or Senators of the Shires or Counties, *Custodes seu Praepositi Comitatus,*[66] of later times called Shireves (who saith this Author *fueront ordeines per veiels Roys quant les Countees demisterent des gards*[67]) and of his Tourns and County Courts: Which Officers and division of Shires continued (as you may read amongst the Laws of those seven Kings) though with much incroachment, during the Heptarchy, as taking one or two Examples for many: Amongst the Laws of King *Ina* it is provided in these Words, *Gif hwa hun righter bidde beforan scirman oth the othrun deman,*[68] the ancient Translation thus, *Si quis rectum sibi roget coram aliquo* Scirman (i. *Praeposito comitatus) vel alio Judice & habere non possit, & accusatus vadium recti dare nolit, emendet* 30 s. *& infra septem noctes faciat ei recti dignum.*[69]

And in another place, *Gif he Eldorman hy, tholige his scire, Qui furem ceperit, vel captum reddiderit, vel ipsum dimiserit, vel furtum celaverit, reddat ipsum furem secundum weram suam, si Eorldermannus, i. Praepositus Comitatus sit,*

England; for some are ecclesiastical, some temporal, and one is mixed: and that is the greatest and most extensive, not so long ago called parliament (borrowing the French name). The greater Anglo-Saxons called it 'witena gemot', that is, a meeting of wise men, and 'geredis', that is, a council, and 'micel synod' (from the Greek word synod), that is, a great meeting. The Latin writers of that and subsequent periods call it the common council, the highest court, the general plea, the great court, the great meeting, the presence of the king, prelates and peers gathered, the common council of the whole realm, etc. And as Livy called the supreme council of Aetolia 'Panetolium', so ought it rightly to be called Pan-anglium. It consists of the king, the clergy, the nobles, and the mayors, knights and burgesses who have been elected, or (as is more significantly said in legal style) the king, the lords spiritual and temporal, and the commons: who represent the body of the whole of England. At certain times it does not exist, for it is proclaimed at the king's pleasure whenever he needs advice concerning difficult and urgent matters, lest any damage be done to the state; and it is dissolved by the same power alone. It has the ultimate and sacrosanct authority in laying down, confirming, abrogating, interpreting and consolidating laws, deciding the more difficult lawsuits between private people, and in all things whatsoever that may belong to the health of the state or to any private matter.]

66. [*Ed.:* keepers or provosts of the counties.]

67. [*Ed.:* were ordained by ancient kings when earls were deprived of the custody [of the counties].]

68. [*Ed.:* If anyone leaves his lord without licence, or steals into another county, and then returns, he shall go back to the place where he was before and make amends of sixty shillings to his lord etc.]

69. [*Ed.:* If anyone should seek justice to be done him before any shire-man (that is, provost of a county), or other judge, and cannot have it, and the accused person will not give a gage of justice, he shall make amends of thirty shillings and within seven months do him such justice as he deserves.]

perdat Comitatum suum nisi Rex parcere velit ei.[70] If the Shireve do it he shall lose the Custody of his Shire or County: And afterwards, *Si quis discedat a domino suo sine licentia, vel in alium Comitatum se furetur, & deinceps inveniatur, redeat illuc ubi antea fuit, & emendet domino suo lx s. &c.*[71]

And albeit the *Saxons* gave this Officer the vulgar Name used to this day, yet it is manifest that the Office was of ancient time before they set any foot in *England.*[72] This word *Shireve* is derived of two *Saxon* words, viz. of *Scyre,* that is, the Shire or County, and *Reve,* that is, *Custos,* or *Praepositus Comitatus,*[73] the Keeper or Gardein of the Shire; and sometime (as you see) they were called Shire-man or Elderman of the Shire. And to this day his Patent is, *Commisimus vobis Custodiam Comitatus.*[74,75] So I agree well with them which affirm that King *Alfred* divided *England* into Shires or Counties, in that he made the most certain division of them; for where, during the time of the Heptarchy, there were many Incroachments one upon another, and many ancient bounds obscured, all that he reformed by his exact partition. But they must also agree with me, that long before the Birth of King *Alfred* this Kingdom had been divided into Shires or Counties. But hereof, at this time, this little shall suffice.

I have in my custody an ancient Record intitled *Kanc' de placito apud Pinendenam inter Lanfrancum Archiepiscopum Cant', & Odonem Baiocensem Episcopum tempore magni Regis* Willielmi *qui* Anglicum *Regnum armis conquisivit:*[76] The effect whereof is, That *Lanfrank* Archbishop of *Canterbury* brought a Writ of right Patent against the said *Odo* of the Manors of *Raculfe, Sandwic', Rateburg', Widetun, Saltwode, cum Burgo Heth ad Saltwode pertinente, Langport, Huoenden, Rokinge, Broche, Detling, Prestitune, Sunderhurst, Earheth, Orpintune, Einsford, &c., una cum libertatibus & pertinentiis de soca, saca, Toll, Team, Flymena, Firmith, Grithbreach, Storsteale, Haunfare, Infangentheof, cum*

---

70. [*Ed.:* If he is an ealdorman, he shall forfeit his shire. He who takes a thief, or renders someone captive, and lets him go, or conceals the theft, shall pay for the thief according to his wergeld. If he is an ealdorman (that is, provost of a county), he shall lose his county, unless the king is willing to spare him.]

71. [*Ed.:* If anyone should seek justice before the shire-man or other judge.]

72. Co. Lit. 109. b. 168. a.

73. [*Ed.:* keeper or provost of the county.]

74. [*Ed.:* we have committed to you the keeping of the county.]

75. Co. Lit. 168.a.

76. [*Ed.:* Kent. Concerning a plea at Pennenden between Lanfranc, archbishop of Canterbury, and Odo, bishop of Bayeux, in the time of the great King William who conquered the English realm with arms.]

omnibus aliis consuetudinibus paribus istis, vel minoribus istis, in terris & in aquis, in sylvis, in viis, & in pratis, & in omnibus aliis rebus infra Civitatem, & extra, & in omnibus aliis locis:[77] Which Writ was removed into the County Court by a Writ called a *Tolt:* and the Record saith, *Quod praecepit Rex Comitatum totum absque mora considere, & omnes Francigenas, & praecipue Anglos in antiquis legibus & consuetudinibus peritos in unum convenire: qui cum convenerint apud Pinendenam pariter considerunt, &c.* Huic placito interfuerunt *Ernestus Episcopus de Rovec', Agelricus Episcopus de Cicestr', vir antiquissimus, & legum terrae sapientissimus, qui ex praecepto Regis advectus fuit, ad ipsas antiquas legum consuetudines discutiendas & edocendas, in una quadriga, Richardus de Tunebreg, Hugo de Monteforti, Willielmus de Acres, Haymo Vicecomes, & alii multi, &c. Barones Regis & ipsius Archiepiscopi, atque illorum Episcoporum homines multi, &c. cum toto isto Comitatu multae & magnae authoritatis viri, &c. Et ab omnibus illis probis & sapientibus hominibus qui affuerunt fuit ita diraciocinatum & etiam a toto Comitatu recordatum atque judicatum, quod sicut ipse Rex tenet suas terras liberas & quietas in suo dominico, ita Archiepiscopus teneat suae terras praedictas omnino liberas & quietas in dominico, &c.*[78] And let not this ancient Judgment in a Writ of Right seem strange: for since that time, and to this day the Judgment for the Tenant in a Writ of Right is, *Quod teneat terram illam, &c. quietam,* or, *in pace, &c.*[79] And under this Record it is thus testified. *Hujus placiti multis testibus multisque rationibus determinatum finem postquam Rex audivit, laudavit, laudansque cum consensu omnium Prin-*

---

77. [*Ed.:* [Following the list of locations], together with the liberties and appurtenances of soke, sake, toll, team, flymenfyrm, grithbreche, [forestel], hamfare, infangthief, and all other customs equivalent to these, or less than these, on land and in water, in woods, in ways, and in meadows, and in all other things within the city and without, and in all other places.]

78. [*Ed.:* that the king commanded the whole county to meet without delay, and that there should be convened all the Frenchmen and especially the English who were learned in the old laws and customs; and they met at Pennenden, and sat down together, etc. At this case were present Arnost, bishop of Rochester, AEthelric, bishop of Chichester, a most elderly man and very wise in the laws of the land, who was brought in a cart by the king's command to discuss and explain the old customs of the laws, Richard de Tonbridge, Hugh de Montfort, William de Acres [Arques], Hamo the sheriff, and many others, etc., the king's barons and his archbishops, and many of the said bishops' men, etc., with the whole of that county, men of much and great authority, etc. And it was decided by all these good and wise men who were present, and also recorded and adjudged by the whole county, that just as the king himself holds his lands freely and quit in his demesne, so the archbishop should hold his aforesaid lands utterly free and quit in his, etc.]

79. [*Ed.:* that he hold the land, etc. quiet, or in peace, etc.]

cipum suorum confirmavit & ut incorruptus perseveraret firmiter praecepit.[80] And the cause of this Controversie is there also expressed in these words. *Tempore magni Regis* Willielmi *qui* Anglicum *Regnum armis conquisivit, & suis ditionibus subjugavit, contigit* Odonem Bajocensem *Episcopum & ejusdem Regis fratrem multo citius quam* Lanfrancum *Archiepiscopum in* Angliam *venire atque in Comitatu de* Chent *cum magna potentia residere, ibique potestatem non modicam exercere. Ac quia illis diebus in Comitatu illo quisquam non erat qui tantae fortitudinis viro resistere posset propter magnam quam habuit potestatem, terras complures de Archiepiscopatu* Cantuar' & *consuetudines nonnullas sibi arripuit, atque usurpans suae dominationi. Postea vero non multo tempore contigit praefatum* Lanfrancum Cadomensis *Ecclesiae Abbatem jussu Regis in* Angliam *quoque venire, atque in Episcopatum* Cantuar', *Deo disponente, totius* Angliae *primatum sublimatum esse, ubi dum aliquandiu resideret, & antiquas Ecclesiae suae terras multas sibi deesse inveniret & suorum negligentia antecessorum illas distributas atque distractas fuisse reperisset, diligenter inquisita & bene cognita veritate, Regem quam citius potuit & non pigre inde requisivit, ut Justicia secundum legem sibi fieret, &c.*[81] And thus much by way of Addition to my former Preface shall suffice.

I have in this ninth Work reported certain Cases which have been adjudged and resolved, together with the Reasons and Causes thereof, to the end the Learned that know the Law may be confirmed, such as know it not may be instructed, the Possessions and Interests of all in general according to Right

---

80. [*Ed.:* Having heard the conclusion of this case, by many witnesses and arguments, the king approved it and, praising it with the consent of all his princes, confirmed it and firmly ordered it to be preserved unbroken thereafter.]

81. [*Ed.:* In the time of the great King William, who conquered the English realm by arms, and subjected it to his authority, it so happened that Odo, bishop of Bayeux, and the said king's brother, arrived in England much earlier than Archbishop Lanfranc and resided in the county of Kent with great power, exercising considerable authority there. And because in those days there was no one in that county who could resist a man of such strength, because of the great power that he had, he seized numerous lands and a good many customs of the archbishopric of Canterbury for himself, and by way of usurpation gained control of them. Not long afterwards, however, the said Lanfranc, abbot of the church of Caen, also came to England by the king's command to be archbishop of Canterbury, by God's arrangement, and supreme primate of all England. He lived there for some time, and found many of the old lands of his church to be missing and distributed and given away by the negligence of his predecessors, and having made diligent enquiry and careful discovery of the truth he went to the king as soon as he could and earnestly asked that justice be done to him according to law, etc.]

strengthened and quieted, Love and Charity between Man and Man continued, unnecessary Suits, the Causes of Contention and Expence, prevented,
and the Reign of our dread Sovereign, for his Zeal of Justice, renowed and
honoured.

And it is very observable out of what root the Doubts and Questions herein
adjudged and resolved did grow: The most difficult whereof do spring out of
these two Roots, either out of Statutes enacted in that supream Court of
Parliament (whereof I have spoken) or out of supposed variety of Opinions
and Rules in our Books. Out of Acts of Parliament principally in two sorts,
either when an ancient Pillar of the Common Law is taken out of it, or when
new remedies are added to it. By the first arise dangers and difficulties, and
by the second the Common Law rightly understood is not bettered, but in
many Causes so fettered, that it is thereby very much weakned. Take one
Example for both; In 5 *Edwardi* 3. 14.[82] Sir *Will. Herle* Chief Justice of the
Court of Common Pleas, saith, That the Statute *De Donis Conditionalibus*[83]
was made in the Reign of King *Edward* the first, (who (saith he) was the most
sage King that ever was) and the Cause of the Statute was to salve the Heritage
in the Blood of them to whom the Gift was made; and yet that Statute shaking
a main Pillar of the Law, that made all Estates of Inheritance Fee simple, no
Wisdom could foresee such and so many mischiefs as upon those fettered
Inheritances followed; but hereof have I given a touch in the Prefaces to my
third and fourth Work; and therefore desiring that this kind of innovation
might be left, I will for this time leave it. Concerning the supposed variety
of Opinions and Rules in our Books, I trust in many Cases herein the studious
Reader shall observe (as in my former Works he hath done) that the Law truly
distinguishing[84] (for *ubi Lex non distinguit nec nos distinguere debemus*)[85] they
be in these Cases well and justly accorded. And I affirm it constantly, That
the Law is not incertain *in Abstracto* but *in Concreto,* and that the incertainty
thereof is *hominis vitium*[86] and not *professionis:*[87] And to speak plainly there

---

82. Co. Lit. 19. a, 392. b. 10 Co. 38. b.

83. [*Ed.:* concerning conditional gifts.]

84. Cawley 132.

85. [*Ed.:* where the law makes no distinction, we ought not to distinguish.]

86. [*Ed.:* the vice of the man, . . .]

87. [*Ed.:* . . . the profession.]

be two Causes of the uncertainty thereof *in Concreto, viz. praepostera lectio* and *praepropera praxis*,[88] preposterous reading, and oversoon practise.

A substantial and a compendious Report of a Case rightly adjudged doth produce three notable effects: 1. It openeth the Understanding of the Reader and Hearer; 2. It breaketh through difficulties, and 3dly, It bringeth home to the hand of the studious, variety of pleasure and profit; I say it doth set open the Windows of the Law to let in that gladsom Light whereby the right reason of the Rule (the Beauty of the Law) may be clearly discerned; it breaketh the thick and hard Shell, whereby with pleasure and ease the sweetness of the kernel may be sensibly tasted, and adorneth with variety of Fruits both pleasant and profitable, the Storehouses of those by whom they were never planted nor warred. Whereunto (in those Cases that be *tortuosi*[89] and of great difficulty, adjudged upon Demurrer or resolved in open Court) no one Man alone with all his true and uttermost labours, nor all the actors in themselves by themselves out of a Court of Justice, nor in Court without solemn Argument, where (I am persuaded) Almighty God openeth and inlargeth the understanding of the desirous of Justice and Right could ever have attained unto. For it is one amongst others of the great honours of the Common Laws, that Cases of great difficulty are never adjudged or resolved *in tenebris* or *sub silentio suppressis rationibus;*[90] but in open Court, and there upon solemn and elaborate Arguments, first at the Bar by the Counsel learned of either party (and if the Case depend in the Court of Common Pleas then by Serjeants at Law only) and after at the Bench by the Judges, where they argue (the puisne Judge beginning and so ascending) *seriatim,*[91] upon certain days openly and purposely prefixed, declaring at large the authorities, reasons and causes of their Judgments and Resolutions in every such particular Case (*habet enim nescio qd' energiae viva vox:*[92]) a reverent and honourable proceeding in Law, a grateful satisfaction to the Parties, and great instruction and direction to the attentive and studious Hearers.

In this, as in the rest of my Works, my chief care and labour hath been for

---

88. [*Ed.*: namely, preposterous reading and premature practice,]
89. [*Ed.*: tortuous.]
90. [*Ed.*: in darkness, or in silence, suppressing the reasons;]
91. [*Ed.*: in order,]
92. [*Ed.*: for the living voice has I know not what efficacy:]

the advancement of truth that the Matter might be justly and faithfully related, and (for avoiding of Obscurity and Novelty) that it might be in a legal and Method and in the Lawyers Dialect plainly delivered, that herein no Authority cited might be wittingly omitted, or coldly applied; no Reason or Argument made on either side willingly impaired; no Mans Reputation directly or indirectly impeached; no Author or Authority cited unreverently disgraced; and that such only as (in mine Opinion) should hereafter be leading Cases for the publick quiet might be imprinted and published. Almighty God (who hath of his great Goodness enabled me hereunto) knoweth that I have not taken these Labours, either for vain Glory or upon presumption of any persuasion of Knowledge: but true it is, that I have been ever desirous to know much; and do acknowledge my self to owe much more to my Profession than all my true and faithful Labours can satisfie: And as I truly confess, that I have no means (for I know my own wants) to quit that Debt, so I faithfully promise never to be found unthankful or unwilling to perform what by my uttermost endeavour shall lie in my power. My desire of the learned Reader, with old *Bracton* (sometime a famous Judge of the Court of Common Pleas (as I find in Record) and a Writer of the Laws) is, *Ut si quid superfluum vel perperam positum in hoc opere invenerit, illud corrigat & emendet, vel conniventibus oculis pertranseat, cum omnia habere in memoria & nulla peccare, divinum sit potius quam humanum.*[93]

Vale.[94]

William Aldred's Case.
(1610) Michaelmas Term, 8 James I
In the Court of King's Bench.
First Published in the *Reports*, volume 9, page 57b.*

> *Ed.:* William Aldred owned the house of Hareleston in Norfolk. Next to the hall and parlor of Aldred's house, Thomas Benton owned a small or-

93. [*Ed.:* Whatever you find has been put in this book superfluously or mistakenly, correct and amend it, or pass it over with your eyes shut, for to remember everything and commit no faults is divine rather than human.]

94. [*Ed.:* Fare[well].]

*[*Ed.:* The initial pleadings are at Trinity 7 Jac. Rot. 2802.]

chard, which he (according to Aldred) maliciously converted to a hog sty in order to vex Aldred. Aldred sued, claiming that the foetid and unpleasant odors of the sty interrupted his enjoyment of his land and was a nuisance. The King's Bench found the swine sty to be a nuisance. Aldred won. The case is particularly important for establishing liability for environmental nuisances, and is an early case in environmental law.

William Aldred brought an action upon the Case against Thomas Benton, which began *Trinity 7 Jacobi, Rot. 2802.* That where the Plaintiff, *29 Septemb. 6 Jac.* was seised of a house, and of a parcel of land in length 31 feet, and in breadth 2 feet and a half, next to the Hall and Parlour of the Plaintiff, of his house aforesaid in *Harleston* in the County of *Norfolk* in fee; and where the Defendant was possessed of a small Orchard on the East part of the said parcel of Land, praed' *Thomas malitiose machinans et intendens ipsum Willhielmum de easuamento et proficuo messuag' et parcell' terrae suorum praed' impedire et deprivare,* the said 29 day of Septemb., *Anno 6 Jacobi quoddam magnum lignile in dicto horto ipsius Thomae construxit et erexit, ac illud adeo exaltavit, &c. quod per ligne illud, &c. tam omnia fenestr. et luminaria ipsius Willihelmi aulae et camerarum suarum, quam ostium ipsius Williehelmi aulae suae praedict. penitus obstupat' fuer., &c. et praed. Thomas ulterius machinans et malitiose intendens ipsum Willihelmum multipliciter praegravare, et ipsum de toto commodo, easimento et proficuo totius messuagii sui praed. penitus deprivare, praed. 29 die Sept. an. 6, supradicto quodd' aedificium pro suibus et porcis suis in horto suo praed' tam prope aulam et conclave ipsius Willihelmi praed. erexit, ac sues et porcos suos in aedificio in horto illo posuit, et ill' ibidem per magnum tempus custodivit, ita quod per | foetidas et insalubres odores sordidorum praedictorum suum et porcorum* [58 a] *praedict' Thomae in aulam et conclavo praed. ac alias partes praed. Messuagii ipsius Willihelmi penetran' et influnent' iidem Willihelmus et famili sui, ac aliae personae in messuagio suo praed. conversantes et existen. absque periculo infectionis in aula et conclavi proed' ac aliis locis messuagi praedicti' continuare seu remanere non potuerunt: praetextu cujus idem Willihelmus totum commodum, usum, easamentum, et proficuum maximae partis messuagii sui praedicti per totum tempus praed' totaliter perdidit et amisit ad damnum ipsius Willihelmi 40. &c.*[1] And

---

1. [*Ed.:* namely, together with all the other profits, rights, benefits and emoluments coming from or in any way belonging to all and singular the said offices, with the other premises, as plainly and fully and

the Defendant pleaded Not guilty, and at the Assises in *Norfolk* he was found guilty of both the said Nusances, and damages assessed. And now it was moved in arrest of Judgment, That the building of the said house for hoggs was necessary for the sustenance of man; and one ought not to be of so delicate nosed, that he cannot endure the sent of hoggs; for *Lex non favet delicatorum votis:*[2] But it was Resolved, That the action for the same (as this case is) was well maintainable; for in a house four things are desired, *habitatio hominis, delectatio inhabitantis, necessitas luminis, et salubritas aeris,*[3] and for Nusance done to three of them an action lieth, *scil.* to the habitation of the house, for that is the principal end of a house. 2. For hindrance of his light, for the old form of action upon the Case was significant, *scil. quod Messuagium horrida tenebritate obscuratum fuit,*[4] therewith agree *7 Edw. 3 50b. 22 Hen. 6 14.* by *Markham, 11 Hen. 4 47.* and to was a Case adjudged in the King's Bench, *Trin. 29 El. Thomas Bland* brought an action upon the Case against *Thomas Moseley,* and declared how that *James Bland* was seised in fee of an ancient house in *Netherousegate* in the Parish of St. *Michael* in the County of the City

---

in as ample a manner and form as Thomas Manners, knight, etc., or any other or other before these times occupying the aforesaid offices, or any of them, had and took them Thomas, maliciously scheming and intending to hinder and deprive him the said William of the easement and profit of the messuage and of part of his aforesaid land, the said 29th day of September, in the sixth year (of the reign of King) James, constructed and erected a large pile of wood (*lignile*) in the said garden of the selfsame Thomas, and made it so high, etc. that by the wood, etc. not only all the windows and lights of the selfsame William of his hall and rooms but also the selfsame William's door of his aforesaid hall were wholly stopped up, etc.; and the aforesaid Thomas, further scheming and maliciously intending greatly to harm the selfsame William, and utterly to deprive him of all the benefit, easement, and profit of the whole of his aforesaid messuage, on the aforesaid twenty-ninth day of September in the above-mentioned sixth year, erected a certain building for his sows and pigs in his aforesaid garden so near to the aforesaid hall and parlour of him the said William, and put his sows and pigs in the building in that garden and kept them there for so long a time, that by the foetid and insalubrious odours of the muck of the aforesaid sows and pigs of the aforesaid Thomas, penetrating and flowing into the hall and parlour and other parts of the messuage of the selfsame William, the same William and his servants, and other persons living in his aforesaid messuage, could not continue or remain in the aforesaid hall and parlour and other places of the same messuage without danger of infection: by virtue whereof the same William has wholly lost and parted with all the benefit, use, easement, and profit of the greatest part of his aforesaid messuage, for the whole time aforesaid, to the damage of the selfsame William of forty pounds, etc.]

2. [*Ed.:* The law does not favour the whims of the dainty:]

3. [*Ed.:* the habitation of man, the delight of the inhabitants, the necessity of light, and the wholesomeness of air,]

4. [*Ed.:* that the messuage was obscured with severe darkness,]

of *York;* and that the said *James,* and all those whose estate he hath in the said house, time out of mind, &c. had and have used to have for them his Tenants, for life, years, and at will, in the West side of the said house seven windows or cleristeries against a piece of land containing half a Rood, in the parish aforesaid, adjoining to the said house, which piece of land time out of mind was without any building, until the 28th day of *September, Anno 28 El.,* and shewed the length and breadth of the said windows for all the time aforesaid, by force of which windows the said *James,* and all those whose estate he hath in the said house time out of mind have used to have for them and their Tenants divers wholesome and necessary easements and commodities, by reason of open Air and light, &c. And that the said *James* the 20th of September Anno. 28 Eliz. demised to the Plaintiff the said house for 3 years; and that the Defendant, maliciously intending | to deprive him of the said easements, [58 b] *et obscurare Messuagium praed. horrida tenebritate, &c.*[5] *20 November Anno. 29 Eliz.* had erected a new building upon the said piece of land, so near to the said seven windows, that the said seven windows were stopped, whereby the Plaintif lost his said easements, &c. *Et maxima pars messuagii praedict' horrida tenebritate obscurata fuit, &c.*[6] In bar of which action the Defendant pleaded, *quod infra praed. civitatem Ebor. talis habetur; et a toto tempore cujus contrarii memoria non existit, habebatur consuetudo, videlicet, quod si quis habuerit fenestras et visum per easdem versus terram vicini sui, vicinus ille visum illarum fenestrarum obstruere super terram illam solebat et posset, sicut melius viderit sibi expedire.*[7] By force of which custom he justified the stopping of the said Windows; and upon that the Plaintiff did demur in Law, and it was adjudged by Sir *Christopher Wray,* Chief Justice, and the whole Court of Kings Bench, that the barr was insufficient in Law to barr the Plaintiff of his action, for two causes. 1. When a man hath a lawful easement, or profit, by prescription time out of mind, &c. another Custom which is also time out of mind cannot take it away, for the one is as ancient as the other: As if one hath a way over the land of *A.* to his Freehold time out of mind by prescription &c. *A.* cannot

---

5. [*Ed.:* and to obscure the aforesaid messuage with severe darkness, etc.]

6. [*Ed.:* And the greater part of the messuage would be obscured with severe darkness, etc.]

7. [*Ed.:* that within the aforesaid city of York there is, and from all the time whereof the memory of man is not the contrary has been, this custom, that is to say, that if any one has windows with a view from the same over the land of his neighbour, that neighbour may, and has been used to, obstruct the view from those windows over his land as might seem most expedient to him.]

allege a prescription or custom to stop the said way, 2. It might be, that before time of memory the owner of the said piece of land hath granted to the owner of the said house to have the said windows, without any stopping of them, and so the prescription might have a lawful beginning: and *Wray,* Chief Justice, then said, that for stopping as well of Air as of Light, an action lieth and damages shall be recovered for them, for both are necessary, for it is said, *et vescitur aura aetherea;* [8] and the said words *horrida tenebritate* are significant, and imply the benefit of light. But he said, That for prospect, which is a matter only of delight, and not of necessity, no action lieth for stopping thereof; and yet it is the great commendation of a house if it have a long and large prospect, *unde dicitur,*

Laudaturque domus longos qui prospicit agros. [9]

But he doth not give actions for such things of delight. And *Solomon* saith, *Ecclesiast. 11. 7. Dulce lumen est et delectabile oculis videre solem.* [10] *Et olium (ut Plutarchus in Conv. 7. Sap. refert.) Rex Aethiopum interrogatus quid optimum? respondebat lucem; quis enim natura duce tenebras non exhorrescit?* [11] and if the stopping of the wholesome Air, give cause of Action, *a fortiori* [12] an Action upon the case lieth in the Case at Barr, for the infecting and corrupting of the Air. And the building of a | Lime-kill is good and profitable, but if it be built so near a house, that when it burneth the smoke thereof entereth into the house, so that none can dwell there, an action lieth for it. So that if a man have a watercourse running in a ditch from the River to his house, for his necessary use, If a Glover set up a Lime-pit for Calves skins, and Sheep skins, so near the said Watercourse, that the corruption of the Lime-pit hath corrupted it, for which cause his Tenants leave the said house, an action upon the case lieth for the same, as it is adjudged in *13 Hen. 7 26b.* and the same stands both with the Rule of Law and Reason, *sc. Prohibetur ne quis faciat in suo quod nocere possit alieno: et sic utere tuo ut alienum non laedas.* [13] See in the

[59 a]

---

8. [*Ed.:* and the heavenly air feeds;]

9. [*Ed.:* whence it is said, A house is praised when it overlooks long fields.]

10. [*Ed.:* Light is sweet, and it is delightful to the eyes to behold the sun.]

11. [*Ed.:* And a king of Ethiopia (as Plutarch recites, in Conv. 7 Sap.), being once asked what was the best thing, answered, the light; for who is not naturally afraid of darkness?]

12. [*Ed.:* so much the more so (or, it follows that).]

13. [*Ed.:* that is, It is prohibited that anyone should do anything in his own land which might harm someone else; and you should so use your own as not to hurt others.]

Book of *Entries tit. Nusance 406 b.* That he who hath a several piscarie in a water shall have an action upon the Case against him who erecteth a Dyehouse, *ac fimos faeditates, et alia sordida extra domum praed. decurrentia in piscariam praed' decurrere fecit, per quod idem proficuum piscariae suae praed. totaliter amisit, &c.*[14] And there is another Precedent against a Dyer, &c. *quod idem Henricus in mansione sua praed. ob metum infectionis per horridum faetorem fumi, foeditatis, et aliorum sordidorum, &c. per magnum tempus morari non audebat.*[15] So in the Case at Bar, forasmuch as the Declaration is, That the Defendant maliciously intending to deprive the Plaintif of the use and profit of his house, did erect a Swine stie *tam prope aulam et conclave ipsius Willielmi, ac sues et porcos suos in aedificio illo posuit, et ill' ibid' per magnum tempus custodivit, ita quod faetidi et insalubres odores sordidorum praed' suum et porcorum praed' Thomae in aulam, &c. penetran' et influen', idem Willielmus ac famuli sui, &c. in messuag' praedict' conversantes existen' absque periculo infectionis in aula, &c. continuare seu remanere non potuerunt, praetextu cujus idem Will' totum commodum, &c. maximae partis praed' messuag' per totum tempus praed' totaliter perdidit.*[16] To which Declaration the Defendant pleaded Not guilty, and was found guilty of the matter in the Declaration, It was adjudged that the Plaintif should recover.

John Lamb's Case.
(1610) Michaelmas Term, 8 James I
In the Court of Star Chamber.
First Published in the *Reports,* volume 9, page 59b.

Ed.: This note case describes requirements for liability for a libel.

14. [*Ed.:* and caused the fetid filth and other muck to flow out of the aforesaid house into the aforesaid fishery, as a result of which the (plaintiff) wholly lost the profit of his aforesaid fishery, etc.]

15. [*Ed.:* that the same Henry for a long time did not dare to remain in his aforesaid mansion house for fear of infection by the horrid stench of the smoke, filth and other muck, etc.]

16. [*Ed.:* so near to the aforesaid hall and parlour of him the said William, and put his sows and pigs in the building in that garden and kept them there for so long a time, that by the fetid and insalubrious odours of the muck of the aforesaid sows and pigs of the aforesaid Thomas, penetrating and flowing into the hall etc., the same William and his servants etc. living in the aforesaid messuage, could not continue or remain in the aforesaid hall, etc. without danger of infection: by virtue whereof the same William had wholly lost all the benefit, etc. of the greatest part of the aforesaid messuage for the whole time aforesaid.]

John Lamb, Proctor of the Ecclesiastical Court exhibited a Bill in the Star-chamber against William Marche, Robert Harrison, and many others of the Town of Northampton, and against Shuchburghe and others, for publishing of two libels. It was Resolved, That every one who shall be convicted in the said Case, either ought to be a contriver of the libel, or a procurer of the contriving of it, or a malicious publisher of it, knowing it to be a Libel, for if any readeth a Libel, the same is not any publishing of it, or if he hear it read, it is no publication of it, for before he read or hear it, he cannot know it to be a Libel, or if he hear, read it, and laugh at it, it is no publishing of it; but if after he hath read or heard it, he repeats the same, or any part of it in the hearing of others, or after that he knoweth it to be a libel, he readeth it to others, the same is an unlawful publishing of it; or if he writes a Copy of it, and do not publish it to others, it is no publication of the Libel; for every one who shall be convicted ought to be a contriver, procurer, or publisher of it, knowing it to be a Libel. But it is great evidence that he published it, when he, knowing it to be a Libel, writeth a Copy of it; if not that afterwards he can prove that he delivered the same to a Magistrate to examine it; for then the subsequent Act doth explain the precedent intent. See Reader, *Bract.*

[60 a] *lib. 3. tract. de | Corona, cap.36. fo. 155. Fiat autem injuria. cum quis pugno percussus fuerit, verberatus, vulneratus seu fustibus caesus; verum etiam cum ei convitium dictum fuerit; vel de eo factum carmen famosum.*[1]

MacKalley's Case.
(In the killing of the Sergeant of London.)
(1611) Easter Term, 9 James I
Before all the Judges of England.
First Published in the *Reports,* volume 9, page 65b.

Ed.: A jury found the following: Richard Fells, a sergeant of the sheriff of London, had been ordered to arrest John Murray for a £500 debt. After arresting Murray one night, Fells was set upon by John Mackalley, John Engles, and Archibald Miller, who tried to rescue Murray. In the fight, Murray called to his friends, "Draw, draw, rogues." MacKalley drew a rapier

---

1. [*Ed.:* A wrong is committed not only when someone is struck with a fist, or beaten or wounded with clubs, but also when he is insulted or made the subject of infamous verses.]

and ran Fells through, killing him. The jury, however, was unsure that this amounted to murder. The justices in the trial were unsure whether the facts amounted to murder or manslaughter. All of the judges of England considered the case and found that the killing of an officer of the law executing process is murder. Mackalley was convicted of murder and hanged. This is an important depiction in its consideration of the requirements of indictments, of arrest, and of the role of the jury as the finder of facts, even allowing them to leave to the judges the inferences to be derived from findings of fact. See also Semayne's Case, p. 135.

By command from the King all the Judges of England were command to meet together to Resolve what the Law was upon a Record (of a special verdict found at the Sessions of Gaol delivery holden at Newgate the fifth day of December, Anno 8 Jacobi) and accordingly all the Judges of England, and Barons of the Exchequer, in the beginning of Hilary Term last past met together, and heard Counsel learned upon the same special verdict, as well of the prisoners, of the King; that is to say, Sergeant Harris the younger; Anthonie Dyet, and Randall Crewe of Counsel with the Prisoners; and Yelverton, Walters, and Coventrie for the King. And the matter was very well argued by Councel on both sides at two several days in the same term; and divers Exceptions were taken to the Indictment, and to the verdict also.

First, against the Indictment five exceptions were taken. 1. Because it appeareth, That the arrest was tortious, and by consequence the killing of the Sergeant could not be murder, but Manslaughter: And they argued that the arrest alledged in the Indictment was tortious, because it was in the night, that is to say, 18 *diem Nov. inter horas quintam et sextam post meridiem,*[1] which appeareth to the Court to be in the Night, and the Night is a time of rest and repose, and not to arrest any one by his body, for thereof would ensue (as in *hoc causa accidit*)[2] bloodshed; for the Officer and Minister of Justice cannot have such assistance, nor the peace cannot be so well kept in the Night, that is to say, *in tenebris,*[3] as in the Day, *in aperta luce:*[4] And the Prisoner

1. [*Ed.:* on the eighteenth day of November between the hours of five and six after mid-day,]
2. [*Ed.:* happened in this case.]
3. [*Ed.:* in the darkness,]
4. [*Ed.:* in the open light,]

cannot know the Officer or Minister of Justice in the Night; nor the Prisoner cannot so soon find sureties for his appearance | in the Night, and thereby avoid his imprisonment, as he may in the day time. And they cited *11 H. 7. 5.* That the Lord shall not distrain for his Rent or Services in the Night. But it was answered by the Councel with the King, and in the end Resolved by all the Judges and Barons of the Exchequer, That the arrest in the Night is lawful, as well at the subjects sute as at the Kings sute; for the Officer or Minister of Justice ought for to arrest him when he can find him; for otherwise perhaps he shall never arrest him, *quia qui male agit, odit lucem;*[5] and if the Officer do not arrest him when he findeth him, and may arrest him, the Plaintif shall have an action upon his Case, and recover all his loss and damages; And it is like to the Case of distress for damage feasant, for which one may distrain in the Night; for otherwise perhaps he shall never distrain the cattel, for they may be taken or escape away and then he cannot distrain them: But in the Case of Rent service it is otherwise; for the Law doth intend that the Tenant will all the day attend upon the Land to pay his Rent, but he is not compellable to attend in the Night, *Vid. 11 H. 7 5a. 10 E. 3 21 12 E. 3. Distresse 17.* and no inconvenience will follow upon it; For although he cannot see the Officer, yet when he heareth him say, I arrest you in the Kings name &c. he ought for to obey him; and if the Officer hath not a lawful warrant, he shall have his action of false imprisonment. And as to the finding of sureties the Law is, That he ought to remain in prison till he finds sureties, be it in the Day time, or in the Night. But great inconvenience will follow on the other side, if those who are indebted to others shall in the Night go at their pleasure without danger of arrest, for then they would become Nightwalkers, and turn the Day into Night in despight of their Creditors. And as the Officer or Minister of Justice may by force of a Warrant directed to him, arrest anyone at the Kings sute either for felony or other crime in the Night, so may he do at a subjects suit; for the King hath no more prerogative as to the time to make an arrest, than a subject: for the arrest is to no other but to the intent to bring the party to Justice. And it appears by the opinion of the Court in the Kings Bench in *Semaigns* Case, in the Fifth Part of my Reports, That the Sherifs may arrest in the Night, as well at the sute of the Subject, as at the Kings sute. And in *Heydons* Case in the Fourth Part of my Reports it is Re-

---

5. [*Ed.:* he (who) does evil hates the light.]

solved, That if one killeth a Watchman in doing his Office, it is Murder, and yet it is done in the Night; and if an affray be made in the Night, and the Constable, or any other, who commeth to aid him to keep the peace be killed, the same is Murder; for when the Constable doth command them in the Kings name to keep | the Peace, although he cannot discern or know him to be the [66 b] Constable, yet at their perils they ought to obey him.

It was also Resolved, that although in truth between five and six of the clock in the ninth of November be part of the Night, yet the Court is not bound *ex Officio*,[6] to take knowledge of it, no more than in the Case of Burglary, without these words, *in nocte ejusdem diei*,[7] or *Noctanter*.[8]

2. It was objected, that Sunday is not *dies juridicus*,[9] and therefore no arrest can be made thereon, but the same is the Sabbath, and therefore therein every one ought to abstain from secular affairs for the better worship and service of God in Spirit and Truth. As to that it was Answered and Resolved, that no judicial act ought to be done on that day, but ministerial acts may be lawfully executed on the Sunday; for otherwise peradventure they shall never be executed; and God permitteth things of necessity to be done that day; and Christ saith in the Gospel, *Bonum est benefacere in Sabbatho*.[10]

3. Another Exception was taken, because it is said in the beginning of the Indictment, *in Curia dicti Dom. Reg in computatorio suo, scituat. in parochia Sanctae Michaelis*[11] in Woodstreet, London, and doth not shew in what Ward the said Parish was, *et non allocatur*;[12] For it is holden in *7 H. 6 36b*. Every Ward in London is an Hundred in a County, and every Parish in London is as a Town in an Hundred, and it is not necessary to set forth in what Hundred a Town no more in what Ward a Parish is; but the same is commonly averred, because that there are divers Parishes in London of one name, and the Ward is added to make distinction of one Parish from another; for which cause it was Resolved, That in the Case at Bar the Indictment was sufficient, notwithstanding the leaving out of the Ward, for it doth not appear to us that

6. [*Ed.:* by reason of office,]
7. [*Ed.:* in the night of the same day,]
8. [*Ed.:* at night.]
9. [*Ed.:* a Law Day, (a day on which judgment may be given).]
10. [*Ed.:* It is good to act well on the Sabbath.]
11. [*Ed.:* in the court of the said lord king in his Compter situated in the parish of St Michael.]
12. [*Ed.:* not allowed.]

there is any other Parish of that name, and this Parish is particularly described, *viz. in Parochia Sancti Michael'* in Wood-street, London. And therewith agreeth the Rule of the Book in *7 H. 6 36b.* for a Bill was ruled good in *Parochia Sancti Laurentii in Judaismo,*[13] omitting the Ward.

The fourth Exception was, because it doth not appear in what Parish the Sherif did commanded Fells the Sergeant to arrest the Defendants; and the same was disallowed by all the Justices; for the words of the Indictment are, *taliter in eadem Curia process. fuit, &c.*[14] and *eadem Curia* fully shewed that the Warrant was made at the same Court mentioned before; and the same was expressly alledged to be holden *in Parochia Sancti Michaelis, &c.*

[67 a]   ❙ 5. It was excepted against the Indictment, *viz.* That the precept was to arrest the Defendant, *si inventus foret infra libertates Civitatis praed'*[15] and the Indictment is *quod in parochia S. Martini Bowyer Rowe in warda de Farringdon infra Londinum praed'*[16] the Sergeant arrested him, so that he hath not pursued the precept, for the precept is *infra libertates*[17] London, and notwithstanding that, the indictment was resolved to be good, for the said Parish and Ward in London shall be intended to be within the liberties of London, for these words liberties of London are more spacious than London, and include in them the City of London itself.

And 9 Exceptions were taken to the verdict. 1. That there is material variance betwixt the Indictment and the Verdict, for the Indictment doth suppose that Piot Sherif of London upon a Plaint entred, made a precept to Fells, Serjeant at Mace to arrest the said MacKalley, the Def.; & by the verdict it appeareth that there was not any such precept made, but that by the custom of London, after the plaint entered, any Sergeant *ex officio* at the request of the Plaintiff may arrest the Defendant *absque aliquo praecepto ore tenus, vel aliter,*[18] so that the Indictment being special, to make this offence Murder, by Construction of Law upon the special matter, without any forethought malice ought to be

---

13. [*Ed.:* in the parish of St Leonard in the Jewry,]

14. [*Ed.:* the process in the same court was such, etc.]

15. [*Ed.:* if (the defendant) should be found within the liberties of the aforesaid city.]

16. [*Ed.:* that in the parish of St. Martin Bowyer Row in the ward of Farringdon within London aforesaid.]

17. [*Ed.:* within the liberties.]

18. [*Ed.:* without any precept, whether by word of mouth or otherwise,]

followed, and proved in Evidence, which is not done in this case. And because the Jurors have not found the said special matter contained in the Indictment, but other matter, Judgement cannot be given against the Prisoners upon this Indictment. To which it was answered, and in the end Resolved, That there was sufficient matter in the verdict pursuant to the matter contained in the Indictment, upon which the Court ought to give judgement of death against the said Prisoners, notwithstanding the said variance, and that for two causes.

1. Because that the Warrant which the Sergeant had to arrest the Defendant was but circumstance, and is not necessary to be precisely pursued in Evidence to be found by the Jury; but it sufficeth if the substance of the matter be found without any such precise regard to circumstance: and therefore, if a man be indicted, that he with a dagger gave another a mortal wound, upon which he died, and in evidence it is proved that he gave the wound with a Sword, Rapier, Baston, or Bill, in that case the Defendant ought to be found guilty, for the substance of the matter is, That the party indicted hath given him a mortal wound, whereof he died, and I the circumstance of the manner [67 b] of the weapon is not material in case of Indictment; and yet such circumstance ought not to be omitted, but some weapon ought to be mentioned in the Indictment. So if A. B. and C. are indicted for killing J. S. and that A. strook him, and that the others were present, procuring, abetting, &c. And upon the Evidence it appeareth, that B. strook him, and that A. and C. were present, &c. in this case the Indictment is not pursued in the circumstance; and yet it is sufficient to maintain the Indictment, for the Evidence doth agree with the effect of the Indictment, and so the variance from the circumstance of the Indictment is not material; for it shall be adjudged in Law the stroke of every of them, and is as strongly the act of the others, as if they all three had holden the weapon, &c. and had altogether strock the dead; and therewith agrees *Plow. Com. 98 a.*

So if one be indicted of the murder of another upon forethought malice, and he is found guilty of Manslaughter, he shall have judgment upon this verdict, for the killing is the substance, and the pretenced malice the manner of it; and when the matter is found, Judgement shall be given thereupon, although the manner be not precisely pursued; and therewith agreeth *Plow. Com. 101.* where it is said, when the substance of the act and the manner of the act, are put in issue together, the Jury find the substance and not the manner, Judgement shall be given for the substance. And I moved all the Judges and Barons, if in this case of killing of a Minister of Justice in the execution of his office, the Indictment might have been general, *sc.* that the prisoners *felonice, voluntarie, et ex malitia, sua proecogitata &c. percusser', &c.*[19] without alleging any special matter; and I conceived that it might well be, for the Evidence would well maintain the Indictment, for as much as in this case the Law doth imply forethought malice. As if a Theef, who offereth to rob a true man, kill him in resisting the thief, the same is murder of forethought malice; Or if one kill another without provocation, and without any forethought malice, which can be proved, the Law will adjudge the same murder, and implieth malice; for by the Law of God every one ought to be in love and charity with all men, and therefore when he killeth another without provocation, the Law implieth malice: and in both these cases they may be indicted generally that they killed of forethought malice, for malice implied by Law, given in Evidence, is sufficient to maintain the general Indictment. So in the case at barr; And in this case of a Sergeant, the Indictment might have been generall, That he feloniously and of his forethought malice killed the said Fells, and the special matter might well have been given in Evidence; | *quod fuit concessum*[20] by all the Judges, and Barons of the Exchequer. The second reason was, because it is expressly alleged in the Indictment, That the said John Mackalley, &c. *eundem Richardum Fells, &c. felonice, voluntarie, et ex malitia sua praecogita, &c. percussit et inforavit, &c.*[21] so that above the special matter which implieth malice, it is expressly contained in the Indictment, that he feloniously and *ex malitia proecogitata* killed the said Fells, and then although the special matter given in Evidence had varied in substance from the special matter contained in the Indictment, yet for as much as it was resolved that the Indictment in this case might be general, for this cause the Evidence, although it doth not agree with the special matter, yet it proveth, that the prisoners killed the said Fells of their forethought malice; and so well maintaineth the Indictment. And that in the end was the opinion of all the Judges and Barons of the Exchequer.

2. Exception was taken to the verdict, That the Custom found by the Jury, that after the plaint entred, the Defendant might be arrested by his body, was

19. [*Ed.:* feloniously, wilfully, and of their malice aforethought, etc., struck, etc.]
20. [*Ed.:* which was granted.]
21. [*Ed.:* feloniously, wilfully, and of his malice aforethought, etc. struck and stabbed, etc., the same Richard Fells, etc.]

against Law, because the Defendant ought to be first summoned before that the warrant in nature of a *Capias*[22] can issue forth, for his body shall not be arrested if he hath sufficient, *et non allocatur;*[23] for it appeareth by the book in *21 E. 4 66b*. That by common experience daily used, that after a plaint entred, by the custom of London, (which is established and confirmed by Parliament) the Defendant may be arrested. And in this case three points were Resolved by all the Judges and Barons of the Exchequer. 1. that although the process be apparently erronious, that yet if the Minister of Justice in the execution thereof be killed, the same is murder. For the Minister is not bound to dispute the authority of the Court, which awardeth the process, but his office is to execute the process: and therefore, if a *Capias* in an action of Debt be awarded against a Baron, or other Peer of the Realm, which is erronious (because their bodie by the Law is privileged in such cases) yet if the Officer be killed in execution thereof, it is murder. So if a *Capias* be awarded where a Distress ought to issue, and in execution thereof the Officer is killed, it is Murder, for as the Sheriff, &c. when he is charged with an Escape shall not take advantage of any Error in the proceeding so the Defendant when he killeth the Sheriff, &c. shall not take advantage of Error in the proceeding. 2. It was Resolved, That if any Magistrate or Minister of Justice, in execution of their office, or in keeping of the peace according to the duty of his office be killed, it is murder, for their contempt and disobedience to the King, and to the Law, for it is *contra potestatem Regis et legis:*[24] and therefore, if a Sheriff, Justice of Peace, Chief Constable, Petit | Constable, Watchman, or any of the [68 b] Kings, Ministers, or any who comes in their aid be killed in doing of their office, it is murder for the cause aforesaid: for when the Officer or Kings Minister by process of Law (be it erroneous or not) arresteth one in the Kings name, or requireth the breakers of the peace to keep the peace in the Kings name, and they notwithstanding disobey the arrest or Commandement in the Kings name, and kill the officer, or the Kings Minister, reason requireth that this killing and slaying shall be an offence in a higher nature than any offence of this nature; and that the same is voluntary, felonious, and murder of forethought malice. And a Watchman by the Law may arrest a Night-walker

22. [*Ed.:* Writ of arrest.]
23. [*Ed.:* and not allowed;]
24. [*Ed.:* against the power of the king and the law:]

4 Hen. 7 2. and if a Watchman arresteth such a one, and he killeth him, the same is murder. *Vide Heydons case* in the Fourth Part of my Reports. And it is true, That the life of a man is much favoured in Law, but the life of the Law it self (which protecteth all in peace and safety) ought to be more favoured, and the execution of the process of Law and of the offices of Conservators of the peace, is the Soul and life of the Law, and the means by which Justice is administered, and the peace of the Realm kept. *Vide 2 R. 3 21.* If the Principal be erroneously attainted, the Accessory shall be put to answer, and shall not take benefit for the saving of his life of the erroneous proceeding against the Principal. 3. It was Resolved, That the Officer or Minister of the Law in the Execution of his office, if he be resisted or assaulted, is not bound to flye to the wall &c. (as other Subjects are) for *Legis minister non tenetur in executione Officii fugere, seu retrocedere.*[25]

3. It was Objected, That the Defendant ought not have been arrested before that the plaint was entered of Record in the Court before the Sheriff, for this same is in truth the Court of Record where the Declaration and pleading shall be. To that it was answered and Resolved by all, That after the plaint entered in the Porters book, and before the entry thereof in the Court before the Sheriff, the Defendant may be arrested by the Custom of London; and therewith agreeth the book in *21 E. 4 66.* in the point. *Vide 9 E. 4 48b.*

4. It was Objected, That the said Arrest found by the verdict was not lawful for the Sergeant in this case ought to have when he arrested him, shewed at whose sute, out of which Court, and for what cause he made the arrest, and in what Court the same is returnable, to the intent, that if it be for any execution, he might pay the money, and free his body, and if it be upon mean process either to agree with the party to put in bayl according to the Law, and to know when he shall appear, as it is Resolved in the *Countess of Rutland's Case,* in the sixth part of my Reports. But in the Case at barr the Sergeant said nothing but I arrest you in the Kings name, at the sute of Mr. Radford, and so the arrest not lawfull, and by consequence the offence is not murder. To *that* it was Answered and Resolved, That it is true that it is holden in the *Countess of Rutland's case,* That the Sheriff, or Serjeant ought upon the arrest shew at whose sute, &c. But the same is to be intended when the party arrested submitteth himself to the arrest, and not when the party (as in this case Murray

[69 a]

25. [*Ed.:* A minister of the law, in the execution of his office, is not expected to run away or draw back.]

did) maketh resistance and interrupteth him, and before he could speak all his words, he was by them mortally wounded and murdred, in which case, the prisoners shall not take advantage of their own wrong. It was also Resolved, That if one knoweth that the Sheriff; &c. hath process to arrest him, and the Sheriff coming to arrest him, the Defendant to prevent the Sheriff to arrest him, kill him with a gun, or any other engine, or weapon, before any arrest made, the same is murder: *a fortiori*,[26] in the case at bar when he knew by the said words, that the Sergeant came to arrest him.

5. Exception was taken, because it was not found by the Verdict, That the said Mackalley *felonice percussit, &c.* but *percussit* only, *et quod iidem Johann' Murray, et Johannes English fuerunt praesentes, auxiliantes, &c.*[27] and doth not say, *felonice; et non allocatur*,[28] for the office of the Jury is to shew the truth of the fact, and to leave the judgement of the Law to the Court; but they have well concluded, And if *super tota materia' praed. videbitur Justic. et Cur. hic, quod praed interfectio dic. Rich. Felles sit murdrum, tunc Jurat. praed. dic. super Sacramentum suum quod praed. Johannes Murray, Johannes Mackalley; et Johannes English sunt culpabiles, et quilibet eorum est culpabilis de murdro praed. Rich. Felles modo et forma prout. per Indictamentum praed. supponitur, &c.*[29] And because the Judges and the Court hath resolved upon the special matter, that it is murder, the Jury have found him guilty of murder contained in the Indictment.

6. It was Objected, That the Sergeant at the time, nor before he arrested shewed the prisoner his Mace; for thereby he is known to be the Minister of the Law, and from thence he hath his name, *scil. serviens ad clavam; Et non allocatur* for two causes. 1. because the Jury have found, That he was *serviens ad clavam dicti Vicecomitis, et juratus, et cognitus, et minister Cur.*[30] And a Bayliff sworn and known needeth not (although the party demand it) shew | his [69 b] warrant, nor any other special Bailif is not bound to shew his warrant without

26. [*Ed.:* so much the more so (or, it follows that).]

27. [*Ed.:* feloniously struck (but) struck (only) and that the same John Murray and John English were present, aiding, etc.]

28. [*Ed.:* feloniously and (the objection is) not allowed.]

29. [*Ed.:* if upon the whole matter aforesaid it shall appear to the justices and the court here that the killing of the said Richard Fells is murder, then the aforesaid jurors say upon their oath that the aforesaid John Murray, John Mackalley and John English are guilty, and each of them is guilty, of the murder of the aforesaid Richard Fells in manner and form as is supposed by the aforesaid indictment, etc.]

30. [*Ed.:* the said sheriff's sergeant-at-mace sworn and known, and a minister of the court.]

demanding of it, *8 E. 4 14. 14 H. 7 9b. 21 H. 7 23.* and where the books speak
of a known Baylif, it is not requisite that he be known to the party who is to
be arrested, but if he be commonly known it is sufficeth. 2. If notice were
requisite, he gave sufficient notice when he said, I arrest you in the Kings
name &c. and the party at his peril ought to obey him; and if he hath no
lawfull warrant, he may have his action of false imprisonment. So that in this
case without Question the Sergeant needeth not to shew his Mace; and if they
shall be driven to shew their Mace, it should be a warning for the party arrested
to flye.

7. Another Exception was taken to the Verdict, because the Custom which
gave to the Sergeant warrant to arrest, was not pursued; for the custom is,
*Quod aliqua persona existens Serviens ad clavam ad requisitionem partis hujus-
modi querelam sic levantis, &c. usa fuit arrestare,*[31] which ought to be taken
that the pleint ought to be entered before the request; but afterwards it is
found that the request was before the pleint, and so the Custom not pursued;
et non allocatur. For by the Custom it is not proved, but that the request may
be as well before as after the pleint entered; and so is the Common usage and
experience.

8. It was Objected, That the verdict was repugnant in itself, for first they
found, that the pleint was entered *de Recordo in Rot. Cur. Computator, in his
verbis, Die Sabbathi* 17 *die Novemb.*[32] and afterwards they found, *quod intratio
praed. in Rot. Cur. praed. facta fuit die Lunae* 19 *die November &c.*[33] And the
jury cannot find any thing against the Record itself. *Vide 11 H. 6 42. 9 H. 6
37. 28 Ass. 34. 47 E. 3 19. 11 H. 4 26. 9 H. 7 3 13 H. 7 14. 33 E. 3. Judgment 255.
Dyer 32 Eliz. 147, &c.* And all that was affirmed for good Law. But that maketh
the Case stronger against the Prisoners, for now the Judges ought to judge
upon a pleint entered of Record *in Cur' Computator.*[34] the Saturday the seventeenth of Novemb. which was before the arrest.

9. Exception was taken to the Verdict, that the entry of the pleint was

31. [*Ed.:* that any person being a sergeant-at-mace, thus raising a plaint at the request of such party,
has been accustomed to arrest,]
32. [*Ed.:* of record in the court-rolls of the Compter in these words, on Saturday the seventeenth day
of November.]
33. [*Ed.:* that the aforesaid entry in the aforesaid court-rolls was made on Monday the nineteenth day
of November, etc.]
34. [*Ed.:* in the court of the Compter.]

without form, and so short and obscure, *quod opus est interprete; et non al-locatur.*[35] For it was found that it was according to the Custom of London; which is but a Remembrance to draw the Declaration at length in the Court of Pleas, which notwithstanding is by Custom sufficient to have the Defendant arrested. And afterwards at the Sessions [of Newgate held] the fifth day of May after this Term, the two Chief Justices openly declared the Resolution of all | the Judges and Barons of the Exchequer, to the great satisfaction and   [70 a] contentment of all there present. And accordingly judgment of death was given against the three Prisoners by the Recorder of London, in the presence of the said two Chief Justices. And the said Mackalley was executed with other Prisoners at Tyborn.

35. [*Ed.:* it is a labour to interpret it; and (this point was) not allowed.]

Part Ten of the *Reports*

The Tenth Part of Coke's *Reports* was published in 1614. It was originally entitled *La dixme part des Reports de Sr. Edw. Coke chivalier, chiefe Justice Dengleteere des plees deste tenus devant le roy mesme assignee, & del Counseil prive d'Estat: des divers resolutions & Jugements donez sur solennes arguments & avec grand deliberation & conference des tresreverend Juges & sages de la ley, de cases en ley queux ne fueront unques resolvs ou adjuges par devant: et les raisons & causes des dits resolutions & Jugements. Publie en la unziesme an de treshaut et tresillustre Jaqves roy Dengleterre, France, & Ireland, & de escosse le 47., le fountain de tout Pietie & Justice, & la vie de la ley.* In English, *The Tenth Part of the Reports of Sir Edward Coke, Knight, Lord Chief Justice of England, of the Pleas assigned to be held before the king Himself, and of the Privy Council of State, of divers Resolutions and Judgments given upon solemn Arguments, and with great deliberation and Conference of the reverend Judges and Sages of the Law, of Cases in law which were never Resolved or Adjudged Before: and the Reasons and Causes thereof. Published in the Eleventh year of the most high and Most Illustrious James, King of England, France, and Ireland, and of Scotland the 47., the Fountain of all Justice, and the life of the Law.* This part covers a wide range of issues, with a number of cases dealing with a corporation's powers and liabilities; the power of particular courts; as well as more issues dealing with estates, leases, and inheritance.

Epigrams from the Title Page:

Deo duce, εὕρηκα.[1]

---

1. [*Ed.:* God, the leader, Eureka.]

Lex tibi quod justum est, Judicis ore, refert.[2]
Jerom. *Justitia non novit Patrem, Matrem, neque Fratrem; personam non accepit, sed Deum imitatur.*[3]

Westm. 2. cap. 39. *Ad Officium Justiciariorum spectat, unicuique coram eis placitanti Jusititiam exhibere.*[4]

(Preface)
Deo, Patriae, Tibi.[5]

At my times of Leisure, after my Publick Services (chearfully taking Industry, mine old Acquaintance, for my Comfort, and aiming at the Good of my dear Country for my comfort) and beginning with this continual and fervent Prayer, *The glorious Majesty of the Lord our God be upon us; oh! prosper thou the Works of our hands upon us, Oh! prosper thou our handy works;*[6] I have, by the most gracious direction and assistance of the Almighty, brought forth and Published this Tenth Work to the view of the Learned and Benevolent Reader.

This part containeth a true and just Report of certain Judgments and Resolutions given in his Majesty's principal Courts of Justice, upon great and mature deliberation, and in Cases of as great Importance and Consequence as in any of my former Commentaries, which I have taken upon me and finished (though it hath been more than difficult to me) to avoid that, the which venerable Verity doth blush at for fear, that is, That she which is the Foundation of Justice should not be hidden and unknown; *Veritas abscondi erubescit; nihil enim magis metuit quam non proferri in publicum, vult se in luce collocari; & quis illam occulat occultetue, quam omnium oculis expositam esse est aequissimum.*[7] Neither is she pleased, when once she is found out and revealed

---

2. [*Ed.:* The law repays you what is just, by the mouth of the judge.]

3. [*Ed.:* St. Jerome: Justice did not know a father, mother, or brother, and did not take on a personality; but it imitates God.]

4. [*Ed.:* It belongs to the office of the justices to do justice to everyone pleading before them.]

5. [*Ed.:* To God, to the Country, to you.]

6. [*Ed.:* Psal. 90. vers. 17.]

7. [*Ed.:* Truth blushes to be hidden, and therefore she fears nothing more than not being related in public, and wants to be placed in the light; and if someone hides or conceals her, it is most equitable to expose her to the eyes of all men.]

to be called into argument and question'd again, as if she were not in Verity indeed; and therefore the Rule is, *Eatenus ratiocinandum est donec Veritas inveniatur; ubi inventa est Veritas, ibi figendum Judicium:*[8] Nay, Sometimes Truth is lost by too much altercation, *nimia altercatione veritas amittitur.*[9] She takes small delight with varnish of Words or garnish of Flowers; for *simplex est sermo, Veritas,* ἁπλὸς ὁ λόγος τῆς ὑληθείας ἔφυ,[10] for her place being between the Heart and the Head doth participate of them both, of the Head for Judgment, and of the Heart for Simplicity. Now whether it be not necessary that the true and just Reasons and Causes of these Judgments and Resolutions, which are not expressed in any Record, for the advancement of Truth and the preventing of Error, in matters of so great Importance and consequence should be plainly and faithfully published to all Posterity, I leave to the Censure of the Learned and Judicious Reader.

Le Case de *Sutton's* Hospital.

    I. I have Reported in the first place (though it be not first in time) the Case of the Hospital of King *James,* founded by *Tho. Sutton* Esq; for that in mine Opinion it doth merit to have the Precedency for two Causes. I. For that it was an Exchequer Chamber Case, where, by the Verdict of the Grand Jury of all the Judges of *England,* it was for the Hospital found *Billa vera.*[11] 2. For that the Foundation of this Hospital is *Opus sine exemplo.*[12] The imitation of things that be evil doth for the most part exceed the Example, but the imitation of good things doth most commonly come far short of the President: But this Work of Charity hath exceeded any Foundation that ever was in the Christian World, nay the Eye of Time it self did never see the like.

The yearly value of the possessions first given.

    For, the first Gift by *Sutton* of Lordships, Manors, Lands and Tenements to continue for ever for the Maintenance hereof, doth amount to the clear yearly value of three thousand five hundred pound, or near thereabouts, and within these few years will be encreased to about the yearly value of five thousand pounds. *Probatio charitatis exhibitio operis.*[13] And besides all this, *Sutton* left to descend to the Plaintiff (a Man of mean quality) the Manor of *Tarbock* in the County of *Lancaster,* consisting of a fair ancient House, two Parks and

---

8. [*Ed.:* Only to argue until the truth is found, and when the truth is found then to give judgment.]
9. [*Ed.:* truth is lost by too much altercation.]
10. [*Ed.:* truth is (in) simple speech.]
11. [*Ed.:* A true bill, or an indictment or other presentment, asserted to by a Grand Jury.]
12. [*Ed.:* a work without precedent.]
13. [*Ed.:* the display [or maintenance] of this work is proof of charity.]

large Demesns, plentifully stored with Timber, of the yearly value of 300 l.
and 50 l. by the year, of Rent of Assise, together with the Rectory of
worth 100 l. *per Annum* within the same County.

The large Revenues of this famous Hospital are to be imployed principally
for four special intents and purposes. I. For the Relief of such worthy and
well esteemed Captains, Commanders and Soldiers, as be unmarried; and have
adventured their Lives in the Wars, for the Service of the Realm, and are fallen
into poverty and impotency. 2. For redeeming of poor Captives, especially
such as are under the miserable Thraldom of Infidels, and constantly keep
their Faith and the profession of true Religion. 3. For the erection of a free
School and maintenance of a Learned School-Master and Usher for training
up of poor Children in good Literature and vertuous Education, and for avoiding of Idleness, the Mother of all Vice and Wickedness. 4. Within this Hospital
there shall be for ever maintained a grave and learned Divine for the Instruction
of all within this Hospital, by Preaching of Gods Holy Word, for the due
celebration of Divine Service, and the Holy Sacraments, and Catechising of
the Youth in the Principles of true Religion; for the accomplishment and
maintenance of which and other godly and charitable Uses, the said Founder
hath left also a very great and large Stock of Mony to his Executors, *Richard
Sutton* Esq; and *John Law* Gent. two faithful, constant, and industrious persons.

This Work of Piety and Charity is founded in the spacious and specious
House called the *Charter-House,* in the Parish of St. *Sepulchre,* in the County
of *Middlesex,* having fair Orchards and Gardens, and containing twenty Acres
within the precinct thereof, so as a Man may say of it, that it is *tanquam Orbis
in Urbe;*[14] a place (as it appeareth by Record and History) ordained of God
for Pious and Charitable Uses. For Sir *Walter Many* of *Henalt* (who was created
by King *Edward the third* Knight of the Garter, for his Service which with
singular commendation he performed in the French Wars) when the pestilence
so reigned in *London,* that the Church-yards were not sufficient to bury the
dead Bodies, especially of the Poor, purchased the place where now this famous
Hospital is erected, and caused the same to be consecrated for the burial of
poor Christians (which, whiles they lived were the Temples of the Holy Ghost)
And the Record telleth you that *Anno Domini* 1349. & *Anno Regni Regis* E.3.23.

To what intents and purposes the Revenues shall be imployed.

---

14. [*Ed.:* as a world within a world;]

Regnante magna Pestilentia consecratum fuit hoc Caemitarium, &c. in quo, &
infra septa ejusdem sepulta fuerunt mortuorum corpora plusquam quinquaginta
millia.[15] But after the Plague by the goodness of the Almighty ceased, the
same Sir *Walter Many*, in the year of our Lord 1371. and in the forty fifth year
of the Reign of King *Edward the third* founded the *Carthusian* Monks there,
who by corruption of speech were vulgarly called the Monks of the *Charter-
house*. So as the Soyl which of ancient Time was given by Sir *Walter Many*,
a Knight and a Soldier, for the Sepulcher of poor Men when they were dead,
is now by *Thomas Sutton* an Esquire, and a Soldier, converted and consecrated
to the Sustenance of the Poor and Impotent whiles they live. And therefore
a Man may truly apply to this place the saying of the Royal Prophet, "Thou
Lord of thy goodness best prepared it for the Poor."[16] And this Case was
Adjudged with the great Applause of all that heard it, or of it, and principally
for four causes. 1. For the honour of our Religion, that hath produced such
a Work of Piety and Charity, as never was in the Christian World for the first
Foundation. 2. For the glory of the Kings Majesty, to whom *ex congruo et*
condigno[17] it is dedicated and beareth his Name. 3. For the increase of Piety
and Charity, *ne homines deterrerentur a piis & bonis operibus:*[18] And, lastly, *ut*
obstruatur os iniqua loquentium.[19] And I dare affirm it, for the honour of our
Religion, that more of such good Works of Piety and Charity have been
founded within this Realm since the beginning of the Reign of our late Queen
Elizabeth of ever blessed Memory, during the glorious Sunshine of the Gospel,
than in many Ages before. And it hath been observed, That (by the blessing
of Almighty God) this Kingdom of *England*, for Piety, Profit and Pleasure,
viz. 1. For this and such other Works of Piety. 2. For the Crowns Inheritances
of Honors, Manors, Lands, &c. and certainty of yearly Profit. And Lastly, for
Forests, Chases, Parks, and other places of pleasure, hath exceeded the greatest
Monarchy in the Christian World.

15. [*Ed.:* In the year of our Lord 1349 and in the twenty-third year of King Edward III, while the great
plague reigned, this cemetery was consecrated, etc., in which and within the bounds whereof were buried
the bodies of more than fifty thousand dead.]

16. *Psal. 68.*

17. [*Ed.:* out of suitability and worthiness.]

18. [*Ed.:* that men should not be deterred from pious and good works.]

19. [*Ed.:* that the mouth which speaks iniquity should be stopped.]

II. Then have I published in *Mary Portingtons* Case, for the general good *Mary Portington's Case.* both of Prince and Country, the honourable Funeral of fond and new-found Perpetuities, a monstrous Brood, carved out of meer Invention, and never known to the ancient Sages of the Law; I say monstrous, for that the Naturalist saith, *Quod monstra generantur propter corruptionem alicujus principii.*[20] And yet I say honourable, for that these Vermin have crept into many honourable Families. At whose solemn Funeral I was present, and accompanied the dead to the Grave of Oblivion, but mourned not, for that the Commonwealth rejoyced, that fettered Freeholds and Inheritances were set at liberty, and many and manifold Inconveniences to the Head and all the Members of the Commonwealth thereby avoided.

III. *Jenning's* Case vouched in *Mary Portington's* Case and doth concern the *Jenning's Case.* common Assurance of the Realm.

IV. And next after cometh *Lampet's* Case, where Perpetuities of Leases for *Lampet's Case.* many thousand years, are by consequence overthrown.

V. The Case of the University of *Oxford* (a Famous Seminary of the Church Case of the University of *Oxford.* and Commonwealth) tendeth to the advancement of Gods true Religion, and in some degree for the better maintenance of a Learned and Religious Ministry, out of both of the Universities of *Cambridge* and *Oxford.*

VI. The Bishop of *Salisbury's* Case against both the diminution of the Pos- Bishop of *Salisbury's* Case. sessions and yearly Revenues of the Archbishops and Bishops of the Realm, and the prejudice of their Successors.

VII. *Whistler's* Case, containing divers material Points for the better con- *Whistler's Case.* struction of Letters Patents of Inheritance in divers Points commonly hapning.

VIII. The Case of the Church-wardens of the Parish of St. *Saviours,* wherein Wardens of St. Saviours. Letters Patents of Leases are well expounded, for the quieting of the Possession of many of the Kings Farmours, and by consequence of the Inheritance and Estates of many others.

IX. The Case of the Court of the *Marshalsea,* wherein the Original Insti- Case of the Court of Marshlesa. tution and Jurisdiction of that Court is clearly manifested. And albeit the Law was well known before in this Case, both by our Book Cases and Records in all succession of Ages: yet as in great Rivers, the courses, windings, fillings in, and out-lets are by experience vulgarly known, whereas the very Fountain and Head it self lie many times hidden and secret, so in this very Case, the Capacity,

---

20. [*Ed.:* that monsters are begotten on account of the corruption of some principle.]

Process and Priviledge of this Court was often resolved in our Books and Years of Terms, and the Jurisdiction commonly known, and yet the true original Institution and Fountain it self lay somewhat deep and obscure, until it was wrought out by Antiquity, which hath so manifested the true sense of the ancient. Acts of Parliament, and the reason of our Books concerning the original and true Jurisdiction of this Court, as the very opposites, being by venerable Antiquity inlightened, are by Reason convinced, and by Authority satisfied; and therefore they are worthy of reprehension which contemn or neglect the study of Antiquity (which is ever accompanied with dignity) as a withered and back-looking curiosity: *multa ignoramus quae non laterent si veterum lectio fuit nobis familiaris:* [21,22] And as the Aluminor spoken of in Law, giveth light and lustre to the letter, or figure to the coloured; so Antiquity doth give light with great grace and ornament, both for the understanding and meaning of the Letter of ancient Acts of Parliament, and of our Book Cases and Authorities in Law. I wish the like were done for all his Majesties Courts of Justice, a matter to them that have orderly read and well observed our Books, and Authorities of Law, of greater labour than difficulty; and yet would the Work greatly tend to the Honour of the Law, and the preventing of many Questions, Suits, and unnecessary Charges and Delays.

Leonard Lovie's Case.

X. *Leonard Lovie's* Case is principally grounded upon the Statutes of 32 H. 8. cap. 1. and 34 Hen. 8. cap. 5. of Wills: which Statutes might seem to be made *ad extorquenda juris-prudentum ingenia,* [23] so many and such intricate and knotty Questions have grown out of those Roots, and yet adding this last Case to the former Cases Reported by me for Exposition of those Statutes, to *Butler* and *Bakers,* in the third Part of my Reports, *fo. 27.* Sir *George Cursons* Case in the sixth Part, *fo. 75.* Sir *Richard Pexals* Case in the eightth Part 83. *Mights* Case *ibidem* 163. *Vigil Parkers ibidem* 173, *&c.* I am perswaded, that if not all, yet the principal scruples and doubts upon those Statutes, are for the general quiet of the whole Realm cleared and resolved. And yet Men of advised and setled Judgments will in their perfect Health provide for their Wives and Children, and by sound advice of Learned Counsel, settle their Estates by

---

21. [*Ed.:* we are unaware of many things which would not be hidden if we were more familiar with reading of the past:]

22. 1 R. 3.c.9.

23. [*Ed.:* to twist the ingenuity of those learned in the law,]

Conveyance in their Life-time, which may, if they will, be revocable at their
pleasure, and not to leave it to stand wholly upon their last Will, which many
times is made when they lye on their Death-Beds (and few Men pinched with
the Messengers of Death, have a disposing Memory) sometimes in hast, and
commonly by slender Advice, and is subject to so many Questions upon concealed Tenures in *Capite,*[24] and other Tenures by Knights Service (in this Eagle-
Eyed World) former Conveyances, and other matters of fact, as in effect they
do for want of due information and instruction, *superare jurisprudentum
artem.*[25] And it is some blemish or touch to a Man well esteemed for his wisdom
and discretion all his Life; to leave a troubled Estate behind him, amongst his
Wife, Children or Kindred after his death. A competent Estate to Wife, Children or Kindred in certainty and quiet, is far better than a greater, accompanied
with Questions and Troubles. But hereof I have given also a light touch in
the end of *Butler* and *Bakers* Case before mentioned; and therefore having
given this Admonition, I will here pass over to the next Case.

XI. Doctor *Leifield's* Case, wherein the Reason of Law is opened, wherefore
Charters and Deeds pleaded, ought to be shewed forth in Court, and a Caveat
given how dangerous it is in Evidence to a Jury to prove Deeds and Writings
by Witnesses without shewing forth; for by that means Deeds that be razed,
interlined, or otherwise adulterated, or utterly insufficient for want of legal
Words, or revocable and void against Fermors and Purchasers, have by concealing and proving the effect of them by disposition of unlearned Men, for
want of good direction passed for good and authentical: And afterwards the
matter coming in question again, and the Court directing upon examination
of the Case, that the Deed ought to be shewed, upon sight thereof the insufficiency appeared, and to the Right prevailed; which I have known both
in the Court of *Common Pleas,* amongst others, *Mich.* 5 *Regis Jacobi,* between
Small and *Blackledge,* and in the Court of Starr-Chamber in the Case between
Green and *Eyer,* and sometime in my Circuit since I was called to be a Judge.

*Dr. Lei-
field's* Case.

XII. *Edward Seymor's* Case, concerning Warranties, a cunning kind of
Learning (I assure you) and very necessary for the Purchasor: For it armeth
him not only with a Sword by Voucher to get the Victory of Recompence by

Seymor's
Case.

---

24. [*Ed.:* (in) chief, (a freehold held directly from the crown).]
25. [*Ed.:* transcend the art of jurisprudence.]

Recovery in Value, but with a Shield to defend a Mans Freehold and Inheritance by way of Rebutter;[26] which Title of the Law is in mine Opinion excellently curious, and curiously excellent. And yet when you have read this Case, you will concur with me, that it was more weighty than difficult.

Beaufage's Case.

XIII. Then cometh in *Beaufage's* Case, as well for the Safety of Sheriffs and their Officers and Ministers, as for avoiding of Extortion *Crimen Expilationis*[27] which in Holy Writ, in that Imprecation against Gods Enemies, is called a cosening Sin, *Let the Extortioner consume that he hath, and let the Stranger spoil his Labour,*[28] Wherein you shall find the Statute of *23 Hen. 6. c. 10.* made for avoiding of Extortion, Perjury and Oppressing, which are for the most part linked together, very well and justaly expounded.

Denbawd's Case.

XIV. Next followeth *Denbawd's* Case, for the just and due granting of *Tales de Circumstantibus*[29] at the Assises for the better expedition of Trials; wherein as well the Sheriffs and their Ministers, as the Parties, their Attornies and followers are to be warned, that by no Practice or Confederacy, directly or indirectly, they procure not partial and affected Freeholders to stand in View, or by any shift to be packed on the *Tales,* whereby Truth and Justice may be subverted, and the necessary Act of *35 Hen. 8. c. 6.* sinisterly abused, for that is an high Offence, and to be punished by a grievous Fine, Imprisonment and other Exemplary Punishment.

Lofield versus Clun.

XV, XX. *Lofield* and *Clun's* Case, touching Reservation of Rents upon Leases for years, *&c,* and how the same shall be confirned, necessary to be known of all Men, because in effect it concerneth all.

Legate's Case.

XVI. Then followeth *Arthur Legate's* Case, against the robbing of Church and Common-Wealth, of the Crown and of the Country, by colour of pestilent Patents of theevish Concealments.

Pilfold versus Cheyney.

XVII, XVIII. After that *Pilfold* and *Cheyney's* Case, concerning the true and legal manner of the assessing and enquiring of damages, *&c.* a necessary kind of Learning, for that many Errors, the Causes of Expence and Delay have been therein often committed.

26. [*Ed.:* An answer to defend against a claim to possess land.]

27. [*Ed.:* the crime of plunder.]

28. [*Ed.:* A quotation from *Psal.* 109. *vers.* 10.]

29. [*Ed.:* Tales of so many of those standing by; a tale being a group of men summoned by the Court to fill an under-staffed venire.]

XIX. Next cometh the Case of the Mayor and Burgesses of *King's Linn* in the County of *Norfolk,* wherein is well discussed what shall be deemed in Law the true name of the Corporation in substance, to the end that Bonds, Covenants, Leases, Grants or Conveyances be not in respect of too much Niceness and Curiosity therein against all Honesty and just Dealing, impeached and overthrown. And to say the truth, I find not in any of our Books from the beginning of the Reign of *Edw.* 3. until the Reign of *Edw.* 6. that any Bond, Lease, Grant or Conveyance have been overthrown by Judgment, in respect of the misnaming of the Corporation, but after a Window was once opened, it is a wonder to consider what light hath been taken by Corporations both Spiritual and Temporal, by Questions and Suits in Law, to avoid their own Leases, Grants and Conveyances, to the hindrance of Multitudes, and undoing of many, under colour of misnaming themselves, it grieveth good Men to remember; *Sed motos praestat componere fluctus.*[30] And this Case is reported for the surety and quiet as well of their Fermors[31] and others claiming from them, as of themselves; for Estates, Covenants and other things made unto them, *ut res magis valeat quam pereat.*[32]

Mayor de Linn's Case.

XXI. Then have you *Osborn's* Case; wherein is at large resolved where false or incongruous Latin, *&c.* shall abate, vitiate or make void Writs, Specialties, Charters, Deeds or Records, and where not.

Osborn's Case.

XXII. *Read* and *Redman's* Case; concerning Summons and Severance, wherein you shall find, when the death of the Party severed shall abate the Writ, and when not; and in some Cases where the death of one of the Plaintiffs, though he be not severed, shall not abate the Original Writ, *&c.*

Read versus *Redman.*

XXIII. *Richard Smith's* Case, in what case a *Quare Impedit* lyeth *de medietate,* &c. *Ecclesiae.*[33]

R. Smith's Case.

XXIV, XXV, XXVI. Then shall you read certain Resolutions upon the Statutes and Commission of Sewers, a necessary kind of Learning to be known, but more necessary (I assure you) to be put in due Execution; and that by colour thereof a private be not privily intended, when the publique is openly pretended. And in those Cases is well discussed what the Commissioners of Sewers may justly and safely do by their Wisdoms and Discretions.

3 Cases sur Stat. de Sewers.

30. [*Ed.:* But it is better to calm the troubled waves (an allusion to Virgil, *Aeneid,* 1. 135.)]
31. [*Ed.:* Fermors are tenants for life or for years; later associated with agricultural holdings.]
32. [*Ed.:* that a thing should rather avail than perish.]
33. [*Ed.:* for the moiety, etc. of a church.]

Scroop's
Case.

XXVII. And lastly *Scroop's* Case, touching a Point of Revocations, very necessary to be known, for that Revocations are grown so frequent; and the Resolution of this one Point may prevent many Controversies, that might have grown out of them, and that most commonly between Brethren and others near of Blood and Alliance.

If any do marvail, that seeing the Matter of every particular Case doth rest in a narrow room, and that my manner of Reporting is summary, relating the effect of all that was said of the one side by it self, and so likewise of the other, beginning ever with the Objections, and concluding with the Resolution and Judgment of the Court, (which I hold to be the best order of Relation) wherefore divers of these Reports are drawn into so great a length; the Cause is apparent, though I allow not of it, that the Questions or Objections moved at the Bar, and the Arguments drawn from Books, Cases and other Authorities in Law be so many, and to say the truth, many Questions are raised rather out of the weight of the Matter, than the difficulty of the Case: For I never saw any Case of great Value proceed quietly without many Exceptions in Arrest of Judgment. The antient order of Arguments by our Serjeants and Apprentices of Law at the Barr is altogether altered. 1. They never cited any Book Case or Authority in particular as is holden in 40 *Edw.* 3. *&c.* But *est tenus ou agree*

Nul livres
cite devant
ceux-jours.

in nostre livres, ou est tenus ou adjudge in termes,[34] or such like, which Order yet remains in Moots at the Bar in the *Inner Temple* to this day. 2. Then was the Citing general, but always true in the particular; and now the Citing is particular, and the Matter many times mistaken in general. 3. In those days few Cases in Law were cited but very pithy and pertinent to the purpose, and those ever pincht most, and now in so long Arguments with such a Farrago of Authorities, it cannot be but there is much refuse, which ever doth weaken or lessen the weight of the Argument. This were easily holpen, if the Matter (which ever lieth in a narrow roomth) were first discerned, and then that every one that argueth at the Bar would either speak to the purpose, or else be short.

But seeing my desire is, and ever hath been, that the Counsel learned, and consequently the Parties might receive satisfaction, for which cause all the Counsel that have argued in the Case to be adjudged, ought to give diligent attendance and attention on those days when the Judges do argue, which are

---

34. [*Ed.:* but it is held or agreed in our books or it is held or agreed in (books of) terms (i.e. the year books).]

ever publickly long before appointed, and prefixed on certain days. I have for that purpose (the pains being mine own, and the Matter not without some fruit) in the Cases of greatest consequence made the larger Report, comprehending the effect of all that was objected and resolved; and yet he may be a good Miner that findeth and followeth the main Veins, though he discovereth not the small and unvaluable Fillets, for there peradventure *materiam superabit opus.*[35] This only I will add as a Caveat to all the Professors of the Law, that seeing their Arguments should tend for the finding out of the true Judgment of Law, for the better execution of Justice, that therein they commit not manifest Injustice; for I am of Opinion that he that wresteth or misapplieth any Text, Book or Authority of the Law against his proper and genuine Sense, yea though it be to confirm a Truth, doth against distributive Justice, which is to give to every one his own. And let not those that heard the Arguments themselves uttered *viva voce,*[36] with the Countenance and Gesture of living Men in the seat of Justice in open Court, fear that when they shall read them privately in a dead Letter, it will want much of the former grace: For though I confess that *habet nescio quam energiam viva vox,*[37] yet when they shall read the effect of all that was spoken at large at several times by several persons, at the Bench and at the Bar by either part, of many and divers Matters collected and united together, and reduced *ad diem*[38] concerning every particular point, it will case them of much labour, and conduce much to the fetling of their Judgment, and that, if I be not deceived, not without a Students delight.

And for that I am intreated to shew as well the times when the *Register,* the *Mirror of Justices, Glanvil, Briton, Fleta,* the *Tales* or *Novae Narrationes, Old Natura Brevium, Littleton* and other Books of the Laws now extant were published, and where the Authors themselves appear not in those Books, who were the Authors of the same, as also the Antiquity of Serjeants at Law: For their satisfaction they shall understand, that first the *Register,* which containeth the Original Writs of the Common Law, is the ancientest Book of the Law; for the Book-Case and Record of 26 *Edw.* 3. *lib. Aff. pl.* 24. proveth directly, that Original Writs of Assise and other Original Writs had been time out of

---

35. [*Ed.:* the task will exceed the matter.]
36. [*Ed.:* orally (literally, "with live voice").]
37. [*Ed.:* the living voice has I know not what efficacy,]
38. [*Ed.:* on the day.]

mind of Man (that is, the beginning whereof cannot be known either by Remembrance, Reading or Record) long before the Conquest, whereof I give here but a light touch, for that I have cited the same more at large in the Preface to the *3d Part of my Commentaries*,[39] and I avoid as much as I can, unpleasing Iterations: And this Book is called *Registrum Cancellariae*[40] in the Statute of *Westm.* 2. *cap.* 24. because that the Chancery is *tanquaem officina Justitiae*,[41] all Original Writs issuing out of that Court: Now, for the Authority thereof, *Bracton, lib.* 5. *Tract' de Exceptionibus, cap.* 17. *fol.* 413. faith thus, *Breve quidem cum sit formatum ad similitudinem regulae Juris, quia breviter & paucis verbis intentionem proferentis exponit & explanat, sicut regula Juris rem quae est, breviter enarrat, &c. Sunt quaedam formata sub certis casibus de cursu & de Communi Concilio totius. Regni concessa & approbata, quae quidem nullatenus mutari poterint absque consensu & voluntate eorum.*[42] Now joyning both these Authorities together a Man may safely conclude, that this Book is most ancient and of greatest Authority. I confess, that by force of Acts of Parliament in succeeding Ages, divers other Writs original in Cases newly happening are (as appeareth in the same) added thereunto. And of these ancient Writs, I will say (as Sir *Th. Smith* a Secretary of State said) that all the Secretaries in Christendom may learn of them to express much Matter in few and significant Words.

For the *Mirror of Justices, Speculum Justiciar'*,[43] the most of it was written long before the Conquest, as by the same appeareth, and yet many things added thereunto by *Horn* a learned and discreet Man (as it is supposed) in the Reign of *Edw.* 1.

Concerning *Glanvil,* he wrote in the Reign of Henry the second as appeareth by this Book; and what he was it appeareth in my Preface to my Eighth Book, a History in my Opinion worthy the reading. And about the same time was the Treatise called the *Old Tenures* made.

39. [*Ed.:* Coke refers here to the third part of the *Reports.*]

40. [*Ed.:* Register of the Chancery.]

41. [*Ed.:* as the workshop of justice,]

42. [*Ed.:* Writs are formulated like rules of law, which briefly and in a few words expound and explain the intention of the maker, just as rules of law briefly state the matter as it is, etc. Some are formed upon certain causes and (issued) of course, and are granted and approved by the common council of the whole realm, and these can in no way be changed without their consent and will.]

43. [*Ed.:* Mirror of Justices, written, probably, circa 1290, although its first printing was long after Coke wrote this preface, in 1642.]

Bracton, as elsewhere I have noted, wrote about the end of the Reign of Henry the third.

Briton composed a learned Work and published the same in 5 *Edw.* I. as appeareth in 35 *H.* 6. by the Commandment of Edward the first (our *Justinian*) the Tenor whereof runneth in the Kings Name, as if it had been written by him, answerable to *Justinians* Institutes, which *Justinian* assumeth to himself, although it were composed by others. This *John Briton* was Bishop of *Hereford*, and of great and profound Judgment in the Common Laws, an excellent Ornament to his Profession; and a Safety and a Solace to himself, *Vide Stamford Praerog. R. 6. &* 21.

Fleta is a Work well written by some learned Lawyer, who being committed to the Prison of the *Fleet*, had leasure to compile it there, and therefore stiled his Book by the name of the *Fleet*, *Fleta*, and concealed his own Name, as in the Preface to his Work appeareth. The Author thereof is unknown, but it apeareth in his Book that he lived in the Reigns of King *Ed.* 2. and *Ed.* 3. *Vide lib.* 1. *cap.* 20. §. *Qui ceperunt, lib.* 2. *cap.* 66. § *Item quod nullus.*[44] But of the certain time when it was first published (for peradventure it had Additions afterwards) there is some Question made: But in seeking after this, I find that this Book took the Name of the Prison of the *Fleet*, and that the *Fleet* took the Name of the River running by it called the *Fleet*.

The Book entituled *Novae* Narationes, vouched and allowed in 39 *H.* 6. 30. by learned *Prisot* and his Companions, Justices of the Court of *Common Pleas*, by the Name of the *Tales*, was published about the beginning of the Reign of King *Edw.* 3. And *Old Natura Brevium* afterwards in the Reign of the same King, for *f.* 100. *b.* the Statute of 5 *Edw.* 3.*c.* 12. is called *le novel statute:* but since, Additions have been made thereunto. Of this Book Sir *Anthony Fitzherbert* in his Proem to his *Natura Brevium* faith as followeth, *Et auxy pur cel intent & purpose, fuit compose per un sage & discreet home un liure appel Natura Brevium.*[45]

Fortescue de laudibus legum Angliae[46] this Book was written in the Reign of King *H.* 6. in commendation of the Laws of *England*, containing withal

---

44. [*Ed.:* See book I, ch. 20, § 'Who took . . .', and Book II, ch. 66, § 'Also that no one . . .'.]

45. [*Ed.:* And also for this intent and purpose there was composed, by a sage and discerning man, a book called *Natura Brevium* (the Nature of Writs).]

46. [*Ed.:* In Praise of the Laws of England.]

much excellent Matter worthy the reading. He wrote also a Book in defence of the Title of King Henry the sixth his Sovereign Lord and Master, to the Crown of *England;* but after out of Truth and Conscience retracted the same, both which I have; wherein he deserved singular commendation, in that he was not amongst the number of those *qui suos amassent Errores,*[47] but yielded to Truth when he found it. This Sir *John Fortescue* was Lord Chief Justice of *England,* and afterwards Lord Chancellor of *England,* and his Posterity remain in great and good account to this day.

Stathom's Abridgment, first published in the Reign of King Henry the sixth by *Stathom* a learned Lawyer of that time: And the *Abridgment of the Book of the Assizes,* published also about the same time, but the Author thereof is unknown.

Littleton's Tenures, a Book of sound and exquisite Learning, comprehending much of the Marrow of the Common Law, written and published by *Thomas Littleton* a grave and learned Judge of the Court of *Common Pleas,* sometimes of the *Inner Temple,* wherein he had great furtherance by Sir *John Prisot* Lord Chief Justice of the Court of *Common Pleas* a famous and expert Lawyer, and other the Sages of the Law who flourished in those days. Of this Book *Hotomon* a Civilian and Canonist in his Commentary *De Verbis Feudalibus, Verbo Feudum,*[48] giveth his Censure, with what Charity or Discretion, judge learned Reader: Stephanus Pasaverinus *excellenti vir ingenio,* &c. *Libellum mihi Anglicanum,* Littletonum *dedit, quo feudorum Anglicanorum jura exponuntur, ita incondite, absurde & inconcinne scriptum, ut facile apparet verum esse quod* Polidorus Virgilius *in Anglicana Historia scribit, stultitiam in eo libro cum malitia & calumniandi studio certare.*[49] Of *Hottoman* and his Author I may justly say, and will say no more, *volentes esse legis doctores, non intelligentes neque quae loquuntur, neque de quibus affirmeant,*[50] and therefore let us leave them among the number of those *qui vituperant quae ignorant.*[51] It is a desperate and dan-

---

47. [*Ed.:* who had liked their errors,]

48. [*Ed.:* Of Feudal Words, the Word Fee.]

49. [*Ed.:* Stephen Pasaverinus, a man of excellent skill, gave me a little English book called Littleton, in which are expounded the feudal laws of England, written so disorderly, absurdly, and inelegantly that it may easily appear to be true what Polydore Virgil wrote in his *History of England,* struggle with the nonsense in this book with ill will and with the inclination of challenge.]

50. [*Ed.:* they want to be doctors of law without knowing what they speak or of what they affirm,]

51. [*Ed.:* who vituperate the things of which they are ignorant.]

gerous Matter for Civilians and Canonists (I speak what I know, and not without just cause) to write either of the Common Laws of *England* which they profess not, or against them which they know not. Sure I am, it were a ridiculous Attempt and Enterprise in me (that because I confess I have read some little part of the Civil and Canon Laws, and that with some good assistance and help) by and by to write either of them or against them. But their Pages are so full of palpable Errors and gross mistakings, as these new Authors are out of our Charity pitied, and their Books out of our Judgment cast away unanswered. Alas, our Books of Law seem to them to be dark and obscure; but no wise Man will impute it to the Laws, but to their Ignorance, who by their sole and superficial Reading of them cannot understand the depth of them. I will not sharpen the Neb of my Pen against them, for that I pity the persons, and wish they had more Discretion, for that I honour their Profession. And for *Littleton's Tenures,* I affirm and will maintain it against all Opposites whatsoever, that it is a Work of as absolute perfection in its kind, and as free from Error, as any Book that I have known to be written of any Human Learning. And the Posterity of this Sage of the Law (unto whom he is a great Ornament) doth flourish unto this day, of whom a Man of great excellency in his Profession hath justly said, that he was a famous Lawyer, &c. to whose Treaty of *Tenures* saith he, the Students of the Common Laws are no less beholding than the Civilians to *Justinian's* Institutes.

Fitzherbert's Abridgment was painfully and elaborately collected and published in 11 *H.* 8. by *Fitzherbert* then Serjeant at Law. And he wrote also another Book called his *Natura Brevium,* an exact Work exquisitely penned, and published in 26 *H.* 8. when he was Sir *Anthony Fitzherbert* Knight, one of the Judges of the Court of *Common Pleas.* About the same time he wrote his Treatise of Justices of the Peace; wherewith the Judges (as I have seen it reported) found fault, for that he therein affirmed that Justices of Peace having by their Commission Authority to hear and determine Felonies, *&c.* could not hear and determine Murder, which (amongst others) they clearly overruled, that Justices of Peace lawfully might do.

Doctor and Student, a Book written in 23 *Hen.* 8. Dialogue-wise between a Doctor of Divinity and a Student of the Common Law, the Authors Name was *S. Germin,* a discreet Man and well read, I assure you, both in the Common Law, and in the Civil and Canon Laws also.

A Book intituled a Treatise made by Divines and other learned in the Laws of the Realm, concerning the Power of the Clergy, and the Laws of the Realm, published in time of King Henry the eighth and after the six and twentieth year of his Reign; for therein the Act of Parliament made in that year is mentioned, which Book I have.

The small Treatises concerning *the manner of keeping Court Baron and Leet, &c. Modus tenendi Hundredum, &c. Returna Brevium, Charta feodi,* &c. and *Ordinances for Fees in the Exchequer* were all published in the end of the Reign of King Henry the eighth.

The Book called the *Diversity of Courts,* was compiled after the 21st year of *H.* 8. for the Statute of 21 *H.* 8. for Restitution of Goods upon Inditement, *&c.* is recited, *fol.* 117. *a.*

Stamford: This Book containeth two parts, one of the Pleas of the Crown, the other of a lesser Volume, of the Prerogative of the King; but the later was first published by Sir *William Stamford* Knight, sometimes of *Grays Inn,* a Man excellently learned in the Common Laws; whose Posterity prosper at this day.

Parkins a little Treatise of certain Titles of the Common Laws, wittily and learnedly composed and published in the Reign of King *Edward* 6. by *John Parkins* an Utterbarister of the *Inner Temple.*

I cannot pretermit the Abridgment of the Statutes, and the Table, to *Fitzherberts* Great Abridgment, and the Book of Entries, profitably and painfully (I assure you) gathered and published in the Reign of the late Queen *Mary,* but especially the first two, tending very much to the case and furtherance of the Professors of the Law, collected by *William Rastal* a Reverend Judge of the Court of Common Pleas, and of great Industry; many things being since added both to his Abridgment of Statutes and to the Book of Entries, who originally was also the Author of the Book called the *Terms of the Law.*

The Lord *Brook's* Abridgment, first published in the 16th year of Queen *Eliz.* This was gathered by Sir *Robert Brook* Knight, Chief Justice of the Court of Common Pleas, for his private use, and was published long after his decease, a worthy and painful work, and an excellent Repertory or Table for the Year Books of the Law: *Sed satius est petere Fontes quam sectari Rivulos.*[52]

Plowden's Commentaries, consisting of two parts, both of them learnedly and curiously polished, and published by himself, the one in the 13th year of Queen *Eliz.* and the other in the 21st year of the same Queen, Works (as they

---

52. [*Ed.:* but it is more satisfactory to seek the sources than to follow the streams.]

well deserve) with all the Professors of the Laws of high account. The Author was an ancient Apprentice of the Law, of the *Middle Temple,* of great Gravity, Knowledge Integrity.

The Lord *Dyer's* Book, containing the fruitful and summary Collections of that Reverend Father of the Law Sir *James Dyer* Knight, late Chief Justice of the Court of Common Pleas, for his private use and remembrance, and never intended by him in this form to be made publique, but were as he left them imprinted after his decease in the 25th year of Queen *Eliz.* the very Original whereof, written with his own Hand, I have.

Lastly, Master *Lambards* Collection of the Office of Justices of the Peace, methodically written, was published towards the end of the Reign of Queen *Elizabeth.*

Concerning the antiquity of Serjeants at Law, it is evident by the Book of the *Mirror of Justices, Justices, lib.* 2. *cap. des Loiers,* which treateth of the Laws of this Realm and the Ministers thereof long before the Conquest, that Serjeants at Law were of ancient times called *Narratores, Countors* or *Counteors,* because the Count or Declaration comprehended the substance of the Original Writ, and the very Foundation of the Suit, of which part, as of the worthiest, they took their denomination, and is all one in effect, with that which in the Civil Law is called *Libellus;* and they lost not that Name in the Reign of King *E. 1.* as it apeareth by the Statute of *W. 1. c. 29. ann. 3 Edw. 1.* for there he is called *Serjeant Countor, Serviens Narrator:* And by the Statute of *Articuli super Chartas, cap. 11. anno 28 E. 1. Nest my a intender que home ne poit aver counsel des countors, & des sages gents pur lour donant;*[53] where under this word [*Countors*] Serjeants at Law are included, and until this day, when any proceeds Serjeant, he doth count in some real Action at the Bar of the Court of Common Pleas; and under these words (*Sages gents*) are included Apprentices at Law: But since the Reign of *E.* 1. they have always been called *Servientes ad legem*[54] for their good Service to the Common-wealth by their sound Advice in Law; and as in ancient time, they that preserved and kept the Peace were called *Servientes pacis* or *ad pacem,*[55] so these Men are called *Servientes legis* or *ad*

---

53. [*Ed.:* It is not to be understood that one may not have counsel of counters and other learned men for their fee,]

54. [*Ed.:* serjeants at law.]

55. [*Ed.:* serjeants of the peace (or) at the peace.]

legem or *in legibus, &c.*[56] And in that ancient Treatise of the *Mirror of Justices ubi supra, Counteurs*[57] are described to be Serjeants skilful in Law of the Realm, which serve the common People to pronounce and defend their Actions in Judgment for their Fee, whose duty is there excellently described. This proveth the great Antiquity of the Serjeants at Law. *Inter placita de Parliament' tent' apud Ashering ann. 19 Edw. 1.*[58] in that great Case of *Thomas de Weylond it is said, Servientes in legibus & consuetudinibus Angliae experti, &c.*[59] and in all our Books of years and terms from the beginning there is mention made of them; as in 1 *Edw. 3. 22. Serjeant le Roy, &c.* and in 1 *Edw. 3. s.* 16. there is mention made of an Apprentice; and he is called an Apprentice of the Law, of this word (*apprender*[60]) for that he ought to be *apprise in la ley,*[61] and hath manifested the same by open reading upon some Statute in that Inn of Court whereof he is Fellow, and is next in degree under a Serjeant. And this Appellation is very ancient, and so is proved *Rotulo Paliamenti in Crastino Epiphaniae, anno 20. Edw. 1. Rot. 5. in dorso,*[62] The Act saith, *De Atturnatis & Apprenticiis, Dominus Rex injuxit Johanni de Mettingham & sociis suis, quod ipsi per eorum discretionem provideant & ordinent certum numerum de quolibet comitatu, &c.*[63] And so is farther provided by a Record, *inter communia Placita tent' in Hustingo London' die Lunae in Festo Sancti Clementiae Papae anno Reg. Edw. 3. post Conquestum 23. viz. Die Jovis proxime ante festum Sancti Gregorii Papae anno Domini 1348. Ego Johannes Tavie Armiger lego animam meam Deo, &c. Item lego omnia tenementa mea cum omnibus pertinentiis quae habeo in parte Australi in Parochia Sancti Andreae, &c. Aliciae Uxori meae ad totum terminum vitae suae, Et quod post decessum praedictae Aliciae totutum illud Hospitium, in quo Apprenticii legis habitare solebant, per Executores meos si superstites fuerint, &c. vendatur, & quod de pecunia inde percepta unus Capellanus idoneus pro anima mea, &c. celebrand', dummodo pecunia illa perseveraverit,*

---

56. [*Ed.:* serjeants of the law, or at law, or in the laws, etc.]

57. [*Ed.:* counters.]

58. [*Ed.:* Amongst the pleas of the parliament held at Ashridge in the nineteenth year of Edward I.]

59. [*Ed.:* serjeants expert in the laws and customs of England, etc.]

60. [*Ed.:* to learn.]

61. [*Ed.:* learned in the law,]

62. [*Ed.:* in the roll of the parliament (held) on the morrow of the Epiphany in the twentieth year of Edward I, roll 5, on the dorse (the reverse side of the roll).]

63. [*Ed.:* Concerning attorneys and apprentices. The lord king enjoins John of Mettingham and his fellows that they should by their discretion provide and ordain a certain number from each county, etc.]

inveniatur. Item lego totum illud tenementum in quo inhabito cum tribus shopis post decessum ipsius Aliciae ad fabricam Ecclesiae Sancti Andreae.[64] Out of this Record I observe three things; first, for the Antiquity of Apprentices of the Law, That the House of Chancery in *Holborn* now called *Tavies Inn,* had been of ancient time, before the 23rd year of Edw. 3., (which is about 264 years past) an House of Court, wherein the Apprentices of the Law were wont to inhabite: 2. For the Antiquity and true Name of that House of Chancery, rightly called *Tavies Inn.* 3. That upon this Will the Case in 13 *R. 2. Tit. Devise Fitzh.* 27. was adjudged, That the Remainder of the House devised to the said *Alice* for life, belonged to the Parson of the Church of *Holborn* and his Sucessors. And in 39 *Edw. 3. f. 47. b.* in a *Quod ei deforceat*[65] *Ingleby, Serjeant,* of Counsel with the Tenant took this Exception; This Writ (saith he) is founded upon a Record precedent, and therefore we pray, that the Demandant may put the Record (whereupon this Writ dependeth) in certain, and in Case of *Attaint* and *scire facias*[66] (which depend upon Records) the Tenant shall have *Oyer* of the Record: *Wilby* and *Shipwith,* This was never any Exception in this place, but we have heard it oftentimes amongst the Apprentices in Houses of Court. And concerning Apprentices of Law thus much shall suffice.

The manner of the Creation of Serjeants is also most ancient; for it is by Writ, which is commonly found in very ancient *Registers,* and continued to this day, in this form, *Rex, &c. Willielmo Herle Salutem; quia de advisamento consilii nostri ordinavimus vos ad statum & gradum Servientis ad legem, in quindena Sancti* Michaelis *proxim' futur, suscipiend', Vobis mandamus firmiter injungentes, quod vos ad statum & gradum praedictum ad diem illum in forma praedicta suscipiend' ordinetis & praeparetis: & hoc sub poena mille librarum.*

64. [*Ed.:* among the common pleas held in the husting of London on Monday, the feast of St. Clement the Pope, in the twenty-third year of King Edward the third after the conquest, in the year of our Lord 1348: I, John Tavie, esquire, bequeath my soul to God, etc. Also I bequeath all my tenements with all the appurtenances which I have in the south part of the parish of St. Andrew, etc. to Alice my wife for the whole term of her life, and that after the decease of the aforesaid Alice all that inn in which the apprentices of the law are used to dwell shall be sold by my executors, if they should survive, etc., and from the money thereby received they should find one suitable chaplain to celebrate for my soul, etc. so long as the money lasts. Also I bequeath all that tenement in which I live, with three shops, after the death of the selfsame Alice, towards the fabric of St. Andrew's church.]

65. [*Ed.:* Writ by which a life tenant or other holders of a limited fee seeks lands lost through nonappearance at an earlier proceeding.]

66. [*Ed.:* Writ to enforce an earlier judgment or other matter of record.]

Teste meipso, &c.[67] wherein for the dignity of him, it is to be observed, 1. That he is called by the King by advice of his Council in that behalf, 2. By the Kings Writ, 3. The Writ is directed to him in the plural number, *vobis,* a special mark of Dignity: 4. That he is called *ad statum & gradum Servientis ad legem:*[68] And in the Act of Parliament of 8 *H.* 6. *cap.* 10. of the Serjeant it is said, *When he taketh the same state upon him.* And in the Act of Parliament of 8 *E.* 4. *cap.* 2. *al creation des Serjeants del Ley, &c.*[69] and Creation is ever applied to Dignity. But it is true, that the said Writ is not put into the printed *Register,* no more than Writs to call any to be a Baron of the Realm or of higher Dignity, for that those Writs originally are only *de gratia Regis;*[70] and such as are published in the printed *Register* are originally *de Jure Legis.*[71] Of the Solemnity of his Call, *viz.* his Hood, Robes, Coif, and other significant Ornaments, of the great and sumptuous Feast they make, of the Rings of Gold they give, of their Attendants, and other great and honourable Ceremonies, I purpose not at this time (being not pertinent to the Question I have in hand) to write any thing at all.

Their ancient Reputation is (I assure my self) the better continued, because they without the least alteration continue the ancient Habits and Ornaments belonging to their state and degree; for most commonly the ancient Reverence of any Profession vanisheth away with change of the ancient Habit, albeit the newer be more costly, courtly and curious. And in the Act of Parliament of 24 *H.* 8. *cap.* 13. he (having both *statum & gradum*[72]) hath the Precedency of divers that sit on the high Bench in a Court of great Eminency in *Westminster-Hall:* But seing there is no Remedy given by Law for Precedency, I (dealing only with matters in Law) mean not to meddle with it: And albeit I have learned more of the Antiquity of this State and Degree in the School of ven-

---

67. [*Ed.:* The king, etc. to William Herle, greeting. Because by the advice of our council we have ordained that you should take upon you the estate and degree of a serjeant at law in the quindene of Michaelmas next following, we command you with firm injunction that you order and prepare yourself to undertake the aforesaid estate and degree at that day in form aforesaid, and this under pain of one thousand pounds. Witness myself, etc.]

68. [*Ed.:* to the estate and degree of a serjeant at law:]

69. [*Ed.:* at the creation of the serjeants of the law, etc.]

70. [*Ed.:* by the king's grace;]

71. [*Ed.:* by right of law.]

72. [*Ed.:* an estate and a degree.]

erable Antiquity, yet hereof thus much for this time shall suffice; *Et valeant qui contabulatis mendaciis antiquitatem superstruunt.*[73]

Of these Serjeants, as of the Seminary of Justice, are chosen Judges; for none can be a Judge, either of the Court of Kings Bench, or of the Common Pleas, or Chief Baron of the Exchequer, unless he be a Serjeant; neither can he be of either of the Serjeants Inns, unless he hath been a Serjeant at Law, for it is not called Judges or Justices Inn, but Serjeants Inn; for I have known Barons of the Exchequer (that were not of the Coif, and yet had judicial places and voices) remain in the Houses of Court whereof they were Fellows, and wore the Habit of Apprentices of the Law.

But I perswade my self you desire to read the Cases whereof I have given you a taste, & *tempus est Veritatis & Justitiae sancta adire penetralia:*[74] And therefore here will take my leave of the good Student, to whom I wish with his increase of reading more and more a delight in this Study, an excellent mean to attain unto augmentation of venerable knowledge (which is one of the ends of my labours) not knowing what better thing to desire for him; and conclude with this Distichon and direction,

> Discendi modus est, dum te nescire videbis:
> Disce, sed assidue; Disce, sed ut sapias.[75]

The Case of Sutton's Hospital.
(1612) Michaelmas Term, 10 James I
In the Court of the King's Bench, before all the Judges of England.
First Published in the *Reports,* volume 10, page 23a.*

Ed.: Parliament passed an act to enable Thomas Sutton to establish a hospital and school in the then-defunct foundation of Charterhouse School. James I granted a license to Sutton to found a hospital for the relief of the

---

73. [*Ed.:* And away with them who strew antiquity with planks of lies.]
74. [*Ed.:* and the time has come to enter the inner sanctum of truth and justice.]
75. [*Ed.:* The manner of learning is, when you see yourself to be ignorant:
       Study, not only to practice; Study that you may be wise.]
*The pleadings of the case are filed at Mich. 10 Jacobi Rot. 574.

needy and a school for the maintenance of poor scholars, appointing Sutton as head of the hospital for life and giving the governors of the school and their successors the license to appoint the head after his death. Sutton purchased the old buildings of Charterhouse in London and established there the Hospital of King James and appointed a master to serve or be dismissed at Sutton's will, (and would be re-established in 1872 in Godalming, Surrey). Richard Sutton and John Lawe were arrested for trespassing on the grounds. They raised many objections to the existence of the foundation in defense. The King's Bench rejected their concerns, in the process inventorying many of the obligations in chartering a corporation, or at least a charitable corporation, making this opinion one of the foundations of the law of corporations. Coke lists the governors established in the charter of the school and hospital, who include not only himself but most of the leading members of the bench.

In the King's Bench Between Simon Baxter, Plaintiff, and Richard Sutton and John Law, Defendants, in an action for trespass, *de eo quod ipsi*[1] 30 May 10 Jac. a Capital Messuage called the Charter-house in the parish of St. Sepulchre, in the County of Middlesex, *freger' & intraver'*[2] upon not guilty pleaded. The whole special matter was found (which you may see at length, Mich. 10. Jacobi Rot. 574, in the Kings Bench). And the same was adjorned out of the Court of the King's Bench by the Judges of the same Court, into the Exchequer Chamber; and was there argued at the Bar by John Walter [of the Inner Temple] Yelverton of Gray's Inn, and by Bacon Solicitor General for the Plaintiff, and for the defendant by Coventry of the Inner Temple, Hutton, Serjeant at Law, and by Hobart, Attorney General. And the Plaintiff's Counsel argued very strongly in general: 1. That there was not any Incorporation created by the King's Letters Patents, dated 22 Junii 9 Jac. Regis. 2. Admitting the incorporation was good; yet there was not any Foundation made by Sutton according to the authority given to him. 3. That the bargain and sale made by Sutton, bearing date 1 Nov. 9 Jac. was utterly void, and by consequence all the said possessions descendible to the Plaintiff. And in the argument of this Case, these points upon these grounds were moved:

1. [*Ed.:* forasmuch as they.]
2. [*Ed.:* broke and entered.]

1. It is Objected that by the Act of Parliament, 9 Feb. 7 Jac. Reg. mentioned in the Record, An Hospital was legally erected and Incorporated, at Hallingbury in the County of Essex; and all the said Manors given to it; and by consequence the said Corporation made after the said | Act by the Letters Patents 22 Junii 9 Jac. Reg. was utterly void. Note reader, the said Act cannot give the said House called the Charter-house, for Sutton purchased it afterwards, viz. 9 May 9 *Jac. Reg.* as appeareth by the record.

1. Objection Postea 24.b.

[23 b]

2. It was Objected that no Hospital was founded by Sutton, and therefore the Incorporation failed; because that Sutton had the King's Licence to Found, Erect and establish an Hospital, which was an act precedent to be performed by Sutton before the Incorporation, which he hath not done; and so he hath not pursued his Licence; which Licence the King might have countermanded; and which was countermanded in Law by the death of Sutton.

2. Objection Postea 25.b.

3. That the King by his Charter cannot name the House and Inheritance of Sutton to be an Hospital, for that would-be to give a name to an Hospital *in alieno solo.*[3]

3. Objection Postea 28.b.

4. The place of every Corporation ought to be certain, for without a certain place there cannot be any Incorporation; but here the Licence to Sutton is to Found an Hospital "at or in the Charter house;" so that he may found it in all or any part of the same house, And therefore till Sutton hath founded it certain, there is not any certainty of the place, and by consequence no Corporation. To which was added, That a place by a known name is not sufficient to support the name of an Incorporation, but the same ought to be described by metes and bounds; And divers precedents were cited and shewed, where the Scite of Hospitals, Priories, &c. were so particularly described.

4. Objection Postea 29.a.

5. The King by his Letters Patents hath intended to make a present Incorporation, and so his words expressly import. 1. "From henceforth, &c." And yet no incorporation can be till Sutton hath named a Master, And the Letters Patents bear date 22 Junii 9 Jac. Reg, And the writing of Nomination 30 Octob. Anno 9, And so the Letters Patents are repugnant in themselves and void.

5. Objection Postea 31.b.

6. Until there be an actual Hospital and poor in it, there cannot be Governours of them, for Governours ought not to be idle, or as Cyphers in Algorisme; for Governours and Government, are *relativa, quae sunt simul tem-*

6. Objection Postea 32.a.

---

3. [*Ed.:* in someone else's soil.]

pore,[4] and as well in his Will as in other Instruments, he has called it many times his intended Hospital.

7. Objection Postea 33.a.

7. To every Corporation a Foundation is requisite; and here is not any Foundation made by Sutton. For first he ought to have *per verba praescripta*

[24 a] *& in terminis terminantibus*[5] | Founded, Erected, and established the said House of Charter-house an Hospital, &c. And the same was likened to Cases of Exchange, *frankalmoigne Dedi, warrantizo,*[6] which are Frank-marriage; *quae sunt verba legalia & incompatibilia, &c.*[7] And divers precedents were shewed to the Justices of building of Hospitals, Schools, &c. wherein the said words of *fundo, erigo, &c.*[8] were used. Secondly, before such lawful foundation made by Sutton, a Stranger could not have given any land or other thing to the Governours. Thirdly, without such Foundation, in time to come it shall not be known who should be the Founder, whereupon confusion would follow.

8. Objection Postea 34.a.

8. The nomination of the Master made by Sutton is void for two reasons; one, that he was named to Master but at will, where he ought to be named for life, in as much as he is to have a free-hold in the Land. Also there ought to be at least an actual Hospital Founded by Sutton according to his Licence, before he could nominate a Master of it; For otherwise it shall be a Mathematical or Utopical Hospital.

9. Objection Postea 34.a.

9. The said bargain and sale made by Sutton to the Governours was void for three causes. 1. That the money which was the consideration thereof was paid by the private persons of the Governours, and therefore the bargain and sale of the Manors &c. cannot enure to them in their politick capacity. 2. The *Habendum*[9] is to the Governours upon trust and confidence; and a body Politick aggregate of many cannot stand seised in trust and confidence to the use of another. 3. Because no Hospital was founded by Sutton according to his Licence; And for all the other Objections made against the Foundation and Incorporation, the said bargain and sale was void, and by consequence all the said Manors descended to the Plaintiff as Cousin and heir to Sutton.

4. [*Ed.:* relative, and exist at the same time.]
5. [*Ed.:* by prescribed words and in certain terms.]
6. [*Ed.:* I have given, I warrant,]
7. [*Ed.:* which are legal words and incompatible, etc.]
8. [*Ed.:* I found, erect, etc.]
9. [*Ed.:* Clause of the grant: "to have".]

10. That no Hospital was Incorporated by the said Letters Patents, and therefore it was objected, That the King could Incorporate them by the name of Governours, &c. of the Hospital, but of an Hospital in Law, or a Legal Hospital, as it was called; For the Governours cannot plead that they are seised *in jure Hospitalis sui,*[10] because in Law there was not any Hospital.

Which brief Report I have made of these Objections, because I think them, or the greater part of them were not worthy to be moved at the Bar, nor remembered at the Bench. And that this Case was by the Justices adjourned into the Exchequer Chamber | more for the weight of the value than for the difficulty of the Law in the case. And the entire Record, as appeareth by the Exceptions, ought to be the Case; which was openly argued in the Exchequer Chamber by all the Judges of England and Barons of the Exchequer, except the Chief Justice of the King's Bench, who was then sick, Sir Robert Houghton, Sir Augustine Nicholls, Sir John Dodderidge, Sir Humfrey Winch, Sir Edward Bromly, Sir John Croke, Sir James Altham, Sir George Snigge, Sir Peter Warburton, Sir Lawrence Tanfield Chief Baron, and Sir Edward Coke, Chief Justice of the Common Pleas. And it was Resolved by them in their arguments (except by Baron Snigge and Justice Croke) that judgment should be given against the Plaintiff, *Et quia rectum est judex sui & obliqui.*[11] A right line maketh discovery not only of that which is right, but of that which is wrong and crooked; and the confirmation of the right and truth is the confutation of error and falshood. I will report the effect of the reasons and causes which affirme and confirme the Resolutions of the Judges, which are of so great authority, perspicuity and gravity, that the Objections need not have any particular answer. And yet for the satisfaction of all men, every one of them shall be particularly answered. And because that this Case doth chiefly depend upon the Letters Patents; And the best Exposition of the King's Charter is upon the consideration of the whole Charter, to expound the Charter by the Charter itself, *verba cartae regiae aeque portant suam expositionem;*[12] and the King's Letters Patents in this case are *viscera causae, & expositio quae ex visceribus causae nascitur, est aptissima & fortissima in lege.*[13] All the parts of the Letters

---

10. [*Ed.:* in right of his hospital.]

11. [*Ed.:* and because right is the judge of itself and of what is crooked.]

12. [*Ed.:* the words of a royal charter in equity bear their own interpretation;]

13. [*Ed.:* the innermost parts (lit. bowels) of the cause, and an exposition which is born in the innermost parts of the cause is the most apt and the strongest in law.]

Patents were considered, and every material part thereof explained according to the true natural sense, which is the best method, upon the consideration of many others, for the more clear Report of this Case.

    The first part of the said Charter viz doth contain a short recital of two things, 1. of the title of the Act of 9 Feb. *anno.* 9. viz "An Act to confirm and enable the erection and establishment of an Hospital and Free Grammar School, given and intended to be given by Thomas Sutton, Esquire." which title proveth that no Hospital was founded by the Act itself; but the scope of the Act was to enable Sutton to erect and establish an Hospital, &c. and therefore the title saith, "intended to be given and performed by Thomas Sutton, Esquire;" And also the same appeareth by divers parts of the body of

the Act, which are all *in futuro & nihil in praesenti.*[14] | Be it enacted, That in the Town of "Halingbury, &c. there may be builded one meet house for abiding of poor people and Scholars, &c." which are words *de futuro*[15] and it is not certain in what part of the Town the House shall be built. 2. "And that the same shall and may be called and named the Hospital of King James;" which are words also *de futuro.* 3. "And that the Lord Arch-Bishop of Canterbury, &c. shall and may be Governour, &c. 4. And that the same Governours, &c. shall for ever hereafter stand and be incorporated:" which words ought to be intended to take effect after the erection of the Hospital, &c. in a certain place, &c. And so the construction is *in futuro,* which well appeareth with the future words following, and may have perpetual succession. 5. "And may for ever hereafter, have, hold, and enjoy, Lordships, Manors, &c. without Licence of Alienation or Licence of Mortmain." By which it appeareth, that this clause is not in effect, but a Licence to give Manors, Lands, &c. holden *in Capite*[16] without other Licence of Alienation, and also without other Licence of Mortmain. But this clause was superfluous and impertinent if the Land should pass by the Act itself, for then no Licence in those cases was requisite. And without question if it were admitted that there was a Corporation, yet no Lands are given to them by those words, *de futuro.* Also although the said Lands were given them, yet the King by his Letters Patent cannot create and incorporate an Hospital in the Charter-house, which was purchased after the

---

14. [*Ed.:* in future, and nothing is in the present.]
15. [*Ed.:* concerning the future.]
16. [*Ed.:* in Chief, that is, a tenancy held directly from the crown.]

Act, and the Action of Trespass in the case at Bar is for Trespass done in the
Charter-house. But it was answered by all the Justices and Barons of the Exchequer (except Justice Croke) that the Act of 9. Jac. doth not Incorporate
the Governours &c. but *in futuro,* which never took nor could now take effect;
and by consequence no Land was or could be given to it. The 2d branch of
the recital is of the purchase of the Charter-house after the Act, which, as it
is there rehearesed, is more fit and commodious than Hallingbury to be converted into an Hospital.

In the second part Sutton is a suitor and petitioner to the King for four
things: 1. "To give Licence to Found, Erect, and establish an Hospital house,
&c. and Free Grammar-School, &c. at or in the Charter-house," wherein hath
been observed the incertainty of the suit, "at or in the Charter-house" or but
of that: after. "2. Incorporate the Governors hereafter named;" so that Sutton
himself doth name the Governours which the King doth Incorporate. 3. By
such name of Incorporation | as is hereafter mentioned to have capacity and
ability, &c. by which also it appeareth that Sutton doth devise and prescribe
the name of the Incorporation; and by all these three clauses it appeareth,
That the suit of Sutton and his express consent was, that the Governours
should be named of the said House called the Charter-house. 4. Sutton was
suitor, "that the Governours, &c. might take in Mortmain for the better maintenance of the said Hospital, Free-school, Preacher," &c.

The third part of the Letters Patent containeth Grants and Acts made by
the King in two manners, sc by way of Licence and by way of Grant; of the
Licences some are requisite; some abundant and not requisite, and some requisite for the sustentation of the poor, &c. and not to the essence of the
Corporation; and of the grants, some are *in praesenti,* and some *in futuro,* and
of each of them some are of necessity, and some explanatory and not of necessity; and those which are of necessity, some are of necessity to the creation
of this body politick, and some to the continuance and preservation of it. And
into those branches the whole Letters Patents are divided, which shall be
observed as they arise and have place in the same Letters Patents. But before
all the Licences and Grants, the King doth prefix a preamble, *sc.* "The King
affecting so good a work, of his Princely disposition and care for the furtherance
thereof, and that the same may take the better effect, &c." (wherein appeareth
the Honour, Charity, and pious disposition of the King) "giveth Licence to
Thomas Sutton, his Heirs, Executors, Administrators, and Assigns, at all times
hereafter at their will and pleasure to place, erect, found and establish at or

The second
branch of
the Char-
ter.

[25 b]

The 3d
part of the
Charter.

The divi-
sion of the
Charter.

in the said house called the Charter-house, one Hospital house, and place of abiding for the finding, sustentation, and relief of poor, aged, maimed, needy, or impotent people, &c. Also to erect, found, &c. one Free-School for the instruction, teaching and maintenance of poor Children or Scholars, &c. And to place and maintain a learned School-master and Usher to teach and instruct the said Children in Grammar. And also one godly and learned preacher, to Preach and teach the Word of God to all the said persons, poor people, and children, members and officers at or in the said house." That in the first place

Answer to 2d objection Antea 23.

doth contain the end of Sutton's piety and charity: for *Sapiens incipit a fine, & quod primum est in intentione ultimum est in executione.*[17] And that was a grand motive to the King of his Royal authority to give him means, *sc.* by Creation of a capable body Politick by way of Incorporation, to have perpetual

[26 a]

succession, to perfect and perpetuate so pious and charitable a work | And that the Incorporation ought to precede the execution of this Licence, is evident by the words and coherence of the Letters Patents, *sc.* For this Licence is *in futuro, sc.* To Thomas Sutton, his Heirs, Executors, Administrators and Assigns, "at all times hereafter at their will and pleasure, &c." so that it is future as well in persons, Heirs, Executors, &c. as in the thing to be done. But when he cometh to the clause of incorporation, he doth it *per verba de praesenti tempore:*[18] "And the said persons and their Successors by the name, &c. We do by these presents for ever hereafter really and fully Incorporate, &c." By which it followeth, that the Incorporation being present, and the execution of this part of the Licence future, the Incorporation ought of necessity precede the execution of the Licence. Then forasmuch as the principal foundation of the scruple was conceived upon these words, "to found, erect, and establish" the true Etymology and genuine sense of them was considered; and *ex vi termini fundare, nihil aliud est quam fundamentum jacere seu ponere, &c.*[19] to lay the foundation of a building; and in this sense the Holy Ghost (which moved Sutton to this work of Piety) in the Scripture taketh it. And therefore in the 3 King. Chap. 6. verse 37. *Fundata est domus anno primo, et Anno* 11 *perfecta fuit domus in omnia opere suo.*[20] And 3 King Chap. 16. Verse

17. [*Ed.:* The wise man begins with the end, and what is first in intention is last in execution.]

18. [*Ed.:* by words of the present tense.]

19. [*Ed.:* by force of the word, to found is nothing other than to lay or place a foundation, etc.]

20. [*Ed.:* 1 Kings, ch. 6, v. 37: In the first [fourth] year was the foundation of the house laid, and in the eleventh year was all the work on the house finished.]

34. *Edificavit in diebus illis Hiel de Bethel Jerico in Abiram primitivo suo fundavit, & in Segub novissimo suo posuit portas.*[21] By which it appeareth that to found, is to lay the foundation of a building, which is the first mechanical part of Architecture. Then when the foundation is laid, then cometh the erection of the House, as it is said by the son of Sirach 49. 15. *Erexit nobis muros, & erexit domus nostras.*[22] And although that the foundation be well laid, and thereupon a building well erected, yet it ought to be well joyned and established, and therefore this word *(establish)* is added to make the building to have continuance. 2 Kings 13. *Stabiliam thronum ejus;*[23] That is, I will make his throne to have perdurance and continuance. So that to Found, Erect, and establish, are *opera laboris, & laboris architector',*[24] and that appeareth by the words of the Charter itself, "The King affecting so good a work," *tam bonum opus:*[25] Also the subsequent words prove it also; "to found, erect, and establish," what? "an Hospital-house." So that it clearly appeareth, that the effect of this Licence is to make fit and to finish and furnish an Hospital-house for the habitation of the poor, &c. See after, Mich. 34 and 35 Eliz. the Case of the Hospital of Bridewell for the exposition of these words, *fundo, erigo, & stabilio,*[26] which is a stronger case than this is. And this word *(place)* in the first place is to be intended, as hath been said, in the last place, *scil.* To place poor in it, | to erect a Free-School for the instruction of youth, and for the maintenance of a Preacher. But how shall this holy and charitable intention (that the same may remain for ever) be produced to an end and effect? The Charter itself shewth it in effect in this manner: It is impossible to take in succession for ever without a capacity; and a capacity to take in succession cannot be without incorporation; and the incorporation cannot be created without the King; for this cause the Charter saith, "And for the maintenance and continuance of the said Hospital, &c. And that the same may take the better effect, That the said persons, &c. be one body Corporate and Politick, to have perpetual succession to endure for ever: We do by these presents for ever [26 b]

21. [*Ed.:* 1 Kings, ch. 16, v. 34: In those days Hiel of Bethel laid the foundation of Jericho in Abiram his firstborn, and in Segub his youngest son he set up the gates.]
22. [*Ed.:* He put up walls for us, and erected our houses (quoting Ecclesiasticus, chap. 49, v. 17.)]
23. [*Ed.:* I will establish his throne.]
24. [*Ed.:* works of labour, and of the labour of builders.]
25. [*Ed.:* so good a work.]
26. [*Ed.:* I found, erect, and establish.]

hereafter fully and really incorporate, &c. to have capacity and ability to take, &c." Without this capacity the end cannot take effect for inhabitants of a Town, or other single persons (who have not capacity to take in succession but only to their singular heirs) have capacity to take an incorporation, and after their incorporation they have capacity to take in succession any lands, tenements, or hereditaments; *unde sequitur,*[27] that the incorporation which giveth capacity ought to precede the giving of any lands, &c. Another licence is given to this new incorporation to take in Mortmain. This Licence is not of necessity, either of the essence of the incorporation, or of the continuance of it; but yet it is requisite for the establishing and maintenance of the end, *scil.* to have the poor sustained, and scholars instructed, &c. For they cannot be maintained without a Revenue, and they cannot take or keep the Revenue (as has been said) without a Licence in Mortmain; and therefore these two, *scil.* Incorporation and Licence in Mortmain ought to precede the donation. For words to Found, Erect, and establish an Hospital-house, cannot be extended to the Incorporation, for that belongeth only to the King, and that the King doth; Nor to any dotation, for as yet (as hath been said) there is not any capacity. *Ergo*[28] it extendeth onely to the building and finishing of the said house to be a fit habitation for poor, &c. Sutton thinking and rethinking, that as well the incorporation as the Licence in Mortmain were in their several degrees requisite to bring his good and charitable purpose to effect, to the end the King should grant that which was onely in his power to grant, and which he himself without the King could not do; he was a suitor to the King to grant him Licence to do that which of himself in respect of the ownership of land he might do without the King, *scil.* To build, finish, and furnish the said house for the habitation of | poor, as well before the Incorporation as after: But to give it possession, &c. as hath been said he could not, and therefore this Licence was but explanatory to declare what Sutton as owner of the Land might do, either with the King's Licence or without the King; and therefore, the King cannot countermand this Licence, because it is but declaratory of that which Sutton might do as owner of the Land without any Licence. And this appeareth by the book in 3 H. 7. Fitz. Grant. 36. the Record whereof I have seen, Between John Buckland, term. Vintner plaintiff, in an action of

[27 a]

27. [*Ed.:* whence it follows,]
28. [*Ed.:* therefore.]

Trespass, and Richard Fowcher, Chaplain Defendant, Sanct. Mich. 2. Hen. 7. Rot. 155., in the King's Bench, and in the Report at large, Termain senth 2 Hen. 7. 13a, 13b. where the case in effect is, That King Henry the fourth by his Letters Patents, Anno 6 *regni sui*,[29] Reciting that Robert Ramsey was seised in Fee of an house in the parish of St. Margaret in London, called the Sun, &c. notwithstanding the Statute of Mortmain, of his especial grace, and for 20 l. gave Licence to Robert Ramsey, that he might give 20 marks rent, going out of the said house, *cuid' capellano divina celebranti ad altare beatae Mar' in eccles. S. Magni London' singul' diebus pro salubri statu preaed' Rob' & Johan' uxor' suae, &c. Habend' & tenend' eid' capellano & successorib' suis capellan' Cantariae praed' divina in eccles. praed' ad altare praed' pro salubri statu, &c. juxta ordinationem praed' Rob. in hac parte faciend' celebrat' imperpet', &c.*[30] And afterwards the said Robert Ramsey by his deed indented 10 Junii 1407, Founded, Ordained, and erected the said Chauntry, and ordained and named one John Meadowe to be the first Chaplain to do the said Divine services; And further by the said deed granted to the said John Meadowe, the first Chaplain, 10 marks of yearly Rent issuing out of the said house, To have to him and his Successors Chaplains of the said Chauntry at four usual Feasts in London to be paid, with clause of distress, to him and his successors; And further appointed by the same deed, That he himself should present to the said Chauntry during his life; and after his decease, that Johanna his wife should present to the same during her life, and after her decease, that the Parson and Church-wardens of the said Church of St. Magnus, and their Successors; and afterwards the said John Meadowe died, and after divers vacations the said Richard Fowcher was presented to the said Chauntry, and for the said Rent behind he entered into the said house the door being open, and took a Cup of the Plaintiff's for a distress, &c. for which taking the action was brought, upon which matters the parties have demurred in Law: And this case was adjourned into the Exchequer Chamber, and there before all the

---

29. [*Ed.:* in the sixth year of his reign,]

30. [*Ed.:* to a certain chaplain celebrating divine service at the altar of the Blessed Mary in the church of St. Magnus, London, every day, for the wholesome estate of the aforesaid Robert and Joan his wife, etc., to have and to hold for ever unto the same chaplain and his successors, being chaplains of the aforesaid chantry and celebrating divine service in the aforesaid church at the aforesaid altar for the wholesome estate, etc., in accordance with the ordinance to be made by the aforesaid Robert in that behalf, etc.]

Judges of England divers Objections were made against this Licence and Grant. 1. That they were *cuidam capellano*,[31] and named none in certain; and when the King's Grant is uncertain it is void; as if the King | licenses one to give 20 marks Rent, *cuid' Abbati*,[32] the Grant is void, because it is incertain. 2. There is not such Chaplain till Robert Ramsey hath named and ordained one, so that it appeareth that the Grant should be to such a one who is not *in rer' natura;*[33] as if the King give Licence to grant to the Mayor and Commonalty of Islington, although the Inhabitants of Islington be afterwards incorporated by the name of Mayor and Commonalty, the Grant is void because there was no such Corporation at the time of the Grant. 3. It was objected that in this case the King hath not made any Incorporation, and Incorporation is a thing to be done only by the King himself; and these words *juxta ordination' per Rob' Ramsey fiendam*,[34] shall not enable the said Ramsey to make an Incorporation, for the King cannot give Licence to any to make an Incorporation, but the said words shall give him power to make ordinances, first touching Masses and other Divine Services. 2. of what manner of habit he shall be, 3. to have perpetual succession, *scil.* elective, presentative, or donative, and that is the effect of the said words, and not to make a Corporation; and the King's Grant shall not be taken by implication; *scil.* by the words to make an Incorporation, and also to give Licence to grant the said Rent, for then the King's Grant shall enure to two intents. 4. Admitting that there shall be an Incorporation by implication; yet the Incorporation ought to be before the Licence, and here the Licence is before the Incorporation, and therefore it is void. 5. The Grant ought to have been that the King gave Licence *facere & erigere Cantar', &c.*[35] and there were not any such words in the Charter; but only Licence to grant a Rent, *&c. cuid' capellano, &c.* 6. The Licence is *secundum ordination' per R. Ramsey fiendam;*[36] and therefore, the King is deceived, because he cannot have knowledge what ordinance it shall be. 7. It was objected that the distress was without warrant and void, because the Licence did extend to grant a Rent onely without mention of any distress. Which objections I

---

31. [*Ed.:* to a certain chaplain,]
32. [*Ed.:* to a certain abbot,]
33. [*Ed.:* in being;]
34. [*Ed.:* in accordance with the ordinance to be made by the aforesaid Robert Ramsey,]
35. [*Ed.:* to make and erect a chantry, etc.]
36. [*Ed.:* in accordance with ordinance to be made by the aforesaid Robert Ramsey;]

have here gathered out of the book Reported at length, 2 Hen. 7. 13a, 13b. and the Reports of Fitz. in 3 Hen. 7. Grant 36, and out of the Record itself.

As to the first and second Objections, it was Resolved, That the Grant was good, for all the Grants of Chauntrys are of such form, *scil. cuid. Capellano,* and although there be not such Chaplain at the time it is not to the purpose; For if the King granteth to the Commonalty of Islington that they shall be Incorporated of a Mayor & Bayliffs, and that they have power to choose one, it is good although the Election of the Mayor is future. So Note Reader, a difference betwixt an estate or interest which none can take without present capacity, and a power, liberty or Franchise, or thing newly created, which may take effect *in futuro.*[37] As to the 3 it was Resolved, That whereas the King by his Charter saith *cuidam Capellano,* it was a sufficient Incorporation; and when he saith in the *Habendum sibi | & successorib'suis,*[38] the same maketh a sufficient succession. And so Note Reader, that this Grant of the King doth enure to three intents, *scil.* to make an Incorporation, to make a succession, and to grant a Rent. As to the 4. it was Resolved, That where the Licence to Found the Chauntry shall be first, and to grant after, that is needeth not, for it is not material which is before, (for the Law shall construe that first to the effect which ought), but here they are *simul & semel.*[39] As to the 5, That in the Licence there were not words of *fundare, erigere, facere;*[40] It was Resolved, That notwithstanding the Grant was good. *Nota,*[41] reader from this, That to the essence of a Chauntry, or other body politic, two things are onely requisite, *scil.* an Incorporation and a gift, and not any words of *fundare, erigere & stabilire,*[42] or words to such effect; for no such words were contained in the grant of Henry the fourth and yet it was adjudged a good Chauntry lawfully incorporated and founded. And if such words had been requisite and necessary in Law, the judgment ought to have been given against the Chauntry, because they were left out in the King's grant. And thereby it appeareth, that in the case at bar, they were explanatory and of abundance: which is a judgment in

[28 a]

37. [*Ed.:* in the future.]
38. [*Ed.:* to have unto him and his successors.]
39. [*Ed.:* at one and the same time.]
40. [*Ed.:* to found, erect, make;]
41. [*Ed.:* Note.]
42. [*Ed.:* to found, erect, and establish,]

the point, by the resolution of all the Judges in the Exchequer Chamber. As to the sixth point, it was resolved that these words, *secundum ordinationem per R. Ramsey fiendam*,[43] import sufficient certainty, *scil.* to make Ramsey to ordain, 1. what Masses and other divine services shall be celebrated, 2. of what habit or order the Chaplain shall be, and 3. whether he shall be elective, presentative, or donative. And by force of these words Ramsey in the case did ordain the same to be presentative by the Rector of the parish of St. Magnus for ever. As to the 7. objection, It appeareth by the Report of Fitzherbert *ubi supra*,[44] that the opinion of the two chief Justices, Hussey and Brian and Starkey, chief Baron, and Fairfax Justice, was, That the distress was without warrant, but Townshend conceived it to be good. But *inspecto recordo*,[45] it was adjudged that the distress was good and well warranted by the grant. For the Chauntry Priest did distrain in the said house for the Rent, and his distress was adjudged lawful, and the Plaintiff barred, And the reasons, as I conceive, were, because the King's Charters, made for the erection of pious and charitable works shall be always taken in the most favourable and beneficial sense; and the most beneficial rent that a man can grant is a rent charge. 2. The distress is a necessary incident to the Rent, for without that the Grantee shall be without remedy: *Verba sunt accipienda cum effectu*,[46] and words are to be taken

[28 b] with the effect. 2 Edw. 3. 3. Which case I have cited at large, because it is | notable and pertinent, and stronger (as I conceive) then the case in question. Secondly, power is given to Sutton "to place a Master of the said Hospital. 3. At all times hereafter to place, erect, found and establish in the said house, &c. one Free-school for instructing youth," (which well expoundeth the pre-

The 4 branch of the Charter the answer to the 3 objection Antea 23.b.   cedent words concerning the Hospital, for these words extend onely to make fit and to finish and furnish a Grammar-school within the said Charter-house) "and a learned Preacher to teach all in the word of God. 4. We do by these presents, ordain, constitute, limit and appoint, That the said House and other the premises shall from henceforth be ever hereafter named incorporated and called the Hospital of King James, founded in the Charter-house, within the County of Middlesex, at the humble petition and at the only costs and charges

43. [*Ed.:* in accordance with the ordinance to be made by Robert Ramsey,]
44. [*Ed.:* in the text above,]
45. [*Ed.:* the record being inspected,]
46. [*Ed.:* words are to be taken with the effect,]

of Thomas Sutton Esquire And the same Hospital and Free-school by the name of the Hospital of King James, &c. We do firmly by these presents erect, found, and establish and confirme, to have continuance for ever." By this clause, the King *in praesenti*[47] giveth the name of the Hospital, but as it appeareth before, Sutton hath devised it, and hath sued to the King to name it accordingly; and that the name of the incorporation itself. (*scil.* At the humble suit of Thomas Sutton,) doth import so that as it is said in 38 E.3.14.b. and 21 E.4.56a, 56b. The name of incorporation is as a proper name or name of baptism: In this case Sutton as God-father giveth the name, and by the same name the King doth baptize the incorporation, By which it appeareth that the objection, That the King cannot give a name to an house which is the Inheritance of another, is not of any value, here Sutton has consented and assented to it, and all the same is done at his humble suit. And this objection doth tend to the dissolution of all ancient Deans and Chapters: For at first, as appeareth in the third part of my Reports in the case of *the Dean and Chapter of Norwich,* All the possessions were to the Bishop, and yet by his assent the Dean and Chapter were incorporate and named of the Cathedral Church, which did then belong to the Bishop only; and afterwards a certain portion was assigned to the Chapter; So that the Chapter was before that they had any possessions; And that is the reason that of common right, the Bishop is Patron of the Prebends that because their possessions were derived from the Bishop, and therefore he was Patron and Founder: And therewith agree 17 E. 3. 40ab., 25 Ass. pl. 8., 10 E. 3. 10., 50 E. 3. 26b., 15 Hen. 7. 11. So that at first the Dean and Chapter were by the assent of the | Bishop incorporated [29 a] and named of the Church Cathedral of the Bishop. And it was said, that questions moved in the Exchequer used to be like spirits which may be raised with much ease, but suppressed and vanquished with much difficulty; but these questions were like ruinous buildings, more easily thrown down then raised and set up. And all the arguments which have been made against this honourable work of charity, are hatched out of meer conceit and invention, without any ground of Law, and such which have any colour were utterly mistaken. And as to the fourth Exception, That the place of every corporation ought to be certain; and Sutton sueth and the King licenceth Sutton to found, erect, &c. an Hospital "at or in the Charter-house," which was incertain; To

Answer to the 4 objection Antea 23.b.

---

47. [*Ed.:* in the present.]

that the Charter expressly answereth That the King by this clause doth ordain, &c. "That the said House and other the premises, shall from henceforth for ever hereafter be, remain, &c. and shall ever hereafter be named and called the Hospital of King James, founded in the Charter house:" So that all the house and premises are baptized by the King by the name of the Hospital, &c. in which is no shadow of incertainty, and therefore Sutton as to the Licence for the mechanical part, which (as has been said) was abundant, to get and finish all or any part of the house for an Hospital, &c. yet all the house itself, Orchards and Gardens &c. are named by the name of the Hospital. And it was observed, That the King by this clause not onely nameth the said house to be an Hospital; but by the name of the Hospital to be erected, founded, established, and confirmed; so that the King nameth it, and leaves the mechanical part to Sutton to perform. And of the same importance is the other Objection, That a known name is not sufficient to found an Hospital, but it ought to be described by metes and bounds, as in divers precedents hath been used; for it appearth in *Willim de Londres' case,* 2 E. 3. 36b. Adam brought a *Scire facias*[48] against Willim de Londres of the manor of E. the Defendant pleaded that he himself is Master of the Hospital of St. Bartholomew and so beareth the name of dignity not named judgment of the writ: to which the Plaintiff replied That which the Defendant Calleth an Hospital is the Manor of East Smithfield, and was a Manor at the time of the fine levied: And it was holden by the Court, That by this Writ he ought to have the Manor, as the Manor was at the time of the fine levied; And whereas the manor was made an Hospital after the fine, by this suit he is to defeat your estate and your name, and accordingly it was ruled that the Writ was good. Which proveth that a manor (which imports more certainty and variety than an house known by a certain name) may be created into an Hospital. And in 15 Ass. pl. 8. *John de Derbie's case,* A Manor made *Corpus praebend'.*[49] The fifth Clause stands upon two Branches: "1. for the better | maintenance and continuance of the said Hospital, &c. and that the same may take the better effect, and that the Revenues may be the better governed and imployed there shall be sixteen Governours, and names fifteen of them by express name, and such person as from time to time shall be Master, to be the first and present governors. 2.

The 5 clause of the Charter.

[29 b]

48. [*Ed.:* Writ to enforce a judgment or other matter of record.]
49. [*Ed.:* A prebendal corporation; usually a charitably or ecclesiastically endowed corporation.]

And the said persons and their successors, by the name of Governours of the Lands, &c. one body incorporate and politick, by that name to have perpetual succession for ever to endure, We do by these presents for ever hereafter really and fully incorporate," and the words of this clause are *verba operativa.*[50] And it is to know, That every Corporation or Incorporation, or body Politick and Incorporate, who are all one, either stand upon one sole person, as the King, Bishop, Parson, &c. or aggregate of many, as Mayor and Commonalty, Dean and Chapter, &c. and these are in the Civil Law are called *Universitas sive Collegium.*[51] Now it is to see what things are of the essence of a Corporation. 1. Lawful authority of Incorporation; and that may be by four means, *scil.* by the Common Law, as the King himself, &c. by authority of Parliament; by the King's Charter (as in this case) and by prescription. The 2. which is of the essence of the Incorporation, are persons to be incorporated, and that in two manners, persons natural, or bodies incorporate and political. 3. A name by which they are Incorporated; as in this case Governors of the Lands. &c. 4. Of a place, for without a place no Incorporation can be made; and here the place is the Charter-house in the County of Middlesex. *Vide* 3 Hen. 6 Det. 20. 17 Edw. 3. 59b. & 45 Edw. 3. 27. 5. By words sufficient in Law, but not restrained to any certain, legal and prescript form of words. And for as much as good pleading is *lapis Lydius,*[52] the touch-stone of the true sense and knowledge of the Common law; the form of pleading of an Incorporation by prescription is to be observed, for in such case he ought to prescribe in every thing which is of the essence of the Incorporation. In the Book of Entries, Quare Impedit 1. the pleading is, *Quoddam Hospitale Sanctae Mariae de Bristow de uno magistro, & conventu a toto tempore, &c. incorporat' fuerunt per nomen Magistri & Conventus Hospitalis Sanct' Mariae de Bristow:*[53] and there it appeareth that: there they purchased Lands and Tenements, and were impleaded without any prescription for the one or the other, because they are incorporated by prescription by a certain name; then to implead and be impleaded, to grant and purchase, are incidents to a body incorporate. M. 15 Hen. 7. Rot. 522. in the Common Pleas there the prescription is *Custos & vicarii collegii vicariorum*

Verba operativa. The division of corporations.

What things are the essence of a corporation

---

50. [*Ed.:* operative words.]

51. [*Ed.:* a university or college (i.e. corporation).]

52. [*Ed.:* a touchstone,]

53. [*Ed.:* a certain hospital of St. Mary of Bristol for a master and convent for all time, etc. were incorporated by the name of the Master and Convent of the Hospital of St. Mary of Bristol.]

[30 a]   *in choro* | *Hereford sunt & a toto tempore, &c. fuerunt incorporat' per nomen Custodis et Vicar' Collegii Vicariorum in Choro Hereford':*[54] and there also they purchased and were impleaded as incidents to the incorporation. Lib' Intrat' tit' Ass. fol. 68. *Magister, fratres, et sorores fraternitatis sive guildae novem ordinum sanctorum Angelorum juxta Brainford*[55] brought an assise: the tenant pleads, *quod in villa de Brainford est quaedam fraternitas incorporata infra tempus memoriae de magistro, fratribus et sororibus novem ordinum Angelorum juxta Brainford Bridge, absque hoc quod habetur aliqua talis fraternitas:* which is reported in 22 Edw. 4. 34a. where the tenant at first pleaded, No such incorporation, and if it be not found, and naught because two bars, and then he pleaded the said plea, *quod est quaedam fraternitas incorporata, &c.*[56] and yet there they were infeoffed by Bocking upon condition, and capable thereof as incident to a corporation. And therewith agreeth *the Bishop of Exeter's case* in the book of Entries, 455. 2 Hen. 7. 17b. the Corporation of Godmanchester 34 Hen. 6 27a, 27b. in the case of the *Hospital of Wycombe. v.* 26 Hen. 8 1. In 9 E. 4. 20a. The Master of the Hospital of Burton S. Lazar prescribed, *quod ipse et omnes praedecessores sui magistri hospitalis praedict' a toto tempore, &c. nominati et cogniti fuerunt, &c. tam per nomen Magistri hospitalis Sancti Lazari de Burton, de ordine Sancti Lazari de Jerusalem in Angliâ, quam per nomen Magistri de Burton Sancti Lazari de Jerusalem in Angliâ:*[57] By which it appeareth that this word *incorporo,* or any derivation thereof is not in Law requisite to create an incorporation, but other equivalent words are sufficient, as *nominati & cogniti:*[58] and therewith agreeth 44 Ass. p. 9. in *The Prior of Plimpton's case,* and 4 Edw. 4. 7b. in the case of the Abbot of Glastenbury,

54. [*Ed.:* The warden and vicars of the college of vicars in the choir of Hereford are, and since time immemorial were, incorporated by the name of the Warden and Vicars of the College of Vicars in the Choir of Hereford:]

55. [*Ed.:* The master, brethren and sisters of the fraternity or guild of the nine orders of holy angels next Brainford. . . .]

56. [*Ed.:* that in the vill of Brainford there is a certain fraternity, incorporated within time of memory, of a master, brethren and sisters of the nine orders of angels next Brainford Bridge, without this that there is any such fraternity: (as the plaintiffs allege). . . . that there is a certain fraternity incorporated, etc.]

57. [*Ed.:* that he and all his predecessors being masters of the aforesaid hospital from time immemorial etc. were named and known etc. both by the name of master of the hospital of St Lazarus of Burton of the order of St Lazarus of Jerusalem in England and also by the name of master of Burton St Lazars of Jerusalem in England:]

58. [*Ed.:* named and known:]

and in none of these Books or Records was any mention made of these words, *fundo, erigo, &c.*[59] or any other like words; for as it hath been said, they are onely declaratory words, and the effect of them may be done by the owner of the land without any grant. And it was well observed, that in old time the Inhabitants or Burgesses of a Town or Borough were incorporated when the King granted to them to have *Gildam Mercatoriam*[60] in the Register 219 b. where the Writ doth recite, *quod cum inter caeteras libertates civibus civitatis Winton' per cartas progenitorum nostrorum quondam Regûm Angliae quas per cartam nostram confirmavimus, concessum sit eisdem, quod nullus eorum qui fuerunt infra gildam mercatoriam placitet extra murum, &c.*[61] where *guilda* signifies *contubernium seu fraternitas incorporata;*[62] And upon that the place of their meetings and assemblies was called the Guild-hall. And I have seen | the [30 b] Charter made by King H. 1. *Textoribus Lond',*[63] by which he granteth to them that they shall have *Gildam Mercatoriam,*[64] and a confirmation of it made by King H. 2. by which Charters they were incorporated. And where the opinion of *Fineux* in 13 H. 8. 3. b. and of *Prisot* in 39 H. 6. 13. b. was cited at the barre, that a corporation aggregate of many cannot be a body only without a Head; the same was utterly denied: For at first most part of the Corporations were a body without any head by force of these words *Gilda Mercatoria*. And that a Corporation aggregate of many may be without a head, see 18 Edw. 2. Annuity 48. 5 Edw. 3. 11. b. 22 Ass. 67. 29 Ass. 17. 2 Hen. 6. 9. 18 Hen. 6. 16ab. 19 Hen. 6. 80. 21 Edw. 4. 55b. 56ab. 7 Edw. 4. 14ab. 2 Maria Dyer 100. And it appeareth by Record that Paulinus the first Archbishop of York, after he had baptised the inhabitants of Nottingham-shire in the River of Trent, founded a Collegiate Church in Southwell of Prebendaries, consecrated to the Virgin Mary, which continueth a body without a head even to this day. See for this word *Guild* or Fraternity in the book of Entries, 68. 37 Edw. 3. cap. 5. 15 R. 2. c. 5. the Statute of 1 Edw. 6. of Chantries. In which three things were observed,

---

59. [*Ed.:* I found, erect, etc.]

60. [*Ed.:* a guild merchant.]

61. [*Ed.:* whereas among other liberties [granted] to the citizens of the city of Winchester by the charters of our forebears, formerly kings of England, which by our charter we have confirmed, it is granted to them that none of them who were in the guild merchant should plead outside the walls, etc.]

62. [*Ed.:* an incorporated company or fraternity.]

63. [*Ed.:* to the dyers of London.]

64. [*Ed.:* a guild merchant.]

Part Ten of the *Reports*

1. how *prudens antiquitas*[65] did always comprehend much matter in a narrow room: 2. that to the creation of an Incorporation the Law had not restrained itself to any prescript and incompatible words: 3. that when a Corporation is duly created, all other incidents are *tacite*[66] annexed to it. And for direct Authority in this point in 22 E. 4. Grants 30. it is holden by Brian chief Justice and Choke, That a Corporation is sufficient without words, to implead or be impleaded, &c. and therefore divers clauses subsequent in the Charters are not of necessity but onely declaratory, and might well have been left out; as 1. by the same to have authority, ability, and capacity to purchase &c. but no clause is added that they may alien, &c. and it needeth not, for it is incident: 2. To sue and be sued, implead and be impleaded, 3. To have a Seal, &c. that is also declaratory, for when they are incorporated they may make or use what seal they will: 4. To restrain them to alien or demise but in certain form; that is an Ordinance testifying the Kings desire, but it is but a precept which doth not bind in Law: 5. The survivors shall be the Corporation, that is a good clause to oust all doubts and questions which might arise, the number being certain: 6. If the Revenues encrease, the same shall be employed to encrease the number of poor, &c. that is but explanatory as appeareth by the *Case of Thetford School* in the 8 part of my Reports, f. 131 ab.: 7. To be visited by the Governors, &c. the same is also explanatory; | For in this case the poore which shall be resident in the house of the Charter-house shall not be incorporated, but certain persons in whom the possessions are vested, who shall not be resident there but onely to have the general, government and ordering of the poor therein; so that this Case is out of the Statutes of 2 Hen. 5 c.l. and 14 Eliz. cap 5. for if no visitor had been appointed by the Charter, the Governors should visit; and the books in 8 E. 3. 28. & 8 Ass. 29. do not gainsay it, where is holden, That if the Hospital be Lay, the Patron shall visit, and if Spiritual, the Bishop shall visit, so that every Hospital is visitable; it is true, but in the Case at the barre the poor of the Hospital are not incorporated, and so no legal hospital. 8. To make Ordinances; the same is requisite for the well ordering and governmenting of the poor, &c. but not to the essence of the incorporation. 9. The exemption from the Ordinary is but declaratory, for being a Lay-incorporation he neither can nor ought to visit. 10. The licence

[31 a]

65. [*Ed.:* prudent antiquity.]
66. [*Ed.:* tacitly.]

to purchase in Mortmain is necessary for the maintenance and support of the poor; for without Revenues they cannot live, and without a licence in Mortmain they cannot lawfully purchase Revenues, and yet it is not of the essence of the Corporation, for the Corporation is perfect without the same; so that by that what hath been said, it appeareth what things *in genere*[67] are requisite to a complete body incorporate, and which are *verba operativa*[68] in this case (which are necessary to be known in every case) the resolution of which it appeareth how necessary it is, that the Law and Experience joyn in hands together.

As to the fifth Objection, That no incorporation was presently made as the Letters Patents import, nor can be till the Master was named, and therefore the Charter is repugnant and void. To that it was answered, That this Objection doth extend to the overthrowing of a great number of Incorporations; for when a Corporation is created by Letters Patents, by the same Patent power is given to them to a choose, master Aldermen, or Bailiffs, or Governours, or the like, and yet they are presently incorporated by the same Letters Patents; and therewith expresly agreeth Plo. Com. 592. in the *Cook's case*, 21 E. 4. 59. & 3 H. 7. Grant. 36. vouched at large before to the first and second Objections. *Vide* 32 E. 3. Aid. 39. 13 E. 4. 8. 16 E. 3. Grant 65. And it is true it is presently by the Letters Patents a Corporation *in abstracto*,[69] but not *in Concreto*,[70] till the naming of the Master. And a Case adjudged in the King's Bench, Mich. 34 & 35 El. rott. 172. *coram reg.*[71] was strongly urged: the governours of the possessions, revenues, and goods *Hospitalis Ed. regis Angliae Sexti*[72] brought a bill of debt against Elias Germaine. The Defendant pleaded, That King Edward the sixth | reciting the care of the city of London for the relief of poor people and infants, *concessit Majori, Civib' et Communitati Lond' Domum mansionalem rocat' Bridewell, &c.*[73] and there the King declareth his intent, that Bridewell shall be founded, erected, &c. an Hospital for the said poor, &c. *idem Rex ut intentio sua melior' capiat effectum*,[74] and to the end the Lands

Answer to the 5th Objection Antea 23b.

[31 b]

67. [*Ed.:* in kind.]
68. [*Fd.:* operative words.]
69. [*Ed.:* in the abstract,]
70. [*Ed.:* in the concrete,]
71. [*Ed.:* before the king (i.e. in the King's Bench).]
72. [*Ed.:* of the hospital of King Edward VI of England.]
73. [*Ed.:* granted to the mayor, citizens and commonalty of London the mansion house called Bridewell, etc.].
74. [*Ed.:* the same king, so that his intention might take better effect.]

which shall be granted to them shall be better governed, *per easd' literas patentes voluit et ordinavit quod Hosp' praed' cum sic fundat' erect' et stabilit' fuer' Hospital' E. 6. Reg' Angl. Christi Bridewell, et S. Tho. Apost' nominetur et appelletur imperpetuum, et quod major' communitas et cives civitat' praed' forent Gubernatores, &c. et quod iidem Gubern' de caetero essent et forent un' corpus corporat' per nomen Gubernat' possess' reventionum et bona' hospital E. Reg' Angl' Christi Bridew. et St. Th'Apost', &c.*[75] and further pleaded, *quod nullum hospital' quale in eisd' lit' pat' mentionat' post confect' praed' literarum pat' sic fundat', erect' et stabilit' fuit, &c.*[76] Upon which the Plaintiff did demurre in law; and upon argument at the barre and bench it was adjudged for the plaintiff. For the said Ordinance, that the said House shall be an Hospital *cum sic fundat' &c. fuer'*[77] is intended onely, of the mechanical part of an actual Hospital, *scil.* of the fitting and finishing of the Hospital, house with poor, &c. And this Hospital in intention onely is sufficient to support the name of a Corporation, and the words *de praesenti, scil. quod iid' gubernat' de caetero essent et forent un' corpus corporat' per nomen, &c.*[78] in law doth incorporate them presently, and shall not stay till there be an actual Hospital, or till the house be fitted or furnished, which is the mechanical part of the Hospital *scil.* for the habitation of the poor; which is the first thing to be observed by the said judgment, *vide* 32 E. 3. Aid. 39. King Edward the third newly founded a Priory and granted to the Monks that they might chuse a Prior, and before that the Prior was chosen W. made a lease to one A. for life, the remainder to the Prior and Convent; and in a *Scire facias,* against A. he pleaded, that W. was seised in Fee and leased to A. the remainder to the Prior and Convent who were newly founded by the King; and because there was not yet a Prior, the right was in

75. [*Ed.:* by the same letters patent willed and ordained that when the aforesaid hospital was so founded, erected and established, it should be named and called for ever King Edward VI of England's Hospital of Christ of Bridewell and St. Thomas the Apostle, and that the mayor, commonalty and citizens of the aforesaid city should be governors, etc., and that the same governors should henceforth be a body corporate by the name of the Governors of the Possessions, Revenues and Goods of King Edward VI of England's Hospital of Christ, Bridewell, and of St. Thomas the Apostle, etc.]

76. [*Ed.:* (and further pleaded) that no such hospital as is mentioned in the same letters patent was so founded, erected and established after the making of the aforesaid letters patent, etc.]

77. [*Ed.:* when it was so founded, etc.]

78. [*Ed.:* of the present (tense), namely, that the same governors henceforth be a body corporate by the name etc.]

the King until, and prayed aid of the King and the aid by award was granted, and a Writ of *Procedend*[79] came, and then A. the Defendant shewed, That after the aid granted there was a Prior made and ordained in whom the right remained, and prayed in aid of the Prior; he was ousted of the aid because he had aid before, which proveth that the remainder in such case is good. The second thing to be observed in the said Judgment in the said case of *The Hospital of Bridewell*, is, that one corporation may be made out of another corporation, sc. the major Citizens, and Commonalty of London, are created in their politick capacity Governours, &c. of the Hospital of Bridewell, 9 E. 3. 18. b. many corporations may be created one out of another, as the Dean and Chapter of Lincoln are a joynt corporation, the Dean by himself is in- corporated, and every of the Prebends is incorporate by himself, and in a case which is so manifest this shall suffice.

Note.

| And as to the sixth Objection, That till an Hospital, be founded that no incorporation can be, for then there shall be idle and mathematical governours. It was answered, That there was an Hospital *in potestate*,[80] and an hospital *in exec*;[81] also an Hospital, *in potentia*[82] and an Hospital, *actu*,[83] An Hospital, *re*,[84] and an Hospital, *nomine*.[85] And as to the creation of an incorporation, an Hospital *potestate, potentia, seu nomine*[86] sufficeth; as one may by Letters Patents be Governour of an Army before there be an army. *Vide* 17 H. 6. Protection 56: And the same agreeth with Philosophy and reason. Aristotle lib. 3. *De generatione* saith, *quod caro gignit carnem;*[87] and that is true *in potestate* but not *actu;* and so any fowl so soon as it is hatcht is *volatilis a volando, quia habet potest' volandi quanquam act' volandi non habet:*[88] So a child as soon as he is born is said *rationalis*,[89] because he hath *potestatem*, although he hath

[32 a]

Answer to the 6th Objection Antea 23b.

---

79. [*Ed.:* Writ requiring an inferior court to render an unspecified judgement.]
80. [*Ed.:* in authority,]
81. [*Ed.:* in execution.]
82. [*Ed.:* in possibility.]
83. [*Ed.:* by impulse,]
84. [*Ed.:* in reality,]
85. [*Ed.:* in name.]
86. [*Ed.:* in authority, in possibility, or in name.]
87. [*Ed.:* that flesh begets flesh;]
88. [*Ed.: volatilis* (fowl), from the word *volando* (flying), because it has the potential ability to fly even though it has not yet the act of flight:]
89. [*Ed.:* rational,]

not, and perhaps never shall have *rationem actu.*[90] And it is also proved by
old Records, and our books also, as in the Book of Enteries. Tit. Annuit 32.
33. *Rex H. 5. quandam domum in quodam loco sive solo apud Shene* (and ab-
butteth and boundeth the soil) *quam vocari et nuncupari voluit Domum Jesu
de Bethlem de Shene, duxit ordinand' et fundand' et domum illam quant' in ipso
fuit fundavit et erexit* (which was but a nominative house, for none was then
built) *et idcirco locum et sol' praed' de Shene ut primar' fundationem dedit, &c.*[91]
by which it appeareth that a void place or soil in which an house is intended
to be built, may by the King's Charter be named a House, and this nominative
house shall be sufficient (as there it was,) to support the name of the incorporation. Also it appeareth by Matthew Paris 64, and *Polydore Virg' Chronic'
Chronicor', &c.*[92] The Hospital of St. Johns of *Jerusalem in England* was incorporated in 14 Hen. 1. of the Templers, by the name of *Magister milit' Templi
et confratres sui in Anglia in an*'[93] 24 *H.* 1. and yet neither the fabrick of the
Temple, nor the house of the hospital, was founded and builded, *sed regnante*[94]
H. 2. of the one *Jordan Biset homo pius et bene nummatus* a holy marshall
monied;[95] and of the other Heraclius Patriarch of Jerusalem were Founders.
Vide Camden's *Britannia* 311, which proveth that a void place to support the
name of a corporation may by the King's Charter be named an Hospital or
Temple, and it is not requisite, that there be always truth in the name of the
Corporation either of an Hospital or of any other body politick. King Henry
the eighth, in the second year of his reign according to the Will of King Henry
the seventh granted to divers Bishops, Thomas Earl, of Arundel, &c. John
Fineux, and Robert Read, Chief Justices, John Young, Master of the Rolls,
&c. who were Executors of King Henry the seventh *quandam peciam terrae
vocat' le Savoy*[96] in the parishes of Saint Clements, and St. Mary le Strand *ad
intentionem quod iidem quoddam hospital', in et super praed' peciam terrae*

---

90. [*Ed.:* reason by impulse.]

91. [*Ed.:* King Henry V caused to be ordained and founded a certain house in a certain place or piece
of soil at Shene which he wished to be called God's House of Bethlehem of Shene, and founded and erected
that house as far as he could . . . and for that purpose gave the place and soil of Shene aforesaid as the first
foundation, etc.]

92. [*Ed.:* Chronicle of Chronicles.]

93. [*Ed.:* Master of the Knights of the Temple and his Brethren in England, in the year.]

94. [*Ed.:* but in the reign of.]

95. [*Ed.:* Jordan Biset, a pious and well moneyed man.]

96. [*Ed.:* a certain piece of land called the Savoy.]

vocat' Savoy erigere, fundare et estabilire possint,[97] 4 H. 8. The King licenseth them *quodd' Hospit' de uno magistro et 5 capellanis super praedict' peciam terr' vocat' le Savoy fundare, & Hospitale cum sic fundation' fuerit,*[98] shall be incorporated by the name *Magister & Capallanorum | Hospital' H. nuper regis Angliae*				[32 b] *7. de Savoy,*[99] and yet in truth it was not an Hospital, in the time of Henry the seventh but in intention onely, and yet the King in his Charter doth call it the Hospital of King Henry the seventh. And the same was admitted to be a good name of incorporation by all those who argued the case betwixt *Mariat et Pascall* upon the incorporation of the said Hospital, Trin. 30 Eliz. in the Exchequer, where the Case was adjudged; or in the Exchequer chamber, where it depended by Writ of Error. And therefore in 44 E. 3. 16. b. Regist. 23. there the Corporation was *Prior Hosp' S. Johan' Jerusal. in Anglia:*[100] and so 9 E. 4. 6. *Hospitale S. Lazari de Jerusal' in Angliâ,* which sufficeth for, the name of the Corporation; although it be but a fiction, *scil.* that either S. John (which was S. John the Evangelist) or Jerusalem was situate in England. So *Magistri milit' Templi Jerusal' in Anglia;*[101] and in the Register, *Prior et frat' Sancti Mariae de monte Carmeli in Anglia*[102] So I have seen a Record, That *Catharine* the first wife of King Henry the eighth had a licence to found a Chauntry by the name of the Chauntry *de monte Calvarie extra Algate London.*[103] And it is great reason that an Hospital in expectancy or intendment, or nomination, shall be sufficient to support the name of an Incorporation, when the Corporation itself is onely *in abstracto,*[104] and resteth only in intendment and consideration of the Law; for a Corporation aggregate of many is invisible, immortal, & resteth only in intendment and consideration of the Law; and therefore in 39 H. 6. 13b. 14 a. Dean and Chapter cannot have predecessor nor successor. 21 E. 4. 27. & 30 E. 3. 15. 6. They may not commit treason, nor be outlawed, nor excommunicate, for they have no souls, neither can they

---

97. [*Ed.:* to the intent that they might erect, found and establish a certain hospital in and upon the aforesaid piece of land called the Savoy,]

98. [*Ed.:* to found a certain hospital of one master and five chaplains upon the aforesaid piece of land called the Savoy, and when the hospital was so founded,]

99. [*Ed.:* the Master and Chaplains of the Hospital of the late King Henry VII of England of Savoy.]

100. [*Ed.:* prior of the Hospital of St. John of Jerusalem in England:]

101. [*Ed.:* Master of the Knights of the Temple of Jerusalem in England.]

102. [*Ed.:* Prior and brethren of St. Mary of Mount Carmel in England.]

103. [*Ed.:* of Mount Calvary without Aldgate, London.]

104. [*Ed.:* in the abstract,]

appear in person, but by Attorney 33 H. 8. Br. Fealty. A Corporation aggregate of many cannot do fealty, for an invisible body cannot be in person, nor can swear, Plow. Com. 213, and *The Lord Berkley's Case* 245, it is not subject to imbecilities, or death of the natural, body, and divers other cases. A thing which is not *in esse* but in apparant expectancy is regarded in Law, as a Bishop who is elect before he be consecrated, an infant in his mother's belly before his birth, &c. 5 E. 2. Bre. 80. 8 E. 2. voucher 237. 38 E. 3. 30. 41 E. 3. 5. 11 E. 3. Quare Impedit 158. So for the name of a Corporation it is sufficient to name a place in England by the name of Jerusalem, mount Calvary, mount Carmel, Bethlehem, &c. *a fortiori,*[105] the name of a spacious and goodly house well and actually buildeth by the name of an Hospital is sufficient; for the same importeth truth and certainty. By which it appeareth, that in the case at barre there was a lawful incorporation of the Governours, &c. created and instituted by the King's Charter, and by consequence as well any person in England, as Sutton, might give and grant to them before any foundation laid, or to be laid by Sutton (as it was imagined he ought to have done before they were capable, &c.) but the same is clearly answered and confuted before; and in truth *haec recitasse, est confutasse.*[106]

[33 a]

Answer to the 7th objection Antea. 23b.

| As to the seventh Objection, it is to know that there are two manner of Foundations, one *fundatio incipiens,*[107] the other *fundatio perficiens,*[108] and therefore *quatenus ad capacitatem, et habilitatem,*[109] the incorporation is metaphorically called the foundation, for that is the beginning, as a foundation *quasi fundamentum capacitatis,*[110] preceding the whole. And therefore in 21 H. 6. 4a. a Writ was brought against John Arden, Abbot of S. John Baptist of Colchester; the Defendant pleaded, that before time of memory foundation was made of the same place *per nomen Abbat. eccl' monast' de S. Joh' de Colchester, &c.*[111] where Foundation is taken for Incorporation, 38 E. 3. 14. 38 E. 3. 28a. 20 H. 6. 27a. & 18 H. 6. 16a. in *The Dean and Canons of Windsor's Case,* and divers other books agree with the same, *Sed quatenus ad dotati-*

---

105. [*Ed.:* so much the more so, or it follows that,]
106. [*Ed.:* to recite this is to confute it.]
107. [*Ed.:* beginning foundation,]
108. [*Ed.:* perfecting foundation,]
109. [*Ed.:* as to the capacity and ability,]
110. [*Ed.:* as it were a foundation of capacity.]
111. [*Ed.:* by the name of the abbot of the monastery of St John of Colchester, etc.]

onem,[112] the first giving of the Revenues is called the Foundation, and who giveth the same is the Founder in law, for *proprie, fundatio est quasi fundi datio*,[113] and the first gift is *fundamentum dotationis seu collationis, et appellatione fundi aedificium et ager continentur;*[114] and that is proved by the Statute of West. 2. c. 41. *Si Abbates, Priores, Custodes Hospital' et aliarum domorum religiosarum fundatarum ab ipso Rege vel a progenitoribus suis alienaver' vel de caetero tenem' domibus ipsis ab ipso vel a progenitoribus suis collata, &c.*[115] In which was observed, that in respect of tenements collated or given by the King, the house was said to be founded by the King, but more fully in the clause following in the said Act, *Si autem domus illa a comite, barone, vel ab aliis fundata fuerit, habeat ille a quo, &c. tenement' sic alienat' collat' fuer' br' e ad recuperand', &c.*[116] where the collation or gift of the Tenements is called the Foundation. And where the Founder bringeth the said Writ *de contra formam collationis*,[117] the Writ of *Praec' quod reddat mesuag' quod eid' domui collat' fuer'*,[118] *vide* 9 H. 7. 26. F. N. B. 211. Old N. B. 142. 38 Ass. p. 22. He who giveth the first lands is the Founder, *quia fundare* in that sense is nothing else but *fundum dare*,[119] and therewith agreeth 14 E. 3. Corrodie 5. In a Writ of Prohibition, where a common person is Founder of an Hospital, the writ as appeareth in the Regis 41a. saith, *Hospitale Sancti Egidii leprosorum de Burton per antecessor' R. filii I. ad sustentation' leprosorum et aliorum pauper' et infirmor' ibid' totum in temporal' et nihil in spiritual' fundat' existit*,[120] and the like Writ where the King is Founder, *cum hospitale nostr' sanctor' Innocentium juxta Lincoln' de fundatione progenitor' nostror' Regûm Angliae, &c. de terris et possessionibus pro sustentatione pauper' et infirmor' in eod' hospital' de-*

---

112. [*Ed.*: but with respect to the endowment,]

113. [*Ed.*: properly, a foundation is as it were the giving of a *fundus*, (piece of ground).]

114. [*Ed.*: the foundation of the endowment or collation, and by the name of *fundus* is contained the building and the field;]

115. [*Ed.*: If abbots, priors, keepers of hospitals and of other religious houses founded by the king himself or his forebears should henceforth alienate the tenements collated to them by himself or his forebears, etc.]

116. [*Ed.*: but if the house was founded by an earl, baron, or other persons, the person by whom, etc. the tenement so alienated was collated shall have a writ to recover it, etc.]

117. [*Ed.*: A writ to recover a gift given to a monastery for charitable purposes and used otherwise.]

118. [*Ed.*: command (the defendant) that he render (to the demandant) the messuage which was collated to the same house.]

119. [*Ed.*: because to found [in that sense giveth nothing else but] a *fundus* (piece of ground).]

120. [*Ed.*: The hospital of St Giles of Burton Lazars was founded by the ancestors of R., son of J., for the support of lepers and other poor and sick people there, as wholly temporal and in no way spiritual.]

gentium dotatum existat:[121] In which it was observed, that where the first Writ saith *fundat'* this Writ calleth it *dotat*,[122] 39 E. 3. 17. The Abbot of Lyra brought a *Scire facias* against the Dean of Woborn, where the Dean said he held of the Patronage (that is of the King's Foundation) and prayed aid of him, and had aid; and there came a Writ of *Procedendo*, and it was challenged because

[33 b]   the Writ said of the Patronage | and not of the Collation, and it was taken all one, 33 E. 3. Aid. 103. *The Dean of Stafford's case,* the Deanry is said to be of the Foundation, and a little after the King's collation 8 Edw. 3. 56. in *Sirach's Case,* by the foundation the land is amortised, *Vide* 4 Edw. 3. Ass. 177. 21 Edw. 3. 60a. 24 Edw. 3. 33. 34a. 44 Edw. 3. 23. 44 Edw. 3. 11.b. 2 Edw. 3. 28. *The Earl of Richmond's case,* 6 Hen. 4, 5. 7 Edw. 4. 12. And therefore it was resolved, That if the King had incorporated the poor of the said Hospitall, Sutton need not have made any instrument comprehending any Foundation or erection, &c. But his gift of the land being the first act had made him Founder, and the very first donation is all the Foundation which is requisite in Law; and to the erection of an Hospital, &c. there is not in law any thing requisite, but incorporation and donation. And in the Report at large I have omitted all the Arguments at length on both sides upon one common ground, where an act to one intent shall enure to divers intents distinct in time; some holding, That the bargain and sale doth amount not only to a Dotation, but also to a Foundation, and others *totis viribus e contra;*[123] for it appeareth to you now without any question, That the first Dotation is the Foundation. And yet in that also a difference is necessary to be well understood; *scil.* when the King expresses the words, designeth the place, appointeth the number, and giveth them a name by his Charter; so that the same is a complete Corporation; there the Founder or Donor hath nothing to do but to make the Dotation without any instrument comprehending these words, *fundo, erigo, stabilio, &c.*[124] or other the like words. For the common person who is the Founder in such case hath nothing to do in the power of incorporation; but when the King by his Charter doth reserve as well the nomination of the persons, as the name of the incorporation to the common person who shall be the Founder, there he ought

---

121. [*Ed.:* whereas our hospital of the Holy Innocents next Lincoln, of the foundation of our forebears, being kings of England, etc., was endowed for the support of the poor and sick staying in the same hospital.]

122. [*Ed.:* founded . . . endowed]

123. [*Ed.:* with all their might to the contrary.]

124. [*Ed.:* I found, erect, establish, etc.]

to name the parties, and to declare by what name they shall be incorporated, and there many times, although it be superfluous, he useth these words, *fundo, erigo, &c.*[125] or the like. And when the common person hath done it and declared it in writing according to his authority, then they are incorporated by the King's Letters Patents, and not by the common person, for he is but an instrument, and the King maketh the Incorporation in such case in the same manner as if all had been comprehended in the Letters Patents themselves: as it is true, that none but the King alone can create or make a Corporation, as it is holden in 49 Edw. 3. 4. 4a. 49 Ass. 8. but, *qui per alium facit, per se ipsum facere videtur.*[126] See for this difference 38 Edw. 3. 14b. 22 Edw. 4. Grant 30. 2 Hen. 7. 13a, 13b. | Grant 36. 20 Hen. 7. 7. And as to the eighth Objection against the nomination of the Master, it was resolved that it was good; For Sutton hath a liberty at his will and pleasure to nominate him; and when he is named, he is Master by force of the Letters Patents, and is now as if he had been named in the Letters Patents themselves at the begining: and the other part of the Objection is answered before.

[34 a]
Answer to
the 8th
Objection.
Ante 24a.

And as to the objections against the bargain and sale, it was first resolved without question, That money given by the Governours or any of them as a private person, is a good consideration to grant the land to them in their politick capacity. But the Indenture importeth that they paid it as Governours and by such name they are acquitted by the Indenture. Also there is twelve pence Rent reserved to Sutton and his heirs, which is a good consideration. 2. Although in the *Habendum*[127] a trust is declared, the same without question cannot make the bargain and sale void, but the conveyance being by bargain and sale, it was wisely done to declare the confidence and trust. And as to the third, the same is clearly answered and resolved as before.

Answer to
the 9th
Objection.
Antea 24a.

And as to the last Objection, *scil.* That in pleading, those Governours cannot plead, that they were seised *in jure hospitalis,*[128] because there was not any Hospital incorporate, nor *in esse,*[129] at the time of the incorporation. To that it was answered, That the pleading shall be that they were seised in their

Answer to
the 10th
Objection,
Antea 24a.

---

125. [*Ed.:* I found, erect, etc.]

126. [*Ed.:* who does something through another is deemed to do it himself.]

127. [*Ed.:* Literally "to have," the clause in the Letters Patent assigning a right to hold the powers for some purpose.]

128. [*Ed.:* in right of the hospital,]

129. [*Ed.:* in being,]

demesne as of Fee *in jure incorporationis suae*,[130] and so it was pleaded in *the Cooks case of London* in Plow. Com. *Vide Fulmerstone's case* also, in Plow. Com. 102. *vide* 7 Edw. 3. the *case of custos altaris*,[131] he counted that he was seised, &c. *in jure altaris*.[132] And as to the precedents which were shewed, it was answered, That there are many clauses inserted in Charters as well of the King as others, *ex consuetudine Clericorum*,[133] which are not *de necessitate legis*,[134] but some declaratory and explanatory, and some prolix and nugatory, but *lex multa proficientia, et preficientia paucis comprehendit*.[135] And all the Judges which argued this case (except the two before-said) did conclude against the Plaintiff, and those two also *mutatâ opinione*[136] did assent to the judgment: so that by the assent of all the said Judges *nullo contradicente*[137] judgment was given against the plaintiff: And the Lord Ellesmere, Lord Chancellour of England, heard all the arguments at the barre and bench did agree in opinion with the Judges: So that this great work of Charity hath tasted of such charity [34 b] which ought to be in Judges, which is declared in the statute I of West. 1. cap. ult. *Summa charitas est facere Justitiam omnibus personis omni tempore quando necesse fuerit*.[138] And there is a good rule for these Governours, and all other Corporations which is expressed in the Statute de Templariis anno 17 Edw. 2. in these words, *Ita semper quod pia et celeberrima voluntas donatorum in omnibus teneatur et expleatur et perpetuo sanctissime perseveret*.[139] And Sir Thomas Fleming, Knight, after the first day this case was argued fell sick, of which Sickness he afterwards died, so as he never argued this case. The said Sir Thomas Fleming was first a Sarjeant at Law, and afterwards Solicitour General to Queen Elizabeth, and to the King that now is for the space of twelve years, and then was preferred to be chief Baron of the Exchequer after the death of Sir William Periam, and then was advanced to be chief Justice of England after the death of Sir John Popham; all which places he discharged

---

130. [*Ed.*: in right of their corporation,]

131. [*Ed.*: keeper of the altar,]

132. [*Ed.*: in right of the altar.]

133. [*Ed.*: by the custom of clerks,]

134. [*Ed.*: legally necessary,]

135. [*Ed.*: the law comprehends many profitable and authoritative things in few words.]

136. [*Ed.*: changing their opinion.]

137. [*Ed.*: no one disagreeing.]

138. [*Ed.*: It is the utmost charity to do justice to all persons at all times when it is needed.]

139. [*Ed.*: provided always that the pious and most esteemed wish of the donors should in every respect be kept and carried out and preserved as sacred for ever.]

with great judgment, integrity and discretion, and he deserved the good opinion of all that knew him, because he was of a sociable and a peaceable nature and disposition.

Which Case I have reported at length for three causes. 1. For the Confirmation of Incorporations founded for works of Piety & Charity in time past. 2. For the better instruction how they may be after so and established that no exception may be taken to them. 3. For the resolving of certain opinions and questions which were moved at the barre, and which might have disturbed the peace of the Law. In the argument of this case many other authorities were cited, *sc.* 2 Edw. 3. 47. 3 Edw. 3. 83. 5 Edw. 3. 144. 7 Edw. 3. 57. 8 Edw. 3. 67. 8 Edw. 3. 208. 18 Edw. 3. 1. 20 Edw. 3. Nonabilite 9. 20 Edw. 3. Corone 225. 21 Edw. 3. 35. 32 Edw. 3. Aid 55. 40 Edw. 3. 28. 44 Ass. 2. 13 R. 2. Breve 643. 11 Hen. 4. 12. 19. 14 Hen. 4. 8. 3 Hen. 6. 28. 7 Hen. 6. 13. 9 Hen. 6. 13, 14. 16. 20 Hen. 6. 7. 21 Hen. 6. 2. 12 Edw. 4. 17. 15 Edw. 4. 1. 21 Edw. 4. 32. 55. 57. Lib. Ent. 112. 6 Hen. 7. 14. 10 Hen. 7. 16. 11 Hen. 7. 9. 11 Hen. 7. 27. 13 Hen. 8. 13. 14 Hen. 8. 29. 32 Hen. 8. br. Corp. 78. 1 Mar. Dye. 98. 7 El. Dy, 81. the case of *The College of Grainstock,* 10 El. Dyer the case of *The College of* Landebrevis, Pl. Com. *Grendon's case* 494. Hil. 16 El. rot. 495. *Sir Fr. Fleming's case* in the Com. Pl.

The names of the governors nominated by Sutton and expressed in the said charter, were, The most Reverend Father in God, George, Archbishop of Canterbury, Thomas Lord Ellesmere, Lord Chancellor of England, Robert Earl of Salisbury, John Bishop of London, Lancelot Bishop of Ely, Sir Edward Coke then Chief Justice of the Common Pleas and now Chief Justice of England, Sir Thomas | Foster, one of the Justices of the Court of Common Pleas, Sir Henry Hobart then the King's Attorney-General, and now Chief Justice of the Court of Common Pleas, John Overal, Dean of the Church of St. Paul in London, George Mountain, Dean of Westminster, Henry Thursby one of the Masters of the Chancery, Jeffery Nightingale, Richard Sutton, John Law, Thomas Brown, and the Master of the said hospital for the time being; and after the death of the said Sir Thomas Foster, one of the Justices of the Court of Common Pleas, (who was a grave and Reverend Judge of great judgment, constancy and integrity) Sir James Altham, Knight, one of the Barons of the Exchequer, was according to the said Charter *unanimi consensu*[140] in his place. And the said Master of the Hospital, which Sutton had nominated *durante*

The Reason of reporting this case at large.

[35 a]

---

140. [*Ed.:* with unanimous consent.]

bene placito,[141] our soveraign Lord the King that now after the death of Sutton, did by his Letters Patents, nominate Master for his life.

The Case of the Isle of Ely.
(1609) Michaelmas Term, 7 James I
Before the Justices of the Court of Common Pleas.
First Published in the *Reports,* volume 10, page 141a.

Ed.: The Commissioners of Sewers decreed that a new, seven-mile-long river should be cut through the fens, and ordered that the new river be paid for by a tax they levied on fifteen towns. The Privy Council referred the case to Coke and the Common Pleas for a determination of whether the Commission had the powers necessary to do this. Coke applied the Parliamentary acts creating the commission and giving it authority and resolved that it only had the power to repair damage to existing watercourses and not to make new ones. Further, it only had the power to assess individuals according to the benefit the individuals reaped from the protection of the sewers.

A Case was referred by the Lords of the Councel to Coke, Chief Justice, Daniel and Foster, Justices of the Court of Common Pleas, concerning a Decree made by the Commissioners of Sewers, for the making of a new River within the Isle of Ely; and in effect the case was such. The Commissioners of Sewers had decreed, That a new River should be cut out of the old River of Owse, and through the main land within the same Isle, for seven miles unto another part of the same River: And for the doing thereof, they had severally taxed as well Fen, Drayton, Samsey, Over-Wivelingham, Rampton, Cottenham, and nine other Towns within the County of Cambridge, out of the Isle, as the Inhabitants of the said Isle, and the tax was general, *sc.* so much of one Town, and so much of another, and *sic de singulis.*[1]

And in this Case two Questions were moved: 1. If the Commissioners of Sewers might by force of their Commission make a new River, or not.

2. If such general taxation upon the Towns was lawful, or not.

---

141. [*Ed.:* during good pleasure,]
1. [*Ed.:* and likewise concerning each.]

As to the first, it is to see what might have been done by the Common Law before any Statute made thereof. And it is to known, That by the Common Law, before the Statute of 6 Hen. 6. cap. 5. the King of Right ought to save and defend his Realm, as well against the Sea, as against the Enemies, that the same be not drowned or wasted: And also to provide, that his Subjects have their passage through the Realm by Bridges and Highways in safety. And therefore if the Sea-walls be broken, | or the Sewers or Gutters are not scoured, [141 b] that the fresh waters cannot have their direct course, the King ought to grant a Commission to enquire and to hear and determine these defaults. Which Commission appeareth in the Register, amongst the Commissions of Oyer and Terminer; in which it is said, *Nos eo quod ratione dignitatis nostrae Regiae ad providend' salvationi Reg' nostri circumquaque sumus stricti, &c.*[2] And with that agreeth the Statute of 6 Hen. 6. cap. 5. and the Statute of 23 Hen. 8. Cap. 5.

And see a notable Precedent Pasch. 44 Edw. 3. Midd. 2. *cor' Rege, praecept' est vicecom' quod distringat A. B. & alios quod ipsi defectus walliarum erga terras suas reparant, et si ipsi sufficientes non fuerunt, quod distrin' omnes tenentes terrar', &c. qui defension', commod', salvamen, vel damnum ratione reparat' seu non reparation' walliae praed' habent seu aliquo modo habere poterint, ita quod quilibet tenentium praed' juxta quantitatem tenurae suae ibid' contributionem praefat' A. B. et aliis ad wallias illas faciend' & reparandas faciant indilate:*[3] Which Record was before any Act of Parliament that limited any form of Commission.

The second thing observable in the said Commission at the Common Law, is this clause, *Ad hujusmodi wallias, fossata, gutterus, sueras, pontes, calceta, et gurgites in locis necessariis reparand' & quotiescunque et ubi necesse fuerit de novo facienda:*[4] By which it appeareth that by the Commission in the Register at the Common Law, that the ancient walls, gutters, or Sewers might be repaired

2. [*Ed.:* Inasmuch as by reason of our royal dignity we are strictly (bound) to provide for the safety of our realm, etc.]

3. [*Ed.:* the sheriff is commanded to distrain A. B. and others that they repair the defects in the seawalls next to their lands, and, if they are not sufficient, to distrain all the tenants of the lands etc. who have or in any way might have defence, benefit, safeguard or damage by reason of the repair or non-repair of the aforesaid walls, so that each of the aforesaid tenants should without delay make contribution to A. B. and the others, according to the quantity of his tenure there, towards making and repairing those walls.]

4. [*Ed.:* For repairing such walls, ditches, gutters, sewers, bridges, causeways and weirs in necessary places, and as often and wherever need arises to renew them.]

or new made; but no new walls, gutters, or Sewers, by force of the said Commission might be made. Then it is to see in what cases the Statutes have made provision in these cases. And it is to know, That the Statute of 6 Hen. 6. cap. 5 doth enlarge the said Commission which was at the Common Law: for where these words (*de novo facienda*)[5] refer onely to old Walls, Gutters, Sewers, &c. the said Act hath these words *& eadem et alia quotiescunque, et ubi necesse fuerit de novo facienda;*[6] which words (*et alia*)[7] being added to the former Commission, give to the Commissioners power to make new Walls, Gutters, Sewers, &c. but this Act did not endure but ten years; and by 18 Hen. 6. cap. 10 the like Commission was established for ten years; and by 23 Hen. 6. cap. 9. for fifteen years; and by 12 Edw. 4. cap. 6. for fifteen years; and by 4 Hen. 7. for twenty-five years; and by 6 Hen. 8. c. 10. for ten years, and until the next Parliament. And afterwards the Statute of 23 Hen. 8. cap. 5. was made, which reciteth none of the former Acts as the others do, but enacteth, That there shall then after a Commission of Sewers "according to the manner, tenor, form, and effect hereafter ensuing," and rehearseth the form of the Commission *de verbo in | verbum:*[8] which Commission omiteth the said words (*& alia*) and followweth the Commission in that point which was at the Common Law. The words of the Act of 23 Hen. 8. being, "And also to reform, repair, and amend the said Walls, Ditches, Banks, Gutters, Sewers, &c. and the same (omitting these words, *and other*) as often, and where need shall be, to make new." And the former clause concerning execution of the former Statute and Ordinances, is restrained with these words (touching the premises,) which refer onely to repair the old Walls or Sewers, or to make them new. And also a subsequent clause, That all and every Statute, &c. heretofore made concerning the premises, (which restraineth that clause *ut supra*[9]) not being contrary to this present Act, nor heretofore repealed, shall stand and be good and effectual for-ever. So that it was Resolved by the Justices, That by force of the said Commission founded upon the Act of 23 Hen. 8. the Commissioners could not make the said new River out of the main land for four causes.

[142 a]

---

5. [*Ed.:* to renew them.]
6. [*Ed.:* and as often and wherever need arises to renew them and make others new;]
7. [*Ed.:* and others.]
8. [*Ed.:* word for word:]
9. [*Ed.:* as above.]

1. That this Act doth prescribe the manner and form of the Commission in express words, which extends onely to the reparation and new making of old walls, gutters, &c.

2. That these words, *et alia,* which were included in the statue of 6 H. 6. and all the said Acts are left out of this commission.

3. All the former Acts were for a time, but this Act which establishes this Commission, is made perpetual by the statute of 3 Edw. 6. c. 8. and therefore it shall be hard to enlarge it beyond the words, and to give power to Commissioners to try inventions at the charges of the Country, which perhaps shall never take good effect, but *via trita est tutissima.*[10]

4. It appeareth by the Register in the writ of *Ad quod damnum,*[11] fo. 252. and F. N. B. 225E. That if an old Ditch or Trench coming from the Sea to a Town, by which Boats or Vessels use to pass to the said Town; now if it is stopped by the outrage of the Sea, and a man would sue to the King to have leave to make a new trench, and to stop the old trench, he ought first to sue *Ad quod damnum,* to know what damage it shall be to the King or others: By which, and by the Writ in the Register *de antiqua trenchea obstruenda et nova facienda seu habenda,*[12] it appeareth that no new trench or river which runneth to the Sea, can be made without the writ of *Ad quod damnum,* and thereupon to obtain the Kings licence to do it. For if any Commissioners might do it *ex officio,*[13] great inconvenience thereupon for private gain as well as for publick damages as stopping of Havens (which are the gates of the Kingdom), | and other common Rivers, as particular nuisance and prejudice to private men, by drowning of their lands and Inheritance, And therefore such new Rivers cannot be made without the Kings Licence, grounded upon a Writ of *Ad quod damnum. See Vide* the Writ of *Ad quod damnum* in such case, *quia optimum.*[14]   [142 b]

But it was resolved, That new Inventions, as of an artificial mill to cast out the water, or of a great River out of the main Land, and other the like, are

10. [*Ed.:* the beaten path is the safest.]

11. [*Ed.:* Royal writ directing the sheriff to ascertain the damage that would be done to a town, if a right to hold a fair is granted in the town.]

12. [*Ed.:* for obstructing an old trench and making or having a new one,]

13. [*Ed.:* by virtue of office,]

14. [*Ed.:* because it is the best.]

not warranted by the said Commission upon the said Act of 23 H. 8. *quia nihil semel inventum est et perfectum;*[15] So when an old Sewer is newly to be made or cleansed, some small alteration in respect of the natural change of the current, or otherwise for the publick good of such place (and so in the like cases) may be made. So when an old wall by the extreme rage of the water is broken, to preserve the lands within the same Level from inundation, another wall, in case of inevitable necessity for the publick good of that part, may be made to defend the people and their Lands within the same Level. For this manner of defence by walling is no new invention, but the old way and mean well approved of by experience, and upon the matter it is but a new making of the old wall in a place by inevitable necessity more fit than the other. But If by the timely reparation of the old wall, the extreme danger may be avoided, no other ought to be made; for *si assuetis mederi possis, nova non sunt tentanda:*[16] but when new inventions are proposed, as is aforesaid, if they are apparently profitable, no owner of the land there will deny to make contribution for his advantage; and then the same ought to be made by a voluntary consent, and not by constraint by force of the said Commission of Sewers upon the said Act of 23 H. 8. But sometimes when a publick good is pretended, a private benefit is intended. And if any such new invention is in truth (*quod raro aut nunquam fit*)[17] good for the Commonwealth, and yet no consent can be obtained for the making of it, then there is no remedy but to complain in Parliament, and there to provide relief, as Sir John Popham, late Chief Justice of England, did, who exhibited a bill in Parliament *anno* 3 Jac. for making a new River in the said Isle, which he himself upon his great charge begun, knowing that without an Act of Parliament, none could be forced by force of the Commission of Sewers, to contribute to such new attempt. But the Bill was utterly rejected.

Also, It was Resolved that none can be taxed towards the reparation, but those who have prejudice, damage, or disadvantage by the said nuisances or defaults, and who may have I benefit and profit by the reformation or removing of them. Also the Tax, Assessment, and charge ought to have these qualities. 1. It ought to be according to the quantity of their lands, tenements, and

[143 a]

---

15. [*Ed.:* nothing is perfect at the time when it is invented;]

16. [*Ed.:* if you can put right the familiar things, you should not try out something new;]

17. [*Ed.:* which is rarely or never done.]

rents, and by number of acres and perches. 2. According to the rate of every persons portion, tenure, or profit, or of the quantity of the Common of pasture, or of fishing, or other commodity. And therefore it was clearly Resolved by them, That the said tax generally of a several sum in gross upon a Town is not warranted by their Commission, but it ought to have been particular, according to the express words, upon every owner or possessor of lands, tenements, rents, &c. observing the qualities aforesaid.

And it is to be observed, That there are three manner of Statutes which concern Sewers: The first consisting *in defendendo et reparando wallias, seweras, &c.*[18] The 2. *in destruendo et amovendo nocumenta, &c.*[19] The 3. which concerneth both the points, *tam in destruendo quam in defendendo.*[20] Of the first sort are Magna Charta, c. 15 & 16. 6 Hen. 6. c. 5. 18 Hen. 6. c. 10. 23 Hen. 6. c. 9. 12 Edw. 4. c. 6. 4 Hen. 7. c. 8. 6 Hen. 8. c. 10. Of the second sort are Magna Charta, c. 23. 25 Edw. 3. c. 4. 45 Edw. 3. c. 4. 1 Hen. 4. c. 12. 9 Hen. 6. c. 9. 12 Edw. 4. c. 7. of the third sort of Statutes, which concern both the former sorts, are 23 Hen. 8. c. 5. 25 Hen. 8. c. 10. 3 Edw. 6. c. 8. and 13 Eliz. c. 9.

---

18. [*Ed.:* defending and repairing walls, sewers, etc.]
19. [*Ed.:* destroying and removing nuisances, etc.]
20. [*Ed.:* both in destroying and in defending.]

Part Eleven of the *Reports*

The Eleventh Part of Coke's *Reports* was published in 1615, and it was the last volume to be published during Coke's lifetime. It was originally published entitled *La unzime part des reports de Sr. Edw. Coke chivalier, chiefe justice Dengleteere des plees destre tenus devant le roy mesme assignee & del Counseil Prive d'Estate, des divers resolutions & judgments donez sur solemnes arguments & avec grand deliberation & conference des tres-reverend judges & sages de la ley, des cases en ley queux ne fueront unques resolve ou adjudges par devant, et les reisons & causes des dits resolutions & judgments. Publié en la unziesme an de treshaut et tresillustre Jaques roy Dengleterre, France, & Ireland, & de escosse le 49. Le fountaine de tout Justice & la vie de la Ley.* In English, *The Eleventh Part of the Reports of Sir Edward Coke, Knight, Lord Chief Justice of England, of the Pleas assigned to be held before the King Himself, and of the Privy Council of State, of divers Resolutions and Judgments given upon solemn Arguments, and with great deliberation and Conference of the reverend Judges and Sages of the Law, of Cases in law which were never Resolved or Adjudged Before, and the Reasons and Causes thereof. Published in the Eleventh year of the most high and Most Illustrious James, King of England, France, and Ireland, and of Scotland the 47., the Fountain of all Justice, and the life of the Law.* The topics essentially are unchanged from prior parts.

Epigrams from the Title Page:

Prov. cap. ii. vers. 3.
Simplicitas justorum diriget eos; & supplantatio perversorum vastabit eos.[1]

---

1. [*Ed.:* The integrity of the upright shall guide them, and the perverseness of wrongdoers shall destroy them [Proverbs, xi. 3].]

Prov. cap. 12. vers. 3.
Non roborabitur homo ex impietate; radix autem justorum non commovebitur.[2]

Compendaria res improbitas, virtus longa.
Compendia, sunt dispendia.[3]

(Preface)
Deo, Patriae, Tibi.[4]

Of writing of many Books, faith Solomon, *there is no end;* which is understood
of such as are written to no end: I mean therefore (Learned Reader) by way
of Preface to propose unto you in few words, the substance of the Cases in
this eleventh Work, whereby you will easily collect the end and scope of the
same.

I. In the first place I report the Case of the Lord *La Ware,* resolved in Parliament holden in the *39th.* year of the Reign of Queen *Elizabeth* wherein
appeareth what Disabilities are personal and temporary, and barreth not the
Heir to claim Honour and Dignity from that Ancestor so disabled, or from
any other Ancestor paramount him; and also what Disablities are in Law
absolute and perpetual.

II. In the second place followeth Auditor *Curles* Case, resolved in the *7th.*
year of the most happy Reign of King *James:* in this case is resolved, That
Judicial Offices cannot be granted in Reversion, but that generally such Grants
by the Common Law of *England* are utterly void, and therefore though this
Case be calculated for the Meridian of the Court of Wards, yet by computation
it may serve for all the Judicial Courts of *England:* a necessary Case I assure
you to be published, and the Law to be put in ure in these days: in which
case are also handled some other particular Points concerning the Office of
the said Auditorship in the Court of Wards.

III. Then cometh in Sir *John Heydon's* Case, adjudged in *Trinity-Term* 10
Regis Jacobi; wherein is perspicuously expressed, where Damages shall be sev-

---

2. [*Ed.:* A man shall not be established by wickedness; but the root of the righteous shall not be moved [Proverbs, xii. 3].]
3. [*Ed.:* Wickedness is short, virtue long. Profits are to be paid for.]
4. [*Ed.:* To God, to the Country, to you.]

erally assessed by the Jurors; and where the first Jury between the Plaintiff and one of the Defendants shall assess Damages for all the Defendants, and where not: whereby all the Books are well reconciled; for want of right Understanding whereof, many Judgments have been arrested, many that have been given, have been overthrown by Writ of Error, to the great charge, delay and vexation of the Party grieved.

IV. After this appeareth the Case of *Priddle* and *Napper* in *Michaelmas-Term* 10 *Jacobi Regis;* and therein is set down what Unity is sufficient within the Statute of 31 *Hen.* 8. to discharge the Land of Tithes, with divers other Points concerning the same.

V. Next after Doctor *Graunts* Case presenteth it self, adjudged *Michaelmas-Term* 11 *Jacobi Regis,* whereby you may see where Parsons and Vicars may have certain Tithes for Houses in Cities, Boroughs, *&c.*

VI. Then you shall read the Case of Sir *Henry Nevil,* adjudged *Michaelmas-Term* 11 *Jacobi Regis:* and understand that a Customary Mannor may be holden by Copy, and that such a Lord may hold Courts, and grant Copies.

VII. Now cast your Eye upon Doctor *Ayrayes* Case, adjudged *Michaelmas-Term* 11 *Regis Jacobi;* wherein you shall perceive what be material misnamings of Corporations, either to avoid their own Grants by mistaking their own Name, or Grants made to them: a Case that concerns the Good and Quiet, not only of Colledges and other Coporations, but of their Farmors, Lessees, and other that claim under them.

VIII. Then is offered to your view *Henry Harpurs* Case, resolved *Trinity-Term* 12 *Jacobi Regis;* wherein Men are directed how the Kings Tenant that holdeth by Knights Service *in Capite,* may dispose two parts of his Lands, *&c.* for the payment of his Debts, advancement of his Wife, preferment of his younger Children, or otherwise according to Law, and leave no trouble or question after his Death, between his Heir and the Devisees; the want of Knowledge whereof hath tended, if not to the undoing, yet to the great hinderance of many Families.

IX. Next to this have I reported *Henry Pigots* Case, adjudged *Trinity-Term* 12 *Jacobi Regis,* to instruct the Reader what alteration of any Deed after the ensealing and delivery, and by whom, avoideth the Deed.

X. By this time I presume you have expected and desired to see the Case of *Alexander Poulter,* that most wickedly and feloniously burnt the good Town of *Newmarket,* who upon consideration of many intricate, and ill penned Statutes, in the end was clearly (as you shall perceive) ousted of his Clergy;

wherein many notable and observable Points concerning Clergy, which by a mean concern the Life of Man, are resolved, *Mich.* 12 *Jacobi.*

XI. And lest there should be error in bringing of a Writ of Error, *Metcalfes* Case, *Michaelmas-Term* 12 *Jacobi* hath gotten the next place: wherein is plainly discussed, upon what Judgment or Award a Writ of Error doth lie, and upon what Judgment or Award it lieth not.

XII. And to avoid error in imposing of Fines upon Contempts in Leets, and other Courts of Record. In the Case of *Richard Godfrey* Esq; is clearly resolved, when the Fine ought to be several, and when joint, and when and how a Fine unlawfully imposed, may be avoided, and when the Lord may distrain for Court Leets, *Mich.* 12 *Jac.*

XIII. The next room *Richard Lifords* Case hath justly gotten, for therein is resolved, what interest the Lessee hath in Timber Trees, when they are not excepted, and what interest in that case the Lessor hath: what and what manner of interest the Lessor hath in Trees excepted, and whether in that case by a general Grant of the Reversion, they pass to the Grantee, and much necessary Learning concerning that Matter, *Mich.* 12 *Jac.*

XIV. Then have you the Case of the Tailleurs of *Ipswich,* a necessary Case for Poor Tradesmen, that many times are by Ordinances made by Incorporations, (whereby the Publick Good is pretended, and Private Respects intended) barred or hindred of the Freedom of their Trade, *Mich.* 12 *Jac.*

XV. *Edward Savels* Case taketh up a very little standing, and shortly sheweth that an *Ejectione firmae,* (that now is grown so common) lieth not for a place known, but of certain Acres of Land, Meadow or Pasture, &c. *Michael.* 12 *Jac.*

XVI. And *Benthams* Case in as few Words as the other, sheweth how in some case the omission of Matter material in a Verdict may be salved, *Mich.* 12 *Jac.*

XVII. I could not keep back Doctor *Fosters* Case, wherein, upon mature consideration had of all the Statutes of Recusants, a clear way is opened, for their just and speedy Conviction according to the Laws. A Case that concerneth the Glory of God, and the Honour of our Religion, *Mich.* 12 *Jac.*

XVIII. And justly doth the Case of *Magdalen-Colledge* in *Cambridge* challenge the next place, which tendeth to the maintenance of Gods true Religion, the advancement of Liberal Arts and Sciences, the supportation of the Ecclesiastical State, the preservation and prosperity of those two famous Sisters, the Universities of *Cambridge* and *Oxford,* and of all the Colledges within the

Realm, and the establishment of Hospitals, and provisions for the Poor, adjudged *Paschae* 13 *Jacobi Regis*.

XIX. And in course of time doth *Lewes Bowles* Case come, wherein is clearly resolved the true operation and sense of the Clause in Leases, without Impeachment of Waste; and what interest the Lessee hath in the Timber of an House prostrated by Tempest, adjudged *Pasch.* 13 *Jac. Regis*.

XX. And though it cometh not in sequence of time, yet the Case of Monopolies cannot come out of time, wherein divers things concerning Monopolies, are clearly resolved, and worthy to be published, *Trin.* 44 *Eliz.*

XXI. And I could not keep back the Earl of *Devonshires* Case, resolved *Hill. 4 Jacobi*, whereby the Prerogative of the King appeareth; That his right of Restitution dieth not by the death of the Party that doth him wrong: the end whereof is, that the Kings Toll may come to the right Mill.

XXII. And lastly, The Case of *J. Bagge*, adjudged *Trin.* 13 *Jac. Regis,* wherein is resolved, where a Writ of Restitution for a Freeman of an Incorporation, being disfranchised, doth lie: and incidently, who have power to disfranchise, and what be sufficient causes of disfranchisement.

This Eleventh Work (Learned Reader) I have published in the tempest of many other important and pressing Business; and therefore could not polish them as I desired.

If I might judge, I should say, that the Matter of these are not inferiour to any of the other. The end of this Edition is, That God may be glorified, his Majesty honoured, the Common Good encreased, the Learned confirmed, and the Student instructed.

The Lord de la Warre's Case.
(1596–1597) 39 Elizabeth I
In the Court of Parliament.
First Published in the *Reports*, volume 11, page 1a.

Ed.: Thomas de la Warre was an hereditary member of the House of Lords. His son, William de la Warre, was barred for his life from holding any hereditary offices or titles, although the Queen had him sit as a puisne member, roughly, as a junior member, in the Lords. William's son Thomas sought to be seated in the Lords. Coke represented de la Warre. In this case, the court construed the nature of a disability from office for life from a permanent disability. Finding William's disability had been personal and not a barrier to his son, and that Thomas could hold more than one title at a time, Thomas was seated as a full member in the Lords.

At the Parliament holden *39 Eliz.* the Case was such: Thomas la Warre, Knight, Lord la Warre, Son and Heir of William, Son and Heir of George, Brother and Heir of Thomas, Son and Heir of Thomas Lord la Warre, exhibited his Petition to the Queen to this effect, That whereas the said Thomas his Great Grand-father was called to Parliament by Writ of Summons, *An.* 3 H. 8. and afterwards the said Thomas the Besayel died; after whose death Thomas his son was called to divers Parliaments by Writs of Summons, and afterwards by Act of Parliament, An. 3 E. 6. for divers causes mentioned in the said Act, it was enacted, That the said William, during his life, should be disabled to claim or enjoy any dignity or Lordship in any Right, Estate, &c. by Discent, Remainder, or otherwise, and afterwards the said Thomas, son of Thomas, died; after whose death, the said William being so disabled, was not called to any Parliament by Writ of Summons, till Queen Elizabeth called him to Parliament by Writ of Summons, and sat as puisne Lord of the Parliament, and, afterwards he died. And now the said Thomas his son being called, this Parliament by Writ of Summons sued to the Queen, that he might have the place in Parliament of his Great Grand-father, viz. between the Lord Berkeley and the Lord Willoughby of Eresby: And the said Petition was endorsed in these words, *Her Majesty hath | commanded me to signify to your* [1 b] *Lordships, That upon the humble suit of the Lord la Warre, she is pleased that the matter shall be considered and determined in the House. Robert Cecil.* Which Petition being read in the Upper House of Parliament, the consideration thereof was committed to the Lord Burghley, Lord Treasurer, and divers other Committees; who at his Chamber in Whitehal, heard the Council Learned on both parties, in the presence of the two Chief Justices, and divers other Justices; and two Objections were made against the Claim of the said Lord la Warre.

1. Forasmuch as his Father was disabled by Act of Parliament to claim the Dignity, the Petitioner could not convey by him who was disabled, as Heir to his Great Grand-father, and by consequence he cannot have the place of his Great Grand-father, but his Fathers place. But it was resolved by the Justices, That there was a difference betwixt a Personal and Temporary disability and a disability absolute and perpetual: As where one is attainted of

Treason and Felony, the same is an absolute and perpetual disability by corruption of Blood, for any of his posterity to claim any Inheritance in Fee-simple, as Heir to him, or to any Ancestor above him: but when one is but disabled by Parliament (without any Attainder) to claim the Dignity for life, the same is a personal disability for his life onely, and his Heir after his death may claim as Heir to him, or to his Ancestors above him.

The second Objection was, That the said William had accepted of a new Creation of the Queen, which dignity newly gained did discend to the Petitioner, which he could not wave, and therefore the Petitioner could not have other place than his Father had. To which it was answered and resolved, That the Acceptance of a new Creation by the said William could not hurt the Petitioner, because the said William was at that time disabled, and in truth was not a Baron, but onely an Esquire; so that when the old and new Dignity discend together, the old shall be preferred. Which resolution was well approved by all the Lords Committees, which was accordingly reported to the Lords of the Parliament, and allowed by them all.

Whereupon it was ordered by the Lords, That the Queen should be acquainted with it by the Lord Keeper of the Great Seal, which was done accordingly, and the Queen confirmed the same also: All which was ordered and entered accordingly; Whereupon, at the same Parliament the Lord De la [2 a] Ware in his Parliament Robes was by the Lord Zouch (supplying | the place of the Lord Willoughby, then within age) and the Lord Berkley also in their robes, brought into the House, and placed in his said place, *viz.* next after the Lord Berkley, Garter King of Arms attending upon them, and doing his office; And I was of Council with the Lord De la Warre.

The Case of the Tailors of Habits &c. of Ipswich.

(1614) Michaelmas Term, 12 James I.
In the Court of King's Bench.
First Published in the *Reports,* volume 11, page 53a.

Ed.: The Corporation of the Tailors of Ipswich was a guild incorporated under a charter from the King, giving them authority to regulate their trade. The guild barred anyone from practicing as a tailor in Ipswich, unless they had been approved by its master and wardens. William Seninge moved to Ipswich and practiced as a tailor. The guild sued Seninge in debt, seeking

£3 13s 4d. The Court of Common Pleas declared that the common law will not allow a man to be prohibited from a lawful trade, the protections of the law are for those in the public trade and not family servants, but that the plaintiffs could recover nothing by their suit. For another case on restraint from the professions, see Dr. Bonham's Case, p. 264, and on the restraint of trade, see Case of the Monopolies, p. 394.

Trin. 11 Jac. Regis in the Kings Bench, *Magistri, Gardiani, et Communitas Scissorum et operatorum pannorum villae Gipwic' in com' Suff',*[1] brought an Action of Debt for three pound, thirteen shillings and four pence against William Shening, and declared, That whereas the King by his Letters Patents had incorporated the Plaintiffs by the said name, and granted to them, That they should have *plenam potestat' et authoritat' facere et constituere rationabiles leges, ordinationes et constitutiones, in script' quae eis viderentur bon', salubr', util', honest' et necessar' secundum eorum discretiones pro bono regimine et gubernatione, &c. societatis praed', &c.*[2] and to set Fines and Amercements for breach of the said Laws, &c. And recited the Statute of 19 Hen. 7. 7. By which it is enacted, That no Master, Wardens, and Society of Crafts and Mysteries, take upon them to make any Acts or Ordinances, nor to execute any Acts or Ordinances, *in exhaeredationem seu diminutionem praerogativae vel aliorum aliquorum, vel contra commune profic' populi, nisi iidem actus et ordinationes examinat' et approbat' furent per Cancellar', Thesaur' Angliae, Capital' Justic' utriusque Banci, vel tres eorum vel aliter coram Justic' Assisae in eorum itineribus, &c. sub poena forisfact' 40l. pro quolibet tempore quo ipsi in contr' facerent.*[3] And afterwards the said Corporation, in the fourth year, made divers Constitutions, and (amongst others) that no person exercising any of the said Trades within

---

1. [*Ed.:* The master, wardens and commonalty of tailors and clothworkers in the vill of Ipswich in the county of Suffolk,]

2. [*Ed.:* full power and authority to make and constitute reasonable laws, ordinances, and constitutions, in writing, which seem to them good, wholesome, useful, honest, and necessary, according to their discretions, for the good rule and governance, etc., of the aforesaid fellowship, etc.]

3. [*Ed.:* to the disinheritance or diminution of the prerogative or of any others, or against the common profit of the people, unless the same acts and ordinances have been examined and approved by the chancellor and treasurer of England, the chief justices of both benches, or three of them, or else before the justices of assize on circuit in those parts etc., on pain of forfeiting forty pounds for each time when they do the contrary.]

the Town of Ipswich *praed'*[4] should keep any Shop or Chamber, or exercise
the said Faculties, or any of them, | or take an Apprentice or Journeyman,
till they had presented them to the said Master and Wardens of the said Society,
for the time being, or any three of them, and should prove that he had served
seven years at the least, as an Apprentice, and before he shall be admitted by
them to be a sufficient Workman; and if any offend in any part thereof, That
he should forfeit and pay to the said Master and Wardens, and Society aforesaid, for every such offence five marks, and to levy the same by Distress, or
Action of Debt, &c. The which (amongst others) was allowed by the Justices
of Assise of the same County, according to the said Act of 19 H. 7. And that
the said William Shening, Tailor, using the trade of a Tailor, after the said
Orders made and ratified as aforesaid, the tenth of October in the tenth year
of the King came to the said Town of Ipswich, and there used the Trade of
a Tailor by the space of twenty days, before he had presented himself to the
said Master and Wardens, or any three of them, or had made proof that he
had served as an Apprentice for seven years in the said Trade, and before he
was admitted by the said Master and Wardens, or any three of them, to be
sufficient a Workman, *per quod actio accrevit eisd' Magistr' Gardian' et Com'*[5]
to have of the said Henry the sum of three pound, thirteen shillings and four
pence.

The Defendant pleaded that he was an Apprentice by the space of seven
years, *viz:* 1 from the first of September, in the first year of the King till the
second of September in the eight year to one Henry Backet in the art of a
Tailor, &c. And that ninth of *September, Anno* 10. Anthony Penny, Esquire
inhabitant in Ipswich, retained him to be his household servant to serve him
for one year; And that within the same time, he by the Commandment of
the said Anthony made divers Clothes and Garments for him, his wife, and
children, as was lawful for him to do, which is the same use and exercise of
the Trade of a Tailor, whereof the Plaintiffs have declared: Upon which the
Plaintiffs did demur in Law. And in this case, upon Argument at the Bar and
Bench, divers points were resolved.

1. That at the Common Law no man might be forbidden to work in any
lawful Trade, for the Law doth abhor idleness, the mother of all evil, *Otium*

[53 b]

---

4. [*Ed.:* aforesaid.]

5. [*Ed.:* whereby an action has accrued to the same master, wardens and commonalty.]

omnium vitiorum mater,[6] and chiefly in young men, who ought to their youth, (which is the time of their sowing) to learn lawful Sciences and Trades, which are profitable to the Commonwealth, and whereof they might gather the fruit in their old age, for idle in youth, poor in age; and therefore the Common Law doth abhor all Monopolies, which forbid any one to work in any lawful Trade; And the same appeareth in 2 Hen. 5. 5b. a Dyer was bound that he should not use the Dyer's craft for two years, and there Hull held, that the Obligation was against the Common Law, and (by God) if the Plaintiff were here, he should go to prison, till he pay a fine to the King: So, and for the same cause. If a Husbandman be bound that he shall not sow his land, the Obligation is against Law. And see 7 Edw. 3. 65b.; If he who taketh upon him to work be unskilful, his ignorance | is a sufficient punishment to him; for, [54 a] *imperitia est maxima mechanicorum poena, et quilibet quaerit in qualibet arte peritos:*[7] And if any one taketh upon him to work, and misdoeth it, an Action upon the Case lieth against him. And the Statute of 5 Eliz. 4., which forbiddeth any person to use or exercise any Craft, Mystery or Occupation, if he hath not been an Apprentice by the space of seven years, was not enacted onely to the intent that Workmen should be skilful, but also that youths should not be nourished in idleness, but trained and brought up in lawful Sciences and Trades: And therefore it appeareth, that without an Act of Parliament, none can be in any wise retained to work in any lawful trade. Also the Common Law doth not forbid any person to use many Arts or Mysteries at his pleasure, *Nemo prohibetur plures negotiationes sive artes exercere,*[8] until it was forbidden by Act of Parliament of 37 Edw. 3. cap. 6. *scil.* That the Artificers and people of Mystery tye every one to one Mystery, and that none use other Mystery but that which he hath chosen; but presently this restraint of Trade and Traffick was found prejudicial to the Commonwealth; and therefore at the next Parliament it was enacted, That all people should be as free as they were at any time before the said Ordinance.

2. That the said restraint of the Defendant, for more than the said Act of 5 Eliz. hath made, was against Law; And therefore for as much as the Statute

6. [*Ed.:* Idleness is the mother of all vices,]

7. [*Ed.:* lack of skill is the greatest punishment for a workman, for in each art everyone looks to those who are skilled:]

8. [*Ed.:* No one is prohibited from exercising several businesses or arts.]

hath not retained him who hath served as a Apprentice for seven years to exercise the Trade of a Tailor; the said Ordinance cannot forbid him to exercise his Trade, till he be presented before them, or till he be allowed by them to be a Workman; for these are against the Freedom and Liberty of the Subject, and are a means of Extortion in drawing moneys to them, either by delay, or some other subtle device, or of oppression of yong Tradesmen, by the old and rich of the same Trade, not suffering them freely to live in their Trade; And all this is against Law, and against the Commonwealth. But Ordinances for the well ordering and government of men of Trade and Mysteries are good, but not to restrain any one in his lawful Mystery.

3. It was resolved, That the said branch of the Act of 5 Eliz. is intended of publick use and exercise of a Trade to all who will come, and not of him who is a private Cook, Tailor, Brewer, Baker, &c. in the house of any for the use of a Family; And therefore if the said Ordinance had been good and agreeable to Law, such private exercise and use had not been within it, for every one may live in such private manner, although he hath never been an Apprentice in the Trade.

[54 b] | 4. It was resolved, That the Statute of 19 Hen. 7. 7. doth not strengthen any of the Ordinances made by any Corporation, with one so allowed and proved as the Statute speaketh, but leaves them to be affirmed as good, or disaffirmed as unlawful by the Law; the only benefit which the Incorporation getteth by such allowance is, That they shall not incur the penalty of forty pound mentioned in the Act, if they put in use any Ordinances which are against the Kings Prerogative, or the common profit of the people. And afterwards Judgment was given, *quod querentes nihil caperent per billam.*[9]

The Case of Monopolies.
(1602) Trinity Term, 44 Elizabeth I
In the Court of King's Bench.
First Published in the *Reports,* volume 11, page 84b.

Ed.: Early in Elizabeth I's reign, a Statute was passed forbidding the importation of playing cards. Later, a monopoly was granted to Ralph Bowes

9. [*Ed.:* that the plaintiffs should take nothing by their bill.]

to manufacture and sell playing cards, or to license others to sell them, in England, for twelve years. At the end of Bowes' monopoly, the queen gave it, and the right to stamp his cards as legal, to Edward Darcy then for twenty-one years, in return for an annual payment of 100 marks. T. Allein, a London haberdasher, sold 180 gross of playing cards, without paying Darcy for the privilege or for the use of his stamp. Darcy sued Allein. Darcy was represented by Dodderidge, Fuller, Fleming, and Coke, as Attorney General, which he was expected to do to defend the queen's privilege in granting monopolies (and in reaping their revenues). Crook, Altham and Tanfield, represented Allien. The King's Bench ruled that the grant was void, because monopolies are against the Common Law, which protects the freedom of trade and liberty of the subject, and against the statutes of Parliament.

This is an unusual report: Coke, at least formally, lost the Case, although his heart was probably not in it. Notice his contrast between the public and private good and the description toward the end of the report of the "odious monopoly" and his contrast of the stated and real purposes of it. For cases on restraint from the professions, see also Dr. Bonham's Case, p. 264, Case of the Tailors of Ipswich, p. 390.

Edward Darcy, Esquire, a Groom of the Chamber to Queen Elizabeth, brought an Action on the Case against Thomas Allein, Haberdasher of London, and declared, That Queen Eliz., *13 Junii, anno 30,* intending that her subjects being able men to exercise Husbandry, should apply themselves thereunto, and that they should not imploy themselves to the making of playing Cards, which had not been any antient manual Occupation within this Realm; and that the making of such a multitude of cards, Card playing was become very frequent, and chiefly amongst servants and apprentices and poor Artificers; and to the end her subjects might apply themselves to more faithful and necessary Trades, by her Letters Patents under the Great Seal of the same did grant unto Ralph Bowes, Esqire, full power, license and authority by himself, his servants, factors and deputies, to provide and buy in any parts beyond the Sea, all such playing Cards as he thought good, and to bring them within this Realm; and to sell and utter them within the same, and that he, his servants, factors and deputies should have and enjoy the whole Trade, Traffic and Merchandize of all playing Cards: And by the said Letters Patents further | granted [85 a] to the said Ralph Bowes, That the said Ralph Bowes his servants, factors, and deputies, and no other should have the making of playing Cards within the

Realm, to have and to hold for twelve years; and by the said Letters Patents the Queene charged and commanded, That no person or persons besides the said Ralph &c. should bring any Cards within the Realm during those twelve years; Nor should buy, sell, or offer to be sold within the said Realm, within the said term any playing Cards, nor should make, or cause to be made any playing Cards within the said Realm, upon pain of the Queens gracious displeasure, and of such fine and punishment as Offenders in the Case of voluntary contempt deserve. And afterwards the Queen, *11 Aug. anno 40 Eliz.* by her Letters Patents reciting the former grants made to Ralph Bowes, granted the Plaintiff, his Executors, Administrators, and their deputies, the same priviledges, authorities, and other the said premisses for one and twenty years after the end of the former time, rendring to the Queen hundred marks *per annum;* And further granted to him a Seal for to mark the Cards. And further declared, That after the end of the said term of twelve yeers, *scil. 30 Junii, an. 42 Eliz.* the Plaintiff caused to be made four hundred grosses of Cards for the necessary uses of the subjects, to be sold within this Realm, and had spent in the working of them 5000 l. and that the Defendant knowing the said grant and prohibition in the Plaintiff's Letters Patents, and other the premisses, *15 Martii, 44 Eliz.* without the Queens License or the Plaintiffs, &c. at Westminster did cause eightie grosses of playing Cards to be made and as well those, as 100 other grosses of playing Cards, of which many were made within the Realm, or brought within the Realm by the Plaintiff, or his servants, factors or deputies, &c. nor marked with his Seal; he had imported within the Realm, and had sold and uttered them to sundry persons unknown, and shewed some in certain, for which the Plaintiff could not utter his playing Cards, &c. *Contra formam praedict' literar' patentium, et in contemptum dictae Dominae Reginae,*[1] whereby the Plaintiff was disabled to pay his farm rent, to the Plaintiffs damages.

The Defendant, besides to one half grosse pleaded, Not Guilty; and as to that he pleaded, that the City of London is an antient city, and within the same, time out of mind there hath been a Society of Haberdashers; and that within the said City there was a Custom, *Quod quaelibet persona de societate* [85 b]   *illa, usus fuit et consuevit emere | vendere, et libere merchandizare omnem rem*

---

1. [*Ed.:* Against the form of the aforesaid letters patent and in contempt of the said lady queen,]

et omnes res merchandizabiles infra hoc regnum Angliae de quocunque, vel qui-buscunque personis, &c.[2] And pleaded, That he was *civis et liber homo de civitate et societate illa,*[3] and sold the said half gross of playing Cards, being made within the Realm, &c. as it was lawful from him to do; upon which the Plaintiffe did demurre in Law.

And this Case was argued at the Bar by Dodderidg, Fuller, Fleming Solicitor, and Coke Attorney-General, for the Plaintiff. And by George Crook, Altham, and Tanfield for the Defendant. And in this Case two general questions were moved and argued at the Bar, arising upon the two distinct grants in the said Letters Patents, *viz.*

1. If the said Grant to the Plaintiff of the sole making of Cards within the Realm were good or not?

2. If the Licence or dispensation to have the sole importation of Foreign Cards granted to the Plaintiffe, were available or not in Law. To the bar, no regard was had, because it was no more then the Common Law would have said, and then no such particular Custome ought to have been alleged, for *in his quae de jure communi omnibus conceduntur, consuetudo alicujus patriae vel loci non est alleganda,*[4] and therewith agreeth 8 Edw. 4. 5a. &c. And although the bar was holden superfluous, yet it shall not turn the Defendant to any prejudice, that he may well take advantage of the insufficiency of the Court.

As to the first question it was argued on the Plaintiffs side, That the said Grant of the sole making of playing Cards within the Realme, was good for three causes:

1. Because the said playing Cards were not any merchandize, or thing concerning Trade of any necessary use, but things of vanity, and the occasion of expence of time, wasting of patrimonies, and of the livings of many, the loss of the service and work of servants, causes of want, which is the mother of wo and perdition, and therefore it belongeth to the Queen (who is *Parens patriae, & paterfamilias totius regni,*[5] and as it is said in 20 Hen. 7. fol. 4.

---

2. [*Ed.:* That every person of that society has been used and accustomed to buy, sell, and trade freely all merchantable property within this realm of England from whatsoever person or persons, etc.]

3. [*Ed.:* a citizen and free man of the city and of that society.]

4. [*Ed.:* in those things that are granted by the Common Law to everyone, the custom of any region or place is not to be alleged.]

5. [*Ed.:* Parent of the country, and the family head of the whole realm,]

Capitalis Justiciarius Angliae)[6] to take away the great abuse, and to take order for the moderate and convenient use of them.

2. In matters of recreation and pleasure the Queen hath a Prerogative given her by the Law to take such order for such moderate use of them as shall seem good to her.

[86 a] 3. The Queen in regard of the great abuse of them, and of the deceit of the subjects by reason of them might utterly suppress them, and by | consequence without injury to any one, she might moderate and suffer them at her pleasure. And the reason of the Law which giveth the King these Prerogatives in matters of recreation and pleasure was, because the greatest part of men are ready to exceed in them. And upon these grounds divers Cases were put; *scil.* That no subject can make a Park, Chase, or Warren within his own Land, for his recreation or pleasure without the Kings grant or license; and if he do it of his own head in a *Quo warranto,*[7] they shall be seised into the King's hands, as it is holden in 3 Edw. 2. Action sur le Statute Br. 48. and 30 Edw. 3. Rot. Pat. The King granted to another all the wild Swans betwixt London Bridg and Oxford.

As the second, It was argued, and strongly urged, That the Queen by her prerogative may dispense with a penal Law, when the forfeiture is popular, or given to the King, And the forfeiture given by the Statute of 3 Edw. 4. cap. 5. in case of bringing of Cards is popular, 2 Hen. 7. 6 b. 11 Hen. 7. 11 b. 13 Hen. 7. 8b. 2 R. 3. 12a. Plow. Com, *Greindon's Case,* 502a, b. 6 Eliz. Dyer. 225. 13 El. 393. 18 Eliz. 352. 33 Hen. 8. Dyer 52. 11 Hen. 4. 76. 13 Edw. 3. Release 36. 43 Ass. pl. 19, 5 Edw. 3. 29. 2 Edw. 3. 6. & 7. F. N. B. 211b.

As to the first it was argued by the Defendants Counsel, and resolved by Popham Chief Justice, *et per totam Curiam,*[8] That the said Grant to the Plaintiff of the sole making of Cards within the Realm was void; and that for two reasons.

1. The same is a Monopoly, and against the Common Law.

2. That it is against divers Acts of Parliament.

Against the Common Law, for four causes

1. All Trades, as well Mechanical, as others, which avoid idleness (the bane

6. [*Ed.:* Chief Justice of England.]
7. [*Ed.:* Writ to enforce limits on a Royal charter.]
8. [*Ed.:* and by the whole court,]

of the Commonwealth) and exercise men and youths in labor for the maintenance of them and their Families, and for the increase of their livings, to serve the Queen if need be were profitable for the Commonwealth; and therefore the grant to the Plaintiff to have the sole making of them is against the Common Law, and the benefit and liberty of the subject; and therewith agreeth Fortescue *in laudibus Legum Angliae,* cap. 26.

And a Case was adjudged in this Court in an Action of Trespass between Davenant & Hurdis Trin. 41 Eliz. Rot. 92. where the Case was, That the Company of Merchant Taylors in London having power by charter to make Ordinances for the better rule and government of the Company, [so that they are consonant to Law and reason,] made an Ordinance, That every Brother of the same Society, who should put any cloath to be dressed by any Clothworker not being a Brother | of the same Society, shall expose one half of his [86 b] cloathes to any Brother of the same Societie, who exercised the Art of a Cloathworker, upon pain of forfeiting ten shillings, &c. and to distrein for it, &c. and it was adjudged, That the Ordinance, although it had the countenance of a Charter, was against the Common Law, because it was against the liberty of the subject; for every subject by the Law hath freedom and liberty to put his cloaths to be dressed by what Clothworker he pleaseth, and cannot be restrained to certain persons, for that in effect shall be a Monopoly; and therefore such Ordinance by color of a charter, or any grant by charter to such effect shall be void.

2. The sole Trade of any Mechanical Artifice, or any other Monopoly is not only a damage and prejudice to those who exercise the same Trade, but also to all other subjects, for the end of all these Monopolies is for the private gain of the Patentees; and although provisions and cautions be added to moderate them; yet *res profecto stulta est nequitiae modus;*[9] it is meer folly to think that there is any measure in mischief or wickedness. And therefore there are three inseparable incidents to every Monopoly against the Commonwealth.

1. That the price of the said commodity shall be raised, for he who hath the sole selling of any commodity, may make the price as he pleaseth. And this word, Monopoly, is said, *Cum unus solus aliquod genus mercaturae universum emit, pretium ad suum libitum statuens.*[10] And the Poet saith,

9. [*Ed.:* it is indeed a useless thing to moderate wickedness;]
10. [*Ed.:* [Monopoly is said], when one single person buys the whole of any kind of merchandise and sets the price at his pleasure.]

Omnia Castor emit, sic fit ut omnia vendat.[11]

And it appeareth by the Writ of *Ad quod damnum,*[12] F. N. B. 222a. That every gift or grant from the King hath this Condition, either expressly or tacitely annexed to it, *Illa quod patria per donationem illam magis solito non oneretur seu gravetur.*[13] And therefore every grant made in grievance and prejudice of the subject is void; and 13 Hen. 4. 14 b. the Kings grant which tendeth to the charge and prejudice of the subject is void.

The second incident to a Monopoly is, That after a Monopoly granted, the Commodity is not so good and merchantable as it was before; for the patentee having the sole trade, regardeth only his private, and not the publicke weale.

3. This same leadeth to the impoverishing of divers Artificers and others, who before by labor of their hands in their Art or Trade had kept themselves and their families, who now of necessity shall be constrained to live in idlenesse and beggary; *vide* Fortescue *ubi supra.*[14] And the Common Law in this point agreeth with the equity of the Law of God, as appeareth in Deut. cap. xxiv.

[87 a] ver. 6. *Non accipies loco | pignoris inferiorem et superiorem molam, quia animam suam apposuit tibi;*[15] You shall not take in pledg the neathet and upper milstone, for the same is his life; by which it appeareth, That every mans Trade doth maintains his life, and therefore he ought not to be deprived or dispossessed of it, no more than of his life. And the same also agreeth with the Civil Law; *Apud Justinianum monopolia non esse intromittenda, quoniam non ad commodum reipublicae sed ad labem detrimentaque pertinent. Monopolia interdixerunt leges civiles, cap. De Monopoliis lege unica. Zeno imperator statuit, ut exercentes monopolia bonis omnibus spoliarentur. Adjecit Zeno, ipsa rescripta imperialia non esse audienda, si cuiquam monopolia concedant.*[16]

11. [*Ed.:* Castor buys everything, so that he may sell everything.]

12. [*Ed.:* Writ directing the sheriff to determine what damage there would be if a Royal charter such as for a fair is granted.]

13. [*Ed.:* that the country should not be more burdened or vexed by that donation than is usual.]

14. [*Ed.:* in the above passage.]

15. [*Ed.:* Do not take the lower and the upper millstone as a pledge, because that would take his life; [Deut., xxiv. 6].]

16. [*Ed.:* For we read in Justinian that monopolies are not to be meddled with, because they do not conduce to the benefit of the common weal but to its ruin and damage. The civil Laws forbid monopolies: in the chapter of monopolies, one and the same Law. The Emperor Zeno ordained that those practising monopolies should be deprived of all their goods. Zeno added that even imperial rescripts were not to be accepted if they granted monopolies to anyone.]

3. The Queen was deceived in her grant, for the Queen as by the preamble appears, intended the same to be for the weal publick, and it shall be imployed for the private good of the Patentee; [and for the prejudice of the weal public];[17] Also the Queen meant that the abuse should be taken away, which shall never be by this Patent, but rather the abuse will be encreased fort the private benefit of the Patentee, and therefore, as it is said in 21 Ed. 3. 46. in the *Earl of Kent's* Case, this grant is void *jure Regio*.[18]

4. This grant is of this first impression, for no such was ever seen to pass [by letters patent][19] under the great Seal of England before this time, and therefore it is a dangerous innovation as well without any or example as without authority of Law, or reason. And it was observed that this grant to the Plaintiff was made for twenty-one years, so that his Executors, Administrators, Wife, or Children, or others inexpert in the Art and Trade shall have this Monopoly. And it cannot be intended, That Edward Darcy Esquire, and Groom of the Queen's Privy Chamber hath any skill in this Mechanical trade in making of Cards, and then it was said, That the Patent made to him was void, for to forbid others to make Cards who have the art and skill, and to give him the onely making of them who hath no skill to make them, shall make the Patent utterly void, *Vide* 9 Ed. 4. 5 b. And although the grant doth extend to his Deputies, and it may be said, he may appoint Deputies who shall be expert; yet if the Grantee himself be unexpert, and the grant be void as to him, he cannot make any Deputy to supply his room, *quia quod per me non possum, nec per alium*.[20] And as to what hath been said, That Playing Cards is a vanity, It is true, if it be abused, but the making of them is no pleasure, but labour and pains. | And it is true that none can make a Park, Chase, or Warren without the Kings licence, for that were *quodam modo*[21] to appropriate those which are *ferae naturae, et nullius in bonis*[22] to himself, and to restrain them of their natural liberty, which he cannot do without the Kings licence: but for hawking, hunting, &c. which are matters of pastime, pleasure, and recreation, there needeth no licence, but every one may in his own land use them at his pleasure [87 b]

17. [*Ed.*: Bracketted text omitted in the 1658 edition.]
18. [*Ed.*: by royal right.]
19. [*Ed.*: Bracketted text omitted in the 1658 edition.]
20. [*Ed.*: because what I cannot do by myself I cannot do through someone else.]
21. [*Ed.*: in a certain manner.]
22. [*Ed.*: of a wild nature, and no one's property.]

without any restraint to be made, if not by Parliament, as appeareth by the Statutes of 11 Hen. 7. c. 17. 23 Eliz. c. 10. 3 Jac. Regis, c. 13. And it is evident by the preamble of the said Act of 3 Edw. 4. c. 4. That the bringing in of forreign Cards was forbidden at the grievous complaint of the poor Artificers Cardmakers, who were not able to live of their trades, if forreign Cards should be brought in; as appeareth by the preamble: By which it appeareth, That the said Act provides remedie for the maintenance of the trade of making Cards, for as much as the same maintain divers families by their labour and industry. And the like Act is made in 1 Hen. 3. cap. 12. And therefore it was resolved, That the Queen could not suppress the making of Cards within the Realm, no more than the making of Dice, Bowls, Balls, Hawks-hoods, Bells, Lewers, Dog-couples, and other like, which are works of labour and art, although they shall be for pleasure, recreation and pastime, and they cannot be suppressed if not by Parliament, nor a man restrained to use any trade but by Parliament. 37 Edw. 3. cap. 16. 5 Eliz. cap. 4. And the playing at Dice and Cards is not forbidden by the Common Law, as appeareth M. 8 & 9 El. Dyer 154 (If not that some be deceived by false Dice or Cards, and there he who is deceived, shall have an Action upon this Case to the deceit) and playing at Cards, Dice, &c. is not *malum in se*,[23] for then the Queen should not suffer, nor license the same to be done. And where King Edward the third in the 39 year of his reign commandeth the exercise of shooting and artillery, and forbiddeth the exercise of casting of stones and barres, and the hand and foot-balles, cock-fighting, & *alios ludos vanos*,[24] as appeareth *in dors' claus' de an.* 39 Edw. 3. *nu.* 23. yet no effect thereof followed, till divers of them were forbidden upon a penalty by divers Acts of Parliament, *viz.* 12 Ric. 2 cap. 6. 11 Hen. 4. cap. 4. 17 Edw. 4. cap. 3. 33 Hen. 8. cap. 9.

Also such charter of a Monopolie, against the freedom of Trade and Traffick, is against divers Acts of Parliament, *scil.* 9 Ed.3. c. 1 & 2. Which for the

[88 a] advancement of the freedom of | Trade and Traffick extendeth to all vendible things, notwithstanding any charter of franchise granted to the contrary, or usage, or custom, or judgment given thereupon; which charters are adjudged by the same Parliament to be of no force, or effect, and made at the request of Prelates, Barons, and Grandees of the Realm, to the oppression of the

---

23. [*Ed.:* wrong in itself,]
24. [*Ed.:* and other useless games,]

Commons. And by the Statute of 25 Ed. 3. cap. 2. It is Enacted, that the Act of 9 E. 3. shall be kept, Holden, and maintained in all points. And it is further thereby enacted, That if any Statute, Charter, Letters Pattents, Proclamation, Command, Usage, Allowance, or judgment be made to the contrary, that the same be utterly void, *vide* Magna Charta cap. 18. 27 Edw. 3. cap. 11, &c.

As to the second question, It was resolved, That the dispensation or licence to have the sole importation and merchandizing of goods (without any limitation or stint) nothstanding the said Act of 3 Edw. 4. is utterly against Law: For it is true, That for as much as an Act of Parliament which generally forbiddeth a thing upon penalty which is popular, or onely given to the King, may be inconvenient to divers particular persons, in respect of person, place, time, &c. And for this cause the Law hath given power to the King, to dispense with particular persons; *Dispensatio mali prohibiti est de jure Domino Regi concessa, propter impossibilitat' praeviden' de omnibus particular', et dispensatio est mali prohib' provida relaxatio, utilitate seu necessitate pensata.*[25] But when the wisdom of the Parliament hath made an Act to restrain *pro bono publico*[26] the bringing in of many foreign manufactures, to the intent that the subjects of the Realm might apply themselves to the making of the said manufactures, &c. And thereby maintain themselves and their family with their handy labor. Now for a private gain to grant the sole importation of them to one, or divers (without any limitation) notwithstanding the said Act is a Monopoly against the common law, and against the end and scope of the same Act; for the same is not to maintain and encrease the labors of the poor Cardmakers within the realm, at whose petition the Act was made, but utterly to take away and overthrow their trade and labours, and that without any reason of necessity, or inconveniency in respect, place or time, and so much the rather because it was granted in reversion for years, as hath been said, but onely for the benefit of a private man, his Executors and Administrators for his particular commodity, and in prejudice of the Commonwealth. And King Edward the third by his Letters Patents, granted to one John Peche the sole importation of Sweet-wine into London, | and at a Parliament holden 50 Edw. 3. this grant [88 b]

---

25. [*Ed.:* Dispensing with things that are wrong by prohibition (i.e. legislation) is rightfully granted to the king, on account of the impossibility of providing for every particular Case; and a dispensation is a release of the prohibited wrong, or a measure of necessity.]

26. [*Ed.:* for the public good.]

was adjudged void, as appeareth in Rot. Parl. an. 50 Edw. 3. Mich. 33. Also admit that such grant or dispensation were good, yet the plaintiff cannot maintain an Action upon the Case against those who bring in any forreign Cards, but the remedie which the Act of 3 Edw. 4. in such Case giveth ought to be pursued. And judgment was given and entered, *quod querens nihil caperet per billam.*[27]

And note, Reader, and well observe the glorious preamble and pretence of this odious monopoly. And it is true *quod privilegia quae re vera sunt in prae-judicium reipublicae, magis tamen speciosa habent frontispicia, et boni publici praetextum, quam bonae et legales concessiones, sed praetextu liciti non debet admitti illicitum.*[28] And our lord the King that now is in a Book which he in zeal to the Law and Justice commanded to be printed Anno 1610. intituled *A Declaration of his Majesties pleasure, &c.* p. 13. hath published, That Monopolies are things against the Lawes of this Realm, and therefore expressly commands that No Suitor presume to move him to grant any of them.

James Bagg's Case.
(1615) Trinity Term, 13 James I
In the Court of King's Bench.
First Published in the *Reports,* volume 11, page 93b.*

Ed.: James Bagg, a burgess of Plymouth, in Devon, was a bit curmudgeonly. He called the mayor "some prince" with not a little sarcasm, as well as calling him a "cozenly knave" whom the council could choose a wiser man to replace. Bagg called another burgess a "knave" and yet another a "seditious fellow." He also suggested that the mayor was exceeding his authority in making merchants take loyalty oaths, after which the merchants refused to take them, provoked wine merchants not to pay a special town wine tax, and suggested that he seek the revocation of the town charter. The Mayor and burgesses voted to amove, or remove, Bagg from office,

---

27. [*Ed.:* that the plaintiff take nothing by his bill.]

28. [*Ed.:* that privileges which in truth are to the prejudice of the common weal nevertheless have more specious frontispieces and pretext of public good than good and lawful grants; but an unlawful thing ought not to be admitted under the pretext of being lawful.]

*The initial pleadings in this case are to be found at 13 Jac. 1 Rot. 23.

and he was disenfranchised. Bagg sued in the King's Bench. The court considered the privileges of citizenship and their protection under the Common Law, Magna Carta, and other Statutes, held that the town could not act on these grounds to remove someone from office or the franchise. Note also the broad claims of jurisdiction to cure errors by officials. For other privileges of citizenship, see also Calvin's Case, p. 166.

James, by the grace of God, of England, Scotland, France, and Ireland, King, defender of the faith, &c. To the Mayor and Commonalty of the borough of Plymouth, in the county of Devon, greeting, &c. Whereas James Bagg, one of the twelve chief burgesses, or magistrates of the borough aforesaid, according to the custom of the borough aforesaid, hitherto used, was duly chosen and made. And whereas the same James, in the office of one of the twelve chief burgesses or magistrates of the borough aforesaid, a long time carried and well governed himself; yet, you the mayor and commonalty of the borough aforesaid, little regarding the aforesaid James, unduly, and without reasonable cause, from the office of one of the twelve chief burgesses and magistrates of the borough aforesaid, unjustly have amoved, in contempt of us, and to the no little damage and grievance of him the said James, and the hurt of his estate, as we, by his complaint, have understood: we therefore to the said James, willing, due, and speedy Justice to be done in this behalf, as is just, command you, and every of you, as heretofore we have commanded you firmly enjoining you, that immediately after the receipt of this writ, the aforesaid James, into the aforesaid office of one of the twelve chief burgesses or magistrates of the borough aforesaid you restore, with all the liberties, privileges, and commodities, to the office aforesaid belonging and appertaining; or that you signify the cause thereof unto us, lest in your default, complaint thereof again to us come: | and how this our writ shall be executed you make [94 a] to appear to us, from the Day of the Holy Trinity, in three weeks, wheresoever we shall be in England, under the penalty of 40l this our writ then sending back to us, &c. Witness E. Coke, at Westminster, the 12th day of June, in the 13th year of our reign, of England, France, and Ireland, and of Scotland the 48th.

By the term of Trinity, in the thirteenth year of King James, Rot. 23. execution of this writ doth appear in a certain schedule to this writ annexed, John Clement, Mayor, the answer of the Mayor and Commonalty of the borough of Plymouth to the writ, to this schedule annexed; according to the command of the writ aforesaid, to the lord the King we most humbly certify, that the Lady Elizabeth, late Queen of England, by her letters patent, sealed with the Great Seal of England, bearing date at Westminster the 28th day of Feb. in the 43d year of her reign, for herself, her heirs and successors, granted to the Mayor and Commonalty of the borough of Plymouth aforesaid, and their successors, (amongst other things), that the mayor and Recorder of the borough aforesaid, for the time being, during the time that they should happen to be in their offices, and also the predecessors of the said mayor then alive, and for the time being, and their successors, should be Justices of the said late Queen, her heirs and successors; to keep the peace in the said borough, and within the limits, precincts, and liberties thereof; and to be kept, and to cause to be conserved and kept, without any command, commission, or warrant for the same to be had, or to be obtained: and further to the said lord the King we certify, that within the borough aforesaid, there is, and from time whereof the memory of man is not to the contrary, there has been a usage and custom, that the mayor and twelve chief burgesses of the same borough, stood, and were of the private council of the borough aforesaid, and twenty-four of the other most discreet burgesses of the borough aforesaid, for the time being, to this chosen and sworn, stood, and were, together with the aforesaid mayor and twelve chief burgesses, of common council of the borough aforesaid, for the regulating and government of the same borough. And that every such burgess who was chosen into the fellowship of the twenty-four burgesses of the common council aforesaid, before he was to be admitted to the said fellowship, should take a corporate oath before the mayor of the same borough, for the time being, that he should carry himself well and honestly, as well towards the mayor of the borough aforesaid, for the time being, as towards the aforesaid twelve chief burgesses of the said borough for the time being, and to them from time to time should shew reverence, and that he should maintain and uphold the liberties and common profit of the borough aforesaid, with his best counsel and advice: | and further we certify, that every one of the aforesaid twelve chief burgesses, from time to time chosen, should be preferred by the mayor of the borough aforesaid, or the rest of the aforesaid twelve chief of the burgesses, or by the greater part of them, for the time being, only without the consent or assent of the aforesaid twenty-four, the other burgesses who are (as before is said) of the common council of the borough aforesaid, to this required. And further we certify, that the aforesaid James Bagg, on the first day of May, in the 32d year of the reign of the Lady Elizabeth,

He ought to have first prescribed that there had been an incorporation of a mayor, &c. from time whereof, &c. *Vide* 22 H. 6. Prescription 47. 6 E. 6. Dyer 71, &c.

Twelve chief burgesses, *de privato consilio burgi,* it would be more aptly said, *de privato consilio majoris et burgensium.*

They do not prescribe or allege any charter that they may disfranchise any of the corporation.

The oath of a chief burgess.

[94 b]

They do not prescribe in this, and yet it is against common right. 1. Die Maii. 32 Eliz. James Bagg chose one of the twenty-four.

late Queen of England, was duly chosen and appointed one of the aforesaid twenty-four of the burgesses of the common council of the borough aforesaid then being, and on the said first day of May, in the 32d year aforesaid, at Plymouth aforesaid, took a corporal oath before the mayor of the borough aforesaid, according to the ancient custom aforesaid, that he the said James would carry himself well and honestly, as well towards the mayor of the borough aforesaid, for the time being, as towards the other twelve chief burgesses of the said borough for the time being, and to them from time to time would shew reverence, and the liberties and common profit of the borough aforesaid would maintain and uphold with his best counsel and advice: and further to the lord the King we certify, that the aforesaid borough of Plymouth is situate so near to the shore and sea-coasts, that by reason thereof, and by reason of the daily meeting there of ships and vessels there coming, as well from the parts beyond the seas, as from elsewhere, many ill-minded men, as well aliens as within born, of evil and perverse conversation, contemners of good government, and disturbers of the peace, in the ships and vessels aforesaid thither coming, in the borough aforesaid, and within the liberties and precincts of the same staying and remaining, are daily found, who can hardly be there brought to the obedience of good rule and government, unless the authority of the mayor of the borough aforesaid for the time being, and of the other chief burgesses aforesaid, with due reverence of the other burgesses and inhabitants of the said borough, be fortified, and the persons of the said chief burgesses, and of the mayor, from the contempt of the vulgar be preserved: and further to the said lord the King we certify, that the aforesaid James Bagg, not ignorant of the premises, little regarding his oath aforesaid, and the authority, as well of the mayor of the borough aforesaid for the time being, as his late predecessors aforesaid, as the other the chief burgesses of the borough aforesaid, setting naught by, and labouring and intending to bring the same authority into contempt: on the first day of May, in the 6th year of the reign of the lord the now King, the said James being then one of the common council of the borough aforesaid, and one of the chief burgesses of the same borough, in the presence of one | Robert TreLawny, then being mayor of the [95 a] borough aforesaid, and of many other of the inhabitants of the borough aforesaid, at Plymouth aforesaid, within the borough aforesaid, contemptuously and malapertly carried himself, as well in gesture as in words, toward the mayor aforesaid; and then and there, to the aforesaid Robert TreLawny, contemptuously and scoffingly, without any reasonable cause, these words following, openly and publicly said and spoke, that is to say, "You, (the aforesaid Robert

These words
are to be repre-
hended; but
are no cause to
disfranchise
him.

TreLawny meaning) are some prince, are you not?" And further to the said
lord the King we certify, that afterwards, that is to say, on the first day of
February, in the 7th year of the reign of the lord the now King, the aforesaid
James Bagg continuing his evil disposition and intention aforesaid, at Plymouth aforesaid, in the presence and hearing of the aforesaid Robert TreLawny,
then being a Justice of the peace of the aforesaid lord the King, within the
borough aforesaid to be kept, by reason of his mayoralty of the borough aforesaid, the year then last past, by virtue of the letters patent aforesaid, and in
the presence and hearing of very many other of the inhabitants of the borough
aforesaid, openly, publicly, and with a loud voice, without any reasonable cause,
these words following, contemptuously, falsely, and scandalously said and

These words
are scornful,
and worthy of
punishment, *sc.*
to bind him to
his good be-
haviour, if they
were published
when the may-
or was sitting
in execution of
his office: but
are no cause to
disfranchise the
delinquent.

spoke, that is to say, "You, (the aforesaid TreLawny meaning) are a cozening
knave;" whereas in truth, the said Robert TreLawny, all his lifetime, honestly,
and from all suspicion of any falsity, fraud, or deceit, lived altogether unsuspected, and in the offices, as well of the mayoralty as of chief burgess of the
borough aforesaid, with praise, carried and governed himself: and further to
the said lord the King we do certify, that on the 20th day of November, in
the 7th year of the reign of the said lord the now King, the aforesaid James
Bagg, continuing his evil disposition and intent aforesaid, at Plymouth aforesaid, seditiously and maliciously stirred up, and persuaded one Thomas Sher-
vil, then being one of the chief burgesses of the borough aforesaid, that he
the said Thomas would join himself with the aforesaid James Bagg in a conspiracy, to amove and depose one John Battersby, then being mayor of the
borough aforesaid, from his office of mayoralty, without any reasonable or

These words
are no cause to
disfranchise
him. 1. Because
nothing was
done and it
might be, that
there was just
cause to re-
move him; and
the cause certi-
fie ought to be
such that it
may appear to
the Court, that
it is a just
cause to dis-
franchise him;
for the party
grieved cannot
have an answer
to it.

Lawful cause, and then and there maliciously and contemptuously spoke to
the aforesaid Thomas Shervill of the aforesaid John Battersby, these words
following, that is to say, "Master mayor (the aforesaid John Battersby meaning)
carrieth himself foolishly in this place; and if you will join with me, we will
turn him out of his mayoralty, and choose a wiser man in his place:" whereas
in truth the aforesaid John Battersby, during the whole time of his mayoralty
aforesaid, in the | executing of his office aforesaid, carried himself well and
discreetly, and with great integrity and gravity. And further to the said lord
the King we certify, that afterwards, that is to say, on the first day of February,
in the 8th year of the reign of the said lord the now King, the aforesaid James

[95 b]

Bagg continuing in his evil disposition and intent aforesaid, at Plymouth afore-

said, in the Guildhall of the borough aforesaid, in the presence of one Thomas
Fowens, then being mayor of the borough aforesaid, in the presence and hearing, as well of the chief burgesses as of the other inhabitants of the borough
aforesaid, scornfully, and without reasonable cause, did speak to the aforesaid
Thomas Fowens these false and injurious words following, that is to say, "Thou   As above.
(the aforesaid Thomas Fowens, then mayor meaning,) art an insolent fellow;"
whereas in truth the said Thomas, in the whole course of his life, bore himself
towards all men honestly, civilly, and with praise. And further to the said lord
the King we certify, that afterwards, that is to say, on the first day of August,
in the 9th year of the reign of the said lord the now King, at Plymouth aforesaid,
in the presence and hearing of the aforesaid Thomas Fowens, and of very
many other of the burgesses of the borough aforesaid, being gathered together
in the Guildhall of the borough aforesaid, the aforesaid James Bagg continuing
his evil disposition and intent aforesaid, divers contemptible words of the
aforesaid Thomas Fowens, then being mayor of the borough aforesaid, with
a loud voice spoke and uttered; upon which the aforesaid Thomas Fowens,
with mild words admonishing the aforesaid James Bagg that he would desist
from uttering such contemptible words aforesaid, the aforesaid James Bagg
thereupon, then and there, that is to say, on the 10th day of August, in the
9th year abovesaid, at Plymouth aforesaid, and in the presence and hearing
of the aforesaid Thomas Fowens, then mayor of the borough aforesaid, and
very many others of the burgesses and inhabitants of the borough aforesaid,
and in contempt and disdain of the said Thomas Fowens, then mayor, turning
the hinder part of his body in an inhuman and uncivil manner towards the
aforesaid Thomas Fowens, scoffingly, contemptuously, and uncivilly, with a
loud voice, said to the aforesaid Thomas Fowens, these words following, that
is to say, ("Come and kiss.") And further to the said lord the King we certify,   This is against
that afterwards, that is to say, on the 20th day of August, in the 9th year of   good manners,
                                                                                      and worthy of
the reign of the lord the now King, at Plymouth aforesaid, the aforesaid James   punishment as
Bagg, with most insolent words, threatened the said Thomas Fowens, then   aforesaid; but
                                                                                      no cause of
being mayor of the borough aforesaid, without any reasonable cause; and then   disfranchise-
and there, to the said John Fowens, threateningly and maliciously spoke these   ment, or of in-
                                                                                      dictment.
words following, | that is to say, "I will make thy neck crack." And further   [96 a]
to the said lord the King we certify, that afterward, that is to say, on the third
day of May, in the 12th year of the reign of the lord the now King, a certain   This is repug-
                                                                                      nant, sc. 3
order and friendly instrument of admonition was made by John Scobb, mayor   Maii and 9
                                                                                      Maii.

of the borough aforesaid, and the greater part of the chief burgesses of the same borough, in these words, that is to say, "the 9th day of May, 1614, the day and year above-written, it was agreed by John Scobb, Mayor, and such other of the masters here underwritten, that if Mr. James Bagg, the elder, do not before the next sessions to be holden within the borough of Plymouth, reconcile himself to the said mayor and his brethren, for such wrongs as he hath committed against them, and withal faithfully promise to demean himself more orderly and temperately for the time to come, that then he shall be clean removed from the Bench, and a new master chosen in his room:" which order or instrument was made and subscribed by the said mayor and nine other of the chief burgesses of the borough aforesaid. And further to the said lord the King we certify, that the aforesaid James Bagg, before the aforesaid next sessions, in the order aforesaid mentioned, did not make any such reconciliation or promise or conformity, as in the order aforesaid is specified, although full notice of the aforesaid order, immediately after the making thereof, and before the aforesaid next sessions was given to him at Plymouth aforesaid. And further to the said lord the King we certify, that afterwards, that is to say, on the 20th day of February, in the 12th year of the reign of the said lord the now King, the aforesaid James Bagg continuing his evil disposition, and in his intent aforesaid, at Plymouth aforesaid, in the Guildhall of the borough aforesaid, in the presence and hearing of John Scobb, one of the chief burgesses of the borough aforesaid, and then being a Justice for the keeping the peace within the borough aforesaid, by virtue of the letters patent aforesaid, by reason of his mayoralty of the borough aforesaid, the year then next before, and in the presence and hearing of the then mayor of the borough aforesaid, and of divers others of the burgesses and inhabitants of that borough, contemptuously these words following, spoke and uttered of the aforesaid John Scobb, openly and publicly, falsely and scandalously, that is to say, "You (the aforesaid John Scobb meaning) are a knave;" whereas the aforesaid John Scobb honestly, I and laudably carried and governed himself. And further to the said lord the King we certify, that afterwards, that is to say, on the 10th day of December last past, the then mayor of the said borough, and divers of the chief burgesses of the borough aforesaid, at Plymouth aforesaid, being assembled together in the alms-house of the said borough, to require and receive an account of the over seers, burgesses of the borough aforesaid, as in times past, and from time whereof the memory of man is not to the contrary, it was used, the aforesaid James Bagg, then and there, in the presence and hearing of the said mayor,

Here it appears that he should be removed by the mayor and nine of the masters; and in the end of the return, it is alleged, that he was removed by the mayor and commonalty, which is repugnant.

As above.

[96 b]

and other of the chief burgesses aforesaid, without any reasonable cause, openly
and publicly said to the said Thomas Shervill, there then present, and one of
the chief burgesses of the borough aforesaid, and for the space of ten years
then last past being, these false and scandalous words following; that is to say,
"You (the said Thomas Shervill meaning) are a seditious fellow;" whereas in   As above.
truth the aforesaid Thomas Shervill always lived unsuspected of any such crime
of sedition, and from time to time in the office of mayor of the borough
aforesaid as in the place and office of chief burgess, honestly, discreetly, and
with great integrity, carried and governed himself. And further to the said lord
the King we certify, that whereas the said lord the King, the   day of
January, in the 12th year of his reign aforesaid, at Westminster in the county
of Middlesex, with the advice of the Lords of his Privy Council of this his
realm of England, ordained and commanded, by public proclamation, and
by letters written under the proper hands of divers of the Lords of his Privy
Council sealed, that none, nor any person whatsoever, should kill or put to
sale any flesh for victuals in the time of Lent then next following, contrary
to the Laws and Statutes of this realm. And that all mayors, and other head
officers, in boroughs and towns corporate, within this kingdom of England,
in the beginning of the time of Lent then next coming, or before, should cause
all victuallers, inn-keepers, keepers of ordinary tables, and alehouse-keepers,
within the precinct of their jurisdiction, to be bounden to the lord the King
by bond, that they should not dress any flesh for victuals all the said time of
Lent, then next following: and whereas afterwards, that is to say, on the 20th
day of February, in the 12th year aforesaid, one John Clement, then, and yet
Mayor of the borough of Plymouth, aforesaid, | according to the duty of his   [97 a]
office, and in obedience of the said ordinance and command of the said lord
the King, sent to all the victuallers, inn-keepers, keepers of ordinary tables,
and alehouse-keepers aforesaid, within the precinct of the borough aforesaid,
that they become bound by their writing obligatory, to the use of the lord
the King, according to the tenor and exigency of the aforesaid ordinance and
command of the said lord the King, and the due execution of the ordinance
aforesaid, in that behalf required and endeavoured to effect within the borough
aforesaid; the aforesaid James Bagg, well knowing the premises, and continuing
his evil disposition and intent aforesaid, at Plymouth aforesaid, endeavouring
and attempting to hinder and make void the due execution of the aforesaid
ordinance and command of the said lord the King; and to that purpose, on
the same 20th day of February, at Plymouth aforesaid, to divers inhabitants

of the borough aforesaid, and other of the King's liege people then being, and having then and there speech with the aforesaid James Bagg, of and upon the business aforesaid, the said James Bagg openly and publicly spoke and uttered these words following, that is to say, "Master Mayor (meaning the said John Clement) doth more herein than he need, and more than he can well answer;" meaning, that the said John Clement, in requiring the aforesaid victuallers, inn-keepers, keepers of ordinary tables, and alehouse-keepers, to become bounden to the use of the said lord the King, according to the aforesaid ordinance and command of the said lord the King, had done more than was needful, and more than he could well answer; by reason of which speech divers victuallers, inn-keepers, keepers of ordinary tables, and alehouse-keepers, dwelling within the aforesaid borough, utterly refused to be bounden to the said lord the King, according to the aforesaid ordinance and command of the said lord the King; and further we certify, that the aforesaid Mayor and Commonalty of the borough of Plymouth, and their predecessors, from time whereof the memory of man is not to the contrary, had and used to have within the borough aforesaid a certain custom of wine, called wine-weight, otherwise wine-wite, payable by every taverner selling wine within the borough aforesaid, of which custom of wine aforesaid the mayor and commonalty for the whole time aforesaid quietly and peaceably were possessed of, until the aforesaid James Bagg, on the 29th day of November, in the 4th year of the reign of the said lord the now King, at Plymouth aforesaid, perfidiously and maliciously practise with William Bently and Thomas Lyde, being taverners and sellers of wine within the borough aforesaid, to them revealing divers secret counsels concerning the common profit of the borough I aforesaid; and them the said William and Thomas then and there persuaded, that they no more should pay the aforesaid custom of wine, called wine weight, otherwise wine-wite, nor any farm or sum of money for the same, to the aforesaid mayor and commonalty, on which very 29th day of November, in the 4th year aforesaid, the aforesaid James Bagg, being then one of the twelve chief burgesses of common council of the borough aforesaid, at Plymouth aforesaid, perfidiously and maliciously spoke to the said William Bently and Thomas Lyde these words, that is to say, "You need not pay the money," (meaning a certain farm by them the said William and Thomas for the custom aforesaid, before then, to the aforesaid mayor and commonalty payable for the wine-weight) "any longer, except you list, for it is not due unto them:" by reason of which perfidious and malicious words the aforesaid William Bently and Thomas Lyde

Margin notes:

This is no cause of disfranchisement without question: also the innuendo is idle and vain.

They have not alleged, that there was a corporation from time whereof, &c.

These words are too general.

[97 b]

The same was but his opinion, which although it be false, is no cause of disfranchisement: and his opinion cannot be a prejudice to their right; the innuendo is vain and idle.

Yet remedy lies for this duty, if they have right to it by the Law.

utterly refused to pay, and yet do refuse, and by reason thereof divers strifes and controversies are risen, and hereafter are like to arise betwixt the aforesaid William Bently and Thomas Lyde, and the aforesaid mayor and commonalty, for the custom of wine aforesaid, and the farm aforesaid, to the great damage and prejudice of the aforesaid mayor and commonalty: and further to the said lord the King we certify, that the aforesaid James Bagg, on the first day of May, in the twelfth year of the reign of the lord the now King, and on divers other days and times then before, at Plymouth aforesaid, perfidiously said to divers inhabitants of the borough aforesaid, and to other the liege people of the said lord the King, upon communication between them and the aforesaid James Bagg then before had, of and concerning the liberties and privileges of the borough aforesaid, "that he (the said James Bagg) would overthrow and make void the charter of the borough aforesaid," meaning the charter aforesaid, by the aforesaid late Queen Elizabeth to the aforesaid mayor and commonalty, as before is said, granted; and that he the said James the liberties and privileges of the borough aforesaid, would call in question, and the same privileges and liberties would overthrow. And further to the lord the King we certify, that afterwards, that is to say, the 17th day of April now last past, the aforesaid James Bagg in the said writ named, for the causes aforesaid, by the mayor and commonalty of the borough aforesaid, from the office of one of the chief burgesses and magistrates of the borough aforesaid, was amoved, &c.

John Clement, Mayor.

Non officit affectus nisi sequatur effectus: and it may be the charter was void in Law, or that it was procured by the lesser number of the burgesses, and then it might be removed; and so he might justify these words.

| Upon the matter aforesaid, and for the causes aforesaid, it was resolved by the Court, That there was not any just cause to remove him; and therefore by the award of the Court, a writ was directed to the Major and Commonalty to restore him. [98 a]

And in this Case, first, it was resolved, That Authority doth belong to the Kings Bench, not only to correct errors in judicial proceedings, but other errors and misdemeanors extra-judicial, tending to the breach of peace, or oppression of the subjects, or to the raising of faction, controversy, debate, or to any manner of misgovernment; so that no wrong or injury, either publick or private, can be done but that the same shall be reformed or punished by the due course of Law.

For the general learning of this and the like Cases, all that was said in the argument of this Case, was divided into these questions.

1. What were sufficient causes to disfranchise a Citizen, Free-man, or Bur-

gess of any City or Borough incorporate, and to discharge him of his freedom and liberty, and what not?

2. How and by whom, and in what manner, such Citizen or Burgess shall be disfranchised?

3. If the return of his removing and disfranchisement, doth carry sufficient matter, but the same is false; what remedy shall be for the party grieved in such Case?

As to the first, it was resolved, That the cause of disfranchisement ought to be grounded upon an Act which is against the duty of a Citizen or Burgess, and to the prejudice of the publick good of the City or Borough whereof he is a Citizen or Burgess, and against his oath which he took when he was sworn a Free-man of the City or Borough; for although one shall not be charged in any Judicial Court for the breach of a general Oath, which he took when he became Officer, Minister, Citizen, Burgess, &c. yet if the act which he doth be against the said duty and trust of his freedom, and to the prejudice of the City or Borough, and also against his oath, it enforces much the cause of his removal, and there is a condition in Law *tacitè*[1] and annexed to his Freedom or Libertie; which if he breaks, he may be disfranchised; but words of Con-

[98 b] tempt, or *contra bonos mores,*[2] although they be against | the Chief Officer, or his brethren, are good causes to punish him, as to commit till he has found Sureties of his Good Behaviour, but not to disfranchise him. So if he intends, or endeavours of himself, or conspires with others, to do a thing against the duty or trust of his freedom, and to the prejudice of the publick good of the City or Borough, but he doth not execute it, it is a good cause to punish him, as is aforesaid, but not to disfranchise him, for *Non officit conatus, nisi sequatur effectus;*[3] and *Non officit affectus, nisi sequatur effectus.*[4] And the reason and cause thereof is, that when a man is a Free-man of a City or Borough, he has a freehold in his freedom for his life, and with others, in their publick capacity, has an inheritance in the lands of the said corporation, and interest in their goods, and perhaps the same concerns his trade and means

1. [*Ed.:* silently.]
2. [*Ed.:* against good morals,]
3. [*Ed.:* An attempt does no harm if it has no effect;]
4. [*Ed.:* A disposition does no harm if it has no effect.]

of living, credit and estimation; and therefore the matter which shall be a cause of his disfranchisement, ought to be an act or a deed, and not a conation, or an indeavour, which he may repent of before the execution of it, and from whence no prejudice doth follow. And those who have offices of trust and confidence shall not forfeit them by endeavours and intentions to do acts, although they declare them by express words, unless the act itself shall ensue, as if one who has the keeping of a park should say, that he will kill all the game within his custody, or will cut down so many trees within the park, but doth not kill any of the game, nor cut down any trees, it is not any forfeiture, *et sic de similibus,*[5] for in all such Cases, either there ought to be an Act, or such a negligence as doth amount to so much *scil.* to the destruction of the game, &c. If a Bishop, Arch-deacon, Parson, &c. fells all the trees, the same is a good cause of deprivation, 2 Hen. 4. 3b. So if a prior aliens the land which he has *in jure domus suae,*[6] it is a cause of deprivation, as appears in 9 Edw. 4. 34. a. If a prior makes dilapidation, it is a good cause to deprive him, as it is held in 29 Edw. 3. 16 a. (20) 28 Hen. 6. 36 a. But if it be but a conation, or endeavour without any act done, in none of those Cases is it any cause of deprivation; for in those Cases, *voluntas non reputatur pro facto.*[7] And if a contempt | (be it of omission or commission) should be a good cause to dis- [99 a] franchise, the best Citizen or Burgess might be, at one time or other, dis-franchised, which would be great cause of faction and contention in cities and boroughs.

As to the second, it was resolved, that no Free-man of any Corporation can be disfranchised by the Corporation, unless they have authority to do it either by the express words of the Charter, or by prescription: but if they have not authority neither by Charter or by prescription, then he ought to be convicted by course of Law before he can be removed; and it appears by Magna Charta, cap. 29. *Nullus liber homo capiatur, vel imprisonetur, aut disseisitur de libero tenemento suo, vel libertatibus, vel liberis consuetudinibus suis, &c. nisi per legale judicium parium suorum, vel per legem terrae,*[8] and if the Corporation have

5. [*Ed.:* and likewise concerning similar things,]
6. [*Ed.:* in right of his house,]
7. [*Ed.:* the will is not to be taken for the deed.]
8. [*Ed.:* No free man shall be taken, or imprisoned, or disseised of his free tenement, or of his liberties or free customs, etc., unless by the Lawful judgment of his peers or by the Law of the land.]

power by Charter or prescription to remove him for a reasonable cause, that will be *per legem terrae;*[9] but if they have no such power, he ought to be convicted *per judicium parium suorum, &c.*[10] as if a Citizen, or Free-man, be attainted of Forgery or Perjury, or conspiracy, at the Kings suit, &c. or of any other crime whereby he is become infamous, upon such attainder they may remove him: So if he be convicted of any such offence which is against the duty and trust of his freedom, and to the publick prejudice of the City or Borough whereof he is free, and against his Oath, as if he has burnt or defaced the charters, or evidences of the City or Borough, or razed or corrupted them, and is thereof convicted and attainted, these and the like are good causes to remove him. And although they have Lawful authority either by Charter or prescription to remove any one from the Freedom, and that they have just cause to remove him; yet it appears by the return, that they have proceeded against him without hearing him answer to what was objected, or that he was not reasonably warned, such removal is void, and shall not bind the party, *quia quicunque aliquid statuerit parte inaudita altera, aequum licet statuerit, haud aequus fuerit,*[11] and such removal is against Justice and right.

As to the third question, if they have power by Charter or prescription to disfranchise one, and afterwards the Judges of the Kings Bench award a Writ to them to restore him, or signifie the cause, &c. and they certifie a sufficient cause to remove him, but it is false; then the Court cannot award a Writ to [99 b] restore him, neither can I any issue be taken thereupon, because the parties are strangers, and have no day in Court; but the party grieved may well have an Action upon the special matter against those who made the Certificate, and aver it to be false; and if it is found for him, and he obtains judgment against them, so that it may appear to the Justices that the causes of the return are false, then they shall award a Writ of Restitution; and this is proved by reason of the Book of 9 Hen. 6. 44 a. where it is held, that upon a *corpus cum causa,*[12] if the cause returned be sufficient, but in truth is false, the Court ought to send back the Prisoner, and he is at no mischief, for if they have no authority, or the cause be false, he may have a Writ of false imprisonment, *vide* Fitz. tit.

9. [*Ed.:* by the Law of the land;]

10. [*Ed.:* by the judgment of his peers, etc.]

11. [*Ed.:* because whoever settles something without hearing the other side, even if he settles it fairly, does not act fairly,]

12. [*Ed.:* A form of habeas corpus, inquiring of the cause of an incarceration.]

Corpus cum causa, 2. the said cause of 9 Hen. 6. 44. well abridged. So in the other, upon such false return, the party grieved may have a special action upon his Case as is aforesaid.

Also if the party grieved, who is so disfranchised, be for the causes of his disfranchisement committed to prison, or if his Shop be shut up, or if with force he be removed out of their assembly, &c. in these and the like Cases he may have an action of false imprisonment, or an action of trespass *quare domum fregit,*[13] or of assault and battery; and in those actions, the causes of his disfranchisement ought to be pleaded, and shall be decided according to Law, 8 Edw. 3. 437. 8 Ass. 29. 31. If a Lay-man is Patron of an Hospital, he may visit it, and depose or deprive the Master for good cause: but if he is deprived without just cause, and by colour thereof is ousted, he shall have an Assize because he has no other remedy; but if the Ordinary deprives a Master who is Ecclesiastical without a cause, he shall not have an Assize, for he has no other remedy by appeal. *Vide* 6 Hen. 7. 14 a. F. N. B. 4 b. 27 Edw. 3. 85. 10 Eliz. Dyer 273. pl. 35.

Also it was resolved, That such return of disfranchisement ought to be certain, so that sufficient matter may appear to the Court to disfranchise the party; and so much the rather, because the party cannot have answer to it, as is said before.

Lastly, it was resolved, that for none of the causes contained in the said Certificate, the said James Bagg by Law ought to be removed; and therefore by the whole Court a Writ was awarded to restore him to his Franchise and Freedom, and so he was.

I Note, Reader, in the Argument of this Case much was said to exhort [100 a] Citizens and Burgesses to yield obedience and reverence to the Magistrates in their Cities and Boroughs, because they derive their authority from the King, and *obedientia est legis essentia,*[14] and therefore it appeareth before, how they shall be punished who commit any contempt against them. But the principal question of this Case was, what Acts were sufficient causes in Law for the Disfranchisement of any Citizen or Burgess, &c.

Leges posteriores priores contrarias abrogant.[15]

---

13. [*Ed.:* [to show] why he broke the close,]
14. [*Ed.:* obedience is the essence of the Law,]
15. [*Ed.:* Later laws abrogate prior and contradictory laws.]

Part Twelve of the *Reports*

The Twelfth Part of the *Reports* was published in 1656, after Coke's death and following the parliamentary restoration to his son of the manuscripts seized by the Crown. It was published in English, in keeping with the new Laws banishing the Law French of Law Books of the Stuart publishers for the plain speaking of the Protectorate of the Commonwealth, as *The Twelfth part of the Reports of Sir Edward Coke, Kt. of Divers Resolutions and Judgments given upon solemn Arguments, and with great Deliberation and Conference with the Learned JUDGES in Cases of Law, the most of them very Famous, being of the Kings especiall Reference, from the* COUNCIL TABLE, *concerning the Prerogative: as for the digging of Salt-peter, Forfeitures, Forrests, Proclamations, &c. and the Jurisdictions of the Admiralty, Common Pleas, Star-Chamber, High Commission, Court of Wards, Chancery. &c. and Expositions and Resolutions concerning Authorities, both Ecclesiasticall and Civill, within this Realm. Also the Formes and Proceedings of Parliaments, both* ENGLAND, *&* IRELAND: *With an Exposition of* Poynings *Law: With Alphabeticall Tables, wherein may be found the Principall Matters contained in this Booke.* The Twelfth Part of the *Reports* was not as polished as those parts that appeared while Coke lived, and it is likely impossible now to discern whether he intended to finish and publish these, or more, of the notes from his manuscript. It is unlikely he intended all of these Cases to be publicly read. Even so, the Case reports are very significant, containing many of Coke's notes on the most politically volatile and constitutionally significant Cases of his career. The cautious acceptance of these notes is typified by the note accompanying its initial publication, by Edward Bulstrode:

> I have perused this Treatise, Intituled, the twelfth part of the REPORTS of Sir *Edward Coke* Knight; and I do, upon my reading thereof, conceive the same to be his *Collections,* and that the Printing of the same (containing very much good, and useful learning) will be for the good of this Nation, and of the Professors of the COMMON LAW.
>
> Edward Bulstrod.
>
> The second of *February,* 1655

Ford and Sheldon's Case.

(1606) Easter Term, 4 James I
In the Exchequer-Chamber.
First Published in the *Reports,* volume 12, page 1.

Ed.: Thomas Ford was a recusant, a person who refused to attend church in violation of the Law, making himself liable for a fine of £20 per month for non-attendance and for other penalties, including forfeiture of his goods. Ford lent money to Sheldon, who gave Ford a deed giving him interests in some of his rents as well as recognizances, which are rather like the modern promissory note, for £21,000. When Ford was convicted of recusancy, the question arose of whether the recognizances, and the debt they represented, could be forfeit to the crown. In the Exchequer before all the judges and Chief Justice Popham of the King's Bench, the court considered that debts are goods, that a penal Law cannot be extended by equity, but that the court construed the recognizances to have been entered in an effort to keep the money that might have been forfeit.

In an information in the Exchequer-Chamber for the King, against Thomas Ford, Esquire, Ralph Sheldon, Esquire, and divers others; the Case was thus.

Thomas Ford was at all times before the Statute of 23 Eliz. a Recusant; and for money lent to Sheldon, some before 23 Eliz. and some after. Ford took a Recognizance in the names of the other Defendants, and took also a grant of a Rent-charge to them in fee, with condition of Redemption by Deed indented: And the Recognizance was conditioned for performance of Covenants in the said Indenture, and afterward the Statute of the 29 Eliz. was made, by which it was enacted, that if default of payment was made in any part of payment (viz.) of 20 l. for every month, &c. And that then and so often the Queens Majesty by processe out of the Exchequer may take, seize, and enjoy all the goods, and two parts, &c. And after the said Act, and before the 34th year of the reign of the late Queen, Ford lent great summs of money to Sheldon, and for assurance of it took a Rent-charge by Deed Indented, with condition of Redemption: and took also several Recognizances in the names of some of the other Defendants, for performance of Covenants, &c. as is aforesaid; which Recognizances did amount in all to the sum of 21,000 l. all which were to the use of the said Ford, and to be at his disposition, and they were forfeited: And afterwards, *viz.* 41 Eliz., Ford was convict of Recusancy, and did not pay 20 l. *per mensem,*[1] according to the Statute. And if upon all this Case the King should have the benefit of these Recognizances, was the question.

And this Case was debated by Counsell learned on both sides in Court. And it was objected by the Counsell of Ford, that if the Recognizance had been acknowledged to Ford himself, they should not be forfeited to the King, for the Statute speaks only of Goods. And Debts are not included within the word (*Goods*). And therefore, if the King grant all the Goods which came to him by the Attainder of J. S., the Patentee shall not have Debts due to him, for that the Grant only extends to Goods in possession, and not to things in action. And this Act is a Penall Law, and shall not be extended by equity.

2. It was objected that these Recognizances were acknowledged good to perform Covenants in an Indenture concerning a Rent-charge: And therefore savers of the realty, and are not within the intention of the said Act, which speaks only of Goods.

3. No fraud or covin appears in the Case; And then forasmuch as no Act of Parliament extends to this Case, it was said, that the Common Law doth not give any benefit to the King: for at the Common Law, in a far stronger [2]   Case, if *Cestuy que use*[2] had been attaint of treason; this use forasmuch | as it was but a trust and confidence, of which the Law did not take notice, it was not forfeited to the King, and could not be granted: and if an Use shall not be forfeited, of which there shall be a *Possessio fratris, &c.*[3] and which shall descend to the heir; *A multo fortiori,*[4] a mere trust and confidence shall not be forfeited.

4. It was objected, that if the Forfeiture in this Case at the Bar accrues to the King, by the Statute of 29 Eliz. it ought to be by force of this word (*Goods*): But that shall not be without question in this Case. For Ford hath not any Goods, but only a mere trust and confidence, which is nothing in consideration of Law.

And the Court cannot adjudge that these Recognizances belong to the King

---

1. [*Ed.:* each month,]

2. [*Ed.:* the person for whose benefit a use has been established.]

3. [*Ed.:* Writ establishing the claim of a half-brother when another sibling has entered the land upon the death of their ancestor.]

4. [*Ed.:* So much the more so,]

by equity of the said Statute, because it is penall: Also one Recognizance was taken in the names of some of the other Defendants, before the Statute of the 29 Eliz. which gave the Forfeiture.

And for that reason, it cannot be imagined that it was to defeat the King of a forfeiture, which then was not *in Esse*,[5] but given afterwards.

As to the first objection, it was answered and resolved by all the Barons and by Popham, Chief Justice of England, and diverse others of the Justices, with whom they conferred, that if the recognizances had been acknowledged to the party himself, that they were given to the King without question for personall actions are as well included within this word, *Goods,* in an Act of Parliament, as Goods in possession. But inasmuch as by the Law things in action cannot be granted over, for that cause by his generall grant, things in action (which only he may grant by his prerogative) without special words passe not for his Prerogative, can never passe by general words. And it was affirmed, that so it had been resolved before, That is to say, that Debts were forfeited to the King by the said Act of the 29 Eliz. And where the Statute saith, "shall take, seize, and enjoy all the Goods, and two parts, &c." Although a debt due to a recusant cannot be taken and seised, yet inasmuch as there is another word, viz. *Enjoy,* the King may well enjoy the Debt; and by process out of the Exchequer levy it; and so "take and seise" refers to two parts of Lands in possession, and *Enjoy* relates to goods.

As to the second objection. It was originally for the loan and forbearance of mony. And as well the Recognizance as the Annuity were made for the security of the payment of the said money: Also when the Recognizances are forfeited, they are but Chattels personal.

As to the third objection, there was Covin[6] apparent: for when he was a Recusant continually after that Statute of the 23 Eliz. and for *that* chargeable to the King, for the forfeiture given by the same Act, it shall be intended that he took these Recognizances in the name of others, with an intent to prevent the King of levying of the Forfeiture: and all the Recognizances, which were taken in other men's names after the said Act, shall be presumed in Law to be so taken, to the intent to defeat the King of his Forfeiture: True it is, that an Use or Trust shall not be forfeited for Treason or other offence by the

---

5. [*Ed.:* in being,]
6. [*Ed.:* A secret agreement to defraud; a conspiracy.]

Common Law, because it is not a thing of which the Common Law taketh any notice, for that *Cestuy que use,* hath neither *Jus in re,*[7] nor *Jus ad rem;*[8] but by the Common Law, when any act is done with an intent and purpose to defraud the King of his lawfull duty, or Forfeiture by the Duty, or Forfeiture by the Common Law, or Act of Parliament, the King shall not be barred of his lawful Duty or Forfeiture *Per obliquum,*[9] which belongs to him by the Law, if the act was made *De directo.*[10]

And therefore if a man Out-lawed buy Goods in the names of others, the King shall have the Goods in the same manner, as if he had taken them directly in his own name: So if any Accountant to the King purchase Lands in the names of others, the King shall seize those lands for mony due unto him. | And this appears by the Case of *Walter Chirton,* Trin. 24 Ed. 3. Rot. 4 in Scaccario, where the Case was, that Walter de Chirton was indebted to the King 1800 l. which he had received of the King's Treasure, and did purchase certain Lands with the Kings money; and by Covin had caused the Vendor to enfeoff his Friends in Fee to defraud the King, and notwithstanding took the Profits himself: and afterwards Walter Chirton was committed to the Fleet for the said Debt. And all the matter was found by Inquisition, and by Judgment the Land was seised into the King's hands *Quousque;*[11] for in case of the King, an act done by Covin, *Per obliquum,* shall be equal to on act done *De directo,* to the party himself; for *Rex fallere non vult, falli autem non potest:*[12] See another President, Trin. 24 Ed. 3. Rot 11. *Ex Recum. Regis,* where one Thomas Favell was Collector of Tithes and Fifteenths, and was seised of certain Lands in Fee-simple, and having diverse Goods and Chattels, *Die intromissionis de collectione et levatione*[13] of Tenths and Fifteenths *Languidus in extremis alienavit tenementa sua et bona et catalla diversis personis,*[14] and died without Heir or Executor. In this case by the Prerogative of the King, Proces was made as well against the Ter-tenants, as against the possessors of the Goods and

[3]

---

7. [*Ed.:* A right in the thing,]
8. [*Ed.:* A right to the thing;]
9. [*Ed.:* By reference; implicitly,]
10. [*Ed.:* By order of the law, explicitly.]
11. [*Ed.:* "until;" a temporary prohibition, an order good until an event, such as payment of a debt.]
12. [*Ed.:* The king does not wish to deceive, and cannot be deceived:]
13. [*Ed.:* On the day of the audit of the collection and levying.]
14. [*Ed.:* in his last illness he alienated his tenements and goods and chattels to various persons,]

Chattells although they were not Executors, &c. *Ad computandum pro collectione praedicta et ad respondendum et satisfaciendum inde Regni, &c. Et hoc per Cancellarium Angliae et Capitales Justiciarios Angliae, et aliorum Justiciariorum utriusque Banci; quod nota bene.*[15]

As to the fourth objection, *Non refert,* whether the duty to accrue to the King by the Common Law, or by Statute; but be it the one way or the other, no subterfuge that the party can use can defeat or defraud the King: and although one of the recognizances was taken before the Statute of 29 Eliz. yet that was to his use, and for that it is in the nature of a Chattell in him, and was taken in the names of others to prevent the Queen of her forfeiture, which she might have by the Act of 23 Eliz.; and although Ford was not convict until 41 Eliz. that is not material, for at all times before that, he was subject to a Forfeiture for his Recusancy.

Case of Non Obstante, or Dispensing Power.
First Published in the *Reports,* volume 12, page 18.

Ed.: In this note, Coke considers the limits on Parliamentary control of the King, and when the King may act in his prerogative notwithstanding an act of Parliament to the contrary. He resolves that Parliament cannot bind the King in a matter within his personal prerogative but it may in all other matters.

Note; a good diversity when the King shall be bound by act of Parliament, so that he cannot dispence with it by any clause of *Non obstante.*[1] No Act can bind the King from any Prerogative which is sole and inseparable to his person, but that he may dispense with it by a *Non obstante;* as a Soveraign power to command any of his Subjects to serve him for the publick Weal; and this solely and inseparably is annexed to his person; and this Royall power cannot be restrained by any act of Parliament, neither in *Thesi,* nor in *Hypothesi,*[2]

15. [*Ed.:* To account for the aforesaid collection and to answer and make satisfaction to the lord king, etc. And this was by the chancellor of England and the chief Justices of England, and the other Justices of both benches: which note well.]

1. [*Ed.:* "Notwithstanding," a clause or writ in which the recipient is excused from some obligation or basis of duty.]

2. [*Ed.:* Statement [or] by Supposition.]

but that the King by his Royall Prerogative may dispense with it; for upon commandment of the King, and obedience of the Subject, doth his government consist; as it is provided by the Statute of 23 Hen. 6. cap. 8. that all Patents made or to be made of any Office of a Sheriff, &c. for term of years, for life, in Fee Simple, or in tail, are void and of no effect, any Clause or Parol *de non obstante,* put, or to be put into such Patents to be made, notwithstanding. And further, whosoever shall take upon him or them to accept or occupy such office of Sheriff by virtue of such Grants or Patents, shall stand perpetually disabled to be or bear the office of Sheriff within any County of England by the same authority; and notwithstanding that by this Act, 1. The Patent is made void. 2. The King is restrained to grant *non obstante.* 3. The Grantee disabled to take the Office; yet the King by his Royall soveraign power of commanding, may command by his Patent, (for such causes as he in his wisdom doth think meet and profitable for himself and the Commonwealth, of which he himself is solely Judge,) to serve him and the Weal publike, as Sheriff of such a County for years, or for life, &c. And so was it resolved by all the Justices of England, in the Exchequer-Chamber, 2 Hen. 7. 66. And so the Royall power to pardon Treasons, Murthers, Rapes, &c. is a Prerogative incident solely and inseparably to the person of the King; and for this *Non obstante* an Act of Parliament to make the Pardon of the King void, and restrain the King to dispense with this by *Non obstante,* and to disable him to whom the Pardon is made to take or plead it, shall not bind the King but that he may dispense with it: and this is well proved by the Act of 13 Ric. 2. Parliament 2. cap. 1. For by this it was enacted, that no Charter of Pardon from henceforth be allowed by whatsoever Justices, for Murther, Treason, Rape of a woman, not specified in the said Charter; and if it be otherwise, be the Charter disallowed.

Note, This was the surest way that the Parliament could take to restrain the King to pardon Murther, unless that he Pardon it by express terms, which they thought the King would not, for they knew that the King could not be restrained by any Act to make a Pardon; for mercy and power to Pardon is a Prerogative incident, solely and inseparably to the person of the King: And it hath oft-times been adjudged that the King can Pardon Murther by generall words without any expresse mention, with *Non obstante,* the said Statute, see [19] 4 Hen. 4. cap. 31. In which it was ordained that no Welshman be Justice, | Chamberlain, Treasurer, Sheriff, Steward, Constable of a Castle, Escheator, Coroner, or chief Forester, nor other Officer whatsoever, nor Keeper of Records, &c. in any part of Wales, notwithstanding any Patent made to the contrary, with clause of *Non obstante licet sit Wallicus natus:*[3] and yet without question, the King may grant this with a *Non obstante.* So Purveyance for the King and his household is incident solely and inseparably to the person of the King, and for this cause the Act of Parliament held in time of H. 3. *De tallagio non concedendo,*[4] tit. Purveyance, in Rastall, which bars the King wholly of Purveyance, is void, as it appears in Co. lib. fol. 69. But in all such cases, although that the King may dispense with Statutes, yet a generall dispensation or grant without *Non obstante* is void; But in things which are not incident solely and inseparably to the person of the King, but belong to every Subject, and may be severed, there an act of Parliament may absolutely bind the King; as if an Act of Parliament to disable any Subjects of the King, to take any Land of his Grant, or any of his Subjects (as Bishops) (as it is done by the Statute 1 Jac. c. 3.) to grant to the King, this is good; for to Grant or take Lands or Tenements is common to every Subject; and for this it is not *Proprium quarto modo,*[5] to Kings, *Scilicet omni soli et semper.*[6] *Vide* the Case of Deans and Chapters upon the Statute of 13 Eliz. *vide* 8 Ric. 2. cap. 2. & 33 Hen. 6. that none shall be Justice of Assise, &c. in the County where he was born or did inhabit; and yet the King with special *Non obstante* may dispense with this, for this belongs to the inseparable Prerogative of the King, *Viz.* his power of commandment to serve, &c.

Q. If High Commissioners Have Power to Imprison.

(1607) Hilary Term, 4 James I
Conference in the Serjeants Inn.
First Published in the *Reports,* volume 12, page 19.

Ed.: In this note, Coke records a debate among the Judges and senior members of the bar over whether the church court, the High Commission, has

3. [*Ed.:* Notwithstanding he was born a Welshman:]
4. [*Ed.:* Concerning the not granting of tallage, which is a delegated power to collect tolls or tax.]
5. [*Ed.:* "appropriate in the fourth manner." Perhaps "fourth branch." The significance of this reference here has so far evaded the editor and all his friends.]
6. [*Ed.:* that is to say, all, only and always.]

> the power to imprison. The Commission is limited only to hearing eccle-
> siastical offenses and only a limited power of incarceration.

Note, Mich. 4 Jac. *post prandium*,[1] there was moved a question amongst the Judges and Serjeants at Serjeants Inne, if the high Commissioners in Ecclesiasticall causes, may by force of their Commission imprison any man or no?

First of all it was resolved, by all, that before the Statute of 1 Eliz. cap. 1. the King might have granted a Commission to hear and determine Ecclesiasticall causes; but then, notwithstanding any clause in their Commission, the Commissioners ought to proceed according to the Ecclesiasticall Law allowed within this Realm, for he cannot alter neither his temporal nor his Ecclesiasticall Laws within this Realm by his Grant or Commission; *Vide Caudrey's Case,* Fifth Report. [And they could not in any case have punished any delinquent by fine or imprisonment unless they had authority so to do by Act of Parliament.][2] Then all the question rests upon the Act of 1 Eliz. which as to this purpose rests upon three branches.

1. Such Commissioners have power to exercise, use, occupy, execute all Jurisdiction Spirituall and Ecclesiasticall.

2. Such Commissioners by force of Letters Patents have power, to visit, reform, &c. all Heresies, &c. which by any manner of Spirituall or Ecclesiasticall power, &c. can, or lawfully may be reformed, &c. so that these branches limit the jurisdiction, and what offences shall be within the Jurisdiction of such Commissioners, by force of Letters Patent of the King; and this is all, and only such offences may lawfully be reformed by the Ecclesiasticall Law.

3. The third branch is, that such Commissioners, after such Commission delivered to them so authorised, shall have power and Lawful authority by virtue of this act, and the said Letters Patent, to exercise, use, and execute all the premises according to the tenor and effect of the said Letters Patent. This branch gives them power to execute their Commission. But it was objected, that this branch doth not give the Queen power, by her Letters Patent, to alter the proceedings of the Ecclesiasticall Law, or gave to the Queen absolute

[20]

---

1. [*Ed.:* after dinner,]
2. [*Ed.:* Bracketed text omitted from 1656 edition.]

power by her Letters Patent to prescribe what manner of proceedings, or punishment concerning the Lands, Goods, or bodies of the Subject; and this appears by the title of the Act restoring to the Crown the ancient Jurisdiction, so that the intent was to make restitution, and not any innovation in the proceeding or punishment: And it was observed that this last branch gave to them power to execute all the Premisses; according to the tenor and effect of the said letters patent, so that these words, "So authorised" in the said Letters Patents, hath relation only to the authority of the Letters Patent, before specified; *Viz.* such as gave to them power to visit, reform, redress, order, correct, and amend all Errors, Heresies, Scismes, Abuses, Contempts, and Enormities whatsoever; which, by any manner of Spirituall or Ecclesiasticall power, can or may lawfully be reformed, &c. These are the tenor and effect of the Letters Patent before remembered; and if any other construction shall be made;

1. It shall be against the express letters, *scilicet*,[3] said Letters Patent.

2. It shall be full of great peril and inconvenience, for then not only imprisonment of body, but confiscation of lands, goods, &c. And some corporall punishment may be imposed for Heresie, Scisme, Incontinence, &c. Also power may be given to them to burn any man for Heresie; which would be against the Common Law of the Land.

[Vide a notable Case adjudged in this point, Hill. 42 El. fol. 389. as to imprisonment, Smith's Case, for at the last Consultation was granted: And at last by the better opinion, as to things committed to them by Commission, they may put fine and imprisonment.][4]

Floyd and Barker.
(1607) Easter Term, 5 James I
In the Court of Star Chamber.
First Published in the *Reports,* volume 12, page 23.

Ed.: This note records the decision of the Chancellor and both Chief Justices that a person acquitted of murder cannot pursue for conspiracy the grand Jury who indicted him, or any of the parties to the proceedings, although he can sue someone who conspired out of court and later swore in court

---

3. [*Ed.:* that is to say,]

4. [*Ed.:* The provenance of this paragraph, from the 1656 edition, is uncertain.]

as a part of a conspiracy. Judges are immune from suit. The Case is an important basis for the Common Law immunity from suit of Judges and counsel.

In this very Term, between Rice ap Evan ap Floyd, and Richard Barker, one of the Justices of the Grand Sessions in the County of Anglesey, and other defendants: It was resolved by Popham and Coke, Chief Justices, the Chief Baron, and Egerton, Lord Chancellor, and all the Court of Star Chamber, that when a grand Inquest indicts one of Murther or Felony, and after the party is acquitted, yet no conspiracy lies for him who is acquitted, against the Indictors, for this that they are returned by the Sheriff by processe of Law to make enquiry of offences upon their Oath, and it is for the service of the King and the Common-wealth. And as it is said in the 10 Eliz. 265. they are compellable to serve the Law, and the Court: and their Indictment or Verdict is matter of Record, and called *Veredictum,*[1] and shall not be avoided by surmise or supposal, and no attaint lies, And for this reason they shall not be impeached, for any conspiracy or practice, before the Indictment: for the Law will not suppose any unindifferent, when he is sworn to serve the King: And with this agrees the Books in 22 Ass. 77. 27. Assise, p. 12. 21 Edw. 3. 17. 16 Hen. 6. 19. 47 Ed. 3. 17. 27 Hen. 8. 2. F. N. B. 115 a. But it is otherwise of a Witnesse, for if he conspire out of the Court, and after swear in the Court, his Oath shall not excuse his conspiracy before; for he is a private person, produced by the party, and not returned by the Sheriff, who is an Officer sworn, and the Jurors are sworn in Court as indifferent persons: And the Law presumes, that every juror will be indifferent when he is sworn; Nor will the Law admit proof against this presumption.

2. It was resolved, that when the party indicted is convict of Felony by another Jury, upon "Not guilty pleaded," there he never shall have a Writ of Conspiracy, but when the party upon his arraignment is *Legitimo modo acquietatus:*[2] but in the case at the Bar, the grand Jury who indicted one William Price for the murder of Hugh ap William, the Jury, who upon not guilty pleaded, convicted him, were charged in the Star Chamber for Conspiracy against him, and indicted and convicted, which manner of Complaint was

1. [*Ed.:* Verdict, (literally, "true statement").]
2. [*Ed.:* In Lawful manner acquitted.]

never seen before: for if the party shall not have a Conspiracy against the Indictors, when the Prisoner is acquitted upon his indictment, *a Multo fortiori*[3] when he is lawfully convict, he shall not charge neither the Grand Inquest by whom he was indicted, nor the Jury who found him guilty: for the Law in such Case doth not give any attaint, for this that he was indicted by the Oath of twelve men at the least, and found guilty by twelve: And in these Cases, the King is the sole party to the proceedings against the Prisoner: but on the other side, when a Jury hath acquitted a Felon or Traitor against manifest proof, there they | may be charged in the Star Chamber, for their partiality   [24] in finding a manifest Offender not guilty, *Ne maleficia remanerent impunita.*[4] And it will be a cause of infinite vexation and occasion of perjury and smothering of great Offences, if such averments and supposals shall be admitted after ordinary and judiciall proceeding: and it will be a means *Ad deterrendos et detrahendos juratores a servitio Regis.*[5]

3. It was resolved that the said Barker who was Judge of Assise, and gave judgment upon the verdict of death, against the said W. P. and the Sheriff who did execute him according to the said Judgment, nor the Justices of Peace who did examine the Offender, and the Witnesses for proof of the Murther before the Judgment, were not to be drawn in question in the Star Chamber, for any Conspiracy, nor any witnesse nor any other person ought to be charged with any Conspiracy in the Star Chamber, or elsewhere, when the party indicted is convicted or attaint of Murther or Felony: and although the Offender upon the Indictment be acquitted, yet the Judge, be he Judge of Assise, or a Justice of Peace, or any other Judge, being Judge by Commission and of Record, and sworn to do Justice, cannot be charged for Conspiracy, for that which he did openly in Court as Judge or Justice of Peace: and the Law will not admit any proof against this vehement and violent presumption of Law, that a Justice sworn to do Justice will do injustice; but if he hath conspired before out of Court, this is extrajudicial; but due examination of Causes out of Court, and inquiring by Testimonies, *Et similia,*[6] is not any Conspiracy, for this he ought to do; but subornation of Witnesses, and false and malicious

---

3. [*Ed.:* so much the more so.]
4. [*Ed.:* That wrongdoing should not remain unpunished.]
5. [*Ed.:* To deter and withdraw jurors from the service of the king.]
6. [*Ed.:* and similar [proofs],]

Persecutions, out of Court, to such whom he knowes will be Indictors, to find any guilty, &c. amounts to an unlawful Conspiracy.

And Records are of so high a nature, that for their sublimity they import verity in themselves; and none shall be received to aver any thing against the Record itself; and in this point the Law is founded upon great reason; for if the Judiciall matters of Record should be drawn in question, by partial and sinister supposals and averments of Offenders, or any on their behalf, there never will be an end of Causes: But Controversies will be infinite; *Et infinitum in jure reprobatur:*[7] and for this it is adjudged in the 47 Ed. 3. 15. that a Judge who hath a Commission, *Viz.* that is of Record, shall not be charged in Conspiracy; which is to be understood of what he did in Court, for the reasons and causes aforesaid: and with this agree the Book, 21 Ed. 4. 67. & 27 Ass. pl. 12. and the reason is for this, that though the party is acquitted, yet the accusing stands with the Record: and accordingly was the Law taken in this Case. But in an Hundred court, or other Court which not of Record, there averment may be taken against their proceedings, for that it is no other than matter *in pais,*[8] and not of Record; as it appears in the 47 Ed. 3. 15. Also one shall never assign for Error, against that which the Court doth as Judges; as to say, that the Jury gave Verdict for the Defendant, and the Court did enter it for the Plaintiff, or to say that the party *who* levied the Fine was dead before the Fine was levied, or such like. *Vide* 1 Hen. 6. 4. 39 Hen. 6. 52. 7 Hen. 7. 4. 11 Hen. 7. 28. 1 Mar. Dyer 89. But in a Writ of false Judgment, the Plaintiff

Averment.

shall have a direct averment against that which the Judges in the Inferior Court have done as Judges, *Quia Recordum non habent*[9] and with this accords 21 Hen. 6. 34. And as a Judge shall not be drawn in question in the Cases aforesaid, at the suit of the parties, no more shall he be charged in the said Cases before any other Judge at the suit of the King. And for this in the 27 Ass. pl. 18. One was indicted and arraigned at the suit of the King, that as he was a Justice of

[25]

Oyer and Terminer,[10] where certain persons were indicted | of Trespass before him, he made an entry of Record, that they were indicted of Felony: And it was adjudged that this Indictment was against the Law, for this that he was

---

7. [*Ed.:* And the infinite is to be disapproved in Law.]
8. [*Ed.:* "on the country," i.e., unsworn, or not a matter of record.]
9. [*Ed.:* Because they have no Record.]
10. [*Ed.:* A county criminal court.]

a Justice by Commission; and that is of Record; and this present act shall be to defeat the Record, *Hoc est*,[11] to aver against that which he did as Judge of Record, which cannot be by the Law. *Vide* 27 Ass. pl. 23. 2 Rich. 3. 9. 28 Ass. pl. 21. 9 Hen. 6. 60. And it was said, that it was the case of one Nudigate, who as a Justice of Peace had Recorded a Force upon a View, which he did as Judge-upon-Record; and a Bill was exhibited against him in this Court, for this, that he had falsely made a Record, where indeed there was not any Force: and by the opinion of Catlyn and Dyer, chief Justices, it was resolved, that that thing, that a Judge doth as Judge of Record, ought not to be drawn in question in this Court.

Note well, that the said matters done at the Bar were not examinable in the Star Chamber; and for this it was ordered and decreed by all the Court, that the said Bill without any answer to it, by the said Richard Barker, shall be taken off the File and cancelled, and utterly defaced: And it was agreed, that insomuch as the Judges of the Realm have the administration of Justice under the King, to all his Subjects, they ought not to be drawn into question for any supposed corruption, which extends to the annihilating of a Record, or of any judiciall proceedings before them, or tending to the Slander of the Justice of the King, which will trench to the scandal of the King himself, except it be before the King himself; For they are only to make an account to God and the King, and not to answer to any suggestion in the Star Chamber; for this would tend to the scandall and subversion of all Justice. And those who are the most sincere, would not be free from continual Calumniations, for which reason the Orator said well, *invigilandum est semper, multae insidiae sunt bonis.*[12]

And the reason and cause why a Judge, for any thing done by him as Judge, by the authority which the King hath committed to him, and as sitting in the seat of the King (concerning his Justice) shall not be drawn in question before any other Judge, for any surmise of corruption, except before the King himself, is for this; the King himself is *De jure* to deliver Justice to all his Subjects; And for this, that he himself cannot do it to all persons, he delegates his power to his Judges, who have the Custody and Guard of the King's oath.

And forasmuch as this concerns the honour and conscience of the King,

---

11. [*Ed.:* That is.]

12. [*Ed.:* one must always be on one's guard, for in good things there are many snares.]

there is great reason that the King himself shall take account of it, and no other.

And Thorp who was drawn in question for corruption, before commissioners, was held against the Law, and upon that he was pardoned; and it is contained in the same Record, *Quod non trahitur in exemplum.*[13] *Vide* the conclusion of the Oath of a Judge. *Vide* the Chronicle of Stow, 18 Edw. 3. 312.

Note, Thomas Weyland, Chief Justice of the Common-bench, Sir Ralph Hengham Justice of the Kings Bench; and the other Justices, were accused of Bribery and Corruption; and their causes were determined in Parliament, where some were banished, and some were fined and imprisoned.

Vide 2 Ed. 3. fol. 27. That the Justices of Trayl-baston[14] (so called for their summary proceeding) were in a manner Justices in Eyre; and their authority was founded upon the Statute of Ragman, which you may see in the old Magna [26] Charta, *Vide* the form of the Commission of the | Trayl-baston, Hollingshead, Chron fol. 312. And note it appears by the said President and Chronicle, that the King did examine the corruption of his Judges before himself in the Parliament, and not by force of any Commission.

Absurdum est affirmare, recredendum esse non judici.[15]

Of Oaths Before an Ecclesiasticall Judge Ex Officio.
(1606) Easter Term, 4 James I.
First Published in the *Reports,* volume 12, page 26.

Ed.: In these notes Coke records the consultation between himself and the Chief Justice Popham of the King's Bench regarding a bill then in Parliament about the procedures for investigations by an ordinary, that is a bishop hearing ecclesiastical Cases in his diocese. Their most important conclusion was that no one may be punished for crimes of thought. There is also important language regarding the Law, that it is the inheritance of the subject and cannot be deprived in any way but by an act of Parliament.

13. [*Ed.:* that it should be drawn into a precedent.]
14. [*Ed.:* Also, "trail-baston," established by the Statute of Rageman of 1276, to punish misdemeanors. By the early fifteenth century, they had been replaced by the commissions of oyer and terminer.]
15. [*Ed.:* It is absurd to affirm that the thing adjudged is to be believed and not the Judges.]

Note, Pasch. 4 Jacobi, In the time of the Parliament, the Lords of the Councell of Whitehall demanded of Popham, Chief Justice and myself, upon motion made by the Commons in Parliament, in what cases the Ordinary may examine any person *Ex officio*[1] upon oath; and, upon good consideration and view of our Books, We answered to the Lords of the Council at another day in the Councell Chamber.

The Ordi-
nary can-
not enforce
a man to
answer gen-
erall Arti-
cles *Ex Of-
ficio.*

"1. That the Ordinary cannot constrain any man, Ecclesiasticall or Temporall, to swear generally to answer to such interrogatories as shall be administered unto him; But ought to deliver to him the Articles upon which he is to be examined, to the intent that he may know whether he ought by the Law to answer to them: and so is the course of the Star-chamber and Chancery; the defendant hath the Copy of the Bill delivered unto him, or otherwise he need not to answer to it.

"2. No man Ecclesiasticall or Temporall shall be examined upon secret thoughts of his heart, or of his secret opinion: But somthing ought to be objected against him what he hath spoken or done. No Lay-man may be examined *Ex officio,* except in two Causes, and that was grounded upon great reason; for Lay-men for the most part are not lettered, wherefore they may easily be inveigled and entrapped, and principally in Heresie and Errors: And this appears by an Ordinance made in the time of Edward I. tit. Prohibition, Rastal."

The words of which Ordinance are, And *Quod non permittant quod alioqui laici in balliva sua in aliquibus locis conveniant, ad aliquas recognitiones per juramenta sua faciendas, nisi in causis matrimonialibus et testamentariis.*[2] And the reason that the Ecclesiasticall Judge shall examine them in these two Cases, is for this; that Contracts of Matrimony, and the Estates of the dead, are many times secret; and they do not concern the shame and infamy of the party, as Adultery, Incontinency, Usury, Simony, Hearing of Mass, Heresie, &c.

And for this cause in these cases, and such like, the Ecclesiasticall Judge ought not to examine *Partem ream,*[3] upon their Oath: for as a civilian said, that this was *inventio diaboli ad destruendas miserorum animas ad infernum:*[4]

---

1. [*Ed.:* Of the office.]
2. [*Ed.:* That they should not permit any laymen in their bailiwick to be convented in any places to make any recognitions by their oaths, except in matrimonial and testamentary causes.]
3. [*Ed.:* The guilty (i.e. accused) party.]
4. [*Ed.:* an invention of the Devil to drag the souls of the wretched down to Hell:]

and in the Register, fol. 36. 6. there is a Prohibition in this form, *Praecipimus tibi quod non permittas quod aliqui laici ad citationem talis Episc' aliquo loco conveniant de caetero ad aliquas recognitiones factas vel sacramenta praestanda,* (the one is the exposition of the other) *nisi in casibus matrimonialibus et testamentariis:* and there is an attachment upon it, *pone per vad' talem Episc': quod sit coram Justiciariis nostris, &c. ostensurum quare fecit summoneri, et per censuras eccles' distringi laicas personas vel laicos homines et foeminas ad comparendum coram eo ad praestandum juramentum pro voluntate sua ipsis invitis* [27] *in grave coronae praejudicium | et dignitatis nostrae Regiae, necnon contra consuetudinem regni nostri; et habeas ibi nomina plegiorum, &c. teste, &c.*[5] by which it doth appear, that this was not only against the said Ordinance, but also against the custome of the Realm, which had been time out of mind, and also in prejudice of the Crown and Dignity of the King: and with this agrees F. N. B. fol. 41. And *vide* the Case reported by the Lord Dyer, (but the Case is not printed,) Trin. 10 Eliz. one Leigh, an Attorney of the Common Pleas, was committed to the Fleet by the High Commissioners in a case Ecclesiasticall, for this, that he had been at Masse, and refused to swear to certain Articles to be proposed to him. And held, that although in such case, Ecclesiasticall Jurisdiction is saved by the Statute of 10 Eliz. yet they ought not in such case to examine upon his Oath: and hereupon he was delivered by all the Court of Common Pleas [upon the return of the matter upon a *habeas corpus.*[6]]

And in Mich. 18 Eliz. Dyer, fol. 175. in *Hind's* case, who would not swear *Commissionariis Eccles' super articulos pro usura, et ea de causa commissus est Gaolae de le Fleet.*[7] He was delivered by *Habeas corpus per totam Curiam.*[8] This was also because they could not imprison.

---

5. [*Ed.:* We command you that you should not permit any laymen at the citation of any bishop henceforth to be convented to make any recognizances or take any oaths . . . except in matrimonial and testamentary causes. (and there is an attachment upon it) Put by gage such and such a bishop that he be before our Justices, etc. to show why he caused lay persons (or lay men and women) to be summoned and to be distrained by the censures of the Church to appear before him to take an oath at his pleasure, against their will, to the grave prejudice of the crown and of our royal dignity, and also against the custom of our realm. And have their the names of the pledges, etc. Witness, etc.]

6. [*Ed.:* Writ to determine the legality of an incarceration. Note also, the bracketed text was omitted from the 1656 edition.]

7. [*Ed.:* Before the ecclesiastical commissioners upon articles for usury, and for that cause was committed to the Fleet gaol.]

8. [*Ed.:* by the whole court.]

Vide le Statute 25 H. 8. cap. 14. Which is declaratory as to this point: It standeth not with the right order of Justice nor good equity, that any person should be convict, and put to the losse of his life, good name, or goods, unless it were by due accusation, and Witnesses, or by presentment, verdict, confession, or processe of Out-lawry, &c. And it is not reasonable that any Ordinary upon suspition conceived of his own fancy, without due accusation or presentment, should put any Subject of this Realm in infamy and slander of Heresie, to the perill of life, losse of good name, or goods; (*et Paulo antea*)[9] the most expert and learned man of this Realm, diligently laying wait upon himself, cannot eschew and avoid penalty and danger, &c. if he should be examined upon such captious interrogatories, as is and hath been accustomed to be ministred by the Ordinaries of this Realm, in Case where they will suspect any man of Heresie: and this was the Judgment of all the said Parliament. See F. N. B. Justice of Peace 72. Lamb, in his Justice of Peace 338. Crompt. in his Justice of Peace 36. 6. In all which it appears, that if any be compelled to answer upon his Oath, where he ought not by the Law, that this is oppression and punishable before a Justice of Peace, a Justice of Assise, &c. for this is an Article of charge, to enquire of all Oppressions: And as to that which was objected, that for a very long time, divers had been examined upon Oath in Ecclesiasticall Courts; as to this it was answered, that it might very well be, and not against Law, for the words of the Treatise or Ordinance, and of the Register, are, *Contra voluntatem eorum, &c.*[10] So that if any assent to it, and take it without exception, that is not *Contra voluntatem eorum,* But to enforce any to take it, who ought not to take it by the Law, is a great oppression; but if any person Ecclesiasticall be charged with any thing which is punishable by our Law, as for usury, &c. there he shall not be examined upon Oath, for this, that his oath is evidence against him at the Common Law, and to do it incurs the penalty of the Statute: but witnesses may be cited to testifie. Register, tit. Consult. F. N. B. 53d. Also by the Statute 2 Hen. 4. cap. 15. it is provided, that *Dictus Diocessanus per se vel per Commissarios suos contra hujusmodi personas, &c. Et ad omne juris effectum, publice et judicialiter procedat et negotium hujusmodi, &c. terminet juxta canonicas sanctiones,* which words, *Juxta Canonicas sanctiones,*[11] give them power to proceed according to their Cannons,

---

9. [*Ed.:* and Paul before, an apparent reference to the trials of St. Paul. Acts 22–28.]

10. [*Ed.:* against their will, etc.]

11. [*Ed.:* the diocesan, by himself or by his commissaries, should proceed publicly and judicially against

and excludes the Common Law; and by pretext of this in the cases mentioned
[28] in the said act, they examined as well Lay-people as | Clerks, upon their Oaths
concerning Heresie, erroneous Opinions, &c. mentioned in the said act in
the Reign of Henry the fourth, Henry the fifth, Henry the sixth, Edward the
fourth, Richard the third, Henry the seventh unto the time of the said Act
of 25 Hen. 8. And for this in the reign of Henry the eighth nor in the reign
of Edward the sixth no layman was examined upon his Oath, except in the
said two Cases of Matrimony and Wills: but in the Raign of Queen Mary,
this Act of 2 Hen. 4. was revived; and then all the Martyrs who were burnt
were examined upon their Oaths: and afterwards by the 10th Eliz. the said
Act of 2 Hen. 4. is repealed, by which the Common-Law is in full force and
effect: And for this cause all the pretence of possession and practice which the
Ecclesiasticall Courts have had is strongly answered by this which hath been
said, that the words of the said Treatise and Register are, *Contra voluntatem
eorum, &c.* And those who have so taken it have assented to it, and that stands
with Law.

Note, that King John[12] after he had murthered his Nephew Arthur, and
Neice Ellenor, the Issue of his elder Brother Geffrey, after he had lost Normandy, Aquitain, and Anjowe, after that his Commons for unjust vexation
disobeyed him, his Nobles revolted from him, the Clergy oppressed by him,
and that he stood excommunicated by the Pope, and his Kingdom interdicted,
he for his protection, granted by his Charter of *13 Maii, anno regni 14.* sub-
mitted himself to the obedience of the Pope: And after in the fourteenth year
of his Raign, as one destitute of all succour and safety, and from day to day
in fear to lose his Crown, by another charter he resigned his Crown and Realm
to the Pope Innocent and his Successors, by the hands of Pandolph his Legate,
and took it of him again to hold of the Pope, which was utterly void, for this,
that the Dignity is an inherent, inseparable to the Royall blood of the King,
and descendable to the next of blood of the King, and cannot be transferred
to another, no more then a Duke, or Earl, or Baron, or other Dignity, may
transfer over their Dignity, for these are incidents inseparable; also the Pope
was an Alien born, and therefore was not capable of Inheritance within En-

---

such persons, etc. to the full effect of the Law, and determine such business, etc. in accordance with the
canonical rules.]

12. Math. Paris, 225, 226, 227, &c.

gland: By colour of which submission and resignation, the Pope and his Successors exacted great summs of the Clergy and Layity of England, *Pro commutandis poenitentiis,*[13] to maintain the height and dignity of the Pope: And for the better inriching of the Coffers of the Pope, Pope Gregory the ninth sent Otho Cardinalis de Carcere Tulliano, into this Realm, when there was indignation betwixt Henry the third and his Nobles, to collect money for the Pope, who did collect infinite summs of money, so that it was said of him, *Quod legatus saginatur bonis Angliae,*[14] which Legate held his Councell at London, anno Domini 1237, and 22 Hen. 3. And for the better finding out Offences which should be redeemed with money, he, with the assent of the Bishops of England there assembled, made divers Cannons, amongst which one was, *Jus jurandi Calumniae in causis ecclesiasticis cujuslibet, et de veritate dicendi in spiritualibus quoque, ut veritas facilius aperiatur et Causae celerius determinentur, Statuimus de Caetero prestari in Regno Angliae secundum Canonicas et legitimas Sanctiones, obtenta in contrarium Consuetudine non obstante, &c.*[15]

By which Cannon it appears that the Law and Custom of England was against this examination of the party Defendant upon his Oath, for it is said, *Statuimus de Caetero prestari in regno Angliae,*[16] so that this was a new Law, and took its effect *De caetero.*[17]

2. *Obtenta in contrarium Consuetudine non obstante.*[18] And this very well agrees with the Register and the said Treatise *De Regia prohibitione,* And the other Authorities, That the Law and Custom of England l was, that Lay-people [29] in criminall causes, be they Ecclesiastical or Temporall, shall not be examined upon their Oath (only in causes matrimoniall and testamentary) otherwise it is of Clerks, as is aforesaid: And for this, that it appears by the said Cannon it self, that this was against the Law and Custom of England; whence it follows that this Cannon shall not bind, for that the Law and Customs of England

---

13. [*Ed.:* For commuting penances,]

14. [*Ed.:* That the legate grew fat on the plenty of England,]

15. [*Ed.:* We have enacted that an oath of accusation in ecclesiastical causes, and also for saying the truth in spiritual matters, so that the truth may more readily appear, and causes be more speedily determined, shall from henceforth be taken in the realm of England in accordance with the canonical and Lawful rules, any custom obtaining to the contrary notwithstanding, etc.]

16. [*Ed.:* We have enacted that from henceforth it shall be taken in England.]

17. [*Ed.:* From henceforth.]

18. [*Ed.:* Any custom obtaining to the contrary notwithstanding.]

cannot be changed without an Act of Parliament, for this, that the Law and Custom of England is the Inheritance of [the subject,][19] which he cannot be deprived of without his assent in Parliament: And it appears in Linwood, cap. Jure jurandi, fol. 8. 6. That Boniface, Bishop of Canterbury, anno 1272. and 57 Hen. 3. a little before the death of that King made this Cannon, *Statuimus quod Laici de subditorum peccatis et excessibus corrigendis per praelatos et judices ecclesiasticas inquiratur ad praestandum de veritate dicenda sacramentum per excommunicationis sententias. Si opus fuerit compellantur impedientes, vero ne hujusmodi juramentum praestetur per interdicae est excommunicatio sententia arceantur.*[20] In which Cannon it is to be observed, that this extends to Lay-people; for, as appears, the Ecclesiastical Judge may examine those of the Clergy upon their Oathes; and note, Linwood, cap. Jure jurando, fol. 6. litera E. saith so. *Hic dicitur causa editionis hujus statuti, viz. Praelati Ecclesiastici procedebant ad inquirendum de criminibus et excessibus subditorum suorum et laïci (nota hic) suffulti potestate dominorum temporalium in hujusmodi inquisitionibus noluerunt jurare de veritate dicenda.*[21]

Note well what the cause was, why Lay-people refused to be examined for Crimes and Excess.

2. It appears, that the Judges of the Common Law by their Prohibition did interdict, &c. as it appears by the Register and the other Authorities; in the time of Edward I. and other Kings, Incroachments were made upon the Subjects, which are here called *Impedimentes,* but now the canon saith *Impellat.*[22]

3. That where by the Law they may examine Lay-people upon their Oath, *In Causis matrimonialibus et testamentariis,*[23] here Boniface makes this Cannon to extend to *Peccata et excessus,*[24] which Cannon was utterly against the Law and Custome of England. In like manner another was made by him at the same time, Linwood, cap. De benef. fol. 231. which Cannon being made di-

---

19. [*Ed.:* Bracketed text omitted from the 1656 edition.]

20. [*Ed.:* We have enacted that laymen (who enquire) of the offences and excesses of subjects, which are to be corrected by bishops and ecclesiastical Judges, may take an oath to speak the truth under sentence of excommunication. If need be hinderers may be compelled . . .]

21. [*Ed.:* Here is stated the reason for the promulgation of this Statute, that is to say, that prelates of the Church proceeded to enquire of the crimes and excesses of their subjects, and laymen (note this), supporting the power of temporal lords, would not swear to say the truth in such inquisitions.]

22. [*Ed.:* Compel.]

23. [*Ed.:* In matrimonial and testamentary causes,]

24. [*Ed.:* Wrongs and excess,]

rectly against the Judges, who did award processe against them, if they did impose any pecuniary pain: And prohibites them the Judges with fear of excommunication, the Cannon being against Law, [the Judges]²⁵ prohibites them notwithstanding this thundering of Excommunication in all ages. And the scope and purpose of the said Cannon was to perplex the Subjects, and to enrich themselves by punishment pecuniary; And this is declared by Act of Parliament made 9 Ed. 2. called Articuli Cleri. *Si praelati imponant Paenam pecuniariam alicui pro peccato, &c. Regia prohibitio locum habet.*²⁶ [Note this.]²⁷

Of Pardons.
(1607) Trinity Term, 5* James I.
Commentary.
First Published in the *Reports,* volume 12, page 29.

> *Ed.:* In this note, Coke describes limits on the king's power to pardon, which may not be used to abrogate guilt but only punishment, which may not be granted in advance of an offense, and which may only be granted for crimes that are *malum prohibitum,* which is to say are wrong as a matter of Law, and not crimes that are *malum in se,* or wrong by their very nature.

Nota, the Law so regards the Weal-publick, that although that the King shall have the suit solely in his name for the redress of it, yet by his pardon he cannot discharge the Offender, for this, that it is not only in prejudice of the King, but in damage of the Subjects. As well for according of infinite Suits they cannot have private actions, and for that reason the Suit is given to the King, not only for himself, but also for all his Subjects, | as if a man ought to repair a Bridge, and for default of reparation it falls into decay: In this case the Suit ought to be in the name of the King, and the King is sole party to the Suit, but for the benefit of all his Subjects. And for this, if the King pardon

Bonum publicum.

[30]

25. [*Ed.:* Bracketed text omitted in the 1656 edition.]

26. [*Ed.:* If prelates impose a pecuniary penalty on anyone for an offence, etc. a royal prohibition shall be available.]

27. [*Ed.:* Bracketed text omitted in the 1656 edition.]

*[*Ed.:* Note the 1656 and 1658 editions record this as "5 Jac. I," which would be 1607. Later editions record this note as dated "7 Jac. I," or 1609.]

it, yet the Offence remains; and in any Suit in the name of the King, for redress of it, the Offender ought (notwithstanding the pardon) to make and repair the Bridge for the benefit of the Weal-publick: but peradventure the pardon shall discharge the Fine for the time past; And with this agrees, 37 Hen. 6. 4. 6. Plow. Com. in *Nicol's Case,* 487. where the words of the Law are; If a Bridge or a High-way is repairable by the Subject, and is in decay, the pardon of the King shall not excuse him which ought to do it, for this, that the other Subjects of the King have interest in it. But note, if the pardon in such case shall discharge the Fine, for inasmuch as the Offence cannot be pardoned, this cannot discharge the Fine, but only for the time before the pardon: but for the time after the pardon, without question the Offender for his default shall be fined and imprisoned; the same Law, and *A multo fortiori*[1] in case of Depopulation; for this is not only an Offence against the King, but against all the Realm; for by this the Realm is enfeebled; idle and dissolute people which are Enemies to the Common-wealth, abound: And for this cause De-population and diminution of Subjects is a greater nuisance and offence to the Weal-publick, than the hindrance of the Subjects in their good and easy passage by any Bridge or High-way: And for this, notwithstanding the pardon of the King, he shall be bound to re-edifie the houses of Husbandry which he hath depopulated, but peradventure for the time before the pardon he shall not be fined, but for the time after without doubt he shall be fined and im-prisoned, for the Offence it self cannot be pardoned, as in the case of a Bridge or High-way; *Quia est malum in se:*[2] But this continues as to the Fine and Imprisonment at all times after the Pardon; but the penalty inflicted by the Statute that may be discharged, *Quia prohibitum.*[3] *Vide* 3 Ed. 3. tit Ass. 443. Where an Abbot was bound to repair a Bridge by Prescription, and after the King by his Charter discharged him, which Charter was allowed in a *Quo warranto.*[4] And after the Abbot was indicted at the Suit of the King, for default of reparation of the said Bridge, and he pleaded the said Charter and allowance: And notwithstanding it was adjudged that he should repair the said Bridge, for this, that although the Suit be in the name of the King for the Offence,

---

1. [*Ed.:* So much the more so.]
2. [*Ed.:* Because it is wrong in itself.]
3. [*Ed.:* Because it is (a wrong only) by reason of prohibition.]
4. [*Ed.:* Writ of right brought by the King against anyone who usurped or exceeded the scope of a franchise or office.]

yet the King cannot discharge it, for this, that it shall be to the prejudice and damage of his subjects: but when the King chargeth his subjects for the making of a bridge, or causey, or wall, &c. there the King may discharge of the pontage, murage, &c. But when one is bound by prescription or tenure, &c. to repair a bridge, &c. there the King cannot discharge of it. And all this appears in the said Book.

And note,[5] if one be bound to the King in a Recognizance for to keep the peace against one and other the Liege people of the King, in this case the King, before the Peace broken cannot pardon or release the Recognizance, as it is agreed in 11 Hen. 4. 43. 37 Hen. 6. 4. 1 Hen. 7. 10. And the reason is, although the recognizance be made to the King solely; yet inasmuch as this is made for the benefit and safety of the subjects of the King, in such Case it cannot be discharged.

Note, no licence can be made to do any thing that is *malum in se*,[6] but *malum prohibitum*[7] may. 11 Hen. 7. 11. 3 Hen. 7. 39 Hen. 6. 39.

Customs, Subsidies, and Impositions.
(Bates's Case).
Commentary.
First Published in the *Reports,* volume 12, page 33.

> *Ed.:* Note of a conference between Coke and Popham, then the Chief Justice of the King's Bench, in which they resolve that the King is limited in placing tariffs and customs on goods entering the kingdom, unless the proceeds are for the benefit of trade, that imports of goods except wool and leather are free of customs under the Common Law, and that money raised in this manner cannot be given to a subject. Taxes for maintenance of public structures should be apportioned to those who benefit from them. Further, they agreed that the King may prohibit a foreigner from entry but only for the public good.

Note, upon conference between Popham, chief Justice, and my self, upon a Judgment given lately in the Exchequer, concerning the imposition of Cur-

Customs, Subsidies, and Impositions.

---

5. Vid. 35 Hen. 6 29 per Fortescue & 16 Ed. 3. grant 53.
6. [*Ed.:* wrong in itself,]
7. [*Ed.:* a wrong [only] by reason of prohibition.]

rants: And upon consideration of our Books, and of Statutes to this purpose: It appeared to us that the rule of the Common Law is in the Register, Title Ad quod Dampnum, and F. N. B. 222a. *quod patria magis solito non oneretur seu gravetur.*[1] Also there is another Rule, that the King may charge his people of this Realm without speciall assent of the Commons, to a thing which may be of profit to the common people, but not to their charge; As it is held in the 13 of Hen. 4. 16. *Et Statutum de Tallagio non concedendo, Nullum Tallagium, seu Auxilium per nos, seu heredes nostros ponatur seu levetur absque voluntate et assensu Parliamenti. Et Magna Charta, cap.* 30. *Omnes Mercatores (Nisi publice antea Prohibiti fuerint) habeant Salvum et securum conductum abire de Anglia et venire in Angliam, et morari et ire per Angliam, tam per terram quam per aquam, ad eniendum et vendendum sine omnibus malis Toluetis per antiquas et rectas consuetudines, praeterquam in Tempore Guerrae;*[2] which Statute hath been confirmed more than thirty times by severall Acts of Parliament, *vide le Statute* 25 Ed. 1. 3 Ed. 1. in turri, 9 Ed. 3. cap. 1, & 2. 14 Ed. 3. 2. 25 Ed. 3. cap. 2. &c. The effect of which is, that every Merchant of this Realm, or other, may freely buy, sell, and passe the Sea with all their Merchandizes, paying the Customs of ancient time used. Queen Mary put an imposition upon Cloathes, which the 1 Eliz. Dyer 165. was moved and not resolved, *vide* 31 Hen. 8. Dyer fol. 43. & 1 Eliz. 165. *Magna Custuma et parva Custuma,*[3] *vide* 9 Hen. 6. 12 & 35. And note there the saying of Babington. Note the 1 Eliz. Dyer 165. there was *Antiqua sive magna Custuma*[4] at the Common Law, *scil.* for Wools, wool-Fels, and Leather, and this was equall to strangers as well as Denizens. And in the time of Ed. 1. a Merchant stranger, grants over the said Customs, 3s. 4d. which is called *Nova seu parva Custuma.*[5]

Upon all which and divers Records which we had seen, it appeared to us, that the King cannot at his pleasure put any Imposition upon any Merchandize

1. [*Ed.:* that the country should not be more burdened or harmed than is usual.]

2. [*Ed.:* The Statute for not granting tallage [provides that] no tallage or aid shall be imposed or levied by us or our heirs without the will and consent of parliament.

And Magna Carta, ch. 30: All merchants (unless they were openly prohibited before) shall have safe and sure conduct to leave England, and come into England, and to stay and go throughout England, both by land and by water, to buy and sell without any evil tolls, by the ancient and rightful customs, except in time of war;]

3. [*Ed.:* Great customs and petty customs,]

4. [*Ed.:* An ancient or great custom.]

5. [*Ed.:* A new or petty custom.]

to be imported into this Kingdom, or exported, unlesse it be for advancement of Trade and Traffic, which is the life of every Island, *Pro bono publico.*[6] As if in foreign parts any imposition is put upon the Merchandizes of our Merchants, *Non pro bono publico,*[7] and for to make equality, for the purpose to advance Trade and Traffick, the King may put an Imposition upon their Merchandizes, for this is not against any of the Statutes which were made for advancement of merchandize, or of the Statutes which were made for advancement of Merchandize, or of the Statute of Magna Charta, cap. 30. which is, *Si aliqui Mercatores de terra contra nos guerrina inveniantur in terra nostra in principio guerrae attachientur, &c. Quo modo mercatores terrae nostrae tractantur qui nunc inveniantur in terra illa, contra nos guerrina: Et si nostra salvi sunt ibi, illi salvi sunt in terra nostra;*[8] for the end of all such restraints is *Salus populi:*[9] And so in the case of Currants, which was now lately adjudged in the Exchequer: also in the case of *Customer Smith,* which was adjudged in the Exchequer, in the reign of Queen Elizabeth both the Impositions were imposed, upon the said reason to make equality, for this was the truth of both cases (*Scil.*) The advancement of Trade and Traffick, and for this cause such Impositions were lawfull.   [34]

And it was clearly resolved by us, that such Impositions so put, cannot be demised or granted to any Subject, for this, that it is to augment and decrease, or be quite taken away upon just occasion for advancement of Merchandize. And this was one of the reasons in *Customer Smiths case,* that it could not be enused; also it was assessed after the Demise.

And although that the King may prohibit any person in some cases with some Commodities to passe out of the Realm, yet this cannot be where the end is private, but where the end is publick, Viz. To restrain the person for this, that, *Quam plurima nobis et Coronae nostrae prejudicialia in partibus exteris*

---

6. [*Ed.:* For the public good.]

7. [*Ed.:* Not for the public good.]

8. [*Ed.:* If any merchants from a land at war with us are found into our land at the beginning of the war, they shall be attached, etc. (until it is known) how the merchants of our land are treated when they are found in the land making war against us; and if our merchants are safe there, they shall be safe in our land.]

9. [*Ed.:* The weal of the people.]

prosequi intendit,[10] and to restrain any Merchandizes either in time of Dearth, or in time of War, for *Necessitas est lex temporis.*[11]

It appeared unto us also, that at the Common Law no Custom was paid, but only for wools, Wool-fels, and Leather, which is called in Magna Charta, *Recta consuetudo;*[12] and all others are there called *Mala tolneta.*[13] which in the Statute De Tallagio non concedendo is called *Male.* And at the beginning of the Raign of Kings, it hath for a long time been used, by authority and consent of Parliament, to grant to the King certain subsidies of Tonnage and Poundage, for term of his life, which began in such form, 2 & 3 Hen. 5. in the 31 Hen. 6. c. 8. & 12 Ed. 4. c. 3. for the Defence of the Realm, and maintenance of certain Wars, by act of Parliament, which proves, that the King by his own power cannot impose it, but by consent of Parliament; but such subsidy of Tonnage and Poundage might be granted by the King so long as he lived; for this, that this is limited and given to the King in certain: But an Imposition put for equality, as hath been said, hath not any certain continuance, but is to be augmented, diminished, or taken away, for the benefit of the Common-wealth: And for that cause it cannot be demised, *vide* 31 Hen. 8. Dyer 43. 1 Mar. D. 92. 1 Eliz. Dyer. 165. 2, & 3 P. & M. D. 128. 12 Eliz. Dyer. 296. 23 Eliz. Dyer. 375. 45 Ed. 3. cap. 4. 27 Ass. pl. 44. Register 192, &c.

Vide M. Ch. cap. 30. they are called *Consuetudines, et per vocabulum artis,*[14] they are called *Custuma, vide le Statute* 51 Hen. 3. Title Exchequer in Rastall: It appears that there were ancient Customs, and those were for Wools, Wool-fels, and Leather, *vide le Statute* 9 Ed. 3. cap. 2. That all Charters and Letters Patents against free Trade and Traffick, made, or to be made, are void.

Vide Fortescue in his Comment of the Lawes of England, cap. 36. fol. 43. *Neque Lex per se vel per ministros suos Tallagia, subsidia, aut quaevis alia onera imponit Legeis suis aut leges eorum mutat, vel novas condit, sine concessione et assensu totius Regni sui in Parliamento suo expresso, &c.*[15] *vide* fol. 13. cap. 9.

---

10. [*Ed.:* That he intends to pursue many things prejudicial to us and to our crown in foreign parts.]

11. [*Ed.:* necessity is the Law of the time.]

12. [*Ed.:* Rightful custom.]

13. [*Ed.:* Evil toll.]

14. [*Ed.:* Customs; and in technical vocabulary.]

15. [*Ed.:* Nor does the king, either by himself or his ministers, impose tallages, subsidies, or any other burdens whatever upon his liege subjects, or change their Laws, or make new ones, without the concession and consent of his whole realm expressed in his parliament, etc.]

And note for the benefit of the Subject, the King may make an Imposition or Toll within the Realm, to repair High-waies, Bridges, and to make Walls for defence: But then the summ imposed ought to be proportionable to the benefit: And this appears the 13 Hen. 4. 16. So the Imposition for equality ought to be for the public good, see the Charter 31 Ed. 1. which is called *Charta mercatoria, ex Rot. mercator. an.* 31 *Ed.* 1. *n.* 42. *Patents* 3 *Ed.* 1. *n.* 1 *et* 9. *de sacco lanae dimidium marcae; lasta coriorum, 1 Mark, &c. Fines* 3 *Ed.* 1. *n.* 24. *intus et non in dorso, vide Rot. Parliament. an.* 13 *Ed.* 3.[16] No new Enhancement of Customs without | common consent: And in 22 Ed. 3. n. 8. against new [35] Customs and Impositions, and that Merchants may freely passe, &c. And in the Parliament An. 8 Hen. 6. n. 29. Amongst the new Impositions granted by Henry the fifth upon Merchandizes coming to Burdeaux: And Parliament 28 Hen. 6. n. 35. the Duke of Somerset accused for causing the King to grant unto Sir Peirce Bracy an Imposition of Wines.

Parl. 9 R. 2. n. 30. against a Patent made to the Lieutenant of the Tower, by colour of which he took Custom of Wine, Oysters, and other Victuals to be void.

29 Ed. 3. 11 n. Ex Rot. Parliamenti, Subsidy of Wools granted for six years, so as during the same time no other aid or imposition be laid upon the Commons.

Parliament 5 Ed. 3. n. 17, 18, 19. against new Impositions upon Staple Commodities, Parl. 22 Ed. 3. n. 31. against Alnage of Worsteds, 5 Ed. 3. n. 163. against all new Impositions, and 5 Ed. 3. n. 191. 38. Ed. 3. n. 26. Rot. Parl. against unreasonable Impositions.

Parl. 7 Ric. 2. n. 35, 36. 9 Ric. 2. n. 30. No Inquisitions or Taxes without consent of Parliament.

Note 2 Ric. 2 Parl. apud Glocestriam, act 25. Subsidy only for defensive Wars, not for invasive, 1 R. 2. Parl. accord. 1 Ric. 3. against Benevolence, *vide* Claus. 4 Ed. 3. n. 22. *bis.*

---

16. [*Ed.:* The Merchants' Charter, from the merchants' rolls of the thirty-first year of Edward I, number 42. Patent (roll) for the third year of Edward I, numbers 1 and 9: for a sack of wool, half a mark; for a last of leather, one mark, and so forth. Fine (rolls) for the third year of Edward I, number 24, inside and not on the dorse. See the rolls of parliament for the thirteenth year of Edward III.]

Buggery.[1]
(1607) Michaelmas Term, 5 James I.
Commentary.
First Published in the *Reports,* volume 12, page 36.

> *Ed.:* This note considers the history and criminalization of certain sexual acts.

Nota, Bugarone Italice, *is a Buggerer, and* Buggerare *is to* buggar, *so Buggary cometh of the Italian word.*

Corone,
Buggery.

The Letter of the Statute of the 25 Hen. 8. cap. 6. If any person shall commit the detestable sin of Buggary with Man-kind, or Beast, &c. it is Felony, which act being repealed by the Statute, 1 Mar. is revived and made perpetuall by 5 Eliz. cap. 17. And he shall lose his Clergy.

It appears by the ancient Authorities of Law, that this was Felony; but they vary in the punishment, for Brit. who writ 5 Ed. 1. cap. 17. saith, that "Sorcerers, Sodomers and Heretics," shall be burned. F. N. B. 269 a. agrees with it: But Flet. lib. 1. cap. 35. *Christiani autem Apostasi, fortilegi & hujus modi & comburi* (in this he agrees with Britton, *Pecorantes et sodomitae terra vivi suffodiantur*).[2]

[37] But in the ancient Book | called the Mirror of Justice vouched in Plowden's Commentaries in *Fogosse's case,* the Crime is more high; for there it is called, *Crimen laesae Majestatis,*[3] a sin horrible, committed against the King: And this is either against the King Celestiall or Terrestrial in three manners: by Heresie, by Buggary, by Sodomy. Note, that Sodomy is with Mankind, and it is Felony by the Statute of 25 Hen. 8.; and therefore the judgment for felony doth now belong to this offence, viz. to be hanged by the neck till he be dead. To make that Offence, *Oportet rem penetrare, et semen naturae emittere, et effundere,* for the Indictment is *Contra ordinationem Creatoris et naturae ordinem rem habuit veneream, dictumque puerum carnaliter cognovit.*[4] Every of which (*rem habuit,*

---

1. [*Ed.:* The word is spelled "Buggary" in the 1656 edition.]

2. [*Ed.:* Apostate Christians should be drawn and burned. . . . Unnatural offenders and sodomites shall be buried alive in the ground.]

3. [*Ed.:* A crime of lèse-majesté (treason).]

4. [*Ed.:* It is requisite to penetrate the 'thing' (*rem*), and to emit and shed the seed of nature, (for the indictment is:) against the ordinance of the Creator and the order of nature, he had venery and carnal knowledge of the said boy.]

et carnaliter cognovit[5]) imply penetration and emission of seed: And so it was held in the case of *Stafford,* who was attaint in the King's Bench and executed. *Paederastes amator puerorum,*[6] whereof the Greek word is, Παιδεραςία, Buggary with boys, *vide* Rot. Parliament. 50 Edw. 3. 58. complained in Parliament that a Lumbard did commit the sin that was not to be named: So in Rape, there ought to be penetration and emission of Seed, *vide* Stamfford fol. 44. Which Statute makes it Felony; he who procures, &c. or receives the Offender, &c. is accessary.

The words of the Statute of West. 1. cap. 34. If a man ravish a woman, 11 Hen. 4. 18. If one aid another to commit Rape, and if he be present, he is principal in the Buggary, &c, *vide* Leviticus 18, 22. and cap. 10, 13. 1 Cor. 6. ver. 9, &c.

Premunire.

(1606) Easter Term, 4 James I.
First Published in the *Reports,* volume 12, page 37.

> *Ed.:* This note discusses Coke's view of the premunire, the writ by which a Common Law court may bar an ecclesiastical court from hearing a case brought by a plaintiff that was in the jurisdiction not of the church court but of the Law court. If the Case begins appropriately in a church court, but as it develops it appears to be more appropriately a Law Case, the Law courts may issue a writ of prohibition against further proceedings in the church court.

Note in the Book of Doctor Cosines, intituled an Answer, &c. to the Abstract, and published 1584. And a Pamphlet now lately published by Doctor Ridley, they would obtrude upon the World, That forasmuch as that now by the act of 10 Eliz. cap. 1. all Spiritual and Ecclesiasticall power within this Realm is annexed to the Crown, and the Law by which they determine causes, which belongs to their Cognizance, is the Ecclesiasticall Law of the King: That for that cause no Premunire lies against any Spirituall Judge for any Cause whatsoever. And some other of their Profession have some other reasons to confirm it.

Premunire. Vide 15 H. 7. 9. Premunire was at the Common Law.

---

5. [*Ed.:* had [venery] and carnally knew.]
6. [*Ed.:* A pederast, a lover of boys.]

1. That when the Statute of Premunire was made, Viz. in the Raign of the Kings Edward the third and Richard the second then the Pope usurped Ecclesiasticall Jurisdiction, although that *De jure*[1] it belonged to the King. And therefore, forasmuch as the King is as well *De facto*,[2] as *De jure,* supream head of all, as well Ecclesiasticall as Temporall; now the Cause being changed the Law is changed also.

2. The conclusion of the Writ of *Premunire* is in *Domini Regis contemptum et praejudicium, et dictae Coronae dignitatum suarum laesionem et exhaeredationem manifestam, et contra formam statuti, &c.*[3] Which proves that the Jurisdictions shall be now severed and united to the Crown; For that which is united to, and derived from the Crown, cannot be said *contra Coronam et dignitatem Regis.*[4]

3. The Court of high Commission is the Court of the King, and is by force of an act of Parliament, and Letters Patents of the King: And for this, although it may be said, that the Consistory Courts are *Curiae episcoporum,*[5] yet the Court by force of high Commission is the Court of the King: And for that reason their proceedings shall not be subject to Premunire.

4. This new Court is erected by act of Parliament, and Letters Patents of the King: And for this, where the Statute of Ric. 2. speaks *De Curia Romana seu alibi, &c.*[6] This (*alibi*) cannot extend to a Court erected by Parliament, Anno 10 Reg. Eliz.

[38]   But to these Objections it was answered and resolved by divers Justices | in this very Term, that without question the Statutes 37 Edw. 3. 16 R. 2. &c. De Premunire, are yet in force: And all such proceedings, by colour of Ecclesiasticall Law before any Ecclesiasticall Judges, who were in danger of Premunire, before the said act 1 Eliz. are now in case of Premunire after the said act; be it before the Commissioners by force of a high Commission, or before Bishops or other Ecclesiasticall Judges: For the said acts of Premunire are not repealed by the said act 1 Eliz.

---

1. [*Ed.:* In Law.]

2. [*Ed.:* As a matter of fact,]

3. [*Ed.:* In contempt and prejudice of the lord king, and to the harm and manifest disinheritance of his said crown and dignity, and against the form of the Statute, etc.]

4. [*Ed.:* against the king's crown and dignity.]

5. [*Ed.:* Bishops' courts.]

6. [*Ed.:* Of the Roman Curia or elsewhere, etc.]

And as to the first and second Objections, it was answered, that true it is, that the Crown of England hath as well Ecclesiasticall as Temporall Jurisdiction, *De jure* annexed to it, as appears by the Resolution in *Cawdries case,* from age to age: And although this was *De jure,* yet when the Pope became so potent and powerfull, he did usurp upon the King's Ecclesiasticall Jurisdiction within this Realm; but this was but meer usurpation (for the King cannot be put out of the possession of any thing which belongs to his Crown:) And for this reason, all the Kings of this Realm *Totis viribus proinde*[7] for the establishment of their temporall Law, by which they inherit the Crown, and by which they govern their Subjects in Peace, and punish those who are rebellious, or who commit great Offences against them and their Crown: And they were always jealous lest any part or point of their temporall Law should be encroached upon: And for this, if the Ecclesiasticall Law usurp any thing upon the temporall Law, this was severely punished: And the Offender esteemed and adjudged an Enemy to the King by the ancient Statutes; and every one might have killed him before the Statute 5 Eliz. and this is the reason for why; although both Jurisdictions belong to the Crown, yet inasmuch as the Crown itself is directed and descendable by the Common Law, and all Treason against the Crown punished by this Law; for this cause, when the Ecclesiasticall Judge usurps upon the Common Law, it is said *Contra Coronam et dignitatem, &c.*[8] And all the Prohibitions directed to the high Commissioners from year to year, from the time of the making of the said Statute 1 Eliz. doth conclude, *Contra Coronam et dignitatem Regiam.*[9]

For, as it was resolved by all the Justices, Pasch. 4 Jac. Regis, *est contra Coronam et dignitatem Regiam,* when any Ecclesiastical Judge doth usurp upon the temporal Law, because as in all those writs it appeareth, the interest or cause of the Subject is drawn *ad aliud examen,* that is, when the Subject ought to have his cause ended by the Common Law, whereunto by Birthright he is inheritable, he is drawn *in aliud examen*[10] (viz.) to be decided and determined by the Ecclesiasticall Law: And this is truly said *Contra Coronam et dignitatem Regiam.*[11] And this appears by all the Prohibitions (which are infinite) which

---

7. [*Ed.:* Provide with all their might.]
8. [*Ed.:* Against the crown and dignity, etc.]
9. [*Ed.:* Against the royal crown and dignity, etc.]
10. [*Ed.:* into another forum.]
11. [*Ed.:* Against the royal crown and dignity.]

have been directed to the high Commissioners and others after the said act
1 Eliz. *A fortiori,* he who offends in *premunire* shall be said to offend *Contra
Coronam et dignitatem regiam:* And this in effect answers to all the aforesaid
Objections; but yet other particular answers shall be given to every of them.

As to the third, although the Court by force of high Commission is the
Court of the King, yet their proceedings are Ecclesiasticall: And for this, if
they usurp upon the Temporall Law, this is the same Offence which was before
the said act of 10 Eliz. For this was the end of all the ancient acts, that the
Temporall Law shall not in any manner be emblemished by any Ecclesiasticall
proceedings.

As to the fourth, although it be a new Court, yet the ancient Statutes extend
to it within this word *Alibi,* and divers new Bishopricks were erected in the
time of Henry the eighth And yet there was never any question, but that |
the ancient Acts of Premunire extended to them.

But to answer to all the Objections aforesaid, founded upon the said Statute
of 1 Eliz. out of the words and meaning of the same act; For whereas the act
1 Eliz. repealed the Statute of 1 & 2 P. M. c. 8. there is an expresse Proviso in
the said act 1 Eliz. that that shall not extend to repeale any clause, matter, or
sentence contained or specified in the 1 & 2 P. M. which in any sort toucheth
or concerneth any matter or cause of *Premunire;* But that all of that, which
doth touch or concern any matter of *Premunire,* shall stand in force and effect:
and the clause of 1 & 2 P. M. which concerns matter of *Premunire,* is such,
every person who by any processe out of any Ecclesiasticall Court of the Realm,
or out of it, or by pretence of any Spirituall Jurisdiction, or otherwise, contrary
to the Lawes of the land, unquiet or molest any man for any thing, parcel of
the possession of any Religious house, shall incur the danger of the act of
Premunire, An. 16 Ric. 2. which proves that as well the act 1 & 2 P. M. as the
act 1 Eliz. which creates the high Commission Court, which refers to the act
of 1 & 2 P. M. intends by express words, that the act of 16 Ric. 2 of Premunire
shall stand in force: Also the act of 1 Eliz. revives the Act of 25 Hen. 8. cap.
10. which makes a *Premunire* in a Dean and Chapter, &c. for not electing,
nor certifying, or not admitting of any Bishop elected; by which it is directly
proved, that the act 1 Eliz. never intended to take away the offence of *Premunire,* but expressly provided for it, as appears by that which hath been said.

But then we are to note in what Cases a Premunire lies, in what not.

And for this, that it is so penal, it is necessary that it should be explained
and made known.

[39]

Prima
Regula.

In all Cases, when the cause originally belongs to the Cognizance of the Regula prima. Ecclesiasticall Court, and suit is prosecuted there, in the same nature as the Cognizance belongs to them (although in truth the cause, all circumstances being disclosed, belongs to the Court of the King, and to be determined by the Common Law) yet no *Premunire* lies in that case, but a Prohibition. As if Tythes are severed from the nine parts, and are carried away: if the Parson sue for the subtraction of these Tythes in the Spirituall Court, this is not within the case of *Premunire;* for it may be that the Plaintiff did not know that they were severed from the nine parts, nor that they were carried away; nor may the Ecclesiasticall Judge know any thing of it: And although that the Defendant pleads this, yet the Ecclesiasticall Court may proceed to try the truth of it without danger, *vide* 10 Hen. 4. 2. according with this opinion; so if a Parson sue for Tythes of Wood, surmising that they were *Silvae caeduae,*[12] under the age of twenty years, where in truth they were above the age of twenty years: (In which case by the Statute of 45 Ed. 3. Tythes ought not to be paid) yet a Prohibition lyeth and no *Premunire.*

But although the cause originally may appertain to the Cognizance of the Regula secunda. Ecclesiasticall Judge, yet if he sue for it in the nature of a Suit, which doth not belong to the Ecclesiasticall Court, but to the Common Law, there a *Premunire* lyeth; as in the case put before: If the Parson after the severing of Tythes, will in any Ecclesiasticall Court within this Realm, sue for carrying away his Tythes severed from the nine parts, which action by matter apparent to the Ecclesiasticall Court, appertains to the Common Law; In such Case both the Actor and the Judge incur the danger of a *Premunire:* And so it was adjudged in 17 Hen. 8. as Spilman reports it: One Turbervile sued a *Premunire* against a Parson, who by citation convened him into the Ecclesiasticall Court within this Realm, | and there Libell'd against him for taking of Tythes which [40] were severed from the nine parts, and the Parson was condemned, and had Judgment that he should be out of the protection of the King, and forfeit all his Lands, Goods, and Chattels, and his body to perpetuall Imprisonment, and damages to the party. So if a Mortuary be delivered to a Parson, and after the party re-take it, if the Parson sue for this as for a Mortuary to him delivered and carried away, he is in case of a *Premunire;* but after the reprisal, if he sue for it as mortuary not executed, in nature of a suit, which belongs to Court

12. [*Ed.:* Coppice-wood.]

Christian, upon the truth of the case there is cause of Prohibition, and no *Premunire* lies, *vide* 10 Hen. 4. 2. So the case which hath been put of suit for tythes of Wood, if the Parson sue for tythes of wood above twenty years growth, so that it appears by the Libell, that the Cognizance of this case doth not belong to Court Christian (viz.) to the Court of the Archbishop of Canterbury, the *Premunire* lies as you may see in the Book of Entries, tit. Dismes, fol. 221. But in the tit. Prohibition, fol. 449. Divisione Dismes, pl. 2, 3, 4, 5, & 6. if the Suit be *Pro silva caedua, &c.* So that as the Suit is framed the Cognizance belongs to Court Christian, although that the truth be otherwise, there a Prohibition lies, and no *Premunire.* For when the cause originally belongs to the Cognizance of the Ecclesiasticall Court, although they hold plea of any incident to it, which belongs to the Common Law, there Prohibition and not *Premunire.*

Regula tertia. When the cause originally belongs to the cognizance of the Common Law, and not to the Ecclesiasticall Court, there although they libell for it according to the course of the Ecclesiasticall Law, yet the *Premunire* lyeth, for this, that this draws the cause which is determinable at the Common Law, *Ad aliud examen,*[13] viz. to be decided by the Civill or Ecclesiasticall Law; and so deprives the Subject of the benefit of the Common Law, which is his birth-right: And with this agrees the Book of Entries, tit. Premunire, fol. 229 b. and 430 a. where it is put for a Rule, *Quod Placita, Querelae, et possessiones terrarum et tenementorum transgr. debitorum et aliorum consimilium infra Regnum Angliae illat. ad Dominum Regem ad Regalem Coronam et dignitates suas specialiter, et non ad forum Ecclesiasticum pertinent. Quidem I. R., &c. machinans Dominum Regem et Coronam et dignitates suas exheredare, et cognitionem quae ad Curiam Domini Regis pertinet, ad aliud examen infra Regnum suum Angliae in Curiam Christianitatis coram A. W. official. &c. trahere, &c. quendam articulum ad prosequendum ipsum R. in eadem Curia Christianitatis coram praefato Officiali pro debito 20 l. et ipsum R. in eadem Curia praefato I. A. inde responsum citari, &c.*[14] So that if the original cause be temporall, although that they proceed

13. [*Ed.:* Into another forum.]

14. [*Ed.:* That whereas pleas, plaints and possessions [*sic*] of lands and tenements, trespasses, debts, and other such like, within the realm of England, belong especially to the lord king and his royal crown and dignities and not to the ecclesiastical court, a certain J.[A.], etc., scheming to disinherit the lord king and his crown and dignities, and to draw the cognizance which belongs to the king's court into another forum within his realm of England, [exhibited] a certain article in court Christian before A. W., official,

by Citation, Libel, &c. in Ecclesiasticall manner, yet this is in danger of *Premunire:* And the reason of this Offence is expressed in the Writ, for this, that he endeavours to draw *Cognitionem (causae,) quae ad Curiam Domini regis pertinet, ad aliud examen,*[15] which is as much as to say, that the Debt, the Cognizance whereof belongs to the Court of the King, and to be determined by the Common Law, he intends by the Originall Suit to draw it to be determined by the Ecclesiasticall Law.

And note, in the Indictment of *Premunire* against Cardinall Wolsey, Mich. 21 Hen. 8. it is said, *Quod praedictus Cardinalis, &c. intend: finaliter antiquissimas Angliae leges penitus subvertere et enervare, universumque hoc Regnum Angliae et ejusdem Angliae populum, legibus imperialibus, vulgo dictis legibus Civilibus et eorum legum Canonibus in perpetuum subjugare | et subjicere, &c.*[16]   [41] and this is included within these words, *Ad aliud examen trahere,*[17] viz. to decide that by the Civill and Ecclesiasticall Lawes, which is determinable by the common Law: And upon this was a notable case in Hil. an. 25 Hen. 8. the case of *Nich. Bishop of Norwich,* against whom, he then being in the custody of the Marshalsey, the Kings Attorney preferred a Bill of *Premunire:* And the matter of the *Premunire* was such. Within Thetford in the County of Norfolk hath been *De tempore cujus, &c.*[18] such Custom, that all Ecclesiasticall Causes arising within that Town should be determined before the Dean of the same Town, who hath within it peculiar Jurisdiction; and that none in the same Town shall be drawn in plea in any other Court Christian for Ecclesiasticall Causes, unless before the same Dean: and if any be against the said Custom drawn in Suit before any other Ecclesiasticall Judge, and this be presented before the Mayor of the same Town, that such party shall forfeit 6s. 8d. And that one such sued in the Consistory of the said Bishop, for a thing arising within the said Town of Thetford, and this was presented before the Mayor, [of Thetford according to the custom,] for which he hath forfeited 6s. 8d. the said Bishop cited the said Mayor to appear before him at his house in Hoxin,

---

etc., to sue the selfsame R. in the same court Christian before the said official for a debt of twenty pounds, and [caused] the said R. to be cited in the same court to answer the said J. A. therein, etc.]

15. [*Ed.:* The cognizance of the cause, which belongs to the lord king's court, into another forum.]

16. [*Ed.:* That said cardinal intended to complete, undermine, and subvert the most ancient laws of England, and to subject and subdue this whole realm of England and the people of this same England to imperial law, commonly called civil law, and to the canons of this law.]

17. [*Ed.:* In another forum.]

18. [*Ed.:* From that time.]

in Suffolk, generally *Pro salute animae*,[19] and upon appearance libelled, *Pro parole*[20] upon all the matter, and enjoyned him upon pain of Excommunication to annul the said Presentment [before a day: and upon a *Premunire* brought for this matter]: And the said Bishop had Counsell learned assigned him; And they objected, that as well the said Presentment as the said Custom were for divers causes void, and therefore it cannot be said, *Contra Coronam et dignitatem Regiam*,[21] nor hath the Bishop drawn the party *Ad aliud examen*, for it ought not to be examined in any Court.

2. They objected, that the Court of the Bishop was not intended within the act of 16 Ric. 2. 32. but *In Curia Romana aut alibi;*[22] and this *alibi* ought not to be intended out of the Realm, but it was resolved by Fitz-James chief Justice, *et per totam Curiam;* That be the Custom and Presentment good or not, this is a temporall thing and determinable by the Common Law, and not examinable in the Spirituall Court; and for this the Bishop in this case hath incurred a *Premunire*.

3. That *Alibi* extends as well to the Courts of the Bishops, and other Ecclesiasticall Courts within this Realm, as elsewhere: And so the Court said, that it had been often times adjudged, upon which the said Bishop (the matter of the Indictment being true) confessed the said Indictment: And upon this appearing the secondary Justice gave Judgment against him, that the said Bishop shall be out of the protection of the King, and that his Lands, Goods, and Chattels should be forfeited to the King, and his body to be imprisoned *Ad voluntatem Regis, &c.*[23]

Nicholas Fuller's Case.
(1607) 5 James I.
In the Court of King's Bench.
First Published in the *Reports*, volume 12, page 41.

Ed.: Coke's notes here describe one of his more famous confrontations with the church courts, in which he asserted the authority of the law courts to

19. [*Ed.:* For the salvation of his soul,]
20. [*Ed.:* By word.]
21. [*Ed.:* Against the royal crown and dignity,]
22. [*Ed.:* In the Roman Curia or elsewhere;]
23. [*Ed.:* According to the will of the king, etc.]

determine the extent of the powers of the church courts. He also specifies that the Law court cannot give a consultation or issue writs when it is not in session, and that a Lawyer in court may be punished for his arguments, in the Law courts if he offends the King or government, and in the church courts if he commits heresy.

In the great case of *Nicholas Fuller* of Grayes Inn, these points were resolved upon conference had with all the Justices and Barons of the Exchequer.

Ecclesiasti-
call Com-
mission.

1. That no Consultation can be granted out of the Term, for this, that it is an award of the Court, and is finall, and cannot be granted by all the Judges out of the Term, nor by any of them within the Term out of Court: And the name of the Writ, Viz. A Writ of Consultation, imports this, that the Court upon consultation amongst them ought to award it.

| 2. That the construction of the Statute 1 Eliz. cap. 1., and of the Letters Patents of high Commission in Ecclesiastical causes founded upon the said Act, belongs to the Judges of the Common Law: For although that the causes, the cognizance of which belongs to them, are merely Spirituall, and the Law by which they proceed is merely Spirituall, yet their authority and power is given to thcm by Act of Parliament, and Letters Patents, the construction of which belongs to temporall Judges: And for this, the consultation which was granted is with this restraint, *Quatenus non agat de authoritate et validitate literarum patentium pro causis Ecclesiasticis vobis vel aliquibus vestrum direct. aut de expositione et interpretatione statuti de anno primo nuper Reginae, &c.*[1] In the same manner as if the King hath a Benefice donative by Letters Patents, although that the Function and Office of the Incumbent be Spirituall, yet inasmuch as he comes to it merely by Letters Patents of the King, he shall not be visitable, not deprivable by any Ecclesiasticall authority, but by the Chancellor of the King, or by Commissioners under the great Seal.

[42]

3. It was resolved when there is any question concerning what power or jurisdiction belongs to Ecclesiastical Judges, in any particular case, the determination of this belongs to the Judges of the Common Law, in what cases

---

1. [*Ed.:* Provided there is no litigation concerning the authority and validity of the letters patent for ecclesiastical causes directed to you or any of you, or concerning the exposition and interpretation of the Statute of the first year of the late queen, etc.]

they have cognizance, and in what not; for if the Ecclesiastical Judges shall have the determination of what things they shall have cognizance, and that all that appertains to their Jurisdiction, which they shall allow to themselves, they will make no difficulty, *Ampliare jurisdictionem suam:*[2] And according to this resolution, Bract. lib. 5. tract. de except. cap. 15. fol. 412. *Cum judex ecclesiasticus prohibitionem a Rege suscepit, supersedere debet in omni casu, saltem donet constiterit in Curia Regia ad quam pertinet jurisdictionem; quia si Judex ecclesiasticus aestimare debet an sua esset jurisdictio, in omni casu indifferenter procederet non obstante Regia prohibitione,*[3] *vide* Entries, fol. 445. There was a question, whether the Court Christian should have cognizance of a Lamp. And a Prohibition was granted, *Quod non procedant in Curia Christianitatis, quousque in Curia nostra discussum fuerit, utrum cognitio placiti illus ad Curiam nostram vel ad forum ecclesiasticum pertineat.*[4] And if the determination of a thing which appears to Court Christian, doth appertain to the Judges of the Common Law, and the Judges of the Common Law have power to grant a Prohibition. And all this appears in our Books, that the Judges of the Common Law shall determine in what cases the Ecclesiastical Judges have power to punish any *Pro laesione fidei,*[5] 2 Hen. 4. fol. 10. 11 Hen. 4. 88. 22 Edw. 4. 20. So of the bounds of Parishes in 5 Hen. 5. 10. 39 Edw. 3. 23. So it belongs to the Judges of the Common Law, to decide who ought to certifie excommunication, and to reject the certificate, when the Ordinary or Commissary is party, 5 Edw. 3. 8. 8 Edw. 3. 69, 70. 18 Edw. 3. 58. 12 Edw. 4. 9 Hen. 7. 1. 10 Hen. 7. 9. For this it was resolved clearly, that if any person slander the authority or power of the high Commissioners, this is to be punished before the Judges of the Common Law, for that the determination of their authority and power which is given to them by the Statute, and the Letters Patents of the King belongs to them, and not to Court Christian: And for this, that the many articles objected against Fuller concerning the slander of their authority

---

2. [*Ed.:* To amplify their jurisdiction:]

3. [*Ed.:* When an ecclesiastical Judge receives a prohibition from the King, he ought to stop in every Case until it has been decided in the King's court to whom the jurisdiction belongs; because if the ecclesiastical Judge should consider whether the jurisdiction is his, he would in every Case proceed indifferently, without regard to the royal prohibition,]

4. [*Ed.:* That they should not proceed in court Christian until it has been decided in our court whether cognizance of that plea belongs to our court or to the ecclesiastical jurisdiction.]

5. [*Ed.:* For breach of faith,]

and power, was solely determinable and punishable before the Judges of the Common Law. One other restraint was added in the consultation: *Et quatenus non agat de aliquibus scandalis, contemptibus, seu aliis rebus, quae ad communem legem aut statuta regni nostri Angliae sunt punienda et determinanda.*[6]

4. It was resolved, that if a Counsellor at Law, in his argument, shall | scandall [43] the King or his Government, Temporall or Ecclesiasticall, this is a Misdemeanor and contempt to the Court; for this he is to be indicted, fined, and imprisoned, and not in Court Christian: But if he publish any Heresy, Schism, or erroneous Opinion in Religion, he may be for this convened before the Ecclesiastical Judges, and there corrected according to the Ecclesiastical Law: for the Rule is, *Quod non est juri consonum quod quis pro aliis quae in Curiis nostris acta sunt, quorum cognitio ad nos pertinet, trahatur in placitum in Curia Christianitatis*[7] as it appears in the Book of Entries, fol. 448. So that the intent is, that Heresie, Schism, or such enormous opinions in Religion, doth not appertain to the Cognizance of temporall Courts: For this cause a Consultation was granted, *Quoad schismata, hereses, et inormiam impiam, vel pernitiosam opinionem in religione, fide, seu doctrina Christiana pie et salubriter stabilita infra regnum nostrum Angliae, quorum cognitio ad forum ecclesiasticum spectat, &c.*[8] *Vide* Mich. 18 Hen. 8. Rot. 78. in Banco Regis. The case was, that a Leet was held *Jovis post festum Sancti Mich. Arch.*[9] 17 Hen. 8. of the Prior of the house of S. John de Bethlehem de Sheine, of his Mannor of Levisham in the County of Surrey, before John Beare the Steward there, a grand Jury was charged to inquire for the King of all Offences inquirable within the said Leet, where one Philip Aldwin, who was Resident within the said Leet, appeared at the said Leet, *Idemque Philippus sciens quandam Margaretam, uxorem Johannis Aldwin apud East Greenwich, infra jurisdictionem Letae praedictae, pluries perantea corpus suum in adulterio vitiose exercuisse, ac volens ipsam Margaretam pro republica in exemplum taliter offendere volentium legitime punire,*

---

6. [*Ed.:* And so long as there is no litigation concerning any slanders, contempts, or other things, which are to be punished and determined at Common Law or by the Statutes of our realm of England.]

7. [*Ed.:* That it is not consonant with Law that anyone should be drawn into plea in court Christian for other things which are litigated in our courts and the cognizance whereof belongs to us.]

8. [*Ed.:* With respect to schismatic beliefs, heresies, and enormous impiety or pernicious opinion in the Christian religion, faith or doctrine, as piously and wholesomely established within our realm of England, the cognizance whereof belongs to the ecclesiastical jurisdiction, etc.]

9. [*Ed.:* On the Thursday after the feast of Michaelmas.]

ad dictam magnam juratam se personaliter exhibuit & eisdem sic juratis de dicta
mala & viciosa vita praefate Margaretae instructionem et informationem veraciter
dedit.[10] Upon which the said Margaret did draw the said Philip into the Court
of the Arch-bishop of Canterbury, and there did libell against him for defamation of Adultery; And that the said Philip said *in hisce anglicanis verbis;*[11]
Margaret Allen is a Whore and a Bawd, and it is not yet three weeks agone
since a man might take a Priest betwixt her legs; which english words were
parcell of the words by which he informed the Grand Inquest at the said Leet:
And upon this he had by award of the Court a Prohibition, by which Writ
it appears, *Quod per leges hujus Regni Angliae omnes & singuli quicunque Domini*
Regis subditi coram quibuscunque ipsius Domini Regis Justiciariis seu quocunque
alio viro judiciali officio seculari fungente in aliqua juratam patriae jurati, vel
ad aliquas instructiones seu informationes alicui hujusmodi jurat in evidentias
dandas comparentes et evidentias dantes, ab omni impetitione et calumnia in
aliqua Curia Christianitatis propterea fienda, quieti et liberi esse debent, et in
perpetuum penitus irreprehen.[12] And by this record it appears, & by the Statute
of 10 Edw. 3. c. 11. by which it is provided, that Indictors of Lay people or
Clerks in Turneys, and after delivering them before Justices shall not be sued
for defamation in Court Christian, but that the Plaintiff who finds himself
grieved shall have a Prohibition formed in the Chancery upon his case, which
was but an affirmance of the common Law, for that the Statute provides only
for Indictors in the Turne only: And yet as well all Indictors in other Courts,
and all Witnesses, and all others who have affairs in the Temporall Courts,
shall not be sued or molested in Court Christian. *vide* Pasch. 6 Eliz. In the
Reports of the Lord Dyer, (which Case is not printed) John Halles in the Case

---

10. [*Ed.:* And the same Philip, knowing that a certain Margaret, wife of John Aldwin, had many times
before then at Greenwich, within the jurisdiction of the aforesaid leet, corruptly used her body in adultery,
and wishing Lawfully to punish the selfsame Margaret for the common good, as an example to others
wishing to offend in such manner, personally exhibited to the same grand Jury and truthfully gave instruction
and information to the same jurors concerning the said evil and vicious life of the said Margaret.]

11. [*Ed.:* in these English words;]

12. [*Ed.:* That by the Laws of this realm of England all and singular the lord king's subjects whatsoever,
being sworn in a Jury of the country before whatsoever Justices of the selfsame lord king, or any other
man whatsoever performing a secular judicial office, or appearing and giving evidence for the instruction
or information of any such juries, ought to be quit and free from any charge or accusation made in any
court Christian on that account, and utterly blameless for ever.]

of marriage, between the Earl of Hereford, and the Lady Katherine Gray, declared his opinion against the sentence given by Commissioners Delegates of the Queen, in a cause ecclesiasticall, under the great Seal: | And that the [44] said Sentence in dis-affirmance of the said marriage was unjust, wicked, and void, and that he thought that the said Judges Delegates had done against their conscience, and could not render any reason for the said sentence: And what offence this was, was referred to divers Judges to consider, by whom upon great deliberation it was resolved, that this offence was a contempt as well against the Queen, as to the Judges; and every of them were punishable by the Common Law, by fine and imprisonment: And that the Queen may upon that sue for it in what Court she shall pleas: for the slander of a Judge in point of his Judgment, be it true or false, is not justifiable, &c. And all this appears by the Report of the Lord Dyer, so that in the said Consultation it was well provided, that the high Commissioners should not intermeddle with any scandall by the Common Law.

5. It was resolved, that when any Libell in Ecclesiasticall Court contains many Articles, if any of them do not belong to the cognizance of Court Christian, a Prohibition may be generally granted; and upon motion made, consultation may be made as to things which do belong to the Spirituall Jurisdiction; for the Writ of consultation with a *Quoad*,[13] is frequent and usuall, but a Prohibition with a *Quoad*, is *Rara avis in terra nigroque simillima Cygno*.[14] And for these reasons it was resolved by all that the Prohibition in the case at the Bar was well granted, which in truth was granted by Fenner and Crook Justices in the time of the Vacation.

Note, these generall Rules concerning Prohibitions *quae sparsim inveniantur in libris nostris.*

Non debet dici tendere in praejudicium ecclesiasticae libertatis quod pro Rege & Repub. necessarium videtur.[15]

Non est juri consonum quod quis super iis quorum cognitio ad nos pertinet in Curia Christianitatis trahetur in placitum.[16]

---

13. [*Ed.:* With respect to.]
14. [*Ed.:* A rare bird in the land, like a black swan.]
15. Articuli Cleri c. 8.
16. Entries 444–447.

Episcopus teneat placitum in Curia Christianitatis de iis quae mere sunt spiritualia.[17]

Prohibeatur de caetero Hospitalariis & Templariis ne de caetero trahant aliquem in placitum coram Conservatoribus privilegiorum de aliqua re cujus cognitio ad forum spectat Regium.[18]

Non concedantur citationes priusquam exprimatur super qua re fieri debet citatio.[19,20]

The knowledge of all cases Testamentary, Matrimony, &c. by the goodnesse of the Princes, and by the Lawes and Customs of the Realm appertain to spiritual Jurisdiction.

6. It was resolved, that this especial consultation, being onely for Heresie, Schism, and erroneous Opinions, &c. that if they convict Fuller of heresie, Schism, or erroneous Opinion, &c. that if he recant the said Heresie, Schism, or erroneous Opinion, that he shall never be punished by Ecclesiastical Law: And after the said consultation granted, the said Commissioners proceeded and convicted Fuller of Schism and erroneous Opinions, and imprisoned him and fined him two hundred pounds: And after in the same Term, Fuller by his Councell moved the Court of Kings Bench to have a *Habeas Corpus et ei conceditur,*[21] upon which Writ the Goaler did return the cause of his detention.

17. Circumspecte agatis, &c.

18. West. 2. cap. 43.

19. [*Ed.:* which are found scattered in our Books:

That which appears necessary for the king and the common weal ought not to be said to tend to the prejudice of the liberty of the Church.

It is not consonant with Law that someone should be drawn in plea in court Christian upon matters whereof the cognizance belongs to us.

A bishop holds plea in court Christian concerning those things that are purely spiritual.

It is forbidden that from henceforth the Hospitallers and Templars should draw anyone in plea before the conservators of their privileges in respect of any matter whereof the cognizance belongs to the royal jurisdiction.

Citations shall not be granted until the matter upon which the citation is to be granted has been expressed.]

20. *Ibidem.*

21. [*Ed.:* have a Writ of Habeas Corpus (or be released) and it was granted.]

Sir Anthony Roper's Case.
(1607) Michaelmas Term, 5 James I.
In the Court of King's Bench.
First Published in the *Reports,* volume 12, page 45.

Ed.: One of the many grants of habeas corpus against the High Commission. Sir Anthony Roper was imprisoned by the church court for failing to release funds for a pension owed from some of his lands to a local vicar. The Justices of the Court of Common Pleas held that this offense was not a heresy or other offense under the Statute giving jurisdiction to the High Commission.

In the case of Sir Anthony Roper, who was drawn before the high Commissioners at the Suit of one Bulbrook the Vicar of Bentley, for a Pension out of a Rectory Impropriate, of which Sir Anthony was seised in fee: And the high Commissioners sentenced the said Sir Anthony to pay that, which he refused; And upon this they committed him to Prison, who in this Term by *Habeas corpus*[1] appeared in Court, upon the return of which Writ the matter did appear: And it was well debated by the Justices, and was resolved, that the said Commissioners had not authority or | commission in the said case, [46] for when the Acts of the 27 Hen. 8. and 31 Hen. 8. of Monasteries had made Parsonages Impropriate, and other Religious Possessions Lay-fee, although that Pensions were saved, yet as it appears by the Preamble of the act of 34 Hen. 8. cap. 16. those to whom the Pensions appertain, had not remedy for the said Pensions, &c. And for this there it is provided, that if the Farmer or Occupier of such Possessions shall wilfully deny the payment of any such Pensions, Portions, Corrodies, Indemnities, Synod Proxies, or any other Profits, whereof any Arch-bishop, Bishop, Arch-deacon, or any other Ecclesiastical person were in possession at, or within ten years next before the time of such dissolution of any such Monastery, &c. that then it shall be lawfull for the said Arch-bishop, Bishop, or other Ecclesiastical person aforesaid, being so denied to be satisfied and paid therof: And having right to the thing in demand, to have such processe, as well against every such person and persons, as so shall deny payment, &c. as against the Church and Churches charged with

---

1. [*Ed.:* Writ determining the legality of an incarceration.]

the same, as heretofore they have lawfully done, and as by, and according to the Lawes of this Realm they may now lawfully do, &c. And if the King hath covenanted to discharge the Patentee, &c. of Pensions, and then suit shall be made for the same in the Court of Augmentations, and not elsewhere; then if the high Commissioners will determine of Pensions, they ought to do it by the act 34 Hen. 8. and the said act gives this expressly to Ordinaries, and their Officials, and the high Commissioners have their authority by the act 1 Eliz. made a long time after.

But it was objected, that the said act 1 Eliz. gave to the Queen, her Heirs and Successors, power to assign Commissioners to exercise and execute all manner of Jurisdiction Spiritual, to visit, reform, &c. all Schism and Heresie, &c. and Enormities which by any manner of Spiritual Jurisdiction can, or lawfully may be reformed. And it was said, that such Spiritual Jurisdiction which the Bishop should have, is transferred to the high Commissioners.

But it was unanimously resolved by Coke, Walmsley, Warburton, Daniel and Foster Justices, that the act 1 Eliz. doth not extend to this case for divers causes, viz.

1. For that the said clause of resignation is not more large then the clause of Restitution; and that the act of 1 Eliz. doth not take away nor alter any act of Parliament, unless those only which are expressly named in the act; and it was resolved that the high Commissioners cannot hold plea for the double value of Tythes carried away before severance, for two causes.

1. For this, that the Statute of 2 Edw. 6. cap. 13. gave the Cognizance of it to Spirituall Judges, which is to be intended of such Spirituall Judges who then were.

2. Substraction of Tythes is injury and no crime, but concerns interest and property: And for this the high Commissioners cannot meddle with it.

2. For that the words of the act 1 Eliz. are (which by any manner of Spirituall Jurisdiction can or lawfully may be reformed). And it appears that these words extend to crime only, and not to cases of Interest betwixt party and party; for the words are: All such Errors, Heresies, &c. which by any manner, &c. so that (such) and (which) are Relatives.

2. This Jurisdiction was given to the Bishops by act of Parliament, viz. by 34 Hen. 8. which is more temporal then spiritual: And for this out of the precedent words 1 Eliz. viz. Spiritual or Ecclesiasticall Jurisdiction, which is

[47]   to be intended of Jurisdictions meerly or purely Spiritual, | but acts of Parliament are more temporall then spirituall.

4. It was not the intent of the act 1 Eliz. which revived the Statute 23 Hen. 8. cap. 9. by which act it is enacted, that none shall be sued out of his Diocesse, &c. that the high Commissioners for private causes shall send for Subjects out of any part of the Realm, and so in effect confound the Jurisdiction of the Ordinary, who is an Officer and Minister so necessary that in divers causes the Courts of the King cannot administer to Subjects without him, &c.

5. If the act of 1 Eliz. had extended to give to high Commissioners power to determine *meum et tuum*,[2] as Pensions, Tythes, Legacies, Matrimonies, Divorces, Administrations, Probates of Testaments, &c. the act would also give the party grieved benefit of appeal, and not give absolute authority to the high Commissioners finally to determine *Meum et tuum,* and to bastardise Issues, &c. without any controlement, for this should be to dissolve the Court of the Ordinary which is so ancient and inevitably necessary in many cases to the administration of Justice, in divers points of it, that without this Justice cannot be executed.

6. The high Commissioners cannot extend themselves but only to Crimes, for the clause which gives to them power to imprison, &c. and to punish, &c. and imprison such Offender, &c. And Offender is only to be intended of him who commits any crime, and not of him who detains Pension, Legacy, Tythes, &c.

Sir Anthony Roper's Case.
(1607) Michaelmas Term, 5 James I.
In the Court of King's Bench.
First Published in the *Reports,* volume 12, page 47.*

Ed.: A different note by Coke of the preceding Case.

Praeceptum fuit Guardiano prisonae Domini Regis de le Fleete, Quod haberet hic; viz. apud Westmonasterium immediate post receptionem hujus brevis corpus Antonii Roper militis in prisona praedicta sub custodia sua detenti, quocunque nomine censeretur, una cum die et causa captionis et detentionis ejusdem Antonii: Et iidem Justiciarii hic, visa causa illa, ulterius fieri fecerint quod de jure et

Hab. Corpus return, and discharge by judgment of the Court.

2. [*Ed.:* mine and thine, (i.e. matters of property).]
*The original pleadings in this case may be found at 5 Jac. Rot. 2254.

secundum legem et consuetudinem regni Domini Regis Angliae fuerit faciendum:
Et modo hic ad hunc diem, scilicet diem Sabbati proximum post octabis Sancti
Mich. isto eodem termino venit praedictus Antonius in propria persona sua sub
Custodia praedicti Guardiani ad barram, hic praedict. et idem Guardianus, tunc
hic mand. Quod ante adventum brevis praedicti, viz. nono die octabis ultimo
praeterito praeditus Anthonius Roper miles reducit se prisonae praedictae praeantea
commissus virtute cujusdam warranti, dati 30 die Junii ultimo praeterit', quod
sequitur in haec verba, viz.[1]

These are in his Majesties name to require and charge you, by vertue of
his high Commission for causes Ecclesiasticall, under the great Seal of England,
to us and others directed, that herewith you receive and take into your Custody
the body of Sir Anthony Roper Knight, and him safely detain Prisoner at this
our commandment, untill we shall give order for his enlargement, signifying
unto you, that the cause of his commitment is, for that there being a certain
cause referred unto us by his Majesties special direction, betwixt him the said
Sir Anthony Roper and John Bulbrook Vicar of Bentley, for that he detained
wrongfully from him the said Vicar, a certain yearly Pension due unto him
from the said Sir Anthony; And being thereupon called before us, and after
[48] full hearing of | the cause in the presence of Sir Anthony and his Councel at
three or four severall times, and at the last adjudged by us to pay the said
Pension, he having somtime of deliberation given unto him by us to consider
therof, hath notwithstanding obstinately disobeyed the said Order, and doth
so still persist: And this shall be your Warrant in that behalf; Given at Lambeth
this thirtieth of June, 1607. *Et quod haec fuit Causa Captionis et detentionis,*
praedicti Antonii in prisona praedicta, corpus tamen praedicti Antonii modo hic
paratus habet prout per breve praedictum sibi praeceptum fuit, &c. super quo,

---

1. [*Ed.*: The warden of the lord king's prison of the Fleet was commanded that he have here, that is
to say, at Westminster, immediately after the receipt of this writ, the body of Anthony Roper, knight,
detained in the aforesaid prison in his custody, by whatever name he should be known, together with the
day and the cause of the taking and detention of the same Anthony, (so that) the same Justices here, having
seen the cause, shall do further whatever by right and according to the Law and custom of the lord king's
realm of England should be done. And now here at this day, namely the Saturday next after the octaves
of Michaelmas this same term, the aforesaid Anthony comes in his own person, being (led) to the bar here
in the custody of the aforesaid warden; and the same warden then sent word here that before the arrival
of the aforesaid writ, namely on the ninth day of October last past, the aforesaid Anthony Roper, knight,
brought himself to the aforesaid prison, having been previously committed by virtue of a certain warrant
dated the thirtieth day of June last past, which follows in these words, that is to say, to wit:]

visis praemissis et per Justiciarios hic plenius examinatis et intellectis, videtur iisdem Justic. hic quod praedicta causa commissionis praedicti Antonii prisonae de Fleet praedict, in retorno praedict: superius specificata minus sufficiens in lege existit ad detinendum praedictum Antonium in prisona praedict. Ideo praedictus Antonius a prisona praedicta per Curiam hic dimittitur, ac idem guardianus de hujusmodi custodia per eandem Curiam hic plene exoneretur, &c.[2] And this was resolved *una voce* by Coke chief Justice, Walmesley, Warberton, Daniell, and Foster Justices, for the causes and reasons afore expressed.

And in the very same Term in *Lanes Case,* a Parson in Norfolk who sued one of his Parishioners before the high Commissioners, for scandaling of him, saying in the Church on the Sabbath before all his Parishioners, That he was a wicked man, and an arrant Knave: Prohibition lyes, for this, that it was not so enormous as the Statute intended. Note, that by express Proviso, the high Commissioners cannot intermeddle with all Heresies, but with exorbitant Heresies, &c. and the other shall be determined before the Ordinary.

The Case of Heresy.
(1600–1601) 43 Elizabeth I
In Conference with Sir John Popham, Chief Justice.
First Published in the *Reports,* volume 12, page 56.*

Ed.: These are Coke's notes of a conference with the Chief Justice of the king's Bench, on the nature of a proceeding for heresy, including the evolution of their procedure, and the problems of indictments brought against Lollards, who were not heretics in the definition by Statute.

---

2. [*Ed.:* And that this was the cause of the taking and detention of the aforesaid Anthony in the aforesaid prison; nevertheless he now has here ready the body of the aforesaid Anthony, as he was commanded by the aforesaid writ, etc. Whereupon, the premises having been seen and fully examined and understood by the Justices here, it seems to the same Justices here that the aforesaid cause of the committal of the aforesaid Anthony to the prison of the Fleet aforesaid as specified above in the aforesaid return is insufficient in Law to detain the aforesaid Anthony in the aforesaid prison. Therefore the aforesaid Anthony is dismissed from the aforesaid prison by the court here, and the same warden fully discharged by the same court here from such custody, etc.]

*There is a most unusual degree of variation among the editions for this report. The text of the 1656 edition is reproduced here. The 1826 report being so much fuller, it is reproduced in whole in the note ** below.

Heresie
upon con-
ference
with Sir
John Po-
pham and
others, An.
43. Eliz.

Note, 2 Mar. title Heresie, Brook *per omnes Justiciarios*[1] & Baker & Hare: The Arch-bishop in his Province, in the Convocation, may and doth use to convict Heresie by the common Law, and then to put them convicted into Ley hands, and then by the Writ, *De haeretico comburendo*[2] they were burnt: But for this, that it was troublesome to call a Convocation of the whole Province, it was ordained by the Statute of 2 Hen. 4. cap. 15. That every Bishop in his Diocesse might convict Hereticks; And if the Sheriff was present, he might deliver the party convict to be burnt, without any Writ *De haeretico comburendo:* But if the Sheriff be absent, or if he be to be burnt in another

**The 1826 edition provides:

The archbishop and other bishops, and other the clergy, at a general synod or convocation might convict a heretic by the Common Law. But for this, that it was troublesome to call a convocation of the whole province, it was ordained by the Statute of 2 Hen. 4. cap. 15. that every bishop in his diocese might convict heretics; and, note, 2 Mary Brook, title Heresy, *per omnes justic*,'[1] and Baker, Chancellor of the Exchequer, and Hare, Master of the Rolls, by that Statute. And if the sheriff was present, he might deliver the party convict to be burnt, without any writ *de haeretico comburendo;*[2] but if the sheriff be absent, or if he be to be burned in another county, then there ought to be a writ *de haeretico comburendo:* and that the Common Law was such, *vide lib. intra,* title Indictment, p. 11. such who there are taken for heretics, some of them, are consonant to true religion. *Vide* 11 Hen. 7. Book of Entries, fol. 3. 19. See Doctor and Student, lib. 2. cap. 29. Cosin 48. 2. See the Statute of 1 and 2 Phil. and Mar. cap. 6. That Ordinaries wanting authority to proceed against heretics, 3 F. N. B. 8. fol. 269. And the writ in the register, which in the new book is omitted, proves this directly, 4 Bracton lib. 3. cap. 2. folio 123, 124. *Concilio Oxoniensi quidam Diaconus convictus fuit de apostasia, sed primo degradatus fuit per Ordinarium:*[3] and true it is, that every Ordinary

[57] may I convent any heretic or schismatic before him, *pro salute animae,*[4] and may degrade him, as Bracton saith, and may enjoin him penance according to the censure of ecclesiastical law; but upon such conviction at Common Law, the party convict shall not be burnt, nor any writ *de haeretico comburendo* lieth upon it; for the Common Law will not commit the decision of a heresy, for the life of a Christian man, to any sole Judge.

The makers of the Act of 1 Eliz. were in doubt what shall be adjudged heresy; and therefore if any person be charged with heresy before the High Commissioners, they have no authority to judge any matter or cause to be heresy, but only such as hath been so adjudged by the authority of canonical scripture, and by the four first general councils, or by any other general council, wherein the same was declared heresy by the express and plain words of canonical scripture, or such as shall hereafter be determined to be heresy by Parliament, with the assent of the convocation; for so it is expressly provided by the said Act of 1 Eliz. And although this Proviso extends only to the High Commissioners; yet seeing in the High

1. [*Ed.:* according to all the judges]

2. [*Ed.:* for burning a heretic;]

3. [*Ed.:* In the council of Oxford a certain deacon was convicted of apostasy, but first he was degraded [from his orders] by the ordinary:]

4. [*Ed.:* for the salvation of his soul,]

County, then there ought to be a Writ *De haeretico comburendo;* And that the Common Law was such, vide lib. intra. title Indictment, pl. 11. who there are taken for Hereticks, some of them are consonant to true Religion, *vide* 11 Hen. 7. Book of Entries, fol. 319. see Dr. & St lib. 2. cap. 29. Cosin. 48. 2.

Commission there be so many bishops, and other divines and learned men, it may serve for a good direction to others, especially to the diocesan, being a sole Judge in so weighty a cause.

At this day the diocesan hath jurisdiction of heresy, and so it hath been put in ure in all Queen Elizabeth's reign: but without the aid of the Act of 2 Hen. 4. cap. 15. the diocesan could imprison no person accused of heresy, but was to proceed against him by the censures of the church; for the bishop of every diocese might convict any for heresy before the Statute 2 Hen. 4. as appears by the preamble of it, but could not imprison, &c.; and now seeing that not only the said Act of 2 Hen. 4. but 25 Hen. 8. cap. 14. are repealed, the diocesan cannot imprison any man accused of heresy, but must proceed against them as he might have done before those Statutes by the censures of the church; as it appears by the said Act of 2 Hen. 4. cap. 15. Likewise the supposed Statute of 5 Rich. 2. cap. 5. and the Statutes of 2 Hen. 5. cap. 7. 25 Hen. 8. cap. 14. 1 and 2 Phil. and Mar. cap. 6. are all repealed so as no Statute made against heretics stands now in force; and at this day no person can be indicated or impeached for heresy before any Temporal Judge or other that hath temporal jurisdiction, as upon perusal of the said Statute appeareth.

There was a Statute supposed to be made in 5 Rich. 2. that commissions should be by the Lord Chancellor made and directed to sheriffs, and others, to arrest such as should be certified into the Chancery by the bishops and prelates, masters of divinity, to be preachers of heresies and notorious errors, their factors, maintainers, and abettors, and to hold them in strong prison, until they will justify themselves to the Law of the Holy Church. By colour of the supposed Act certain persons that held that images were not to be worshipped, &c. were holden in strong prison, until they (to redeem their vexation) miserably yielded before these masters of divinity to take an oath, and did swear to worship images, which was against the moral and eternal Law of Almighty God. We have said by colour of the said supposed Statute, &c. not only in respect of the said opinion, but in respect also, that the said supposed Act was in truth never any Act of Parliament, thought it was entered in the Rolls of the Parliament, for that the Commons never gave their consent thereunto. And therefore in the next Parliament, (though it was entered in the Rolls of the Parliament) for that the Commons never gave their consent thereunto, therefore in the next Parliament, the Commons preferred a bill, reciting the said supposed Act, and constantly affirmed, that they never assented thereunto, and therefore desired that the said supposed Statute might be aniented and declared to be void; for they protested, that it was never their intent to be justified by, and to bind themselves and successors I to the prelates, more than their ancestors had done in times past; and hereunto the King [58] gave his Royal assent in these words, *Pleist au Roy.*[5] And mark well the manner of the penning of the Act; for seeing the Commons did not assent thereunto, the words of the Act be, "it is ordained and assented in this present Parliament, that, &c." And so it was, being but by the King and the Lords. [Or rather, by the craft of the bishops and the then chancellor.]

It is to be known that of ancient time, when any Acts of Parliament were made to the end the same might be published and understood, and especially before the use of printing came into England, (after the Parliament was ended) the Acts of Parliament were ingrossed into parchment and bundled up together with a writ in the King's name, under the Great Seal, to the sheriff of every county, sometimes in Latin,

5. [*Ed.:* At the pleasure of the king.]

see the Statute of 1 & 2. P.M. cap. 6. That Ordinaries wanting authority to proceed against Hereticks, 3. F. N. B. fol. 269. And the Writ in the Register, which in the new Writ is omitted proves this directly, 4. Bracton, lib. 3. cap. 9. fol. 123, 124. *Concilio Oxoniensi quidam Diaconus convictus fuit de Apostasia, sed primo degradatus fuit per Ordinarium:*[3] And true it is, that every Ordinary may convent any Heretick or Schismatick before him, *Pro salute animae,*[4] and may degrade him, as Bracton saith, and may injoyn him penance according to the censure of Ecclesiasticall Law: But upon such conviction at Common Law, the party convict shall not be burnt, nor any Writ *De haeretico com-*

---

and sometimes in French, to command the sheriff to proclaim the said Statutes within his bailiwick, as well within liberties as without. And this was the course of Parliamentary proceedings, before printing came in use in England, and it continued after we had the print till the reign of Hen. 7.

Note, at the Parliament holden in 5 Rich. 2. John Braibrooke, Bishop of London, being Lord Chancellor of England, caused the said ordinance of the King and Lords to be inserted into the Parliamentary writ of proclamation to be proclaimed amongst the Acts of Parliament, which writ I have seen, the purclose of which writ, after the recital of the Acts directed to the Sheriff of N., is in these words, *Nos volentes dictas concordias, sive ordinationes in omnibus et singulis suis articulis inviolabiliter observari, tibi praecipimus quod praedictas concordias sive ordinationes in locis infra balivam tuam, ubi melius expedire volueris, tam infra libertates, quam extra, publice proclamari et teneri facias juxta formam praenotatam. Teste Rege apud Westm.* 26 *Maii, anno regni Regis, R.* 2. 5.[6]

But in the Parliamentary proclamation of the Acts passed in anno 6 Rich. 2. the said Act of 6 Rich. 2. whereby the said supposed Act of 5 Rich. 2. was declared to be void, is omitted; and afterwards the said supposed Act of 5 Rich. 2. was continually printed, and the said Act of 6 Rich. 2 hath by the craft of the prelates been ever from time to time kept from the print.

Certain men called Lollards were indicated for heresy upon the Statute 2 Hen. 4. for these opinions, viz. *Quod non est meritorium ad Sanctum Thomam nec ad Sanctum Mariam de Walsingham peregrinari ? Nec imagines crucifix et aliorum sanctorum adorare. 3. Nulli sacerdoti confiteri nisi soli Deo, &c.*[7] Which opinions were so far from heresy, as the makers of the Statute of 1 Eliz. had great cause to limit what heresy was.

6. [*Ed.:* We, wishing the said accords or ordinances to be inviolably observed in all and singular their points, command you that you publicly proclaim the aforesaid accords and ordinances in those places within your bailiwick where you think fit, both within liberties and without, and cause them to be kept according to the aforementioned form. Witness the king at Westminster on the twenty-sixth day of May in the fifth year the reign of King Richard II.]

7. [*Ed.:* [1] that it is not meritorious to make pilgrimages to St. Thomas or to St. Mary of Walsingham; (2) nor to adore images of the crucifix and of other saints; (3) no priests to be allowed except by God alone, etc.]

---

3. [*Ed.:* At a council at Oxford a certain deacon was convicted of heresy, but first he was degraded by the Ordinary:]

4. [*Ed.:* For the salvation of his soul,]

burendo lyeth upon it; for the Common Law will not commit the Disseison of a Heresie, for the life of a Christian man, to any sole Judge.

Nota, The makers of the act of 1 Eliz. were in doubt what shall be deemed Heresie, Schism, or Schismaticall Opinion: And for this on purpuse the Statute 10 Eliz. provides that nothing shall be deemed Heresie by any of the Commissioners, by vertue of the high Commission, but what had been determined for Heresie by one of the four generall Councils, or expresly by the word of God, or Parliament, and will not leave it to so many of the Bishops and high Divines who are Commissioners, to determine what was Heresie: without question it cannot be thought reasonable that this shall be left without any limitation to one only Bishop, but to a generall Convocation; for *Plus vident oculi quam oculus,*[5] see Fox in Ed. 6. Tyne the Ordinary convicted none but by commission, and it appears by Bracton, *vide supra,* & Britton, who writ in 5 Edw. 1. lib. 1. cap. 17. That an Heretick shall be burnt for Heresie, but he doth not speak of the manner of conviction: See Horne in Myrrour of Justice; And true it is, that is appears by the preamble of the Statute, 2 Hen. 4. that the Ordinary hath Cognizance of Heresie: And this is true, as it hath been said, *Pro salute animae;* but not to burn the Heretick before that Statute: And with this agrees the Statute, 2 Hen. 5. cap. 7. 23 Hen. 7. 9. 25 Hen. 8. cap. 14. which recites the mischief, and the said act 2 Hen. 4. introduceth, *scil.* That a man incurs the losse of his life, good fame, or goods, upon naked suspition without due examination and testimony, or presentment, *viz.* Confession, &c. Also that the words in the said Act, *viz.* Cannonical Functions, were to generall and incertain; Also that it was not defined by the said act what was Heresie, the said Act repeals the act, 2 Hen. 4. & 2 Hen. 5. and the same act 25 Hen. 8. gives power to the Ordinary to proceed in other form and manner then the Statute 2 Hen. 4. hath provided, *viz.* That the Ordinary shall only proceed upon presentment or indictment of Heresies, or upon an accusation of two lawfull witnesses, and not otherwise. Also the Ordinary cannot burn the Heretick without the Kings Writ *De haeretico comburendo,* so that the proceeding in that Commencement and end was altered by the Statute 25 Hen. 8. and where this Statute sayes, Ordinaries having power to examine Heresies, this restrains it to Ordinaries themselves and not to Suffragans, Commissaries, &c. Then came the Statute of 1 Edw. 6. cap. 12. and

5. [*Ed.:* Two eyes can see better than one,]

that repealed, 5 Ric. 2. 2 Hen. 5. & 25 Hen. 8. but not the 2 Hen. 4. by expresse words, but by generall words, *viz.* All Statutes concerning matter of Religion: then came the Statute 1, & 2. P & M. cap. 6. and revived the Statute 2 Hen. 4. amongst others, by the reviver of which, without more, the Statute of 25 Hen. 8. loseth its force, so that the Ordinary may proceed upon bare suspition, and burn in any case without the Kings Writ: But by the act 1, & 2. P. & M cap. 8. after divers acts expresly repealed, *Scil.* 21 Hen. 8. 23 Hen. 8. 24 Hen 8. 27. Hen. 8. but the act of the 25 Hen. 8. cap. 14. was not expresly repealed, for this was repealed before by the act 1 Edw. 6. and yet in the end of that long and prolix Act, there is a generall clause which is sufficient of it self to repeal the Act of 25 Hen. 8. cap. 14. without more, *Scil.* the Ecclesiasticall Jurisdiction of the Arch-bishop and Ordinary to be in the same Estate, for processe of Suits, punishment of crimes, and execution of Church censures, with knowledge of Causes belonging to the same; and as large in these points as the said Jurisdiction was the twentieth year of the Raign of Hen. 8. by which Clause without question the Act of the 25. of Hen. 8. cap. 14. was repealed; then came the Statute of 1 Eliz. cap. 1. and by this the said Act of the 1, & 2. Phil. & Mar. is repealed, except such branches as after in the Act is excepted: And after divers acts particularly are repealed by the Act 1, & 2. Phil. & Mar. and are revived by 1 Eliz: particularly: And after in the same act of 1 Eliz. it is enacted, that all other Statutes repealed by the said act of Repeal of 1, & 2. Phil. & Mar. and not in this act specially revived shall remain repealed: But the act 25 Hen. 8. cap. 14. was not particularly revived, and therefore is repealed; And after it is enacted by the Statute of 1 Eliz. that the said act 1, & 2. Phil. & Mar. of reviving of three Acts for punishment of Heresies, and the said three Acts themselves shall be repealed, so that now at the Common Law none can be burnt for Heresie, but by conviction at a Convocation, for the Statute of 2 Hen. 4. cap. 15. and 25 Hen. 8. 14. are now repealed, and no regard was had to the said Doctor Cosins, in his Apology pag. 48. That he heard the two chief Justices, &c. for he doth not touch any time, or persons, &c. And it may very well be that they said, That cognizance of Heresie belongs to Ordinaries *Quatenus*[6] to penance, but not *Quatenus* to losse of life.

Note also, that by the said Writ in the Register, it appears that Hereticks

6. [*Ed.:* [Who are only] commanded.]

convict ought first to abjure, so that it may be said *Omnes infra ovile*,[7] and after relapsed into the same Heresie, there he shall suffer death: And with this accords Fitzh. but *quaere de hoc*.[8]

Note, divers were convicted in the time of Queen Eliz. upon the Statute of 2. Hen. 4. for the order and form of 25 Hen. 8. was not observed, both which acts are repealed; So William Newburgess. lib 2. cap. 13. *de haeretico comburendo* in France.

Note, the High Commission may punish Heresies, and upon their conviction a Writ *De haeretico comburendo*. See the Act 6. Ric. 2. by which the Commons disavowed their assent to the act of 5 Ric. 2. That Hereticks shall be imprisoned, &c. upon the Certificate of the Bishops, &c. and there the Commons declared, that it was not their intent to be justified, nor bound themselves, nor their Successors to Prelates, more then their Ancestors had done in time past.

Note well, the act 5 Ric. 2. was contrived by the Prelates in the name of the Commons, wheras they never assented: And this private act of 6 Ric. 2. not Printed, nor was it after divers Parliaments, as it may appear before.

Langdale's Case.
Prohibition.
(1608) Michaelmas Term, 6 James I.
In the Court of Common Pleas.
First Published in the *Reports*, volume 12, page 58.

Ed.: This is one of several notes in this part of the Reports discussing the travails of Marmaduke Langdale, whose ex-wife, Joan, sued him before the High Commission for failing to pay alimony. He sought a prohibition from Common Pleas even though he had no suit then pending before it. The court awarded the prohibition anyway. These notes detail the forms and rationale for prohibitions to the ecclesiastical court.

7. [*Ed.:* All within the fold,]
8. [*Ed.:* investigate the matter.]

Prohibi-
tion.

    In the case of *Langdale* in this very Term, in a Prohibition to the high Commissioners, two points were moved; The one, if a *Feme-covert*[1] may sue for Alimony before the high Commissioners. The other, if the Court of Common Pleas may grant a Prohibition, when no Plea is pendent in the Common Pleas: As in this case no Plea can there depend betwixt Husband and Wife. And forasmuch as this concerns the Jurisdiction of the Court, this was first of all debated, divers objections were made against it.

    1. That this Court hath not Jurisdiction to hold Plea without an Original, unlesse it be by priviledge of an Attorney, Officer, or Clerk of the Court, [59] unlesse that it be in an especiall case, viz. when there is an action | there depending for the same cause; then it was agreed that a Prohibition shall be awarded out of the Common Pleas, in respect that the Court hath an action there depending for the same cause, and so being possessed of the cause, it gave the Court Jurisdiction to award Prohibition out of the same Court: And for that the Prohibition ought to recite, *Quod cum tale placitum pendet, &c.*[2] and the Defendant *Pendente placito praedicto,*[3] hath pursued in Court Christian: And with this accords, as hath been said, F. N. B. 43 g. where it is said, that if a man be sued in the Common Pleas for a Trespasse, if the Plaintiff also sue in Court Christian for the same cause, the Defendant may shew this in the Common Pleas, and shall have a Prohibition then directed to the Judges: And so alwaies when the matter is pendent in the Common Pleas, if suit be for the same cause in Court Christian, he shall have a Prohibition: But a man shall have a Prohibition out of the Chancery, or Kings Bench upon his surmise, surmising that he is sued in Court Christian for a temporall cause; And 2 Edw. 4. 11. 6. was cited, where it is held that *Ne admittas,*[4] which is a Prohibition, doth not lye unlesse that the *Quare impedit*[5] be pendent.

    And it was answered and resolved by Coke chief Justice, Warburton, Daniel, and Foster, Justices, that the Common Pleas may award a Prohibition, although that no Suit be there pendent, for this, that the Common Pleas is the principall Court of Common Law for Common Pleas: For it belongs to the Jurisdiction of the Common Pleas to determine all Common Pleas.

---

1. [*Ed.:* Married woman.]
2. [*Ed.:* But when such plea is pending, etc.]
3. [*Ed.:* While the aforesaid plea was depending,]
4. [*Ed.:* Writ to prohibit a bishop from admitting a clerk to contested benefice or other office.]
5. [*Ed.:* Writ to recover a presentment, or right to appoint a clerk to benefice or advowson.]

Quia communia placita non sequantur Curiam nostram,[6] as it is enacted by Magna Charta, which hath thirty times been confirmed by other acts of Parliament: Then if the Ecclesiasticall Judges incroach upon the Jurisdiction of the Common Pleas to hold Plea of any thing against the Common Law of the Land, or of any thing triable by the Law, there the Principle Court of Common Law shall grant a Prohibition, and that without Originall Writ, for divers causes.

1. For that no Originall Writ which issues out of Chancery is retornable or into the Kings Bench or Common Pleas, but is directed to Judge, or party, or both, and is not retornable: But it appears in the Register, that if the Prohibition be contemned, then the Chancellor may award an Attachment to punish this contempt, retornable or in the Common Pleas, or in the Kings Bench: But an Attachment in such case is but as a Judiciall Writ; And this appears by the Register, fol. 33. And if the Attachment in such case be retornable into the Common Pleas, &c. the Plaintiff in the Declaration shall make mention of an Originall Writ in the Chancery, and of the contempt, &c. as appears in a notable President.

2. There was great reason that no Originall Writ of Prohibition shall be returnable, for the Common Law was a Prohibition in it self, and he who did incroach upon the Jurisdiction of it incurred a contempt: And with this agrees our Books, as 9 Hen. 6. 56. in Attachment upon a Prohibition in the Common Pleas, William Babington then chief Justice of the Bench, concerning a Suit in Court Christian of tythes of grosse Trees: And there Fulthorp the Serjeant took exception to the Count, for this, that the Plaintiff in his Count did not declare upon any Statute nor that any Prohibition, *Scil.* Original Writ was directed unto him: And there it is held that the Statute of 45 Edw. 3. and the Common Law also was a Prohibition in it self: And thus the rule of the Book, 19 Hen. 6. 54. Prohibition, for this, that one had sued in a Court Baron against the Common Law; And there Ascue said, the Statute is a Prohibition in it self, so it is held I in 8 Ric. 2. title Attachment sur Prohibition, 15. Note, by [60] Clopton in the Common Pleas, who then was a Serjeant, that if a Plea be held in Court Christian, which belongs to the Court of the King, without any Prohibition *in facto,* the Plaintiff shall have an Attachment upon a Prohibition, for this, that the Law is a Prohibition in it self, for by the Law they

---

6. [*Ed.:* Common pleas shall not follow our court,]

ought to hold no Plea, but that which doth belong to their Jurisdiction, *Quod fuit concessum, &c.*[7] Register 77. Estrepment. *Praecipimus quod inhibeas, &c.*[8] F. N. B. 259. Regist. 112. *Supersedeas*[9] to a Court Baron, for holding plea *Vi et armis,* or above forty shillings: And F. N. B. a Writ of Consultation is as much an originall as a Prohibition, yet the Common Pleas hath granted infinite Consultations, *ergo*[10] Prohibitions, *Qui habet jurisdictionem absolvendi, habet jurisdictionem ligandi:*[11] And one Writ is as Originall as the other.

Note, there are many severall Writs of expresse Prohibitions, *Scil.* Prohibitions with this word *Prohibemus vobis,*[12] and Letters in nature of Prohibitions, as *Supersedeas,* by which it is commanded, *Quod supersed in placito praedicto:*[13] And Injunction is a Prohibition, and also in its nature, for the words are an Injunction to the party, not to the Judge; And a *Supersedeas* is to an Officer or Judge, not to the party.

Prohibition of wast returnable out of Chancery, *Quia retornabile.*[14] Express prohibitions are in two manners, the one founded upon a Suggestion, the other upon Record; upon suggestion where plea is pendent, and yet the suggestion is the foundation, for it is not so without a plea pendent, but is founded upon Record when no plea is pendent, as shall be said hereafter: For Prohibitions founded upon Record, *Ne admittas, &c.* ought to re-cite the plea pendent, for all those which are founded upon Record ought to recite a plea pendent. So a Writ to the Bishop to admit a Clark, is a Judiciall *Latitat,*[15] as Dyer defends it: And as to the Book of 2 Edw. 4. it is well agreed, that this doth not lye in the Common Pleas, unlesse a *Quare impedit* be depending, for this ought to recite a Writ to be depending, and it should be against reason to restrain any to present, or to make Wast by Estrepment,[16] unlesse that a Writ be pendent: And as to the opinion of Fitzherbert, it was affirmed for good Law, for every one agrees it, that if a plea be pendent in the Common

7. [*Ed.:* Which was granted, etc.]

8. [*Ed.:* We command that you inhibit, etc.]

9. [*Ed.:* Writ staying the proceedings of an inferior court.]

10. [*Ed.:* therefore.]

11. [*Ed.:* He who has jurisdiction to absolve, has jurisdiction to bind:]

12. [*Ed.:* We prohibit you.]

13. [*Ed.:* That you surcease in the aforesaid plea.]

14. [*Ed.:* Because it is returnable.]

15. [*Ed.:* Writ of general summons, not restricted to service in one place.]

16. [*Ed.:* Spoil or waste by a life Tenant to the determine of the reversioner or remainderman.]

Pleas, then a Prohibition there lies, and the pendency or not pendency of a plea is not materiall for divers causes.

1. The pendency of a Plea may give a priviledge to the party, but no Jurisdiction to the Court in collaterall Suit: And there is a diversity betwixt Priviledge of Court, and Jurisdiction of Court, for a Plea pendent may give priviledge to the party, *Eundo, redeundo & morando,*[17] but doth not give Jurisdiction to the Court to hold plea by Bill by collaterall Suit against any other, as an Officer, Attorney or Clerk may.

2. The Prohibition in such a case where plea is pendent is no processe Judiciall upon the Record, for it is a collaterall Suit.

3. If the Common Pleas, which is the proper Court for Common Pleas, cannot grant a Prohibition without a Plea pendent; certainly the Kings Bench, which holds plea of Common Pleas by secondary means, cannot do it: And so the Archbishop of Canterbury in his Articles concerning Prohibitions holds, that neither the one Court nor the other may grant Prohibitions in such a case: But inasmuch as the Common Law is in stead of an Originall, as hath been said, both Courts may grant it.

4. Infinite Presidents may be shewn of Prohibitions out of the Common Pleas, without recitall of any plea pendent, as is agreed on the other part: And true it is, that it ought to be, if the Court hath not Jurisdiction | to grant any   [61] without plea pendent. Every petty Clerk of the Common Law shall have by his priviledge a Prohibition without plea pendent; *a fortiori,*[18] the Common Law it self may prohibite any one, who against the Common Law shall incroach upon its Jurisdiction, and enquire of things done against the Jurisdiction of the Court. Plea pendent is cause of priviledge and not of Jurisdiction, 4 Edw. 4. 37. 37 Hen. 8. 4. Action or information upon the Statute of 2 Hen. 5. cap. 5. is but an information to the Court of wrong done to the Common Law, for this, that no Originall Writ lies, as upon penall Law, upon *Malum prohibitum,* this is *Malum in se de quo Curia intelligi & informari voluit.*[19]

5. A President is in 22 Edw. 4. where a prohibition was granted out of the Common Pleas, for that the Plaintiff might have a Writ of false Judgment at

---

17. [*Ed.:* literally, "In going, remaining or returning," a privilege from arrest for debt.]

18. [*Ed.:* so much the more so,]

19. [*Ed.:* a wrong as a result of prohibition . . . a wrong in itself, whereof the court wishes to be told and informed.]

the Common Law: The Record it self agrees with the Report, for the words of the Record are,

6. That Officers and Clerks, as well in the Common Pleas, as in the Exchequer, and Farmers of the King in the Exchequer, may have by priviledge of Court a Prohibition without Originall: *a fortiori,* the Law it self shall have greater priviledge then an Officer or Clerk, and certainly to enforce the party to bring an action will be a means to multiply Suits to no end, for the Law it self in 4 Edw. 4. fol. 37. if any man upon the Statute of 2 Hen. 5. for not delivering of a Libell, be brought into the Common Pleas: And if he cannot have a Prohibition without such Suit, this shall be a cause, as hath been said, to multiply Suits, and is against the publick Weal; For he will bring his action upon the Statute before that he will be deprived of his Prohibition, and by that he gives himself cause of Prohibition; every Prohibition is as well at the Suit of the King as of the party, as is held in 28 Edw. 3. 97. false Latine shall not abate, nor excommunication in the plaint is no plea: For this is the Suit of the King, as well for his Jurisdiction as for the party, who by Law may choose his Court, 15 Edw. 3. title Corrody 4. The King may sue for this contempt where he pleaseth.

Note, that although the Originall cause was in the Kings Bench for Corrody, Excommunication is no plea in disability of the Plaintiff, because it is the Suit of the King for contempt to his Law. *vide* 21 Hen. 7. 71. Kelway 6. in *quare non admisit,*[20] 4 Edw. 4. 37. for not delivery of a Libell in the Common Pleas, and then he shall have a Prohibition by all the Justices: so upon the Statute of 2 Edw. 6. c. 13. for suing for Tythes where there is a prescription, &c. And this shall be to introduce multiplication of Suits, when himself gives cause of Prohibition, 38 Hen. 6. 14. 22 Edw. 4. 20. 13 Edw. 3. title Prohibition, 11. after a Judgment in the Common Pleas, after which the Patron sues the Recoverer in Chancery, surmising equity, Attachment upon a Prohibition out of the Common Pleas, yet no Plea pendent.

Note, the Reporter reported this Attachment to issue out of the Common Pleas, for the Chancellor would not prohibite him.

32 Hen. 6. 34. An Attorney in the Palace assaulted and menaced, the Court shall take a Bill and enquire of it, 4 Edw. 4. 36, 37. there a Prohibition without view of Libell, for this, that action was pendent, Statham Prohibition 3.

---

20. [*Ed.:* why he did not admit (apparently a heading in Kelway).]

Prohibition super Articulos,[21] title Prohibition plea 5. gives a Prohibition before, *scil. Coram Justiciariis nostris apud West.*[22] *vide* F. N. B. fol. 69 b. in a Writ of *Pone, Register indic. coram Justiciariis nostris apud West.*[23] is the Common Pleas, F. N. B. 64 d. 38 Edw. 3. 14. Statute 2 Edw. 6. cap. 13. such Courts grant Prohibitions who have used to grant them: *Hales Case* in | my Reports.   [62] Note the reason that many Prohibitions were granted in the Kings Bench, for that no Writ of Error lies but in Plaint.

Mouse's Case.

(1608) Michaelmas Term, 6 James I.
First Published in the *Reports,* volume 12, page 63.

> *Ed.:* A note Case. A ferryman was carrying forty-seven people, including a fellow named Mouse, when a storm blew up and threatened the barge. A fellow passenger threw over all of the cargo to save the barge, including Mouse's casket, with £113 inside. Mouse sued but lost. In Cases of necessity, anyone may act to save lives and there is no liability to them, although there may be liability against the ferryman.

In an action of Trespasse brought by Mouse, for a Casket, and a hundred & thirteen pounds, taken and carried away; the Case was, the Ferry-man of Gravesend took forty seven Passengers into his Barge, to passe to London, and Mouse was one of them, and the Barge being upon the water, a great Tempest hapned, and a strong wind, so that the Barge and all the passengers were in danger to be drowned, if a Hogshead of Wine and other ponderous things were not cast out, for the safeguard of the lives of the men: It was resolved *per totam Curiam,*[1] that in case of necessity, for the saving of the lives of the passengers, it was lawfull to the Defendant being a passenger to cast the Casket of the Plaintiff out of the Barge, with the other things in it, for *Quod quis ob tutelam corporis sui fecerit, jure id fecisse videtur,*[2] to which the

---

21. [*Ed.:* Prohibition upon the articles.]

22. [*Ed.:* that is to say, before our Justices at Westminster.]

23. [*Ed.:* Put on the register before our Justices at Westminster.]

1. [*Ed.:* by the whole court,]

2. [*Ed.:* Whatever someone does to protect his body, is deemed to be done rightfully,]

Defendant pleads all this speciall matter; and the Plaintiff replies, *De injuria sua propria absque tali causa:*[3] And the first day of this Term, this Issue was tried, and it was proved directly, that if the things had not been cast out of the Barge, the passengers had been drowned: And that *Levandi causa,*[4] they were ejected; some by one passenger and some by another; And upon this the Plaintiff was non-suit.

It was also resolved, that although the Ferry-man sur-charge the Barge, yet for safety of the lives of Passengers in such a time and accident of necessity, it is lawfull for any passenger to cast the things out of the Barge: And the Owners shall have their remedy upon the sur-charge against the Ferry-man, for the fault was in him upon the sur-charge; but if no sur-charge was, but the danger accrued only by the act of God, as by Tempest, no default being in the Ferry-man, every one ought to bear his losse for the safeguard of the life of a man, for *Interest Reipublicae quod homines conserventur,*[5] 8 Edw. 4. 23, &c. 12 Hen. 8. 15. 28 Hen. 8. Dyer 36. plucking down of a house in time of fire, &c. And this *Pro bono publico, & conservatio vitae hominis est bonum publicum.*[6] So if a Tempest arise in the Sea, *Levandi navis causa,*[7] and for salvation of the lives of men, it may be lawfull for Passengers to cast over the Merchandizes, &c.

Prohibitions del Roy.
(1607) Michaelmas Term, 5 James I.
In Conference Before the King.
First Published in the *Reports,* volume 12, page 63.

Ed.: These are Coke's notes of a conference in which he and his fellow Judges informed the King that he does not have the privilege to personally decide a Case at Law. The Law requires an artificial logic, in which he is not skilled. The Law, also, protects the King. These were not the answers the King was expecting; James was a strong proponent of the divine right of monarchy and saw little merit to being beholden to the Law. Other

---

3. [*Ed.:* Of his own wrong without such cause:]
4. [*Ed.:* In order to lighten the load,]
5. [*Ed.:* It is in the interest of the common weal that men should be saved.]
6. [*Ed.:* For the public good; and the preservation of a man's life is a public good.]
7. [*Ed.:* In order to lighten the ship,]

reports of this conference do not depict Coke in as cool a light. Even so, this report was widely circulated after its publication. This opinion reflects remarks in Bracton and Fleta, earlier Law Books, but no one had been quite so bold in presenting the ideas to a monarch. As a cornerstone of modern notions of the rule of Law and an independent judiciary, the report is one of the most important Law opinions in the history of the Common Law.

Note, upon Sunday the 10th of November, in this same Term, the King, upon complaint made to him by Bancroft, the Archbishop of Canterbury, concerning Prohibitions, the King was informed, that when the question was made of what matters the Ecclesiastical Judges have Cognizance, either upon the exposition of the Statutes concerning tithes, or any other thing Ecclesiastical, or upon the Statute 1 Eliz. concerning the high Commission, or in any other case in which there is not express authority in Law, the King himself may decide it in his Royall person; and that the Judges are but the delegates of the King, and that the King may take what Causes he shall please to determine, from the determination of the Judges, and may determine them himself. And the Archbishop said, that this was clear in Divinity, that such Authority belongs to the King by the Word of God in the Scripture. To which it was answered by me, in the presence, and with the clear consent of all the Judges of England, and Barons of the Exchequer, that the King in his own person I cannot adjudge any case, either criminall, as Treason, Felony, &c. or   [64] betwixt party and party, concerning his Inheritance, Chattels, or Goods, &c. but this ought to be determined and adjudged in some Court of Justice, according to the Law and Custom of England, and always Judgments are given, *Ideo consideratum est per Curiam,*[1] so that the Court gives the Judgment: And the King hath his Court, viz. in the upper house of Parliament, in which he with his Lords is the supream Judge over all other Judges; for if Error be in the Common Pleas, that may be reversed in the King's Bench: And if the Court of King's Bench err, that may be reversed in the upper house of Parliament, by the King, with the assent of the Lords Spirituall and Temporall, without the Commons: And in this respect the King is called the chief Justice, 20 Hen. 7. 7 a. by Brudnell:[2] And it appears in our Books, that the King may

1. [*Ed.:* Therefore it is decided by the court,]
2. 2 Ric. 3. 9. 21 Hen. 7. 8.

sit in the Star Chamber, but this was to consult with the Justices, upon certain questions proposed to them, and not *in Judicio;*[3] so in the King's Bench he may sit, but the Court gives the Judgment: And it is commonly said in our Books, that the King is alwaies present in Court in the Judgment of Law; and upon this he cannot be non-suit: But the Judgments are always given *Per Curiam;*[4] and the Judges are sworn to execute Justice according to Law and Custom of England. And it appears by the Acts of Parliament of 2 Edw. 3. cap. 9. 2 Edw. 3. cap. 1. That neither by the great Seal, nor by the little Seal, Justice shall be delayed; *ergo,* the King cannot take any cause out of any of his Courts, and give Judgment upon it himself,[5] but in his own cause he may stay it, as it doth appear, 11 Hen. 4. 8. And the Judges informed the King, that no King after the conquest assumed to himself to give any Judgment in any cause whatsoever, which concerned the administration of Justice within this Realm, but these were solely determined in the Courts of Justice: And the King cannot arrest any man, as the Book is in 1 Hen. 7. 4. for the party cannot have remedy against the King; so if the King give any Judgment, what remedy can the party have, *vide* 39 Ed. 3. 14. One who had a Judgment reversed before the Councill of State; it was held utterly void for that it was not a place where Judgment may be reversed, *vide* 1 Hen. 7. 4. Hussey chief Justice, who was Attorney to Edward the fourth reports that Sir John Markham, chief Justice, said to King Edward the fourth that the King cannot arrest a man for suspicion of Treason or Felony, as others of his Lieges may; for that if it be a wrong to the party grieved, he can have no remedy: and it was greatly marvelled that the Arch-bishop durst inform the King, that such absolute power and authority, as is aforesaid, belonged to the King by the word of God, *vide* 4 Hen. 4. cap. 22. which being translated into Latin, the effect is, *Judicia in Curia Regis reddita non annihilentur, sed stet judicium in suo robore quousque per judicium Curiae Regis tanquam erroneum, &c. vide West.* 2. *cap. 5. vide le Stat. de Marlbridge, cap.* 1. *Provisum est, concordatum et concessum, quod tam majores quam minores justitiam habeant et recipiant in Curia Domini Regis, et vide le Stat. de Magna Charta,*[6] *cap. 29. 25 Ed. 3. cap. 5.* None may

---

3. [*Ed.:* in the way of judgment.]

4. [*Ed.:* By the court.]

5. 17 Hen. 6. 14. 39 Edw. 3. 14.

6. [*Ed.:* Judgments given in the king's courts shall not be annulled (elsewhere), but a judgment shall stand in its force until (it is annulled) by judgment of the king's court as erroneous, etc. See Westminster

be taken by petition or suggestion made to our Lord the King or his Council, unless by Judgment: And 43 Ed. 3. cap. 3. no man shall be put to answer without presentment before the Justices, matter of Record, or by due process, or by writ Originall, according to the ancient Law of the Land: And if any thing be done against it, it shall be void in Law and held for Error, *vide* 28 Ed. 3. c. 3. 37 Ed. 3. cap. 18, *vide* 17 Ric. 2. *ex rotulis Parliamenti in Turri, act.* 10.[7] A controversy of Land between parties was heard by the King, and sentence given, which was repealed for this, that it did belong to the Common Law: Then the King said, that he thought the | Law was founded upon reason, and   [65] that he and others had reason, as well as the Judges: To which it was answered by me, that true it was, that God had endowed his Majesty with excellent Science, and great endowments of nature; but his Majesty was not learned in the Lawes of his Realm of England, and causes which concern the life, or inheritance, or goods, or fortunes of his Subjects; they are not to be decided by naturall reason but by the artificiall reason and judgment of Law, which Law is an act which requires long study and experience, before that a man can attain to the cognizance of it; And that the Law was the Golden met-wand and measure to try the Causes of the Subjects; and which protected his Majesty in safety and peace: With which the King was greatly offended, and said, that then he should be under the Law, which was Treason to affirm, as he said; To which I said, that Bracton saith, *Quod Rex non debet esse sub homine, sed sub Deo et Lege.*[8]*

The Lord Aburgaveney's Case.
In the Parliament.
First Published in the *Reports,* volume 12, page 70.

Ed.: This is a note of a judicial conference which resolved a question referred to it by members of the House of Lords, whether a man is made a baron

---

II, ch. 5. See the Statute of Marlborough, ch. 1: It is provided and agreed, and granted, that both great and small should have and receive Justice in the king's court. And see the Statute of Magna Carta.]

7. [*Ed.:* out of the rolls of parliament in the Tower.]

8. [*Ed.:* The king ought not to be under any man, but under God and the Law.]

*[Note (in 1703 edition), Bracton and Fleta both affirm, *Rex libert superiore in regno Deum et legem. Item curiam suam, i.e. comites et barones, &c.*]

or noble on the making of a writ, the delivery of the writ, or being seated in Parliament by command of the writ. The Judges rule that he must sit, although the ennoblement of a baron created by the king by letters patent under the Great Seal is created once the letters are made. This Case foreshadows some of the technical problems at the heart of the later U.S. Case of *Marbury v. Madison.*

The Writ doth not make a Peere, &c.

In the Parliament a question was made by the Lord of Northampton, Lord privy Seale, in the upper house of Parliament; That one Edward Nevil, the father of Edward Nevil, Lord of Aburgaveney, which now is, in the 2, and 3. of Queen Mary, was called by Writ to Parliament, and died before the Parliament: If he was a Baron, or no, and so ought to be named, was the question; and it was resolved by the Lord Chancellor, the two chief Justices, chief Baron, and divers other Justices there present, that the direction and delivery of the Writ did not make a Baron or Noble, until he did come to the Parliament, and there sit, according to the commandment of the Writ, for until that, the Writ did not take its effect, & the words of the Writ were wel penned, which are, *Rex & Regina, &c. Edwardo Nevil de Aburgaveny Chivalier, quia de advisamento & assensu consilii nostri pro quibusdam arduis, & urgentibus negotiis statum & defensionem regni nostri Angliae concernentibus, quoddam Parliamentum nostrum apud Westmonasterium, 21 die Octobris proximo futuro teneri ordinavimus, & ibidem vobiscum, ac cum Praelatis, Magnatibus & Proceribus dicti regni nostri colloquium habere & tractatum: vobis in fide & Ligeantia, quibus nobis tenemini, firmiter jungendo mandamus, quod consideratis dictorum negotiorum arduitate & periculis iminentibus, cessante excusatione quacunque, dictis die & loco personaliter intersitis nobiscum, ac cum Praelatis, Magnatibus ac Proceribus supradictis, super dictis negotiis tractaturis, vestrumque consilium impensur. & hoc sicut nobis, &c.*[1] And in the 35 Hen. 6. 46. and other Books,

---

1. [*Ed.:* The king and queen, etc. to Edward Nevil of Aburgaveney, knight. Because, by the advice and consent of our council, we have ordained our certain parliament to be held at Westminster on the twenty-first day of October next coming, for certain arduous and urgent business concerning the estate and defence of our realm of England, there to have discussion and treaty with you and with the prelates, great men and peers of our said realm: we, firmly enjoining, command you upon the faith and allegiance which you bear unto us that, considering the arduousness and imminent dangers of the said business, that you, leaving aside all excuses whatsoever, be there personally at the said day and place, with us and with the prelates, great men and peers mentioned above, to treat and give your advice upon the said business, and this as you, etc.]

he is called a Peer of Parliament, the which he cannot be until he sit in Parliament, and he cannot be of the Parliament until the Parliament begin: And forasmuch as he hath been made a Peer of Parliament by Writ (by which implicitly he is a Baron) the Writ hath not its operation and effect, until he sit in Parliament, there to consult with the King and the other Nobles of the Realm; which command of the King by his *Supersedeas*[2] may be countermanded, or the said Edward Nevil might have excused himself to the King, or he might have waived it, and submitted himself to his Fine, as one who is destrained to be a Knight, or one learned in the Law is called to be a Serjeant, the Writ cannot make him a Knight, or a Serjeant; And when one is called by Writ to Parliament, the order is, that he be apparrelled in his Parliament Robes, and his Writ is openly read in the upper house, and he is brought into his place by two Lords of Parliament, and then he is adjudged in Law, *Inter pares Regni,*[3] that is to say, *Ut cum olim Senatores e censu eligebantur, sic Barones apud nos habiti fuerint, qui per integram Baroniam terras suas tenebant, sive 13. feoda militum, & tertiam partem unius Feodi militis, quolibet Feodo computato ad 20 l. quae faciunt 400 marcas denarii erat valentia unius Baroniae integrae, & qui terras & redditus ad hanc valentiam habuerint, ad Parliamentum summoniri solebant;*[4] So that by this it appears, that every one who hath an entire Barony may have of right and of course a Writ to be summoned to Parliament, for without Writ none can sit in Parliament: And with this agrees our Books, for *Una voce*[5] they agree, that none can sit in Parliament as Peer of the Realm, without matter of Record, and if Issue be taken, whether a Baron or no Baron, Earl or no earl, this shall not be tryed *per paiis,*[6] but by the Record, by which it appears, that he was a Peer of Parliament, for without matter of Record he cannot be a peer of Parliament, | 35 Hen. 6. 46. 48 Edw. 3. 30 b. 48 Ass. pl. 6. 22 Ass. pl. 24. Register, 287. *Henricus tertius post magnas perturbationes & enormes exactiones inter ipsum Regem, Simonem de Monte forti, & alios Barones motas & susceptas, statuit & ordinavit, quod omnes illi Comites & Barones regni* [71]

---

2. [*Ed.:* Writ staying proceedings in a lower court.]

3. [*Ed.:* Among the peers of the realm,]

4. [*Ed.:* Just as senators were once chosen for their wealth, so amongst us there were barons who held their lands by a whole barony, or thirteen knight's fees and the third part of a knight's fee, each fee being reckoned at twenty pounds, which makes four hundred marks and one penny to be the value of one whole barony; and whoever had lands and rents to this value was usually summoned to parliament.]

5. [*Ed.:* with one voice.]

6. [*Ed.:* on the country, or unsworn.]

Angliae, quibus ipse Rex dignatus est brevia summonitionis dirigere, venirent ad Parliamentum, & non alii nisi forte dominus Rex alia illa brevia eis dirigere voluisset:[7] Which Act or Statute continues in force to this day, so that now none, although that he hath an entire Barony, can have a Writ of Summons to Parliament without the King's Warrant, under the privy Seal at least.

But if the King create any Baron by Letters Patents under the great Seal to him and to his Heirs, or to him and to his Heirs of his body, or for life, &c. there he is a noble man presently, for so he is expressly created by Letters Patents of the King, which cannot be countermanded: And he ought to have a Writ of Summons to Parliament of right and of course, and he shall be tryed by his Peers, if he shall be arraigned before any Parliament, but so shall not he be who is called by Writ, until he sits in Parliament, which is the diversity.

Richard the second created John Beauchamp of Holt, Baron of Kidderminster, by Letters Patents, dated 10. Oct. 11. year of his Raign, where all others before him were created by Writ.

Of Convocations.

(1610) Trinity Term, 8 James I.

First Published in the *Reports,* volume 12, page 72.

Ed.: These notes are of a judicial conference in which the limits of the powers of a Church Convocation are discussed. Particularly, the convocation cannot change the requirements of Common Law, Statute, or custom.

Convocation.

Note, it was resolved by the two chief Justices and divers other Justices, at a Committee before the Lords in the same Parliament, on divers points concerning the authority of a Convocation.

1. That a Convocation cannot assemble at their Convocation without the assent of the King.

2. That after their assembly they cannot confer together to constitute any Cannons without licence *del Roy.*

---

7. [*Ed.:* Henry III, after the great disturbances and enormous accusations moved and begun between the selfsame king, Simon de Montfort, and other barons, enacted and ordained that all those earls and barons of the realm of England to whom the selfsame king thinks it worthy to direct writs of summons shall come to the parliament, and no others, unless the lord king will direct other writs to them:]

3. When they upon conference conclude any Cannons, yet they cannot execute any of their Cannons without Royall assent.

4. They cannot execute any after Royall assent, but with these four limitations:

1. That they be not against the Prerogative of the King.

2. Nor against the Common Law.

3. Nor gainst any Statute Law.

4. Nor against any Custome of the Realm.

And all this appears by the Statute 25 Hen. 8. cap. 19. and this was but an affirmance of what was before the said Statute, for that it appears by the 19 Edw. 3. title *Quare non Admisit,* 7. where it is held, that if a Cannon Law be against the Law of the Land, the Bishop ought to obey the commandment of the King, according to the Law of the Land, 10 Hen. 7. 17. there is a Cannon that no Spirituall person shall be put to answer before a secular Judge; But this does not bind, because it is against the Common Law: And it appears by the Statute of Merton cap. 9. that they in case of Bastardy, were enforced to certifie against the Law of the church, that *Nati ante matrimonium fuerint Bastardi, quia Ecclesia habet tales pro legitimis, & rogaverunt omnes Episcopi Magnates quod consentirent, quod qui nati fuerint | ante matrimonium essent legitimi,*[1] which proves, that the Cannon Law in this point being repugnant to the Law of the Land, was not of any force: And for this, they implored the aid of the Parliament, *Et omnes Comites & Barones una voce responderunt, quod nolumus leges Angliae mutari, quae huc usque usitatae sunt et approbatae.*[2]

2 Hen. 6. 13. A Convocation may make Constitutions, by which those of the Spiritualty shall be bound, for this, that they all, or by representation, or in person, are present, but not the temporalty.

21 Edw. 4. 47. The Convocation is spirituall, and all their Constitutions are Spirituall. *Vide* the Records in the tower of 18 Hen. 8. 8 Edw. 1. 25 Edw. 1. 11 Edw. 2. and 15 Edw. 2.

Prohibitio Regis ne Clerus in Congregatione sua, &c. attemptet contra jus seu Coronam: alia, ne quod statuat in Concilio suo in prejudicium Regis seu legis,

[73]

---

1. [*Ed.:* Those born before marriage were bastards, because the Church regards them as legitimate; and all the bishops asked the great men whether they would consent that those who were born before marriage should be legitimate,]

2. [*Ed.:* And all the earls and barons answered with once voice, "We will not change the Laws of England which have until now been used and approved."]

&c.[3] By which it appears, that they can do nothing against the Law of the Land; for every part of the Law, be it Common Law, or Statute Law, cannot be abrogated nor altered without an Act of Parliament, to which every one shall be party, except for Spirituall Causes, or which concern Spirituall persons, if it be against the Prerogative of the King and the Common Law.

Proclamations.

(1610) Michaelmas Term, 8 James I.
In Conference Before the Lord Treasurer.
First Published in the *Reports,* volume 12, page 74.

Ed.: These are Coke's notes of a conference with the Privy Council, in which the King and Council sought an opinion on the authority of the King to pass proclamations to restrict building in London or to regulate the trade in starch, which was particularly in demand for the clothing of the well to do, as it was necessary for ruffed collars. Coke, with Chief Justice Fleming, Chief Baron Tanfield, and Baron Altham, initially refused to answer without consulting other Judges. Later, Coke answered, saying that the King can only require subjects to obey the Law, but he could not extend his prerogative beyond its legal bounds, could not create new crimes, and could not enlarge the criminal jurisdiction of Star Chamber. It was one of Coke's most significant attacks on the royal prerogative.

Memorand. That upon Thursday, 20 Sept 8 Regis Jacobi, I was sent for to attend the Lord Chancellor, Lord Treasurer, Lord privy Seal, and the Chancellor of the Dutchy; there being present the Attorney, the Solicitor, and Recorder: And two questions were moved to me by the Lord Treasurer; the one if the King by his Proclamation may prohibit new Buildings in and about London, &c. The other, if the King may prohibit the making of Starch of Wheat; And the Lord Treasurer said, that these were preferred to the King as grievances, and against the Law and Justice: And the King hath answered, that

---

3. [*Ed.:* The king's prohibition that the clergy in their convocation, etc. should not attempt anything against his right or crown. And another, that they make no enactment in their council in prejudice of the king or the Law, etc.]

he will confer with his privy Council, and his Judges, and then he will do right to them; To which I answered that these questions were of great importance. 2. That this concerned the answer of the King to the body, *viz.* to the Commons of the house of Parliament. 3. That I did not hear of these questions untill this morning at nine of the Clock: for the grievances were preferred, and the answer made when I was in my Circuit. And lastly, both the Proclamations, which now were shewed, were promulgated, anno 5 Jac. after my time of Attorney-ship: And for these reasons I did humbly desire them that I might have conference with my Brethren the Judges about the answer of the King, & then to make an advised answer according to law and reason. To which the Lord Chancellor said, that every President had first a commencement, and that he would advise the Judges to maintain the power and Prerogative of the King; and in cases in which there is no authority and President, to leave it to the King to order in it according to his wisdome, and for the good of his Subjects, or otherwise the King would be no more than the Duke of Venice; And that the King was so much restrained in his Prerogative, that it was to be feared the bonds would be broken: And the Lord privy Seal said, that the Physitian was not alwaies bound to a president, but to apply his Medecine according to the quality of the disease: And all concluded that it should be necessary at that time to confirm the Kings Prerogative with our Opinions, although that there were not any former President or Authority in Law, for every President ought to have a Commencement.

| To which I answered, That true it is, that every President hath a Com- [75] mencement, but when Authority and President is wanting, there is need of great considerations, before that any thing of novelty shall be established, and to provide that this be not against the Law of the Land: for I said, that the King cannot change any part of the Common Law, nor create any Offence by his Proclamation, which was not an Offence before, without Parliament. But at this time I only desired to have time of consideration and conference with my Brothers, for *Deliberandum est diu, quod statuendum est semel;*[1] To which the Solicitor said, that divers Sentences were given in the Star Chamber upon the Proclamation against building, and that I my self had given sentence in divers cases for the said Proclamation: to which I answered, that Presidents

---

1. [*Ed.:* It requires a long time to deliberate concerning something which is laid down in an instant;]

were to be seen, and consideration to be had of this upon conference with my Brethren, for that *Melius est recurrere, quam male currere;*[2] And that Indictment concludes, *Contra leges & statuta;*[3] but I never heard an Indictment to conclude, *Contra Regiam Proclamationem.*[4] At last my motion was allowed, and the Lords appointed the two chief Justices, chief Baron, and Baron Altham to have consideration of it.

Note, the King by his Proclamation, or other waies, cannot change any part of the Common Law, or Statute Law, or the Customs of the Realm, 11 Hen. 4. 37. Fortescue in laudibus Angliae legum, cap. 9. 18 Edw. 4. 35, 36, &c. 31 Hen. 8. cap. 8. *hic infra:* Also the King cannot create any Offence by his Prohibition or Proclamation, which was not an Offence before, for that was to change the Law, and to make an Offence which was not, for *Ubi non est lex, ibi non est transgressio, ergo,*[5] that which cannot be punished without proclamation, cannot be punished with it. *Vide* le Stat. 31 Hen. 8. cap. 8. which Act gives more power to the King then he had before, and yet there it is declared, that proclamation shall not alter the Law, Statutes, or Customs of the Realm, or impeach any in his Inheritance, Goods, body, life, &c. But if a man shall be indicted for a contempt against a Proclamation, he shall be fined and imprisoned, and so impeached in his body and goods, *vide* Fortescue, cap. 9. 18. 34. 36. 37, &c.

But a thing which is punishable by the Law, by fine and imprisonment, if the King prohibit it by his Proclamation, before that he will punish it, and so warn his Subjects of the peril of it, there if he commit it after, this as a Circumstance aggravates the Offence; But he by Proclamation cannot make a thing unlawful, which was permitted by the Law before: And this was well proved by the ancient and continuall forms of Indictments, for all Indictments conclude, *Contra legem & consuetudinem Angliae,*[6] or *Contra leges & statuta, &c.*[7] but never was seen any Indictment to conclude *Contra Regiam proclamationem.*[8]

---

2. [*Ed.:* It is better to run back than to keep running astray;]
3. [*Ed.:* Against the Laws and Statutes;]
4. [*Ed.:* Against the royal proclamation.]
5. [*Ed.:* Where there is no Law, there is no trespass; therefore,]
6. [*Ed.:* Against the Law and custom of England.]
7. [*Ed.:* Against the Laws and Statutes, etc.]
8. [*Ed.:* Against the royal proclamation, etc.]

So in all cases the King out of his providence, and to prevent dangers, which it will be too late to prevent afterwards, he may prohibit them before, which will aggravate the Offence if it be afterwards committed: And as it is a grand Prerogative of the King to make Proclamation (for no Subject can make it without authority from the King, or lawfull Custom) upon pain of fine and imprisonment, as it is held in the 22 Hen. 8. Procl. B. but we do finde divers Precedents of Proclamations which are utterly against Law and reason, and for that void, for, *Quae contra rationem juris introducta sunt non debent trahi in consequentiam.*[9]

An Act was made, by which Forraigners were licensed to Merchandize within London, Hen. 4. by Proclamation prohibited the execution of it, and that it should be in suspence *Usque ad proximum Parliamentium,*[10] which was against Law, *vide dors. claus.* 8 Hen. 4. Proclamat. in London. But 9 Hen. 4. | An Act of Parliament was made, That all the Irish people should depart the   [76] Realm, and go into Ireland before the feast of the Nativity of the blessed Lady, upon pain of death, which was absolutely *in terrorem,* and was utterly against the Law.

Hollinshed 722. An. Dom: 1546. 37 Hen. 8. the Whore-houses, called the stews, were suppressed by Proclamation, and sound of Trumpet, &c.

In the same Term it was resolved by the two chief Justices, chief Baron, and Baron Altham, upon conference betwixt the Lords of the privy Council and them, that the King by his Proclamation cannot create any Offence which was not an Offence before, for then he may alter the Law of the Land by his Proclamation in a high point, for if he may create an Offence where none is, upon that ensues fine and imprisonment: Also the Law of England is divided into three parts, Common Law, Statute Law, and Custom; But the Kings Proclamation is none of them: Also *Malum, aut est malum in se, aut prohibitum,*[11] that which is against Law is *malum in se; malum prohibitum*[12] is such an Offence as is prohibited by Act of Parliament, and not by Proclamation.

Also it was resolved, that the King hath no Prerogative, but that which the Law of the Land allows him.

---

9. [*Ed.:* Whatever is brought in contrary to the reason of the Law ought not to be treated with consequence.]

10. [*Ed.:* Until the next parliament,]

11. [*Ed.:* A wrong is either wrong in itself, or a wrong by reason of [statutory] prohibition,]

12. [*Ed.:* a wrong in itself; a wrong by reason of prohibition.]

But the King for Prevention of Offences, may by Proclamation admonish his Subjects that they keep the Lawes, and do not offend them, upon punishment to be inflicted by the Law, &c.

Lastly, if the offence be not punishable in the Star Chamber, the Prohibition of it by Proclamation cannot make it punishable there: And after this resolution, no Proclamation imposing Fine and Imprisonment, was afterwards made, &c.

Thomlinson's Case.
(1605) Hillary Term, 2 James I.
In the Court of Common Pleas.
First Published in the *Reports,* volume 12, page 104.

> *Ed.:* A note on a grant of a writ of habeas corpus to a litigant arrested by the Court of Admiralty for failing to give evidence in a Case filed before it, but which did not happen on the sea and was not in its jurisdiction. A note by the editors of the first edition suggests that this opinion was written for insertion into Part Seven of the *Reports,* but Coke withdrew it on the command of the King.

Theodore Thomlinson had brought an action of Account for Goods against one Philips in the Common Pleas, and thereupon Philips sued Thomlinson in the Court of the Admiralty, supposing the Goods to have been received in forain parts beyond the Seas: and the said Thomlinson being committed for refusing to answer upon his Oath to some Interrogatories there proposed to him, brought his *Habeas Corpus,*[1] which was returned thus, *Ego William Pope Marescallus supremae Curiae Admiralitatis Angliae Dom. Justic. Sereniss. Reginae nostrae in brevi huic Schedulae annex. specificat. Certific. quod infra vocat. Theodore Thomlinson ante advent. istius brevis capt. fuit & custodiae meae commiss. ex eo quod dictus Theodorus Thomlinson vinculo sacramenti coram Judice Admiralitatis Angliae astrictus ab respondend. quibusdam articulis contra eum in dictâ cur' dat' &c. sub poena quinque librarum &c. contumaciter examen suum*

13. [*Ed.:* The tribune of the people interrogating.]
1. [*Ed.:* Writ to ascertain the legality of an incarceration.]

subire recusavit, Idcirco, &c.[2] And it was resolved by the Court of Common Pleas.

1. That the Court of Admiralty hath no Cognizance of things done beyond Sea, And this appears plainly by the Statute of 13 Ric. 2. cap. 5. the words of which Statute are, that the Admirals and their Deputies shall not meddle from henceforth of any thing done within the Realm, but only of a thing done upon the Sea, *Vide* 19 Hen. 6. fol. 7. For things transitory done beyond the Seas, are either triable in the Kings Courts, or the party grieved may have his remedy before the Justices where the Fact was done beyond Seas.

2. That the proceedings in the Court of the Admiralty are according to the course of the Civill Law, and therefore the Court is not of Record, and by consequence cannot assesse any Fine in such case, as Judges of a Court of Record may do.

3. That the Return above mentioned was insufficient, as being too generall, because it is not specified for what cause or matter Thomlinson was examined, so as it might appear that the Interrogatories were of such things, as were within their Jurisdiction, and that the party ought by Law to answer upon his Oath, for otherwise he might very well refuse.

This case was intended to have been inserted by my Lord Coke into his 7th. Report, but not then published, because the King commanded that it should not be Printed, but the Judges resolved ut supra.

Walter Chute's Case.

(1614) Easter Term, 12 James I.
In Conference in Serjeants' Inn.
First Published in the *Reports,* volume 12, page 116.

Ed.: This is a note of an unusual judicial conference in which they considered the legality of the King's creating a variety of offices, particularly

---

2. [*Ed.:* I, William Pope, marshal of the supreme court of Admiralty of England, certify unto the lords Justices of our most serene queen specified in the writ annexed to this schedule that the within-named Theodore Thomlinson was taken and committed to my custody, before the arrival of this writ, forasmuch as the said Theodore Thomlinson was constrained by the bond of an oath to answer before the Judge of the Admiralty of England upon certain articles given against him in the same court, etc. on pain of five pounds, etc., and contemptuously refused to undergo his examination. Whereupon, etc.]

one for Walter Chute to register aliens. The Judges held that it would be illegal for the King to create the office, because it would be more for private gain than for public benefit. This is an important limit imposed by Law on royal patronage and so on royal revenue.

New erect-
ed office
void.

Walter Chute Sewer to the King, did exhibit a Petition to the King, that for the safety of the Realm, and the security of strangers within the Realm, that the King would vouchsafe to erect a new Office of Registering of all strangers within the Realm, except Merchant-strangers, to be kept at London, and to grant the said Office to the Petitioner, with a reasonable Fee, or without a Fee: And that all strangers, except Merchant-strangers, might depart the Realm within a certain convenient time, if they do not repair to the said Register, and take a Billet under the Registers hand: Which Petition the Lords of the Councel did refer to me, by their honourable Letters of the 13. of Novem. 1613, that I calling to me Counsel learned in the Law, should consider what the Law is in that behalf, and how it may stand with conveniency and policy of State, to put the same in execution, and by whom it ought to be performed: And upon conference had with the Justices of the Common Pleas, and the other Justices and Barons of Serjeants Inne Fleetstreet; It was resolved, that the erections of such new Offices, for the benefit of a private man was against all Law, of what nature soever: And therefore where one Captain Lee did make suit to the King to have a new office to make Inventory of Goods of those who died testate or intestate; It was resolved by the Lord Chancellor and my self, that such Grant shall be utterly void, although no certain person hath it, and that this was against Common Law, and the Statute of 21 Hen. 8. In

[117]

like manner, another sued I to have the Registering of Birth-dates, and the time of the death of each person within the Realm, and that it might be on Record and authenticall: So Mich. 19 Jac. To make a new Office in the upper Bench, for the only making of all Latitats at the suit of the Lord Daubigny, and after him of the Lord John Hungerford, and others, was resolved to be void. So Littletons suit, to name an Officer to be a generall Register, or rather Tabler or Indexer of all Judgements, for Debts and Damages, Recognizances, Bils, Obligations to the King, Deeds inrolled, Fines upon Offenders in the Star Chamber, and other Courts whatsoever: and this was pretended to be for the benefit of the Purchaser, and the ready finding of Records; and to such purpose was made the Statute of the 27 Eliz. for inrolling of Statutes; but the Suit was rejected by the two chief Justices and others: for every Court shall choose Officers either by Law or Prescription: the Law or Custom may not be changed without a Parliament; and so it was resolved Hil. 12 Jac. Regis; and divers other such inventions were resolved to be against Law and Record.

As to the second, in the case of Sir Walter Chute, concerning the conveniency or inconveniency of it, it was resolved, that it was inconvenient for divers causes. 1. For a private man to have private ends. 2. The numbring of Strangers by a private man would infer a Terror, and the King and Princes of other Countries will take offence at it, and will do the like to the Kings Subjects. 3. It is to be considered what breach it will be to former Treaties.

As to the third, in the case of Sir Walter Chute, that may be performed without any inconvenience; and so it was devised by the Lord Burleigh, and other Lords of the Councel: An. 37 Eliz. viz. To write Letters to the Mayors, Bayliffs, or other head Officers of every City, Borough, or Town, where any strangers are resident, to certifie how many strangers, and of what quality are in their Cities, &c. the which they are to know in respect of their Inhabitants, and Contributions to the poor, and other charges, and this may be done without any writing.

Which Suit being made to the Lords, was well approved by them, and the Suit utterly disallowed the 3. Dec. An. 3 Hen. 8. Commission granted to divers, to certifie the number of Strangers, Artificers, with the number of their Servants within London, and the Suburbs thereof, &c. according to the Statutes. See *Candishs Case,* 29 El. for making of all Writs of *Supersedeas* in the Kings Bench.

13 Eliz. A grant of an Office of Thomas Knivet, to examine all his Majesties Auditors and Clerks of the Pipe concerning their Offices for years: It was resolved by the Court to be against Law, for it belongs to the Barons who are Judges; and it is also an Invocation in a Court of Justice. 25 Eliz: A Grant of an Office to Thomas Leichfield to examine all deceits false allowances of the Queens officers for eight years, resolved to be void.

The making of *Subpoenas* in Chancery anciently belonged to the six Clerks: The late Queens Majesty granted the same by Patent to one particular man.

The keeping and filing of Affidavits in Chancery anciently belonged to the Register. The Kings Majesty, that now is, granted the same to one particular man.

The erecting and putting down of Innes hath been anciently in the power of the Justice of Peace. His Majesty hath given that power by Patent to a particular man.

[118] | The taking of the Depositions, and all other proceedings, before and by the Commission which hath used to be taken and kept by the Commissioners themselves, or some Clerk of their appointment; his Majesty hath granted the same by Patent to one particular man.

The King by his Letters Patents granted to Simon Darlington the Office of Alveger and limited what Fees he should take.

The sole drawing, writing, and ingrossing of all Licences and Pardons was granted to Edward Bacon Gent. with the Fee that had formerly been taken, and a Restraint for all others, &c.

The Offices of *Subpoenas* was granted to Thomas George and others during life, with the fee of 2s. and a restraint that no others presume to make those Writs.

The Office of making and registering all manner of assurances and Policies, &c. was, by Letters Patents granted to Richard Gandler Gent. with such fees as the Lord Major and others should rate, with power to rate fees, and a restraint of all others, &c. which was during pleasure, and afterwards to him and others during lives.

The Office of writing Tallies and Counter-Tallies granted to Sir Vincent Skinner.

Quare.   The office of ingrossing Patents to the great Seal, and an encrease of fees granted late to Sir Richard Young, and Mr. Pye.

Sir Stephen Procter's [Proctor's] Case.
(1614) Easter Term, 12 James I.
In Conference in Star Chamber.
First Published in the *Reports,* volume 12, page 118.

> *Ed.:* Note of a judicial conference in Star Chamber, on the result when Judges are evenly divided on a judgment. The Common Law courts did not enter judgment unless there was a majority. The Chief Justices held that the matter for the Star Chamber should be resolved according to its own precedents. Coke recites only two, which are not utterly conclusive.

Judges divided in the Star Chamber.   In an Information preferred in the Star Chamber by the Attorney-generall, against Stephen Procter, Berkenhead, and others, for Scandall and Conspiracy of the Earl of Northampton, and the Lord Wooton. At the hearing of this case, were present eight Lords, *Scil.* The chief Baron, the two chief Justices, two Bishops, one Baron, the Chancellor of the Exchequer, and the Lord Chancellor: And the three chief Justices, and the Temporall Baron condemned Sir Stephen Procter, and fined and imprisoned him: But the Lord Chancellor, the two Bishops, and the Chancellor of the Exchequer acquitted him. And the question was, if Sir Stephen Procter shall be condemned or acquitted; and it seemed to some of the Clerks *prima facie*,[1] that the better shall be taken for the King, and that he shall be condemned, but others were of the contrary opinion; and hereupon the matter was referred to the two chief Justices, calling to their assistance the Kings learned Councel: And first they resolved, that this question must be determined by the Presidents of the Court of Star Chamber, for that Court is against the rule and order of all other Courts, for in the Kings Bench, the Common Pleas, or the Exchequer, or in the Exchequer Chamber, where all the Justices are assembled, if the Justices are equally divided, no judgment can be given. And so it is in the Court of Parliament; and therefore this course ought to be warranted by the custom of the Court: And as to that, two Presidents only were produced for the maintenance of the said Custom, Viz. One in the Hilary Term, 39 El. between Gibson Plaintiff, and Griffith and others Defendants, where the Complaint was for a Riot, and at the hearing of the Case, there was eight present, four gave their judgements that the Defendants were guilty, but the other four, whereof the Lord Chancellor was one, pronounced | the Defendants not guilty, and no sentence of [119] condemnation was ever entered, because the Lord Chancellor was one of the four who acquitted them. The other was Hil. 45 Eliz. In an information by the Attorney-general against Katherne and others, for forging of a Will, and a Misdemeanor for procuring a fraudulent Deed to defeat the Queen of her Escheat: And eight were in presence at the hearing of the Cause, whereof four found the Defendants guilty of Forgery, and did inflict the punishment according to the Statute of the 5 Eliz. but the others, whereof the Lord Chancellor was one, gave sentence, that the Defendants were guilty of the Misdemeanor, and not of the Forgery, and imposed a fine of 500 l. only, which decree was entered according to the Lord Chancellors voice, although the sentence on the other side was more beneficiall for the King, and no other president could be found in this case, the which I have reported this Term.

---

1. [*Ed.:* on the face of it,]

Exaction of Benevolence.
First Published in the *Reports*, volume 12, page 119.

Ed.: In this note case, Coke described the precedents for the monarch requesting gifts from wealthy nobles to fund various projects when there was no money left from the last Parliamentary supply, or grant of taxes. Because the benevolences were technically voluntary, they were lawful. This case has a considerable significance as a predecessor decision to the Five Knights' Case and the Petition of Right.

Concerning Benevolence.

Note, the exaction under the good name of Benevolence began in this manner.

When King Edward the fourth, had a Subsedy granted to him in the 12 Edw. 4. by Parliament, because he could have no more by Parliament, and without a Parliament he could not have any Subsedy to be levied of the Lands and Goods of the Subject, he invented this shift or device, in which three things are to be observed.

1. The cause.

2. The Invention.

3. The Successe.

1. The Duke of Burgandy, who had married Margaret, the Sister of Edward the fourth solicited King Edward to joyn in War with him against the French King, to which the King easily consented, because he sought revenge against the French King for aiding the Earl of Warwick, Queen Margaret, and Prince Edward, and their party, and therefore, to make War against the French King, was the cause.[1]

2. The invention was, The King called before him at severall times a great number of the wealthiest of his Subjects, to declare to them his necessity, and his purpose to levy War for the honour and safety of the Kingdom, and demanded of each of them a certain summ of money, and the King treated with them, with such great grace and clemency, and with such gentle prayer to assist him in his necessity, for the honour of the Realm, that they very freely yeelded to his request, for the honour and safety of the Realm. Amongst the rest, there was a Widow of a very good Estate, of whom the King meerly asked

---

1. Hollingshead, 11 Edw. 4 694. Stow. 701.

what she would willingly give him for the maintenance of his Wars; By my faith, quoth she, for your lovely countenance sake, you shall have twenty pound, which was more then the King expected; the King thanked her, and vouchsafed to kisse her, upon which she presently swore he should have twenty pounds more.

3. The successe and event was: That wheras the King called this a Benevolence to please the people, yet many of the people did much grudge at it, and called it a Malevolence.

Primo Ed. 5. in the Oration of the Duke of Buckingham in Guild hall in London, he inveighed, amongst other things, against this Taxation under the name of Benevolence. 1 Ric. 3. cap. 2. the Subjects of the Realm shall not be charged with such charge or imposition called Benevolence, which tendeth to the subversion of the Law, and destruction of Commonalty, as appears in the Preamble (where any such charge). And that such exaction before taken, under the name of benevolence, shall not be drawn into example | to make [120] such or the like charge, but shall be damned and adnulled for ever: But it appears by the Preamble, that this was against the wil and liberty of the Subject, but a free-wil offering is not restrained.

An. 6 Hen. 7. The King declared in Parliament, that he had just cause of War against the French King, which for the causes there shewn was approved, and for that he desired a Benevolence towards the maintenance of it; and every one promised his helping hand, the which the King greatly commended; and to the intent that the poorer sort might be spared, he demanded it by way of a Benevolence, according to the example of Edward the fourth and published, that he would by their open hands measure their benevolent hearts; and he who gives but a little, according to his gift.

By this means he collected great summs of money, with some grudge for the extremity shewn by the Commissioners, 11 Hen. 7. cap. 20. An Act was made for levying of that Benevolence, according to their assent, but only of such as assented.

An: 20 Hen. 7. A Commission to levy what was granted by 11 Hen. 7.

Note, that 15 Hen. 8. a Commission under the great Seal, called a Commission of Anticipation, to collect the Subsidy before the day.[2]

An: 16 Hen. 8. For War with France, a Benevolence levied by Commission

2. Stow 880.

with great Curses and Imprecations against the Council, and with successe, for it was to levy a sixth part of the value in money or Plate against the good will of the Subject.

An: 26 Hen. 8. Another Benevolence levied by Commission for maintenance of War against France, with ill successe, for it was exacted of the Subject against his good will. But if the Subjects of their free will, without any compulsion, will give to the King for publick uses any summs of money, this is not prohibited by any Statute.

And the Statute 11 Hen. 7. cap. 18. proves this, where the Parliament compels them who have freely granted any thing to the King for publick use, to pay it.

Feb. An: 40 Eliz. It was resolved by all the Justices and Barons, that a free Grant to the Queen without coercion is lawfull, and accordingly they granted to the Queen, *Quod nota bene, quia, &c.*[3]

---

3. [*Ed.:* which note well, because, etc.]

Part Thirteen of the *Reports*

The Thirteenth Part of Coke's *Reports* was published in 1659 under the initial title of the publisher, *Certain Select Cases in Law,* Reported by Sir EDWARD COKE, Knight, Late Lord Chief Justice of ENGLAND And one of His Majesties Council of State: Translated out of a Manuscript written with his own hand. Never before Published. In later editions of the *Reports,* it was bound in under the title *The Thirteenth Part of the Reports published from the notes of Sir Edward Coke, Knight. after his Death.* The reports in this part were drawn from the same manuscript as those in Part Twelve.

(Preface)
To The Reader.

READER,

It may seem altogether an unnecessary work to say any thing in the praise and vindication of that Person and his Labours, which have had no less then the generall approbation of a whole Nation convened in Parliament: For if King Theodorick in Cassiodore could affirme, *Neque enim dignus est a quopiam redargui qui nostro judicio meretur absolvi,*[1] That no man ought to be reproved whom his Prince commends. How much rather then should men forbear to censure those and their Works which have had the greatest allowance and attestation a Senate could give, and to acquiesce and rest satisfied in that judgement? Such respect and allowance hath been given to the learned Works of the late Honourable and Venerable Chiefe Justice, Sir Edward Coke, whose Person in his life time was reverenced as an Oracle, and his Works (since his decease) cyted as Authentick Authorities, even by the Reverend Judges them-

---

1. [*Ed.:* For neither is it worthy in any place to reprove someone who in our judgment deserves to be absolved.]

selves. The acceptance his Books (already extant) have found with all knowing Persons, hath given me the confidence to commend to the publick view some Remains of his, under his owne hand-writing, which have not yet appeared to the World, yet (like true and genuine Eaglets) are well able to behold and bear the light: They are of the same Piece and Woofe with his former Works, and in respect of their owne native worth, and the reference they bear to their Author, cannot be too highly valued: Though, in respect of their quantity and number, the Reports are but few; yet, as the skilfull Jeweller will not lose so much as the very filings of rich and precious mettals; and the very fragments were commanded to be kept where a Miracle had been wrought, *Propter miraculi claritatem et evidentiam:*[2] So these small parcels, being part of those vast and immense labours of their Author, great almost to a Miracle (if I may be allowed the comparison:), were there no other use to be made of them (as there is very much, for they manifest and declare to the Reader many secret and abstruse points in Law, not ordinarily to be met with in other Books so fully and amply related) deserve a publication, and to be preserved in the respects and memories of Learned men, and especially the Professors of the Law; and to that end they are now brought to light and published. If any should doubt of the truth of these Reports of Sir Edward Coke, they may see the originall Manuscript in French, written with his own hand, at Henry Twyfords Shop in Vine-Court Middle Temple.

Farewell.

J.G.

---

2. [*Ed.:* On account of the clarity and distinctness of the miracle:]

Prohibitions.

(1609) Hilary Term, 6 James I
In Conference before the King.
First Published in the *Reports,* volume 13, page 30.

Ed.: These are Coke's notes of another conference in which he defended the prohibitions issued against the local court held by the Lord President of York, only one term after his last conference. Coke chronicles typical prohibitions to the King's satisfaction. See De Modo Decimandi, p. 505.

Upon Wednesday, being Ashwednesday, the   day of February, 1606. A great Complaint was made by the President of York unto the King, That the Judges of the Common Law had, in contempt of the Command of the King the last Term, granted sixty or fifty Prohibitions at the least out of the Common-Pleas, to the President and Councel of York after the sixth day of February, and named three in particular, (*scil.*) between Bell and Thawptes, another between Snell and Huet, and another in an Information of a Riotous Rescue preferred by English Bill by the Attorney General against Christopher Dickenson, one of the Sheriffs of York, and divers others, in rescuing of one William Watson out of the Custody of the Deputy of one of the Pursuivants of the same Councel who had arrested the said Watson by force of a Commission of Rebellion awarded by the President and Councel, which Prohibition in the said Information was (as was affirmed) denied upon a motion made in the Kings Bench the last Term, and yet granted by us. And the King sent for me to answer to that Complaint: and I onely, all the rest of the Justices being absent, waited upon the King in the Chamber neer the Gallery; Who, in the presence of Egerton Lord Chancellor, the Earl of Salisbury Lord Treasurer, the Lord of Northampton Lord Privy Seal, the Earl of Suffolk Lord Chamberlain, the Earl of Worcester, the Archbishop of Canterbury, the Lord Wotton, and others of his Councel, rehearsed to me the Complaint aforesaid: and I perceived well, that upon the | said Information he had conceived great [31] displeasure against the Judges of the Common Pleas, and chiefly against me; To which I (having the Copy of the Complaint sent to me by the Lord Treasurer the Sabbath day before) answered in this manner, That I had, with as much brevity as the time would permit, made search in the Offices of the Preignothories of the Common Pleas: and as to the said Cases between Bell and Thawptes, and Snell and Huet, no such could be found: but my intent was not to take advantage of a Misprisal: and the truth was, that the sixth day of February the Court of Common Pleas had granted a Prohibition to the President and Councel of York, between Lock Plaintiff, and Bell and others Defendants: and that was, a Replevyn in English was granted by the said President and Councel, which I affirmed was utterly against Law: For at the Common Law no Replevyn ought to be made, but by Original Writ directed to the Sheriff. And the Statute of Marlbridg cap. 21. and West. 1. cap. 17. hath authorized the Sheriff upon Plaint made to him, to make a Replevyn; and all that appeareth by the said Statutes, and by the Books of 29 Edw. 3. 21. 8 Eliz. Dyer 245. And the King neither by his Instructions had made the President and Councel Sheriffs, nor could grant to them power to make a Replevyn against the Law, nor against the said Acts of Parliament; but the same ought to be made by the Sheriff. And all that was affirmed by the Lord Chancellor for very good Law: And I say, that it might well be that we have granted other Prohibitions in other Cases of English Replevyns. Another Prohibition I confess we have granted between Sir Bethel Knight, now Sheriff of the County of York, as Executor to one Stephenson, who had made him and another his Executors, and preferred an English Bill against Chambers, and divers others in the nature of an Action upon the Case, upon a Trover and Conversion in the life of the Testator of goods and Chattels, to the value of 1000 l. and because the other Executor would not joyn with him, although he was named in the Bill, he had not any remedy at the Common Law, he prayed remedy there in Equity: and I say, that the President and Councel have not any authority to proceed in that Case, for divers causes.

1. Because there is an express limitation in their Commission, that they shall not hold plea between party and party &c. unless both parties, or one of them, *tanta paupertate sunt gravati*,[1] that they cannot sue at the Common Law: and in that case the Plaintiff was a Knight, and Sheriff, and a man of great ability.

2. By that Suit the King was deceived of his Fine, for he ought to have had 200 l. Fine, because that the damages amounted to 4000 l. and that was one of the causes that the Sheriff began his Suit there, and not at the Common

---

1. [*Ed.:* are grieved with such poverty,]

Law: another cause was, that their Decrees which they take upon them are final and uncontroulable, either by Error, or any other remedy. And yet the President is a Nobleman, but not learned in the Law; and those which are of the Councel there, although that they have the countenance of Law, yet they are not learned in the Law; and nevertheless they take upon them final and uncontroulable Decrees in matters of great importance: For if they may deny Relief to any at their pleasure without controulment, so they may do it by their final Decrees without Error, Appeal, or other remedy: which is not so in the Kings Courts where there are five Judges; for they can deny Justice to none who hath Right, nor give any Judgment, but the same is controulable by a Writ of Error, &c. I And if we shall not grant Prohibitions in Cases where [32] they hold Plea without authority, then the subjects shall be wrongfully oppressed without Law, and we denyed to do them Justice: And their ignorance in the Law appeared by their allowance of that Suit, *scil.* That the one Executor had no remedy by the Common Law, because the other would not joyn in suit with him at the Common Law: whereas every one learned in the Law knoweth, that summons and severance lieth in any Suit brought as Executors: and this also in that particular Case was affirmed by the Lord Chancellor; and he much inveighed against Actions brought there upon Trover and Conversion, and said, that they could not be found in our ancient Books.

Another Prohibition I confess we have granted, between the L. Wharton, who by English Bill sued before the Councel, Banks, Buttermere, and others, for fishing in his several Fishings in Darwent in the County of C. in the nature of an Action of Trespass at the Common Law, to his damage of 200 l. and for the causes next before recited, and because the same was meerly determinable at the Common Law, we granted a Prohibition, and that also was allowed by the Lord Chancellor. And as to the case of Information upon the Riotous Rescous, I having forgotten to speak to that, the King himself asked what the Case was? to whom I answered, that the case was, That one exhibited a Bill there in the nature of an Action of Debt, upon a *Mutuatus*[2] against Watson, who upon his Oath affirmed, that he had satisfied the Plaintiff, and that he owed him nothing, and yet because the Defendant did not deny the Debt, the Councel decreed the same against him, and upon that Decree the Pursuivant was sent to arrest the said Watson, who arrested him upon which

2. [*Ed.:* Action to collect a debt not much under seal.]

the Rescous was made: and because that the Suit was in the nature of an Action of Debt upon a *Mutuatus* at the Common Law, and the Defendant at the Common Law might have waged his Law, of which the Defendant ought not to be barred by that English Bill, *quia beneficium juris nemini est auferendum:*[3] the Prohibition was granted; and that was affirmed also by the Lord Chancellor: whereupon I concluded, that if the principal cause doth not belong unto them, all their proceedings was *coram non Judice,*[4] and then no Rescous could be done: but the Lord Chancellor said, that though the same cannot be a Rescous, yet it was a Riot, which might be punished there: which I denyed, unless it were by course of Law by force of a Commission of Oyer and Terminer, and not by an English Bill: but to give the King full satisfaction in that point, the truth is, the said Case was debated in Court, and the Court inclined to grant a Prohibition in the said case; but the same was stayed to be better advised upon, so as no Prohibition was ever under Seal in the said Case.

Also I confess, that we have granted divers Prohibitions to stay Suits there by English Bill upon penal Statutes: for the manner of prosecution, as well for the Action, Proces, &c. as for the count, is to be pursued, and cannot be altered; and therefore without question the Councel in such cases cannot hold Plea, which was also affirmed by the Lord Chancellor. And I said, that it was resolved in the Reign of Queen Eliz. in *Parots Case,* and now lately in the Case of *the President and Councel of Wales,* That no Court of Equity can be erected at this day without Act of Parliament, for the reasons and causes in the Report of the said *Case of Parot.*

[33]　　　And the King was well satisfied with these reasons and causes of | our proceedings, who of his Grace gave me his Royall hand, and I departed from thence in his favour. And the surmise of the Number, and that the Prohibition in the said Case in the Information was denied in the Kings Bench, was utterly denied: for the same was moved when two Judges were in Court, who gave not any opinion therein, but required Serjeant Hutton who moved it, to move the same again when the Court was full, &c.

---

3. [*Ed.:* because the benefit of the Law is not to be taken away from anyone:]
4. [*Ed.:* beyond its jurisdiction,]

The Case de Modo Decimandi,[1] and of Prohibitions, debated before the Kings Majesty.

(1609) Trinity Term, 7 James I
In Conference before the King.
First Published in the *Reports,* volume 13, page 37.

Ed.: These are Coke's notes on the three-day debate on prohibitions held in 1609, before the King and Council, between the bishops and Lawyers of the civil Law, and the Common Law Judges over whether attempts by priests to collect tithes that are due de modo decimandi, or according to custom, can be brought in the ecclesiastical courts, or whether they must be brought in the Law courts. The debates are illustrative of the dispute between the Law and the church that was then ranging on several fronts.

Richard, Archbishop of Canterbury, accompanyed with the Bishop of London, the Bishop of Bathe and Wells, the Bishop of Rochester, and divers Doctors of the Civil and Canon Law, as Dr. Dunn Judg of the Arches, Dr. Bennet Judg of the Prerogative, Dr. James, Dr. Martin, and divers other Doctors of the Civil and Canon Law came attending upon them to the King to Whitehall the Thursday, Friday, and Saturday after Easter-Term, in the Councel-Chamber; where the Chief Justice, and I my self, Daniel Judg of the Common-Pleas, and Williams Judg of the Kings-Bench, by the command of the King attended also: where the King being assisted with his Privy Councel, all sitting at the Councel-Table, spake as a most gracious, good, and excellent Soveraign, to this effect: As I would not suffer any novelty or Innovations in my Courts of Justice Ecclesiastical and Temporal; so I will not have any of the Laws, which have had judicial allowances in the times of the Kings of England before him, to be forgotten, but to be put in execution. And for as much as upon the contentions between the Ecclesiastical and Temporal Courts great trouble, inconvenience and loss may arise to the subjects of both parts, namely when the controversie ariseth upon the jurisdiction of my Courts of ordinary Justice; and because I am the head of Justice immediately under God, and knowing what hurt may grow to my Subjects of both sides, when no

---

1. [*Ed.:* Of the custom of tithing,]

private case, but when the Jurisdictions of my Courts are drawn in question, which in effect concerneth all my Subjects, I thought that it stood with the Office of a King, which God hath committed to me, to hear the controversies between the Bishops and other of his Clergy, and the Judges of the Laws of England, and to take Order, that for the good and quiet of his Subjects, that the one do not encroach upon the other, but that every of them hold themselves within their natural and local jurisdiction, without encroachment or usurpation the one upon the other. And he said, that the onely question then to be disputed was, If a Parson, or a Vicar of a Parish, sueth one of his Parish in the Spiritual Court for Tythes in kinde, or Lay-fee, and the Defendant alledgeth a custom or prescription *De modo Decimandi,* if that custom or prescription, *De modo Decimandi,* shall be tryed and determined before the Judg Ecclesiastical where the Suit is begun; or a Prohibition Lyeth, to try the same by the common Law. And the King directed, that we who were Judges should declare the reasons and causes of our proceedings, and that he would hear the authorities in the Law which we had to warrant our proceedings in granting of Prohibition in cases of *Modo Decimandi.* But the Archbishop of Canterbury kneeled before the King, and desired him, that he would hear him and others who are provided to speak in the case for the good of the Church of England: and the Archbishop himself inveighed much against two things:

[38] 1. That a *Modus Decimandi* should be | tryed by a Jury, because that they themselves claim more or less *modum Decimandi;* so as in effect they were Tryors in their own cause, or in the like cases. 2. He inveighed much the precipitate and hasty Tryals by Juries: and after him Doctor Bennet, Judg of the Prerogative Court, made a large Invection against Prohibitions *in Causis ecclesiasticis:*[2] and that both Jurisdictions as well ecclesiastical as temporal, were derived from the King; and all that which he spake out of the Book which Dr. Ridley hath lately published, I omit as impertinent: and he made five Reasons, why they should try *Modum Decimandi.*

And the first and principal Reason was out of the Register, fo. 58. *quia non est consonans rationi, quod cognitio accessarii in Curia Christianitatis impediatur ubi cognitio Causae principalis ad forum Ecclesiasticum noscitur pertinere.*[3] And

---

2. [*Ed.:* in ecclesiastical causes.]

3. [*Ed.:* because it is not consonant with reason that the cognizance of an incidental matter in court

the principal cause is Right of Tythes, and the Plea of *Modo Decimandi* sounds in satisfaction of Tythes; and therefore the Conusance of the original cause, (*scil.*) the Right of Tythes appertaining to them, the Conusance of the bar of Tythes, which he said was but the accessary, and as it were dependant upon it, appertained also to them. And whereas it is said in the *Bishop of Winchesters Case,* in the second part of my Reports, and 8 Edw. 4. 14. that they would not accept of any Plea in discharge of Tythes in the Spiritual Court, he said, that they would allow such Pleas in the Spiritual Court, and commonly had allowed them; and therefore he said, that that was the Mystery of iniquity founded upon a false and feigned foundation, and humbly desired the reformation of that Error, for they would allow *Modum Decimandi* being duly proved before them.

2. There was great inconveniency, that Lay-men should be Tryers of their own Customs, if a *Modus Decimandi* should be Tryed by Jurors; for they shall be upon the matter Jurors in their own cause.

3. That the custom of *Modo Decimandi* is of Ecclesiastical Jurisdiction and Conusance, for it is a manner of Tything, and all manner of Tything belongs to Ecclesiastical Jurisdiction: and therefore he said, that the Judges, in their Answer to certain Objections made by the Archbishop of Canterbury, have confessed, that suit may be had in Spiritual Courts *pro modo Decimandi;* and therefore the same is of Ecclesiastical Conusance; and by consequence it shall be tryed before the Ecclesiastical Judges: for if the Right of Tythes be of Ecclesiastical Conusance, and the satisfaction also for them of the same Jurisdiction, the same shall be tryed in the Ecclesiastical Court.

4. In the Prohibitions of *Modus Decimandi* averment is taken, That although the Plaintiff in the Prohibition offereth to prove *Modum Decimandi,* the Ecclesiastical Court doth refuse to allow of it, which was confessed to be a good cause of Prohibition: But he said, they would allow the Plea *De Modo Decimandi* in the Spiritual Court, and therefore *cessante causa cessabit & effectus,*[4] and no Prohibition shall lie in the Case.

5. He said, that he can shew many consultations granted in the cause *De Modo Decimandi,* and a Consultation is of greater force then a Prohibition;

Christian should be hindered where it is known that the cognizance of the principal cause belongs to the ecclesiastical jurisdiction.]

4. [*Ed.:* when the cause ceases, the effect ceases also,]

for Consultation, as the word imports, is made with the Court with consultation and deliberation. And Bacon, Solicitor-General, being (as it is said) assigned with the Clergy by the King, argued before the King, and in effect said less then Doctor Bennet said before: but he vouched 1 Ric. 3. 4. the Opinion of Hussey, when the Original ought to begin in the Spiritual Court,

[39]   and afterwards a I thing cometh in issue which is tryable in our Law, yet it shall be tryed by their Law: As if a man sueth for a Horse devised to him, and the Defendant saith, that the Devisor gave to him the said Horse, the same shall be tryed there. And the Register 57 and 58. If a man be condemned in Expences in the Spiritual Court for laying violent hands upon a Clark, and afterwards the Defendant pays the costs, and gets an Acquittance, and yet the Plaintiff sueth him against his Acquittance for the Costs, and he obtains a Prohibition, for that Acquittances and Deeds are to be determined in our Law, he shall have a Consultation, because that the principal belongeth to them. 38 Edw. 3. 5. Right of Tythes between two spiritual persons shall be determined in the Ecclesiastical Court. And 38 Edw. 3. 6. where the Right of Tythes comes in debate between two spiritual persons, the one claiming the Tythes as of common Right within his Parish, and the other claiming to be discharged by real composition, the Ecclesiastical Court shall have Jurisdiction of it.

And the said Judges made humble suit to the King, That for as much as they perceived that the King in his Princely Wisdom did detest Innovations and Novelties, that he would vouchsafe to suffer them with his gracious favor, to inform him of one Innovation and Novelty which they conceived would tend to the hinderance of the good administration and execution of Justice within his Realm.

Your Majesty, for the great zeal which you have to Justice, and for the due administration thereof, hath constituted and made fourteen Judges, to whom you have committed not onely the administration of Ordinary Justice of the Realm, but *crimina laesae Majestatis,*[5] touching your Royal person, for the legal proceeding: also in Parliament we are called by Writ, to give to your Majesty and to the Lords of the Parliament our advice and counsel, when we are required: We two chief Justices sit in the Star-Chamber, and are oftentimes called into the Chancery, Court of Wards, and other High Courts of Justice: we in our Circuits do visit twice in the year your Realm, and execute Justice

5. [*Ed.:* (jurisdiction over) the crime of lèse-majesté (treason).]

according to your Laws: and if we who are your publique Judges receive any diminution of such reverence and respect in our places, which our predecessors had, we shall not be able to do you such acceptable service as they did, without having such reverence and respect as Judges ought to have. The state of this Question is not *in statu deliberativo,*[6] but *in statu judiciali;*[7] it is not disputed *de bono,*[8] but *de vero, non de Lege fienda, sed de Lege lata;*[9] not to frame or devise new Laws, but to inform your Majesty what your Law of England is: and therefore it was never seen before, that when the Question is of the Law, that your Judges of the Law have been made Disputants with him who is inferior to them, who day by day plead before them at their several Courts at Westminster; and although we are not afraid to dispute with Mr. Bennet and Mr. Bacon, yet this example being *primae impressionis,*[10] and your Majesty detesting Novelties and innovations, we leave it to your Grace and Princely consideration, whether your Majesty will permit our answering *in hoc statu judiciali,*[11] upon your publique Judges of the Realm? But in Obedience to your Majesties command, We, with your Majesties gracious favor, in most humble manner will inform your Majesty touching the said Question, which we, and our predecessors before us, have oftentimes adjudged upon judicial proceedings in your Courts of Justice at Westminster: which Judgments cannot be reversed or examined for any Error in Law, if | not by a Writ of Error in [40] a more high and supream Court of Justice, upon legal and judicial proceedings: and that is the ancient Law of England, as appeareth by the Statute of 4 Hen. 4. cap. 22.

And we being commanded to proceed, all that which was said by us, the Judges, was to this effect, That the Tryal *De Modo Decimandi* ought to be by the Common Law by a Jury of twelve men, it appeareth in three manners: First, by the Common Law: Secondly, by Acts of Parliament: And lastly, by infinite judgments and judicial proceedings long times past without any impeachment or interruption.

But first it is to see, What is a *Modus Decimandi? Modus Decimandi* is,

---

6. [*Ed.:* in a deliberative state,]
7. [*Ed.:* in a judicial state;]
8. [*Ed.:* for the good of it;]
9. [*Ed.:* for truth, not to make Law but to lay down what it is;]
10. [*Ed.:* [a Case] of first impression,]
11. [*Ed.:* in this judicial state,]

when Lands, Tenements, or Hereditaments have been given to the Parson and
his successors, or an annual certain sum, or other profit, always, time out of
minde, to the Parson and his successors, in full satisfaction and discharge of
all the Tythes in kinde in such a place: and such manner of Tything is now
confessed by the other party to be a good bar of the Tythes in kinde.

1. That *Modus Decimandi* shall be tryed by the Common Law, that is, that
all satisfactions given in discharge of Tythes shall be tryed by the Common
Law: and therefore put that which is the most common case, That the Lord
of the Mannor of Dale prescribes to give to the Parson 40s. yearly, in full
satisfaction and discharge of all Tythes growing and renewing within the Mannor of Dale, at the Feast of Easter: The Parson sueth the Lord of the Mannor
of Dale for his Tythes of his Mannor in kinde, and he in Bar prescribes in
manner *ut supra:*[12] The Question is, if the Lord of the Mannor of Dale may
upon that have a Prohibition, for if the Prohibition lyeth, then the Spiritual
Court ought not to try it; for the end of the Prohibition is, That they do not
try that which belongs to the Tryal of the Common Law; the words of the
Prohibition being, that they would draw the same *ad aliud examen.*[13]

First, the Law of England is divided into Common-Law, Statute-Law, and
Customs of England: and therefore the Customs of England are to be tryed
by the Tryal which the Law of England doth appoint.

Secondly, Prescriptions by the Law of the Holy Church, and by the Common Law, differ in the times of limitation; and therefore Prescriptions and
Customs of England shall be tryed by the Common Law. See 20 Hen. 6. fo.
17. 19 E. 3. Jurisdiction 28. The Bishop of Winchester brought a Writ of
Annuity against the Archdeacon of Surry, and declared, how that he and his
successors were seised by the hands of the Defendant by title of Prescription,
and the Defendant demanded Judgment, if the Court would hold Jurisdiction
being between spiritual persons, &c. Stone Justice, Be assured, that upon title
of prescription we will here hold Jurisdiction; and upon that, Wilby chief
Justice gave the Rule, Answer: Upon which it follows, that if a *Modus Decimandi,* which is an annual sum for Tythes by prescription, comes in debate
between spiritual persons, that the same shall be tryed here: For the Rule of
the Book is general, (*scil.*) upon title of prescription, we will hold Jurisdiction,

12. [*Ed.:* as above:]
13. [*Ed.:* into another forum.]

and that is fortified with an Asseveration, *Know assuredly;* as if he should say, that it is so certain, that it is without question. 32 Edw. 3. Jurisd. 26. There was a Vicar who had onely Tythes and Oblations, and an Abbot claimed an Annuity or Pension of him by prescription: and it was adjudged, that the same I prescription, although it was betwixt spiritual persons, should be tryed by [41] the Common Law: *Vide* 22 Hen. 6. 46 and 47. A prescription, that an Abby time out of minde had found a Chaplain in his Chappel to say Divine Service, and to minister Sacraments, tryed at the Common Law.

3. See the Record of 25 Hen. 3. cited in the case of *Modus Decimandi* before: and see Register fo. 38. when Lands are given in satisfaction and discharge of Tythes.

4. See the Statute of Circumspecte agatis, *Decimae debitae seu consuetae,*[14] which proves that Tythes in kinde, and a *Modus* by custom, &c.

5. 8 Edw. 4. 14. and Fitz. N. B. 41 g. A Prohibition lieth for Lands given in discharge of Tythes. 28 Edw. 3. 97. a. There Suit was for Tythes, and a Prohibition lieth, and so abridged by the Book, which of necessity ought to be upon matter *De Modo Decimandi,* or discharge.

6.[15] 7 Edw. 6. 79. If Tythes are sold for mony, by the sale the things spiritual are made temporal, and so in the case *De Modo Decimandi,* 42 Edw. 3. 12. agrees.

7. 22 Edw. 3. 2. Because an Appropriation is mixt with the Temporalty, (*scil.*) the King's Letters Patents, the same ought to be shewed how, &c. otherwise of that which is meer Temporal: and so it is of real composition, in which the Patron ought to joyn: *Vide* 11 Hen. 4. 85. Composition by writing, that the one shall have the Tythes, and the other shall have mony, the Suit shall be at the Common Law.

Secondly, By Acts of Parliament.

1. The said Act of *Circumspecte agatis,* which giveth power to the Ecclesiastical Judg to sue for Tythes due first in kinde, or by custom, *i.e. Modus Decimandi:* so as by authority of that Act, although that the yearly sum soundeth in the Temporalty, which was payd by Custom in discharge of Tythes, yet because the same cometh in the place of Tythes, and by constitution, the Tythes are changed into mony, and the Parson hath not any remedy for the

---

14. [*Ed.:* Tithes due or accustomed,]

15. [*Ed.:* The 1659 edition misnumbers this and the next paragraph "7" and "8."]

same, which is the *Modus Decimandi* at the Common Law; for that cause the Act is clear, that the same was a doubt at the Common Law: And the Statute of *Articuli Cleri,* cap. 1. If corporal pennance be changed *in poenam pecuniariam,*[16] for that pain Suit lieth in the Spiritual Court: For see Mich. 8 Hen. 3. Rot. 6. in Thesaur'. A Prohibition lieth *pro eo quod Rector de Chesterton exigit de Hagone de Logis de certa portione pro Decimis Molendinarum;*[17] so as it appeareth, it was a doubt before the said Statute, if Suit lay in the Spiritual Court *de Modo Decimandi.* And by the Statute of 27 Hen. 8. cap. 20. it is provided and enacted, That every of the subjects of this Realm, according to the Ecclesiastical Laws of the Church, and after the laudable usages and customs of the Parish, &c. shall yield and pay his Tythes, Offerings, and other duties: and that for subtraction of any of the said Tythes, offerings, or other duties, the Parson, &c. may by due Proces of the Kings Ecclesiastical Laws, convent the person offending before a competent Judg, having authority to hear and determine the Right of Tythes, and also to compel him to yeild the duties, *i.e.* as well *Modus Decimandi,* by laudable usage or Custom of the Parish, as Tythes in kinde: and with that in effect agrees the Statute of 32 Hen. 8. cap. 7. By the Statute of 2 Edw. 3. cap. 13. it is enacted, That every of the Kings Subjects shall from henceforth, truly and justly, without fraud or guile, divide, &c. and pay all manner of their predial Tythes in their proper kinde, [42] as they rise | and happen in such manner and form as they have been of Right yielded and payd within forty years next before the making of this Act, or of Right and Custom ought to have been payd.

And after in the same Act there is this clause and Proviso, Provided always, and be it enacted, That no person shall be sued, or otherwise compelled to yield, give, or pay any manner of Tythes for any Mannors, Lands, Tenements, or Hereditaments, which by the Laws and Statutes of this Realm, or by any priviledg or prescription, are not chargeable with the payment of any such Tythes, or that be discharged by any compositions real. And afterwards, there is another Branch in the said Act; And be it further enacted, That if any person do subtract or withdraw any manner of Tythes, Obventions, Profits, Com-

16. [*Ed.:* into pecuniary penalty.]

17. [*Ed.:* forasmuch as the rector of Chesterton demanded a certain portion from Hugh de Logis for tithes of mills.]

modities, or other Duties before mentioned (which extends to Custom of Tything, *i.e. Modus Decimandi,* mentioned before in the Act, &c.) that then the party so substracting, &c. may be convented and sued in the Kings Ecclesiastical Court, &c. And upon the said Branch, which is the Negative, That no person shall be sued for any Tythes of any Lands which are not chargeable with the payment of such Tythes by any Law, Statute, Priviledg, Prescription, or Real Composition. And always when an Act of Parliament commands or prohibits any Court, be it Temporal or Spiritual, to do any thing temporal or spiritual, if the Statute be not obeyed, a Prohibition lieth: as upon the Statute *de articulis super Cartas,* ca. 4. *Quod Communia Placita non tenentur in Scaccario:*[18] a Prohibition lieth to the Court of Exchequer, if the Barons hold a Common-Plea there, as appeareth in the Register 187. b. So upon the Statute of West. 2. *Quod inquisitiones quae magnae sunt examinationis non capiantur in patria;*[19] a Prohibition lieth to the Justices of *Nisi Prius.* So upon the Statute of *Articuli super Cartas,* cap. 7. *Quod Constabularius Castr.* Dover, *non teneat Placitum forinsecum quod non tangit Custodiam Castri,*[20] Register 185.[21] So upon the same Statute, cap. 3. *Quod Senescallus et Mariscallus non teneant Placita de libero tenemento, de debito, conventione,*[22] *&c.* a Prohibition lieth, 185. And yet by none of these Statutes, no Prohibition or *Supersedeas*[23] is given by express words of the Statute. So upon the Statutes 13 Ric. 2. cap. 3. 15 Ric. 2. cap. 2. 2 Hen. 4. cap. 11. by which it is provided, That Admirals do not meddle with any thing done within the Realm, but onely with things done upon the Seas, &c. a Prohibition lieth to the Court of Admiralty.

So upon the Statute of West. 2. cap. 43. against Hospitalers and Templers, if they do against the same Statute, Regist. 39 a. So upon the Statute *de Prohibitione regia, Ne laici ad citationem Episcopi conveniant ad recognitionem fa-*

---

18. [*Ed.:* That common pleas should not be held in the Exchequer.]

19. [*Ed.:* That inquisitions which require great examination should not be taken in the country.]

20. [*Ed.:* That the constable of Dover Castle should not hold a foreign plea which does not touch the keeping of the castle.]

21. See Lib. Entr. 450, a Prohibition was upon the Statute that one shall not maintain; and so upon every penal Law. See F. N. B. 39. b. Prohibition to the Common Pleas upon the Stat. of Magna Charta that they do not proceed in a Writ of *Praecipe in Capite,* where the Land is not holden of the King. 1 & 2 Eliz. Dyer 170, 171. Prohibition upon the Statute of barrenes, and pettit is onely prohibited by implication.

22. [*Ed.:* That the steward and marshal should not hold pleas of freehold, debt, covenant, etc.]

23. [*Ed.:* Writ from a superior court to an inferior court to stay proceedings.]

ciend. vel Sacrament. praestanda nisi in casubus matrimonialibus & Testamen-tariis,[24] a Prohibition lieth. Regist. 36. b. And so upon the Statute of 2 Hen. 5. cap. 3. at what time the Libel is grantable by the Law, that it be granted and delivered to the party without difficulty, if the Ecclesiastical Judg, when the cause which depends before him is meer Ecclesiastical, denyeth the Libel, a Prohibition lieth, because that he doth is against the Statute; and yet no Prohibition by any express words is given by the Statute. And upon the same Statute the Case was in 4 Edw. 4. 37. Pierce Peckam took Letters of Admin-istration of the Goods of Rose Brown of the Bishop of London, and afterwards T. T. sued to Thomas Archbishop of Canterbury, That because the said Rose Brown had Goods within his Diocess, he prayed Letters of Administration to be committed to him, upon which the Bishop granted him Letters of Ad-
[43]　ministration, and afterwards | T. T. libelled in the Spiritual Court of the Arch-bishop in the Arches against Pierce Peckam, to whom the Bishop of London had committed Letters of Administration to repeal the same: and Pierce Peckam, according to the said Statute, prayed a Copy of the Libel exhibited against him, and could not have it, and thereupon he sued a Prohibition, and upon that an Attachment: And there Catesby Serjeant moved the Court, that a Prohibition did not lie, for two causes: 1. That the Statute gives that the Libel shall be delivered, but doth not say that the Plea in the Spiritual Court shall surcease by Prohibition. 2. The Statute is not intended of matter meer spiritual, as that case is, to try the Prerogative and the Liberty of the Archbishop of Canterbury and the Bishop of London, in committing of Administrations. And there Danby Chief Justice, If you will not deliver the Libel according to the Statute, you do wrong, which wrong is a temporal matter, and punishable at the Common Law; and therefore in this case the party shall have a special Prohibition out of this Court, reciting the matter, and the Statute aforesaid, commanding them to surcease, until he had the Copy of the Libel delivered unto him: which case is a stronger case then the case at the Bar, for that Statute is in the Affirmative, and the said Act of 2 Edw. 6. cap. 13. is in the Negative, *scil.* That no Suit shall be for any Tythes of any Land in kinde where there is *Modus Decimandi,* for that is the effect of the said Act, as to that point. And always after the said Act, in every Term in the whole Reigns of King

---

24. [*Ed.:* concerning the royal prohibition, that laymen be not convented at the citation of a bishop to make recognitions or take oaths except in matrimonial and testamentary causes,]

Edward the sixth, Queen Mary, and Queen Elizabeth, until this day, Prohibitions have been granted *in Causa Modi Decimandi,* and Judgments given
upon many of them, and all the same without question made to the contrary.
And accordingly all the Judges resolved in 7 Edw. 6. Dyer 79. *Et contemporanea
expositio est optima & fortissima in lege, & a communi observantia non est re-
cedendum, & minime mutanda sunt quae certam habuerunt interpretationem.*[25]

And as to the first Objection, That the Plea of *Modus Decimandi* is but
accessary unto the Right of Tythes; it was resolved, that the same was of no
force, for three causes:

1. In this case, admitting that there is a *Modus Decimandi,* then by the
Custom, and by the Act of 2 Edw. 6. and the other Acts, the Tythes in kinde
are extinct and discharged; for one and the same Land cannot be subject to
two manner of Tythes, but the *Modus Decimandi* is all the Tythe with which
the Land is chargeable: As if a Horse or other thing valuable be given in
satisfaction of the Duty, the Duty is extinct and gone: and it shall be intended,
that the *Modus Decimandi* began at the first by real composition, by which
the Lands were discharged of the Tythes, and a yearly sum in satisfaction of
them assigned to the Parson, &c. So as in this case there is neither Principal
nor Accessary, but an Identity of the same thing.

2. The Statute of 2 Edw. 6. being a Prohibition in it self, and that in the
Negative, If the Ecclesiastical Judg doth against it, a Prohibition lieth, as it
appeareth clearly before.

3. Although that the Rule be general, yet it appeareth by the Register it
self, that a *Modus Decimandi* is out of it; for there is a Prohibition *in Causa
Modi Decimandi,* when Lands are given in satisfaction of the Tythes.

As to the second Objection, it was answered and resolved, That that was
from, or out of the Question; for *status Quaestionis non est | deliberativus sed
judicialis,*[26] what was fit and convenient, but what the Law is: and yet it was
said, It shall be more inconvenient to have an Ecclesiastical Judg, who is not
sworn to do Justice, to give sentence in a case between a man of the Clergy
and a Lay-man, then for twelve men sworn to give their Verdict upon hearing
of Witnesses *viva voce,*[27] before an indifferent Judg, who is sworn to do Right

[44]

25. [*Ed.:* And contemporary exposition is the best and strongest in Law. and one should not go back
on common observation; and things which have had a certain interpretation are not to be changed.]
26. [*Ed.:* the state of the question is not deliberative but judicial.]
27. [*Ed.:* orally (Literally, with living voice).]

and Justice to both parties: But convenient or inconvenient is not the Question: Also they have in the Spiritual Court such infinite exceptions to Witnesses, that it is at the Will of the Judg with which party he shall give his sentence.

As to the third Objection, it was answered and resolved: First, That *satisfactio pecuniaria*[28] of it self is Temporal: But for as much as the Parson hath not remedy *pro Modo Decimandi* at the Common Law, the Parson by force of the Acts cited before might sue *pro Modo Decimandi* in the Ecclesiastical Court: but that doth not prove, That if he sueth for Tythes in kinde, which are utterly extinct, and the Land discharged of them, that upon the Plea *de Modo Decimandi,* that a Prohibition should not lie, for that without all question appeareth by all that which before hath been said, that a Prohibition doth lie. See also 12 Hen. 7. 24 b. Where the original cause is Spiritual, and they proceed upon a Temporal, a Prohibition lieth. See 39 Edw. 3. 22 Edw. 4. Consultation, That right of Tythes which is meerly ecclesiastical, yet if the question ariseth of the limits of a Parish, a Prohibition lieth: and this case of the limits of a Parish was granted by the Lord Chancellor, and not denyed by the other side.

As to the Objection, That an Averment is taken of the refusal of the Plea *de Modo Decimandi;* it was answered and resolved, That the same is of no force for divers causes:

1. It is onely to Enforce the contempt.

2. If the Spiritual Court ought to have the Tryal *de Modo Decimandi,* then the refusal of acceptance of such a Plea should give cause of Appeal, and not of Prohibition: as if an Excommunication, Divorce, Heresie, Simony, &c. be pleaded there, and the Plea refused, the same gives no cause of Prohibition: as, if they deny any Plea, meer spiritual Appeal, and no Prohibition lieth.

3. From the beginning of the Law, no Issue was ever taken upon the refusal of the plea *in Causa Modi Decimandi,* nor any Consultation ever granted to them, because they did not refuse, but allowed the plea.

4. The refusal is no part of the matter issuable or material in the plea; for the same is no part of the suggestion which onely is the substance of the plea: and therefore the *Modus Decimandi* is proved by two Witnesses, according to the Statute of 2 Edw. 6. cap. 13. and not the refusal, which proveth, that the *Modus Decimandi* is onely the matter of the suggestion, and not the refusal.

---

28. [*Ed.:* pecuniary satisfaction.]

5. All the said five matters of Discharge of Tythes mentioned in the said Branch of the Act of 2 Edw. 6. being contained within a suggestion, ought to be proved by two Witnesses, and so have been always from the time of the making of the said Act; and therefore the Statute of 2 Edw. 6. clearly intended, that Prohibitions should be granted in such causes.

6. Although that they would allow *bona fide de Modo Decimandi*,[29] without refusal, yet if the Parson sueth there for Tythes in kinde, when the *Modus*[30] is proved, the same being expressly prohibited by the I Act of 2 Edw. 6. a   [45] Prohibition lieth, although the *Modus* be spiritual, as appeareth by the said Book of 4 Edw. 4. 37. and other the cases aforesaid.

And afterwards, in the third day of debate of this case before his gracious Majesty, Dr. Bennet and Dr. Martin had reserved divers consultations granted *in Causa Modi Decimandi,* thinking that those would make a great impression in the Opinion of the King: and thereupon they said, That Consultations were the Judgments of Courts had upon deliberation, whereas Prohibitions were onely granted upon surmises: And they shewed four Presidents:

One, where three joyntly sued a Prohibition in the case of *Modo Decimandi,* and the Consultation saith, *Pro eo quod suggestio materiaque in eodem contenta minus sufficiens in Lege existit, &c.*[31]

2. Another *in Causa Modi Decimandi,* to be payd to the Parson or Vicar.

3. Where the Parson sued for Tythes in kinde, and the Defendant alleged *Modus Decimandi* to be payd to the Vicar.

The fourth, where the Parson libelled for Tythe Wool, and the defendant alleged a custom, to reap corn, and to make it into sheaves, and to set forth the tenth sheaf at his charges, and likewise of Hay, to sever it from the nine cocks at his charge, in full satisfaction of the Tythes of the Corn, Hay, and Wool.

To which I answered, and humbly desired the Kings Majesty to observe that these have been reserved for the last, and center point of their proof: And by them your Majesty shall observe these things:

1. That the Kings Courts do them Justice, when with their consciences and oaths they can.

---

29. [*Ed.:* an agreed scheme for tithing, in good faith.]
30. [*Ed.:* scheme.]
31. [*Ed.:* Forasmuch as the suggestion and the matter therein contained is insufficient in Law, etc.]

2. That all the said Cases are clear in the Judgment of those who are learned in the Laws, that Consultation ought by the Law to be granted.

For as unto the first president, the case upon their own shewing appeareth to be, Three persons joyned in one Prohibition for three several parcels of Land, each of which had a several manner of Tything; and for that cause they could not joyn, when their interests were several; and therefore a Consultation was granted.

As to the second president, The manner of Tything was alledged to be payd to the Parson or Vicar, which was altogether uncertain.

As to the third president, The *Modus* never came in debate, but whether the Tythes did belong to the Parson or Vicar? which being betwixt two spiritual persons, the Ecclesiastical Court shall have Jurisdiction: and therewith agreeth 38 Edw. 3. 6. cited before by Bacon: and also there the Prior was of the Order of the Cistertians; for if the Tythes originally belonged to the Parson, any recompence for them shall not bar the Parson.

As to the last president, the same was upon the matter of a Custom of a *Modus Decimandi* for Wool: for to pay the Tythe of Corn or Hay in kinde, in satisfaction of Corn, Hay and Wool, cannot be a satisfaction for the Wool; for the other two were due of common right: And all this Appeareth in the Consultations themselves, which they shew, but understand not. To which the Bishop of London said, that the words of the Consultation were, *Quod suggestio praedicta materiaq; in eadem contenta minus sufficiens in Lege existet, &c.*[32] so as *materia* cannot be referred to form, and therefore it ought to extend to the *Modus Decimandi*.

[46]   I To which I answered, That when the matter is insufficiently or uncertainly alleged, the matter it self faileth; for matter ought to be alleged in a good sentence: and although the matter be in truth sufficient, yet if it were insufficiently alleged, the plea wanteth matter. And the Lord Treasurer said openly to them, that he admired that they would alledg such things which made more against them than any thing which had been said. And when the King relied upon the said Prohibition in the Register, when Land is given in discharge of Tythes, the Lord Chancellor said, that that was not like to this case; for there, by the gift of the Land in discharge of Tythes, the Tythes were actually discharged: but in the case *De Modo Decimandi,* an annual sum is payd for

32. [*Ed.:* That the aforesaid suggestion and the matter therein contained is insufficient in Law, etc.]

the Tythes, and the Land remains charged with the Tythes, but ought to be discharged by plea *de Modo Decimandi:* All which was utterly denyed by me; for the Land was as absolutely discharged of the Tythes *in casu de Modo Decimandi,* when an annual sum ought to be payd, as where Land is given: for all the Records and presidents of Prohibition in such cases are, That such a sum had been always, &c. payd *in plenam contentationem, satisfactionem & exonerationem omnium & singularium Decimarum, &c.*[33] And although that the sum be not payd, yet the Parson cannot sue for Tythes in kind, but for the mony: for, as it hath been said before, the Custom and the said Acts of Parliament (where there is a lawful manner of Tything) hath discharged the Lands from Tythes in kinde, and prohibited, that no suit shall be for them. And although that now (as it hath been said) the Parsons, &c. may sue in the Spiritual Court *pro Modo Decimandi,* yet without question, at the first, the annual payment of mony was as Temporal, as annual profits of Lands were: All which the King heard with much patience. And the Lord Chancellor answered not to that which I had answered him in, &c.

And after that his most excellent Majesty, with all his Councel, had for three days together heard the allegations on both sides, He said, That he would maintain the Law of England, and that his Judges should have as great respect from all his Subjects as their predecessors had had: And for the matter, he said, That for any thing that had been said on the part of the Clergy, that he was not satisfied: and advised us his Judges to confer amongst our selves, and that nothing be encroached upon the Ecclesiastical Jurisdiction, and that they keep themselves within their lawful Jurisdiction, without unjust vexation and molestation done to his Subjects, and without delay or hindering of Justice. And this was the end of these three days consultations.

And note, That Dr. Bennet in his discourse inveighed much against the opinion in 8 Edw. 4. 14. and in my Reports in *Wrights Case,* That the Ecclesiastical Judg would not allow a *Modus Decimandi;* and said, That that was the mystery of iniquity, and that they would allow it. And the King asked, for what cause it was so said in the said Books? To which I answered, that it appeareth in Linwood, who was Dean of the Arches, and of profound knowledg in the Canon and Civil Law, and who wrote in the Reign of King Henry the sixth, a little before the said Case in 8 Edw. 4. in his title *de Decimis, cap.*

33. [*Ed.:* in full contentment, satisfaction, and discharge of and singular the tithes, etc.]

Quoniam propter, &c. fo. 139 b. *Quod Decimae solvantur, &c. absque ulla dim-inutione:* and in the gloss it is said, *Quod Consuetudo de non Decimando, aut de non bene Decimando non valet.*[34] And that being written by a great Canonist of England, was the cause of the said saying in 8 Edw. 4. that they would not allow the said plea *de Modo Decimandi;* for always the *Modus | Decimandi* is lesse in value then the Tithes in specie, and then the same is against their Canon; *Quod decimae solvantur absque diminutione, & quod consuetudo de non plene Decimando non valet.*[35] And it seemed to the King, that that Book was a good Cause for them in the time of King Edward the fourth to say, as they had said; but I said, That I did not relie upon that, but upon the grounds aforesaid, (*scil.*) The Common Law, Statute-Laws, and the continuall and infinite judgements and judiciall proceedings, and that if any Canon or Con-stitution be against the same, such Canon and Constitution, &c. is void by the Statute of 25 Hen. 8. Cap. 19. which see and note: For all Canons, Con-stitutions, &c. against the Prerogative of the King, the common Laws, Statutes, or Customs of the Realm are void.

Lastly, the King said; That the high Commission ought not to meddle with any thing but that which is enormious and exorbitant, and cannot permit the ordinary Proces of the Ecclesiasticall Law; and which the same Law cannot punish. And that was the cause of the institution of the same Commission, and therefore, although every offence, *ex vi termini*,[36] is enormious, yet in the Statute it is to be intended of such an offence, is *extra omnem normam*,[37] as Heresie, Schisme, Incest, and the like great offences: For the King said, That it was not reason that the high Commission should have conusance of common offences, but to leave them to Ordinaries, *scil.* because, that the party cannot have any appeal in case the high Commission shall determine of it. And the King thought that two high Commissions, for either Province one, should be sufficient for all England, and no more.

[47] appears in left margin.

---

34. [*Ed.:* and in the Gloss it is said that a custom of not tithing, or of not tithing in full, does not avail.]

35. [*Ed.:* That tithes be paid, etc. without any dimunition, and that a custom of not tithing, or of not tithing in full, does not avail.]

36. [*Ed.:* by force of the term,]

37. [*Ed.:* outside every rule,]